PSYCHIATRIC
CASUALTIES

PSYCHIATRIC CASUALTIES

HOW AND WHY THE MILITARY

IGNORES THE FULL COST OF WAR

MARK C. RUSSELL AND **CHARLES FIGLEY**

COLUMBIA UNIVERSITY PRESS

NEW YORK

Columbia University Press
Publishers Since 1893
New York   Chichester, West Sussex
cup.columbia.edu

Library of Congress Cataloging-in-Publication Data
Names: Russell, Mark C. (Mark Charles), 1960- author. | Figley, Charles R., 1944- author.
Title: Psychiatric casualties : how and why the military ignores the full cost of war /
    Mark Russell and Charles Figley.
Other titles: How and why the military ignores the full cost of war
Description: New York : Columbia University Press, [2021] | Includes bibliographical references
    and index. |
Identifiers: LCCN 2020030645 (print) | LCCN 2020030646 (ebook) | ISBN 9780231187763
    (hardback) | ISBN 9780231187770 (trade paperback) | ISBN 9780231547451 (ebook)
Subjects: LCSH: Soldiers—Mental health services—United States—Evaluation. |
    United States—Armed Forces—Medical care—Evaluation. | Veterans—Mental health
    services—United States—Evaluation. | Military psychiatry—United States—History.
Classification: LCC UH629.3 .R87 2021 (print) | LCC UH629.3 (ebook) | DDC
    362.2088/35500973—dc23
LC record available at https://lccn.loc.gov/2020030645
LC ebook record available at https://lccn.loc.gov/2020030646

Cover design: Elliott S. Cairns
Cover image: Master1305/Shutterstock.com

This book is dedicated to generations of service members and their families who suffered needlessly for their country. The suffering was due to the U.S. military's chronic neglect of mental healthcare, perpetuating a preventable cycle of wartime mental health crises since World War I. May this book convince our government and military leaders to join the battle for full mental health parity with medical health and end this tragic cycle for future American generations who will protect us all.

CONTENTS

PREFACE

D esperate cries of "medic!" evoke an automatic response from the military to urgently bind the predictable physical realities of warfare. No questioning the authenticity of the fallen soldier's medical wounds, or the military's sacred obligation to do everything within its power to provide the best medical care possible to save or restore the lives of those sent in harm's way. No speculation about a marine's toughness, moral integrity, motives, loyalty, courage, or preexisting contributions to their medical wounding. It would likewise be unthinkable to ridicule, shame, blame, punish, incarcerate, or kill our sailors and airmen bearing tangible evidence of their sacrifice.

The U.S. government and American people would be morally outraged if the military entered a war completely unprepared to meet even the basic medical needs of its warrior class—certainly heads would roll and leaders be held accountable—as they should be! And if the U.S. military ever went to war with grossly inadequate numbers of well-trained medical providers or an insufficient treatment facilities, shamed and stigmatized injured warriors, denied family members proper care, or caused a major public health crisis including mass death by prematurely discharging hundreds of thousands of untreated wounded veterans each year, leaving it up to individual combatants, their families, and charities to pick-up the pieces, we the people would demand the national news media and Congress to forcefully investigate the reasons why and fix it!

After all, the inevitable consequence of going to war is that people will be maimed and people will die. So, whenever the country decides to get into a war, the very least the politicians, heads of state, free press, military leaders, and American citizens can and should demand is that we do everything humanly possible to implement Abraham Lincoln's pledge from his second inaugural address: "To bind up the nation's wounds; to care for him who shall have borne the battle, and for his widow, and his orphan."

Fortunately, for the most part, our government and military does an *excellent* job in honoring its promise to care for the medical wounds of war as evidence by a 97 percent survival rate from battlefield injuries. In fact, military medicine has been a trendsetter, providing cutting-edge advances in medical technology, lifesaving procedures, and rehabilitation that have helped countless veterans and their civilian counterparts alike—both at home and abroad.

THE REST OF THE STORY

Tragically, the predictable outcomes of human warfare have never been limited to bodily injury—a lesson relearned by the U.S. military during the Second World War (WWII): "Each moment of combat imposes a strain so great that men will break down in direct relation to the intensity and duration of their exposure. Thus psychiatric casualties are as inevitable as gunshot and shrapnel wounds in warfare."[1] In fact, as we detail later, since WWII, more American combatants have become neuropsychiatric casualties than those both killed and medically wounded combined, and these psychiatric conditions are the top cause for military attrition and costly pension disability.

Despite these realities, how does the military and society treat its warriors with "invisible" injuries? Do these casualties receive the same sense of urgency, priority setting, planning, and preparation to provide the optimal care in restoring and saving lives of those whose sacrifices are less visible? Some may argue that unlike medical wounds, people don't die from emotional injuries, so of course treatment is unequal. Well, that may be true initially, but a disturbing historical trend of veteran deaths by suicide has outpaced those killed in action since the Vietnam War, and this trend has continued in earnest today. That inconvenient fact aside, veterans succumbing to war stress injuries routinely have endured ridicule, blame, shame, punishment, incarceration, execution, and critical questioning of their toughness, moral integrity, courage, loyalty, and preexisting responsibility for their injuries. And when a congressionally mandated military task force on mental health (2007) finally admitted six years into a shooting war that we entered the current conflicts in Afghanistan and Iraq completely unprepared to meet even basic mental needs during "peacetime" (even as war-military leaders were congratulated and promoted), there was no ceremonial head rolling or accountability. Despite the steady deluge of media stories of a rampant public health crisis characterized by a war veteran suicide epidemic, untreated PTSD, immoral discharges for misconduct and personality disorder, and more than 214 government studies of military mental healthcare, not a single Congressional hearing or major news investigation has investigated the reasons "why" this and every war generation since the First World War has endured these self-inflicted crises and or examined how to end the tragic cycle. This is especially problematic given that the military has extensive documentation from its "lessons learned" providing a clear blueprint of how to best meet wartime needs.

PURPOSE OF THE BOOK

In this book, we examine the rich, often tragic, and thus "dark" history of how the military has managed or mismanaged its mental health problem. We shed critical light on the underlying reasons for the status quo and begin a discussion on concrete, practical solutions to end the generational cycle of mental health neglect and crisis. It is our deepest conviction that if the U.S. military can ever get on the "right side" of the mental health issue and truly become a world leader in advancing the mental health sciences in actual deeds, and not words, then the rest of U.S. society and citizens from other countries will stand to reap great benefits, just as we have from military medicine.

ACKNOWLEDGMENTS

We would like to acknowledge first those who have been forced to endure the preventable anguish resulting from exposure to the terrible and humiliating tactics we describe in the book. Thanks to these men and women who served our country honorably, including the individual mental health providers. They were nearly always understaffed and undertrained in standards of care for these injuries. Thanks to the military families for caring for their loved ones and overcoming the challenges they have faced as military and veteran families as well as their own and other family members. We also want to acknowledge our families who have endured us during the many years it has taken to research, write, and publish our findings. Finally, we would like to personally thank Stephen Wesley and Christian Winting at Columbia University Press for their remarkable skills in transforming our academic, jargon-laden prose into a sound and coherent story that makes it compelling to nearly everyone. Thank you all.

PSYCHIATRIC CASUALTIES

INTRODUCTION

THE GENESIS OF THE MILITARY'S
MENTAL HEALTH DILEMMA

Each moment of combat imposes a strain so great that men will break down in direct relation to the intensity and duration of their exposure. Thus psychiatric casualties are as inevitable as gunshot and shrapnel wounds in warfare.
J. APPEL AND G. BEEBE, "PREVENTIVE PSYCHIATRY"

The tragic, predictable outcomes of modern warfare are an all too familiar reality for those serving in the military and their families, as well as civilian populations caught in the proverbial crosshairs. Consequently, multitudes of human beings will inevitably be killed, physically maimed or sickened, made refugees, and/or psychiatrically and morally injured during or after any war. The military's certainty of psychiatric casualties, as reflected in our opening quote from Appel and Beebe, U.S. Army colonels during the Second World War (WWII), is especially poignant given the technological advances in weaponry designed to kill, maim, and terrify. Few exposed to the horrors of interpersonal violence, death, and destruction enjoy immunity and return home unscathed.

Until our species can attain the utopian ideal of global tolerance and peaceful coexistence, war is a certainty. In fact, since the twentieth century, generations of Americans have been exposed to the ravages of war about every twelve years. Therefore, it is incumbent upon political and military leaders to exercise due diligence in properly planning for and preparing to meet the inevitable wartime medical, social, and mental health needs of the warrior class who are required to sacrifice life, limb, mind, and soul to implement the political decision to war.

LEARNING THE LESSONS OF WAR

Those who cannot remember the past are condemned to repeat it!
GEORGE SANTAYANA, 1905

Few would disagree with Santayana's pronouncement—particularly those in the profession of defending the national trust.[1] Learning historical lessons has traditionally been viewed as invaluable for preparing future military leaders.[2] Wars are won or lost—people may live or die—by how adeptly battlefield lessons are incorporated. Thus it has long been military doctrine to systematically and thoroughly analyze and integrate combat lessons by establishing "a system for the collection, analysis, dissemination, and implementation of combat, training, and materiel testing experiences with associated combat relevant lessons learned into Department of the Army (DoA) doctrine, organization, research, development, acquisition, training, planning, and other appropriate activities. It creates a system to serve in both peace and wartime as the focal point for the collection, analysis, dissemination, and implementation of combat relevant lessons learned which will enhance the army's ability to perform its missions."[3] The U.S. Army defines "lessons learned" as "Validated knowledge and experience derived from observations and historical study of military training exercises and combat operations."[4] The magnitude of how seriously the military regards learning war lessons is made evident by the number of dedicated policies, programs, and agencies, including the Joint Center for Lessons Learned, Center for Army Lessons Learned, Navy Lessons Learned System, Air Force Offices of Lessons Learned, Center of Military History, and Marine Corps Center for Lessons Learned (e.g., see http://www.au.af.mil/au/awc/awcgate/awc-lesn.htm).

LEARNING MEDICAL LESSONS OF WAR

Following the Korean War, Army Surgeon General Hal B. Jennings Jr., writes, "It behooves us to learn from past experience and apply lessons learned in preparing and planning for military operations or contingencies of the future. Therefore, I commend this volume to Army Medical Department planners and believe the information will be an invaluable tool."[5] When it comes to heeding the medical lessons of war, it is established

Department of Defense (DoD) policy that the service surgeons general "participate in development and implementation of medical materiel adaptations identified by combat and exercises observations relevant to assigned functional areas as follows: a. Combat relevant health care, doctrine, training, organization, and leadership development issues, and b. Medical and dental materiel."[6] Indeed, each military medical department has its own lessons learned policies and dedicated programs such as the Army Medical Lessons Learned System, Navy Medical Lessons Learned System, and the Air Force Medical Service Exchange.

Consequently, the history of military medicine reveals impressive progression in medical advancements gleaned largely from incorporating hard-won battlefield lessons.[7] Military medicine has steadily evolved into providing world-class, cutting-edge services in hygiene, disease prevention, mass casualty triage, emergency medicine, medical transportation, trauma surgery, amputee prosthetics, and burn care.[8] Direct benefit to the private sector is transparent and profound. The overall success from the military's investment in learning from postwar medical analyses and research is best exemplified by the stunning evolution of survivability rates: 97 percent of severely wounded twenty-first-century combatants survive in contrast to 3 percent in the armies of Alexander.[9] Consequently, medical epidemics of yellow fever, malaria, dysentery, and tuberculosis that once plagued military populations have been relegated to the history books. Today, we do not hear of major medical crises afflicting veterans, other than widespread barriers to timely care.

LEARNING THE PSYCHIATRIC LESSONS OF WAR

Each of the military medical departments (Air Force, Army, and Navy/Marine Corps) is responsible for provision of mental health services to its respective service personnel and family members during times of peace and war. Although not explicitly stated in the military's medical lessons learned policies,[10] each medical department is accountable for ensuring that psychiatric lessons, like medical lessons, are properly implemented before, during, and after mobilization for war. Evidence of learning war trauma lessons is relatively straightforward. The clearest proof of actual lessons learned is the absence of forgetting or ignoring basic tenets for meeting wartime mental health needs and preventing catastrophe.

Not widely known by the American public is that psychiatric casualties since WWII have eclipsed the *combined* numbers of personnel both killed in action (KIA) and medically wounded in action (WIA; see figure 0.1). For instance, during WWII a stunning total of 1,076,245 U.S. personnel were either KIA (405,399) or WIA (670,846),[11] whereas an equally staggering 1,253,000 American service members were admitted to hospitals for war stress injury (Army: 1,103,000; Navy/Marine Corps: 150,000).[12] What makes the WWII trend even more alarming is the fact the U.S. War Department (now the DoD) psychiatrically screened and rejected more than 1.6 million purportedly predisposed war neurotics from entering the military and another 1 million from deploying to war zones.[13] In other words, the U.S. military entered WWII with the psychiatrically strongest, most resilient, and healthiest fighting force ever assembled. Yet even this virtual battalion of Captain Americas succumbed to war stress injuries at a higher rate than those killed or wounded in the war.

Fast-forward to the twenty-first century and the trend becomes more apparent, with 936,283 military personnel[14] and 685,540 veterans, respectively, treated for psychiatric conditions by the Department of Veterans Affairs (VA).[15] These men and women served during Operation Iraqi Freedom (OIF), Operation Enduring Freedom (OEF) Operation New Dawn (OND), Operation Inherent Resolve (OIR), and Operation Freedom's Sentinel (OFS), and their numbers far exceed the combined total of 58,586 U.S. military personnel either KIA (5,435) or WIA (53,151).[16] In 2016, the VA inexplicably ceased its annual healthcare utilization reporting, which had been publicly accessible and contained detailed statistics, including total numbers of Global War on Terrorism (GWOT) veterans diagnosed and treated for a variety of service-related mental health conditions beyond post-traumatic stress disorder (PTSD). Nevertheless, based on the VA's 2015 statistics alone, the alarming yet mostly invisible trend of psychiatric casualties far outpacing medically wounded and combat deaths is staggering.

However, psychiatric diagnostic stats inadequately describe the full scope of the short- and long-term suffering that individual veterans and their families must endure, such as the undesired loss of a military career, unemployment, homelessness, medically unexplained physical conditions, moral injury, domestic violence, legal prosecution, stigma, substance abuse, divorce, incarceration, vicarious traumatization, and premature death, including suicide, that has affected more than 5,648 families of GWOT-era veterans (see table 0.1).

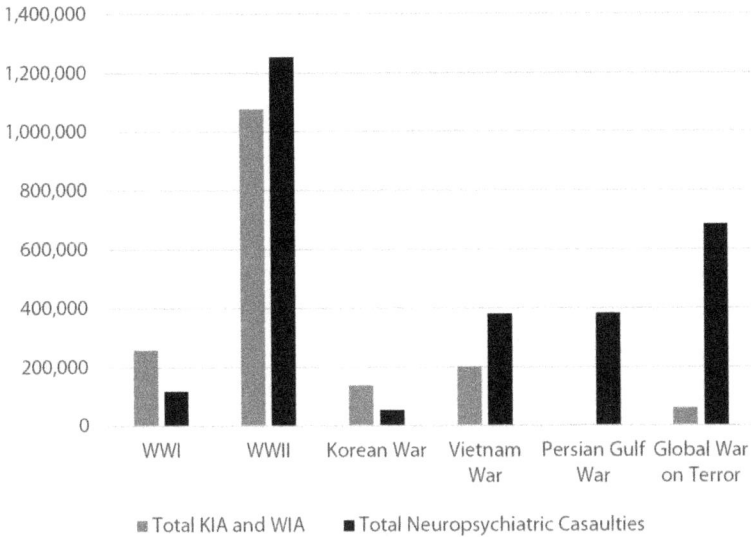

FIGURE 0.1 Comparing U.S. military neuropsychiatric and nonpsychiatric casualty rates.

SOURCES: DATA ON KIA AND WIA (CONGRESSIONAL RESEARCH SERVICE, *AMERICAN WAR AND MILITARY OPERATIONS CASUALTIES: LISTS AND STATISTICS* [WASHINGTON, DC: CONGRESSIONAL RESEARCH SERVICE, FEBRUARY 26, 2010]), EXCEPT GLOBAL WAR ON TERROR (GWOT) (HTTP://WWW.DEFENSE.GOV/NEWS /CASUALTY.PDF).

Data on neuropsychiatric (NP) rates for WWI (Department of Veterans Affairs, 1959), NP disability pensions only; WWII (Brill, 1966; B. H. Chermol, "Wounds Without Scars: Treatment of Battle Fatigue in the U.S. Armed Forces in the Second World War," *Military Affairs: The Journal of Military History, Including Theory and Technology* 49 [1985]: 9–12), per Veterans Administration, *Annual Report of the Director of Veterans Affairs-1947* [Washington, DC: U.S. Government Printing Office, 1947], the greatest number of NP disability pensions for WWII veterans is 474,395; Korean War (Veterans Administration, *Annual Report of the Director of Veterans Affairs-1959* [Washington, DC: U.S. Government Printing Office, 1959]), NP disability pensions only; Vietnam War and Persian Gulf War [Veterans Benefits Administration, *Annual Benefits Report FY2015* [Washington, DC: U.S. Department of Veterans' Affairs, 2015]), PTSD disability pensions only; GWOT (Veterans Benefits Administration, *Annual Benefits Report FY2015* [Washington, DC: U.S. Department of Veterans' Affairs, 2015]), total veterans who received VA mental healthcare; 580,720 GWOT veterans are receiving PTSD disability pensions (Veterans Benefits Administration, *Annual Benefits Report FY2018* [Washington, DC: U.S. Department of Veterans' Affairs, 2019]). In 2016, the VA stopped publishing raw psychiatric data via annual healthcare utilization reports.

INVESTIGATING WARTIME BEHAVIORAL HEALTH CRISES

After a decade-long review of official U.S. military documents, government reports, declassified studies, newspaper articles, and other primary sources, we published the first-ever investigation into answering two seminal questions: (1) Is there a verifiable generational cycle of wartime mental health crises? (2) To what extent, if any, are these crises self-inflicted and preventable (short of ending all future wars, which we have already established remains elusive)? Results of our analysis were conclusive and overwhelming. We provide here a brief overview of the major findings. Readers wanting greater detail are encouraged to read our initial reports.

DEFINING WARTIME MENTAL HEALTH CRISES

We define wartime mental health crises as "a sentinel public health event whereby mental health demand of the military population demonstrably exceeds the mental health system's capacity to provide adequate access to timely, effective mental health and social support services during and/or after a period of war resulting in escalating unmet needs that endangers the health and safety of large numbers of individual members, families, and society."[17]

WHAT IS THE EVIDENCE OF A GENERATIONAL CYCLE OF WARTIME BEHAVIORAL HEALTH CRISES

Through an exhaustive review, we found irrefutable evidence of a pattern of postwar American mental health crises since WWI as determined by prevalence of large numbers of psychiatric casualties (see figure 0.1) coinciding with ample government and newspaper reports of unmet mental health needs with national news headlines for every war starting from the American Civil War.[18] These headlines are eerily similar to contemporary reports of unmet mental health needs.[19] That said, wartime behavioral health crises are not unique to the United States, with similar reports from the United Kingdom, Canada, Germany, France, and Israel, among others. However, for practical purposes, we will stick with the American narrative.

ARE WARTIME MENTAL HEALTH CRISES PREVENTABLE?

Once a decision is made to go to war, to what extent can we prevent mental health crises? This is an infinitely more complicated and multifaceted question. After all, if psychiatric casualties are just as inevitable as being killed or physically wounded in war, how realistic is it to try to avert problems like PTSD and suicide?

The term "preventable" is not used to convey a Pollyannaish sentiment that all war stress injuries like PTSD or suicide can be avoided any more than we can prevent combatants from being KIA or WIA. For example, despite military medicine's unheralded success in achieving a 3 percent mortality rate, some combatants will always suffer or die from physical wounds, infections, and illness. In essence, military medicine has generally eliminated the unnecessary or "preventable" suffering and death from the physical consequences of war by steadfast commitment and adherence to learning its battlefield medical lessons of war. Similarly, to the extent the U.S. military demonstrates its commitment to learning from its own psychiatric lessons of war, we can assert that unnecessary or preventable suffering and premature death has been avoided. In other words, *we did our very best to implement what we knew should be and should not be done to avoid unnecessary harm.* Conversely, evidence of the military's neglect of and/or failure to properly learn its war trauma lessons represents a self-inflicted harming of service members suffering and possibly dying from untreated or inadequately treated war stress injuries, as well as a clear breach of trust and duty owed to war fighters and their families—it is the gross neglect and/or incompetence that directly results in the "preventable" aspect of mental health crises. In other words, *we knew what should and should not be done, but chose to ignore it despite knowing the potential harm.*

TEN FOUNDATIONAL WAR TRAUMA LESSONS

In our initial analyses, we first examined the U.S. military's official lessons learned reports from WWI to the Persian Gulf War[20] and the current Afghanistan/Iraq wars[21] to determine what the military itself has documented about wartime behavioral health services. Military medicine acknowledges the immense value of knowing the history of war stress injuries:

"The past can enable mental health professionals to avoid mistakes made earlier and to devise new ways to deal with modern stress."[22] We and our colleague Kristen Robertson identified ten foundational or superordinate lessons learned that are essential to meeting basic mental health and social needs during times of peace and war:

1. War inevitably causes a legitimate spectrum of war stress injury.
2. Adequate research, planning, and preparation are indispensable during war and peace.
3. A large cadre of well-trained mental health specialists is compulsory.
4. A holistic public health approach to war stress injuries necessitates close collaboration with the private sector along with full parity between medical and mental health services.
5. Effective mental health services demand empowered leadership of an independent, unified, organizational structure (e.g., "Behavioral Health Corps") providing integrated, well-coordinated continuity of care equal to medical services.
6. Elimination of mental health stigma, barriers of care, and disparity is a priority leadership issue at all levels directly impacting individual, family, and military readiness.
7. Ensure ready access to high-quality mental health services including definitive care prior to military separation or discharge.
8. Families must receive adequate mental health and social support during and after military service.
9. Accurate, regular monitoring and reporting are crucial for timely, effective management of mental health needs.
10. Robust dedicated mental health "lessons learned" policy and programs are integral to meeting present and future needs and prevent crisis.[23]

ACKNOWLEDGING REPETITIVE FAILURE TO LEARN WAR TRAUMA LESSONS

Aside from a single book chapter on "The Psychiatric Lessons of War" in the army's *Textbook of Military Medicine: War Psychiatry*,[24] there is no identifiable resource describing what the lessons of war trauma are or any evidence of their being successfully learned. In fact, the opposite is true. For example, within the military's war psychiatry textbook, the history of managing war stress casualties is aptly summarized under the heading "Lessons Learned/Relearned, Lessons Available but Not Learned."[25] It is highly uncharacteristic for sophisticated armed forces like the U.S. Army to blatantly and repeatedly neglect the lessons of war. In stark contrast to well-defined military policies and dedicated lessons learned centers for incorporating tactical and medical lessons, there exists no official policy or central repository in which psychiatric lessons are explicitly collected, identified, and reported, nor are they regularly incorporated into training, or monitored for compliance throughout military medicine. Here's a sampling of the military's admission to ignoring its war trauma lessons:

WWI

The next most important lesson is that of preparing, in advance of an urgent need, a comprehensive plan for establishing special military hospitals and using existing civil facilities for treating mental disease in a manner that will serve the army effectively and at the same time safeguard the interests of the soldiers, of the government and of the community.[26]

Although the total number of American troops in France in January, 1918, was only approximately 203,000, the caring for mental patients had already become a problem. It was obvious at the outset that such patients could not be cared for in the individual American base hospitals scattered throughout France, partly because of the lack in some of them of medical officers, nurses, or enlisted personnel who had had experience in the actual care and treatment of patients suffering from acute mental disorders, but chiefly because of the absence of any special facilities for treatment.[27]

WWII

In retrospect . . . the concepts and practices as developed by combat psychiatry in World War II, generally, rediscovered, confirmed, and further elaborated upon the largely forgotten or ignored lessons learned by the Allied armies, including the American Expeditionary Forces in World War I. Thus, the lessons of World War II combat psychiatry . . . should be regarded as relearned and consolidated insights.[28]

Further, and most important, there was the documented history of World War I, as well as accounts from other previous wars, which provided abundant evidence that combat would produce large numbers of psychiatric casualties. Despite the foregoing data that were available to responsible authorities, there was no effective plan or real preparation for the utilization of psychiatry by the Army in World War II. Facilities for the care and treatment of psychiatric cases were only barely sufficient for the small PEACETIME Army.[29]

KOREAN WAR

In sharp contrast to the prompt application of psychiatry at the division level, psychiatric efforts at the Army level were meager and ineffective. It was evident that a need to support division psychiatry by a second echelon of psychiatry at the Army level was not recognized although such a need was first demonstrated in World War I and in World War II.[30]

VIETNAM WAR

In addition to providing an impetus for accurate diagnosis, the demands for treatment of large numbers of traumatized veterans spurred the development of effective treatments both for reactions that occurred on the battlefield, as well as those that occurred outside the war zone. Particularly following WWI and WWII great gains were made in diagnosing and treating stress reactions. Sad to say, many of these lessons were forgotten and had to be relearned with Vietnam veterans.[31]

PERSIAN GULF WAR

The mental health personnel deployed to the Gulf War were often not adequately trained as individuals or units, they were not well equipped, in many cases doctrine was not followed . . . We were not ready. Our challenge is to develop and implement a peacetime mental health program that will allow us rapidly to transition to war. American soldiers deserve no less.[32]

Finally, six years into the first American war of the twenty-first century—collectively known as the global war on terror—the congressionally mandated DoD Task Force on Mental Health (TF-MH) reported chronic deficiencies:

The Task Force arrived at a single finding underpinning all others: The Military Health System lacks the fiscal resources and the fully-trained personnel to fulfill its mission to support psychological health in peacetime or fulfill the enhanced requirements imposed during times of conflict.[33]

They urgently pleaded to Congress:

The time for action is now. The human and financial costs of un-addressed problems will rise dramatically over time. Our nation learned this lesson, at a tragic cost, in the years following the Vietnam War. Fully investing in prevention, early intervention, and effective treatment are responsibilities incumbent upon us as we endeavor to fulfill our obligation to our military service members.[34]

CONSEQUENCES FOR IGNORING FOUNDATIONAL WAR TRAUMA LESSONS

Failure to implement a single foundational lesson can have a cascading effect that significantly erodes capability to meet basic needs.[35] Predictable outcomes include higher incidence of unmet mental health and social needs, difficulty with social reintegration, suicide spikes, chronic comorbid injuries, and disability, all within the context of clear erosion of system capacity to meet needs (staffing shortages, attrition, delayed access to care, etc.). Sustained neglect, prolonged warfare, delayed recognition, and continued disregarding of foundational psychiatric lessons will always devolve into costly mental health catastrophes, posing significant long-term harm, costs, and public health risks.[36]

Veterans have been compensated for wounds and injury since 1636 when the Pilgrims at Plymouth passed the first pension law in America: "Any man who should be sent forth as a soldier and return maimed should be maintained competently by the colony during his life."[37] However, the primary motive for veteran compensation has always been military recruitment and prevention of mass desertion.[38] Harvard economist Linda Bilmes estimated an overall $1 trillion price tag for the American government in regard to disability compensation and VA treatment for OEF/OIF/OND veterans.[39]

Government concerns over the financial costs of war stress injury are primarily focused on disability pensions and treatment, as well as fears over malingering, all of which can threaten the government's ability to recruit and retain a fighting force and jeopardize its economic standing.[40] As the volume and costs of disability pensions increased for psychological conditions, so too did government scrutiny and efforts to tighten regulations. For instance, after WWI, seventy-two thousand veterans were discharged for neuropsychiatric conditions, despite psychiatric screenings at enlistment, and forty thousand sought disability benefits.[41] Consequently, government and military officials attributed most of the neuropsychiatric problems to predisposition and fraud, resulting in the 1921 amendment of the War Risk Insurance Act that excluded conditions that were believed to have existed before military service.[42] In other words, prior to 1921, the overriding presumption in military pension laws was that any injury or condition incurred on active duty was compensable.[43] During WWII, the IOM reported an estimated 1.3 million service members were treated for a neuropsychiatric condition and more than five hundred thousand U.S. Army soldiers were discharged for psychiatric disability in spite of extensive psychiatric screenings at enlistment.[44] Consequently, per the IOM: "Policy makers were also concerned with preventing the national economy from slumping into a postwar recession or even depression."[45] In the twenty-first-century wars in Afghanistan and Iraq, government concerns regarding skyrocketing rates of PTSD disability claims resurrected the unresolved debates about the legitimacy of war stress injury. For instance, a 2005 investigation by the VA Office of the Inspector General reported the number of beneficiaries receiving compensation for PTSD increased by 79.5 percent from 120,265 to 215,871 from 1999 to 2004, and PTSD disability pensions increased 148.8 percent from $1.72 billion to $4.28 billion, while compensation for all other disability categories only increased by 41.7 percent.[46] In 2019, there are 580,720 GWOT veterans receiving service-connected compensation for PTSD alone.[47] Government concerns led the VA to commission the IOM because

in particular, compensation claims for PTSD have attracted attention because of the increasing numbers of claims in recent years and because diagnosing PTSD is more subjective than is the case with many of the other disorders that VA administers benefits for.[48]

In short, the IOM was charged to review whether the diagnostic construct of PTSD was evidence based and to advise on more stringent criteria and procedures for accurately diagnosing PTSD.[49]

The Congressional Budget Office reported that in 2013, some 3.5 million out of 22 million living U.S. veterans received disability compensation for medical and mental health conditions.[50] Spending on veterans' disability benefits nearly tripled since fiscal year 2000, from $20 billion in 2000 to $54 billion in 2013, with a forecasted total $64 billion in 2015.[51] The most common disability categories are musculoskeletal (36 percent), hearing related (13 percent), and skin related (11 percent), with PTSD accounting for 4 percent of pensions. However, over the next forty years, PTSD disability pension costs will likely increase from $355 billion to $534 billion, depending on the duration and intensity of U.S. military deployments.[52]

Table 0.1 reflects the Congressional Budget Office's (CBO, 2012) cost estimate for VA treatment from only 2004 to 2009 for OEF/OIF/OND veterans diagnosed with PTSD and traumatic brain injury (TBI). The combined total cost for veterans diagnosed with PTSD, TBI, or both is estimated to be $2,220 million in comparison to $1,450 million for veterans seeking VA treatment without PTSD or TBI.[53] What about other mental health conditions? The CBO estimates the average annual cost of VA treatment for mental health conditions other than PTSD or TBI is $4,300 per veteran. During FY2004–FY2009 the VA spent $3.7 billion on the first four years of mental health treatment in general, 60 percent of which ($2.2 billion) was spent only for veterans diagnosed with PTSD and/or TBI.

TABLE 0.1 VA costs of treating OEF/OIF/OND veterans with PTSD and TBI

CONDITION	AVERAGE ANNUAL COST PER PATIENT	NUMBER OF OEF/OIF/OND VETERANS TREATED BY VA (FY2004–FY2009)	TOTAL COST (MILLIONS OF DOLLARS) (FY2004–FY2009)
PTSD only	$8,300	103,500	$1,420
TBI only	$11,700	8,700	$130
Both PTSD and TBI	$13,800	26,600	$670
No PTSD or TBI	$2,400	358,000	$1,450

Source: Congressional Budget Office, *The Veterans Health Administration's Treatment of PTSD and Traumatic Brain Injury Among Recent Combat Veterans, February 2012.* (Washington, DC: Congressional Budget Office, February 2012).

Looking at the most recently published utilization data, the VA reported 685,540 or 57.2 percent of all OEF/OIF/OND veterans in 2015 were receiving VA treatment benefits for a mental health diagnosis.[54] Based on the CBO's cost estimates,[55] the VA spent about $12.8 million to treat 297,828 OEF/OIF/OND veterans for a non-PTSD mental health condition[56] and an additional $30.2 million to treat 364,894 veterans diagnosed with PTSD for a combined total of $43 million.[57] Per Bilmes:

> The most striking finding is that veterans from Iraq and Afghanistan are utilizing VA medical services and applying for disability benefits at much higher rates than in previous wars. The higher medical use is the result of several factors, including: a) higher survival rates for seriously wounded troops; b) higher incidence of PTSD and other mental health ailments; c) more veterans who are willing to seek treatment and apply for benefits for mental health problems; d) more generous medical benefits, more presumptive conditions, and higher benefits in some categories.[58]

Moreover, the long-term ripple effect of societal costs from war stress injury typically expands three to four decades after a war ends.[59] The crude estimates of disability pension and treatment costs ensure that the trend will continue, with the healthcare costs after the war far exceeding the cost of the war itself.

THE ELEPHANT IN THE ROOM: *WHY* THE MILITARY NEGLECTS ITS WAR TRAUMA LESSONS

The underlying causes of wartime mental health crises are inherently complex and multifactorial. Preliminary investigations into present and past wartime behavioral health crises reveal a clear pattern of self-inflicted and largely preventable crises caused primarily by the military's repetitive neglect and failure to learn from its own documented lessons of war trauma.[60] Since WWI, the world's greatest military powers engaged in rigorous, impassioned debates to explain and, more importantly, to determine how to end a deplorable psychiatric casualty trend that existentially threatened the military's capacity to fulfill its mission to fight and win wars and posed a risk of financial bankruptcy at home. These so-called trauma-pension debates have been written about extensively and initially emerged from controversy regarding liability torts from railroad and other industry accidents.[61] The majority of military and government leaders, as well as military historians, blamed the "unmanly" military trend on both the morally corrosive cultural influence of psychiatry, which pathologizes normal combat stress reactions, diagnosing these reactions as shell shock and traumatic neuroses, and the generally weakening influence of the modern culture of trauma, which emphasizes victimhood over the customary stiff upper lip resilience.[62]

On the other hand, military leaders who dealt firsthand with war stress injury provide an alternative viewpoint: "Undoubtedly, the most important lesson learned by psychiatry in World War II was the failure of responsible military authorities, during mobilization and early phases of hostilities, to appreciate the inevitability of large-scale psychiatric disorders under conditions of modern warfare,"[63] attributing primary etiology of war stress injuries to exposure to toxic war stress and assigning responsibility to the military to properly plan and prepare for these equally legitimate and predictable wounds of war.

Origins of the word "dilemma" can be traced to the 1520s, from the Late Latin and Greek *dilemma*, or "double proposition," a technical term in rhetoric referring to situations in which someone is forced to choose between two unfavorable alternatives.[64] From the military's perspective, the dilemma involving military mental health can essentially be boiled down to two undesirable propositions, each representing one part of the military's twofold mission: (1) Support the force health protection mission by openly acknowledging and committing to learning from the psychiatric realities of war—thus running the risk of catastrophic failure to fulfill the war-fighting mission (e.g., mass "evacuation syndromes") and potential financial ruin; or (2) support the war-fighting mission by actively ignoring and avoiding fully learning the psychiatric lessons of war to sustain the immediate ability to fight and win wars—thus perpetuating a generational cycle of preventable wartime behavioral health crises harming millions of veterans and their families, as well as society.[65]

EVACUATION SYNDROME

According to the *Textbook on War Psychiatry*, an evacuation syndrome "develops in combat or in field training exercises when through accident or ignorance an evacuation route, usually through medical channels, opens to the rear for soldiers displaying [a] certain constellation of symptoms and signs."[66] The army authors elaborate on WWI evacuation syndromes: "An initial trickle of soldiers turned into a flood, and very soon this inappropriate evacuation of men—for symptoms only—turned into a significant source of manpower loss."[67] Consequently, the military has an inherent, deep-seated fear of mass hysteria, evacuation, and attrition that directly threaten its war-fighting mission. This causal explanation for evacuation syndromes sheds light on the military's ambivalence toward mental health:

> It is important to remember that most psychiatric casualties are soldiers who, because of the influence of negative psychological, social, and phys-iological factors, unconsciously seek a medical exit from combat. Most cases, therefore, will mimic features of other medical disorders that would be "legitimate" forms of escape from combat, thus becoming "evacuation syndromes." Improperly treated through evacuation, the symptoms may persist or worsen, developing characteristics of traumatic neurosis (chronic post-traumatic stress disorder).[68]

At the heart of the mental health dilemma are the competing demands and responsibilities placed on military commanders to look out for the welfare of individual service members and their families, while maintaining unit morale and readiness to accomplish mission priority one, to fight and win wars. During war, individual physical safety and mental well-being regu-larly take a backseat to the unit and mission. For example, during WWI, twenty-two-year-old Army Private McCubin was diagnosed with "shell shock" after exposure to twenty-six days of continuous shelling but faced the death penalty after his court-martial conviction for cowardice.[69] The private appealed for leniency, and even his company commander recommended mercy, but the commanding general rejected the appeal, noting: "If toleration be shown to private soldiers who deliberately decline to face dan-ger, all the qualities which we desire will become debased and degraded."[70] Private McCubin was executed. By most measures, the general's insensitive response was cruel and unjust. Would he have executed a disabled soldier suffering from a shrapnel or gunshot wound? However, what if the general was correct, and leniency results in entire units refusing to fight (aka "evac-uation syndrome")? Such mass attrition may cause greater casualties. Those in the military do not have the luxury of debating and claiming the moral high ground.

Counterbalancing the present negative war narrative are reports indicating not all news is bad. A recent *U.S. Time* article by the Pentagon's chief psychiatric consultant, "Military Mental Health's Wins and Losses Since the Iraq Invasion," describes several unprecedented accomplishments this century, including extensive deployment health screenings, annual frontline assessments by mental health advisory teams, a plethora of educational resources for service personnel and family members, greater emphasis on resilience training, and funding of treatment research.[71] Additional noteworthy initiatives include publication of the first-ever PTSD practice guideline,[72] the proliferation of VA/DoD treatment applications for smartphones, greatly increased access to crisis services (e.g., Veterans Crisis Line), the rollout of standardized training and dissemination of evidence-based PTSD treatments, revamping military transition assistance programs, societal and media support of returning veterans, and unprecedented numbers of nonprofit agencies to fill the void in veterans' social reintegration services. Positive portrayals by the national media include headlines such as "Military Study Finds Benefits in Mental Health Screening,"[73] "Senate Approves Amendment to Expand Mental Health Care,"[74] "Study Seeks Biomarkers for Invisible War Scars,"[75] "For Veterans, a Surge of New Treatments for Trauma,"[76] and "Army Seeks to Improve Troop Resilience as Suicides Increase."[77]

In all, these last accomplishments clearly demonstrate that this generation, like past war generations, has reacted to a wartime mental health crisis with the compassionate, sincere sense of urgency it deserves. Our focus on the ontogenesis of generational crises should not in any way detract from the herculean individual efforts within military populations, government, and the private sector to respond to the crisis.

THE DARKER SIDE OF MILITARY MENTAL HEALTHCARE

As a whole, the nation deserves great credit in the positive ways it has demonstrated support to its current warrior class, especially those bearing tangible evidence of their sacrifice. As a country, we honor our heroes. The unrecognized chasm in the level and type of institutional and public sustenance for the millions of veterans and family members in this and every previous American war suffering from less-visible wounds, however, is profound. As previously asserted, a debt of gratitude is owed to military mental healthcare from its direct beneficiaries, the mental health professions, and the broader society. Yet a full understanding of the mental health narrative requires us to also acknowledge a darker and generally unvoiced aspect of the military's struggle to resolve its mental health dilemma that continues to present day.

After an extensive review of the literature on war stress, we have identified ten overarching strategies or approaches the military has implemented in order to eliminate, minimize, or conceal its mental health problem: (1) cruel and inhumane handling; (2) legal prosecution, incarceration, and executions; (3) weaponizing stigma to humiliate, ridicule, and shame into submission; (4) denying the psychological realities of war; (5) screening and preventing weakness; (6) delay, deception, and watchful waiting; (7) bad paper discharges; (8) diffusion of responsibility and accountability; (9) inadequate, experimental, and harmful treatments; and (10) perpetuating neglect and self-inflicted crises.

Our book has three primary purposes: (1) to generate public awareness about the nature and causes of preventable wartime crises and the military's attempts to resolve its mental health dilemma, (2) to identify constructive solutions to improve the quality of mental healthcare inside and outside the military, and (3) to end the generational cycle of neglect and self-inflicted harm. Our analysis is not a bashing of the military or the people who serve, nor is it about political decisions to war. It is truly intended to be the first-ever honest self-reflection of military mental healthcare, where we have been, and where we need to go.

1

A WAR TO DIE FOR

CASUALTY TRENDS OF MODERN WARFARE

S ir Francis Bacon once said, "History makes men wise."
Military mental healthcare history appears to ignore lessons
learned. "It's like generals don't know shit about combat stress," was
a common attitude I have hear from combat vets. It is time the generals are
educated about the history of combat stress and the costs of killing.

Military mental health is a story of self-inflicted generational crises. This
crisis is deeply rooted in the inherent dilemma of the military's dual, sometimes competing missions. On one hand, the military has the mission of
winning battles. On the other, the military has the mission of protecting the
mental and physical health of its war fighters. The emotional injuries and
their prevention and treatment have been challenging for the U.S. military.
As we will learn, the military has a tendency to avoid talking about death,
killing, or injury of self or others. War planners rarely focus on adequate
mental health services. War injuries associated with any traumatic stress or
psychiatric disability are viewed, implicitly or explicitly, as a discipline problem; a fake or pseudo-illness caused primarily by an individual preexisting
weakness, cowardice, or malingering; or a by-product of the corrosive
modern (weakening) influences of psychiatry and the societal "culture of
victimization" and compensation.

Naturally, how militaries and governments deal with emotionally injured
war fighters and handles its documented war trauma lessons learned depends
heavily on which side of the trauma-pension debate is embraced. In the context of war, the military is routinely faced with choosing to honor its duty
to safeguard the health and well-being of service-members in favor of the
warfighting mission-giving rise to military medicine. The prime objective

of military medicine is to *preserve the fighting force* by preventing illness and healing physical wounds—the intersection of the military's warfighting and force health protection missions. Modern industrial warfare and the ensuing epidemic rise of psychiatric casualties, however, have threatened the military's warfighting mission and have led to the introduction of mental health services. Herein lies the seeds of the military's mental health dilemma. What has motivated the military to accept or tolerate something as antithetical to its mission as mental healthcare and individual weakness (breakdown) within the rank and file? Is it a humane gesture born out of enlightenment from the psychological realities of modern warfare or a desperate measure of self-preservation resulting in a callous disregard for the health of combatants?

Appreciating the historical context of military mental healthcare and these trauma-pension debates is crucial to understanding the strident forces that are maintaining the status quo and resisting organizational change—those that are perpetuating the generational cycle of this self-inflicted wartime mental health crises. We begin this chapter by framing the military's dilemma.

THE MILITARY'S COMPETING MISSIONS

In 1775, the Continental Congress authorized the establishment of the American Continental Army (June 14, 1775), Navy (October 13, 1775), and Marine Corps (November 10, 1775) to fight for American independence. In 1789, the Department of War or War Department was established, and as its title suggests, the primary mission then and now is *to fight and win wars*. In 1780, the U.S. Coast Guard was established, followed by a permanent Department of Navy in 1789, and the Department of Air Force on September 18, 1947. After World War II (WWII), the War Department was rebranded with more politically correct titles such as the National Military Establishment (NME or *enemy*) and the Department of Defense (DoD) in 1949.

Today, the DoD describes itself as

America's oldest and largest government agency. With over 1.3 million men and women on active duty, and 742,000 civilian personnel, we are the nation's largest employer. Another 826 thousand serve in the National Guard and Reserve forces. More than 2 million military retirees and their family members receive benefits.[1]

The DoD's primary mission is "to provide the military forces needed to deter war and to protect the security of our country."[2] Carl von Clausewitz, in his book *On War*, described war in general as a political instrument and offered two types of war and related objectives: (1) "war to achieve limited aims" and (2) war to "disarm" the enemy or "to render [him] politically helpless or militarily impotent."[3] Others make a distinction between symmetrical wars (e.g., U.S. Civil War with large distinguishable armies) and asymmetrical or guerilla-type warfare (e.g., American Revolution). Whatever the type or objective, the military's mission is to fight and win. Consequently, the predictable physical outcome of war is that combatants (and often noncombatants) are wounded and killed. Military historians, however, are quick to point out that most war fighters die from disease and infection. Therefore, the world's militaries readily adopted a secondary mission to preserve the fighting force by preventing unnecessary attrition or loss of manpower from disease and injury.

Military historian Richard A. Gabriel wrote two seminal texts on war and medicine, *Man and Wound in the Ancient World*[4] and *Between Flesh and Steel*,[5] tracing the chronological history of the military-medicine relationship from 4000 B.C.E. to present day and its dramatic impact in advancing the medical field at large. Just as today, medical care of wounded warriors was critical for an army to sustain its ability to fight and win wars even in times of antiquity. The quality of military medical care, however, has always depended on the general level of medical knowledge within a given society. The Sumerian Army (2400 B.C.E.) was the first to systematically provide medical care to its soldiers, but formal institutions of military medicine were possible only with the advent of well-organized armies of Assyria and Rome, the latter establishing a permanent Roman Legion *Medical Corps*, combat medics, battle surgeons, and military hospitals by Augustus Caesar (27 B.C.E.). Gabriel dispels modern misperception of ancient medicine as too primitive to be of import, describing how the Sumerians (2500 B.C.E.) and Egyptians (1700 B.C.E.) placed equal importance of the mind and body in healing wounded soldiers.[6] According to Gabriel, "The primary goal of military medicine, then as now, is to reduce manpower loss caused by enemy actions and to save the lives of as many soldiers as possible so they can live to fight again."[7] Sanitation, disease prevention, and treatment of illness and wounds reflect the military's evolving force protection mission as more combatants died from disease and infections than in actual combat in every war until WWI.

On July 27, 1775, the Continental Congress created a medical service for a twenty-thousand-man army. As in ancient times, disease and infection killed more colonial troops than combat in a 9:1 ratio.[8] In 1777, George Washington ordered the first-ever army-wide inoculation to prevent disease (smallpox) as recommended by his new surgeon general, Dr. Benjamin Rush, a signer of the Declaration and the so-called father of American psychiatry. In 1798, the navy's medical department was created. In 1847, Congress authorized medical officers to receive military ranks for the first time. The army began the War of 1812 with no medical department, but in 1818, Congress included a permanent Army Medical Department (AMEDD) in a military reorganization act. In early 1862, Congress expanded and reorganized the AMEDD, giving the army surgeon general an actual general-officer rank for the first time. That same year, the AMEDD directed the keeping of detailed medical records, later compiled into a massive five-volume medical history of the Civil War—the first detailed history of war's medical effects, including psychiatric disability. The U.S. Army's penchant for detailed psychiatric statistics ended during the Korean War (see chapter 6). Jonathan Letterman, medical director of the Army of the Potomac, led epochal reforms, including reorganizing the medical field supply, a system of forward hospitals, and an AMEDD-controlled ambulance corps. His field-hospital and ambulance evacuation ideas are followed in essence even today.

As the twentieth century began, the AMEDD was again restructured. New branches were added to the AMEDD, including the Nurse Corps. Women had long cared for U.S. soldiers. During the Civil War, women served in the hospitals of both armies. Dorothea Dix, famed for work with the mentally ill, was superintendent of women nurses for the Union Army. Clara Barton, founder of the American Red Cross, recruited volunteers. In 1922, Congress authorized "relative rank." Nurses wore officer insignia, but legally they were still not commissioned officers. The same law that let women into the army authorized appointment of contract dental surgeons. In 1908, dentists were admitted to the AMEDD; in 1911, a true Dental Corps was created; and in 1917, their status, pay, and benefits were equalized with army doctors. Later acts created the Veterinary Corps who were responsible not only for military animals but also for the wholesomeness of army food. This was preventive medicine, as was the new emphasis on sanitation. Preventive medicine was a factor in victory. This was the first major war in which mortality from communicable disease was lower than that from battle wounds. The motor ambulance added a new level of mobility to the evacuation techniques established by Letterman. High death rates of army pilots sparked study of aviation medicine. In 1947, Congress created the Medical Service Corps (MSC) to absorb the Medical Administrative Corps, Sanitary

Corps, and Pharmacy Corps. The MSC today is the corps of medical admin-istrators, scientists, and certain health-care specialties, including military psychologists, occupational therapists, and social workers. In 1949, Air Force medicine became an independent service. In 1951, the first helicopter ambu-lance unit began operations in Korea. Now wounded warriors could reach a sterile, fully-equipped hospital in minutes. A 1967 law removed limits on promotion of Army Medical Specialist Corps and Army Nurse Corps offi-cers, equalizing the promotion and retirement rules of these mostly female corps in line with other AMEDD corps.

MILITARY AND MEDICAL DILEMMAS

The marriage between medicine and the military presents a number of dilemmas. Since antiquity, the military has regarded medical specialists with some suspicion as being willing or inadvertent accomplices to war-weary or malingering soldiers who feign physical ailments to avoid combat. Yet, the effectiveness of military medicine to prevent attrition can make or break a military operation. On the flipside, military medical providers must endure personal moral conflicts of violating their Hippocratic oaths by healing soldiers only to send them back to the frontlines where they might perish, as well as criticism from civilian medical organizations about their moral complicity to protracting war (e.g., Vietnam War). Consequently, the merg-ing of the warrior and healer professions invites tension between individual and organizational allegiances to the respective mission: war fighters take life, whereas healers save lives. Moreover, warfare tactics often require com-manders, regardless of genuine concern about troop well-being, to make difficult life-and-death decisions. For instance, use of military deception or feigning tactics that knowingly result in the deaths of an entire unit reflects painful dilemmas a battlefield commander may face to end a battle and thereby save more lives.

Military medicine's contribution to both warfighting and force health protection missions is undeniable. Perhaps most important, the military's commitment to documenting and learning its wartime medical lessons has led to significant breakthroughs in advancing the medical sciences at sig-nificant benefit to the private sector. In ancient warfare, only the wounded of the victors received treatment. A comparative analysis of wounded and

TABLE 1.1 Battle Mortality from Antiquity to the Twenty-First Century

ERA	WAR	TOTAL MEDICALLY WOUNDED	MORTALITY
1194–1184 B.C.E.	Trojan War	213	90%
264–146 B.C.E.	Punic Wars	180	91%
1775–1783	American Revolution	10,633	42%
1861–1865	U.S. Civil War (Union)	422,295	33%
1917–1918	World War I	257,404	21%
1941–1945	World War II	963,403	30%
1950–1953	Korean War	137,025	25%
1964–1975	Vietnam War	200,727	24%
1990–1991	First Gulf War	614	24%
2001–2012	Operation Enduring Freedom–Operation Iraqi Freedom	10,369	10%

Source: Richard Gabriel, *Between Flesh and Steel: A History of Military Medicine from the Middle Ages to the War in Afghanistan* (Washington DC: Potomac Books, 2013).

killed combatants of ancient and modern times highlights the lethality of modern warfare. For instance, a victorious ancient army could expect to suffer 5.5 percent dead and 6 percent wounded compared with today's U.S. military, which experiences 17.6 percent dead and 41.8 percent wounded (table 1.1).[9]

WHERE DOES MILITARY MENTAL HEALTHCARE COME INTO THE PICTURE?

The idea that a soldier of previously sound mind could be so emotionally disturbed by combat that he could no longer function was not entertained [prior to the twentieth century]; that he might suffer long-term psychological consequences of battle was also dismissed.

E. JONES AND S. WESSELY, "A PARADIGM SHIFT IN THE CONCEPTUALIZATION OF PSYCHOLOGICAL TRAUMA IN THE 20TH CENTURY"

Many misconceptions, distortions, and deceptions have been promulgated by the military and ill-informed academics. One is about the historical scope of the military's mental health dilemma, such as questioning the validity of PTSD, the first diagnosis of the impact of post-traumatic stress.[10] The debates raged on through the first twenty years of its existence as the first trauma diagnosis. This provided a useful excuse to avoid studying incidence and prevalence of PTSD in war fighters. There was "reasonable doubt" of the legitimacy of psychological injury legal claims. These PTSD and trauma-pension debates are inseparably intertwined with military and mental healthcare. A chronological retelling of the military mental healthcare story allows for a greater appreciation of the varied societal, economic, political, and military forces at play that have shaped the past, current, and future landscape.

To further create the impression of a recent twentieth-century phenomena, some notable historians have argued that the *first traces* of war-stress injury did not emerge until the Russo-Japanese War (1904–1905), emphasizing that "as a result, it was believed by British military physicians that 'no war neuroses were observed in the Boer War'."[11] In addition to being factually wrong, this belief was extraordinarily presumptuous (e.g., how does anyone know what pre-twentieth-century soldiers actually believed or how they reacted to war?). Moreover, the projected sentiment of how unfathomable an idea that healthy soldiers could breakdown from war stress explains persistent convictions that only cowards, malingerers, and predisposed weaklings would breakdown, which was complicit with morally corrupt psychiatrists and lawyers. Is the spectacle of war-stress injury a twentieth-century invention, as some claim? Hippocrates (400 B.C.E.) offered the first Western diagnostic classification scheme for psychological disorders, such as hysteria, melancholy, insanity, and mania, but we are left to conjecture about prevalence of these conditions in ancient Greek warriors. Hippocrates noted, however, that "whenever people of the mountains or plains or prairies were sent to another country a terrible perturbation always followed them."[12]

SEVENTEENTH AND EIGHTEENTH CENTURIES

The first identifiable war syndrome called *nostalgia* was reported by Johannes Hofer in 1678, which resembled German, Spanish, and French case reports describing a range of psychophysical symptoms, including persistent obsessive thinking of home, melancholia, anxiety, hallucinations, heart palpitations, and intense surges of fear or dread of future threats sometimes resulting in death by active or passive suicide by people of "all temperaments, weak and strong, are more or less susceptible."[13] Because most *nostalgia* cases involved conscripted Swiss soldiers during the seventeenth and eighteenth centuries, it was believed to be primarily a Swiss disease.[14] In 1774, Jasper reported thousands of Scottish soldiers with *homesickness illness* had died with parallel incidences documented among English, Laplander, Celts, French and Austrian soldiers.[15]

The earliest recognition for treatment of war-stressed veterans can be traced back to 1706 when Peter the Great established a clinic in Vyborg to care for mentally exhausted soldiers. This was followed by specialized psychiatric hospitals and asylums established in 1761 by Catherine the Great to provide humane treatment for mentally ill veterans and citizens alike.[16] After the American Revolutionary War, Dr. Rush's (1781) medical memoirs *Medical Inquiries and Observations upon the Diseases of the Mind* became the first textbook on psychiatry published in America leading the American Psychiatric Association (APA; founded in 1844) to anoint Rush the so-called father of American psychiatry. In his 1781 book, Rush describes the tragic story of two identical twin Continental officers who "served with bravery and distinction" without any previous psychiatric history. After the war, the brothers returned home to their wives and families. Living in separate towns, the twin officers each developed "morbid melancholia" from memories of the war and both committed suicide within weeks of each other.

NINETEENTH CENTURY: INDUSTRIALIZATION AND THE START OF THE TRAUMA-PENSION WARS

The nineteenth century marked the beginning of the Industrial Age with significant technological advances in weaponry and delivery systems matched against outdated battlefield tactics. This was the beginning of modern warfare, which reached unprecedented heights (or lows depending on one's perspective) in the terrorizing and killing of human beings. By the end of the century, psychiatric-related attrition and disability compensation would emerge as a simmering issue within the world's military powers as well as within general society when industrial accidents ignited the so-called trauma-pension debates. In 1852, the U.S. military's experience during the early eighteenth century, including the American-Indian Wars (1811–1890), War of 1812 (1812–1815), and Mexican War (1846–1848), compelled the U.S. Congress to establish the Government Hospital for the Insane in Washington D.C., to provide "the most humane care and enlightened curative treatments for the insane of the Army and Navy," indicating an early recognition of the military's mental health problem.

THE CRIMEAN WAR (1853-1855)

The Crimean War was a mini–world war with the British and Russian militaries as the main protagonists. Each side got a taste of the psychological toll that resulted from industrialized warfare. After the war in 1859 the Russian Chief Military-Sanitary Committee established a military psychiatric school dedicated to train Russian military psychiatrists and study war-stress injuries and their treatment. Such research and training were deemed essential by the Russian military to prepare the army for future wars.[17] Additionally, in 1863 the first British Army created a specialty hospital for war-stress injuries in Netley, England. At Netley, W. C. Maclean conducted his inaugural study of 5,500 Crimean War veterans diagnosed with "irritable heart."[18] Both the opening of the Netley facility and Maclean's irritable heart study followed the American lead.

PRE-TWENTIETH-CENTURY ORIGINS OF MILITARY MENTAL HEALTHCARE AND FRONTLINE PSYCHIATRY

Military efforts to prevent attrition from psychiatric breakdown by use of brief respite (e.g., rest, food, shelter), occupational therapy, massage, and mild electric shock while limiting evacuation to distant hospitals can be traced back to the Russian Army during the Crimean War (1853–1856).[19] After the Crimean War, the Russian Chief Military-Sanitary Committee established the first military psychiatric school in 1859 dedicated to training military psychiatrists and study war-stress injuries and their treatment.[20] The emerging field of combat psychiatry was considered by pre–Soviet Russian military to be essential in preparing for future wars.[21]

THE U.S. CIVIL WAR (1861–1865)

The first major field trials on the psychophysical impact of modern industrialized warfare was the American Civil War, which introduced technological advances in artillery, transportation, ironclads, submarines, machine guns, and aerial surveillance. The U.S. Civil War remains the bloodiest American war with an estimated 498,332 battlefield casualties.[22] This tragic war compelled the nation to recognize the emotional toll of warfare as Civil War–era physicians were ill-prepared and overwhelmed by large numbers of psychophysical maladies defying logical explanation.[23] Union Army Surgeon General William A. Hammond adopted a progressive holistic medical paradigm of mind–body unitary theory that essentially equated physical wounds with psychiatric conditions, like irritable heart, and also established the U.S. Army Hospital for Diseases of the Nervous System in 1862 Philadelphia (later known as Turner Lane), which was dedicated to the research and treatment of nervous disorders. At Turner Lane, S. Weir Mitchell, the father of American neurology developed the resting cure, whereby war-stress casualties were administered seclusion, rest, ample nourishment, and mild electrical stimulation to replenish depleted nerve force. Emphasis was placed on the physician's use of persuasion by appealing to a soldier's strengths and masculinity for eventual return to duty (RTD). Occupational therapy was employed for recuperating soldiers to maintain their military identity by engaging in menial labor just behind the frontlines rather than receiving automatic military discharge. In 1864, Union Army physician Jacob M. DaCosta reported 33 percent of two hundred soldiers with irritable heart were successfully treated and RTD using Mitchell's resting cure,[24] making it the first ever clinical trial for war-stress injury. The emerging frontline policy of attitude and convalescence utilized firm expectations of recovery and RTD, thus helping to avoid malingering and a feared mass exodus.[25] Unfortunately, the history of military mental healthcare is largely one of forgetting and rediscovering the lessons of war trauma.[26]

INDUSTRIALIZATION AND EMERGENCE OF
TRAUMA-PENSION DEBATES

Before WWI, the predominant medico-legal paradigm of traumatic stress injuries in Western society was an authentic, compensable injury to the

central nervous system caused primarily by exposure to extreme environmental events.[27] Early post-traumatic conceptualizations like British physician John Erichsen's railway spine (1864), American physician George
Beard's traumatic neurasthenia (1869), and German neurologist Hermann
Oppenheim's traumatic neuroses all posited legitimate brain injury caused
by traumatic events.[28] Subsequently, the British Legislative Act of 1864
and the 1889 German Imperial Insurance Office Act established the legal
precedent granting traumatic or accident neuroses the status of actionable
conditions, whereby responsible companies were held liable to provide
compensation.[29] Industries fearing mass fraud, hired reputable physicians
to discredit the authenticity of traumatic neuroses in favor of a paradigm of
hysteria, emphasizing pseudo-illness, predisposed weakness, and malingering.[30] In 1900, the Hartmannbund Association of German Doctors for the
Protection of Economic Interests was formed to combat state welfare legislation and the insurance societies linked to physicians.[31] Medical politics were
dominated by the struggle with insurance societies branding traumatic neuroses as a disaster with grave consequences for Germany's economy, public
health, and national strength.[32] For example, in 1911, the leading German
Army psychiatrist Robert Gaupp expressed his dualistic view of predisposed
hysteria stating that individuals who succumbed "lacked a firm mechanism
of inhibition seen in particular women, effeminate men, children, the
uneducated, and those outside Western Europe who were more likely to
lose self-control and react to stimuli by 'fleeing into' hysterical symptoms."[33]
The paradigm of traumatic neuroses was slowly losing ground to the socio-
culturally more palatable predisposed hysteria concepts warning against the
iatrogenic effects of pensions. The trauma-pension, mind-body controversy,
however, did not reach critical-mass until the outbreak of world war.

THE MILITARY'S UNLEARNED WAR TRAUMA LESSONS

During the Boer War (1899–1902), British surgeon Morgan Finucane (1900)
gave the following detailed account of hospitalized soldiers: "the clinical
fact of most interest undoubtedly is the large number of cases of functional
impairment of nerve sense and motor power, associated with psychical
symptoms akin to nervous shock or those observed after railway accidents."[34]
Drawing a transparent link to earlier conceptualizations of post-traumatic
disorders of Erichsen (1864) and Oppenheim (1888), Finucane added that
"it is likely that in the near future the country will be deprived of a large

number of our most capable and experienced men if the cases continue to occur in such frequency."[35] This, along with Jones report that functional cardiac symptoms or disordered actions of heart were a major cause of incapacitation during the Boer War—with 41 percent of hospitalized soldiers discharged from the military,[36] offers stark refutation to the assertion of psychiatry impunity before WWI.

In 1912, the British Army conducted a study on the incidence of mental disease from 1886 to 1908 revealing a dose response to war-stress exposure: "the amount of the increase is proportional to the duration of campaign," predicting that "we shall have to deal with a larger percentage of mental disease the hitherto."[37] This, coupled with the U.S. Army's 1917 report, revealed the military's foreknowledge of a mental health dilemma: "There is a strong suspicion that the high insanity rate in the Spanish-American War and the Boer War, and perhaps earlier conflicts, was due, in part at least, to failure to recognize the real nature of the severe neuroses, which are grouped under the term "shell shock" in this war."[38].

EVACUATION SYNDROMES

According to the U.S. Army's *Textbook on War Psychiatry*, an evacuation syndrome "develops in combat or in field training exercises when through accident or ignorance an evacuation route, usually through medical channels, opens to the rear for soldiers displaying certain constellation of symptoms and signs."[39] The army authors elaborate on WWI evacuation syndromes: "An initial trickle of soldiers turned into a flood, and very soon this inappropriate evacuation of men—for symptoms only—turned into a significant source of manpower loss."[40] The military's causal explanation for evacuation syndromes offers invaluable insight into its ambivalence toward mental health:

It is important to remember that most psychiatric casualties are soldiers who, because of the influence of negative psychological, social, and physiological factors, unconsciously seek a medical exit from combat. Most cases, therefore, will mimic features of other medical disorders that would be "legitimate" forms of escape from combat, thus becoming "evacuation syndromes." Improperly treated through evacuation, the symptoms may persist or worsen, developing characteristics of traumatic neurosis (chronic post-traumatic stress disorder).[41]

EXTENDING THE TRAUMA-PENSION AND MIND-BODY DEBATES TO WAR-STRESS INJURIES

Toward the end of the first year of WWI, European militaries and their governments hotly debated the legitimacy of war-stress injuries and their compensation, as well as how best to deal with the societal threats posed by mass psychiatric attrition. During the 1914 Berlin Society of Psychiatry and Nervous Illness meeting, famed German neurologist Hermann Oppenheim, a staunch proponent of the legitimacy of traumatic neuroses, argued that

> the war has taught us and will continue to teach us (1) that just as before there are traumatic neuroses; (2) that they are not always covered by the concept of hysteria; and (3) that they are really the product of trauma and not goal-oriented, well-cultivated pseudo illness.[42]

In response, German Army psychiatrist Robert Gaupp (1911) declared that "the most important duty of the neurologist and psychiatrist is to protect the Reich from proliferations of mental invalids and war pension recipients."[43] Gaupp was referencing the new diagnosis of pension-seeking neuroses believed to harm veterans.[44]

The military's innovative response to evacuation syndromes during and since WWI, included preventing psychiatric evacuations by deploying mental health specialists to implement what is today referred to as the combat and operational stress control (COSC) doctrine.[45] The military's COSC policy entails providing brief respite and restorative interventions with the explicit expectation that 95 percent of psychiatric casualties will be RTD to their frontline units until either they complete their deployment or their mental health deteriorates, resulting in gross incapacitation (e.g., psychosis) or imminent danger to self or others.[46] A comprehensive review of the military's frontline psychiatry COSC policies demonstrates its unquestionable effectiveness in preventing psychiatric evacuations.[47] A recent review of the long-term effects of the military's unchallenged one-hundred-year policy, however, offers a stark contradiction to official military propaganda promoting the health benefits for service members and their families.[48] Later, we will further examine this particular stratagem in dealing with the mental health dilemma.

REDISCOVERING THE PSYCHIATRIC REALITIES OF WAR DURING WWI

By mid-1914, early into WWI, every major warring power had witnessed an unprecedented number of evacuations because of psychiatric breakdown. Hundreds of thousands of military officers and enlisted members alike were being discharged, sent home, and given disability pensions for afflictions like shell shock and traumatic neuroses.[49] European governments and their military departments became increasingly alarmed by the epidemic of war-stress casualties. These casualties existentially endangered the military's capacity to fight and win wars as well as produced skyrocketing disability pension costs that threatened to bankrupt economies.[50] The ensuing trauma-pension debate intensified.

As the WWI battles of 1916 intensified (i.e., The Somme), unmatched numbers of war neuroses occurred, further elevating the trauma-pension debate into a German state of emergency.[51] Consequently, the military on both sides found itself in a classic double-bind whereby if they openly acknowledge the psychological toll from modern warfare as a legitimate outcome akin to physical sacrifices, then this inevitably would lead to mass evacuation syndromes and possible bankruptcy—thus resulting in systemic failure to sustain warfighting, let alone win the war. At a September 1916 Munich War Congress of the German Association for Psychiatry and Neurological Association, medical history was made. European powers replaced the holistic, authentic post-traumatic stress paradigm (e.g., traumatic neuroses) espoused by Oppenheim and others, with an effeminate paradigm of war hysteria, a pseudo illness caused primarily by predisposed individual weakness, cowardice, malingering, and pension-seeking.[52] The impact of the military's 1916 paradigmatic change cannot be overstated, as recently acknowledged by the Department of Navy and U.S. Marine Corps:

> After 1916, the medical model of combat stress was replaced by the idea of shell shock. Shell shock was considered a temporary and reversible response to stress that would always resolve with no more than a little rest and encouragement. It was then believed to be caused not by literal damage to the brain, but by a weakness of character brought out by the dangers and hardships of war.[53]

Consequently, after 1916, a uniformed frontline mental health doctrine emerged with strict prohibition against psychiatric labeling, evacuation, discharge, and pensioning.[54] In addition, aggressive methods replaced ineffectual gentle approaches in treating war hysteria, such as increasing battlefield executions, legal prosecution, public shaming, faradization (electric shock), and the Kauffman cure (severe electric shocks) to reduce incidence of cowardice resulting in claims of 90 percent RTD to the frontlines.[55] The Allied powers took similar concerted actions to end the perceived existential threats to their military and society caused by evacuation syndromes. For example, in 1916, the British Army Council issued a directive replacing shell shock diagnosis with a Not Yet Diagnosed (Nervous) (NYDN) classification because of concerns about rampant attrition and pensions for malingerers.[56] Efforts to increase social pressure on combatants to avoid seeking psychiatric care included the intentional weaponization of stigma with labels of cowardice, followed by intensifying the use of proven strategies to deal with weakness, as well as full implementation of frontline psychiatry doctrine. By the time the U.S. military entered WWI in 1918, it was prepared to manage its mental health dilemma by adopting the European frontline psychiatry doctrine.[57] Justification for the new NYDN classification scheme is apparent in the U.S. Army's summary of its lessons learned:

> Soldiers in World War I who were called "shell shocked" indeed acted as though they had sustained a shock to the central nervous system and the diagnosis of "war neurosis" conveyed chronic or severe mental illnesses. This problem was remedied when medical personnel were instructed to tag such casualties as NYD (nervous) which gave soldiers nothing definite to cling to and no suggestion had been made to help them in formulating their disorder into something that was generally recognized as incapacitating and requiring hospital treatment, thus honorably releasing them from combat duty.[58]

Naturally, stigma associated with war-stress injuries greatly intensified and has served as an invaluable tool in managing the military's mental health dilemma, as we discuss later.

When WWI began, the mental health fields of psychiatry (1808) and psychology (1879) were still in their infancy and desperate for external validation in academic and medical circles. Epidemic numbers of psychiatric casualties, as well as negative publicity regarding psychiatric attrition and pension costs for returning shell shocked veterans, created the perfect storm that forced frantic military leaders to solicit the services of so-called mental health specialists that many regarded as frauds.[59] Ambiguity toward mental health in both military and civilian sectors was widespread, as articulated by British Secretary of Navy and future Prime Minister Winston Churchill (1942): "I am sure it would be sensible to restrict as much as possible the work of these gentlemen, who are capable of doing an immense amount of harm with what may very easily degenerate into charlatanry."[60] The military's distrust and antipathy toward psychiatry was clearly demonstrated when WWI ended. Most warring powers, including the United States, expeditiously purged its mental health programs and specialists from the military.[61] Begrudgingly, the same warring powers were compelled to reconstitute their mental health services to deal with WWII evacuation syndromes.

THE AMERICAN EXPERIENCE OF MENTAL HEALTHCARE IN WWI

Some 4.7 million Americans fought in WWI. Of these, 53,402 were killed in action (KIA) and 204,002 were medically wounded in action (WIA) (Congressional Research Services, 2010).[62] A total of 70,158 draftees were psychiatrically screened and rejected for service to prevent war-stress casualties—the first mass use of psychological testing.[63]

Documentation of the American Army's WWI experience is excellent, whereas data on Navy/Marine Corps and the Veterans Administration (VA) is meager. Despite only six months of exposure to WWI combat, 106,000 American soldiers were hospitalized as neuropsychiatric casualties.[64] In all, seventy-two thousand soldiers were discharged from the military for neuropsychiatric conditions, with forty thousand claiming disability,[65] but only 2.8 percent allegedly determined to be caused by combat.[66] An additional 8,640 cases of "nervous and mental diseases" were diagnosed by the U.S. Army but not discharged. In 1918 alone, 24.4 percent of deployed soldiers and sailors were evacuated to the United States for "nervous or mental disorders," and more than twenty thousand were psychiatrically discharged.

Before entering WWI, the U.S. Army adapted the European model of developing a continuum of psychiatric services in the war zone aimed

primarily to prevent manpower attrition.[67] This so-called forward psychiatry, provided brief respites to acute stress casualties coupled with a clear
expectation of eventual return to their frontline units.[68] Consequently, about
65 percent of acute war-stress casualties were returned to the war, which
was heralded as a major success.[69] According to the Institute of Medicine
(IOM), "by WWI, experts had estimated that "the insanity rate of men in the
Army increases nearly 300 percent in time of war.""[70] In 1918, a specialized
treatment center for war neuroses was established at the army hospital in
Plattsburg, New York, to meet the growing demand, and those deemed
"incurable," or who exceeded family capacity to care, were institutionalized at St. Elizabeth's Home in Washington, DC. During 1918 alone, twenty
thousand veterans resided in nine federally funded homes for disabled
soldiers, with another twelve thousand in state-run homes.[71]

Media reports indicated that the size of the crisis continued to expand
well after the 1919 WWI armistice. At the same time, the mental health
system appeared to be inundated. For instance, in a September 14, 1919, *New
York Times* article, "War's Big Lesson in Mental and Nervous Diseases," the
U.S. Army Chief of Section of Neurology and Psychiatry, Surgeon General's
Office warned public health officials that "Up to May 1, 1919, the army
returned to the civil community approximately 72,000 of these . . . nervously
handicapped men . . ." and that

> it would seem that that great lesson of the war as far as neurology and
> psychiatry is concerned, is that our communities contain definite fixed
> quotas of crippling and multiplying diseases for the control of which no
> adequate provision exists, and that the sufferers from these conditions are
> handicapped in their relations to society, and that many of them burden
> and injure it. We have now a unique opportunity to change our attitude and
> improve our policies in these matters.

In 1921, the *New York Times* reported "400 Ex-Soldiers New York
Suicides"[72] indicating a crisis in one city alone—the headline continues that
"Dr. Salmon So Charges in Testimony, Lack of Care of Mentally Disabled
Veterans," and a year later "Veterans' Suicide Average Two a Day," followed
by a 1923 headline "26,000 Veterans Now in Hospital: Alarming Increase
Is Reported in Neuro-Psychiatric and Tuberculosis Cases."[73] By 1927,
47 percent of all veterans treated by the U.S. Veteran's Bureau were diagnosed
with neuropsychiatric conditions.[74]

Subsequent news headlines revealed a greatly incapacitated mental health system: "Colonel Paul V. McNutt, National Commander of the American Legion: Declared that the Needs of Disabled Veterans were Becoming an Increasingly Difficult Problem because of the Failure of Congress to Provide Adequate Funding"; followed by "Insane War Veterans Reported Increasing: Legions Rehabilitation Body Told Number Exceeds Hospital Facilities"[75]; and "Veteran's Claims Cut by 57 Percent: Reviewing Boards Disallow 29,995 of 51,213 Disability Cases Nervous Diseases Found More Frequent in Cities."[76] According to subsequent reports, by 1944, almost half of the sixty-seven thousand inpatient beds in VA hospitals were occupied by WWI war-stress casualties.

Presidential and congressional concerns of possible mental health deficiencies can be inferred by headlines, including "Bonus First or Disabled? By Henry L. Stimson Chairman Joint Committee for Aid to Veterans"[77] and "Says Veterans Lack Psychiatric Relief: McNutt Declares Disabled Men Are In Jails, As Hospitals Are Not Available."[78] Government interventions to address systemic deficiencies include the 1917 War Risk Insurance Act; Vocational Rehabilitation Law of 1918; and the World War Adjustment Act in 1924. In 1921, Public Law 67–47 consolidated three veteran's related agencies into the "Veteran's Bureau," with 140 new regional centers to meet veteran's wartime needs, and in 1930, the VA was created to further consolidate government support for veterans.[79]

Swank and Marchand's classic study[80] of WWI infantry soldiers revealed that "within 60 consecutive days of combat," 98 percent of soldiers "become psychiatric casualties of some kind, whether of combat exhaustion, acute anxiety state or depression" and the other 2 percent had "predisposition to an "aggressive psychopathic personality."[81] The following statements provide additional evidence of a mental health system unprepared to effectively manage war-stress casualties:

> The next most important lesson is that of preparing, in advance of an urgent need, a comprehensive plan for establishing special military hospitals and using existing civil facilities for treating mental disease in a manner that will serve the army effectively and at the same time safeguard the interests of the soldiers, of the government and of the community.[82]

Although the total number of American troops in France in January, 1918, was only approximately 203,000, the caring for mental patients had already become a problem. It was obvious at the outset that such patients could not be cared for in the individual American base hospitals scattered throughout France, partly because of the lack in some of them of medical officers, nurses, or enlisted personnel who had had experience in the actual care and treatment of patients suffering from acute mental disorders, but chiefly because of the absence of any special facilities for treatment[83]

Notably, "American involvement in WWI produced a total of 69,000 disabled neuropsychiatry causalities costing the government over $1 billion in disability pensions, so selection standards were raised."[84]

TOLERATING PSYCHIATRY IN WWI TO REDUCE ATTRITION AND PENSIONS

In 1915, the British Army commissioned famed psychologist Lieutenant Colonel Charles M. Myers who coined the controversial term shell shock,[85] while observing the French Army's medical use of frontline psychiatric interventions to achieve a 91 percent RTD.[86] Myers studied British hospital disposition records and noted the correlation of lower RTD rates the greater the distance soldiers were evacuated from the front.[87] He went on to improve upon the French system by developing an echelon of respite and restorative treatment deploying mental health professionals to the war zone to prevent attrition.[88]

PROVING THE VALUE AND BENEFIT OF PSYCHIATRY TO THE MILITARY

British frontline psychiatry programs initially reported promising results with more than 31 percent of war-stress casualties RTD that eventually improved to 90 percent RTD.[89] The remaining cadre of war-stress casualties was assigned to neuropsychiatric rehabilitation centers at or near the war zone, implementing the new military policy of prohibiting psychiatric evacuation, discharge, and pensioning except in the most extreme cases of obvious, chronic, and profound decompensation.[90] In 1917, the American Expeditionary Forces sent army psychiatrist Major Thomas Salmon to observe British efforts to manage the psychiatric problem in preparation for the U.S. entry into the war in 1918. Salmon adopted the European system of echelon of restorative care.[91] He was the first to introduce a number of other innovations, including the frontline policy of avoiding psychiatric labeling (e.g., shell shock), evacuation, and discharge; as well as mandating simple, immediate treatment at the frontlines with clear expectation of RTD. K L. Artiss later coined the acronym PIE (proximity, at or near the frontlines; immediacy, as soon as possible after developing a combat stress reaction (CSR); expectancy, expected RTD after brief respite versus evacuation) to formalize military doctrine.[92] Throughout WWI, the U.S. military reported RTD rates of 65–90 percent as a result of its frontline psychiatry doctrine, thus demonstrating how mental health disciplines could benefit the military mission.[93]

INITIAL MISTRUST OF FRONTLINE PSYCHIATRY AND MENTAL HEALTH SERVICES

Jones et al., however, reexamined historical records at the Convalescent NYDN Depot, which admitted 66,800 British soldiers between August 1917 and January 1919 and reported very few war-stress casualties actually returned to their fighting units in contradiction to the military's past claims. Furthermore, after reanalyzing medical records from the PIE unit at 4 Stationary Hospital, only 606 British soldiers (19. 6 percent) were RTD with a significant number believed to have relapsed. The authors concluded that a 19.6 percent combatant RTD was considerably lower than previously claimed by the military.[94] British Army leaders began to doubt the validity of frontline psychiatry claims, prompting an internal investigation by the army's chief neurology consultant Gordon Holmes who played a pivotal role in establishing frontline psychiatry.[95] After auditing three frontline psychiatry centers in 1917, Holmes reported an 80 percent RTD rate within three weeks in contrast to 30–40 percent at base hospitals in France, and only 4–5 percent RTD in UK hospitals.

These findings appeared to reaffirm frontline psychiatry's value to the military in preserving the fighting force. In addition, Holmes reported only 10 percent of soldiers RTD subsequently relapsed for shell shock, but then he proceeded to close several PIE units.[96] Nevertheless, an empirical foundation was built during WWI establishing the efficacy of frontline psychiatry doctrine as an invaluable tool for the military to end evacuation syndromes.

The status quo has been aptly summarized by the Department of Navy and U.S. Marine Corps:

Prior to 1916, stress casualties, such as "shell shock," were believed to be true medical injuries caused by physical disruption in the brain as a result of nearby artillery blasts. They were treated like any other physical injury, without the burdens of social stigma or personal blame, and many were evacuated from theater on both sides of the war.[97]

However,

After 1916, the medical model of combat stress was replaced by the idea of shell shock. Shell shock was considered a temporary and reversible response to stress that would always resolve with no more than a little rest and encouragement. It was then believed to be caused not by literal damage to the brain, but by a weakness of character brought out by the dangers and hardships of war.[98]

PSYCHIATRY'S SHORT-LIVED VICTORY

During the so-called interwar period between WWI and WWII, the demonstrated successes of WWI frontline psychiatry programs in terms of RTD and preventing psychiatric attrition was either ignored or intentionally disregarded following military and government investigations into the economic and political fallout from the military's massive psychiatric problem. As noted earlier, seventy-two thousand U.S. soldiers were discharged for neuropsychiatric conditions with forty thousand claiming disability[99] after just three months of exposure to modern warfare. Conclusions by investigative commissions almost universally blamed preexisting individual weaknesses and the corrosive influence of psychiatry (i.e., psychiatric diagnosing, disability pensions), as well as inadequate military training, leadership, and unit morale.[100] The potential contributory role of the military's frontline psychiatric policies in regards to postwar prevalence of psychiatric disability and pensions was never entertained.

Consequently, European and American militaries disbanded their mental health services, including all frontline psychiatry programs and personnel, and embarked instead on unprecedented, comprehensive psychiatric screening programs. The intent was to prevent predisposed war hysterics from infiltrating the armed forces in that "prominent civil and military medical authorities pointed out that World War I had demonstrated the necessity and feasibility of psychiatric screening in eliminating overt and covert mental disorders prior to entry in the military service."[101] From the military's perspective, the only real value of mental health specialists was to prevent their future clientele from contaminating the military. Rigorous military discipline, training, unit cohesion, and leadership would take care of the rest.[102]

WWII AND RELEARNING THE REALITIES OF MODERN WAR

In all, from 1942 to 1945, despite rejecting more than 1,680,000 psychiatrically predisposed or even remotely defective inductees, rates 7.6 times higher than WWI,[103] psychiatric discharges during WWII were significantly higher. There were more than 1,103,000 U.S. Army and 150,000 U.S. Navy/Marine Corps psychiatric hospital admissions, resulting in 504,000 (72 percent) Army and 100,000 (67 percent) Navy/Marine Corps personnel being psychiatrically discharged.[104] In September 1943 alone, more soldiers were discharged from the army (112,500) than accessed (118,600) with the majority for psychiatric reasons, which raised considerable alarm among war planners[105] and prompting Chief of Staff General George C. Marshall to abandon the extensive predisposition screening policy in 1943 because it could cost them the war.[106] Thus, the military rediscovered the truth about the universal vulnerability of individuals exposed to the toxic effects of modern warfare.

As for frontline psychiatry, during the 1942 North Africa Tunisian Campaign, 20–34 percent of all nonfatal U.S. battle casualties were psychiatric in nature and 97 percent of these cases were evacuated out of the war zone.[107] During the 1942 Guadalcanal invasion, 40 percent of the First Division Marine evacuees were psychiatric casualties.[108] In March 1943, U.S. Army Captain Frederick Hanson utilizing "brief periods of sedation and rest along with the techniques of suggestion and ventilation, demonstrated that 30 percent of acute psychiatric casualties could be returned-to-duty (RTD) within 30 hours from a forward treatment area." Later that year, Hanson reported that 70 percent of 494 neuropsychiatric casualties were RTD after forty-eight hours. As a result, in April 1943, General Omar Bradley issued a directive establishing a holding period of seven days for psychiatric patients at evacuation hospitals, disavowing psychiatric labeling, and advocating use of the term "exhaustion" for all combat psychiatric cases.[109]

In June 1943, U.S. Army issued *Circular Letter No. 17, Neuropsychiatric Treatment in the Combat Zone*, stating the following:

> The problem of neuropsychiatric disabilities under modern battle conditions has been a serious one. Approximately 20 percent of all nonfatal casualties are psychiatric in origin. Trial under actual field conditions in the Tunisian campaign has shown that 60 percent of the total neuropsychiatric casualties can be returned to effective combat duty within 3 or 4 days if they are treated within the combat zone.[110]

Overall, throughout WWII, reports were common of 80 to 90 percent stress casualties RTD to war zones. Thus, the U.S. military relearned the benefits of frontline psychiatry in furthering its mission to conserve the force.

A total of 16,112,566 Americans, or nearly 9 percent of the population, served during the five years of WWII—approximately four million served in combat zones with 405,399 KIA and another 670,846 medically WIA.[111] Mass pre-war psychiatric screenings was utilized to reject a total of 1,767,900 purportedly predisposed, constitutionally weak, and defective volunteer candidates vulnerable to nervous breakdown within eleven years of combat.[112]

At the outset of the American's 1941 entrance into WWII, the war-stress injury rate was 20–34 percent of total casualties with only 3 percent RTD. Of the 1,103,000 army admissions, 648,500 were diagnosed with "psychoneurosis" (akin to anxiety, depression, and PTSD constructs), 67,642 with "psychosis," 43,339 with "alcoholism or drug addiction," 66,455 with "immaturity reaction" (akin to adjustment disorder, but includes 250 diagnoses of "pathological personality"), 2,715 as "asocial and antisocial personality types" (akin to personality disorder), 28,871 as "disorders of intelligence," 5,455 with "pathological sexuality," and 64,638 diagnosed as "other psychiatric disorders."[113] In addition, there were 156,345 diagnoses of "other neurological disorder" (including 8,565 diagnoses for "blast concussion" or "posttraumatic encephalopathy" akin to TBI), and 18,077 diagnoses of "epilepsy" (some possibly MUPS), along with 1,864 diagnoses of "paralysis, other, and unspecified," 5,201 diagnoses of "neuralgia," and 20,268 diagnoses of "miscellaneous disorders of the nervous system" akin to possible MUPS.[114]

In total, 504,000 Army and 100,000 Navy/Marine Corps were given psychiatric discharges and awarded disability pensions,[115] as the *New York Times* reported in "500,000 Discharged As Psychiatric Cases."[116] A 1952 follow-up study with 1,475 WWII vets reported high rates of somatic complaints, including insomnia (31.9 percent), headache (42.8 percent), irritability (48.6 percent), concentration (20.1 percent), restlessness (45.4 percent), gastrointestinal (41.7 percent), cardiovascular (21.9 percent), and musculoskeletal (34.8 percent) issues.[117] Suicide rates of WWII veterans is unknown at this time. A 2010 news article, however, reports that "Suicide Rates Soar Among WWII Vets, Records Show: Older Veterans Twice as Likely to Take Their Own Lives as Those Returning from Iraq and Afghanistan."[118]

The 1944 *Washington Post* article, "U.S. Owes Veterans Better Psychiatric Aide," summarizes a three-day U.S. Senate subcommittee hearing on Wartime Health and Education, stating, "they showed by their testimony that conditions of modern war confronted the country with a serious problem in the treatment, training, and re-adaptation of many victims of wartime mental and emotional disturbances."[119] One year later, a 1945 *Washington Post* article headline cautioned, "Thousands of GIs temporarily disabled during the war now stand to become permanently crippled during the peace . . . Is the problem so urgent? It is," and reported that "there are more than half a million World War II veterans currently drawing pensions for disabilities."[120] The 1945 article refers to national concerns over acute shortages of psychiatric personnel, high veteran unemployment rates, the VA's delay in expanding neuropsychiatric services, the negative impact of persistent mental health stigma, and greatly unprepared communities to assist returning veterans and their families, which all have contributed to a military mental health crisis.[121] Furthermore, media reports like "Communities Held Failing Veterans: Social Service Experts Find a Lack of Help in Solving Readjustment Problems"[122]; "Plan Urged to Get New Psychiatrists: $100,000,000 for Training to Meet War Veteran Needs"[123]; and "Veterans Seeking Psychiatric Help: But Most Must Wait Months Even for Screening Tests Survey in City Shows"[124] signify significant unmet wartime needs.

According to VA historians, "Many of the returning veterans needed treatment of medical and psychological problems resulting from their war experience. Veterans with psychiatric disorders occupied 58 percent of VA hospital beds at the end of 1946."[125] As Baker and Pickren observed, however, "the shortage of trained mental health workers in the VA" caused newly developed "mental hygiene clinics" to be "immediately overwhelmed with service demands far beyond the capacity of their personnel and space to provide such services," leading the authors to conclude "it was clear that no matter how the various service components were arranged, there were simply not enough personnel to meet the demands."[126]

Early presidential concerns over the plight of WWII-era mental health-care is clearly reflected by President Roosevelt's 1944 Executive Order to his Secretary of War (akin to DoD), that "it should be the responsibility of the military authorities to insure that no overseas casualty is discharged from the armed forces until he has received the maximum benefits of hospitalization and convalescent facilities which must include physical and psychological rehabilitation, vocational guidance, prevocational training, and resocialization."[127] Congress became extensively involved in address-ing broad systemic and societal deficiencies in meeting wartime demand, noted in such news headlines as "The Veteran: House Veterans Committee Deflects Inquiry on Medical Care of Soldiers"[128] and "Psychiatrists Ask Rise in VA Funds: Deterioration of Services to Veterans Is Alternative, Congress Is Warned."[129] This involvement was furthered with the passage of landmark legislation like (1) the Servicemen's Readjustment Act of 1944 (the GI Bill); (2) the National Neuropsychiatric Institute Act of 1945, which sought to eliminate the disparity between mental and physical health with the creation of the National Institute of Mental Health; and (3) Public Law 79-293, To Establish a Department of Medicine and Surgery, 1946, which ultimately led to the creation of the VA's Neuropsychiatry Division in 1948, along with mass employment and training of clinical and counseling psychologists to address national shortages.[130]

Documentation of war trauma lessons is extensive and clearly indicates significant incapacity to adequately meet wartime mental health needs because of the failure to learn from previous generations of psychiatric lessons. For example, according to Albert Glass, the army's chief neuropsy-chiatry consultant, "Undoubtedly, the most important lesson learned by psychiatry in World War II was the failure of responsible military author-ities, during mobilization and early phases of hostilities, to appreciate the inevitability of large-scale psychiatric disorders under conditions of modern warfare."[131] As N. Q. Brill has noted, "From the beginning, there was a short-age of trained psychiatrists, neurologists, psychiatric nurses, attendants, aides, social workers, psychologists, occupational therapists, and recreational therapists."[132] As for the VA,

Similarly, the number of psychiatrists in the VA after World War II was simply too small to deal with the increased needs for treatment . . . It was this shortage of mental health professionals that prompted both the VA and the National Institute of Mental Health (NIMH) to generously fund training more a massive expansion of the mental health field after World War II.[133]

PARADIGM SHIFT TOWARD UNIVERSAL VULNERABILITY AND NORMALIZING TRANSIENT BREAKDOWN

The hard realities on the ground compelled military leaders to reconcile their faulty etiologic paradigm of hysteria and omnipotent power afforded to military discipline, training, and leadership to prevent psychiatric breakdown. In November 1943, Chief of the Army General Marshall ended the social experiment to screen out predisposed weakness and reintroduced mental health specialists and frontline psychiatry into the rank and file.[134] In addition, military researchers reaffirmed a dosage effect from combat exposure wherein seasoned veterans were breaking down, on average, after eighty to ninety combat days. This prompted U.S. Army psychiatrists to observe that "one of our cultural myths has been that only weaklings break down psychologically [and that] strong men with the will to do so can keep going indefinitely."

The military's 1943 paradigm of exhaustion was explicitly intended to replace the psychiatric diagnosis of psychoneuroses and marked a partial reversal of the 1916 paradigm of war hysteria, which had attributed psychiatric breakdown primarily to individual predisposed weakness, cowardice, greed, or faulty leadership. Consequently, a middle-of-the-road view was created that normalized acute, transient psychiatric breakdown but maintained the stigmatizing paradigm of hysteria for chronic conditions. In October 1945, the U.S. Army introduced the new diagnosis "transient personality reactions," which included combat exhaustion and acute situational maladjustments from noncombat stressors.[135] The APA renamed this diagnosis "gross stress reaction" in its *Diagnostic and Statistical Manual of Mental Disorders* (DSM).[136] The revised traumatic stress paradigm gave credence to a universal adaptation to extreme stress (i.e., war, natural disasters) wherein anyone's coping capacity could be exceeded, and temporary emotional breakdown would occur. Inherent predispositions, personality disorder, or malingering were not invoked in this formulation unless symptoms became chronic and resistant to treatment. Subsequent terms like combat exhaustion, battle fatigue, combat fatigue, fliers' fatigue, operational fatigue, combat stress reactions, and combat operational stress reactions represent a continuation of the WWII paradigm.

In short, just as the 1916 paradigm shift to hysteria suited the military's narrative in WWI to stigmatize psychiatric breakdown and end evacuation syndromes, the revised WWII paradigm of universal transient gross stress reaction justified the military's frontline psychiatry doctrine to conserve the fighting force. In so doing, it also limited disability pensions by attributing chronic war-stress injury to preexisting weakness, personality disorder, or malingering, all of which exacerbated stigma and barriers to seeking care.

CONTINUING EVOLUTION OF FRONTLINE PSYCHIATRY IN THE TWENTIETH CENTURY

The U.S. Army's *Textbook of Military Medicine: War Psychiatry* cites the Korean War (1950–1955) as further validation of the frontline psychiatry doctrine.[137] The abruptness of the Korean War caught U.S. military medical planners off guard, and no psychiatrists or consultation services were readily available. Consequently, nearly 90 percent or more of psychiatric casualties were evacuated out of the war zone, about twenty per week from June to October 1950.[138] By October 1950, a three-echelon frontline treatment system was developed under Mental Hygiene Consultation Services utilizing PIE principles that resulted in 50–70 percent RTD.[139] By the war's end, "Most reports describe a return to duty rate of 60 to 90 percent. Significantly, there were few 'repeaters' among those diagnosed with combat stress, treated, and returned to duty. Reports from 1951 to 1952 state that 5 to 10 percent were 'neuropsychiatric repeaters'."[140] In regards to possible benefits to individual service members, military authors cite that before reconstituting frontline psychiatry in October 1950, only 50 percent of evacuated psychiatric casualties maintained their military careers and were RTD in noncombat roles.[141] Again, similar to the world wars, no military studies were conducted comparing clinical outcomes of military personnel RTD with outcomes of those evacuated and treated for war-stress injury.

KOREAN WAR

Some 6.8 million American men and women served during the Korean War, 33,739 were KIA, and 103,284 were medically WIA.[142] An estimated

848,000 Korean War veterans also served in other war periods: 171,000 in both WWII and Vietnam, 404,000 only in WWII, and 273,000 only in Vietnam.[143]

Distinct from previous modern American wars, evidence of a mental health crisis in the Korean War–era is modest at this time—perhaps an artifact of the relative paucity of neuropsychiatric documentation during this war or an accurate reflection of the times. The army's war-stress casualty statistics are reported only as ratios of annual incident number per one thousand per average troop strength, or as percentages, which varied significantly throughout the war. For instance, as Glass reports, "Admissions for psychiatric disorders during July 1950 occurred at a rate of 209/1,000/year the highest in the Korean War to which was associated the highest KIA rate (769.04), the second highest WIA rate (950.97)"[144] and relates that in October of that same year, "the psychiatric admission rate for October of 34.21/1,000/year."[145] According to the army's official medical postwar analysis, there were a total of 13,515 army hospital admissions for unspecified "psychiatric disorders," along with 1,688 disability discharges credited to "impairment and disease of nervous system," including 322 for "encephalopathy due to trauma" (akin to TBI) and 91 for "neuralgia" (akin to chronic pain)—notably, neuropsychiatric discharges were either omitted or did not occur.[146] Overall, the diagnosis of "symptoms and ill-defined conditions" (possibly akin to MUPS) was the second-leading cause of all army hospital admissions, with rates of forty-five per one thousand (division personnel) and forty per one thousand (nondivision personnel) recorded, whereas "psychiatric disorders" were the fourth-leading cause for all hospital admissions with rates of thirty-six per one thousand (division personnel) and twenty-five per one thousand (nondivision personnel) reported. A total of 38,481 army personnel received outpatient neuropsychiatry treatment in Korea.[147]

In short, unlike WWI and WWII counterparts, the Korean War cohort began the trend of avoiding detailed reporting of war-stress casualties, especially absolute or total numbers of neuropsychiatric admissions, discharges, or disability pensions. Medical postwar analysis reveals that psychiatric conditions represented more than 9 percent of disease admissions for division troops, producing an overall estimated rate of thirty-six per one thousand average strength per year, compared with 5 percent for nondivision troops or twenty-five per one thousand per year.[148] There was a total of 13,585 reported psychiatric hospital admissions (unspecified by type) along with

1,781 admissions for "concussion" (akin to TBI).[149] A total of 131 suicides and 101 homicides among U.S. Army personnel in Korea was reported during 1950–1953, resulting in a suicide rate among active-duty Korean War soldiers of eleven per one hundred thousand.[150]

References to high incidence of substance abuse, depression, and misconduct stress behaviors are made by Jones, "To an extent the situation resembled that of the nostalgic soldiers of prior centuries. In these circumstances the soldier sought relief in alcohol abuse (and, in coastal areas, in drug abuse) and sexual stimulation. These often resulted in disciplinary infractions." For example, U.S. Army psychiatrists observed that as incident rates of frost bite arose, the number of psychiatric casualties decreased — raising suspicions of self-infliction.[151] Fontana and Rosenheck examined 5,138 war-zone veterans seeking VA treatment (320 WWII, 199 Korean, and 4,619 Vietnam vets) and reported data from both veterans and their clinicians indicating a significant positive relationship between traumatic war experiences and current psychiatric symptoms across all three wars. In particular, killing was related significantly to all symptom categories in all cohorts, suggesting that responsibility for killing another human being is the single most pervasive, traumatic experience of war, with the role of observer and failure as well as exposure to combat in general following closely.[152] In 1956, a total of fourteen thousand veterans received VA group psychotherapy services and six thousand received individual counseling.[153]

As but five years had elapsed, WWII war trauma lessons were still known, and the principle of forward psychiatry (promptly returning soldiers with acute stress injuries to their frontline units after brief respite) was soon implemented Colonel Glass, who literally wrote the book on WWII lessons learned.[154] Nevertheless, Korean War–era media headlines suggest the possible inability to meet these social reintegration needs: "640,000 in WWII: Army All Out in Study of Psycho Cases,"[155] "Korean Veterans Seek Homes,"[156] "Rise in Neurotic Seamen Called Challenge to Merchant Marine,"[157] "Korean Veterans Due for Benefits: 200,000 Expected to Collect Unemployment Aide,"[158] and "Psychiatry Panel Scores VA Policy: Physicians at Parlay Say Incentives Are Lacking for Hospital Staff."[159] Moreover, according to VA historians, "Suicide of veterans became of great concern to the VA during the 1950s when the rate of suicide among veterans both within the VA hospital system and outside it, already higher than in the non-veteran populations, suddenly increased alarmingly over the pre-WWII rates."[160] The post–Korean War suicide trend sparked the VA's first research program into veteran's suicide—finding, among other factors, a link between suicide and the psychotropic medications thorazine and rauwolfia.[161]

The extent of presidential and congressional actions to address wartime mental health deficiencies during the Korean War era pales in comparison to WWI and WWII. A number of notable mental health–related government interventions did occur, however, including the creation of (1) the 1956 Bradley Commission: The President's Commission on Veteran's Pensions; (2) the Department of Veteran's Benefits, which was established in 1953 within the VA to coordinate veteran's education, training, and disability benefits; (3) the Psychiatric Evaluation Program, which was created in 1955 to study effective treatment of patients with psychiatric disorders; and (4) To Consolidate Into One Act All of the Laws Administered by the Veterans' Administration, and for Other Purposes, Public Law 85–857, September 2, 1958, which added research to the VA's Department of Medicine and Surgery mission.

Although not nearly as extensive as WWI and WWII documentation, some indication of the strained capacity to meet mental health demands has been substantiated by the Uniformed Services University of the Health Sciences:

> During the initial months of the Korean War, psychiatric facilities in Japan inappropriately evacuated many psychiatric cases to the ZI (Zone of Interior) because "Limited Service" of World War II had been abolished in 1947. Also, the neuropsychiatry (NP) staff during this early period were meager and lacked sophistication in combat psychiatry.[162]

In addition,

> In sharp contrast to the prompt application of psychiatry at the division level, psychiatric efforts at the Army level were meager and ineffective. It was evident that a need to support division psychiatry by a second echelon of psychiatry at the Army level was not recognized although such a need was first demonstrated in World War I and in World War II. This lack of recognition was unfortunate since two qualified psychiatrists were available in Eighth Army to provide the professional nucleus for a second echelon Army level psychiatric facility.[163]

And, notably, as reported in a 1951 *Report to Surgeon General U.S Army on Tour of Medical Installations of Far East Command*,

> nearly all of the psychiatrists sent to Korea were quite junior. Some consultants stress the young psychiatrist's lack of training:' The suggestion was made by several medical officers that it would have been more useful to them to have had more indoctrination into the principles of combat psychiatry and to have learned more about the treatment and disposition of such patients.[164]

THE VIETNAM WAR

More than 8.5 million individuals served in the U.S. Armed Forces during the Vietnam era, 1964–1973, with about 3.14 million serving in Southeast Asia.[165] Of the latter number, almost one million saw active combat or were exposed to hostile, life-threatening situations. Some 47,410 American military personnel were KIA and 153,303 were medically WIA.[166]

The history of frontline psychiatry has been well documented for the war in Vietnam.[167] Of particular import, military medical leaders credited frontline psychiatry as being responsible for historically low rates of war-stress casualties identified in the war zone with more than 90 percent RTD and a meager 2–5 percent of total evacuated casualties identified as neuropsychiatric.[168] Findings from a congressionally mandated study, however, reported that millions of Vietnam veterans did experience PTSD, including 30 percent of combat veterans.[169] These findings were in stark contradiction to the military's narrative of psychiatric victory over war-stress injury in news media stories of veterans experiencing depression, substance abuse, traumatic grief, moral pain, medically unexplained physical conditions, interpersonal violence, incarceration, homelessness, and suicide.[170] Consequently, accusations of widespread malingering and politically motivated antiwar therapists[171] were countered by claims of military and governmental betrayal and efforts to avoid pension costs,[172] thus recycling the generational trauma-pension debates born out of WWI.

Recently, however, the U.S. military has amended its historical interpretation of the lessons of Vietnam in regard to the controversy over psychiatric casualties reported in the war zone versus on the home front. For instance,

Camp notes that "the incidence of soldiers hospitalized or excused from duty status—ranged between 12 per 1,000 per year and 16.5 per 1,000 per year. Although this record appears very favorable compared to rates for the Korean War (73/1,000/year) and World War II (28–101/1,000/year), it is misleading."[173] The author elaborates: "Not only does this rate address only one measure of soldier psychological and behavioral dysfunction, but in averaging 8 years of experience it also minimizes the fourfold increase in the last few years of the war and disguises the problems that ultimately emerged."[174] In addition, some Vietnam-era army psychiatrists openly questioned whether frontline psychiatry doctrine bore some responsibility for the vast numbers of delayed presentation.[175] Needless to say, no military research has been conducted that compared outcomes for frontline psychiatry RTD with psychiatric evacuations and treatment.

Official army medical postwar analysis has singled out neuropsychiatric conditions as a "major problem."[176] Following the Korean War trend, however, the depth of Vietnam-era documentation of war-stress casualties has been progressively thinner compared with WWI and WWII—staying clear from reporting absolute numbers unlike the detailed records for medically WIA. Although extensive reviews of war-stress casualties during the Vietnam era have been conducted, revealing several noteworthy themes,[177] records containing absolute numbers of war-stress casualties in the Vietnam era are sparse, as commented on by previous researchers.[178] A rare 1988 study on marines, reported 8,828 psychiatric admissions in Vietnam from 1965 to 1971, with a war-stress casualty rate of 35.3 per 1,000 per years, exceeding KIA rates.[179] "Personality disorder" was reported as the most frequent psychiatric diagnosis, followed by "anxiety neuroses," and "acute situational maladjustment,"[180] but no specific data have been furnished.

As previously stated, the absence of centralized, transparent, and accurate reporting of military mental health demand not only prohibits organizational leaders to properly plan and react to meeting wartime needs but also aggravates the perceived and actual crisis. This assertion is best exemplified by the impassioned controversy surrounding the Vietnam era, wherein military and academic postwar analyses routinely report that "the incidence of neuropsychiatric illness in U.S. Army troops in Vietnam is lower than any recorded in previous conflicts,"[181]—frequently citing that only 2–5 percent of total casualties were neuropsychiatric in nature.[182] These analyses are in dramatic discordance with a postwar psychiatric landscape of an estimated 250,000[183] to 2 million[184] Vietnam veterans suffering from PTSD, and an additional 9,000 to 150,000[185] reported suicides. Consequently, there has been no shortage of speculation as to the reasons for such wildly discrepant claims, granting fertile ground to select data to confirm a wide-range of biases.

A related theme in the literature pertains to the relatively low (2–5 percent) rates of classic ("combat exhaustion" or "combat fatigue") war-stress casualties attributed to a twelve-month rotation policy intended to reduce war-stress exposure.[186] This rate stands in stark contrast to the exceedingly high incidence of "character and behavior disorders," which includes diagnoses such as personality disorder, substance abuse, and "indiscipline" (akin to misconduct stress behaviors) as well as to a similar temporal rise in the "psychosis" diagnosis. For example, army neuropsychiatric diagnostic rates in Vietnam gradually increased each successive year from 1965 to 1970. For example, the diagnosis of "psychosis" increased from 1.6 (1965) to 3.8 (1970) per 1,000; "psychoneurosis" from 2.3 (1965) to 3.3 (1970) per 1,000; "character and behavior disorders" (akin to personality disorder) from 3.1 (1965) to 8.1 (1970) per 1,000; and "other psychiatric conditions" from 3.8 (1965) to 8.5 (1970).[187]

SUBSTANCE ABUSE

In regard to drug abuse, Army Surgeon General Neel has reported the following:

> One of the unique problems that faced the Medical Department in Vietnam was the drug milieu into which the American soldier was immersed, both on and off duty, upon arrival in the theater. The growth of illicit drug use within the Army kept pace with that in the larger society, but the ready availability of marijuana, barbiturates, amphetamines, heroin, opium, and other substances in Vietnam.[188]

The surgeon general continued: "Comprehensive statistics are not available, but preliminary work based upon sample surveys of soldiers entering and leaving the combat zone indicates that illegal drug use is widespread."[189] For instance, results from an anonymous questionnaire given to soldiers departing Vietnam in 1967, indicated 29 percent reported using marijuana.[190] Stanton declared that from 1967 to 1971, the proportion of enlisted soldiers smoking marijuana "heavily" (twenty or more times) in Vietnam increased from 7 percent to 34 percent, while the proportion of "habitual" users (more than two hundred times) stabilized at 17 percent to 18 percent between 1969 and 1971.[191] Baker reported seventy-five opiate deaths in Vietnam within a three-month span in 1970,[192] and by October 1971, an estimated "44 percent of all lower ranking enlisted men (E-1 to E-4) were using heroin and half of these may have been addicted . . . By 1971 more soldiers were being evacuated from Vietnam for drug use than for war wounds."[193]

Another common theme in this era was the nontraditional inverse casualty trend whereby psychiatric admissions and evacuations greatly increased toward the end of the war, as WIA and KIA rates substantially decreased,[194] thereby raising suspicion about the legitimacy of referring to these conditions as war-stress casualties.[195] For example, army psychiatric hospital admissions steadily increased from 11.7 per 1,000 (1965), to 13.3 (1968), 15.8 (1969), and 25.1 per 1,000 (1970)[196], and jumped to 129 per 1,000 per year (60 percent of evacuations) by April 1972—the majority of which were for drug dependence.[197] During those same rates, WIA rates decreased from a peak of 120.4 (1968) to 87.6 (1969) to 52.9 (1970).[198]

MISCONDUCT STRESS BEHAVIORS

Another major finding from the Vietnam experience is relearning the lessons of the American Civil War, WWI, WWII, and the Korean War regarding the differential impact of misconduct stress behaviors.[199] Vietnam-era *Army Field Manual 8–5139* termed these behaviors "misconduct combat stress reactions"[200] associated with "low-intensity" warfare and the effects of chronic war-related stress on rear echelon noncombat personnel, also referred to as "nostalgic" or "garrison" casualties (venereal diseases, substance abuse, indiscipline, personality disorders).[201] Indiscipline can range from relatively minor acts of omission or insubordination, such as failure to take preventive hygiene measures in Korea leading to frostbite or chloroquine-primaquine in Vietnam resulting in malaria, to commission of serious acts of disobedience (mutiny), homicide (e.g., "fragging"—killing or injuring by a fragmentation grenade), and even atrocity (My Lai). For instance, of 823 psychiatric casualties from the Third Marine Division from February to October 1967, only 11.8 percent were diagnosed as combat stress reactions, 30 percent were diagnosed as personality disorders, likely to be evacuated.[202] Moreover, Linden reported a progressive increase in the number of courts martial for insubordination and assaults (including murder) during the Vietnam War.[203] For example, after President Nixon announced withdrawal plans on June 9, 1969, fragging increased from 0.3 per 1,000 per year in 1969 to 1.7 per 1,000 per year in 1971.[204]

EVIDENCE OF OTHER WAR-STRESS INJURY

Since WWI, the military has been concerned with chronic stress effects on aviators called "flying fatigue" or "operational fatigue," which is identical to war-stress injuries in nonaviators. According to Neel, "No problem, however, was more common yet more elusive than that of flyer fatigue. It became more pronounced after 1965 when the buildup of U.S. forces gained momentum and remained a significant limiting factor in the conduct of airmobile operations,"[205] yet statistical data are unavailable. Military suicide rates are unknown; however, in 1988, the Centers for Disease Control and Prevention (CDC) confirmed that nine thousand veterans had committed suicide. Regarding functional somatic or MUPS conditions, the military, of course, did not keep track. Diarrheal diseases during the Vietnam War, however, were among the "major problems" identified by army medicine, which is consistent with other war generations, as well as a high incidence of potential functional MUPS (akin to irritable bowel syndrome). For instance, in 1965, the average theater-wide annual rate for this type of disease was 69 per 1,000 per year; in 1969, it was 35 per 1,000 per year (compare this with WWII rates of 55 to 129 cases per year per 1,000 troop strength).[206] To be clear, there are multiple reported causes of diarrheal diseases, and therefore, it would be erroneous to label all such cases as entirely MUPS. Shay eloquently documented case studies of traumatic grief and moral injury in Vietnam combat veterans, but prevalence is unknown. During the Vietnam War, 12–14 percent of all combat casualties had a TBI.[207] Caveness et al. initiated an extensive longitudinal National Institutes of Health Vietnam Head Injury Study (VHIS) in 1974, with 1,221 Vietnam veterans who sustained TBI between 1967 and 1970.[208]

POSTWAR MENTAL HEALTH ANALYSES

In 1972, the VA's annual report to Congress indicated that mental health demands were progressively escalating, remarking that its seventy-three mental hygiene clinics alone provided treatment to more than sixty thousand Vietnam veterans with more than one and a quarter million treatment visits per year.[209] In light of the discordant reports of Vietnam veteran's mental health needs, in 1983, Congress mandated the National Vietnam Veterans Readjustment Study (NVVRS) through Public Law 98–160 to "establish the prevalence and incidence of PTSD and other psychological problems in readjusting to civilian life."[210] In 1988, the NVVRS reported 479,000 male (15.2 percent) and 7,166 female (8.5 percent) veterans currently met the criteria for PTSD, with a lifetime prevalence of 30.6 percent or 960,000 male vets and 26.9 percent or 1,900 female vets.[211] Aside from PTSD diagnosis, the NVVRS found that 38 percent of veterans divorced within six-months; 40 percent of homeless men were Vietnam vets; 15 percent of vets were unemployed; and Vietnam veterans were 65 percent more likely to commit suicide.[212] In 2007, Dohrenwend et al. reexamined the NVVRS data, leading to revised estimates of 18.7 percent lifetime PTSD prevalence and current rates of 9.2 percent.[213]

Media reports during the Vietnam War era provide a strong implications of an unprepared and overwhelmed mental health system. For instance, the 1972 *New York Times* article, "Postwar Shock Besets Veterans of Vietnam," reported serious social problems and noted that "there is evidence that the problem is more pervasive than has been acknowledged by the Government, and may indeed be building to a social problem of serious magnitude."[214] And noted further that "the best and most effective treatment of the PVS (post-Vietnam syndrome), when it is detected, would appear to be sympathetic counseling . . . but the professional staffs have been strained by the rising number of veterans seeing help."[215] In 1967, only a small number of the VA's eighty thousand hospital beds were occupied by Vietnam veterans; by 1972, more than fifty thousand psychiatric inpatients from Vietnam had been cared for and a larger number sought help in outpatient clinics. Additional news headlines like "Addiction in Vietnam Spurs Nixon and Congress to Take Drastic New Steps" and "Delayed Trauma in Veterans Cited,"[216] "Angry Vietnam Veterans Charging Federal Policies Ignore Their Needs: They See Neglect and Inaction by the Administration in Jobs, Education, Healthcare and Counseling,"[217] and "Aid Urged for Vietnam Veterans"[218] appear to reinforce the perception of a system incapable of meeting wartime demands.

The sheer number of executive and congressional corrective actions offers additional evidence of broad system deficiencies. During the 1970s, Congress passed special legislation to fund significant expansion of VA mental health resources to meet growing wartime demand, which one can assume represents previously unmet need. For instance, "mental hygiene clinics" grew from 70 (1970) to 131 (1981), "day treatment centers" from 36 (1970) to 73 (1981), and "day hospitals" increased from 9 (1970) to 39 (1981); in addition, substance abuse treatment centers expanded as well, from 30 (1970) to 113 (1981).[219]

By 1988, to address the wartime need, the VA had instituted thirty-one residential PTSD programs, sixty-five general outpatient PTSD clinics, and thirty specially funded PTSD clinical team programs.[220] Multiple efforts were made to either shed impartial light on veteran's needs in the vacuum of reliable data or to address systemic inadequacy, including the Report to the President from The President's Commission on Mental Health;[221] the Veterans Health Care Amendments of 1979, Public Law 96–22,[222] which initially established 90 VA Centers that Congress expanded to 189 by 1985, wherein 371,000 Vietnam veterans and 80,000 family members received counseling;[223] the 1981 Legacies of Vietnam Study;[224] the IOM's Veterans and Agent Orange: Health Effects of Herbicides used in Vietnam;[225] the congressionally mandated 1983 investigation into the $9 million NVVRS;[226] and the CDC's Vietnam Experiences Study.[227] In 1989, the VA finally was elevated to a Cabinet-level department, symbolizing the national importance of veteran's affairs.

POSTWAR CONTROVERSY

The most lingering, controversial theme emerging from the Vietnam-era harkens back to impassioned 1916 debates over the very nature, cause, and authenticity of war-stress injuries.[228] At center front are efforts to explain the discrepant trends in neuropsychiatric casualty rates, especially the significant delayed presentation after the war. Renner places primary responsibility for the trends of diagnosing "character and behavior disorders" like personality disorder and rampant drug abuse on the need to deflate or hide the war-stress casualty rates until returning home.[229] Others have remarked about the Vietnam era's individual rotation policy, whereby individuals entered and departed deployed units on jet transports and often returned to a rejecting home environment, which violated prior war trauma lessons of the importance of group cohesion and social support.[230] Some have accused the military and government of maliciously intending to deny the toxicity of war on veteran's health, or to simply avoid paying compensation, whereas others have attributed these discordant records as evidence of widespread fraud and malingering.[231] Scholarly treatises have attributed the apparent Vietnam War anomaly to American antiwar political activism within a modern era "culture of trauma," which is embedded in the unprecedented and invalid PTSD construct,[232] whereas others have ascribed this anomaly to the belief that war stress alone is to blame.[233]

In keeping with the post–Korean War trend, there is a paucity of official military post-Vietnam lessons learned analysis. Several documented lessons, however, have indicated an initial lack of preparation or resources that could negatively affect the capacity to meet wartime needs. For instance, Huffman reports that "the man least trained and most junior in rank became (for some months) the sole representative of Army psychiatry in the only combat zone of the United States Army,"[234] and Jones "contends that the casualties of such low-intensity, intermittent campaigns are similar to nostalgic casualties of the American Civil War and of prior wars."[235] Looking at *Trauma and the Vietnam War Generation*, Kulka et al. find that

> In addition to providing an impetus for accurate diagnosis, the demands for treatment of large numbers of traumatized veterans spurred the development of effective treatments both for reactions that occurred on the battlefield, as well as those that occurred outside the war zone. Particularly following WWI and WWII great gains were made in diagnosing and treating stress reactions. Sad to say, many of these lessons were forgotten and had to be relearned with Vietnam veterans.[236]

Jones continues, "Vietnam revealed the limits of World War II type psychiatric treatment policy in a low-intensity, prolonged, unpopular conflict. Such conflicts, if they cannot be avoided, must be approached with primary prevention as the focus," adding,

> Although successful treatments for low-intensity combat stress casualties were developed as early as the Napoleonic Wars, circumstances can prevent the application of remedies. For example, during the Vietnam War the 1-year rotation policy, ostensibly for the purpose of preventing psychiatric casualties due to cumulative stress, the policy of rotating commanders out of combat units after 6 (and later only 3) months in order to give more officers combat experience, and the policy of individual replacement of losses rather than unit replacements all interacted to impair unit cohesion which might have prevented some of the nostalgic casualties.[237]

PARADIGM CONFLICT OF PTSD AND TRANSIENT
GROSS STRESS REACTION

Moreover, heated controversies ensued after the 1980 adoption of a PTSD diagnostic construct by the APA[238] that reattributed the primary cause of injury to traumatic stress exposure versus individual weakness.[239] For instance, military historians opined that before 1980, "the idea that a soldier of previously sound mind could be so emotionally disturbed by combat that he could no longer function was not entertained; that he might suffer long-term psychological consequences of battle was also dismissed."[240] The hotly contested PTSD debates have been reviewed elsewhere.[241] From the military's perspective, legitimizing chronic war-stress injury as primarily caused by traumatic stress exposure versus hysteria or predisposed weakness significantly undermines its paradigm of transient personality or gross stress reactions, destigmatizes chronic stress-related conditions, and opens a virtual floodgate of pension-seekers. In response, although bound to adhere to current professional standards of medical and psychiatric practice, such as the DSM and PTSD, the military has largely resisted change to its paradigm of stigmatizing hysteria for chronic stress injury. For example, per the U.S. Army's *Textbook of Military Medicine: War Psychiatry*, chronic PTSD occurs "in those with social and biological predispositions in whom the stressor is meaningful when social supports are inadequate"[242] and that "other mechanisms such as positive reinforcement (secondary gain in Freud's model) seem more important in the chronic maintenance of symptoms."[243]

FIRST PERSIAN GULF WAR

Between August 1990 and July 1991, 697,000 U.S. military personnel were deployed for twelve months to participate in Operations Desert Shield and Desert Storm (ODS), including a three-day ground war ending on February 27, 1991, that resulted in 148 American service members KIA and 467 medically WIA.

Unfortunately, the trend of progressively inadequate documentation was magnified by the Persian Gulf War cohort. Unlike its predecessors, this war cohort did not compile (or make accessible) a central repository for documenting medical (or neuropsychiatric) postwar statistics and lessons learned analyses. Instead, it opted to upload a host of disparate journal articles to its website.[244] Nonetheless, for the first time, postwar information from all of the service branches is centrally available; however, essential neuropsychiatric statistics is entirely absent. Consequently, comparatively less is known about the scope of immediate wartime mental health demands of the Persian Gulf War cohort than of any previous war generation since the American Civil War. At best, the following information is sketchy and woefully incomplete.

During ODS, psychiatric casualties represented nearly 7 percent of all medical evacuations, including a total of 476 army war-stress casualties.[245] The IOM was commissioned to conduct a comprehensive study of the health consequences of Persian Gulf War.[246] Assessing the military mental health demand relies exclusively on inconsistent survey methodology conducted by diverse agencies. One VA study of recently deployed military personnel found 9 percent of female and 4 percent of male service members endorsed PTSD diagnostic criteria within five-days of returning home. RAND[247] and IOM[248] conducted an extensive review of Gulf War epidemiological data and generally critiqued the data for overall low quality. Absolute numbers of war-stress casualties either from the DoD or VA were not cited in any of a dozen national studies. Instead, varied prevalence estimates of a handful of psychiatric diagnoses like PTSD, depression, panic disorder, anxiety disorder, and substance abuse are reported in the form of various sample percentages, making it difficult to gauge if wartime resources are adequate.

Generally speaking, PTSD rates for military personnel ranged from 1.9 percent to 9 percent, with most studies showing deployed vets having two to three times greater likelihood of having PTSD and depression than nondeployed peers.[249] Upon returning home, however, an estimated 34 percent of ODS veterans reported significant psychological distress, including feeling dazed, numb, agitated, and estranged and reporting difficulty making emotional contact and participating in practical life problems.[250] As of December 31, 2004, the VA reported a total of 1,514 Gulf War veterans had committed suicide, exceeding the 148 personnel KIA. A study of DoD postwar hospitalization for mental disorders (June 1991 to September 1993) reported that 50 percent were for alcohol-related disorders.[251]

A new controversial war syndrome (Gulf War Illness) characterized by diverse MUPS emerged, involving more than seventy thousand to seven hundred thousand ODS veterans. In regards to MUPS, according to IOM, "every study reviewed by this committee found that veterans of the Gulf War reported higher rates of nearly all symptoms examined than their nondeployed counterparts."[252] For example, results from a VA study revealed the prevalence of MUPS in Gulf War vets: headache (54 percent), sleep disturbance (47 percent), joint pain (45 percent), back pain (44 percent), fatigue (38 percent), and heartburn (37 percent). Low, but higher, rates of fibromyalgia, chronic fatigue syndrome, gastrointestinal problems, multiple chemical sensitivity, dermatologic conditions, and arthralgias (joint pain) were observed for deployed relative to nondeployed veterans.[253] In addition, 40 percent of ODS veterans reported significant family and marital distress ten years after returning home.[254]

According to the Office of the Inspector General (OIG), DoD, the military's Gulf War–era system for managing war-stress casualties "did not adequately support planning for combat stress casualties" and the "DoD has identified and corrected the deficiency."[255] Furthermore, the OIG's postwar audit of the DoD's existing structural processes for ensuring adequate planning, implementation, and training related to prevention, early identification, and treatment of war-stress casualties led to the principle conclusion that "no central point of contact exists in DoD for handling combat stress control issues; and insufficient joint doctrine exists addressing combat stress control."[256] The OIG audit shed further light on wartime capacity during the previously concluded Gulf War, adding that "at the Service level, the combat stress control programs offered by the Navy (includes Marine Corps) and the Air Force are inadequate to support their members."[257]

Media reports support these findings, including "Stress Follows Troops Home From Gulf,"[258] "Gulf War Taking Toll at Home,"[259] and "Gulf Veterans Still Paying the Price: Some Troops Count Jobs, Marriages, and Health Among War's Casualties."[260] In addition to this steady flow of critical media reports, further possible signs of the military's lack of preparedness to meet veteran's needs in regards to the estimated seven hundred thousand personnel complaining of MUPS include the extent of retrospective research into Gulf War Illness. This research has been complicated by the systemic lack of pre- and postdeployment health screening to determine the potential etiologic role of war stress. A strong indication of the broad systemic failure in meeting wartime demand is evident eight years after the Gulf War when the Government Accountability Office (GAO) concluded that "results of the research and investigation activities are accruing slowly and basic questions about the causes, course of development, and treatments of Gulf War veterans' illnesses remain unanswered."[261]

Earlier in 1995, the IOM concluded that "no single comprehensive data system exists that enable researchers to track the health of Persian Gulf War veterans both while on active duty and after separation."[262] A follow-up by the GAO cited ongoing fragmentation and inadequate coordination between VA, DoD, and the Department of Health and Human Services as principle factors, despite an interagency Persian Gulf Veterans' Coordinating Board established in 1994. In terms of cost of the crisis, from 1997 to 1998 alone, the VA and DoD spent more than $121 million on research and investigation into Gulf War veterans' illnesses.[263]

Concerns over Persian Gulf War mental health demand and capacity to meet wartime needs spurred a plethora of investigations, including research by GAO, IOM, OIG, DoD, and RAND.[264] Additionally, presidential and legislative action was required, including 1991 Public Law 102–25, Persian Gulf Service and PTSD,[265] which required DoD and VA to assess PTSD treatment and other rehabilitation resources; the 1991 National Defense Authorization Act, Public Law 102-190,[266] which mandated the DoD establish a Persian Gulf Registry to track all deployed service member's health status; the 1992 Persian Gulf War Veterans' Health Status, Public Law 102-585,[267] which mandated the VA to establish a Gulf War Veterans Health Registry; the 1996 Presidential Advisory Committee on Gulf War Veterans' Illnesses;[268] the 1998 Persian Gulf War Veterans Act, Public Law 105-277;[269] The Veterans Programs Enhancement Act, Public Law 105–368;[270] and the 1992 mandate to create the Defense and Veterans Head Injury Program (DVBIC).

According to *The Gulf War and Mental Health*, the army's postwar conclusions was that

> most of the division mental health sections arrived in Saudi Arabia deficient in personnel, appropriate training, supplies, and equipment. They all had a great deal to overcome. There was sufficient time before the start of the ground war to fix many problems, but lack of readiness prevented some of the sections from adequately supporting their divisions during the prolonged Desert Shield phase of the Gulf War.[271]

Similarly, the Journal of the U.S. Army Medical Department reported that

> Corps and division mental health teams (and the evacuation hospitals) did not have to cope with large numbers of battle fatigue casualties. If significant casualties had occurred, these teams would have found it very difficult

to carry out their mission. They were not adequately staffed, equipped or trained in peace-time to perform their wartime role. The world is a dangerous place and the Army must be prepared today for tomorrow's conflict. As highlighted here, lessons learned in SWA (Southwest Asia) provide a reference point from which to prepare for this inevitability.[272]

These self-reflections indicate significant deficiencies in critical areas of planning, preparation, and training that one can conclude would greatly limit capacity to meet wartime needs.

Overall, it appears that known and estimated mental health demand, along with candid self-critical lessons learned appraisals, as well as news media accounts, and numerous presidential and congressionally initiated corrective actions, all suggest a greater than 50 percent likelihood of at least a moderate wartime behavioral health crisis. The Persian Gulf War crisis appears to be greater in magnitude, scope (the number and diversity of major problems), and duration, than the Korean War era, but it pales in comparison to mental health catastrophes suffered in the WWI, WWII, and Vietnam War eras. This appears to be largely a function of the Gulf War's distinction as the shortest and least bloody American conflict in the past century. Moreover, it remains unclear what proportion of veterans with Gulf War Illness might be attributable to either a primary or secondary feature of war-stress injury. Emerging trends during the Persian Gulf War crisis match those of recent generations in terms of greatly diminished transparency in recordkeeping and ignoring fundamental war trauma lessons, such as the need to adequately plan and prepare for inevitable war-stress casualties and the need for adequate numbers of well-trained specialists, to name but two.

The Persian Gulf War (1990–1991) reinvigorated the trauma-pension debate as five hundred thousand U.S. military personnel participated in ODS, involving a four-day ground war. Like previous wars, frontline psychiatry was utilized as the prime treatment of war-stress injury. Martin and Cline's lessons learned from the Persian Gulf War cite problems with organization, coordination, mobility, staffing, and training of the military's combat stress control program.[273] The military author's expressed dissatisfaction with the reported 90 percent RTD and 3–5 percent psychiatric evacuation rates, critiquing military leaders for inconsistent application of frontline principles, resulting in a lower-than-expected RTD rate and higher-than-desired evacuations.[274] About six to twelve months after returning home, 34 percent of ODS veterans reported significant psychological distress, including dazed feelings, numbing, agitation, and estrangement, as well as difficulty making emotional contact and participating in practical life problems.[275] Approximately eighteen months after returning home, PTSD rates jumped to 9.4 percent for men and 19.8 percent for women. Even more perplexing was Gulf War Illness, consisting of a diverse pattern of medically unexplained physical symptoms, that may have affected more than one hundred thousand Gulf War veterans.[276] Similar to prior wars, no research has been conducted to compare the administrative or clinical outcomes of military personnel evacuated or RTD through frontline psychiatry.

GLOBAL WAR ON TERROR AND TWENTY-FIRST-CENTURY MILITARY PARADIGM ON WAR-STRESS INJURY

Essentially, since WWII there has been little change in the dominant paradigm of war-stress injury within twenty-first-century Western militaries. The current paradigm continues to reflect a mind-body dichotomy, emphasizing holistic, universal, nonpredisposed, and "normalized" acute or temporary disability from war stress considered to be legitimate and morally indistinguishable from acute physical injuries.[277] In contrast, chronic war-stress injury continues to be viewed by the military in dualistic, predisposed psychiatric formulations,[278] which is consistent with 1916-era so-called war hysteria.

THE MILITARY'S MENTAL HEALTH DILEMMA

Gabriel reported that most ancient combatants were not killed when fighting in formation, but that the "real killers on the ancient battlefield was fear,"[279] explaining that "as stress increased, the probably that someone would lose his nerve and run increased." Seeing soldiers run often led to panics within units. It was while these terrified combatants were running away that the real killing began, especially when chariots and calvary were employed. This interesting historical anecdote has important ramifications for the military's reflexive assault against emotional and moral weakness, whatever the cause.

Origins of the word dilemma can be traced to the 1520s, from late Latin and Greek dilemma or "double proposition," a technical term in rhetoric referring to situations in which someone is forced to choose between two unfavorable alternatives.[280] From the military's perspective, the dilemma involving military mental health can be boiled down to two undesirable proposition, each representing the military's twofold mission: (1) a force health protection mission by openly acknowledging and committing to learning from the psychiatric realities of war, and thus running the risk of catastrophic failure to fulfill its warfighting mission (e.g., mass evacuation syndromes) and potential financial ruin; or (2) a war-fighting mission by actively ignoring and avoiding fully learning the psychiatric lessons of war to sustain the immediate ability to fight and win wars, and thus perpetuating a generational cycle of preventable wartime behavioral health crises harming millions of veterans and their families as well as society.[281]

ATTEMPTED SOLUTIONS TO RESOLVE THE MILITARY'S MENTAL HEALTH DILEMMA

From the military's perspective, one might argue that the early attempts to treat mental injuries humanely on par with physical wounds at the outset of WWI were directly responsible for intolerable evacuation syndromes. Consequently, alternatives strategies for dealing with its mental health dilemma not only are justified but also are the sole viable answer to a perplexing problem. The truth is, however, that the historical record clearly reveals the military's episodic flirtation with more "positive" or enlightened approaches toward mentally wounded combatants has been exceptionally brief and incomplete at best,[282] in particular when compared with its reliance on "darker" or less humane approaches, as we will discuss.

TEN HARMFUL MILITARY STRATEGIES TO MANAGE ITS MENTAL HEALTH DILEMMA

After an extensive review of the literature on war stress, we have identified ten overarching strategies or approaches the military has implemented to eliminate, minimize, or conceal its mental health problem: (1) Cruel and Inhumane Handling; (2) Legal Prosecution, Incarceration, and Executions; (3) Weaponizing Stigma to Humiliate, Ridicule, and Shame into Submission; (4) Denying the Psychological Realities of War; (5) Screening and Purging Weakness to Prevent War-Stress Injury; (6) Delay, Deception, and Delay; (7) Faulty Diagnosis and Backdoor Discharges; (8) Maintaining Diffusion of Responsibility and Unaccountability; (9) Inadequate, Experimental, and Harmful Treatments; and (10) Perpetuating Neglect, Indifference, and Self-Inflicted Crises. Any one or combination of these ten avoidant strategies would prohibit the military to fulfill its force health protection mission in regards to meeting the basic mental health needs of service members and their families, thus perpetuating the generational cycle of self-inflicted and preventable public health crises.

In chapter 2, we examine the scope and costs associated with the current mental health crisis as an illustration of the price we pay for neglecting our war trauma lessons.

2

THE DARK SIDE OF MILITARY MENTAL HEALTH

A HISTORY OF SELF-INFLICTED WOUNDS

A single finding underpinning all others: The Military Health System lacks the fiscal resources and the fully trained personnel to fulfill its mission to support psychological health in peacetime or fulfill the enhanced requirements imposed during times of conflict.

DEPARTMENT OF DEFENSE TASK FORCE ON MENTAL HEALTH, *AN ACHIEVABLE VISION*

Through its review, the committee found that PTSD management in DoD appear to be local, ad hoc, incremental, and crisis-driven, with little planning devoted to the development of a long-range, population-based approach for this disorder by either the Office of the Assistant Secretary of Defense for Health Affairs (OASD(HA) or any of the service branches.

INSTITUTE OF MEDICINE, *TREATMENT FOR POSTTRAUMATIC STRESS DISORDER IN MILITARY AND VETERAN POPULATIONS*

Alone, neither of these pronouncements on military mental health-care will cause most Americans to bat an eye. Their true significance is perhaps salient only to those who have experienced them. The first quotation comes from the military's greatly delayed compulsory mental health review, six years into the wars in Iraq and Afghanistan. The second came seven years after the Department of Defense (DoD) and Congress were supposed to have fixed military mental health.

What are the real-life implications for neglecting the basic lessons of war trauma? How many lives actually are affected? How does exposure to violence from war affect people and their families? The neurotoxic effects of war stress do not discriminate by race, ethnicity, religion, gender, sexual orientation, political party, age, service branch, or role. War is the great equalizer.

To date, the breadth and scope of the so-called invisible wounds of war have never received a full reckoning. Most studies, whether academic or commissioned by the government or investigated by the press, cite the prevalence of a small handful of sensationalized diagnoses—post-traumatic stress disorder (PTSD), depression, traumatic brain injury (TBI), generalized anxiety, and suicide—and believe they have provided a comprehensive snapshot of our wartime mental health crisis. That is like counting all the cars in Idaho to estimate how many automobiles there are in the United States.

The spectrum of war injuries—not just of the body but also of the mind—is vast. Our lofty goal for this chapter is to take a complete look at the scope of the wartime crises of past and present.

THE SPECTRUM OF WAR AND TRAUMATIC STRESS INJURIES

It has long been known that war neuroses do not constitute a clinical entity with characteristic and invariable symptoms. Instead there is a wide variety of syndromes, the symptoms of which vary greatly.
R. R. GRINKEL AND J. P. SPIEGEL, *WAR NEUROSES IN NORTH AFRICA*

This quote is taken from a previously classified U.S. Army report during World War II. Unfortunately, U.S. psychiatrists advocating for PTSD diagnosis in 1980 did not read this, and thus the cyclical trauma-pension wars continued. Nearly every written historical account of war or combat stress, regardless of when or where it was written, describes a similar range of stress injuries that can best be divided into three broad classifications: neuropsychiatric conditions, medically unexplained physical conditions, and psychosocial, spiritual, and conduct-related conditions. We'll describe each briefly, but before doing so, it's worth examining the army's own classification scheme as well as how closely it parallels the statistics that have come out of the DoD and Veterans Administration (VA). These classifications are free-floating anxiety, somatic regression, psychosomatic visceral disturbances, conversion symptoms, depressions, neuroses complicating cerebral concussion (TBI), exhaustion states, fatigue, psychoses, and malingering.

TABLE 2.1 Number of GWOT Veterans Receiving VA Mental Healthcare Up to 2015

DIAGNOSIS	KOREA	VIETNAM	GWOT
Any mental health disorder (except dementia)	109,028	1,100,729	959,235
Post-traumatic stress disorder	12,604	399,572	458,496
Bipolar disorder	2,716	57,304	72,258
Depression	56,047	584,926	573,467
Substance use disorder	12,105	318,679	262,565
Anxiety disorder	29,519	280,499	366,880
Schizophrenia	2,891	50,059	22,622

NEUROPSYCHIATRIC CONDITIONS

Neuropsychiatric diagnoses encompass an exceptionally broad array of potential diagnoses for returning service members, including but not limited to PTSD, acute stress disorder (ASD), major depression disorder, bipolar disorder, generalized anxiety disorder, substance use disorders (SUDs), psychotic-related disorders, impulse-control disorders, traumatic brain injury (TBI), somatic illness disorders, dissociative disorders, eating disorders, sleep disorders, intermittent explosive disorder, and personality disorders (PDs). Table 2.1 shows the partial spectrum of war-stress injury diagnoses in veterans of Korea, Vietnam, and the current Global War on Terror (GWOT)—clearly revealing that PTSD represents only a sliver of the trauma spectrum.

MEDICALLY UNEXPLAINED PHYSICAL SYMPTOMS

The label medically unexplained physical symptoms (MUPS) is itself enough to scare anyone away. But MUPS is also called war syndrome, psychosomatic illness, or hysteria. The DoD currently lumps it into the large, unwieldy category of so-called symptoms, signs, and ill-defined (SSID) conditions. Today, veterans may receive a wide range of quasi-medical labels—everything from irritable bowel syndrome to post-traumatic headaches (PTHAs) to chronic fatigue syndrome to fibromyalgia to atypical cardiac pain, idiopathic (pseudo) seizures, phantom limbs, and chronic pain syndrome.

PSYCHOSOCIAL, SPIRITUAL, AND LEGAL MANIFESTATIONS OF WAR-STRESS INJURY

The psychological toll of human warfare, as evidenced by each generational mental health crisis, far exceeds the mere prevalence of neuropsychiatric and psychosomatic labels. To understand the actual scope and breadth of wartime mental health needs and the psychological costs of modern war, we must examine the prevalence of a wide range of known psychosocial, spiritual, and legal manifestations of war-stress injury that are not covered by diagnostic codes. These include post-traumatic anger, moral injury, suicidal and parasuicidal behaviors, traumatic and complicated grief, and misconduct stress behaviors, as well as the behavioral effects of chronic war-stress injury, such as divorce, interpersonal violence, domestic violence, child abuse, homelessness, unemployment, and incarceration.

THE WARRIOR CLASS

Military personnel do not go to war and return home in a vacuum. War-stress injury touches those closest to war veterans—their families and children, and even their caretakers. Although we focus on active-duty, reserve, and national guard in the Air Force, Army, Marine Corps, and Navy, we also must include civilians who deploy as military contractors, not to mention American diplomatic corps, law enforcement, intelligence personnel, and embedded journalists. We will not delve into the ripple effect of untreated war-stress injury or so-called collateral damage. For our purposes, we'll concentrate on the warrior class.

THE DANGER OF UNDER- AND OVERREPORTING WARTIME NEEDS

The virtues of accurate, timely, and transparent reporting of wartime mental health demand are obvious. They afford leaders an opportunity to make decisive corrective actions to prevent or mitigate a crisis, and they evade the intrinsic harm of grossly underestimating and underpreparing for the inevitable injuries of war. Perhaps not as obvious, yet of particular concern to veterans, is the possible danger of public backlash from overreporting or even just the reporting of postwar adjustment problems. Media portrayals of the emotionally "damaged" and unstable war veteran can fuel public fears, stigma, and discriminatory bias. For instance, the higher-than-average unemployment rates of veterans are often attributed to media coverage of veteran PTSD, suicide, and misconduct.[1]

Falsely equating a diagnosis of a war-stress injury with permanent disability and impaired functioning, however, reflects a widespread misconception, one that is exacerbated by antiquated stigma. To be certain, resilience does not mean the absence of war-stress injury, just as it does not mean the absence of medical wounds. Concerns over public backlash from accurate reporting of our veteran's mental health needs indicate out-of-date cultural beliefs that only make the crisis worse. If true, then emphasis should be placed on public education and the elimination of this harmful mental health stigma and disparity. Conversely, avoiding an honest accounting of the full spectrum of war-stress injury only reinforces this stigma and perpetuates the crisis. Accurate monitoring of wartime needs can lead to effective planning, preparation, and proper resourcing of the mental health system, thus preventing crisis. Prioritizing war stress and medical casualties hypothetically could produce psychological benefits commensurate with medical services (consider that the last irrefutable military medical crisis was a tuberculosis outbreak among WWI veterans).[2]

We can see a distinct consequence of the fragmented, inept monitoring of wartime mental health needs in the widely discrepant estimates of the prevalence of postdeployment conditions like PTSD, depression, and generalized anxiety. Some sources estimate it at 5 percent,[3] whereas others have estimated that as many as "38 percent of Soldiers and 31 percent of Marines report psychological symptoms. Among members of the National Guard, the figure rises to 49 percent."[4]

THE MOST COMMON REASON WARRIORS AND FAMILY MEMBERS SEEK CARE

Mental health is consistently the number-one reason for military attrition and active-duty hospitalizations and is the third most-cited reason for all outpatient medical record encounters throughout the DoD. It's also the top reason military children are seen in military medical facilities (31.5 percent), with respiratory illness the next most frequent diagnosed medical condition (12.6 percent). Mental health is also the number-one reason for hospitalizing military family members (53.2 percent) with the next closest medical reason being perinatal care (9.9) and injury (4.9 percent).[5]

Table 2.2 offers further evidence of the trauma spectrum and a snapshot of the active-duty personnel and discharged veterans who actively seek mental healthcare. The DoD's statistics are misleading—they make no distinction between deployment-related conditions and people who may be diagnosed with multiple conditions. That said, these statistics do offer a glimpse into the military's mental health needs, even if the data grossly underestimate the actual demand by failing to account for personnel who, to avoid stigma or reprisal, go around military medicine and instead go to the DoD's community counseling centers, DoD contractors, chaplains, or civilian clinicians, all of which are completely invisible to military medicine and the DoD.

TRACKING MENTAL HEALTH INJURIES AS WARTIME CASUALTIES

The military defines a casualty as "a service member who is [or] has been classified as deceased, wounded, ill, or injured."[6] After every war, military medical departments publish their lessons learned. These extensive postwar analyses have been conducted specifically on "neuropsychiatric casualty" rates, given the well-documented and highly publicized problems of returning veterans with war-stress injuries from every war in the twentieth century.

Unlike medical wounds, the prevalence of the equally inevitable and exponentially higher war-stress casualties is not centrally tracked and thus is virtually unknown. In fact, nowhere throughout the vast network of DoD, Veterans Health Administration (VA), and federal health agencies like the Centers for Disease Control and Prevention (CDC), is the current number of known or estimated war-stress casualties reported for this relatively finite (less than half of 1 percent) military population, and that includes high-profile service-connected conditions like PTSD.[7]

UNDERSTANDING THE HEALTHY-WARRIOR EFFECT

Comparing rates of suicide and psychiatric conditions in the military versus civilian population be done cautiously in light of the *healthy-warrior effect*.

TABLE 2.2 Cumulative Number of GWOT-Personnel Diagnosed with Neuropsychiatric Condition by DoD and VA, 2001–2015

DIAGNOSIS	DOD	VA
Adjustment disorders	1,028,969	NR
Post-traumatic stress disorder	177,471	458,496
Anxiety disorder	683,001	366,880
Mood-related disorders	760,892	645,725
Substance use disorder	506,057	318,679
Psychotic-related disorders	32,599	202,705
Somatoform disorders	24,966	NR
Personality disorders	81,017	NR
Sexual-related disorders	NR	45,998
Other mental health disorders	685,038	959,235
Traumatic brain injury	375,230	37,970
Total	**3,513,987**	**3,035,688**

Source: Armed Forces Health Surveillance Center (AFHSC), "Substance Use Disorders in the U.S. Armed Forces, 2000–2011," *Medical Surveillance Monthly Report* 19, no. 11 (November 2012): 11–16; Armed Forces Health Surveillance Center (AFHSC), "Medical Evacuations from Operation Iraqi Freedom/Operation New Dawn, Active and Reserve Components, U.S. Armed Forces, 2003–2011," *Medical Surveillance Monthly Report* 19, no. 2 (February 2012): 18–21; Armed Forces Health Surveillance Center (AFHSC), "Health Care Experiences Prior to Suicide and Self-Inflicted Injury, Active Component, U.S. Armed Forces, 2001–2011," *Medical Surveillance Monthly Report* 19, no. 2 (February 2012): 2–6; Armed Forces Health Surveillance Center (AFHSC), "Hospitalizations Among Members of the Active Component, U.S. Armed Forces, 2011," *Medical Surveillance Monthly Report* 19, no. 4 (April 2012): 10–16; Armed Forces Health Surveillance Center (AFHSC), "Hospitalizations Among Members of the Active Component, U.S. Armed Forces, 2010," *Medical Surveillance Monthly Report* 18, no. 4 (April 2011): 8–15; Armed Forces Health Surveillance Center (AFHSC), "Hospitalizations for Mental Disorders, Active Components, U.S. Armed Forces, January 2000–December 2009," *Medical Surveillance Monthly Report* 17, no. 11 (November 2010): 14–16; Armed Forces Health Surveillance Center (AFHSC), "Mental Disorders and Mental Health Problems, Active Component, U.S. Armed Forces, 2000–2011," *Medical Surveillance Monthly Report* 19, no. 16 (June 2012): 11–17, cited in T. Servies, Z. Hu, A. Eick-Cost, and J. L. Otto, "Substance Use Disorders in the U.S. Armed Forces, 2000–2011," *Medical Surveillance Monthly Report* 19, no. 11 (November 2012): 11–16; VA Annual Healthcare Utilization Report (2015/2017).

Note: NR, not reported.

An unknown number of active-duty and veterans will have more than one diagnosis. DoD data include diagnosis only by military medicine, excluding mental health services provided by military community (family) counseling centers, pastoral care (chaplains), military life consultants and other contractors, Vet centers, and outsourcing to non-DoD civilian providers.

Unlike civilians, military personnel are subject to extensive health screenings before and during military service. The majority of non-war-related psychiatric discharges occur within a year of entry into service. After the Vietnam military drug epidemic, the military implemented extensive drug testing, and nearly every aspect of a service member's behavior is under scrutiny. This includes exercise, diet, and social competency. In short, service members in general, and those who deploy to war zones in particular, represent an unusually healthy segment of American society.[8] Given that fact, the wartime prevalence of health conditions should be weighted accordingly. During WWII, the American military's unprecedented mass psychiatric screening program rejected more than 1.6 million purportedly predisposed war neurotics who might breakdown after eleven years of combat.[9] Consequently, when 1.3 million WWII veterans become neuropsychiatric casualties,[10] including hundreds of the most battle-tested and hardy of military leaders with "old sergeant's syndrome,"[11] the military should have learned its lesson about the pathogenic effects of war stress.

A COMPREHENSIVE SURVEY OF WARTIME MENTAL HEALTH NEEDS

Now that we've framed the military's mental health issue, it is time to direct our attention to the matter at hand. Who is affected by the military's negligence? What follows is the single-most comprehensive picture of the military's mental health needs.

There is inherent truth in the cliché, "No one returns from war unscathed." Common perceptions of the term *resilience* often misconstrue this to mean the absence of mental health problems despite exposure to adversity. In fact, resilience is the capacity to bounce back, to persevere, to keep going even in the face of problems. One can have PTSD and be resilient at the same time. In fact, veterans with PTSD are often the epitome of resilience. Most returning veterans are resilient, especially the millions who live with war-stress injury. Another reason we open with resilience is that discussions of veteran mental health and social reintegration are often unfairly chock full of stereotypes of emotionally damaged veterans. They fail to recognize resilience, and the adaptive experiences of veterans, including the forming of close social ties; a brotherhood or sisterhood they may never experience again; developing a deep sense of pride, esprit de corps, and existential purpose; experiencing the profound satisfaction of personal growth and sacrifice; and having accomplished one's mission.[12]

According to a Joint Mental Health Advisory Team report, more than half of returning service members endorsed the statement, "I feel pride from my accomplishments during this deployment"; 63.2 percent agreed that "This deployment has made me more confident in my abilities"; and 24.9 percent related to "I deal with stress better because of this deployment."[13] It is a mistake, however, to confuse resilience with the absence of war-stress injury or to equate that injury with severe or permanent disability.

THE ELEPHANT IN THE ROOM: MILITARY AND VETERAN SUICIDES

Every day, approximately twenty-two American veterans commit suicide totaling over 8,000 vet suicides each year. I repeat, 8,000 veteran suicides each year.
SENATOR JOHNNY ISAKSON (R-GA), FEBRUARY 2, 2015

In 2012, the VA revised its estimates to "only" twenty American veteran suicides each day. Both the VA and DoD, but especially the latter, were reluctant to admit the existence of a suicide epidemic. They claimed that war and multiple deployments had nothing to do with why active-duty and veterans committed suicide. The military knew it had a suicide problem as far back as 2001, after a series of suicides and homicide-suicides within the Army Special Forces Afghanistan veterans. These service members were the best of the best in terms of training, morale, and psychological resilience. The matter was brushed aside. It took high-profile military suicides for Congress to finally act. With the passing of the Joshua Omvig Veterans Suicide Prevention Act[14] and the Clay Hunt Act,[15] Congress compelled the VA and DoD to start tracking suicides. Eventually, they established crisis hotlines, a flurry of suicide prevention research and programs, and centralized agencies like today's Defense Suicide Prevention Office (DSPO), which is responsible for overseeing the DoD's suicide problem.

In 1812, the former surgeon general of the Continental Army and cosigner of the Declaration of Independence, Benjamin Rush, often referred to as the "father of American psychiatry," reported the tragic suicide of two distinguished army captains, identical twins, who "both served with honour during the war . . . were cheerful, sociable . . . happy in their families and . . . independent in their property." They succumbed to "melancholy" shortly upon returning home from the American Revolution.

Historically, the total number of wartime suicides for a given generation is always unknown, for the same reasons then as today. Nevertheless, most war cohorts report a high incidence of suicide. Directly after WWI, America saw news headlines like "400 Ex-Soldiers New York Suicides,"[16] and "Veterans Suicides Average Two a Day."[17] From April to July 1940, there were twenty-six army suicides,[18] but otherwise, the prevalence of WWII-era suicides is unknown. A recent news article, "Suicide Rates Soar Among WWII Vets, Records Show," posits that older veterans are twice as likely to commit suicide than Operation Enduring Freedom/Operation Iraqi Freedom (OEF/OIF) vets.[19] During the Korean War, a reported 131 soldiers committed suicide, at an incidence rate of 11 per 100,000,[20] but no data exist for other service branches or after military discharge. VA historians Baker and Pickren observed that "suicide of veterans became of great concern to the VA during the 1950s, when the rate of suicide among veterans both within the VA hospital system and outside it, already higher than in the nonveteran population, suddenly increased alarmingly over the pre-World War II rates."[21]

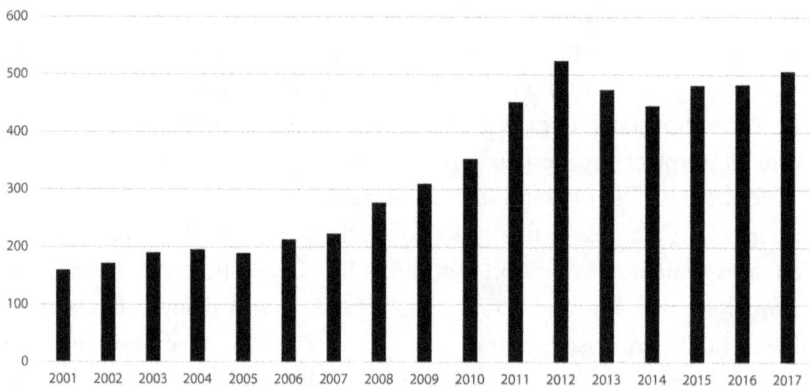

FIGURE 2.1 DoD reported suicide trend of active duty, reserve, and national guard, 2001–2017.

SOURCES: CY2001–2010: COL (RET) ELSPETH CAMERON RITCHIE, MD, MPH; CHIEF CLINICAL OFFICER; DEPARTMENT OF MENTAL HEALTH; *PSYCHOLOGICAL CONSEQUENCES OF THE LONG WAR WORKSHOP ON IMPROVING THE HEALTH, SAFETY AND WELL-BEING OF YOUNG ADULT* (WASHINGTON DC); CY 2011–2017: DEPARTMENT OF DEFENSE (DOD), *SUICIDE EVENT REPORTS: CALENDAR YEAR 2017 ANNUAL REPORT* (WASHINGTON, DC: DEFENSE HEALTH AGENCY, 2017), HTTPS://WWW.PDHEALTH.MIL/RESEARCH-ANALYTICS /DEPARTMENT-DEFENSE-SUICIDE-EVENT-REPORT-DODSER

The post–Korean War suicide trend sparked the VA's first research program into veteran suicide, which found a link to the new psychotropic medications Thorazine (chlorpromazine) and Rauwolfia alkaloids (antihypertensives).[22]

In the Vietnam era, active-military suicide data were unavailable, but media reports revealed concerning trends, like "Suicide Risk Double for Viet Veterans."[23] According to the CDC,[24] total mortality in the five years after discharge was 17 percent higher in Vietnam veterans, and this excess mortality was due to external causes (including suicide). In 1988, the CDC testified before Congress that nine thousand Vietnam War veterans had committed suicide, but others have cited figures as high as twenty thousand to one hundred and fifty thousand.[25] This number is well over the 47,410 service members killed in action. Veterans of the Persian Gulf War fared no better: as of December 31, 2004, the VA reported a total of 1,514 suicides, multiple times greater than the 148 military personnel killed in action.[26]

THE MILITARY SUICIDE EPIDEMIC

In the twenty-first century, wartime suicide has once again emerged as a major national concern. Military suicides eclipsed the total number of service members killed in action in Afghanistan and Iraq combined, and that is counting only those who commit suicide during active duty or reserve status, and not the estimated twenty to twenty-one veterans killed by suicide every day who have been discharged from the military. Between 2001 to 2010, a total of 25,357 active-duty service members engaged in suicidal or parasuicidal behaviors.[27] According to the army's top psychiatrist, from 2001 to 2013, a total of 3,096 military personnel successfully committed suicide.[28] And 19,955 military personnel received inpatient or outpatient diagnosis of intentionally self-inflicted injury or poisoning; 3,463 were identified as "likely self-harm" after hospitalization for injury or poisoning with a concurrent mental health diagnosis.[29] Recent studies have shown one in five treatment-seeking OEF/OIF veterans reported contemplating suicide.[30]

On the frontlines, 11 percent of deployed soldiers and 11.6 percent marines reported suicidal ideation in 2010,[31] and 30 percent of a sample of soldiers seen for mental health appointments had considered suicide within the past month.[32] A particularly high-risk period is the first five years when veterans transition out of the military and back into civilian life. Among 3,069 male Navy and Marine Corps personnel transitioning to civilian life, 7 percent (sailors = 5.3 percent, marines = 9.0 percent) reported suicidal or self-harming ideation during the previous thirty days of transitioning to civilian life.[33] In 2010, the Department of Veterans Affairs reported that an estimated 950 veterans received treatment for attempted suicide each month during their two-year study. Of these same veterans, an estimated 7 percent committed suicide, and another 11 percent attempted suicide again within nine months. According to the Department of Veterans Affairs, an average of eight thousand veterans commit suicide each year.[34]

Despite anecdotal accounts of the apparent link between war and suicide, researchers have repeatedly claimed no clear association exists.[35] Given the incoherent status of government monitoring, due caution is warranted. Research comparing deployed cohorts with nondeployed cohorts to control for the effects of firsthand exposure to war stress must be aware of inherent stressors within nondeployed military populations, like exposure to potentially traumatic occupational hazards (disaster relief, training accidents). For example, in 1994, the *Washington Post* reported on three suicides among troops in Haiti, but that referred to military personnel deployed on peace-keeping operations.[36]

Both the DoD and VA publicly recognize the most commonly overlooked, yet inevitable manifestation of war-stress injuries are functional somatic conditions or "war syndromes," currently called MUPS, and diagnosed as SSIDs. This catchall diagnosis, which includes MUPS, captures medical uncertainty pending the examination results of patients who later may receive a medical diagnosis.[37] The VA aptly warns that SSID diagnoses are not indicative of war-related MUPS.[38] In the wake of Persian Gulf War illness, however, a comprehensive reevaluation of veterans initially given a SSID diagnosis found that 45 percent of the cases revealed evidence of a previously undetected primary or secondary mental health condition.[39]

Appreciating the physical toll of stress is vital: many individuals—whether because of their cultural idiom of distress, gender, fear of stigma, or just how they metabolize stress—are prone to complain about insomnia, headaches, fatigue, chronic pain, irritable bowel, bruxism, sexual dysfunction, seizures, and anything and everything else other than their emotional symptoms. The VA and DoD, however, pay only lip service to war-related MUPS. Contrary to the VA/DoD's MUPS clinical practice guidelines, these symptoms are not screened, diagnosed, or treated,. Table 2.3 provides a glance at the potential prevalence of MUPS—nearly four million active-duty and more than seven hundred thousand veterans with service-connected health issues have been

TABLE 2.3 Prevalence of Possible MUPS-Related Diagnoses Among Active-Duty Personnel

CONDITION	SURVEILLANCE	PREVALENCE	SOURCE
Functional gastrointestinal disorders[a]	2005–2014	53,438	AFHSC (2016): 10–15
Chronic pain syndrome	2007–2014	20,419	AFHSC (2015), 16–19
Seizure[b]	2008–2016	814 deployed 16,257 nondeployed	AFHSC (2017), 12–19
Chronic fatigue syndrome	2007–2016	211,213	AFHSC (2017), 23–32
Insomnia-related motor vehicle accidents	2007–2016	172,062	AFHSC (2017), 2–11
Headaches[c]	2003–2016	864,906	AFHSC (2001–2016)
Eating Disorders	2004–2013	3,527	AFHSC (2014)
Symptoms, Signs, and Ill-Defined Illness[d]	2003–2016	3,959,954	AFHSC (2001–2016)
Symptoms, Signs, and Ill-Defined Illness	2002–2015	715,263	VA (2015)

Source: Armed Forces Health Surveillance Center (AFHSC), *Medical Surveillance Monthly Reports* 24, no. 12 (2017): 2–11; Armed Forces Health Surveillance Center (AFHSC), *Medical Surveillance Monthly Reports* 24, no. 12 (2017): 12–19; Armed Forces Health Surveillance Center (AFHSC), *Medical Surveillance Monthly Reports* 24, no. 12 (2017): 23–32; Armed Forces Health Surveillance Center (AFHSC), *Medical Surveillance Monthly Reports* 23, no. 6 (2016): 10–15; Armed Forces Health Surveillance Center (AFHSC), *Medical Surveillance Monthly Reports* 22, no. 12 (2015): 16–19; Armed Forces Health Surveillance Center (AFHSC), *Medical Surveillance Monthly Reports* (2014); Armed Forces Health Surveillance Center (AFHSC), *Medical Surveillance Monthly Reports* (2001–2016); Department of Veterans Affairs (VA), *Analysis of VA Health Care Utilization Among Operation Enduring Freedom, Operation Iraqi Freedom, and Operation New Dawn Veterans, from 1st Qtr FY 2002 Through 1st Qtr FY 2015*, Epidemiology Program, Post-Deployment Health Group, Office of Public Health, Veterans Health Administration (Washington, DC: Department of Veterans Affairs, 2015), www.publichealth.va.gov/epidemiology.

Note: [a]Cases of irritable bowel syndrome (IBS) (ICD-9: 564.1), functional diarrhea (FD) (ICD-9: 564.5), functional constipation (FC) (ICD-9: 564.0), and dyspepsia (D) (ICD-9: 536.8). [b]Seizure events include an unknown number of stress-related pseudo-seizures. [c]Headaches are total headaches diagnosed; an unknown number are post-traumatic headaches (PTHA). [d]SSID is composed of 190 somatic symptom codes for which a medical diagnosis has yet to be determined. An unknown portion of SSIDs will be stress-related MUPS.

diagnosed with SSID. If the army's estimates are correct that 45 percent of SSID are psychogenic in origin, that means more than three hundred thousand veterans and nearly two million active-duty personnel may be expressing their psychological turmoil in physical terms, with an unknown number of those symptoms resulting from to war-stress injury.

After the Persian Gulf War, the Institute of Medicine (IOM) completed an extensive review of the scientific literature on war stress and health, and concluded this: "Chronic stress can lead to adverse health outcomes that affect multiple body systems such as the CNS, endocrine, immune, gastrointestinal and cardiovascular systems."[40] Despite the robust findings of MUPS-related war stress casualties, this large segment of the spectrum of war-stress injury routinely evades epidemiological accounting. The combined influence of deeply entrenched stigma and this "warrior culture" ensure the likely prominence of MUPS over psychiatric stress casualties in military populations.[41] This is exactly why the military must follow its own MUPS practice guidelines.

POST-TRAUMATIC HEADACHES

PTHA is significantly associated with combat exposure with a reported prevalence in 30 to 90 percent of veterans diagnosed with TBI or PTSD. Afari et al. found that PTSD symptoms independently predicted PTHA among combat veterans, who were four times more likely to report PTHA than noncombat veterans. From 2001 to 2015, the DoD reported some 864,906 service members were diagnosed with headaches, but it is unclear how many of these may be PTHA-related diagnoses.

HISTORICAL PRECEDENTS

War produces inexplicable somatic conditions, including MUPS.[42] For example, official army medical records during the American Civil War (1861–1865), which predate the fields of psychiatry, neurology, and psychology, reveal that at least twelve hundred Union Army soldiers received disability discharges in 1863 for "irritable heart" syndrome.[43] They suffered inexplicable fatigue, sweating, joint pain, headache, anxious agitation, and diarrhea, which doctors of the time viewed as an organic response to battle stress. By 1888, there were about twenty-six thousand disability pensions for "diseases of the heart";[44] 5,547 cases and seventy-four deaths resulting from depression, anorexia, and chronic fatigue symptoms associated with "nostalgia"; more than eighty thousand cases of "headaches"; nearly sixty-five thousand cases of "neuralgia" (akin to chronic pain); and 160,000 soldiers diagnosed with "constipation and diarrhea" with an unknown number "functional" in nature (akin to irritable bowel syndrome).[45] During WWI,

TABLE 2.4 Incidence of Psychosomatic Complaints During WWII

PHYSICAL COMPLAINT (MEDICAL SPECIALTY WARD)	TOTAL GROUP	COMBAT VETERANS	NONCOMBAT TROOPS
Gastrointestinal	29.7%	85.4%	4.6%
Orthopedic	23.5%	88.5%	11.5%
Multiple symptoms	17.3%	84.3%	15.7%
Cardiovascular	15.9%	88.1%	11.9%
Headache	8.1%	86.6%	13.4%
Genitourinary	5.4%	80.0%	20.0%

Source: W. C. Menninger, *Reactions to Combat: Psychiatry in a Troubled World* (New York, NY: MacMillan, 1948), 156.

out of just under seventy thousand American soldiers receiving psychiatric disability pension, there were sixty-three cases of "shell shock," nearly two thousand cases of "neurocirculatory asthenia" (akin to "irritable heart"), and about seven thousand cases of "nervous diseases and injuries" (including tic, tremor, mutism), and more than six thousand cases of "epilepsy" (an unknown number of which were MUPS).[46]

The prevalence of MUPS in WWII veterans reveals equally high rates of somatic complaints, including insomnia (31.9 percent), headache (42.8 percent), irritability (48.6 percent), poor concentration (20.1 percent), restlessness (45.4 percent), gastrointestinal (41.7 percent), cardiovascular (21.9 percent), and musculoskeletal (34.8 percent).[47] Menninger conducted a study on U.S. hospitals during WWII.[48] Table 2.4 gives the results of Menninger's research indicating a clear relationship between combat exposure and the likelihood of being admitted to medical, nonpsychiatric wards. Similarly, Palmer reviewed war-related "dyspepsia," or peptic ulcer, in WWII and Vietnam, and found that between 1942 and 1945, more than fifty thousand WWII army personnel were discharged from the military for ulcer disease.[49] In 1969, during Vietnam, an estimated three thousand soldiers suffered ulcer disease, and ten cases each month required evacuation. During the Korean War, the second-most-frequent cause of army hospital admissions was classified as "symptoms and ill-defined conditions."[50] During the Persian Gulf War (1990–1991), more than six hundred thousand of

690,000 deployed personnel complained of MUPS (e.g., chronic fatigue, pain). Reports that up to 45 percent of deployed Gulf War veterans may have MUPS prompted the VA/DoD to create clinical practice guidelines for MUPS.

In 2013, the VA reported that MUPS "such as chronic pain and fatigue, are common in the general and Veteran population" and that "Chronic Fatigue Syndrome (CFS), Fibromyalgia (FM) and Irritable Bowel Syndrome (IBS) are among the most commonly diagnosed medically unexplained conditions."[51]There are, however, many more potential MUPS diagnoses, including noncardiac chest pain, pseudo-seizures, and multiple chemical sensitivity, just to name a few. A The IOM's report on VA rates of service-connected disability diagnoses before OEF (1999) to 2006, provides a rare glimpse into the association between war and MUPS. For instance, diagnoses of "fibromyalgia" increased more than 300 percent from 1999 to 2006; "irritable bowel syndrome" rose 68.6 percent; and "lumbosacral or cervical strain" diagnosis increased by 46.8 percent.[52]

Today, the DoD and VA do not track the total or estimated prevalence of MUPS-related war stress casualties, and so statistics are completely unknown. In fiscal year 2010, DoD reported SSID was the diagnosis given in 1.7 million medical visits, and in 2001 and 2012, the VA reported that 55.8 percent or 590,446 treatment-seeking OEF/OIF/OND veterans received SSID diagnoses. Other studies on MUPS in the current war cohort indicate a high frequency of somatic complaints, including 75 percent reporting fatigue, 70 percent sleep difficulties, 42 percent headaches, 50 percent joint pain, and 23 percent gastrointestinal symptoms.[53] OEF/OIF veterans with and without a diagnosed mental health condition were treated in the VA for 222 types of medical conditions.[54]

Of those medical conditions, Babson and Feldner reviewed the literature on post-traumatic sleep disturbance—described as both a hallmark symptom of PTSD, and a potential etiologic factor.[55] For instance, 71 percent of returning OIF personnel screened as (PTSD positive, and even 26 percent of those PTSD negative) reported problems sleeping,[56] and changes in sleep patterns, including fragmented rapid eye movement sleep, are strongly associated with early development of PTSD.[57] In 2010, nearly two hundred thousand service member military outpatient visits were coded for the diagnosis of "organic sleep disorder."[58] This comes at a cost: the DoD reported near the same number of active-duty personnel with primary insomnia were involved in car accidents between 2007 and 2016.[59]

THE SPECTRUM OF NEUROPSYCHIATRIC DIAGNOSES

Historical and cultural influences of wartime mental health diagnosis have been reviewed.[60] Notwithstanding the ever-changing labels, the constellation of underlying symptoms and signs of the human stress response are relatively inconsistent. Every war generation is faced with the dilemma of whether and how to diagnose the casualties of war stress, and from this, we have a wide range of inconsistent labeling. War veterans have been subject to a wide range of psychiatric diagnoses, whether accurate or not.

In the Union Army, during the first two war years, nearly fourteen hundred soldiers were diagnosed with "insanity." By the end of the third year, 1863, fifteen thousand were treated in the Government Hospital for the Insane. Some 80 percent were diagnosed with "mania," and the rest with "dementia," "melancholia," and "monomania." By the end of the Civil War, fifteen hundred were psychiatrically discharged for "insanity."[61] During World War II, the spectrum of psychiatric diagnoses expanded: Of 1.1 million army neuropsychiatric admissions, nearly seven hundred thousand soldiers were diagnosed with "psychoneurosis" (that era's version of anxiety, depression, and PTSD constructs). Nearly seventy thousand were diagnosed with "psychosis," more than forty thousand with "alcoholism or drug addiction," sixty-six thousand with "immaturity reaction" (like adjustment disorder, but including 250 diagnoses of "pathological personality"), nearly three thousand as "asocial and antisocial personality types" (like PD), nearly thirty thousand with "disorders of intelligence," more than five thousand with "pathological sexuality," and the rest with "other psychiatric disorders."[62]

Today, war veterans are subject to an even wider range of possible psychiatric diagnoses. Table 2.5 shows the DoD's annual report of absolute numbers of service members given a psychiatric diagnosis from 2000 (before war) to 2016. Before the 2001 Afghanistan invasion, some 104,000 personnel were diagnosed through military medicine, compared with 288,000 in 2016. Unfortunately, the military data do not separate out deployed from non-deployed personnel. Table 2.5 reflects only a portion of the actual mental health demand, those available through military medicine records, and does not include the vast numbers of personnel who actively avoid mental health treatment through the military's community counseling centers, mental health contractors, or civilian providers outside the military. Inexplicably, PTSD and TBI rates are also excluded by the Armed Forces Health

TABLE 2.5 Prevalence of Psychiatric-Related Diagnosis Among Active-Duty Population, 2000–2016

DIAGNOSIS	2000	2001	2002	*2003	2004	2005	2006	2007	2008	2009	2010	2011	2012	2013	2014	2015	2016	TOTAL (2000–2016)
Anxiety disorders	7,112	7,728	8,983	18,927	22,203	25,367	28,433	39,024	45,072	54,218	60,729	68,672	76,989	76,829	75,445	73,030	71,069	683,001
Adjustment disorders	28,393	30,148	30,206	36,855	39,230	37,649	42,090	51,616	60,017	71,440	79,500	89,563	96,701	87,579	81,250	80,939	85,793	1,028,969
Mood disorders	18,450	18,651	19,760	35,288	38,605	37,994	40,040	45,166	48,003	56,426	58,653	61,996	62,887	59,332	56,471	53,178	49,992	760,892
Substance abuse disorders	21,744	22,655	23,484	27,515	27,609	25,632	29,151	30,171	32,199	38,353	39,117	36,276	35,897	31,826	28,685	27,268	28,475	506,057
All other mental disorders	18,006	17,567	16,865	22,548	26,522	28,470	39,286	42,974	43,801	50,550	57,231	57,021	59,856	56,429	52,712	49,241	45,959	685,038
Psychotic disorders	1,613	1,534	1,193	1,229	1,236	1,145	1,460	1,664	1,372	2,118	2,359	3,007	3,070	2,829	2,525	2,238	2,007	32,599
Somatoform disorders	N/A	N/A	N/A	1,416	1,591	1,610	1,375	1,392	1,424	1,649	1,666	1,880	2,042	2,455	2,326	2,048	2,092	24,966
Personality disorders	9,195	8,181	8,241	5,987	5,627	5,388	5,161	4,961	3,735	3,507	3,073	3,410	2,929	2,669	2,770	3,018	3,165	81,017
Total	104,513	106,464	108,732	149,765	152,623	163,255	186,996	216,968	235,623	278,261	302,328	321,825	340,371	319,848	302,184	290,960	288,552	3,802,539

TABLE 2.6 Prevalence of Psychiatric Diagnoses in GWOT VA Treatment-Seeking Veterans

DIAGNOSIS	2001–2012	2002–2015	2016	2017	2018 (FOIA)
Post-traumatic stress disorder	239,094	393,139	NR	NR	458,496
Anxiety disorders	161,510	309,232	NR	NR	366,880
Mood disorders	184,404	321,365	NR	NR	645,725
Psychotic-related disorders	111,199	202,705	NR	NR	22,622 (schizophrenia only)
Substance use disorders	118,438	219,143	NR	NR	262,565
Sexual-related disorders	26,788	45,998	NR	NR	NR
Other mental health	32,268	60,980	NR	NR	959,235
Traumatic brain injury	28,828	37,970	NR	NR	NR
Total number of veterans diagnosed with mental health condition	**444,505 (53.3%)**	**708,062**	NR	NR	**2,715,523**

Source: Department of Veterans Affairs, *Analysis of VA Health Care Utilization Among Operation Enduring Freedom, Operation Iraqi Freedom, and Operation New Dawn Veterans, from 1st Qtr FY 2002 Through 3rd Qtr FY 2012* (Washington, DC: Veterans Affairs, 2012); VA Annual Healthcare Utilization Report 2016; 2018 FOIA request by authors.

Note: NR, not reported.

Surveillance Center's annual reports, although PTSD is likely included in the catchall "all other" category.

We can separate out the non-service-connected mental health conditions in the military from those we might refer to as war-stress injury in the VA data. Table 2.1 provides a partial glimpse of the spectrum across three major American wars. Regarding the GWOT, table 2.6 illustrates that war veterans are likely to manifest a broad array of mental health conditions, not just PTSD.

PREVALENCE OF MODERN-DAY TRAUMATIC NEUROSES: ASD AND PTSD

Within military circles, being diagnosed with PTS-"D" (disorder) is viewed widely as a death blow for one's career, which is why many avoid detection or disclosure. But war is only one way to acquire ASD/PTSD. The former diagnosis, ASD, refers to a short-term PTS-response. If it persists longer than one month, psychiatrists diagnose it as PTSD. This is a common side-effect of the occupational hazards of military service: combat, but also motor vehicle accidents, captivity, military training accidents, sexual trauma, terrorism, and even disaster relief or humanitarian missions. Consequently, the military is uniquely positioned to be the world leader in addressing traumatic stress.

Table 2.7 provides a snapshot of the immediate deployment-related mental health needs of service members, including ASD/PTSD diagnosis, and Table 2.8 gives the annual prevalence of both combat and non-combat-related PTSD and TBI.

Research has shown again and again that PTSD diagnosis is significantly associated with an extremely broad group of psychiatric, medical, and MUPS conditions. It is often attended by depression, suicide, substance abuse, poor physical health, relationship problems, chronic pain, sleep disturbance, and anger problems. This is especially the case the longer it goes untreated. As the IOM summarizes, "In the brain, there is evidence of structural and functional changes resulting directly from chronic or severe stress. The changes are associated with alterations of the most profound functions of the brain: memory and decision-making," and that "profound effects on multiple organ systems . . . the continuation of altered physiologic states over months and years contribute to the accumulation of adverse long-term health consequences."[63] This is why every expert practice guideline strongly recommends early identification and intervention—it can prevent the accumulation of health problems. Unfortunately, as long as the military ignores these problems, the costs in money and quality of life will only spiral.

SEXUAL DYSFUNCTION

Few studies have examined sexual dysfunction in returning veterans. From 2001 to 2015, the VA reported 45,998 GWOT veterans were diagnosed with sexual-related problems. Sexual problems are most often attributed to PTSD and depression. The IOM[64] reviewed one small study of combat veterans that found 85 percent of male veterans with PTSD had erectile dysfunction—compared with only 25 percent of those without PTSD. Nunnink et al. reported that 30.5 percent of 197 OIF/OEF veterans reported sexual problems. Hirsch evaluated sexual dysfunction in fifty-three male OIF and OEF veterans and found diminished libido (n = 39), erectile dysfunction

TABLE 2.7 Frontline Mental Health Burden: U.S. Army MHAT Surveys, 2003–2013

SOURCE	SAMPLE	ASD/PTSD	ANY MENTAL HEALTH (PTSD, DEPRESSION, ANXIETY)	CONCUSSIVE INJURY WITH LOSS OF CONSCIOUSNESS	PERCENT SUICIDAL IDEATION (SI) AND NUMBER OF COMPLETED SUICIDES	NUMBER (%) OF PERSONNEL SCREENED POSITIVE FOR MH AND RECEIVED COSC OR BH IN WAR ZONE
2003 MHAT-I OIF	Army N = 750	15%	17%	No data	17% SI N = 24 complete	27% Soldiers positive MH screen
2006 MHAT-IV OIF	Army N = 1,320 Marine N = 447	17% Army 14% Marine	20% Army 15% Marine	No data	18% SI N = 14 Army complete N = 2 Marine complete	42% Soldiers positive MH screen 15% Marines positive MH screen
2008 MHAT-V OIF	Army N = 2195	16%	Deployment no.: 1st: 11%; 2nd: 19%; 3rd: 27%	12%	15% SI N = 34 complete	No data
2009 MHAT-VI OIF	Army N = 1260	11%	14%	No data	12% SI N = 34 complete	No data
2010 Joint MHAT-7 OEF	Marine N = 335	17%	19%	12%	12% SI N = 6 complete	No data
2013 Joint MHAT-9 OEF	Army N = 849	9%	10%	4%	9% SI N = 2	18% overall

Source: Mental Health Advisory Team-I (MHAT-1), *MHAT Operation Iraqi Freedom 16 December 2003* (Washington, DC: U.S. Army Surgeon General, 2003); MHAT-II (MHAT-II), *Operation Iraqi Freedom-II, Mental Health Advisory Team* (MHAT-II), *20 January 2005* (Washington, DC: U.S. Army Surgeon General, 2005); Mental Health Advisory Team-III (MHAT-III), *Mental Health Advisory Team* (MHAT-III), *Operation Iraqi Freedom 04–06, 29 May 2006* (Washington, DC: Office of the Surgeon Multinational Force-Iraq & Office of the Surgeon General, United States Army Medical Command, 2006); Mental Health Advisory Team-IV (MHAT-IV), *Mental Health Advisory Team (MHAT-IV) Operation Iraqi Freedom 05–07, 17 November 2006* (Washington, DC: Office of the Surgeon Multinational Force-Iraq & Office of the Surgeon General, United States Army Medical Command, 2006); MHAT 2007; Mental Health Advisory Team-V (MHAT-V), *Mental Health Advisory Team (MHAT-V) Operation Enduring Freedom 06–08, 14 February 2008* (Washington, DC: Office of the Surgeon Multinational Force-Iraq & Office of the Surgeon General, United States Army Medical Command, 2008); Mental Health Advisory Team-VI (MHAT-VI), *Mental Health Advisory Team (MHAT-6) Operation Enduring Freedom 2009 Afghanistan, November 6, 2009b* (Washington, DC: Office of the Command Surgeon US Forces Afghanistan (USFOR-A) and Office of the Surgeon General, United States Army Medical Command, 2009); MHAT 2012; Joint Mental Health Advisory Team-7 (Joint MHAT-7), *Operation Enduring Freedom 2010 Afghanistan; MHAT 2012*; Joint Mental Health Advisory Team-8 (Joint MHAT-8), *Operation Enduring Freedom 2013 Afghanistan (12 August 2013. (Office of the Surgeon General United States Army Medical Command and Office of the Command Surgeon HQ, USCENTCOM and Office of the Command Surgeon U.S. Forces Afghanistan (USFOR-A), 2013).

TABLE 2.8 Number of Service Members Reported Diagnosed with PTSD or TBI by Military Medicine, 2000–2017

DIAGNOSIS	2000[a]	2001	2002	2003[b]	2004	2005	2006	2007	2008	2009	2010	2011	2012	2013	2014	2015 PARTIAL	2016	2017	TOTAL
PTSD: new cases nondeployed Deployed	1,612	1,705	1,749	1,746	2,145	2,298	2,145	2,596	2,883	2,975	2,984	3,135	3,244	3,414	3,442	1,191	NR	NR	39,264
PTSD: new deployed	N/A	N/A	90	978	3,566	6,688	7,570	11,609	14,332	13,984	14,839	16,024	17,773	14,452	12,570	3,732	NR	NR	138,207
PTSD total	1,612	1,705	1,839	2,724	5,711	8,986	9,715	14,205	17,215	16,959	17,823	19,159	21,017	17,866	16,012	4,923	NR	NR	177,471
TBI	10,959	11,619	12,407	12,815	14,468	15,528	17,022	23,221	28,479	28,895	29,367	32,838	30,650	27,452	25,068	22,694	18,311	13,437	375,230
Total PTSD and TBI	12,571	13,324	14,246	15,539	20,179	24,514	26,737	37,426	45,694	45,845	47,190	51,997	51,667	45,318	41,080	27,617	N/A	N/A	552,701

Source: PTSD data: Congressional Research Service (2016) based on Armed Forces Health Surveillance Center data (2001–2015); TBI data: Department of Defense, Defence and Veterans Brain Injury Center, "DoD Worldwide Numbers for TBI," : http://dvbic.dcoe.mil/dod-worldwide-numbers-tbi; PTSD, TBI rates: Armed Forces Health Surveillance Center.

Note: [a]Pre-war rates; [b]Iraq invasion starts.

(n = 26), and ejaculatory dysfunction (n = 8).[65] Unrecognized sexual problems are critical when war veterans return home and they and their romantic partners have to unexpectedly deal with intimacy issues—creating just another interference with postdeployment or post-military adjustment.

PREVALENCE OF PERSONALITY DISORDERS

During WWII, the prevailing belief was that exposure to war stress intensified one's existing personality traits, but it did not create new traits. Diagnosing a PD requires clear evidence of inflexible, maladaptive personality traits that cause a pattern of problematic adjustment, usually evident in adolescence. In other words, one does not develop a PD on the battlefield. Since WWI, a personality-type diagnosis could get one discharged, and it soon became a weapon for commanders to get rid of their discipline problems quickly. Diagnosing PD is not new to the twenty-first-century military. For example, during WWI, more than six thousand army personnel were diagnosed with "constitutional psychopathic states," a precursor to what we now call PD.[66] In WWII, two hundred and fifty soldiers were diagnosed with "pathological personality," and twenty-seven hundred were diagnosed with "asocial and antisocial personality types."[67] This trend reportedly increased significantly during the Korean and Vietnam wars, but absolute totals are unavailable.[68]

According to the Government Accountability Office (GAO), DoD data from November 2001 through June 2007 revealed that twenty-eight hundred returning war veterans were among twenty-six thousand service members administratively separated on the basis of having a PD—essentially a diagnosis of "preexisting" disability incompatible with military service (see chapter 9). The significance of the GAO finding is that administratively separated personnel are generally ineligible for disability pension and VA treatment benefits, which is referred to as a "backdoor discharge"—the military has subsequently amended its PD policy.[69] From 2000 to 2011, a total of 81,017 active-duty service members were diagnosed with PD by military healthcare; it is unknown how many were also war veterans (see chapter 9).

"MORAL INJURY" OR PERPETRATOR TRAUMA

An all-too frequently overlooked psychological, even spiritual, effect of war is the act or witness of killing. Grossman called the killing of one's own species as the "universal phobia."[70] Litz et al. conducted an extensive review of the concept of "moral injury" defined as "perpetrating, failing to prevent, bearing witness to, or learning about acts that transgress deeply held moral beliefs and expectations."[71] The "moral injury" construct is controversial among war veterans who fear moral backlash for performing their duty.

In their examination of just over five thousand war zone veterans seeking VA treatment, Fontana and Rosenheck concluded that the agent of killing related significantly to all symptom categories in all cohorts, suggesting that responsibility for killing another human being is the single most pervasive, traumatic experience of war. Following close behind this experience is observing a killing and exposure to combat in general.[72] The duration and severity of PTSD symptoms in Vietnam combat veterans is closely associated with their exposure to human death, which may cause more harm than the threat of personal death from combat.[73] Exposure to "grotesque death," abusive violence, and atrocities—for instance, friendly fire or the death of children—increased the risk of PTSD.[74] After controlling for combat exposure, 151 Vietnam vets' endorsement of atrocity exposure was significantly related to the severity of their PTSD symptoms and guilt.[75] Guilt about combat actions was the strongest predictor of suicidal ideation and attempts. In particular, many suicidal veterans in their study reported killing women and children out of fear or anger. Fontana et al. found that killing or failing to prevent death motivated suicide attempts.[76]

The current war cohort has a high frequency of exposure to potential moral injury: 56.1 percent of deployed marines and 48.4 percent of soldiers reported killing combatants in 2010,[77] and 69 percent of returning deployers reported injuring a woman or child.[78] Among nearly three thousand OIF soldiers who reported killing, 2.8 percent reported suicidal ideation.[79] If we know about the frequency and type of combat experiences, we can better anticipate wartime demands. Veterans seeking counseling for moral injury–specific difficulties may be more likely to do so through chaplains or spiritual leaders rather than through mental healthcare providers.

PREVALENCE OF TRAUMATIC GRIEF REACTION

According to the VA's *Iraq War Clinician's Guide Second Edition* "Traumatic grief refers to the experience of the sudden loss of a significant and close attachment. Having a close buddy, identification with soldiers in the unit, and experiencing multiple losses were the strongest predictors of grief symptoms in the above sample of Vietnam veterans."[80] Despite its clinical prominence, research on the prevalence of traumatic grief reaction (TGR), complicated bereavement, prolonged grief disorder, or whatever label one wants to use in war veterans is rare. Shay offers many eloquent examples of TGR in Vietnam combat veterans grieving the death or severe wounding of combat buddies.[81] Pivar and Field reviewed TGR in war veterans, reporting the intensity of grief symptoms — even after thirty years — was similar to grieving spouses.[82] Pivar observes, "if left untreated, [it] can continue unabated and increases the distress load of veterans," adding that "the existence of a distinct and intense set of grief symptoms indicates the need for clinical attention to grief in the treatment plan."[83]

A sample of Vietnam veterans treated for PTSD proved that TGR as a war stress injury can be distinct from psychiatric conditions like PTSD, depression, and generalized anxiety, but it is often overlooked.[84] An extensive review of Persian Gulf War veterans by RAND cited a study of fifty-six soldiers involved in a deadly "friendly fire" incident, finding 29 percent still had nightmares and 38 percent reported increased alcohol use after four months.[85] Soldiers assigned to "graves registry" reported more current and lifetime psychiatric disorder.

Today, the incidence of TGR is not tracked and thus is unknown. Studies of TGR reveal that of more than twenty thousand active-duty members screened positive for PTSD, almost 80 percent reported witnessing people being wounded or killed or engaging in direct combat, 86 percent knew a fellow service member who was shot or wounded,[86] and 79 percent of deployed marines reported the death of a unit member.[87] Additionally, 50 percent of OIF soldiers and 57 percent OIF marines reported handling human remains,[88] a significant risk factor identified in Vietnam[89] and Persian Gulf War veterans.[90]

According to the DoD, "The well-being of one's family affects a service member throughout his or her career and plays an integral role in readiness to deploy in a moment's notice." The realities of the all-volunteer army are that about half are married and the other half are moving toward (or returning to) marriage. In *Families Under Fire*, Everson and Figley relay story after story of military families, awaiting the return of their husband, child, or grandchild while carrying on at home. Spouses suddenly become a single-parent household and figure out a way to manage day to day.[91]

Steady increases in the tempo of military operations beginning long before the current conflict have placed more demands on families, and the current operational load can be taxing for even the most resilient families.[92] Generations of postwar analyses of war-stress casualties have routinely ignored the potential "ripple effect" on military family members.[93] In an all-volunteer military, unhappy spouses and children lead to career changes. Most studies of all branches find that families are for the most part happy being a military family, satisfied with military services for families, and instilled with a sense of pride.

In 1944, Despert conducted a review of children's mental health during WWII and found that most, but not all, appeared resilient. Dekel and Goldblatt reviewed the intergenerational effects of war on spouses and children of veterans diagnosed with PTSD or a related condition from WWII, Korea, and Vietnam, and concluded that the greater the father's level of distress, PTSD symptoms, or violence, the greater distress and symptoms appeared in family members.[94] Beckham et al. examined children of Vietnam War veterans, finding that many children of fathers with PTSD reported notable difficulty, including 40 percent who used drugs, 35 percent with behavioral problems, 15 percent with violent behavior problems, 45 percent with significant signs of secondary PTSD, and 83 percent reporting elevated hostility scores.[95] The spouses do not escape this either. A reported 38 percent of Vietnam War veterans divorced after six months of homecoming.[96] Jordan et al. studied Vietnam War vets and spouses or coresident partners, finding that veterans with PTSD had more severe problems with family adjustment, parenting skills, and violent behavior.[97] Some 40 percent of Persian Gulf War veterans reported significant family and marital distress a year after returning home.

In 2014, 1.8 million American children lived in military families, representing just a fraction of those exposed directly to parents' wartime deployments over the past fifteen years. Wadsworth et al. reviewed the effects of deployments on military children and discovered elevations in risk-taking and impulsive behaviors and more mental health problems, especially during deployment. From 2000 through 2011, nearly one hundred thousand military personnel were diagnosed with a "partner relational problem," almost forty thousand with a "family circumstance problem," and more than twenty thousand with "maltreatment related problem" (e.g., abuse).[98] From 2000 to 2007, the Air Force's Family Advocacy Program reported thirty-three thousand cases of substantiated spouse abuse and thirty-two thousand cases of child abuse—most of which was emotional abuse (55 percent), followed by neglect (46 percent), and multiple forms of maltreatment (45 percent). An additional 37 percent reported physical abuse. In today's cohort, 5.9 percent of deployed marines reported pending separation or divorce, and rates of marital discord are steadily increasing. In 2003, 12 percent reported marital problems; between 2004 and 2006, 24 percent did so; and between 2005 and 2007, 25 percent of soldiers and 23 percent of marines reported martial problems.[99] Children and spouses use significantly more mental health services during deployments.[100]

TRAUMATIC BRAIN INJURY

In 2007, the DoD Task Force on Mental Health intimated that the principle reason for its mental health system's collapse was the unanticipated demands of two so-called signature injuries: PTSD and TBI. Although diagnostic labels have evolved, both PTSD and TBI have been the focus of concern since the twentieth century. Early detection of injury is critical in TBI patient management.[101] According to the IOM, cooccurring psychiatric conditions are reported in 49 percent of moderate to severe TBI and in 34 percent of mild TBI cases.[102]

TBI has been a documented medical concern going back to the armies of Napoleon, who first described "wind contusions" following artillery shell explosions.[103] Studies of TBI have been conducted after every major war since the twentieth century. An estimated 10 percent of WWI-era shell-shock cases were later determined to be "shell concussions."[104] Across every war, we have seen the prevalence of TBI. In WWI, 337 army personnel were diagnosed with "brain injury.".[105] In WWII, 8,500 were diagnosed with "blast concussion" or "posttraumatic encephalopathy."[106] During the Korean War, more than three hundred soldiers were diagnosed with "encephalopathy due to trauma" and more than seventeen hundred were admitted to the hospital for "concussion"[107]—and nearly five hundred Navy and Marine Corps veterans had cases of "craniocerebral injuries." During the Vietnam War, 12 to 14 percent of all combat casualties were reportedly diagnosed with TBI.[108] A longitudinal National Institutes of Health Vietnam Head Injury Study in 1974 found more than twelve hundred Vietnam veterans diagnosed with a traumatic brain injury between 1967 and 1970. After the Persian Gulf War, Congress mandated the establishment of the current Defense and Veterans Head Injury Program (DVBIC) in 1992, "to integrate specialized TBI care, research and education across military and veteran medical care systems."

Today, a total of 375,000 military personnel and nearly 38,000 veterans[109] have been diagnosed with TBI (see table 2.8). All patients admitted to Walter Reed Army Medical Center between January 2003 and February 2005 who had been exposed to blasts were routinely evaluated for brain injury, and 59 percent were found to suffer TBI. Of those injuries, 56 percent were moderate or severe, and 44 percent were mild.[110] The GAO reported disturbing trends: 57 percent of marines deployed to Afghanistan received no TBI screenings despite reporting a head injury after an improvised explosive device (IED) blast, and 42 percent who reported losing consciousness after an IED blast also received no TBI screening.[111]

The DVBIC is the DoD's research Center of Excellence for TBI. In 2011, it began publicly reporting military TBI rates. As noted in table 2.8, a total of 375,000 service members have been diagnosed with TBI, with 80 percent rated "mild" TBI (mTBI). TBI is significantly associated with a variety of cooccurring conditions, such as PTSD, depression, SUD, sleep disturbance, post-traumatic anger and interpersonal violence, and suicide. Repeat mTBI and severe TBI were found to be associated with increased severity of psychiatric symptoms and suicide after seven years, as well as lifetime risk of an Alzheimer's-like condition called chronic traumatic encephalopathy. In 2013, the IOM reported that 19.5 to 44 percent of veterans with TBI also had PTSD.[112]

MALINGERING AND FACTITIOUS DISORDERS

Malingering is the intentional fabrication or exaggeration of mental or physical symptoms by a person motivated by external incentives, for instance, to avoid military duty, work, or incarceration, or for financial compensation or drugs. Factitious disorders and illnesses are like malingering with respect to the fabrication of symptoms, but these individuals seek to assume "sick roles," like hospitalization, medical evaluation, and treatment. From 1998 to 2012, the army identified more than five thousand service members who received a diagnosis of malingering or factitious illness, 168 of those during deployment.[113]

SUBSTANCE USE DISORDERS

It is well documented that the stress of war has always been associated with substance abuse, both during and particularly after war.[114]

Historically, the use of alcohol, drugs, and tobacco has been common in the military. Alcoholism and opiate addiction were major concerns in the Union Army—more than fifty-five hundred soldiers were hospitalized for inebriation, 110 of whom died of alcohol poisoning. There were almost four thousand cases of delirium tremens, of which 450 proved fatal. And there were more than nine hundred cases of chronic alcoholism, forty-five of which were lethal.[115] In the Civil War, the unlimited and unmonitored prescription of morphine, heroin, and cocaine to treat physical wounds and medically unexplained pain symptoms (like functional rheumatism) was widespread. This led to the unintended consequences of causing drug addiction to grow rampant among thousands of veterans. During WWI, more than four thousand deployed soldiers were discharged for "alcoholism or drug addiction"[116]; that number grew to forty-three thousand in WWII.[117] In the Korean War, the incidence of SUD was reported to be "high," but the number was never specified.[118] During the Vietnam War, however, SUD was by far the most extensive. Stanton reported that from 1967 to 1971, the proportion of enlisted soldiers smoking marijuana "heavily" (twenty or more times) in Vietnam increased from 7 percent to 34 percent, whereas the proportion of "habitual" users (more than two hundred times) stabilized at between 17 percent and 18 percent between 1969 and 1971.[119] In 1970, four hundred soldiers were admitted for drug overdose in Vietnam hospitals.[120] Baker cited seventy-five opiate deaths in Vietnam within a three-month span in 1970, and by October 1971, an estimated "44 percent of all lower ranking enlisted men (E-1 to E-4) were using heroin and half of these may have been addicted.[121] By 1971, more soldiers were being evacuated from Vietnam for drug use than medically WIA [wounded in action]."[122] The Persian Gulf War cohort similarly reported a high, but unspecified, incidence of SUD. In 1981, the DoD adopted a zero-tolerance policy for illicit drugs, and began mandatory, random urinalysis and enacted stricter policies against drinking to disentangle the warrior mythos from alcohol abuse.[123] Then, as now, increases in military alcohol use may be a form of self-medicating to cope with untreated war-stress injury.

The IOM has reported that since the start of OEF/OIF "alcohol abuse among returning military personnel has spiked. In 2008, nearly half of active duty service members reported binge drinking."[124] In today's cohort, from 2000 to 2016, a reported half-million active military personnel (see table 2.8) and more than three hundred thousand VA-treatment-seeking GWOT veterans (see table 2.8) have been diagnosed with an SUD. Estimates of military alcohol abuse range from 12 percent to 40 percent, including 36 percent of the National Guard. But the majority of these cases are untreated.[125] Since OEF, a twelve-year surveillance period revealed more than seventy thousand service members had been diagnosed with drug abuse (excluding alcohol), the most frequent of which was marijuana. News media reports of prescription drug abuse and pain killers, and heightened concerns around the overprescription of psychotropic medications to deployed personnel are concerning. Some 14 percent of OIF deployed soldiers surveyed on the frontlines reported taking psychotropic medications,[126] and 12 percent reported illicit drug use, including prescription medication abuse in the past thirty days, as reflected in an increasing trend for opioid-related diagnoses since 2002. Prescription drug misuse by active-duty personnel doubled from 2 percent in 2002 to 4 percent in 2005, and as of 2008, had spiked to 11 percent.[127]

THE MENTAL HEALTH NEEDS OF MEDICALLY WOUNDED VETERANS

The government's commitment to care for the medical wounds of the military is highlighted in the VA's motto: "to care for him who shall have borne the battle and for his widow, and his orphan." This is an adaption of Lincoln's famous Second Inaugural refrain, to "bind the wounds of war." We see it again in the Military Health System's mission "to ensure delivery of world-class health care to all DoD service members, retirees, and their families." High rates of neuropsychiatric conditions, however, continue to be reported for those who have been wounded in action (WIA).

An archival examination of nearly eighteen thousand military and medical records of Civil War veterans revealed a 64 percent increase in "nervous disorder" diagnoses among wounded Union Army veterans compared with those not wounded.[128] During the Korean War, a study of wounded soldiers found 56 percent who were admitted to orthopedic wards reported neuropsychiatric symptoms upon impromptu psychiatric interview.[129] The prevalence of PTSD among WIA Vietnam veterans was more than 30 percent. One-third of Purple Heart recipients suffered from PTSD, whereas only 15 percent of nonwounded veterans did.[130] Many of the estimated fifty thousand Civil War veterans described inexplicable sensations from amputated limbs attributed to a ghost or hallucination, eventually leading to the terms causalgia (nerve injury) and phantom limb. Currently, the prevalence of phantom limb pain (PLP) or phantom limb sensation (PLS) is virtually universal, occurring in between 50 percent and 90 percent of amputees,[131] with reports of chronic incidence varying from 10 percent to 78 percent.[132]

As of February 2018, a total of fifty-two thousand military and DoD civilians have been medically wounded in action. More than 30 percent of evacuated OIF active-duty WIA veterans reported excessive dissociation, PTSD, or depression symptoms that warranted mental health evaluation.[133] Rates of depression and PTSD among 613 severely WIA service members increased significantly between the initial one-month postinjury assessment (in which 4.2 percent had PTSD symptoms and 4.4 percent had depression) to seven months postinjury (in which 12 percent had PTSD and 9.3 percent met criteria for depression). About fifty thousand veterans of Iraq and Afghanistan are considered to be polytrauma patients, meaning they have suffered multiple traumatic injuries. That includes more than sixteen hundred personnel with severe TBI and more than a thousand with severe burns.

In 2009, Congress legislated the creation of the Extremity Trauma and Amputation Center of Excellence (EACE), a joint enterprise between the DoD and VA to optimize the quality of life of service members and veterans who sustained extremity trauma or amputation. As of October 2015, there were approximately twenty-six thousand such cases. These injuries ranged in severity and complexity, but nearly half involved the legs. From 2001 to 2015, EACE documented more than sixteen hundred GWOT veterans with major limb amputations. Of these individuals, 69 percent suffered a single limb loss injury, and 31 percent had lost multiple limbs. Another 52 percent of these military amputees have been diagnosed with PTSD. It was not until 2016 that the military went an entire year in the GWOT without a traumatic amputation.

MISCONDUCT STRESS BEHAVIORS

The Department of the Army describes a range of maladaptive stress reactions, from minor to serious violations of military law and the Law of Land Warfare. Most often these occur in poorly trained soldiers, but even the "good and heroic, under extreme stress may also engage in misconduct." This behavior can include mutilating the enemy dead, mistreating prisoners, looting, rape, malingering, refusing combat, self-inflicted wounds, desertion, torture, and the intentional killing of noncombatants.[134] Indiscipline can consist of relatively minor acts of omission or insubordination—such as the failure to take preventive hygiene measures in Korea, which led to frost-bite, or failing to take chloroquine-primaquine in Vietnam, which resulted in malaria. It also can be the commission of serious acts of disobedience, mutiny, homicide, "fragging," and even atrocity (e.g., the My Lai massacre in Vietnam).

To be clear, war atrocities have occurred in every major human war, by all combatants, and the commission of atrocities does not automatically equate to war stress injury, nor is the presence of war stress injury a justifi-cation for atrocity. Since the Civil War, the legal system has struggled with the culpability in soldiers accused of atrocity and misconduct who also show evidence of severe war-stress injury. Jones reported one such lesson from the Korean and Vietnam Wars: "Low-intensity garrison (guerilla) warfare can produce 'nostalgic' types of combat reactions that include alcohol and drug abuse, depression, and suicide. The mental health worker needs to be aware of the variety of stress responses that result from different types of combat."[135]

The Union Army executed 267 soldiers, about forty-five per year coming from nine hundred courts-martial convictions. More than half were exe-cuted for desertion, 25 percent for homicide, 10 percent for rape or mutiny, and the rest for thievery or espionage. During WWI ,the American Army executed thirty-five soldiers for the rape or murder of civilians.[136] In WWII, there were 1.7 million courts-martial, which constituted a third of all crim-inal cases in America from 1941 to 1946, including twenty-one thousand cases of "desertion," resulting in the last American execution for desertion in 1945 of a combat soldier diagnosed with "psychoneuroses." These WWII-era atrocities led to executions of more than one hundred American soldiers for the rape or murder of civilians.

Army psychiatrists in Korea observed that as incidence rates of frostbite rose, the number of neuropsychiatric casualties decreased—which raised suspicions that this frostbite was self-inflicted.[137] There were 101 reported homicides within the U.S. Army in Korea between 1950 and 1953,[138] and an estimated 163 unarmed Korean women, children, and elderly refugees were killed by U.S. forces at No Gun Ri in 1950.[139] During the Vietnam War, Linden reported a progressive increase in the number of courts-martial for insubordination and assaults, including murder, exemplified by incidents of "fragging."[140] These had increased from just 0.3 per 1,000 people in 1969 to 1.7 per 1,000 in 1971.[141] A reported 320 atrocities by American military personnel were substantiated by the Vietnam War Crimes Working Group, which was commissioned after the 1968 My Lai Massacre of as many as five hundred unarmed Vietnamese, including many women and children.[142]

As in other wars, especially low-intensity guerilla-type warfare like in Iraq and Afghanistan, there has been a high incidence of misconduct stress behaviors by American personnel, ranging from inappropriate handling of American and enemy combatant dead, to prisoner torture and sexual abuse,[143] as well as several substantiated incidents of rape and homicide of unarmed civilians, including children. The number of court-martial or incidents of atrocity is unknown at this time. In 2014, the Associated Press reported a total of twenty-eight thousand soldiers were discharged for misconduct since the Iraq War.[144] Frontline military surveys reveal that soldiers and marines with diagnosed with mental health problems were reported as more likely to mistreat noncombatants.[145] One study showed that deployed marines with PTSD were eleven times more likely to be discharged for misconduct behaviors than their peers without PTSD.[146] A study by Street et al. on military sexual trauma found that 52 percent of active-duty female and 29 percent of male personnel reported "offensive sexual behavior" and 9 percent of female and 3 percent of male soldiers reported "sexual coercion." In 2011, the U.S. Army noted a 64 percent increase in violent sexual crimes since 2006. By August 2010, 260 American military personnel died from "self-inflicted wounds" while deployed to Iraq and Afghanistan. Suicide remains a violation of military law and unsuccessful attempters are subject to discipline. For instance, in 2012, the U.S. Court of Appeals for the Armed Forces heard the appeal of Marine Private Lazzaric Caldwell who received a bad-conduct discharge and six-month sentence from a courts-marital conviction for violating Article 134 "prejudicial to good order and discipline" after slitting his wrists. Private Caldwell was diagnosed with PTSD and depression before his 2010 suicide attempt. Under public pressure, the Court of Appeals overturned the conviction, but self-inflicted injury (including suicide attempts) remains a chargeable form of misconduct stress (see chapter 4).

POST-TRAUMATIC ANGER AND INTERPERSONAL VIOLENCE

Irritability and postwar anger problems that occasionally escalates into violence have been reported in every generation of war veterans. In the context of combat, anger and aggression are normative responses to threats.[147] Such responses are not only adaptive to war but also modeled and reinforced through military training.[148] Social reintegration transitions from deployment to after military discharge are critical periods of adjustment, wherein violence against oneself or others may arise, and it is perhaps then that individual and family support is most important.

The government's study of the effects of the Vietnam War, "Legacies of Vietnam," found 24 percent of vets who saw heavy combat were later arrested for criminal offenses, compared with 17 percent of other veterans of other wars and 14 percent of nonveterans.[149] A study by Jordan et al. found that approximately one-third of Gulf War–era veterans with PTSD were perpetrators of partner violence in the previous year.[150]

A 2012 army-wide study of twenty thousand soldiers found length of deployment was positively correlated with the severity of self-reported interpersonal violence perpetration in the year after deployment.[151] The longer they were deployed, the more likely they were to abuse their wives or husbands when they returned. One sample found that OEF/OIF veterans with PTSD self-reported irritability or anger as their highest symptom, with 29 percent of reports rated as "quite a bit" or "extreme."[152] Another study reported 70 percent of veterans with PTSD reported impulsive aggressiveness, compared with just 29 percent of veterans without PTSD.[153] Another sample of male combat veterans found that 33 percent reported physical aggression toward a partner and 91 percent reported psychologic aggression toward a partner. Furthermore, veterans who did not have partners reported general physical aggression.[154] Data from the National Comorbidity Survey revealed 21 percent of current partner abuse was indirectly attributable to combat exposure-mediated by PTSD.[155] Table 2.9 reveals a relatively stable level of aggressive behaviors when combatants return home, providing a small window for intervention.

This behavior, and behavior like it, often puts veterans in jail. A 2008 New York Times article reported 121 cases of OEF/OIF veterans who were charged with homicide after returning home from war.[156] According to the Bureau of Justice Statistics, on any given day, 9.4 percent—or 223,000—of the inmates in the country's prisons and jails are veterans.[157] An estimated 4.5 percent of veterans in state and federal prisons served in OEF/OIF. After the Vietnam War in 1982, the New York Times reported "Jailed veterans case brings post-Vietnam problem into focus,"[158] harkening back to a 1929 headline "Says Veterans Lack Psychiatric Relief: McNutt Declares Disabled Men Are In Jails, As Hospitals Are Not Available." Studies today have argued that incarceration rates of veterans are no greater than rates of nonveterans.

TABLE 2.9 Aggression of Active Duty and National Guard Following Deployment

TYPE OF AGGRESSION	3 MONTHS	12 MONTHS
Angry: kicked, smashed, punched something	41%	40%
Threatened another with physical violence	40%	35%
Got into fight and hit someone	17%	18%

Source: Thomas et al. (2010).

MENTAL HEALTH NEEDS OF PRISONERS OF WAR

In 1992, the IOM completed a literature review on the long-term health effects of WWII and Korean War prisoners of war (POW), finding consistently higher rates of psychiatric illness among them than among non-POW veterans. The same was found among prisoners of the Civil War, who suffered comorbid physical, nervous disease, and mortality rates.[159] Goldstein et al. reported 29 percent of WWII POWs in Japan still met PTSD criteria forty years after their release. Lifetime PTSD rates in 426 POWs during WWII and Korean War were reported as high as 70 percent, with current rates of 20 to 40 percent.[160] There are no reported twenty-first-century POWs, but the mental health demand for veteran POWs and their families must be anticipated by future war planners.

CHRONICITY AND COMORBIDITY

Universal expert consensus calls for early identification and intervention of war-stress injuries to avert long-term adverse health and functioning consequences from chronic disability. Researchers have repeatedly observed that upward of 80 to 90 percent of ASD diagnoses will convert to PTSD.[161] A 2010 army frontline survey identified 15 percent of deployed soldiers and 16 percent of marines met ASD criteria, and those prevalence rates increased with multiple deployments.[162] The risk of long-term disability and impairment has been shown to increase overtime: chronicity breeds comorbidity.

An estimated 50 to 80 percent of patients with PTSD also meet criteria for additional psychiatric disorder or MUPS.[163] Stability of MUPS in

390 Persian Gulf War veterans over a five-year period revealed no significant changes in number or severity of symptoms over time.[164] A recent VA
study found 32 percent of female and 20 percent of male OEF/OIF veterans
who suffer with PTSD had ten or more diagnosed medical ailments—only
11 percent of female and 7 percent of male veterans without PTSD or other
psychiatric condition had that many.[165]

UNEMPLOYMENT

Another common, yet controversial, indicator of postwar readjustment is
unemployment. The press has reported on the jobless problems of returning veterans since the Civil War. A 1934 New York Times headline "Says
Economy Drives Veterans to Suicide: R.W. Means Appeals to a House
Committee for a Broader Interpretation of the Law." Throughout the duration of war, the unemployment rate among veterans fluctuates, but typically
it is higher once war ends and mass military demobilization begins, when
hundreds of thousands of service members are discharged in a short window
of time.[166] As of 2011, according to the U.S. Department of Labor, unemployment rates for OEF/OIF veterans stood at 4.5 percent overall, but reached
21.9 percent for veterans between the ages of eighteen and twenty-four,
which is likely the majority.

HOMELESSNESS

Following the Gulf War, a 1994 New York Times article reported, "The Department of Veterans Affairs estimates that up to 250,000 of the nation's veterans
are homeless." In 2004, the VA provided mental health treatment to just over
forty thousand homeless veterans.[167] According to the National Council for
Homeless Veterans (2009), there are more than 194,000 homeless veterans.
Of those, 33 percent were deployed to war zones; 89 percent received an honorable discharge; 76 percent suffer mental health, alcohol, or drug problems;
and 17 percent are post–Vietnam Era (just 2 percent are OEF/OIF veterans).

   The VA has made inroads into reducing veteran homelessness. Fewer
GWOT veterans are homeless than of previous war cohorts. Unfortunately,
two-thirds of homeless GWOT veterans have PTSD—a much higher rate
than in earlier cohorts of homeless veterans, who have PTSD rates between

8 and 13 percent. Across thirty-one studies on veterans experiencing home-lessness published from 1987 to 2014, the strongest and most consistent risk factors were SUDs and mental illness, followed by low income.

THE COST OF INCREASED HEALTHCARE

The severity of PTSD symptoms can ruin one's health. It is strongly related to cardiovascular problems,[168] IBS,[169] CFS,[170] chronic pain,[171] somatization,[172] and altered immune responses. In 2007, American military epidemiologists reported a high frequency of somatic complaints in OIF veterans with PTSD: more than 75 percent reported fatigue, 70 percent reported sleep difficulties, 42 percent reported headaches, 50 percent reported joint pain, and 23 percent reported gastrointestinal symptoms[173] and elevated incidence of diarrhea. In contrast, 28 percent of non-PTSD OIF veterans reported chronic fatigue and 70 percent confirmed sleep difficulties,[174] and 86 percent of 283 cardiology referrals for OIF veterans with PTSD revealed no organic basis.

CARETAKER COMPASSION STRESS

The military has long been aware of the secondary effects from trauma. For instance, during WWI, the term "shell shocked by proxy" was attributed to legendary British Army psychiatrist William H. R. Rivers, who himself began mimicking his shell-shocked patients' symptoms. According to Nickerson and Shea:

> We learn from Rivers the capacity of patients to teach us, and when need be, to heal us. The act of listening to individuals is fundamental, and it is not passive. It implies a willingness to be changed by what we hear. Otherwise one no longer listened attentively enough to the individual voice. There was a real danger, he thought, that in the end the stories would become one story, the voices blend into a single cry of pain.

During WWII, U.S. Army psychiatrist Albert J. Glass warned:

> The psychiatrist himself is likely to become weary and emotionally exhausted . . . each case a decision that may mean life or death for the

soldier must be reached . . . he may identify himself with his patients and see them as all equally deserving of evacuation; or . . . adopt a harsh policy, assume a severe and caustic manner.

In 2013, RAND reported an estimated 275,000 to one million caretakers of wounded GWOT veterans, including 63,000 seriously disabled. "Spouses, parents, and siblings of wounded troops face increased stress, greater risk of heart disease, compromised immune functions, and a host of other health threats because of the physical and emotional demands of caring for their infirm loved ones." The report continued: "Despite the need, no national strategy for supporting military caregivers exists. Government agencies and other organizations are trying to help, but most programs are in their infancy and inadequate to meet the need of this growing population."

This is one more example of the military failing to learn its war trauma lessons and the collateral damage of its negligence. Compassion stress may affect 40 percent to 80 percent of caregivers.[175] In 1978, one of this book's authors, American Vietnam veteran and psychologist Charles R. Figley, coined the term "secondary catastrophic stress reactions," which he later reformulated as "secondary traumatic stress" (STS). This was later confirmed by studies on the children of Vietnam veterans.[176] Recent army surveys of deployed behavioral health personnel revealed 33 percent reported "burnout."[177] A high incidence of "compassion fatigue" also has been reported by military psychologists,[178] military chaplains,[179] VA counselors,[180] and family caregivers.[181] Thirty-six percent of wives of PTSD-affected veterans meet the criteria for STS disorder. They report significantly higher levels of STS symptoms compared with the wives of veterans without PTSD. Also, wives of PTSD-affected veterans report having more psychological difficulties and lower perceived quality of life compared with the other two groups.

As this overview has proved, exposure to war has always affected humans—their minds, they bodies, and even their souls—in ways that are so much more than significant than PTSD, TBI, and suicide. This trauma continues to affect veterans and their families. Now that we have covered the financial costs of refusing to learn these war trauma lessons and the price our soldiers continue to pay, we are ready to uncover the ten harmful strategies responsible for this mess and what prevents the military from addressing its mental health dilemma.

3

CRUEL AND INHUMANE HANDLING

THE FIRST DARK-SIDE STRATEGY

It is interesting to note that one of the principal symptoms manifested by these feebleminded soldiers was the wandering spell, which lasted for hours in some instances, and the soldier would be found away from his unit in a more or less dazed condition.

Many of these mental defectives were court-martialed for desertion and often punished when, as a matter of fact, they were totally irresponsible for the acts committed.

AMERICAN EXPEDITIONARY FORCES DURING WORLD WAR I

The U.S. military and the rest of the world's armed forces have insisted from the beginning that stern discipline was the most effective way to handle all forms of personnel weakness, especially war-stress injury. Why? Because they believed that harsh discipline bred strength and beat out weakness, whether it be desertion or the weakness of refusing to fight, disrespecting an officer, cowering, or trembling in fear. Extolling harsh, sometimes cruel punishments in front of the rank-and-file has always been a commander's reflexive weapon to intimidate the soldiers into submission at the expense of the unfortunate few.

THE CASE FOR MILITARY DISCIPLINE

In 1757, then–Lieutenant Colonel George Washington observed, "Discipline is the soul of an Army. It makes small numbers formidable; procures success to the *weak*, and esteem to all." More combatants were killed in ancient battles when they broke formation and fled than in direct conflict. Disobedience, overt fear, running away, and the panic of an unnerved (or undisciplined) few has long been associated with disaster for militaries. They believe *weakness*—freezing-up, refusing to fight, straggling, insubordination, disobedience, desertion, madness, hysterical paralysis, self-inflicted wounds, cowardice, physical or emotional exhaustion, exposure to chronic excessive or traumatic stress, malingering, grief—is their greatest enemy.

Military leaders learn early and often that tolerating indiscipline invites contagion. Consequently, throughout history, commanders have resorted to public demonstrations of harsh and sometimes cruel discipline to punish the weak—regardless of the source of their so-called weakness—to intimidate the ranks.

MISCONDUCT STRESS BEHAVIORS

The Department of the Army describes a range of maladaptive stress reactions, from minor to serious violations of military law, most often occurring in poorly trained soldiers. They note, however, that the "good and heroic, under extreme stress may also engage in misconduct" even in highly cohesive well-trained and led units.[1]

For example, according to previously classified military documents, the first-ever U.S. special forces unit was organized during World War II (WWII) and consisted of 2,639 officers and enlisted personnel.[2] On its first mission, fifty-three Rangers were killed and 91 percent of this highly decorated unit received awards, including 1,214 Purple Hearts after 240 days of intensive, continuous combat. After deployment, however, 10 percent of the force was convicted of various misconducts and court-martialed.[3] Under the extreme stress of prolonged combat, some of the force had fallen into misconduct stress behaviors: mutilating enemy dead, not taking prisoners, looting, rape, malingering, refusing to fight, taking drugs, self-inflicting wounds, fragging, desertion, torture, and intentionally killing noncombatants.[4]

From 2002 through 2006, the average annual rate of army prosecutions of desertion tripled compared with the five years before the war.[5] In 2006 alone, more than three thousand soldiers deserted, compared with just over two thousand in 2004. In total, the U.S. Army court-martialed twice as many soldiers for desertion and other unauthorized absences as it did on average each pre-war year from 1997 to 2001. From 2003 to 2007, 109 soldiers were convicted of going absence without leave (AWOL) or deserting war zones in Iraq or Afghanistan.

The *New York Times* interviewed two Army combat veterans charged with desertion:

> James and Ronnie, who both have five years of service, suffer from post-traumatic stress disorder and abuse alcohol to self-medicate, said Dr. David M. Walker, a former Air Force psychiatrist who has examined both men. With help from lawyers, James and Ronnie returned to Fort Bliss on Tuesday.
>
> They were charged with desertion and face courts-martial and possibly a few months in a military brig. "If I could stay in the military, get help, that's what I want," said Ronnie, who completed an 18-month combat tour in Kirkuk, Iraq, with the 25th Infantry Division in 2004.[6]

MILITARY ORDER AND DISCIPLINE

The military's ability to effectively fight and win wars often hinges on its aptitude to impose discipline with a carrot and a stick. Clear rewards for compliance are contrasted with equally transparent punishment for transgressions. Military codes have always authorized punishment for disciplinary infractions to ensure good order and discipline. By the late 1700s, the British Articles of War prohibited conduct prejudicial to "good order and military discipline," which was adopted into the American Military's Uniformed Code of Military Justice (UCMJ). Today, the U.S. Army defines military discipline this way:

> Military discipline is founded upon self-discipline, respect for properly constituted authority, and the embracing of the professional Army ethic.
>
> While military discipline is the result of effective training, it is affected by every feature of military life.
>
> It is manifested in individuals and units by cohesion, bonding, and a spirit of teamwork; by smartness of appearance and action; by cleanliness and maintenance of dress, equipment, and quarters; by deference to seniors and mutual respect between senior and subordinate personnel; by the prompt and willing execution of both the letter and spirit of the legal orders of their lawful commanders; and by fairness, justice, and equity for all Soldiers.[7]

When it comes to meting out discipline, "commanding officers exercise broad disciplinary powers" that range from being verbally reprimanded or fined, to having privileges restricted or food rations reduced, to being given extra instruction or duties, to having a demotion in rank or a possible administrative separation or court-martial depending on the nature and severity of the offense. This is a far cry from the physicality of military discipline that was fairly routine up to the Vietnam War.

PUNISHING WEAKNESS TO MAINTAIN MILITARY DISCIPLINE AND GOOD ORDER

To prevent desertion or insubordination, the Roman legion sentenced those found guilty of such to *fustuarium*: the stoning or beating to death with clubs in front of the entire legion.[8] During the Roman Republic, if a cohort of soldiers was found guilty of mutiny, desertion, or cowardice, they would be sentenced to *decimation*: the cohort would split into groups of ten soldiers, and each soldier would draw lots—the losing soldier was killed by the other nine.

From the sixteenth to eighteenth centuries, the British Royal Navy implemented public floggings to punish and avert future expressions of military weakness. British crews from the fleet would gather weekly to hear offenses read aloud, and the condemned sailor's bare back was lashed in front of the entire ship's company.[9] The sailor would be whipped with a cat-'o-nine-tails, nine waxed cords of thin rope with a knot on the end of each strand. Afterward, the accused was dragged below ship to have salt rubbed into his wounds—a painful practice to prevent infection.[10] By 1750, the maximum number of lashes was limited to a dozen, but flogging was not banned completely until the 1880s. The Russian Army reintroduced flogging during World War I (WWI) to curtail desertion and cowardice.[11]

Since the time of Napoleon, massive modern militaries relied increasingly on volunteer armies of conscripted citizens and faced a new dilemma: How to prevent war stress–related escape behaviors spurred by the progressively destructive effects of industrial war.

The numbers of deserters, malingerers (e.g., "rheumatism fakers"), and veterans executed with war-stress injury in any historic era is unknowable. How many of the soldiers who deserted the battlefield had a war-stress injury is pure speculation, but ample historical evidence suggests that many were battle-seasoned veterans, including senior enlisted and officers during the American Civil War and the Boer War.[12] During the Vietnam War, thirty-three thousand U.S. Army personnel deserted in 1971 alone, but the prevalence of war-stress injury was unreported.[13]

Discipline problems during the Civil War, as in other wars, ranged from insubordination, theft, and drunk and disorderly behavior to more serious offenses, like murder and desertion. There were an estimated three hundred thousand deserters between the Union and Confederate armies, and an unknown but larger number of soldiers who fell behind while marching with their units.[14] Punishment for lesser offenses might involve digging and filling up latrines or burying dead horses. For more serious offenses, however, there was more creativity to punish the accused and, perhaps more important, instill fear in would-be copycats.

Sometimes, offenders were branded with hot irons on the forehead, cheek, hand, or hip with a letter ("C" for cowardice, "D" for deserter). Other times, in a practice called *barreling*, they were made to stand on a barrel for hours wearing a sign detailing their crime and balancing a log on their shoulders or made to march around the camp wearing a barrel. Or they might be bucked and gagged, in which case the soldier had to sit for six to twelve hours with a gag in his mouth, his knees raised, and his arms outstretched. In some cases, a thin log would be passed under the offender's knees and over his elbows and his hands and ankles would be tied so that he could not move. Or, especially for the crime of desertion, a soldier's legs would be shackled with a short iron chain to a cannonball weighing more than thirty pounds.

DISTINGUISHING COWARDICE AND OTHER WEAKNESS FROM WAR-STRESS INJURY

Marlowe highlights the historical military dichotomy of human adaptation to war stress as a *flight* or *fight* response.[15] Combatants either exhibit constitutional weakness or *cowardice* by physically deserting the battlefield or they exhibit constitutional heroism and join the fight despite their fear. We would add the *freeze*—the dissociative response—as another human response to fear, violence, and death. Consider the trembling, mute, and immobilized WWI soldier disobeying orders to charge across a machine-gun-riddled no-man's land.

To be certain, we are not suggesting that all or even most acts of desertion or indiscipline are products of war-stress injury and should be treated with leniency. Nor are we implying that cowardice does not actually exists—it does, and military leaders are right to be concerned about behavioral contagion if indiscipline is not properly addressed. What we are saying is that the military has often ignored the distinction between acts motivated by cowardice and acts motivated by war-stress injury, opting instead to punish and deter.

But historical precedents of enlightened military leaders who recognized war-stress injury exist. For instance, the Greek historian Herodotus reported that in 480 B.C.E., King Leonidas dismissed two of his handpicked three hundred Spartan warriors before the battle of Thermopylae who had demonstrated signs of emotional distress from early fighting, recognizing "they had no heart for the fight and were unwilling to take their share of the danger."[16] During WWII, the U.S. Army estimated 15 percent of soldiers who deserted or went AWOL had psychiatric problems. Such high incidence was confirmed in an army study reporting sixty-three of one hundred soldiers who had been incarcerated for going AWOL were diagnosed with a mental disorder. In a separate U.S. Army investigation of more than two thousand incarcerated soldiers, 82.3 percent of soldiers disciplined for AWOL and 97 percent of soldiers incarcerated for desertion did so following at least four months of intense combat.[17] In sum, it is equal folly to exaggerate emotional breakdown as evidence of cowardice deserving punishment as opposed to therapeutic intervention

The dichotomy between cowardice and bravery in the face of war stress is seriously undermined by what military physicians and researchers call "old sergeant's syndrome."[18] Throughout military history, there is ample documentation of chronic war-stress injury within the military's most battle-seasoned, highly trained, and well-respected leaders.[19] For example, Sobel examined one hundred WWII U.S. Army noncommissioned officers who were "old" in combat experience and identified old sergeant syndrome or Guadalcanal twitch: "For these men were among the best and most effective of the trained and disciplined combat infantry soldiers"[20] who developed abnormal tremulousness, excessive startle, severe anxiety, sweating, dyspepsia, depression, loss of self-confidence, and guilt with a highly uncharacteristic tendency to be the "first to get in and last to leave a foxhole." Military research on frontline psychiatry treatment of one hundred cases of old sergeant syndrome proved futile, and 100 percent of those returned to duty (RTD) relapsed within less than ten hours to three combat days despite their attempts to remain on the battlefront with long-term disposition of reassignment to noncombat jobs in the backlines or discharge.[21] Battle-tested infantry leaders were not the only vulnerable group.

The aviator's equivalent of old sergeant's syndrome was called "flier's fatigue" or "operational fatigue." In the 1949 movie *Twelve O' Clock High*, a combat-seasoned WWII Army Air Corps bomber squadron commander succumbs to flier's fatigue—similar to combat fatigue—after replacing the former squad leader after he was impaired by the same affliction. Flier's fatigue and battle deaths were highest for bomber crews with fewer than 25 percent completing a full tour of duty and high relapse rates with the majority requiring further treatment after their tour.[22] Yet, even these proven combat veterans were not immune from accusations of "being yellow" once they succumbed to the effects of war stress.[23]

Even the military's most elite special forces deployed to Iraq and Afghanistan have reported a high prevalence of war-stress injury, like post-traumatic stress disorder (PTSD).[24] These findings suggest that the severe and continuous deployments, dangerous operations, and war cause mental health decline that leads to medical decline and the risk of a mental health crisis.

HARSH PUNISHMENT OF COMBATANTS WITH WAR-STRESS INJURY

The military tradition of extolling discipline to correct undesired behavior and send poignant warnings to the masses has a long history. Flogging, whipping, solitary confinement, running the gauntlet, tarring and feathering, and shackling were all fairly standard physical punishments used even by military leaders like General George Washington to combat cowardice and mass desertions.[25] Following the War of 1812, the deputy inspector general of army hospitals described medical examinations from flogging: "I have seen several instances of men who have received five hundred lashes . . . and I am aware of one soldier who received seven hundred lashes and drummed out of the corps."[26] Other military leaders, however, including Washington's surgeon general, Benjamin Rush, argued for more compassionate treatment of mentally ill combatants.[27]

Regarding corporal punishment of mentally ill soldiers, Marshall warned: "Insanity has been frequently feigned by soldiers who wished to obtain their discharge . . . but it is also true, and the fact is a melancholy one, that real insanity has been mistaken for feigned, and the patients treated and punished as imposters."[28] Marshall poignantly recalled the tragic case of an enlisted soldier with eleven years of service who developed symptoms of mental alienation (insanity) but was repeatedly accused of malingering and denied proper treatment. After five courts-martial convictions resulting in five incidents of severe public flogging, the soldier's untreated mental illness worsened. He eventually received a less-than-honorable discharge, but his mental health deteriorated still and shortly thereafter he "committed suicide by drinking a quantity of sulphuric acid."[29]

During the U.S. Civil War and WWI, war-stress casualties who were either incapable or unwilling to continue to fight were often subject to "Field Punishment One"—that is, binding personnel accused of cowardice to a tree, fence post, or barbed-wire fencing within an active battlefield to motivate others to not shirk their duties.[30] Overly stressed soldiers needing a respite often were assigned "occupational therapy," which consisted of grueling, tedious, often distasteful labor, like cleaning latrines. The intention was to have the troops view returning to the frontlines as imminently more desirable. The consequence was to prevent the combatants from receiving the sufficient rest and relief so critical to building resilience to additional combat stress injuries.

Anecdotal reports of physical abuse of those with combat stress injuries in the military are abundant. Perhaps the most notorious incident was in Polermo, Italy (1946), when news reporters observed WWII legend, U.S. Army General George C. Patton repeatedly slapping and threatening hospitalized "battle-fatigued" soldiers with a loaded revolver for having the audacity to lay next to the "honorably wounded." Although Patton's exploits might be over the top even by military standards, he was expressing a widely held antipathy toward mental health and the mentally unhealthy.[31]

THE CAGING OF SOLDIERS RETURNING FROM THE PACIFIC WAR

An unsurprising but tremendously disturbing finding was reported by WWII army investigators that encapsulates the cruelty that military personnel often faced whose injury was emotional or spiritual in nature rather than physical. In 1943, the U.S. Army's Office of the Inspector General (OIG) investigated the treatment of American marines and soldiers returning on "liberty ships" from intense fighting in the Pacific. Thousands of war veterans were returning home confined in the bowels of these ships in wire-mesh cages. These cages measured six feet by three and were three feet high, thus prohibiting occupants from sitting, which the official OIG report appropriately labelled as "quite inhumane." The inspector general's report further revealed that the "transportation of this type of patient, understood so little, and feared so much, would be too difficult for medical and attendant personnel to control disturbed patients, so orders were issued to place shock machines for electroconvulsive therapy"[32] in case these veterans protested too much or became too emotionally distraught over their quarters.

Kessler reports WWII abuses of U.S. marines and soldiers diagnosed with war-stress injury during ship transportation to San Francisco from the Pacific theater.[33] In 1943, an army investigator wrote, "Returning Army transports carried most of the mental cases and the latter were relegated to an undesirable section of the ship which was poorly lighted and ventilated . . . fundamentals of care such as nutrition and water balance was neglected, morphine was used as a sedative."[34] Kessler goes on to report that despite official recommendations to remove the stigma created by the letters "NP" (neuropsychiatric) boldly written on a veteran's identification tag, nothing changed. NP was widely "looked upon by men so designated as social pariahs to the consequent grief and consternation of the psychiatric patients."[35] Thus, dating back to America's first war, the approach to those suffering from war-stress injury was neglect.

Given the deplorable treatment that some veterans with war-stress injury endured, it should come as no surprise that a number of these veterans never made it home. From April 1944 through October 1944, just under three thousand U.S. veterans diagnosed with war-stress injury were transported by ship from the Pacific theater. Nineteen of them died. All but one of the deceased was reportedly diagnosed as "psychotic."[36] Official causes of death: nine drowned (usually from jumping overboard), one hanged himself, one died of diphtheria, three died of cardiac conditions, one died of malnutrition, one died of pyelonephritis, and two died of unknown causes.[37] What role did being caged like animals for weeks, deprived of basic decency, humiliated, rejected, and isolated play in their deaths? The OIG reported that the caged veterans were periodically escorted to the ship deck for fresh air, but is it any wonder that people nine jumped ship and drowned instead of returning to their cages?

The investigators concluded that "in retrospect, it seems unconscionable that such abuses and inhumanities, as have already been enumerated,
could occur in the first place."[38] These abuses included severe overcrowd-
ing, no ventilation, no access to the decks, physical restraints, chains, and
chronic exposure to air temperatures averaging 105°F to 110°F during the
fourteen-day trip.[39] We have not been able to locate the records on who, if
anyone, was held accountable for the deaths.

THE CRUELTY OF PHYSICAL NEGLECT, ISOLATION, AND ABANDONMENT

During WWI, psychiatric casualties were admitted to the "isolation-insane
building," which was "a long rectangular building with windows and doors
heavily barred on the outside and heavily screened on the inside, the interior
broken into small cell-like structures stoutly maintained."[40] This practice
continued into WWII, during which such personnel were labeled as psychiatric casualties, systematically segregated from those with medical wounds,
and sometimes subjected to brutal, often inhumane treatment that led to
their untimely death.[41]

In modern wars, there is no widespread physical maltreatment of
war-stress casualties, but isolated reports of abuse continue to emerge.
For example, in 2010, the House Oversight Committee heard testimony
about an army sergeant with twelve years of military service who suffered
migraine headaches, vision loss, anger episodes, and suicidal ideation
stemming from the concussive effects of a mortar blast during an Iraq
deployment. His partial blindness was diagnosed as a preexisting personality disorder, subject to military discharge and potential loss of VA treatment
benefits.[42] After rejecting the diagnosis, the sergeant was allegedly confined
in a closet and monitored around the clock by armed guards who kept
him awake—keeping the lights on and blasting heavy metal music through
the night.[43] When the sergeant tried to escape, he was reportedly pinned
down, injected with sleeping medication, and dragged back to the closet.
He signed the personality disorder discharge papers after enduring a month
of such treatment.[44]

We would never tolerate the past physical abuses of veterans with war-
stress injury. The mentally ill veteran even today, however, is subject to
considerable cruelty, neglect, isolation, and abandonment.

EXPLAINING THE MILITARY'S CRUELTY TOWARD
THE PSYCHIATRICALLY DISABLED VETERAN

What is it about mental illness that brings out the worst? In 1973, the U.S. Navy published a commissioned study on "dehumanization" in institutional settings.[45] The study was led by legendary American psychologist Philip Zimbardo, the researcher behind the infamous Stanford Prison Experiment in 1971, which was also funded by the navy.

The study defined dehumanization as "producing a decreased awareness of the human attributes of others and a loss of humanity in interpersonal interactions. People stop perceiving others as having the same feelings, impulses, thoughts, and purposes in life that they do, and thus psychologically eliminate any human qualities that these others might share with them."[46] As a consequence, "people are less likely to perceive and respond to the personal identify of other people, and are more likely to treat them as if they were not human beings."[47] A dehumanized orientation toward the psychiatrically injured can serve as an adaptive defense against emotional responses that normally would disturb someone. By not responding to the human qualities of other people, it is easier to act inhumanely toward them. It also is easier to be callous or rude, to ignore their demands and pleas, to use them for one's own purposes, and even to harm or destroy them if they are irritating or frustrating.[48]

The navy's research identified four situations in which people are more likely to adopt a dehumanized perception of others. First, dehumanization in self-defense, which is the "detached concern" that many helping professionals, such as physicians and therapists, adopt to maintain some psychological distancing while aiding others in pain. Second, socially imposed dehumanization, which occurs in work situations when the job requires a level of dehumanizing in dealing with large numbers of people — for instance, dealing with college students during registration or prisoners or mental patients during institutional mealtimes. Third, dehumanization for self-gratification, which reflects purely selfish needs for gratifying a desire for personal power or satisfaction of impulses toward lust in the use of others solely for personal gain, pleasure, or entertainment — like soliciting prostitutes.

The fourth scenario of dehumanization the navy identified was dehumanization as a means to an end — that is, viewing groups of people as obstacles in achievement of their goals, either because these others oppose them, cause them additional problems, or simply are "in the way." By perceiving such people in a dehumanized manner as "the enemy," "a threat to security," or "inferior," it becomes less of a problem to take action against them in the name of some greater cause, like winning the war. Thus, the suffering, injury, or destruction of these people is justified as a means toward a "noble" end.[49] Examples given include nuclear bombing of Japanese cities, Nazi mass murder of Jews, or denial of medical treatment to black men with syphilis (the controversial Tuskegee study) to study the course of disease. Does the military's dehumanization of psychiatrically injured service members fall within these lines?

The growing theme thus far in this book is that the military has never accepted that service members may suffer from neuropsychiatric illness caused by war. Part of this lack of acceptance is the result of the military culture of good order and discipline. This culture found ways of punishing weakness. The Civil War provided new methods for maintaining discipline and order: branding, barreling, buckling, gagging, and shackling. Although this type of cruelty toward soldiers is unacceptable today, the struggle to manage human behavior in the face of war-stress injury continues, as does the high postwar suicide rate.

4

LEGAL PROSECUTION, INCARCERATION, AND EXECUTIONS OF MENTAL ILLNESS

THE SECOND DARK-SIDE STRATEGY

Many of these soldiers witnessed horrible events; they saw friends die; they lost limbs and faces; they went without sleep or food for days at a time. They have dealt with the same demons as the accused, and yet they have resisted alcohol and drugs. The accused is asking you to hold him to a different standard.

Send a message to the others who have suffered. Give them a reason to stay the course and resist the temptation. Don't let Sergeant K use PTSD as an excuse to violate the law and put others at risk.

This time, he damaged a wall. Next time, who knows? The Government asks for a Dishonorable Discharge and three years confinement, because justice demands as much.

E. R. SEAMONE, "RECLAIMING THE REHABILITATIVE ETHIC IN MILITARY JUSTICE"

During times of war, military leaders are confronted with a problem: how to discipline personnel who violate military law (i.e., the Uniformed Code of Military Justice, UCMJ). Commanders are responsible for maintaining morale, discipline, and good order within their units. To allow criminal misconduct to go unpunished is to send an untenable message that could metastasize into widespread indiscipline in the ranks. So, historically, commanders have erred on the side of setting an example of personnel who either cannot or will not fight. Often these commanders award excessive punishments—including executions—as a way to keep others in line.

In contrast, the enlightened commander must consider whether misconduct is rooted in a war-stress injury like post-traumatic stress disorder (PTSD). Behavior like freezing under fire, desertion, excessive aggression, substance abuse, social isolation, poor hygiene, oversleeping, recklessness, tardiness, and suicide attempts are common features of war-stress injury—and also are grounds for frequent legal actions against military personnel. During World War II (WWII), the U.S. Army reported that out of a sample of five thousand general prisoners, more than two thousand were incarcerated for absence without leave (AWOL), desertion, and misbehavior before the enemy after an average of four months of intense combat. Within this group of incarcerated combat veterans, neuropsychiatric problems were cited in 79.3 percent of cases.[1]

The commander's dilemma is even harder when the offender is an otherwise-valuable, proven leader with a clean record of honorable service and no prior history of discipline problems. Most commanders appear to do a reasonable job weighing factors such as the individual's past performance, deployment history, and the nature and severity of the alleged offenses in determining a fair and proper legal disposition. During World War I (WWI) and WWII, the U.S. military implemented highly successful progressive legal forms emphasizing suspended sentences in favor of rehabilitation, treatment, and restoration to duty that predate today's Veterans Treatment Courts.[2]

Ample evidence also indicates, however, that the military is all too ready to abuse the legal system to manage its mental health problem.[3] In 2014, a Vietnam War veteran brought a civil suit to amend his discharge. After completing two honorable tours of duty, fighting in four separate campaigns in Vietnam, and earning an Air Medal with Valor Device for heroism, John Doe was given an Undesirable Discharge after a 1973 conviction for threatening and hitting fellow soldiers. John Doe was later diagnosed with PTSD by a civilian therapist, but his Undesirable Discharge prohibits government employment and VA benefits like disability compensation, PTSD treatment, healthcare, education, and benefits for surviving family members.[4] In the following sections, we review the military's legal system and options available to commanders in dealing with misconduct of war veterans.

The connection between war-stress exposure and future criminality is the same as it has been in most major wars. In its 2009 *Porter v. McCollum* opinion, the unanimous Supreme Court cited early studies of this connection in support of the nation's "long tradition of according leniency to veterans in recognition of their service, especially for those who fought on the front lines."

Desertions, disobedience, freezing, misconduct stress behaviors, and other forms of "weakness" can jeopardize the efficiency of fighting units, and therefore, they present serious and legitimate concerns for the military. During WWII, there were 1.7 million courts-martials, which accounted for a third of all criminal cases in America between 1941 and 1946. Of these, twenty-one thousand were cases of "desertion," one of which even resulted in the last American execution for desertion in 1945. The soldier in question had been diagnosed with "psychoneuroses." Legal prosecution for cowardice is not brought against only those soldiers who physically leave the battlefield, but also those who flee psychologically. Anecdotal reports of the so-called freeze response to extreme stress are readily apparent in military records, but it comes under many different names, including war hysteria, shell shock, conversion reaction, and dissociation disorder. How many of these immobilized soldiers were prosecuted for cowardice is unknowable, but we should expect such overt demonstrations of weakness would be dealt with harshly.

The stress of war has always been associated with a high incidence of substance use disorder (SUD),[5] a phenomenon well documented by every generation both during and particularly after war. Alcoholism and opiate addiction were major concerns within the Union Army, where more than five thousand soldiers were hospitalized for inebriation, more than a hundred of whom died from alcohol poisoning.[6] During WWI, more than four thousand deployed soldiers were discharged for "alcoholism or drug addiction,"[7] ten times that number in WWII.[8] During the Korean War, SUD was reported to be "high," but the exact number was unspecified.[9] In Vietnam, substance use was by far the most extensive. From 1967 to 1971, the proportion of enlisted soldiers smoking marijuana "heavily" (twenty or more times) in Vietnam increased from 7 percent to 34 percent, whereas the proportion of "habitual" users stabilized at between 17 percent and 18 percent from 1969 to 1971. The same holds true for contemporary veterans. For instance, the Institute of Medicine (IOM) reported that since the start of Operation Enduring Freedom and Operation Iraqi Freedom (OEF/OIF), "alcohol abuse among returning military personnel has spiked. In 2008, nearly half of active duty service members reported binge drinking."[10] In today's cohort, from 2000 to 2011, a reported more than three hundred thousand active military personnel[11] and two hundred thousand veterans[12] have been diagnosed with SUDs.

Combat veterans struggling with substance use are extremely vulnerable to legal prosecution under the UCMJ for a range of circumstances, including driving under the influence, public intoxication, conduct unbecoming, unauthorized absence, illicit drug use, or prescription drug abuse. The military's zero-tolerance policy for drug use results in nearly automatic discharges for first timers, regardless of rank and past performance, as do repeated alcohol-related incidents. Per the Department of Navy, "The Navy's policy on drug abuse is 'zero tolerance.' Navy members determined to be using, possessing, promoting, manufacturing, or distributing drugs and/or drug abuse paraphernalia shall be disciplined as appropriate and processed for ADSEP [administrative separation] as required."[13]

The actual number of current war veterans prosecuted for SUD is unknown. In 2007, National Public Radio reported that since the Iraq invasion of 2003, the U.S. Army had discharged almost 20 percent more soldiers for "misconduct," including twice as many soldiers for drug abuse than it had in the same period before the war for "having behavior issues that are potentially linked to PTSD than they did before the war."[14] The number of enlisted soldiers prosecuted and discharged out of the U.S. Army for drugs, alcohol, crimes, and other misconduct soared from 5,600 at the peak of the Iraq war in 2007 to more than 11,000 in 2013, while the number of discharged army officers tripled in 2013.[15] Unfortunately, no hard data are available on the number of Afghanistan or Iraq veterans prosecuted for SUD, nor how many of those may have had war-stress injury.

If not drugs, it might be violence. War veterans of every generation have suffered anger problems that occasionally have escalated into violence in which they are injured or have injured others. In the context of combat, anger and aggression are normative responses to threats.[16] Such responses are not only adaptive to war but also have been extensively modeled and reinforced through military training.[17] The trouble is reintegrating the battle-ready soldier into peaceful society. Social reintegration transitions from deployment and after military discharge are adjustment periods during which eruptions of violence against soldiers or those around them are more likely and when individual and family support is most critical. In 1977, the U.S. government funded a study on the effects of the Vietnam War, called the "Legacies of Vietnam." They found that 24 percent of veterans who saw heavy combat were later arrested for criminal offenses, compared with just 17 percent of other-era veterans and 14 percent of nonveterans. Another study in 1992 found that approximately one-third of Gulf War–era veterans with PTSD had perpetrated partner abuse in the previous year. In today's cohort, an army-wide study of twenty-thousand OEF/OIF soldiers found length of deployment was positively correlated with the severity of self-reported interpersonal violence perpetration in the year after deployment.[18]

Another study of veterans of Iraq and Afghanistan with PTSD found self-reported irritability and anger to be the highest symptom, with 29 percent of reports rated as "quite a bit" or "extreme."[19] Another study found 70 percent of veterans with PTSD reported impulsive aggressiveness, compared with just 29 percent of veterans without PTSD.[20] Another more recent study estimated that one-third of veterans seeking PTSD treatment reported perpetrating partner violence.[21]

In addition to predicting PTSD, high combat exposure predicts war-zone misconduct: those soldiers who see the most combat are the most likely to later perpetrate violence against themselves, their spouse, and others.[22] A 2010 study on psychosocial predictors of military misconduct reported that almost 11 percent of a sample of twenty thousand marines deployed to Iraq and Afghanistan between 2002 and 2007 received either bad-conduct discharges or demotions in rank from misconduct.[23] The most frequently cited reasons for bad-conduct discharges were drug abuse, frequent contact with civil or military authorities, and court-martial convictions.[24]

What accounts for this misconduct? We find it to be most common in the younger and less mentally healthy personnel. The strongest predictor for bad conduct discharge was age at first combat deployment (eighteen to twenty-one) and psychiatric diagnosis. Marines diagnosed with a psychiatric disorder after combat were nine times more likely to receive a bad conduct discharge than marines who were not diagnosed.[25] Table 2 shows a clear trend of an increasing number of other-than-honorable (OTH) separations for misconduct as the duration of the war increases. Similar data was not found for the other branches of the military (see table 2), but we assume the same holds true across the armed forces.

During WWII, 102 American soldiers were tried, convicted, and executed for the rape and murder of civilians. How many of them involved war-stress injury we do not know. U.S. Army psychiatrists in Korea observed that as incidence rates of frostbite rose, the number of neuropsychiatric casualties decreased, raising suspicions of self-infliction.[26] During WWII, U.S. Army researchers reported that "misbehavior before the enemy, violation of Article of War 75, is an extremely serious military crime, heavily punished by a General Courts-Martial. It is committed in nearly all cases by combat soldiers." They further found that neuropsychiatric problems were evident in over 80 percent of nearly six hundred combat veterans convicted of Article 75.

In addition, there were 101 reported homicides within the U.S. Army in Korea from 1950 to 1953,[27] and an estimated 163 unarmed Korean women, children, and elderly refugees were killed by U.S. forces at No Gun Ri in 1950.[28] During Vietnam, Linden reported a progressive increase in the number of courts-martial for insubordination and assaults (including murder), exemplified by "fragging" incidents that more than quintupling from 1969 to 1971.[29]

A reported 320 atrocities by U/S? military personnel were substantiated by an army task force (i.e., the Vietnam War Crimes Working Group) created after the 1968 My Lai Massacre wherein 347 to 504 unarmed Vietnamese were murdered, including many women and children.[30] Research on Vietnam War veterans reported statistically significant association between combat exposure and post-military-service antisocial behavior,[31] along with exposure to war atrocities and interpersonal violence.[32]

As in other wars, especially low-intensity (guerilla-type) warfare like Iraq and Afghanistan, there has been a high incidence of misconduct stress behaviors by American personnel, ranging from inappropriate handling of American and enemy combatant dead to prisoner torture and sexual abuse, as we saw in the 2004 Abu Ghraib incident. Many incidents of rape and homicide of unarmed civilians, including children, are substantiated. Because the military does not track its legal prosecution of mentally injured combatants, the total number of courts-martial and "bad paper discharges" related to misconduct stress behavior is unknown. In 2014, the Associated Press reported a total of twenty-eight thousand soldiers were discharged for misconduct since the Iraq War. From 2003 to 2013, the U.S. Army discharged 20 percent more soldiers for "misconduct," 40 percent more for personality disorder, and 50 percent more for drug abuse, including eleven thousand enlisted soldiers in 2013 alone.[33] We can reasonably assume a large number of combat personnel have been prosecuted and received punitive discharges for war-stress injuries like misconduct stress behaviors.

The purpose of military law, according to the UCMJ, is to "promote justice, to assist in maintaining good order and discipline in the armed forces, to promote efficiency and effectiveness in the military establishment, and thereby to strengthen the national security of the United States."[34] Commanders are given significant roles in the military justice system because discipline is essential to mission readiness. At the same time, safeguards, such as the right to trial and appeal, are intended to protect against abuse of authority.[35]

According to the *Manual of Courts-Martial*, the three levels of courts-martial (i.e., summary, special, and general) depend on the nature and severity of the alleged offenses. The summary court-martial is used for lower-level offenses similar to nonjudicial punishment, but the individual's commander believes warrants sterner punishment. But similar to nonjudicial punishment, the commander acts as judge and jury, although more legal due-process protections are granted to individuals.[36] Special and general courts-martial each invoke the full legal protections, rules of evidence, and procedures of a standard trial, typically with a military defense and prosecuting attorneys and presided by a military judge. The difference between special and general courts-marital pertains to the seriousness of the offense and severity of punishment.

Military separation or discharges characterized as OTH, bad-conduct, and dishonorable are often referred to as bad paper discharges, because they dissolve military pensions, VA benefits (like treatment), and GI Bill eligibility. As a result, they significantly affect future civilian employment and other civil rights. The term "bad paper discharge" also is used for general (Under Honorable) administrative separations that may have no legal charges attached—like personality disorder, adjustment disorder, alcohol rehabilitation failure, and sleep walking—yet can have the same lifelong impact on war veterans as an OTH discharge. Some courts have found such discharges overly punitive because they stigmatize the service member's reputation, impede their future employment, and serve as prima facie evidence against the service member's character, patriotism, and loyalty.[37]

PROSECUTION OF MILITARY PERSONNEL WITH WAR-STRESS INJURY

Many of our returning veterans and service members experience life-changing events, some of which may cause them to react in adverse ways and get into trouble with the law.[38]

Human adaptation to war stress is historically associated with a predictably broad spectrum of potential neuropsychiatric diagnoses, medically unexplained physical symptoms, behavioral changes, and misconduct stress behaviors.[39] After a comprehensive review of the scientific literature on the long-term adverse health effects and deployment-related stress, the IOM drew the following conclusion:

> In the brain, there is evidence of structural and functional changes resulting directly from chronic or severe stress. The changes are associated with alterations of the most profound functions of the brain: memory and

decision-making. They are also associated with symptoms of fear and anxiety, and they might sensitize the brain to substances of abuse and increase the risk of substance-use disorders.[40]

Service members returning from deployment to war zones are at significant risk for behaviors often associated with exposure to war stress but that could become the focus of legal difficulties. Contemporary frontline surveys reveal that deployed soldiers and marines diagnosed with mental health problems were more likely to mistreat noncombatants in violation of the UCMJ.[41] Another study showed that deployed marines with PTSD were eleven times more likely to be discharged for misconduct than their peers without PTSD.[42]

Perhaps not surprisingly, the military does not routinely track or report on the number of service members legally prosecuted who are war veterans, or those who also may be diagnosed with a war-stress injury. The army's post-WWII analysis, however, revealed that from 1942 to 1945, 56 percent of a sample of twenty-three thousand soldiers incarcerated after courts-martial convictions were diagnosed with psychiatric conditions.[43] Nonetheless, reports on the frequency of discipline and legal dispositions of military personnel (e.g., courts-marital convictions, misconduct separations) for any historical era are inherently flawed because we cannot know how many cases involved veterans suffering from war-stress injury. The following presentation in no way suggests that war veterans with or without war-stress injury should not be disciplined or discharged. All we can say is that the military often mishandles at least some war veterans based on the frequency of disposition.

THE MILITARY'S UNETHICAL LEGAL REVOLVING DOOR

Many courts-martial are problem-generating—rather than problem-solving— courts when they preclude treatment considerations as tangential matters, lack a coherent framework for evaluating the benefit of treatment vice incarceration, and result in punitive discharges that preclude offenders from future VA treatment.
E. R. SEAMONE, "RECLAIMING THE REHABILITATIVE ETHIC IN MILITARY JUSTICE"

The military justice system's punitive approach toward emotionally injured war veterans is part and parcel of the Department of Defense's (DoD) habit ignoring the lessons of war trauma learned by its WWI and WWII predecessors. The present-day policy disavows responsibility for the provision of mental health treatment and rehabilitation for veterans in the criminal justice system and lets the Department of Veterans Affairs (VA) and private sector worry about it. Consequently, military personnel and veterans with untreated mental health conditions are at significant risk for legal issues,[44] which creates a pattern called the revolving door.

A recent *Military Law Review* article aptly summarizes the military justice system's punitive handling of stress-injured defendants. First, accused service members with suspected or confirmed mental conditions are referred to psychiatric sanity boards that focus only on fitness to stand trial and rarely make treatment recommendations. Then, military conviction and incarceration generally prohibit access to adequate mental healthcare. Third, bad paper discharges bar the majority of emotionally injured veterans from accessing critically needed VA treatment benefits and affect future employability. Last, the Department of Homeland Security has cited national security threats from discharged untreated combat veterans who have been taught to overcome instinctual resistance toward killing who are actively being recruited by homegrown terrorists.[45]

Even the sentencing standards used by the current military justice system is scripted rather than individualized, and it is heavily skewed toward punishment rather than treatment. This raises serious ethical worries that

> even though an accused who has been cleared by a sanity board may appreciate the wrongfulness of his acts, this does not alleviate the concern that his mental condition contributed in some palpable way to the offense or that the offense would not have occurred in the absence of the service-connected psychological influence.[46]

Commanders, judges, and panels also need to be wary that past mental illnesses connected to military service likely will continue if service members are not helped to develop the "necessary cognitive tools."[47]

VETERANS TREATMENT COURTS

After more than a decade of sustained combat operations in Iraq and Afghanistan, the civilian justice system developed the Veteran Treatment Court (VTC) to target the mental health conditions underlying some criminal conduct by veterans. They accomplish this through an interdisciplinary treatment team that is presently absent in today's military justice system.[48] Recall *Porter v. McCollum*, the unanimous Supreme Court ruling on a Korean War veteran:

> Our Nation has a long tradition of according leniency to veterans in recognition of their service, especially for those who fought on the front lines as Porter did. Moreover, the relevance of Porter's extensive combat experience is not only that he served honorably under extreme hardship and gruesome conditions, but also that the jury might find mitigating the intense stress and mental and emotional toll that combat took on Porter.[49]

In response to a crisis of discharged veterans with untreated war-stress injury facing prosecution in civilian courts, Judge Robert Russell from Buffalo, New York, established the first VTC in 2008. The program he established "provides veterans suffering from substance abuse issues, alcoholism, mental health issues, and emotional disabilities with treatment, academic and vocational training, job skills, and placement services," as well as "ancillary services . . . such as housing, transportation, medical, dental, and other supportive services."[50]

These courts use therapy rather than incarceration, a sentencing structure modeled after civilian drug and mental health courts emphasizing interventions addressing the underlying causes of legal transgressions by suspending sentences in favor of treatment and social support. In 2010, the Buffalo VTC diverted the prosecution of a thirty-two-year-old married veteran diagnosed with PTSD after three combat tours who was charged with assaulting VA staff. This became "the first criminal case nationwide to be transferred from federal court to a local veteran's treatment court where the goal is to treat— rather than simply punish."[51]

After their documented success in rehabilitating mentally ill veterans, President Barack Obama recommended greatly expanding civilian VTCs. Chairman of the Joint Chiefs of Staff Admiral Mike Mullen later said, "VTCs are having a significant impact across the country. I have seen these courts make a real difference, giving our veterans a second chance, and significantly improving their quality of life." Still, the military's strong public support of the VTC's problem-solving approach raises the question: Why does the DoD maintain a more punitive tack to its mental health dilemma?

Recent media and political attention to VTCs belie the fact that similar problem-solving legal approaches were instituted after every major

American engagement since the Civil War. The military developed its first specialized courts-martial rehabilitation programs, which included limited mental health services, during WWI. In these disciplinary barracks, convicted personnel received rehabilitative interventions in lieu of suspended sentences and bad paper discharges. Per the U.S. Army judge advocate general, the explicit purpose of the DB was "to give the man a certain period of time in which by positive action he can evidence his reformation and be restored to the service without the stigma of a dishonorable discharge appearing upon his record."[52] Although the DB programs were open to the general military prison population, the influx of convicted veterans with war-stress injury spurred the development of mental healthcare services. As the army surgeon general reported,

> Fort Leavenworth Disciplinary Barracks. As a result of this, many cases of mental diseases were discovered among delinquents and the charges against them either were dropped and discharged on disability initiated, or, if the case was tried and sentence imposed, the findings of the court were approved, including discharge, and the confinement was omitted.
>
> For example, during the summer of 1918 the commanding officer of one of the camps in the United States was facing serious difficulties on the charges of neglect of duty about to be brought by the Inspector General of the Army. He had been frequently absent from his post, was lax in the enforcement of discipline, did not have the details of his command well in hand, organized an excessive number of entertainments, etc.
>
> Examination by a psychiatrist revealed a mild manic state, and upon the psychiatrist's report the charges were dropped and sick leave of six months was granted, at the expiration of which this officer had made a perfect recovery.
>
> Had a psychiatrist not been available, the matter would have ended quite differently, as the mental symptoms were not sufficiently pronounced to have justified the dropping of the charges, except on the recommendation of an expert. If the officer had been tried he would certainly have been convicted, which would have been a gross injustice to him, and would have postponed his recovery indefinitely.[53]

By most standards, the WWI-era legal problem-solving approach was successful. Army Staff Judge Advocate Major George V. Strong would later remark, "Like the Navy, in the great majority of these cases—'over 80 percent'—the Army program worked, with many restores later being discharged as non-commissioned officers with a character 'Excellent'."[54]

Overall, an estimated 20 percent of military prisoners sentenced to dishonorable discharge were restored to active-duty through the DB.[55] Although preventing personnel attrition was an important motivation for this judicial problem-solving approach, the primary goal according to the Navy judge advocate general was to avoid "turning [a military offender] adrift without the credentials generally necessary to secure honest employment in civil life."[56]

Following WWI, restoration to duty remained the objective of the military justice system, but the responsibility for that restoration was split with local military prisons. As war-stress casualties escalated during WWII, the military established Mental Hygiene Units (MHU) at Service Command Rehab Centers (SCRC). These units aimed to understand and rehabilitate war trauma through, for instance, group therapy.[57] Near the end of WWII, the Army's Fifth SCRC instituted a progressive mental health program called "total therapeutic push," which embodied the modern VTC philosophy of "therapeutic jurisprudence" by orienting toward therapy rather than retribution.[58] Both officers and enlisted personnel prosecuted for misconduct after returning from combat received six weeks of intensive therapy at SCRC MHUs and then were evaluated for whether they could be returned to duty, reclassified, or discharged.[59] Accordingly, the military justice system had the responsibility to "differentiate between the cause and effect relationship" and to base treatment on "sound mental hygiene principles" and discharge decisions on more "careful study and analysis of the factors involved" in their offenses."[60]

An analysis of SCRC records between 1940 and 1946 indicated that the army restored more than half of punitively discharged soldiers to honorable active-duty status—and did so with a subsequent recidivism rate of only 12 percent.[61] The Navy and Marine Corps rehabilitated 75 percent of sixteen thousand punitively discharged offenders to honorable service.[62] For all of these service members, their discharges had been wiped clean, helping not only the military but also the families and communities who depended on their future employability and good name.[63] Per Seamone, "It is significant that, within this specialized correctional setting, trainees actually received more therapy time than psychiatric battlefield casualties received during their rehabilitation period in mental hygiene units."[64] Consider this example from psychologists Major Harry Freedman and Major Michael J. Rockmore during WWII:

> One soldier suffered shrapnel wounds and lost several of his "closest buddies" in severe combat conditions in the North African Theater. He then lived in a state where "I didn't give a damn whether I lived or not."

Following a series of unauthorized absences, alcohol-induced rampages, and an occasion when he pleaded for the military police to shoot him, the Army adopted a treatment-based approach: "After a course of treatment this soldier was returned to duty of a limited nature within the continental limits of the United States." Accordingly, "[t]he Army recognized [the relationship between his lack of treatment and his criminal behavior] and treated him as a soldier-patient.

The reward was that a combat-experienced soldier continued to render effective service where otherwise a stockade prisoner might have been the only result.[65]

Seamone identified two critical WWII legal lessons: (1) the use of therapeutic intervention and conditional sentencing to address underlying problems; and (2) the need to expand and adapt a court-martial procedure when addressing offenders with combat trauma.[66]

In 1951, the U.S. Air Force established the 3320th Corrections and Rehabilitation Squadron. Throughout the early years of the Vietnam War, the 3320th and other service Discharge Remission Programs worked to suspend punitive discharges of convicts with combat fatigue in favor of comprehensive and individualized treatment. However, 1973 marked not only the end of conscription and the beginning of the all-volunteer force but also introduced the concept of "quality force"[67] or what today is often called the "zero-defect military." The quality force doctrine essentially ended the military justice system's commitment to rehabilitation and brought back the culture of discharge. Consequently, the latter years of the Vietnam War saw punitive discharges of veterans dramatically escalate, for offenses as petty as drug use and other nonviolent misconduct stress behaviors.[68] Today, only the Air Force maintains a viable legal restoration program.[69]

EXECUTING MENTALLY ILL COMBATANTS

The military has long upheld the practice of executing soldiers for cowardice as an example to others, regardless of whether their refusal to fight was psychopathological or an intentional act of disobedience. In the Union Army, nearly three hundred executions were handed down from nine hundred courts-martial convictions. More than half of those soldiers were executed for desertion (though two hundred thousand actually did desert), a quarter for homicide, 10 percent for rape or mutiny, and the rest for thievery or espionage. During WWI, the American Army executed thirty-five soldiers for the rape or murder of civilians[70] and an unknown number for cowardice.

At least three thousand British soldiers were sentenced to death for cowardice, desertion or malingering. More than three hundred of them were actually executed.[71] When one WWI soldier diagnosed with "shell shock" was court-martialed, his evaluating army physician retorted, "I went to the trial determined to give him no help of any sort, for I detest this type, I really hoped that he would be shot, as indeed anticipated by all of us."[72] At least three of twenty-three executed Canadian soldiers also had confirmed shell shock diagnosis.[73]

Throughout WWII, forty thousand U.S. soldiers were charged with desertion.[74] Of these, nearly three thousand were tried by general courts-martial for desertion, and forty-nine were sentences to death. A total of 102 U.S. soldiers were executed in WWII for rape or unprovoked murder of civilians— how many of those offenders suffered from war-stress injury, we do not know. In fact, the only U.S. service member executed solely for a military offence (desertion in the face of the enemy) since the U.S. Civil War and the last ever since, was twenty-four-year-old U.S. Army Private Eddie D. Slovik in 1945.[75] Private Slovik was diagnosed by an army division neuropsychiatrist with "psychoneuroses" (a precursor to PTSD) after an extended artillery bombardment during the Battle of the Bulge.[76] Slovik had just arrived to his unit in time for the bombardment, and afterward he informed his commander of his intent to desert if not reassigned.[77] Private Slovik explained during his two-hour general courts-martial on November 11, 1944, "They were shelling the town and we were told to dig in for the night. The following morning they were shelling us again. I was so scared, nerves and trembling, that at the time the other replacements moved out, I couldn't move."[78]

Private Slovik's psychiatric diagnosis, however, did not constitute a legal defense of insanity and so he was convicted and sentenced to death. Slovik's military attorney appealed to General Eisenhower who confirmed the execution order on December 23, 1944, noting that it was necessary to discourage further desertions.[79] On January 31, 1945, Private Slovik was tied to a post, blindfolded, and shot multiple times by his fellow unit members. He died slowly. He would be the last American soldier executed with a known or knowable war-stress injury since the U.S. Civil War. The last executed service member was killed in 1961 when twenty-six-year-old Army Private John Bennett was hanged for the rape and attempted murder of an eleven-year-old

Austrian girl. Bennett was an African American who had a reported history of mental health problems not disclosed during his trials. His execution raises the specter of racial disparity, since WWII when fifty-five of seventy executed American soldiers were black, even though African Americans constituted less than 10 percent of the army.

In contrast to VTC and the military's now-defunct diversionary treatment programs, today's military justice system is to punish and deter, handing down discharges that preclude mental health treatment and intensify stigma. As Seamone reported in 2011,

> The military justice system is at odds . . . with itself—in the way it under-mines the stated sentencing philosophy of rehabilitation of the offender, the way it erodes the professional ethic by denying core values, and the way it defies the moral obligation to advance the interests of both the veteran and the society he will rejoin.[80]

This failure hearkens back to pre-WWI arguments against problem-solving programs, which claimed "the Army is not a reformatory for its own criminals or for criminals from civil life, and it cannot be made one without doing great damage to the service!"[81]

5

HUMILIATE, RIDICULE, AND SHAME INTO SUBMISSION

THE THIRD DARK-SIDE STRATEGY

The greatest weapon against the so-called "battle fatigue" is ridicule. If soldiers would realize that a large proportion of men allegedly suffering from battle fatigue are really using an easy way out, they would be less sympathetic.

Any man who says he has battle fatigue is avoiding danger, and forcing on those who have more hardihood than himself the obligation of meeting it.

If soldiers would make fun of those who begin to show battle fatigue, they would prevent its spread, and also save the man who allows himself to malinger by this means from an afterlife of humiliation and regret.

GENERAL GEORGE S. PATTON JR.

The military has a long-storied tradition of deploying shame, guilt, and ridicule coupled with humiliating public displays of cruelty to deal with its mental health dilemma. Such tactics have included branding the letters "C" (for cowardice) or "W" (for worthlessness) with hot irons into soldiers, flogging them or stripping them naked and forcing them to march around camp wearing only a barrel, or subjecting them to Field Punishment One (see chapter 3).

Modern militaries have witnessed a significant escalation in psychiatric casualties that eclipses both those killed and wounded since World War II (WWII). At the same time, political correctness has "disarmed" them from physically mistreating those casualties of war stress. Legal prosecutions are often long and costly, and while individual bad paper discharges offer a cheaper and more efficient alternative, their effect as a public deterrent is limited. So modern militaries have felt compelled to greatly expand and weaponize stigma as a subtler but no less harmful strategy against their mental health epidemic.

STIGMA

Stigma is a brand or stain. Psychologists have identified three sources of mental health stigma. The first is institutional stigma caused by a policy that either intentionally or unintentionally "restricts opportunities and hinder the options of people with mental illness."[1] The second is public stigma, which reflects bias against mental health issues, either from family or the broader society. The third is self-stigma, the internalization of negative attitudes and beliefs toward oneself.[2]

Psychiatrically disabled veterans without visible war wounds have regularly been branded cowards and deserters by the U.S. military. The intent was to ridicule, shame, or punish those who might undermine military authority and cow those who might contemplate following suite.[3] We can see this in the language around was-stress injuries in the military. Debilitated veterans are characterized as inherently defective, weak, or unmanly (e.g., male hysteric, psycho, Section 8, war hysteric, wussy, limp-dick, personality disorder), as immoral frauds attempting to avoid combat (e.g., evacuation neurotic, slacker, malingerer), or as profiteers seeking disability payment (e.g., goldbricker, pension neurotic, illness-seeker, dreg on society, leech).[4]

According to Brigadier General William Menninger, the U.S. Army's chief consultant of neuropsychiatry during WWII,

> There was a tendency to stigmatize the neuropsychiatric patient as being a failure. When the case was not physical, then the individual was variously regarded as perverse, subversive, unwilling, weak, dumb. He was likely to be labeled as a "quitter," "an eight ball," "gold brick," or any of numerous other vernaculars disparaging terms.[5]

A recent attempt to compare stigma in the military and the private sector led RAND investigators to conclude, "Within the military, stigma is largely conceptualized and assessed as a barrier to care," making direct comparisons with the general population nearly impossible.[6] The effects of institutionalized stigma or "barriers to care" not only deter individuals from seeking mental health treatment but even from disclosing symptoms. Disclosing symptoms even to one's spouse[7] risks promotion and retention within the military, especially officer ranks. Stigma-driven barriers to care in the military predictably result in far more diagnoses of war-stress injury after military discharge, a trend already underway that thus far has been met with accusations of mass fraud.[8]

RECOGNIZING THE NEED TO ELIMINATE
MENTAL HEALTH STIGMA

After a war ends, the military invariably reflects on its psychiatric lessons learned and cites the need to eliminate the disparity, prejudice, and stigma associated with mental health. The U.S. Army's official lessons learned after WWI calls upon the military to end mental health stigma and disparity:

> The greatest obstacle to neuropsychiatry in both civil and military practice has been the barrier that tends to separate nervous and mental diseases from all other diseases, and it was thought by some that, in so far as the Military Establishment was concerned, the greatest good, both to the practice of neuropsychiatry and to the patients who were dependent upon it, would be accomplished if a determined effort were made to break through this barrier and to place the mental patient on a par with patients incapacitated by reason of other diseases.[9]

Similar conclusions were reached by the army after WWII about improved medical training:

> If medical practice is ever to progress to the ideal of psychosomatic medicine, it will require the reorientation of medical training and of all practitioners so that equal emphasis is placed upon the roles of the psyche and of the soma in all illness.[10]

And repeated in 2004:

> Reducing the perception of stigma and the barriers to care among military personnel is a priority for research and a priority for the policymakers, clinicians, and leaders who are involved in providing care to those who have served in the armed forces.[11]

As well as in 2007:

> In the military, stigma represents a critical failure of the community that prevents service members and their families from getting the help they need just when they may need it most.
>
> Every military leader bears responsibility for addressing stigma; leaders who fail to do so reduce the effectiveness of the service members they lead.[12]

The military is aware it must eliminate the policies and practices that perpetuate the stigma that prevents service members from getting needed support. Military mental health practitioners and administrators within the military know better than anyone about these problems. But this has been an uphill battle to convince the military leadership.

WEAPONIZING STIGMA

The military's episodic reflections on the need to eliminate harmful stigmas is laudable, but the record shows it generally is more invested in maintaining and intensifying that stigma as a way to deal with mental health problem. Scholars have described the evolution of weaponizing combat stress as the intentional development of tactics and war-fighting strategies aimed primarily at demoralizing, terrorizing, and debilitating the enemy with stress casualties. In a similar vein, the military has purposefully weaponized stigma against internal threats posed by psychologically injured warriors.

In 2010, navy medical leaders admitted that the military's frontline psychiatry policies intensified mental health stigma and barriers to care by deliberately misattributing the primary cause of war-stress injury as being the result of individual weakness and predisposition rather than to the known deleterious dosage effects of stress. As a result, military mental health providers began acting under

> two comforting, though dangerous, assumptions—that any Service member who is not complaining doesn't need attention and deployed Marines or Sailors who say they are "good to go" after developing stress problems can be safely considered psychologically well and fit without further medical monitoring or care.[13]

These assumptions led to military mental health providers purposefully intensifying social stigma to erect barriers for seeking mental healthcare and to prevent attrition. Mental health providers operated under a model that a morally weak character leads to significant problems because of stress. The Department of Navy and U.S. Marine Corps noted, "Under this character weakness model, marines or sailors who fail to return to full functioning after experiencing combat or operational stress should be considered for an administrative separation for a personality disorder rather than a medical evaluation board."[14] Navy medical leaders have acknowledged that this assumption and basis for evaluation is scientifically unsound.

> *Confessing to the injurious impact from weaponized stigma:*
> The social stigma surrounding stress problems may have contributed to lower numbers of stressed Service members seeking treatment that might result in medical evacuation, but this stigmatizing conception of combat stress and psychological health has also discouraged Marines and Sailors from ever seeking professional help for stress problems of any kind. Without early treatment, problems are more likely to become chronic and entrenched.[15]

We next examine specific examples of the military's propensity to weaponize its greatest weapon in dealing with its vexing mental health problem.

LACKING MORAL FIBER

Before caving in to public pressure, the modern militaries of WWII made no attempt to disguise their weaponization of stigma. This is perhaps best illustrated with the British and American militaries' use of the highly potent label lacking moral fiber (LMF), and their formal written policies intended to suppress the masses succumbing to or disclosing mental health conditions. Reported usage of the LMF label within the twenty-first-century UK military is a direct testament of the durability of the military's weaponization of stigma to reduce the prevalence of war-stress injury.[16] In 1940, the famed British Royal Air Force (RAF) adopted a formal policy to curb escalating psychiatric casualty rates and disability pensions. They imposed severe penalties, such as immediate transfer or discharge, and publicly shamed those branded LMF by their commanders. Often this was done in front of their peers who were unable or unwilling to fly without a valid medical reason.[17] Intended to be harsh and punitive toward morally corrupt service members (e.g., LMF discharges are roughly equivalent to OTH separations today), the main purpose of the UK's LMF policy was to intimidate the group.

The context for the UK's weaponization of stigma was to reduce psychiatric attrition, but why was attrition a matter of concern? In 1942 alone, the UK's Bomber Command estimated that the chance of surviving a single tour was 44 percent, with only a 19.5 percent chance of completing a second without being killed or wounded in action.[18] Additionally, Bomber Command suffered about six thousand psychiatric casualties. Of those, between 1,000 and 1,200 were labeled LMF. The stigmatizing policy did not discriminate between the jittery novice flier or the battle wary pilot on his third or fourth tour. Nor did the amount or type of combat exposure matter as well as whether the service member was physically wounded.

British military historian Edgar Jones concluded, "The calculated use of stigma gave the policy force." This was evidenced by a statement from the RAF's Air Commodore, calling out "the dangers of too lenient treatment of failures, from whatever cause, owing to the possible undermining effect on other officers striving to maintain their morale."[19]

One RAF pilot suffered transient paralysis and mutism after his twentieth combat mission. He was quickly labeled LMF. He described how his commander reacted to him:

I was allowed no more contact with the crew and had to pack all my kit for immediate departure. No goodbyes or anything, and these men were like my family.

Before leaving I was summoned before the Commanding Officer for the severest dressing down of my career when he left me in no doubt of the seriousness of the affair:

I had let the side down and turned my back in the face of the enemy, an action for which soldiers had been shot in the First World War, he said.[20]

Enlisted aircrew members often were reassigned to ground combat units, whereas officers typically were ordered to Not Yet Diagnosed Neuropsychiatric (NYDN) centers. These centers were established in 1916 to eliminate psychiatric attrition from WWI-era shell shock.[21] Upon admission to NYDN hospitals, the LMF-branded personnel would endure further shaming by standing at attention in front of unit members while their Flying Badges and rank markings were stripped from their uniforms. If personnel did not return to full duty after their "treatment" at NYDN centers, they would be given less-than-honorable discharges that significantly hurt future employment. Jones reports an annual rate of 160 to 240 LMF cases that resulted in a total of more than 2,700 cases among British aircrew personnel, mostly pilots.[22] Near the end of WWII, the RAF got rid of its LMF policy "to avoid embarrassing the government,"[23] but it remained a stigmatizing label through the 1960s and, in some ways, persists today.

In 2002, a group of British soldiers sued the Ministry of Defense for inadequate mental healthcare. They argued that the military had done little to change stigma. The High Court Justice apparently agreed. "No doubt there could have been more rapid change," the Court wrote, and "No doubt more could have been done to address the persistent stigma attaching to psychiatric/psychological disorder, particularly in the ranks."[24] Jones, however, adds, "Others have argued that a measure of stigma is needed to prevent both conscious and unconscious resort to psychological disorders as an exit from situations of personal danger."[25] Who are these "others" to whom Jones alludes? Surely, military and government officials would be reluctant to unilaterally stop wielding stigma to discipline their troops.

U.S. MILITARY POLICIES AND WEAPONIZING STIGMA

In 1947, legendary American general George S. Patton explained the army's use of stigma during WWII: "The greatest weapon against the so-called 'battle fatigue' is ridicule." We could easily dismiss this as a misrepresentation of official military policy if it was not echoed by the highest ranking military commander. "To the specialists, the psychoneurotic is a hospital patient," said U.S. Army WWII chief of staff, General George C. Marshall, continuing that

> to the average line officer, he is a malingerer. Actually, he is a man who is either unwilling, unable, or slow to adjust himself to some or all phases of military life, and in consequence, he develops an imaginary ailment which in time becomes so fixed in his mind as to bring about mental pain and sickness.[26]

The stigma exacerbating attitudes of many of the military's top leaders became formally institutionalized.

Reducing exorbitant manpower attrition and costs caused by evacuations of psychiatric casualties during WWI led to the military's hundred-year-old frontline psychiatry, or combat and operational stress control (COSC), doctrines that were permanently institutionalized after WWII. Essentially, the military has designed a policy that provides a measure of brief restorative interventions and strictly prohibits psychiatric treatment and evacuation with the explicit expectation that upward of 95 percent of stress casualties will be returned to duty (RTD).[27]

The military's justification of its RTD policy is multilayered but includes the prevention of harmful stigma: "Evacuees had to deal with the stigma and shame of evacuation out of the theater. However, if psychological casualties were treated at forward locations with brief supportive therapy and the expectation of return to duty, between 60 percent and 80 percent were able to continue as soldiers."[28] A recent review seriously undermines the military's claim of stigma-reducing benefits,[29] but more important to our current purpose, is this question: How does the military systematically employ stigma to achieve its goals?

The military's weaponization of stigma to reduce psychiatric attrition is central to its frontline doctrine and its bedrock principle of *expectancy*, whereby medical and mental health practitioners are instructed to persuade the soldier-patient of certain realities of their situation—that is, what they should expect. This includes the transient, normal nature of their fear and abject certainty of their recovery and RTD after a brief convalescence. The military's frontline policies, however, represent a much more sophisticated and subtle variant of the UK's LMF. In fact, the expressed purpose of frontline psychiatry is to destigmatize combatants by avoiding psychiatric diagnosis, evacuation, and treatment.[30] Instead, military leaders and healthcare specialists are required to persuade war-stressed veterans of the reasons why they must RTD as soon as possible, which is to avert the highly stigmatizing moral, personal, and social consequences.

Military mental healthcare providers and commanding officers often use persuasion, exhortation, reinforcement, encouragement, and reassurance to compel patients to RTD. In using persuasion, the medical officer, having assured himself that the condition is functional, persuades the patient to make the effort necessary to overcome the disability. Medical officers user their authority and bring into play all of the moral suasion they can, appealing to patients' social self-esteem to them him cooperate and put forth a real effort of will. If moral persuasion fails, then the medical officer would default to more forcible methods, and according to certain witnesses, even threats would be justified in certain cases.[31]

Exhortation is commonly used even before medical personnel are involved. Often, commanding officers make an appeal to the soldier concerning the necessity of aiding comrades on the line or simply asking whether the soldier had actually gone so far as to abandon them. In instances of exhortation, nearly half of all men presenting with anxiety were RTD within six hours.[32] Commanding officers also would use words and phrases that would be familiar to the soldier to be most effective. The importance of the war and the consequences of defeat to them and their families were stressed, and appeals were made to their sense of duty, pride, and loyalty to comrades, unit, and country.[33]

Another tactic that commanding officers might use is reinforcement, urging the patient to stay with his buddies, not to be a coward, and to fulfill his soldierly duty. Commanding officers and medical personnel also appeal to a soldier's patriotic motivation, pride in self and the unit, and to all aspects of personal determination to fulfill a commitment.[34]

Mental healthcare providers also give immediate, explicit reassurance to the soldier. They explain that they suffer from battle fatigue, a temporary condition that will improve quickly. They actively reassure the patient that it is neither cowardice nor sickness but rather a normal reaction to terribly severe conditions.

AMERICAN LMF POLICY

Similar to WWI, the U.S. military in WWII quickly adopted policies of European allies to deal with its mental health problem. According to U.S. Army *Circular No. 24 American Expeditionary Forces, France*:

> It would seem then that we should profit as far as we can from the experience of the French in this matter. Check the development of neurosis by denying its existence at the start.
>
> The treatment of the patients should be calmative and restorative and any appearance of such symptoms as tremors, paralysis, etc., should be rigidly discouraged.
>
> This idea should run through the whole personnel of the hospital. At first it should be affected by gentle persuasion, but if the patients persist in the production of hysterical symptoms sterner measures should be resorted to.[35]

For instance, within eight months of the U.S. Eighth Army Air Forces arriving in England to begin bombing operations over Germany, thirty-five LMF cases were identified as "psychological failure."[36] The Eighth Army Air Force Commander proposed a less-pejorative label (i.e., "Temperamental Unsuitability") that the U.S. Army Air Force officially adopted as policy in 1942.[37] The initial U.S. policy emphasized treatment and rehabilitation, eventually changing the label to an even less stigmatizing term: "Primary Flying Fatigue." But by the end of 1942, more than 250 new cases of emotionally disturbed aircrew were identified, including 166 pilots.[38]

From mid-1943 through the end of the war, more than two thousand American airmen became psychiatric casualties, resulting in the widespread use of the infinitely more stigmatizing terms LMF and the Americanized "lack of intestinal fortitude" within the U.S. military. In all, about 1,200 American pilots and aircrew were branded with the LMF label. Dispositions varied from temporary reassignment, psychiatric treatment, and courts-martial. One battle-tested but overstressed American pilot in the Ninety-Fifth Bomb Wing was sentenced to confined hard labor and was given a less-than-honorable discharge after being convicted for "misbehaving before the enemy" when he refused to fly. Another enlisted crewmember received two years of hard labor and a dishonorable discharge for disobeying an order to fly soon after his unit had sustained heavy casualties.[39]

The following legal case provides a telling example of the U.S. military's weaponization of stigma and the silencing effect such punishments would expectedly have on military members as a whole who may experience war-stress injury:

Second Lieutenant, 412 Bombardment Squadron. This twenty-nine-year-old navigator had five combat missions. He was performing satisfactorily until he was wounded in the right arm when his plane was badly damaging on the fifth mission.

He was hospitalized for three weeks, developed tension symptoms, was unable to perform his duties on subsequent practice missions, and asked to be grounded. He was found to be tense, depressed, and to show evidence of weight loss. He had an excellent record, went to college for two years, held good jobs, was well motivated towards flying and did well as a navigator.

The Central Medical Board qualified him in October 1943 because it was not felt that he was suffering from "operational exhaustion." He was recommended for an *Other than Honorable Discharge* by the Reclassification Board.[40]

After WWII, the U.S. Army Eighth Air Force commanding general boasted that only about 1,200 airmen were permanently removed from flying because of psychiatric reasons.[41] This prompted one American historian to quip, "Even more significant, despite an overall casualty rate approaching 50 percent, much less than 1 percent of flyers were grounded for alleged cowardice."[42] From the military's perspective, a successful mental health policy has always been measured in terms of preserving manpower numbers, not improving the mental health and well-being of war-stressed combatants.[43]

EVIDENCE OF CONTEMPORARY WEAPONIZATION OF STIGMA

In today's military, no overt policies employ stigma to manage mental health. In fact, current Department of Defense (DoD) directives espouse considerable antistigma rhetoric. One must look, however, at what the military is actually doing to eliminate stigma, such as at the policies that reinforce stigma, as well as organizational barriers to seeking care. The military's weaponization of stigma is evident in its proclivity to prosecute, incarcerate, and execute emotionally injured war veterans. This includes bad paper discharges, which have increased significantly since the Vietnam War. All of these stigma-enabling efforts send clear and powerful signals throughout the military: the repercussions are dire for those with war-stress injuries.

In 2004, U.S. Army researchers found that 73 percent of soldiers returning from Iraq who screened positive for a mental health condition like post-traumatic stress disorder (PTSD) reported not seeking mental health treatment.[44] The landmark study provided an unprecedented insight not only into the level of oppressive stigma returning personnel must endure but also the efficacy of the military's stigmatizing policies. For instance, 22 percent of spouses and 77 percent of their active-duty partners reported they would not seek mental healthcare for fear of being seen as weak;

TABLE 5.1 Military Studies on Stigma and Organizational Barriers to Care

SURVEY QUESTION	SCREENED POSITIVE FOR MH DISORDER IRAQ	SCREENED POSITIVE FOR MH DISORDER AFGHANISTAN	NOT SCREENED POSITIVE FOR MH DISORDER AFGHANISTAN
I would be seen as weak	65%	47%	23%
It would harm my career	50%	40%	17%
My unit leadership might treat me differently	63%	39%	22%
My leaders would blame me for the problem	51%	36%	14%
There would be difficulty getting time off work for treatment	55%	46%	17%

Source: M. C. Russell and C. R. Figley, "Do the Military's Frontline Psychiatry/Combat Operational Stress Control Programs Benefit Veterans? Part Two: Systematic Review of the Evidence," *Psychological Injury and Law* 10 (2017): 24–71.

21 percent of spouses and 56 percent of their soldier partners cited concerns about harm to the active-duty member's career.[45] Table 5.1 highlights some of the questions and responses reported by the army's frontline researchers in regards to stigma.

In 2007, the Department of Defense committed to reverse these harmful trends:

> Our Center of Excellence will work with the Military Departments to develop and execute an anti-stigma campaign, using some of the best and brightest minds in the Military, Federal family, and civilian professional community to ensure the right tools are created and used to reduce stigma associated with seeking mental health care when needed and at the earliest possible time.[46]

The military has reported an encouraging trend that levels of perceived stigma and barriers appear to be gradually declining. For example, in 2013, only 40 percent (down from 50 percent) of deployed soldiers screening positive for PTSD said they would not seek mental healthcare because it would harm their career. Since the 2007 pronouncement, dozens of commissioned studies, DoD task forces, and government oversight investigations have been conducted, often with overlapping findings and corrective actions for the military to achieve its stated goal to eliminate stigma.[47]

In 2012, the Institute of Medicine reached the following conclusion about the military leadership's commitment to actually eliminate stigma and organizationally induced barriers:

> In DoD and each service branch, leaders at all levels of the chain of command are not consistently held accountable for implementing policies and programs to manage PTSD effectively, including those aimed at reducing stigma and overcoming barriers to accessing care. In each service branch, there is no overarching authority to establish and enforce policies for the entire spectrum of PTSD management activities.[48]

Nine years after the DoD committed itself to ending stigma in the military, the Government Accountability Office (GAO) reported the following:

> The DoD is not well positioned to measure the progress of its mental health care stigma reduction efforts for several reasons. First, DOD has not clearly defined the barriers to care it generally understands as "mental health care stigma" and does not have related goals or performance measures to track progress.
>
> Second, GAO's review found that multiple DOD- and service-sponsored surveys that contain questions to gauge stigma use inconsistent methods, which precludes the analysis of trends over time in order to determine effectiveness of stigma reduction efforts.[49]

Moreover, both the GAO and an independent RAND study reported 203 specific DOD policies that served as organizational barriers to seeking mental healthcare by promoting stigma.[50] For instance, "an Army policy requires verification that a soldier has no record of emotional or mental instability to be eligible for recruiting duty."[51] Despite all the politically correct pronouncements and incremental changes, the fact is that military leadership is not interested in divesting itself from a weapon as effective as stigma. That means that "no single entity is coordinating department-wide efforts to reduce stigma."[52]

Consequently, the likelihood that stigma and its organizational obstructions will be significantly reduced by the military in the foreseeable future is remote. "Without a clear definition for 'mental healthcare stigma' with goals and measures, along with a coordinating entity to oversee program and policy efforts and data collection and analysis," the GAO reported, "the Department of Defense does not have assurance that its efforts are effective and that resources are most efficiently allocated."[53]

THE SLIPPERY SLOPE

Since 2008, the military has rolled out a host of specialized trainings aimed at reducing psychiatric attrition by teaching service personnel and their families empirically derived cognitive and behavioral coping skills before, during, and after deployment to remain psychologically resilient. One of these programs, Battlemind, discusses it this way:

> Battlemind is a Soldiers inner strength to face adversity, fear, and hardship during combat with confidence and resolution. In essence it is psychological resiliency. The objective of Battlemind training is to develop psychological resiliency which contributes to a Soldiers will and spirit to fight and win in combat, thereby reducing combat stress reactions and symptoms.

The stated intent of DoD's seventy-seven disconnected resiliency programs — which often bear strong names like Battlemind, Comprehensive Soldier Fitness, Spiritual Warrior Resilience, Landing Gear, Warrior Resilience and Thriving, Passport Toward Success, and PRIDE — is to destigmatize mental health conditions and encourage help-seeking by ensuring that "all soldiers have the necessary skills to successfully transition home."

In 2011, RAND reviewed the effectiveness of DoD's resiliency trainings in reducing stigma and preventing war-stress injury as advertised. They were not impressed:

> No standard measures of resilience or outcomes were used across resilience programs. We found that only five of the twenty-three programs had conducted formal assessments of their effectiveness. Because of this, there is limited evidence available as to how well the programs are working or would work if they were implemented in the military. Where evidence is available, the effects appear to be positive but modest.

In conclusion, RAND researchers opined, "Since strength is already an inherent value within the military culture, promoting psychological resilience as a form of strength is a natural fit." Yes, it may be a natural fit with the military focus on strength, but what does it say then about service personnel and their families who, despite receiving x hours of strength-building training, still break down (as they assuredly will)? What will these *training failures* and those around them think about their obvious lack of "inner strength to face adversity, fear, and hardship"? They were taught how to cope and be resilient, yet they failed. Why? Were they too weak to begin with? Were they secretly cowards? After all, now it is documented that they received the evidence-based skill training.

Messaging equating resilience with strength sends a clear signal to the rank and file, that nonresilience—also called mental illness—is weakness. Although academics will beg to differ, and rightly so, to the average marine or soldier, the only way a warrior is respected as resilient and strong is to avoid a mental health diagnosis. This is precisely the desired result of weaponizing stigma. Although many leaders promoting resilience-propaganda may have good intentions, the military's newfound messaging offers them cover—that is, plausible deniability that their intent was harmful while simultaneously silencing those who may need help.

WHY HAS MILITARY MENTAL HEALTH STIGMA PERSISTED?

The military mental health stigma has persisted because it helps the all-volunteer military sustain a high level of readiness by protecting the fighting force from the exorbitant costs associated with psychiatric attrition, treatment, and discharge.

Imagine a time when military personnel feel completely unencumbered to disclose post-traumatic stress during and after deployments without any career repercussions. Instead of shame, ridicule, and rejection military, leaders and healthcare personnel openly encourage and positively reinforce health-seeking behaviors. In this utopia, mental health and physical health are indispensable sides of the same coin. Sound ideal? It is not from the military's perspective. A slow trickle of deployed personnel leaving the frontlines becomes a torrid evacuation syndrome caused by mass hysteria and liberal psychiatric evacuation policies. Who will pay for treatment? Who will be left to fight? How will the morale of those remaining on the frontlines erode?

Eventually, even the hardiest start to question whether it is worth staying and dying when they see their emotionally injured friends leave the battlefield, possibly with a Purple Heart and a disability pension. Warrior Transition Units back home are swollen beyond capacity with divisions of temporary disabled personnel and skyrocketing pension costs threaten the financial stability of the country. Given that the modern-day trend of psychiatric casualties far outpace the total of combatants wounded or killed in action,[54] this scenario is the military's version of hell.

The recurring explanation used by the military for persistent stigma is that such antiquated and prejudicial beliefs exist in mainstream culture.[55] This truism is rarely challenged. The logical implication is that American society is responsible for taking the lead in changing cultural bias against mental illness. In other words, the military is passively at the mercy of mainstream culture. It must be pointed out, however, that the military has a long and storied tradition of assertively working to eradicate undesirable and dysfunctional cultural belief systems. For instance, the military has zero-tolerance policies for drug use, racial discrimination, sexism, and sexual harassment.[56] According to the DoD's directive on diversity and civil right protection, it is policy that "Programs or activities conducted by, or that receive financial assistance from, the Department of Defense shall not unlawfully discriminate against individuals on the basis of race, color, national origin, sex, religion, age, or disability."[57]

Not so for mental health stigma and discrimination. Annually, the military strictly monitors compliance with its equal opportunity policies and commanders are held accountable for noncompliance. Random drug testing and regular physical fitness testing support the military's commitment to curb unproductive cultural habits. In fact, the military's dedication to counter mainstream culture's less favorable attributes can be so effective that individuals are successfully taught to override their individualistic mind-set and life-preservation instinct and display amazing acts of heroism and self-sacrifice.

Although prejudice and discrimination continue to persist in the military, there can be no dispute over the military's general effectiveness in changing its culture even while civilian culture lagged behind. What can be argued is that the military is not actually committed to changing the culture around stigma and mental health. And why should it be? From the military's perspective, abandoning its weaponization of stigma is akin to unilaterally forsaking automatic rifles. Both are potentially disastrous unforced errors from the military's perspective. The military's worst fears, however, lack any factual or evidence-based support. Like all fundamental war trauma lessons, the military refuses to implement what it says is required to eliminate harmful stigma and barriers to care. Modern psychiatric casualty trends prove that weaponizing stigma has not been a winning strategy for the war veteran, their family, the military, or society.

6

DENYING THE PSYCHIATRIC REALITY OF WAR

THE FOURTH DARK-SIDE STRATEGY

As in the etiology of any neurosis, constitutional factors and the individu-
al's life history, including the genetic background of his personality, are very
important. Yet many observers have given these factors undue weight.

The realities of war, including the nature of army "society" and traumatic stim-
uli, cooperate to produce a potential war neurosis in every soldier-when a neurotic
breakdown is precipitated, which constitutes an illness and requires treatment.

R. R. GRINKER AND J. P. SPIEGEL, *WAR NEUROSES IN NORTH AFRICA*

The fourth strategy in the history of military mental health is the simple denial that a crisis exists. Our systematic review revealed several types of denial and this is where our analysis begins. First, we have just a few words about the concept of denial.

Denial is the "refusal to admit the truth or reality."[1] In a psychiatric sense, Anna Freud described denial (or *verleugnung*) as a primitive unconscious defense mechanism instinctively employed by children and psychotics to protect the ego from internal and external threats. For Freud, denial occurs when individuals reject a reality that is too uncomfortable to accept, insisting it is untrue despite overwhelming evidence to the contrary.

One can engage in simple denial, such as denying the reality of an unpleasant fact, like the tobacco industry denying the link between smoking and lung cancer. *Minimization* is to admit the fact but deny its seriousness—a tactic we see in the politics around global warming. In either case, Freud considered denial a mechanism of the immature mind.[2] Its short-term benefits ultimately end in long-term failure. The denier can never effectively learn from and adapt to reality. Modern psychologists consider denial a process of protecting oneself from the unpleasant or frightening aspects of an external reality that undermine motivations and intentions to protect oneself from a potential threat.[3]

ADAPTIVE AND MALADAPTIVE DENIAL

Whether denial and other repression strategies may be considered adaptive or maladaptive depends on the context and degree. For instance, moderate levels of denial in lung cancer patients—"I'm going to beat this!"—may improve their perception of health and physical functioning compared with patients with low-level denial who morbidly focus on actual survival odds or those with high-level denial who may avoid treatment altogether.

Likewise, when it comes to the military, we can distinguish between adaptive and maladaptive denial. Denying the psychological and physical realities of warfare in the heat of battle is often adaptive from the perspective of an individual soldier—it lets him or her survive and focus on the mission. Such denial is maladaptive, however, when warfighters deny serious signs of their own war-stress injury, like suicidal or homicidal thoughts or when military leaders weaponize stigma. This is especially true when military organizations and their governments systematically deny that war-stress injuries are authentic consequences of war as much as gunshot and shrapnel wounds are.

Avoidance denial and *optimistic denial* are different.[4] Avoidance denial makes one highly anxious about perceived vulnerability and threats of harm and engage in threat reduction behaviors by avoiding protective actions. In contrast, optimistic denial is to deny one's vulnerability to future threats and therefore to downplay the risk of harm. Within the military, we find abundant evidence of both types of denial that largely coincide with the length of wartime mental health crises. At war's outset, each military cohort regularly demonstrates optimistic denial in the exaggerated confidence of its mental health policies to reduce the numbers of psychiatric casualties and ignoring the documented lessons of previous wartime needs.

During the Vietnam War, the military prematurely proclaimed victory over neuropsychiatric illness: "The incidence of neuropsychiatric illness in U.S. Army troops in Vietnam is lower than any recorded in previous conflicts." We all know how that turned out. As war persists and the inevitable mental health crisis emerges—largely due to the military's lack of preparation— military leaders become increasingly nervous about the imminent barrage of bad press and congressional scrutiny.[5] This is when the military customarily uses avoidance denial or reactive strategies to cope with a self-inflicted crisis and thus continuing to avoid learning its war trauma lessons.

MILITARY USE OF DENIAL TO COPE WITH ITS MENTAL HEALTH DILEMMA

Each moment of combat imposes a strain so great that men will break down in direct relation to the intensity and duration of their exposure. Thus, psychiatric casualties are as inevitable as gunshot and shrapnel wounds in warfare.
J. APPEL AND G. BEEBE, "PREVENTIVE PSYCHIATRY"

Since the twentieth century, the military has reflexively employed denial as a primitive yet central tactic in its initial dealings with the mental health dilemma. The military's denial of the psychological realities of war manifests in four critical interrelated ways: (1) denying the inevitability of large numbers of psychiatric casualties from modern warfare; (2) denying the inherent need to adequately plan and prepare to meet wartime mental health needs; (3) denying the primary etiological role of exposure to war stress as a legitimate cause of a spectrum of stress injury; and (4) denying organizational responsibility to meet mental health needs.

Lieutenant Colonel A. G. Kay analyzed the effect of industrialized war from 1886 to 1908 on the British Army and found significant associations between increased rates of war-stress injury and duration of exposure: "The amount of the increase is proportional to the duration of campaign"[6] and intensity of combat. Kay discussed "the conditions of modern warfare calling large numbers of men into action, the tremendous endurance, physical and mental required, and the widely destructive effect of modern artillery fire," and forewarned military leaders about the future toxic effects of twentieth-century war: "We shall have to deal with a larger percentage of mental disease the hitherto."[7] Kay's prophetic warning is routinely ignored by war planners intent on denying the psychological realities of modern warfare ("only a small percentage succumbs and takes flight into sickness").[8] These realities are left only to be relearned the hard way:

The war has taught us and will continue to teach us (1) that just as before there are traumatic neuroses; (2) that they are not always covered by the concept of hysteria; and (3) that they are really the product of trauma and not goal-oriented, well cultivated pseudo illness.[9]

The psychological realities of modern industrialized warfare that Oppenheim and Appel and Beebe[10] aptly summarized for their respective cohorts were clearly evident long before World War I (WWI):

> There is a strong suspicion that the high insanity rate in the Spanish-American War and the Boer War, and perhaps in earlier conflicts, was due, in part at least, to failure to recognize the real nature of the severe neuroses, which are grouped under the term "shell shock" in this war.[11]

And they were tragically repeated after World War II (WWII):

> Undoubtedly, the most important lesson learned by psychiatry in World War II was the failure of responsible military authorities, during mobilization and early phases of hostilities, to appreciate the inevitability of large-scale psychiatric disorders under conditions of modern warfare.[12].

As military historians Jones and Wessely argue, however, before the twentieth century, "The idea that a soldier of previously sound mind could be so emotionally disturbed by combat that he could no longer function was not entertained; that he might suffer long-term psychological consequences of battle was also dismissed."[13]

Yet, psychiatric realities could no longer be rationally denied by credible authorities, as Salmon notes: "Today the enormous number of these cases among some of Europe's best fighting men is leading to a revision of the medical and popular attitude toward functional nervous diseases."[14]

If psychosis is a complete break from reality and denial is a primitive defense against descending into psychotic despair, then no other suitable diagnosis can explain the military's inability to appreciate the size and scope of wartime mental health needs than denial. Consider the military's efforts to minimize reality, as stated by the assistant secretary of defense health affairs: "Of the 10 percent or so who have PTSD, most will recover with time, patience and love. Some will need more."[15]

The army's senior psychiatrist, a brigadier general, recounted the preparation for the 2003 invasion of Iraq: "We were not allowed to talk of the unseen wounds of war—we were not allowed to prepare for the unseen wounds." These observations were later validated by the Department of Defense (DoD) Task Force on Mental Health: "Despite the dedicated work of its members, the current system is not structured to address these new challenges, leaving many psychological health needs unmet. Without a fundamental realignment of services, this situation will worsen."[16]

It is evident how deeply entrenched the military's denial is around its promise to care for psychiatric casualties by its persistence despite immense public criticism. Consider the findings independent studies like the Institute of Medicine (IOM), concluded after thirteen years of war: "PTSD management appears to be local, ad hoc, incremental, and crisis-driven, with little planning devoted to the development of a long range, population-based approach for the disorder by either the Office of the Assistant Secretary of Defense for Health Affairs or any of the service branches."[17]

Perhaps the most visible demonstration of military denial is its repeated post-hoc admission of abject failure to properly plan and prepare for the predictable psychological outcomes of war. A certain degree of latitude can be given to WWI-era leaders who failed to heed prior lessons of war trauma—the sheer magnitude of WWI psychiatric casualties was unprecedented in human history. The documentation and dissemination of those psychiatric realities began in earnest after WWI, however, and future war planners had no excuse. As Colonel Albert Glass reports, "there was the documented history of World War I, as well as accounts from other previous wars, which provided abundant evidence that combat would produce large numbers of psychiatric casualties."[18]

What beside the primitive psychological defense of denial can explain how the U.S. military—which prides itself as an ardent student of history—would confess after WWII that "despite the foregoing data that were available to responsible authorities, there was no effective plan or real preparation for the utilization of psychiatry by the army in WWII. Facilities for the care and treatment of psychiatric cases were only barely sufficient for the small peacetime Army."[19]

According to Glass,

> psychiatric disorders proved to be a major source of manpower loss to the U.S. Army in World War II. At the beginning of the war, a potential loss of this magnitude was neither expected nor planned for by military authorities in general or the Medical Department in particular. It was not until February 1942 that a psychiatrist was assigned to the Surgeon General's Office.[20]

The best illustration of the military's failure not to repeat the errors of the past may be found in the massive two-volume report issued by the U.S.

Army surgeon general. It took twenty-one years to write this 2,038-page report about the lessons of WWII. It was intended to halt future leaders from denying the realities of war: "With this information so readily available, there can be little excuse for repetition of error in future wars, should they occur."[21]

Certainly no one expected this pattern of denial, crisis, and relearning to continue after WWII, especially in the military. After the last major American war of the twentieth century, the Persian Gulf War, we again saw a similar admission of the military's denial in preparation. Martin claims that "they (mental healthcare providers) were not adequately staffed, equipped or trained in peace-time to perform their wartime role. . . . As highlighted here, lessons learned in SWA (Southwest Asia) provide a reference point from which to prepare for this inevitability."[22]

The military's tenacious denial of and unapologetic failure to cope with its mental health dilemma appears unencumbered by morality or time. Leaping forward to the first major wars of the twenty-first century, on June 16, 2007, a congressionally mandated DoD Task Force on Mental Health publicly unveiled its findings. The task force found that the "Military Health System lacks the fiscal resources and the fully trained personnel to fulfill its mission to support psychological health in peacetime or fulfill the enhanced requirements imposed during times of conflict."[23]

Six years into the Afghanistan and Iraq wars, the DoD again revealed its repeated failure to adequately plan and prepare, announcing ninety-nine corrective actions covering every fundamental lesson of war trauma, from staffing and training to treatment, prevention, stigma, and reintegration. The DoD pleaded for urgent action for the sake of thousands of neglected soldiers.[24] Amid congratulations and promotions was the unspoken consequence of the military's denial: escalating rates of PTSD, suicide, traumatic brain injury (TBI), substance abuse, misconduct stress behaviors, legal prosecutions, and caregiver distress.[25]

In addition to grossly underestimating the inevitable high volume of war-stress casualties and forsaking proper planning to meet wartime mental health needs, the military also routinely denies the primary cause of this injury: exposure to war stress. "It should always be remembered," writes Glass, "that modern war produces two unique types of casualties in large numbers; namely, injuries and psychiatric disorders, both of which are caused by traumatic forces set forth by a changing and hostile environment."[26] Glass also writes that "when finally, psychiatric casualties were regarded as legitimate consequence of battle stress and strain, it became possible to prepare adequately for their prevention and treatment."[27]

These historical anecdotes have robust empirical support. The IOM reports, for example,

> In the brain, there is evidence of structural and functional changes resulting directly from chronic or severe stress. The changes are associated with alterations of the most profound functions of the brain: memory and decision-making. They are also associated with symptoms of fear and anxiety, and they might sensitize the brain to substances of abuse and increase the risk of substance-use disorders.[28]

At the beginning of WWII, most military authorities and many psychiatrists, including civilian consultants to the armed services, believed that psychiatric disorders did not occur to a significant extent in "normal" people but rather arose primarily in the minority population deemed to be "weaklings" or those who had underlying emotional instability that predisposed them to psychiatric illness.[29]

The U.S. Army's *Textbook on War Psychiatry* explains that PTSD occurs "in those with social and biological predispositions in whom the stressor is meaningful when social supports are inadequate."[30] If the military truly has learned that war produces a legitimate spectrum of injury, we should expect it would behave accordingly. Evidence would support adequate planning, staffing, and treatment in the same way the military cares for predictable physical wounds. Military clinicians and researchers would regularly screen and track the full spectrum of injury instead of only a handful of conditions, as it currently does.[31] They would not tolerate stigma and barriers to care, and they certainly would never have weaponized these to reduce help-seeking. In other words, evidence is overwhelming that the military has avoided learning its lesson that war-stress injury is a legitimate and predictable outcome from war.

DENIAL OF ORGANIZATIONAL RESPONSIBILITY

Those who deny responsibility usually are attempting to avoid potential pain by shifting attention away from themselves.[32] This type of denial involves avoiding personal responsibility by (1) blaming or shifting culpability;

(2) attempting to minimize the effects or results of an action appear to be less harmful than in actuality; (3) justifying actions by attempting to make that choice look proper because of their perception of what is right; and (4) acting in a regressive or childish way (e.g., whining, temper tantrum).

Historically, the military has frequently exercised the strategy of shifting blame for war-stress injury on every factor other than war itself, including but not limited to individual predisposed weakness and amoral pension-seeking; disability compensation and pensions or "pension-seeking neurosis," corrosive influence of psychiatry and mental health providers in general, weakening influence of the modern "culture of trauma and victimhood," politically motivated antiwar advocates and psychiatrists, overly lenient and ineffectual unit leaders, inadequate military training and discipline, sensationalized media coverage, insufficient congressional support, and shifting the responsibility for treatment to the Department of Veterans Affairs (VA).

For example, the U.S. military often defers responsibility for definitive mental healthcare to the VA or private sector.[33] Upon learning of the WWII crisis characterized by mass untreated psychiatric casualties discharged by the military, President Franklin D. Roosevelt authored a December 4, 1944, directive to the secretary of war clarifying the military's responsibility:

My dear Mr. Secretary:

I am deeply concerned over the physical and emotional condition of disabled men returning from the war. I feel, as I know you do, that the ultimate ought to be done for them to return them as useful citizens—useful not only to themselves but to the community.

I wish you would issue instructions to the effect that it should be the responsibility of the military authorities to insure that no overseas casualty is discharged from the armed forces until he has received the maximum benefits of hospitalization and convalescent facilities which must include physical and psychological rehabilitation, vocational guidance, prevocational training, and resocialization.

Very sincerely yours,
Franklin Delano Roosevelt[34]

The commander-in-chief's order was a 180-degree reversal of the military's policy and practice of essentially no treatment and discharge to "maximum benefit" of mental health treatment and retention before separation.[35] Toward the end of WWI, however, the U.S. military was also assigned responsibility for treatment of its psychiatric casualties before discharge. "As the war proceeded," according to Colonel Thomas Salmon, M.C., and Sergeant Norman Fenton,

> it was considered desirable to require that all mental cases be treated for a reasonable period in the military hospitals. Directions recommended in June, 1918, sent out November 20, 1918, provided that all except cases which were evidently incurable should be treated in the military hospitals for a period of at least four months, unless recovery took place sooner.[36]

In 2012, President Obama's executive order echoed his predecessor's effort to compel the military to accept its responsibility for caring of mentally ill combatants. "Our efforts also must focus on both outreach to veterans and their families and the provision of high quality mental health treatment to those in need," he said. "Coordination between the Departments of Veterans Affairs and Defense during service members' transition to civilian life is essential to achieving these goals."[37]

If the military's policy was to accept responsibility for treating its war-stressed personnel, there would be no need for executive actions by the commander-in-chief.

ATTEMPTS TO MINIMIZE HARMFUL EFFECTS

The best example of this stratagem is the military's frontline combat operational stress-control policy. This century-old policy promotes the military's claim of the long-term health benefits to deployed personnel and their families of repeatedly returning traumatized soldiers to combat units. They are to remain downrange until they are either severely incapacitated (e.g., psychotic) or present imminent danger to self or others.

A perfect illustration of this avoidance stratagem is when the military was confronted by the Government Accountability Office (GAO) in 2006 regarding its PTSD prevention and treatment programs. The GAO reviewed the DoD's PTSD screening policies that mandate postdeployment health assessment screenings intended for early identification and intervention. According to the GAO, "A joint VA/DOD guideline states that service-members who respond positively to three or four of the questions may be at risk for PTSD." [38] Postdeployment health assessment (PDHA) screenings typically are conducted by nonphysicians, often enlisted medics or physician assistants or sometimes general practitioners. These specialties most often refer to specialists like neurology and psychiatry for positive screenings of a high-risk health problem like PTSD. The GAO, however, found that the military failed to refer 78 percent of returning Operation Enduring Freedom/Operation Iraqi Freedom veterans who were at highest risk for PTSD (endorsing three to four out of four symptoms) to a mental health specialist in compliance with the purpose of its screening policy.[39] That mental health referral would evaluate whether someone actually had PTSD and warranted treatment.

When confronted, the military responded by denying responsibility with a string of deeply strained justifications for not referring high-risk patients to a specialist. They noted the "potential risks associated with false positive" and said, "no medical intervention is without risks. The general premise of medical practice is that the benefits should outweigh the risks. In terms of PTSD, the risks are associated with potentially issuing a diagnosis of PTSD for an individual who has no diagnosable mental health disorder."[40]

In other words, the military prefers that a nonphysician or generalist assess a high-risk condition like PTSD. The military attempts to covers its bases: "In making a clinical determination associated with a mental health referral, the risks of false positive must always be weighed against the accuracy of clinical judgement. Watchful waiting may be more appropriate in situations in which the clinician is not sure about a diagnosis or the severity of symptoms."[41]

The PDHA screener may never see the service member again, but is encouraged to wait versus refer to a specialist. This means that it is entirely up to the service member to reengage the medical system when their symptoms worsen, are in crisis, or attempt suicide. This type of reactionary policy contradicts the entire reason for conducting proactive screenings in the first place—a tragic example of institutional denial.

THE HARM OF DENIAL

We have seen a laundry list of cases in which the military employed its strategy: to deny, deny, deny. And the consequences have been harmful.

The military's entrenched culture denies millions of veterans and their families essential mental health services—a direct violation of its force health protection duty. The military has extensively documented the critical import of early identification and intervention for war-stress injury. Salmon writes, "First, that it is not only in accordance with the best scientific practice to treat soldiers suffering with war neuroses as early and as effectively as possible but to do so is an important contribution toward the conservation of manpower and military morale."[42] Today's U.S. Army reaffirms this foundational requirement: "Once mental disorder symptoms emerge, the most effective strategy for ensuring recovery lies in the prompt application of evidence-based treatments.[43]

In 2004, the VA and DoD published their joint practice guidelines for managing post-traumatic stress that included expert consensus recommendations for use of the identified evidence-based treatments.[44] The practice guidelines were updated in 2010 and explicitly state the necessity of timely PTSD treatment: "The clinically significant symptoms cause significant distress or impairment in social, occupational, or other important areas of functioning. The symptoms last more than three months after exposure to trauma. Chronic PTSD is unlikely to improve without effective treatment."[45]

In fact, untreated war-stress injury is invariably likely to metastasize into an infinite number of cooccurring problems, such as substance abuse, depression, suicide, chronic pain, interpersonal violence, and divorce.

Military denial is the moral equivalent of exposing soldiers to known carcinogens and then intentionally denying them access to timely identification and lifesaving treatment. Consequently, the vast majority of war veterans never receive appropriate mental healthcare until it boils over into personal crisis, often long-after discharge.[46] Indirect effects from the military's denial strategies include exorbitant costs of personnel attrition and replacement on the military-side, as well as the escalating costs of disability compensation and societal ripple effects from repetitive major public health crises.

We are unaware of any previous investigations into the military's reliance on denial as a defense mechanism in dealing with its mental health dilemma. The extent to which the military's propensity to deny the psychiatric realities of war reflects an unconscious or intentional process is open to debate. Clearly, a disconnect exists between the public knowledge that war results in psychiatric casualties and the DoD's systemic failure to provide even peacetime levels of mental health services. The irrational and highly uncharacteristic nature of the discordant behavior by the military can be attributed only to denial or gross negligence with malice and forethought.[47] For the military to endure repeated organizational embarrassment, shame, and public disdain for failing to live by its moral code to do right by millions of service personnel and their families, we must assume its denial strategies offer a tremendous payoff.

INSTITUTIONALIZED RESISTANCE TO ORGANIZATIONAL CHANGE

Institutionalized resistance is defined by Agocs as "the pattern of organizational behavior that decision makers in organizations employ to actively deny, reject, refuse to implement, repress or even dismantle change proposals and initiatives." According to him, it also "entails a range of behaviors: refusal to engage in joint problem-solving, refusal to seek common ground, silencing of advocates for change, sabotage, the use of sanctions, and another repressive acts."[48]

The closest example we can find of this stratagem is the military's kneejerk response to a whistleblower who filed a grievance with the DoD Inspector's Office in 2005,[49] detailing a mental health crisis the military actively wanted to deny. In retaliation, top military officials disseminated a Public Affairs Guidance[50] expressly designed to refute claims of a crisis of inadequate staffing and treatment that were latter validated by the DoD Task Force.[51] The officials then exacted retribution against said whistleblowers by denying military promotion and threatening the service member's career.[52]

Perhaps the military's resistance and denial are so institutionalized because it fears that acknowledging the mental health crisis would cripple its capacity to fight and win wars because of attrition through mass evacuation syndromes and depleted finances from the costs of meeting wartime mental health needs. Or perhaps it fears that the competing costs and resources for mental health services will fatally detract from military readiness, like weapon procurement. Or perhaps the military is afraid that expanding disability pensions will bankrupt society or that admitting the crisis would undermine military recruitment and retention efforts to sustain an all-volunteer force. Or perhaps it is simply cultural antipathy and deeply held personal beliefs, biases, and fears toward mental health, in general, and its clientele and practitioners, in particular.

7

PURGING WEAKNESS

THE FIFTH DARK-SIDE STRATEGY

In the beginning of World War II, military authorities, both lay and medical, believed that psychiatric disorders occurred only in predisposed individuals— weaklings. This led to the endorsement of and the reliance upon the policy of psychiatric screening. As the war progressed, these authorities discovered that most mental disorders occurred in "normal" men and that screening was ineffective in preventing the occurrence of such conditions.

J. APPEL AND G. BEEBE, "PREVENTIVE PSYCHIATRY"

Appel and Beebe's commentary gives the appearance that the military has finally learned a fundamental war trauma lesson: that exposure to the neurotoxic effects of warfare is often the primary cause of stress injury.

Not so fast. According to the U.S. Army's *Textbook of Military Medicine: War Psychiatry*, chronic post-traumatic stress disorder (PTSD) occurs "in those with social and biological predispositions in whom the stressor is meaningful when social supports are inadequate,"[1] noting that "other mechanisms such as positive reinforcement (secondary gain in Freud's model) seem more important in the chronic maintenance of symptoms."[2] The army concludes that "whatever the theory of causation, PTSD symptoms appear to be relatively universal given a severe enough stressor; however, it is not the presence of symptoms but the psychological purposes they serve that determines the degree of disability."[3]

Such sentiment contradicts the lessons learned from the World War I (WWI) trauma lessons and the World War II (WWII) cohort: "The war has taught us and will continue to teach us (1) that just as before there are traumatic neuroses; (2) that they are not always covered by the concept of hysteria; and (3) that they are really the product of trauma and not goal-oriented, well cultivated pseudo illness."[4]

Throughout history, the military has searched for explanations of the escalating trends of psychiatric attrition and disability and the correct policies to resolve its mental health dilemma. Invariably, the finger eventually points to the inherent weakness of modern combatants, inadequate military training and unit leadership, the morally corrosive influence of mental health specialists, and the weakening effects of contemporary society, media, and its culture of victimhood.[5] In other words, any and every conceivable reason has been given to explain psychiatric attrition and disabilities other than exposure to the neurotoxic effects of industrialized human warfare.

To implement its false narrative, the military has used various prevention and purging strategies to eliminate "weakness." These purges have included psychiatric screening and rejection at time of accession; psychiatric evaluations of active-duty personnel leading to legal or administrative bad paper separations for behavior like misconduct or personality disorder; restricting the influence of military mental healthcare providers; and revamping military training, discipline, and leadership to include building morale, cohesion, and resiliency. In chapter 4, we discussed the harmful purging habits of the military to rid itself of war-stressed combatants through bad paper and backdoor discharges, a theme we return to in chapter 9. In this chapter, we focus on the other purging and prevention approaches designed to avoid learning war trauma lessons.

PSYCHIATRIC SCREENING, REJECTION, AND MORE SCREENING

Military institutions have traditionally screened out candidates who lacked the requisite physical standards to endure the rigor of military training and service. During the Civil War, Union Army Surgeon General Hammond instituted a policy requiring candidates to be at least twenty-two years old, with the idea that this would prevent physical and mental health breakdowns. But extending the military's screening policy to emotional or psychological weakness was not widespread until WWI.

In 1917, as the military prepared to enter WWI, Major Thomas Salmon, an army psychiatrist, was sent to Europe to establish American policies that would prevent large-scale psychiatric casualties and pension costs already experienced by allies. Salmon noted the importance of psychiatric screening in his report:

> For the United States, this experience carries important lessons. Most important than all others is the result of careless recruiting. The problem of dealing with mental diseases in the army—difficult at best—has been made still more so by accepting large numbers of recruits, who had been in institutions for the insane or were of demonstrably psychopathic make-up.[6]

His informed view on the ongoing debate about the primary cause for war-stress injury being cumulative exposure to war stress or predisposed weakness, however, led him to conclude as follows:

> Although an excessive incidence of mental diseases has been noted in all recent wars, it is only the present one that functional nervous diseases have constituted a major medical military problem. As every nation and race engaged is suffering severely from these disorders, it is apparent that new conditions of warfare are chiefly responsible for their prevalence.[7]

He recommended rejecting candidates with a known history or propensity of being "insane, feebleminded, psychopathic, and neuropathic"[8] to save the country millions of dollars in pensions.

The U.S. Army's comprehensive psychiatric screening program was ground-breaking. It consisted of the creation of Army Alpha and nonverbal Beta tests (precursors to intelligence testing), measuring both literate and illiterate candidates, and the first standardized personality test by Robert Woodworth. Consequently, the U.S. Army rejected more than seventy thousand candidates for psychiatric reasons and another fifteen thousand soldiers were discharged prior to deploying for demonstrating psychiatric weakness.

By 1918, the American military also had adopted the Allies' frontline psychiatry policy, which was explicitly designed to prevent psychiatric attrition, treatment, and pensioning by emphasizing brief convalescences for stress-injured combatants near the frontlines, avoiding diagnostic labels, and insisting soldiers return to duty. Specialized treatment centers that were staffed with psychiatrists and other mental health specialists to provide specialty care near the frontlines were developed, as per Salmon's recommendation. This specialized center was a "special military hospital using existing civil facilities for treating mental disease in a manner that will serve the army effectively and at the same time safeguard the interests of the soldiers, of the government and of the community."[9]

Today, the military routinely touts its hundred-year-old WWI-era front-line psychiatry policy, now called "combat and operational stress control," as exceptionally successful in reducing rampant psychiatric attrition that once threatened the Western alliance's ability to win the war.[10]

Objectively, the U.S. military's WWI effort to prevent psychiatric casualties and disability pensions by screening out predisposed weakness was a massive failure. After only six months of exposure to actual combat, more than one hundred thousand psychiatrically screened soldiers were hospitalized as neuropsychiatric casualties—compared with just over two hundred thousand medically wounded.[11] In all, seventy-two thousand soldiers were discharged from the military for neuropsychiatric conditions; thirty-six thousand claimed permanent disability[12] costing the government more than $1 billion in disability pensions.[13] An additional 8,600 cases of "nervous and mental diseases" were diagnosed by the U.S. Army but were not discharged. In 1918 alone, 24 percent of deployed soldiers and sailors were evacuated to the United States for "nervous or mental disorders," and more than twenty thousand were psychiatrically discharged. Overall, about 2 percent of soldiers were found to exhibit some form of war-stress injury:

- 11,443 diagnosed with "psychoneuroses" (akin to PTSD, anxiety, and depression constructs, including 219 diagnoses of "traumatic neurosis" a direct precursor of PTSD);
- 7,910 diagnosed with "psychoses," including 51 diagnosed with "traumatic psychoses," a precursor of PTSD;
- 4,170 diagnosed with alcoholism or drug addiction;
- 6,196 diagnosed as "constitutional psychopathic states" (akin to personality disorder);
- 21,858 diagnosed as "mental deficiency";
- 6,916 diagnosed with "nervous diseases and injuries" (akin to possible MUPS), including diagnoses, such as:
  - tics (243);
  - sciatica (137);
  - neuritis (222);
  - injury to nervous system (554), includes 337 diagnosed with "brain injury" akin to possible TBI;

- tremor (243);
- other forms (902); and
- epilepsy (6,388) (can be indicative of MUPS)
- delinquency (1,498) cases or stress misconduct stress behaviors.[14]

It is certainly possible, however, that matters could have been worse for the United States if not for its purging efforts. Nonetheless, WWI appeared to support Oppenheim's conclusion that "the war has taught us and will continue to teach us (1) that just as before there are traumatic neuroses; (2) that they are not always covered by the concept of hysteria; and (3) that they are really the product of trauma and not goal-oriented, well cultivated pseudo-illness."[15]

That said, despite ample evidence to the contrary, conclusions by military investigative commissions tasked with recommending lessons learned to avoid a repeat of the dishonorable spectacle of war-stress injury almost universally blamed preexisting individual weaknesses, the corrosive influence of psychiatry (psychiatric diagnosing, disability pensions), and inadequate military training, leadership, and unit morale.[16] Anything and everything was responsible except for war itself. The *Report of the War Office Committee of Enquiry Into "Shell Shock"* reads as follows:

> On the influence of war stress and shell shock in the production of insanity, the WWI commission observed: "Most witnesses were of opinion that the stress of war rarely produced insanity in the stable man, but that it acted, as is commonly observed with other forms of stress, as a factor upon those who by predisposition were liable to breakdown. Heredity, environment, training, and education in childhood are the dominant factors concerned in the evolution of the mental as of the physical personality and in consequence the predisposition to mental and nervous disorders of the adult is to a great extent determined before he becomes a soldier. This predisposition plays an immense part in the incidence of shell shock."[17]

THE SO-CALLED INTERWAR YEARS

The interwar period stretches from the end of WWI in 1918 to the official beginning of WWII in 1939. Although it may have reflected the end of the shooting war, the military's war on mental health was just beginning. Military historian Ben Shepard best summarizes the military's reported lessons learned from WWI and its need to purge weakness for future war-fighting:

> There should be no excuse given for the establishment of a belief that a functional nervous disability constitutes a right to compensation. This is a hard saying. It may seem cruel that those whose sufferings are real, whose illness has been brought on by enemy action and very likely in the course of patriotic service should be treated with such apparent callousness. But there can be no doubt that in an overwhelming proportion of cases, these patients succumb to 'shock' because they get something out of it.
>
> To give them this reward is not ultimately a benefit to them because it encourages the weaker tendencies in their character. The nation cannot call on its citizens for courage and sacrifice and, at the same time, state by implication that an unconscious cowardice or an unconscious dishonesty will be rewarded.[18]

Shepard's appeal is an insight into the military's thinking about its mental health dilemma. Having diagnosed the problem for unprecedented numbers and costs associated with war-stress injury, post-WWI military powers all took concerted action to eliminate psychiatry from its rank and file; to aggressively screen out and reject the psychologically weak and predisposed; to prevent or significantly reduce psychiatric disability pensions; and to significantly ramp up military discipline, vigorous training, unit morale building, and leadership development. It did so to strengthen individual resistance against the erosive softening effects of modern culture that encourages cowardice, weakness, and pseudo-psychiatric illness.

Since WWI, the military's standards for training, discipline, and leadership instruction have evolved in response to its mental health dilemma—with greater emphasis being placed on improving unit morale and cohesion and mandatory resiliency training designed to avert psychiatric attrition.

The military regularly avows that the Special Forces have historically produced the highest levels of cohesion, morale, and leadership—and the lowest rates of psychiatric casualties.[19] These claims add credence to the health-promoting value of preventing psychiatric evacuations. Israeli Defense Forces (IDF) researchers reported similarly low PTSD rates in decorated veterans,[20] which implies membership in elite groups may be a protective variable.

We should be cautious, however, about overinterpreting the protective benefits of cohesion, especially in light of the stigma active-duty elite personnel experience in self-disclosing stress symptoms. For instance, a recent anonymous survey of U.S. Army Special Operations Forces personnel revealed PTSD rates of 16 to 20 percent, nearly doubling the prevalence rate reported by regular army soldiers and contradicting assertions of the hyperresilience of elite soldiers.[21] According to the U.S. Army's summary of the 1982 Lebanon War, "Despite high morale and a good deal of attention given by command to morale and the factors maintaining it, the IDF still suffered relatively high rates of psychiatric casualties."[22]

Without doubt, factors like cohesion, morale, and leadership can support the mental health of deployed service members. But this does not automatically translate to better long-term health outcomes for personnel returning to duty after experiencing war-stress injury or who are diagnosed with psychological disorder in war zones. Researchers often make the distinction between delayed presentation and delayed onset in regards to PTSD with the former often involving the toleration versus absence of symptoms.[23]

For instance, IDF researchers found so-called delayed onset of PTSD in 16.5 percent of combat veterans after leaving military service who were never diagnosed with combat stress reaction (CSR) while on active duty.[24] Another IDF study used the term "hidden PTSD" to account for 16 percent of combat veterans who refused to self-disclose symptoms largely out of fear of stigma and career reprisal.[25] Several scholars have attributed significant escalation in veterans diagnosed with mental health problems after military service to phenomena like diminished levels of protective social support and lower fear of career reprisal.[26] Therefore, it is reasonable to assume that at least in some, if not many cases, the immediate protective benefit of unit support, cohesion, and leadership even in the military's elite forces may erode after personnel relocate to other units, retire, or separate from the military.

CONTEMPORARY RESEARCH ON UNIT COHESION AND SOCIAL SUPPORT

Research on the protective benefits of unit cohesion and deployment-related social support appears to be mixed. Most empirical findings of predictors for combat PTSD report that social support from family, friends, and community is the most reliable indicator of resilience.[27] Recent military studies from the United Kingdom[28] and United States,[29] however, indicate high levels of unit cohesion is associated with lower probability of postdeployment mental health diagnoses. This includes PTSD, with the exception of one U.S. finding that only the deployment variable of high morale was a significant buffer against combat PTSD, not unit cohesion or patriotism.[30]

Han et al. concluded that postdeployment social support was a stronger buffer against combat-PTSD than unit social support during deployment.[31] Others have observed that low levels of perceived social support both during and after deployment is significantly related to mental health problems.[32] Needless to say, the relative protective benefit from unit cohesion, morale, leadership, and social support is not in question.

The real question is whether the military's emphasis on preventing war-stress injury by enhancing protective factors coupled with its purging of any measurable type of weakness is sufficient to reverse wartime psychiatric trends?

PURGING MILITARY MENTAL HEALTHCARE

Infused with confidence by post-WWI commission reports, European and American militaries disbanded their mental health services, including all frontline psychiatry programs and mental health personnel. The intent was to prevent predisposed war hysterics from infiltrating the armed forces in the first place. "Prominent civil and military medical authorities," writes Glass, "pointed out that World War I had demonstrated the necessity and feasibility of psychiatric screening in eliminating overt and covert mental disorders prior to entry in the military services."[33]

From the military's perspective, the only real value of mental health specialists was to conduct the preinduction screenings and allow the military's rigorous military discipline, training, unit cohesion, and leadership to take care of the rest.[34] In historian Ben Shepard's book *A War of Nerves*, he details how the military's mental health dilemma often is attributed to modern society's *culture of trauma* and the ascendancy of psychiatry. The military believed these had a corrosive moral and psychological weakening influence, which purportedly reinforces self-indulgence, victimization, and persistent illness-seeking behavior that undermines soldier's stiff upper lip. Getting rid of the shrinks was to eliminate half of the problem. Now all the military needed was to prevent the emotionally vulnerable from contaminating the rank and file, and that will end the mental health dilemma once and for all.

DOUBLING-DOWN ON PURGING PREDISPOSED WEAKNESS

After WWI, the military doubled down on its effort to screen out potential troublemakers, hysterics, cowards, and future pensioners by significantly broadening the criteria for rejection to include any known, conceivable, or hypothesized potential risk factor. In other words, the unprecedented psychiatry problem of WWI was largely caused because the psychiatric screenings casting too narrow a net.

In 1941, famed psychiatrist Harry Stack Sullivan was appointed as chief neuropsychiatric consultant to the Selective Service and tasked with developing a more robust purging program with different levels of medical and psychiatric examinations, including extensive review of legal, medical, family, and psychiatric records; standardized intelligence testing; and various psychiatric questionnaires all designed to reject anyone with a greater-than-average chance of breakdown. D. W. Orr reported the objectives of neuropsychiatric screenings was to disqualify the obviously psychopathic or psychiatrically unfit just as with Salmon's program in 1917.[35] His program, however, went further to

> eliminate (1) those men with more subtle personality disorders missed by previous examiners; (2) men whose present personality makeup suggests that they may break under the special stresses and strains of camp life; and even beyond these, (3) men who may be expected to develop some type of neuropsychiatric disorder at any time during the next eleven years.[36]

The list of disqualifying predisposing or preexisting risk factors was extensive and varied. The reasons ranged from the reasonable (e.g., intellectual deficit, history of epilepsy, current or past psychiatric history, active substance abuse, incarceration history, enuresis, current medical conditions, frequent medical illness) to the absurd, like any history of medical hospitalizations, shyness, speech impediment, extended family psychiatric or substance abuse history, tendency to worry, repeating a grade, parental divorce, adoption, school suspension, limited dating experiences, unstable work history, or any other hypothesized "neurotic" tendencies. The policy suggested they followed an old cliché: when in doubt, reject.[37]

Considerable public consternation ensued as large numbers of patriotic volunteers were rejected because they appeared to be nervous or effeminate, had sweaty palms, showed tenseness, had hand tremors, or answered affirmatively to questions like "Do you worry?" or "Are you nervous?" or "Do you have headaches or stomach troubles?" As the war progressed, consequent manpower shortages alarmed military leaders who authorized a series of revisions to selection standards.[38]

For those deemed psychologically hardy enough to pass the initial psychiatric screening, service personnel were under constant monitoring from basic training to the point of possible deployment. Signs of emotional, moral, or behavioral weakness led to the purging of another million soldiers. It is not widely known by the American public, but the United States entered WWII with the most psychiatrically tested, emotionally healthy, and resilient armed forces the world has ever known. The Greatest Generation was conceptually a virtual army of super soldiers. Unlike Vietnam, Korea, and Iraq, WWII is widely heralded as a so-called good war. It was backed by overwhelming domestic support, and service members returned as liberators and heroes.

Still, the American's grand social engineering and psychiatric experiment proved nothing short of a colossal failure.

During the North African campaign, between 1941 and 1943, for example, the American military, supposedly devoid of inherently predisposed, constitutionally weak, morally defective service personnel was faced with grim unlearned lessons of the reality of modern warfare. At the outset, psychiatric rates of 20 to 34 percent of total casualties materialized. Only 3 percent returned to duty. During the 1942 Guadalcanal invasion, 40 percent of First Division Marine evacuees were psychiatric casualties. In all, from 1942 to 1945, despite purging more than two million predisposed defective Americans, psychiatric casualties were eight times higher than in WWI.[39]

WWII psychiatric rates climbed before the end of the war. As table 7.1 shows, more than one million army and 150,000 navy and marine personnel were admitted to psychiatric hospitals, resulting in more than half a million army and 110,000 navy psychiatric discharges.[40] In September 1943 alone, more soldiers were discharged from the army (112,500) than accessed (118,600). The majority of these were psychiatric discharges, prompting Chief of Staff General George C. Marshall to abandon the extensive predisposition screening policy in 1943 — screening out potential service members was costing the war.[41]

In 1943, significant modifications were made in the psychiatric selection criteria. Many induction stations reexamined applicants they previously

TABLE 7.1 Prevalence of Neuropsychiatric Screening Rejections and Disability Discharges

WAR	TOTAL REJECTED AT ACCESSION	TOTAL REJECTED AT MOBILIZATION	GRAND TOTAL REJECTED	TOTAL DISABILITY DISCHARGES
World War I	70,158	15,247	85,405	43,706
World War II	1,846,000	Unknown	1,846,000	375,333

Source: I. C. Berlien and R. W. Waggoner, "Selection and Induction," in *Zone of Interior*, Vol I. of *Medical Department United States Army, Neuropsychiatry in World War II*, ed. A. J. Glass and R. J. Bernucci (Washington, DC: Office of the Surgeon General, Department of the Army, 1966).

rejected and found more than 50 percent were now acceptable.[42] Follow-up investigations into attrition rates of these previously disqualified "predisposed" soldiers revealed 80 percent remained on active duty after one year,[43] and many served for longer at satisfactory performance levels.[44]

In another study, 56 percent of previously rejected predisposed registrants were inducted. A separate study of veterans previously disqualified followed up one year after induction and found 84 percent still on active duty—the rest were discharged or killed in action.[45]

What accounts for the failure of mass psychiatric screenings? Some have offered that it could be the lack of adequately trained psychiatric staff to conduct screenings, variability in screening instruments and procedures used, dishonest self-disclosures, or insufficient time to perform psychiatric examinations.[46] Although these factors may explain how some false negatives later developing postwar disorders could have slipped through the cracks, 1.2 million hospital admissions still resulted in six hundred thousand neuropsychiatric discharges of soldiers who had passed excessively stringent inclusion. This reveals a fatally flawed hypothesis on the relative etiologic contribution of predispositions in warfare. As a footnote on American purging efforts, WWII marked the beginning of a trend in which the total number of neuropsychiatric casualties first outnumbered the combined total of combatants killed and wounded. This further shows that exposure to war stress alone is the single-best explanation for war-stress injury, far and above any other risk or predisposing factor.

After WWII, each military service continued to experiment with different psychiatric screening and personality tests to measure service suitability. One psychologist followed 134 navy recruits retained after being screened as psychiatrically predisposed and unfit for military duty—and found that 70 percent were performing satisfactorily two years later, compared with 86 percent of a control group.[47]

At present, the three components of psychiatric screenings for military accession are as follows: (1) estimates of intellectual potential via the Armed Services Vocational Aptitude Battery (ASVAB) used since 1976; (2) measures of educational achievement, high school graduation, or an equivalent test; and (3) a review of medical screening forms and general psychiatric examination during the entrance physical evaluation at military induction centers intended to identify and disqualify inductees only with clear psychiatric illness.[48] Regarding current attempts of screening for predisposed personalities, the U.S. Army's Office of the Surgeon General's psychiatric consultant reports, "Supplemental psychiatric evaluations and written screening tools were abandoned after postwar assessments. These assessments demonstrated their poor predictive power in evaluating service capacity of recruits for a combat environment."[49]

In 1862, Union Army Surgeon General Hammond reported soldiers younger than twenty were at high risk of breakdown. In WW I, Alfred Wolfshohn conducted one of the earliest studies on predispositions in postwar disorders by comparing a hundred "war neurotics" matched with a control group of a hundred veterans wounded in action, finding 75 percent of war neurotics, but none of the controls had a family history of psychoneurosis (i.e., nervousness, alcoholism, epilepsy, and insanity). Other studies of WWI and WWII veterans have reported that 45 to 70 percent of those with postwar disorders were predisposed from familial psychopathology.

SCIENTIFIC REVIEWS ON CAUSES AND RISK FACTORS FOR COMBAT-RELATED PTSD

Table 7.2 contains systematic literature reviews and meta-analyses of etiologic predictors for combat-related PTSD. With rare exceptions,[50] this research almost universally cites the level of combat exposure as being the single-greatest predictor and risk factor for war-stress injury, like PTSD.[51] In other studies, the variable of peri-traumatic dissociation assumes the mantel, which is an indirect measure of the level of exposure to traumatic stimuli.[52]

TABLE 7.2 Meta-Analyses and Systematic Review of Risk Factors for Combat-Related PTSD

STUDY	DESIGN	SAMPLE	MAJOR FINDINGS	LIMITATIONS
Kulka, Schlenger, Fairbank, Hough, Jordan, Marmar, and Weiss, 1990[a]	National Vietnam Veterans Readjustment Study: national probability sampling and interview research: preliminary validation, clinical interviews, and family interviews	N = 3,016 total interviews: n = 344 Vietnam theater vets; n = 474 spouse interviews; n = 96 Vietnam-era vets	Exposure to war stress significantly related to combat PTSD independent of precombat predisposing factors; PTSD significantly higher in Vietnam theater vets versus Vietnam-era vets; premilitary childhood adversity; depression and substance abuse higher in Vietnam theater vets dosage effect of level of combat exposure and severity of postwar readjustment problems; readjustment problems significantly related to war-stress exposure, PTSD, substance abuse, and service-connected disability	Nonrandomization retrospective analysis; verification of reported combat exposure of Vietnam theater vets
Ozer, Best, Lipsey, and Weiss, 2003[b]	Meta-analysis of studies on predictors of adult PTSD	68 studies met inclusion criteria, 17 involving military veterans: 7 predictors: prior trauma, prior psychological adjustment, family mental health history, perceived life threat, post-trauma social support, peri-traumatic emotional response, and peri-traumatic dissociation	All predictors yielded significant effect sizes; peri-traumatic dissociation strongest predictor; social support had small to medium effect; weakest predictors were family history, prior trauma, and prior adjustment	Over-reliance on retrospective self-report; self-report and recall bias; lack of prospective studies; variability in defining and measuring variables; level of exposure (combat) was not analyzed

(continued)

TABLE 7.2 (continued)

STUDY	DESIGN	SAMPLE	MAJOR FINDINGS	LIMITATIONS
Ramchand, Rudavsky, Grant, Tanielian, and Jayconx, 2015[c]	Review of literature 2009 to 2014 on risk factors for combat-related PTSD and other mental health diagnoses in military personnel deployed to Iraq and Afghanistan; also analyzed treatment-seeking versus non-treatment-seeking samples	48 U.S. studies on military personnel; 56 studies on U.S. veterans; 10 non-U.S. studies on military personnel; 4 studies on non-U.S. veterans	0–48 percent PTSD rates in non-treatment-seeking samples; 2–68 percent in treatment-seeking samples; 4–45 percent depression rates in deployed samples; 4–60 percent alcohol abuse in deployed samples; combat exposure was strongest predictor of all mental health problems; multiple deployments increase PTSD; lower social support during and after deployment increase risk in mental health problems; <50 percent who reported they need treatment, receive it; combat-PTSD significantly related to poor physical health, suicidal ideation, dying by suicide, depression, substance abuse, aggression, and criminal outcomes	Many studies do not control for combat exposure; significant variation in methodological rigor and measurement; inadequate longitudinal data
Brewin, Andrews, and Valentine, 2000[d]	Meta-analysis of risk factors for PTSD	77 studies on military (n = 28) and nonmilitary populations	Trauma severity was strongest risk factor during and after trauma followed by lack of social support and post-trauma life stress; weak effects for pretrauma factors	Heterogeneity of studies in regard to sampling, design, measurement, statistical analysis, and resulting effects

Elbogen et al., 2012[e]	Cross-sectional, random sampling for national survey by Department of Veterans Affairs	$N = 1,388$ (56 percent) of 3,000 U.S. OEF/OIF veterans completed mailed surveys	20 percent met PTSD criteria and 27 percent alcohol abuse; 33 percent report violent acts in community; 11 percent severe violence; increase risk of violence linked to combat exposure (CE), younger age, PTSD, alcohol, criminal arrest; decreased risk of violence linked to older age, level of social support, and resilience	Generalizability limited by design; lacking longitudinal assessment of protective factors; target of violence not assessed; no reporting level of violence experienced during deployment
Phillips et al., 2010[f]	Prospective study of demographic, pretrauma risk factors, and deployment risk factors before and after deployment	706 U.S. Marine recruits evaluated before and after deployment and combat stress exposure	10.8 percent diagnosed with new onset PTSD; combat exposure type (e.g., threat of death, exposure to violence) was strongest predictor of PTSD than other deployment, postdeployment, and pretrauma risk factors; level of postdeployment social support reduces risk of PTSD	Sampling bias of self-selected volunteers; use of nonanonymous surveys; low response rate (13 percent); ceiling effects from stigma and fears of career reprisal; PTSD symptoms not assessed before deployment
Pietrzak et al., 2009[g]	Retrospective, nonrandomized mailing of surveys to 1,000 veterans	28.5 percent response ($n = 272$) from U.S. OEF/OIF veterans 1–4 years after military discharge	Resilience scores correlated negatively to PTSD, depression, and psychosocial problems; CE correlated negatively with postdeployment social support and correlated positively for PTSD, depression, and social problems; resilience mediated unit support and PTSD and depression; unit support predicted increased postdeployment social support	Sampling bias; report and recall bias from retrospective self-report; limited generalizability because of low response rate; limited assessment of spectrum of war-stress injury (e.g., substance abuse)

(continued)

TABLE 7.2 (continued)

STUDY	DESIGN	SAMPLE	MAJOR FINDINGS	LIMITATIONS
Zohar et al., 2008[h]	Semiprospective study of demographic, premilitary, precombat factors, and military risk factors assessed 2 years before military service and after deployment	2,362 Israeli war veterans diagnosed with combat-related PTSD, matched with 2,323 veterans not diagnosed with PTSD	Social functioning, motivation, training, premilitary/pretrauma risk factors all found to be insignificant in predicting PTSD	Ceiling effect from stigma, e.g., hidden PTSD in control group in which 16 percent eventually were diagnosed with PTSD; combat exposure type, intensity, and duration not assessed
Xue et al., 2015[i]	Meta-analysis of combat PTSD risk factors	32 studies accepted out of 2,657 screened; 27 risk factors evaluated	Level of combat exposure greatest risk factor for combat PTSD; psychiatric history, life stress, and pretrauma history not significant predictors; inconsistent but strong finding of postdeployment social support and lower PTSD risk	Heterogeneity of studies in regard to sampling, design, measurement, statistical analysis, and resulting effects; inclusion of observational studies only relying on self-report

Sources:

[a] R. A. Kulka et al., *Trauma and the Vietnam War Generation: Report of Findings from the National Vietnam Veterans Readjustment Study* (New York, NY: Brunner/Mazel, 1990).

[b] E. J. Ozer, S. R. Best, T. L. Lipsey, and D. S. Weis, "Predictors of Posttraumatic Stress Disorder and Symptoms in Adults: A Meta-Analysis," *Psychology Bulletin* 129, no. 1 (2003): 52–73.

[c] R. Ramchand, R. Rudavsky, S. Grant, T. Tanielian, and L. Jaycoux, "Prevalence of, Risk Factors for, and Consequences of Posttraumatic Stress Disorder and Other Mental Health Problems in Military Populations Deployed to Iraq and Afghanistan," *Current Psychiatry Report* 17 (2015): 1–11.

[d] C. R. Brewin, B. Andrews, and J. D. Valentine, "Meta-analysis of Risk Factors for Posttraumatic Stress Disorder in Trauma-Exposed Adults." *Journal of Consulting and Clinical Psychology.* 68, no. 5 (2000): 748–766.

[e] E. B. Elbogen et al., "Protective Factors and Risk Modification of Violence in Iraq and Afghanistan," *Journal of Clinical Psychiatry* 73, no. 6 (2012): 767–773.

[f] C. J. Phillips, C. A. LeardMann, G. R. Gumbs, and B. Smith, "Risk Factors for Posttraumatic Stress Disorder Among Deployed US Male Marines," *BMC Psychiatry* 10 (2010): 1–11.

[g] R. H. Pietrzak et al., "Psychosocial Buffers of Traumatic Stress, Depressive Symptoms, and Psychosocial Difficulties in Veterans of Operations Enduring Freedom and Iraqi Freedom: The Role of Resilience, Unit Support, and Post-Deployment Social Support," *Journal of Special Operations Medicine* 9, no. 3 (2009): 74–78.

[h] Zohar et al., 2008

[i] C. Xue, Y. Ge, B. Tang, Y. Liu, P. Yang, M. Wang, and L. Zhang, "A Meta-analysis of Risk Factors for Combat-Related PTSD Among Military Personnel and Veterans," *PLOS One* 10, no. 3 (2015): 1–11.

After analyzing a host of premilitary, military, and post-military variables linked to the development of combat PTSD, the National Vietnam Veterans Readjustment Study (NVVRS) report concluded,

> Taken together, these results are consistent with a model of PTSD that posits a role for individual vulnerability (potentially including biological, psychological and socio-demographic factors) and a role for exposure to environmental factors (specifically, war zone stressors) in determining who among theater veterans gets PTSD. However, it is clear that exposure to war zone stress makes a substantial contribution to the development of PTSD in war veterans that is independent of a broad range of potential predisposing factors.[53]

A reanalysis of NVVRS data revealed even stronger evidence of a dosage effect from war-stress exposure.[54] The reasonable conclusion from etiologic studies cited in table 7.2 is that any assertion that war-stress injury is caused by inherent predisposed weakness is both historically and empirically false. The other more probably causes are noted in the following section and throughout the remainder of this book.

RESEARCH ON HARMFUL EFFECTS OF DEPLOYMENT LENGTH AND MULTIPLE DEPLOYMENTS

Beebe and Appel have reported that the highest risk for breakdown for newcomers in a war zone is within the first five to twenty-one days of combat. Seasoned veterans crash on average after eighty to ninety combat days. This effect of deployment length prompted army psychiatrists to observe: "One of our cultural myths has been that only weaklings break down psychologically (and that) strong men with the will to do so can keep going indefinitely."[55]

Subsequent reviews since WWII have established a consistent linear relationship between duration and intensity of combat-related stressors and psychophysical breakdown.[56] According to the findings of research on Israeli soldiers with a previous history of CSR, for example, these soldiers were 57 percent more likely to experience CSR in the next war, 67 percent more likely to experience CSR if they participated in two wars, and 83 percent more likely to experience CSR if they participated in three wars.[57]

Vietnam War veterans serving thirteen-month combat tours or longer were more likely to have PTSD than those who served one year or less.[58]

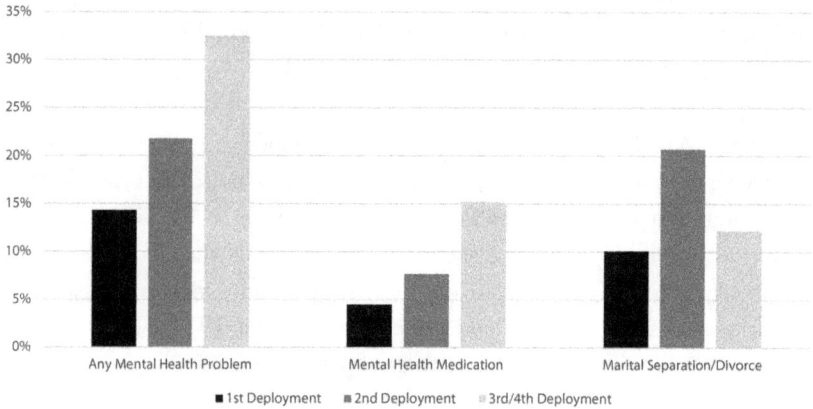

FIGURE 7.1 Cumulative impact of multiple deployments on mental health.

SOURCE: JOINT MENTAL HEALTH ADVISORY TEAM-7 (JOINT MHAT-7), *OPERATION ENDURING FREEDOM 2010 AFGHANISTAN (22 FEBRUARY 2011)* (WASHINGTON, DC: OFFICE OF THE SURGEON GENERAL UNITED STATES ARMY MEDICAL COMMAND AND OFFICE OF THE COMMAND SURGEON HQ, USCENTCOM AND OFFICE OF THE COMMAND SURGEON U.S. FORCES AFGHANISTAN (USFOR-A), 2011).

In today's cohort, an army-wide study of twenty-thousand soldiers found that length of deployment was positively correlated with the severity of self-reported interpersonal violence perpetration in the year after deployment.[59]

The 2003 British High Court ruled that "it was known that a linear relationship exists between the acute reaction to combat stress and the duration and intensity of combat." Figure 7.1 offers a visual analysis of the characteristic dose response effects on several mental health-related outcomes in regards to multiple deployments.

Amy Adler et al. examined more than three thousand U.S. military personnel deployed to the Balkan theater for NATO peacekeeping missions and found that length of deployment was significantly associated with greater severity of PTSD and depression symptoms in male service members. Kline et al. analyzed anonymous pre-deployment surveys from 2,500 National Guard members deploying to Iraq in 2008. They found that 25 percent of those who reported at least one previous deployment were three times more likely to screen positive for PTSD and major depression than those deployed for the first time. Moreover, they were twice as likely to report chronic pain and were more than 90 percent likely to score below population norms on physical health functioning.

Of six studies published between 2009 to 2014 assessing the effects of multiple deployments on service members deployed to Iraq or Afghanistan, five reported the number of deployments significantly increase PTSD prevalence.[60] Research on the resilience factor of *benefit finding*—the ability to ascribe meaning to enduring high stress of combat—is associated with the initial reduction in combat PTSD rates of two thousand U.S. soldiers deployed to Iraq. Yet, the protective element was found to significantly erode after nine to twelve months into the deployment as well as in subsequent deployments.

Cumulative length of deployment longer than three years was significantly associated with multiple physical symptoms, PTSD, and other mental illness in UK military personnel as well as with problems at home, interpersonal conflict, and family troubles. In 2003, the Ministry of Defense implemented deployment policy changes largely because of the class action that strictly limits deployment length and cumulative exposure.[61]

In 2007, 22 percent of UK deployed personnel had tour lengths longer than the recommended guidelines threshold of thirteen months or less in the previous three years, resulting in significant adverse health outcomes. This led British military researchers to conclude: "Consistency of our findings for all the outcomes assessed was remarkable, providing empirical evidence of the damaging effect of overstretch—i.e., the pace of military deployments." Under recent pressure by the ministry to relax its deployment limitations, UK researchers reviewed more than a hundred studies on the effect of number and cumulative length of deployments between 2002 and 2014, identifying ten studies deemed suitable.

Five other studies have reported significant associations of increased PTSD rates with the number of deployments. Two studies showed no association, with mixed findings on mood disorders, alcohol misuse, anxiety and somatic symptoms. Yet, this apparent inconsistency in findings was attributed to measurement errors and variations in defining and measuring combat exposure, health outcomes, and deployment roles, along with inadequate long-term data and probable ceiling effects resulting from stigma associated with identifiable self-reports.

A series of prospective analyses on the impact of U.S. deployment and combat stress exposure recently compared large samples of military personnel on a host of physical and mental health–related outcomes before and after deployment to assess the impact of that deployment (see table 7.3). According to these analyses, exposure to combat stress significantly increased the risk of new onset PTSD, depression, disordered eating, traumatic brain

TABLE 7.3 Prospective Research on the Health Effects of Deployment and Combat Stress Exposure in U.S. Military Personnel

STUDY	SAMPLE	OUTCOME	MEASURES	DESIGN	MAJOR FINDINGS	LIMITATIONS
McCutchan, Liu, LeardMann, Smith, Boyko et al., 2016[a]	N = 75,934 U.S. military assessed three different time periods divided into deployed with combat exposure (CE); deployed without CE, and no deployment	New onset multiple physical symptoms (MPS)	PHQ-15 Somatoform Disorders subscale PCL-C CE	Randomly selected sample baseline assessments before deployment and psotdeployment	Deployed personnel significantly more likely to report MPS at each time point compared with control; 10 percent of deployed with CE with new onset MPS at baseline, increased to 13 percent in 2007	Potential sampling bias; Uncertainty of temporal relationship between deployment and MPS; Unable to specify if MPS are medically unexplained
Crain, Larson, Highfill-McRoy, and Schmied, 2011[b]	N = 63,890 U.S. Marines on first combat deployment; n = 3,258 with a predeployment mental health diagnosis; n = 60,632 control group with no mental health diagnosis	New onset mental health diagnoses	Medical record review; career outcome: demotion and discharge rates 6 months after deployment	Nonrandom predeployment- and 6-month postdeployment screening for mental health diagnosis	Predeployment diagnosis was significant risk factor for postdeployment diagnosis; 15 percent of preexisting diagnosed with new onset versus 5 percent control; 8 percent of preexisting and 4 percent of control demoted in rank; 7 percent of preexisting and 3 percent of control discharged	Severity of combat exposure not assessed; no data on combat operations stress reaction (COSR) or use frontline psychiatry; no data on preexisting diagnoses; No standardized assessment of mental health status; No data on new onset diagnoses and career outcomes

Study	Sample	Outcome	Measures	Assessment timing	Findings	Limitations
Nash, Boasso, Steenkamp, Larson, Lubin, and Litz, 2015[c]	N = 867 U.S. Marines deployed to Afghanistan with high CE; n = 673 deployed Marines with low CE	New onset PTSD and depression and preexisting symptoms	CAPS PCL-M BDI-II BAI WHODAS LEC CTQ DRRI Brief COPE PDEQ	Baseline assessment 1 month before deployment and 1, 5, and 8 months postdeployment	13 percent new onset PTSD; 8 percent reported high PTSD at predeployment: preexisting 69 percent met PTSD criteria predeployment, decreased to 50 percent at 8 months; 79 percent overall reported low-stable symptom trajectory across cycle	Nonrandom selection; males only; older marines excluded (more likely to have previous deployments); follow-up limited to 8 months
Jacobson et al. 2008[d]	N = 48,481 U.S. military: deployed with CE (n = 5531); deployed but no CE (n = 5561); nondeployed (n = 37,310)	New onset alcohol abuse; binge drinking; and heavy drinking	Frequency and intensity of weekly drinking PHQ CAGE Holmes-Rahe CE survey	Randomly selected sample baseline assessments before deployment and on average 1 year postdeployment	New onset drinking outcomes highest in active-duty exposed to combat; combat exposure significantly associated with greater new onset alcohol problems in National Guard and reservists with combat exposure versus those who did not deploy	Representativeness of sample; potential bias of less healthy nondeployed comparison group; recall bias of self-reported drinking; ceiling effect from stigma and fear of career reprisal
Boyko et al. 2010[e]	N = 44,754 U.S. military: deployed with CE (n = 4813); deployed but no CE (n = 4908); nondeployed (n = 33,624)	New onset diabetes	Self-report of diabetes diagnoses after deployment; review of Department of Defense (DoD) medical database for new diagnosis of diabetes PHQ PCL-C CE survey	Randomly selected sample baseline assessments before deployment and up to 3 years postdeployment	PTSD diagnosis significantly related to new onset diabetes; diabetes not significantly linked to deployment, with or without CE; two or more deployments and separation from the service significantly linked to diabetes	Bias in medical records of Reserves and National Guard who do not use DoD or Department of Veterans Affairs (VA) healthcare; deployment group without CE had lower risk of diabetes; no objective assessment of diabetes

(continued)

TABLE 7.3 *(Continued)*

STUDY	SAMPLE	OUTCOME	MEASURES	DESIGN	MAJOR FINDINGS	LIMITATIONS
Wells et al., 2010[f]	N = 40,219 U.S. military: deployed with CE (n = 4719); deployed but no CE (n = 4831); nondeployed (n = 30,669)	New onset depression	PHQ SF-36V PCL-C CAGE CE survey	Randomly selected sample baseline assessments before deployment and on average 349 days postdeployment	Deployed men and women with CE had significant increase in new onset depression (5.7 percent and 15.7 percent, respectively) compared with nondeployers (3.9 percent and 7.7 percent) and the deployed but no CE group (2.3 percent and 5.9 percent)	Potential unrepresentativeness of sample; nonspecific measures of combat-related PTSD; limited CE questions; ceiling effect of stigma and fear of career reprisal
Smith et al. 2010[g]	N = 50,184 U.S. military: deployed (n = 11,942) compared with nondeployed (n = 38,176)	New onset PTSD	PCL-C CE survey Smoking and drinking questions	Randomly selected sample baseline assessments before deployment and on average 2.7 years postdeployment	New onset PTSD using specific DSM-IV criteria and more sensitive criteria significantly associated with deployment and CE (7.6 percent and 8.7 percent) as compared with deployed without CE (1.4 percent and 2.1 percent), and nondeployers (2.3 percent and 3.0 percent); threefold increase in PTSD in deployers with CE; CE significantly linked to new onset PTSD	Potential unrepresentativeness of sample; nonspecific measures of combat-related PTSD; ceiling effect of stigma and fear of career reprisal; report and recall bias
Seelig et al., 2010[h]	N = 41,225 U.S. military: follow-up survey during deployment (n = 1770); follow-up survey postdeployment (n = 9264), before follow-up survey of nondeployed (n = 30,190)	New onset sleep disturbance	Holms-Rahe CE Survey PHQ PCL-C CAGE Sleep duration	Randomly selected sample baseline assessments before deployment and at least 2 weeks postdeployment	Deployed personnel significantly more likely to report sleep disturbance versus nondeployers; CE significantly increased odds of sleep problems; deployed personnel with CE were 52 percent to 74 percent more likely to report sleep problems versus no CE groups	Potential unrepresentativeness of sample; nonspecific measures of combat-related PTSD; ceiling effect of stigma and fear of career reprisal; no objective measure of sleep duration and quality

Study	Sample	Measures	Outcomes	Design	Findings	Limitations
Wang et al., 2015	N = 29,314 married U.S. military at time of deployment compared with recently divorced (n = 1545) and those who stayed married (n = 27,769)	Self-report of marital status; PCL-C; CAGE; PHQ; Physical component summary; Mental component summary	New onset marital divorce and physical and mental health problems	Randomly selected sample baseline assessments before deployment and on average 3 years postdeployment	5.3 percent (n = 1545) military personnel divorced compared with no divorce (n = 27,769); divorce and all outcomes (physical, mental, behavioral) all significantly linked to CE; divorce associated with being female, young, enlisted, active-duty, low education, reports of poor physical and mental health	Potential unrepresentativeness of sample; nonspecific measures of combat-related PTSD; no data on length of marriage or children; no measure of marital satisfaction at predeployment; ceiling effect of stigma; report and recall bias
LeardMann et al., 2008	N = 5410 U.S. military deployed with CE without predeployment history of PTSD symptoms	SF-36V; PCL-C; CAGE	New onset PTSD and predeployment physical health problems	Randomly selected sample baseline assessments before deployment and 2-3 years postdeployment	58 percent of new onset PTSD ranked in lowest 15 percent on predeployment mental and physical health status; 7.3 percent (n = 395) new onset PTSD based on PCL criteria; 8.6 percent (n = 457) new onset PTSD diagnosed by physician	Potential unrepresentativeness of sample; report and recall bias; nonspecific measures of combat-related PTSD and deployment trauma
Jacobson et al., 2009ˣ	N = 42,174 U.S. military: men n = 33,578 and women n = 12,641 were assigned to one of three groups: deployed with CE; deployed but no CE; and nondeployed	Holmes-Rahe; PCL-C; CAGE; PHQ	New onset disordered eating (e.g., extreme weight gain or loss.)	Randomly selected sample baseline assessments before deployment and on average 2.7 years postdeployment	New onset disordered eating highest in deployed and CE group; 5.2 percent women reported postdeployment disordered eating with 63 percent (n = 2174) new onset; 3.9 percent men reported postdeployment disordered eating with 67 percent (n = 3,532) new onset	Potential unrepresentativeness of sample; nonspecific measures of combat-related PTSD and CE; differentiation of new onset because of CE versus episodic nature; did not assess purging behaviors; ceiling effects of stigma

(continued)

TABLE 7.3 (Continued)

STUDY	SAMPLE	OUTCOME	MEASURES	DESIGN	MAJOR FINDINGS	LIMITATIONS
Granado et al., 2015[l]	N = 36,061 U.S. military: deployed with CE (n = 4,444: 1 CE event n = 586; >1 CE event n = 3858; deployed but no CE (n = 4,385; nondeployed (n = 27,232)	New onset hypertension	SF-36V Physical and mental health component summary Behavioral outcomes (smoking, body mass index, alcohol) DoD medical record review	Randomly selected sample baseline assessments before deployment and on average 2.7 years postdeployment	6.1 percent (n = 2,345) deployers with multiple CE reported new onset hypertension; nondeployers reported higher rate of new onset hypertension than deployers (with and without CE); deployers with multiple CE highest risk for new onset	Bias of nondeployers may have more health problems; report and recall bias; selection bias against deployers with CE in remote areas and excluded from survey
Smith et al., 2009[m]	N = 46,077 U.S. military: deployed (n = 10,753) compared with nondeployed (n = 35,324)	New onset respiratory illness	DoD medical dbase records PHQ PCL-C CAGE	Randomly selected sample baseline assessments before deployment and on average 2.7 years postdeployment	Deployers (14 percent) had higher rate of respiratory symptoms versus nondeployers (10 percent); no significant new onset illness associated with deployment	Bias of nondeployers may have more health problems; report and recall bias; ceiling effects of stigma and fears of career reprisal; CE not assessed
Crum-Ciaflone et al., 2015[n]	N = 35,465 U.S. military: deployed with CE (n = 12,280); deployed but no CE (n = 10,602); nondeployed (n = 37,143)	New onset coronary heart disease (CHD) and PTSD	DoD medical dbase records PHQ PCL-C CAGE	Randomly selected sample baseline assessments before deployment and on average 5.6 years postdeployment	1.0 percent (n = 657) new onset CHD; increase odds of new onset CHD in deployers with CE; CHD linked to PTSD before deployment only (n = 900 previously deployed)	Bias of nondeployers may have more health problems; report and recall bias; ceiling effects of stigma and fears of career reprisal

| Stein et al., 2015[o] | N = 4,645 U.S. soldiers deployed to Afghanistan | New onset traumatic brain injury (TBI) and other PTSD and other mental health problems | CIDI-SC PCL-C Columbia suicide severity rating scale | Assessed 1–2 months predeployment; redeployment; and 3 and 9 months postdeployment | 18 percent reported mild TBI; 1.2 percent >mild TBI; after adjustment to predeployment risk factors, deployment acquired TBI significantly increases risk of PTSD, generalized anxiety, depression at 9 months; elevated suicide risk at 3 months | Bias of self-report on clinical outcomes; lack objective measures of TBI; moderate and severe TBI not tracked because most likely hospitalized; nonanonymous surveys; ceiling effect of stigma and fear of career reprisal |

Note: BAI: Beck Anxiety Inventory; BDI-II: Beck Depression Inventory-Second Edition; CAPS: Clinician Administered PTSD Scale; CIDI-SC: Composite International Diagnostic Interview Screening Subscales; CTQ: Childhood Trauma Questionnaire; DRRI: Deployment Risk and Resilience Inventory; Holmes-Rahe: Holmes-Rahe Social Adjustment Scale; LEC: Life Events Checklist; PCL-C: PTSD Checklist-Civilian Version; PDEQ: Peritraumatic Dissociative Experiences Questionnaire; PHQ: Patient Health Questionnaire; SF-36V: Medical Outcomes Study Short Form 36-item Health Survey for Veterans; WHODAS: World Health Organization Disability Assessment Scale-II.

Sources:

[a] P. Mccutchan, X. Liu, C. A. LeardMann, T. Smith, E. Boyko, K. Gore, M. C. Freed, C. C. Engel, "Deployment, Combat, and Risk of Multiple Physical Symptoms in the US Military: A Prospective Cohort Study," *Annals of Epidemiology* 26, no. 2 (2016), DOI:10.1016/j.annepidem.2015.12.001.

[b] Crain, Larson, Highfill-McRoy, and Schmied (2011).

[c] W. P. Nash, A. M. Boasso, M. M. Steenkamp, J. L. Larson, R. E. Lubin, and B. T. Litz, "Posttraumatic Stress in Deployed Marines: Prospective Trajectories of Early Adaptation," *Journal of Abnormal Psychology* 124, no. 1 (2015): 155–171.

[d] Jacobson et al. 2008.

[e] Boyko et al. (2010).

[f] Wells et al. (2010).

[g] Smith et al. (2010).

[h] A. D. Seelig, I. G. Jacobson, C. J. Donoho, D. W. Trone, N.C. Crum-Cianflone, and T. J. Balkin, "Sleep and Health Resilience Metrics in a Large Military Cohort," *Sleep* 39, no. 5 (2010): 1111–1120.

[i] Wang et al. (2015).

[j] LeardMann et al. (2008).

[k] Jacobson et al. (2009).

[l] Granado et al. (2015).

[m] T. C. Smith, C. A. LeardMann, B. Smith, I. G. Jacobson, and M. A. K. Ryan, "Postdeployment Hospitalizations Among Service Members Deployed in Support of the Operations in Iraq and Afghanistan," *Annals of Epidemiology* 19, no. 9 (2009): 603–612.

[n] Crum-Ciaflone et al. (2015).

[o] Stein et al. (2015).

injury, coronary heart disease, hypertension, respiratory illness, multiple physical health complaints, marital conflict and divorce, sleep disturbance, and substance abuse.[62]

A frontline psychiatry policy emphasizing returning to duty can reasonably be said to substantially aggravate the risk to the health and well-being of individuals suffering from one or more of these issues during or after deployment and who are repeatedly returned to duty until their health status deteriorates into more serious, disabling injury.

The evidence is overwhelmingly clear: *predisposed weakness theory* is a myth with no substantial evidence to support it. War deployment and the combat environment account for neuropsychiatric casualties. The corrosive influence of psychiatry—psychiatric diagnosing and disability pensions—as well as inadequate military training, leadership, unit morale, and exposure to high intensity combat are the real causes of these casualties.

It is not the widely held belief by the military and general society that these stress injuries are generally the result of personal weakness, predisposition, or greed. These beliefs continue to the great harm of those who joined the military to protect the nation and their fellow Americans. Such bias is not only factually inaccurate but also reinforces weaponized stigma, creates barriers to care, and is deeply disrespectful of the sacrifices of the men and women sent into harm's way.

8

DELAY, DECEIVE, AND DELAY AGAIN

THE SIXTH DARK-SIDE STRATEGY

On June 16, 2007, after six years of public statements and sworn testimony to the contrary, the Department of Defense (DoD) reported that "the Military Health System lacks the fiscal resources and the fully-trained personnel to fulfill its mission to support psychological health in peacetime or fulfill the enhanced requirements imposed during times of conflict," caused by the military's chronic neglect, deception, and procrastination.[1] As early as 2004, senior military and congressional leaders knew of the mental health discrepancies and the corrective actions that could avoid a crisis.[2] The forewarnings included a widely circulated DoD Inspector General's grievance against the military in January 2006 documenting rampant organizational failure in staffing, training, treatment, monitoring, family support, stigma, and organization.[3] The report echoed charges by past mental health officers: "A frequent comment by frustrated and harassed psychiatrists during World War II was that responsible authorities failed to heed the lessons learned by psychiatry in World War I."[4]

The military's ability to win wars requires the defeat of its adversaries on the battlefield and its ability to win public support at home. Since World War I (WWI), the military has been embroiled in national controversies over large numbers of veterans returning with unmet mental health needs and skyrocketing pension costs that either threaten or erode public support.[5] Consequently, the military has been forced to develop public relations campaigns designed to manage the narrative around these issues to sustain public backing long enough to win the pertinent war.

Manipulating the public narrative is another example of an overarching strategy to avoid dealing with the psychological realities of war. The military avoids the issue through delay, deception, and delay in three, sometimes overlapping stages. First, it avoids initial disclosure or recognition of wartime mental health needs or crisis through publicity blackouts. Second, it deceives the public by promulgating propaganda designed to deny the existence and scope of a mental health crisis. Third, it delays full commitment to and implementation of externally mandated changes by engaging in tactical appeasement, half measures, or other forms of partial compliance.

AVOIDING PUBLIC DISCLOSURE OF THE RECOGNITION OF MENTAL HEALTH NEEDS

Transparency about the size, scope, and costs of wartime mental health needs would result in serious public questioning of the comparative benefits of prosecuting a war. Therefore, the military strives to maintain public ignorance about the psychological realities of war to sustain public support. The military accomplishes its goal to maintain ignorance in a variety of ways, such as enacting public relations (PR) polices that completely or partially prohibit verbal or written public disclosures about the extent of its mental health problem,[6] and restricting the tracking and disclosure of injuries to a handful of psychiatric diagnoses (e.g., post-traumatic stress disorder, traumatic brain injury).[7] It also has ensured that no single centralized agency is responsible for tracking and reporting mental health needs throughout the DoD.[8] The military has published prevalence data that are intentionally vague,[9] thus avoiding publishing real-time data on mental health casualties, disability pensions, and other issues.

The DoD does publish real-time casualty statistics through a centralized database maintained by the Defense Casualty Analysis System (DCAS),[10] which includes data for military and DoD civilian personnel deaths, injuries, and illnesses for combat and noncombat reasons (e.g., accidents, illness, self-inflicted injuries). According to the DCAS, "Reports are used by DoD organizations, external government agencies, both houses of Congress, the President, the news media, and the general public. The data contained in this site can be used to understand trends in casualties."[11] The DCAS, however, does not track or report on the prevalence of war-stress injuries despite the fact that psychiatric casualties outnumber the combined total of medically wounded and killed in action since the World War II (WWII).[12]

The military's use of PR blackout policies to avoid public disclosure of its mental health problem was evident during WWII. The director of the Bureau of Public Relations and other high-ranking officials distributed the following memorandum on April 28, 1944:

Subject: Statistical information by percentages, rates, or numbers of neuropsychiatric casualties in the armed services is *classified*. The release of statistical information as indicated above constitutes a violation of AR 380–5 and
Article 76, Navy Regulations. The following policy will govern all Army and
Navy releases for publication of information concerning neuropsychiatric
casualties of the Armed Forces.

All material on this subject will be checked for accuracy by the Surgeon
General's Office, U.S. Army, before final clearance by the Review Branch,
War Department Bureau of Public Relations.[13]

Public outcry over the unexpectedly high volume of psychiatrically injured
soldiers returning from the war led to a September 23, 1944, inquiry by
the inspector general "concerning the handling and diagnosis of psychoneurotics within the Army."[14] The inspector general openly criticized the
military's blackout policy, forcing the chair of the Board of Declassification
of Medical and Scientific Reports of the Surgeon General's Office to issue
a 1945 memorandum requiring "full publicity of the psychiatric problem
should be given in a factual manner."[15] Yet even as WWII ended and the
country turned its attention toward helping reintegrate millions of veterans,
the military's publicity blackout was resolute. A June 29, 1945, memo explicitly forebode publication of "statistics (percentages, rates, numbers, names
or identifiable photographs) of Neuropsychiatric Casualties."

In response, the army's chief neuropsychiatry consultant, Brigadier
General Menninger wrote that "the public relations and publicity policy
with regard to neuropsychiatry involve a problem of great magnitude. . . .
There is an urgent need for frank and extended publication in this field.
By a liberal policy of public education, the War Department can give its
support and aid to those veterans discharged for neuropsychiatric causes."[16]

Brigadier General Menninger would go on to conclude that it is crucial
to establish

full-time public relations officer in this field (neuropsychiatry) with the
authority of the War Department to release such information as seemed
indicated. Only by such methods can impending problems be attacked
aggressively and the public educated, thereby avoiding the experience of
this war and the common welfare of communities ignored.[17]

Today, the military's effort to avoid public disclosure of its mental health
crisis is evident both from covert, circumstantial evidence and its overt

written policies. That the DoD does not have a single agency responsible for maintaining and reporting accurate mental health prevalence data (e.g., not just reporting military medical records) constitutes a publicity blackout. The DoD's Armed Forces Health Surveillance Center and the Deployment Health Center[18] can provide only mental health data gleaned from service members who are seen by military medicine and does not capture any data from the other agencies responsible for providing mental health services, such as base community counseling centers.[19]

The Institute of Medicine (IOM) has repeatedly called on the DoD to "dedicate funding, staffing, and logistical support for data analysis and evaluation."[20] Yet multiple comprehensive independent reviews have reported that "in many cases, however, the response [of the DoD and VA] does not match the magnitude of the problems, and many readjustment needs are unmet or unknown."[21] Consequently, prevalence estimates for war-stress injury since the outset of the Afghanistan and Iraq Wars have been limited to a handful of psychiatric diagnoses, including, most notably, post-traumatic stress disorder (PTSD), depression, generalized anxiety, substance abuse, and traumatic brain injury (TBI).[22] The vacuum of any centralized reporting by the DoD has been filled by a plethora of research studies within and outside the DoD and VA that report varying prevalence rates (2 percent to 60 percent) of specific postdeployment diagnoses.[23] Anyone is free to selectively generate statistics to fit their pet theory, and this causes the chaos and controversy that provides the DoD with plausible deniability. Consider this: no controversy or confusion surrounds the number of personnel with traumatic limb amputation, positive HIV status, pregnancy, or other medical conditions, because a single agency with a centralized database is accountable for taking care of physical medical needs.

Amid concerns over public reaction to a mental health crisis, the military ignored a foundational PR lesson from WWII calling for transparency. On May 23, 2006, the DoD published a PR guide, called Public Affairs Guidance (PAG), "To coordinate accurate talking points and messages about the mental health of Soldiers returning from OIF/OEF for all military and VA spokespersons."[24]

DESIRED EFFECTS

In the PAG, the army lays out clear rules for adhering to official policy, regardless of rank. The guide states that "all Army spokespersons whether they are PAOs (public affairs officers), commanders, chaplains, healthcare providers, etc., will speak accurately and with one voice on the issue of mental health and deployed and returning Soldiers." Moreover, the guide claims that this single voice belongs not just to the army but also to other branches and divisions of the U.S. military, such as the "National Guard Bureau (NGB), U.S. Army Reserve (USAR) and Department of Veterans Affairs (VA)." The guide demands that all military personnel "establish and demonstrate to the American public that . . . the majority of soldiers returning from OIF and OEF [Operation Iraqi Freedom and Operation Enduring Freedom] are mentally healthy and transition home successfully" and that "the Army and VA are prepared to provide them the best health care possible" for the few who may need short-term treatment."[25]

In addition to these policies, the PAG lists "key talking points" such as the following: (1) "Unique to this war, is that military leadership is taking a proactive approach"; (2) "The military is doing a number of things to reduce stigma and improve access to care"; (3) "There are numerous opportunities for reserve and National Guard to receive immediate attention"; and (4) "They [army leaders] are proactively addressing mental health needs of Soldiers with early intervention and working to build resilience."[26] Each of these areas was reported as chronically and seriously deficient by the DoD Task Force on Mental Health (TF-MH), which was co-chaired by the army surgeon general. The army's 2006 PR policy reflects a coordinated partial publicity ban intended to delay full disclosure about the actual size and scope of a mental health crisis that only a year later it described as needing immediate action. The 2007 task force called for "fully investing in prevention, early intervention, and effective treatment . . . to fulfill our obligation to our military service members."[27]

PUBLIC DECEPTION AND PROPAGANDA

Military efforts to confuse or deceive government officials and the public about the presence or scope of mental health crises can be detected in the calculated decision made since the Korean War to avoid collecting or publishing actual numbers of psychiatric casualties; in senior military officials releasing distorted, incomplete, or inaccurate statements to the media, Congress, and military populations; and in the military's issuance of written coordinated PR policies or propaganda that contain known or knowable falsehoods with intention to deceive.

Those interested in the history of military mental healthcare can readily access the U.S. army's WWI[28] and WWII[29] lessons learned analyses. Each volume provides detailed statistical accounting of the psychiatric realities of war so that future generations would not forget the extent of the mental impact. Transparent and complete data are available on the number of soldiers diagnosed with specific neuropsychiatric conditions, those admitted to neuropsychiatric hospitals, those psychiatrically screened and rejected, and those who received psychiatric discharges. Importantly, this level of transparency is missing for the navy and marine corps during the two world wars.[30] Nevertheless, after admitting culpability to a self-inflicted mental health crisis caused by ignoring WWI lessons, the army painstakingly compiled two data-filled volumes of WWII psychiatric lessons learned. More than 1,948 pages detail what is required to meet wartime mental health needs, with U.S. Army Surgeon General Leonard D. Heaton sternly warning: "With this information so readily available, there can be little excuse for repetition of error in future wars, should they occur."[31]

Tragically, those lessons have been ignored repeatedly.[32] Equally troubling, however, is that the military appears to have made a calculated decision to avoid duplicating the transparency of the WWII cohort, opting instead for little to no recording of its psychiatric lessons and purposeful use of vague statistics. Consequently, individuals seeking similar detailed accounting of the psychological effects of the Korean War, the Vietnam War, the Persian Gulf War, and the Global War on Terror will be bitterly disappointed.[33]

Statistical data on the prevalence of war-stress injuries are typically limited to an incidence ratio of X per one thousand average troop strength for a specific month, year, or region. Researchers then must locate records of troop strength unique to the formula. For example, the Vietnam War cohort reported the prevalence of certain psychiatric casualties like psychosis increased from 1.6 (1965) to 3.8 (1970) per one thousand average annual troop strength and psychoneurosis from 2.3 (1965) to 3.3 (1970) per one thousand average annual troop strength. The cohort, however, provided no data on absolute or total numbers.[34] This poor data collection is not simply happenstance, but rather is a calculated effort; note that the military collected the absolute numbers to derive its ratios but chose only to report ratios.

Similarly, no official reports of the prevalence of mental health problems in the Persian Gulf War exist. As of 2015, both the VA and DoD no longer provide public access to aggregate numbers for deployment-related conditions like PTSD. In fact, the DoD's annual surveillance of Deployment-Related Conditions of Special Interest excludes PTSD but tracks medical conditions like TBI, pulmonary embolism, amputations, heterotopic ossification, and Leishmaniasis. In short, the military's deceptive recordkeeping practices treat these conditions as if they do not exist.

The military also pursues individualized deception through senior officials. These deceptions are evident when top leaders submit verbal or written statements on the status of mental healthcare, which the military then quickly shows to be inaccurate. Senior military officials (civilian and active duty) have ready access to aggregate data and reports on most aspects of mental healthcare (e.g., staffing levels, attrition rates) or can ask for this data to be gathered. Although one would expect that the senior military officials who make these statements should have accurate information, it is possible for human error. For instance, readers are encouraged to review official statements by top military leaders to national news media[35] and congressional testimony from 2004 to 2007, and to compare the factual bases of those statement with the June 2007 DoD TF-MH findings.

In one such instance, many DoD officials gave testimony on May 24, 2007, at a congressional hearing[36] that clearly contradicted the June 16, 2007, DoD TF-MH report on the catastrophic systemwide failure in every aspect of mental healthcare (e.g., chronic, severe staffing shortages, inadequate access to timely, quality treatment). Representative Darrell Issa's pointed questioning is informative. After hearing public testimony by a deputy secretary of defense who oversees military medicine that "the military health system is second to none in its ability to deliver timely, quality mental health, and behavioral care. In addition, walk-in appointments are available in virtually all military mental health clinics around the world."[37] Rep. Issa alluded to a preview of the DoD TF-MH[38] findings and retorted that he was "a little surprised that there were quite as many of them as there were, terms like robust and touting surveillance programs, pre-deployment health assessments since 1998, mental health care in theater, the use of multi-faith chaplains, etc." He went on to say, "I was a little surprised that, in light of what we are looking at here and some potential for falling through the cracks, that it was sort of, gee, this thing says nothing is broken."[39] Issa also directly questioned the staffing shortages that went unresolved,

> I am going through the math and saying I bet you don't have 400 psychiatrists and psychologists . . . why is it you are *not* asking for these kind of resources? . . . Again, I am going to go on to General Pollock, but I would really hope when you testify before Congress you come with the problems, not just the superlatives.[40]

As noted at the start of the chapter, the DoD finally reported on the major mental health crisis in the military in 2007, despite having knowledge of the required corrections since 2004. Rather than proactively addressing obvious mental health deficiencies, on January, 23, 2007, the U.S. Navy issued the PAG: "All Navy spokespersons whether they are PAOs [public affairs officers], commanders, chaplains, health care providers, etc., will speak accurately and with one voice on the issue of mental health and deployed and returning Sailors and Marines."[41] The U.S. Navy rationalized the PAG by citing an article in *Stars and Stripes* in which Navy psychologist CDR Mark Russell foresaw a "perfect storm brewing in the military's mental health care system."[42] This article was later picked up by *USA Today* and disseminated widely. As a result, the PAG issued by the navy claimed that "Navy Medicine's goal is to ensure that every returning sailor and marine receives any necessary mental health care services as early as possible—providing prevention and treatment services as early as possible is the best way to prevent the long-term effects of war."[43] The PAG also asserted a much more proactive approach than the 2007 task force on mental health portrayed, claiming that "Navy and Marine Corps leadership . . . are proactively addressing mental health needs with early intervention and working to build resilience prior to combat deployments."[44] The PAG also asserted that Navy Medicine was more capable than ever to provide care for its service members, continually evaluating its care and increasing its providers and portals to care.

Five months later, the DoD TF-MH (co-chaired by the navy surgeon general) contradicted the navy's official messaging.[45] On February 28, 2007, navy headquarters issued a memorandum to eliminate its military social work billets—this action was reversed after the June 2007 DoD TF-MH findings were published. The task force clearly stated "the number of active duty mental health professionals is insufficient and likely to decrease without substantial intervention."[46] The U.S. Navy's PAG represents deceptive propaganda: the PR policy explicitly disputed unwanted, albeit accurate news media reports by providing information that senior officials either knew or should have known to be false to sway public opinion.[47]

Not only has the military perpetuated deception through vague or missing data, misleading statements from senior officials, and contradictory statements, it also silences those who would reveal the truth. In 2012, the army suspended several doctors at Joint Base Lewis-McChord who unethically changed the PTSD diagnoses of soldiers to nonservice-connected psychiatric conditions like personality disorder and adjustment disorder to reduce pension costs.[48] The army also suspended the retired army psychiatrist who informed Congress and the media about these unethical diagnostic practices.[49] Similarly, several army mental health clinicians claimed retribution after informing the media about wrongful misconduct discharge of soldiers diagnosed with PTSD and TBI at Fort Carson, Colorado,[50] and a senior navy psychologist reported reprisal after speaking out against the current mental health crisis.[51] Taken together, these deceptions reflect an alarming trend that likely affects other insiders from coming forward.

DELAY THROUGH APPEASEMENT, HALF MEASURES, AND PARTIAL COMPLIANCE

When a mental health crisis can no longer be denied, Congress and the president customarily dictate reforms through legislation[52] or executive orders.[53] A particularly artful strategy for delay is to give the public the appearance of concern, commitment, and compliance while delaying full implementation. For instance, amid rampant reports of unmet mental health needs and suicides, in October 2005, Congress mandated the DoD to establish a mental health task force.[54]

The DoD has exhibited a lack of enthusiasm to take up the compulsory review; it took the military until May 2006 to establish the congressionally mandated task force and then another thirteen months to disclose its findings in June 2007.[55] The military's procrastination ensured that hundreds of thousands of war veterans received either no or grossly substandard mental healthcare before discharge. Moreover, the DoD's tactics contradict the false sense of urgency its mental health task force espoused: "the immediacy of these needs imparts a sense of urgency to this report. As such, the Task Force urges the Department of Defense to adopt a similar sense of urgency in rapidly developing and implementing a plan of action."

It is common for compliance with externally mandated remedial actions on military mental healthcare to take years, likely in the hope that interest will wane. From 2005 to 2009, Congress mandated three different task forces on mental health issues (Mental Health, 2005; Suicide Prevention, 2008, and Recovering Warriors Transition, 2009). Yet each task force took an average of two years to present their report (Mental Health, 2007; Suicide Prevention, 2010; Recovering Warriors Transition, 2011). Comparatively, in

TABLE 8.1 Timeline for DoD Task Forces

TASK FORCE	DATE OF CONGRESSIONAL MANDATE	DATE OF DOD REPORT
DoD Task Force on Mental Health	2005	2007
DoD Task Force on Suicide Prevention	2008	2010
DoD Task Force on Traumatic Brain Injury	2007	2007
DoD Task Force on Recovering Warriors Transition	2009	2011

2007, the army surgeon general initiated a task force on TBI with a strict five-month deadline; the report was delivered on time (see table 8.1).

Clearly, military officials react to external mental health mandates with great hesitation. In contrast, when a general or an admiral wants a review of a serious medical issue, it is accomplished without haste (see table 8.1). Without a designated flag or general officer in charge of mental healthcare, fragmented and dysfunctional efforts undoubtedly will be repeated during subsequent American military engagements.

Inordinate delays have been employed in regard to other issues the military wants to avoid, such as investigations into the use of Agent Orange, experimental LSD and radiation exposure, and Gulf War Illness. Most recently, the Government Accountability Office (GAO) conducted multiple investigations describing the DoD's incremental and partial compliance with mandatory changes to its personality disorder discharge policy concluding that

> the military services lack separation policies that address all of DOD's eight requirements for separating service members with non-disability mental conditions . . . Most of the services reported by fiscal year 2012 that they were not compliant with all eight requirements and many of the 20 reports contained incomplete and inconsistent information.

Additionally, the GAO was tasked with reassessing the DoD's compliance with repeated recommendations by six separate independent commissioned studies and DoD task forces to reduce stigma and organizational barriers to care. The GAO concluded that the "DOD has efforts underway to improve perceptions about mental health care for service-members and, to a comparably limited extent, deployed civilians." The report, however, also stated that the GAO "has not clarified or updated certain policy provisions that may contribute to mental health care stigma" and that "certain policies are unclear or out-of-date and limit career opportunities for individuals who have sought mental health care." Ultimately, "a 2014 RAND Corporation report identified 203 DOD policies that may contribute to stigma," and concluded that the "DoD is not well positioned to measure the progress of its mental health care stigma reduction efforts."

The military implements these delay strategies to avoid expending resources toward a mental health problem that it does not feel responsible for and does not want to spend money on. Moreover, delaying recognition and action allows the military to transfer costs of mental healthcare to the Department of Veterans Affairs (VA) and the private sector. The hope is that the war will end before the military is forced to transform its mental health policies.

In addition to these delays, in an effort to defer legitimate change, the military simply appeases external bodies when charged with change. For example, seven years after the DoD TF-MH[56] had published its recommended overhaul of military mental healthcare, multiple government-sponsored studies were conducted on DoD's mental health system as a whole[57] and on specific program components, including psychological health and traumatic brain injuries[58]; PTSD assessment and treatment,[59] suicide prevention; substance abuse[60]; and prevention, resilience, and reintegration services.[61] Yet the military has not always complied with the recommended corrective actions.[62]

A year after the Iraq invasion, the VA and DoD published its first clinical practice guidelines for PTSD in which four evidence-based psychotherapies were identified and highly recommended for returning combatants: prolonged exposure, stress-inoculation training, cognitive therapy, and eye movement desensitization and reprocessing.[63] Yet insiders reported grossly deficient military mental health staffing and treatment.[64] Congress mandated[65] that the military ensures that

> each member of the Armed Forces who incurs a traumatic brain injury or posttraumatic stress disorder during service shall . . . be enrolled in the program[66] . . . and be provided the highest quality, evidence-based care . . . and be rehabilitated to the fullest extent possible using up-to-date evidence-based practices.[67]

In response, the Office of the Assistant Secretary of Defense published a clinical training policy to "ensure that mental health professionals apply evidence-based psychotherapies . . . when treating Service members with PTSD and acute stress disorder." The DoD proceeded to create a mirage of compliance by establishing a plethora of disjointed and unmonitored programs. Persistent negative media reports spurred Congress to commission RAND to reinvestigate the military's mental health services. In 2011, RAND completed a thorough review of military mental healthcare system,[68] revealing the military's mostly superficial or half-hearted effort to meet wartime mental health needs:

> The proliferation of programs creates a high risk of a poor investment of DoD resources. Our report suggests that there is significant duplication of effort, both within and across branches of service. Without a centralized evidence base, we remain uncertain as a nation about which approaches work, which are ineffective, and which are—despite the best intent of their originators—potentially harmful to service members and their families.[69]

In a report prepared for the Office of the Secretary of Defense Center for Military Health Policy Research, R. M. Weinick and colleagues expressed skepticism of the value of a multitude of programs within and across branches without a centralized evidence base. As a result, the country has remained uncertain about which programs work and why and which programs potentially may be harmful.

In April 2012, the U.S. Army published its treatment policy intended to appease the relevant powers: "The availability of consistent evidence-based assessment and treatment services for PTSD is a high priority for the U.S. Army Medical Department."

The issues for the DoD did not end there; the GAO reported unresolved persistent problems with the military's data of mental health expenditures: "We found, however, that the O&M funding data that DOD provided for all four reports on PH and TBI activities are not reliable. . . . In the present study, we have again found that O&M figures for DCOE and funding and obligations data provided by TRICARE Management Activity are unreliable."

President Obama was forced to intervene, and on August 31, 2012, he issued an executive order—"Improving Access to Mental Health Services for Veterans, Service Members, and Military Families"—charging military officials to "take steps to meet the current and future demand for mental health and substance abuse treatment."[70] The military's superficial overtures, however, reflect yet another example of their tendency to delay through appeasement; the service members' timely access to mental health treatments continued to receive negative scrutiny.[71] The IOM reported that "there are over 21 specialized PTSD

outpatient programs throughout the service branches and no data were available on access to these programs, the number of patients that they serve, or
how service members are prioritized for admission."[72]

In a separate IOM study, the assessment of the military's commitment to
comply with congressional and executive mandates was even more telling:
"The committee has serious concerns about inadequate and untimely
clinical follow-up and low rates of delivery of evidence-based treatments,
particularly psychotherapies to treat PTSD and depression." The military's
selective compliance with previous mental health mandates was also noted:

> However, DoD and the service branches lack data on whether the guideline
> is being used by providers to inform treatment decisions. They do not track
> and evaluate the types of treatments that patients receive or their outcomes
> although efforts to do so have begun, for example, the Army's Behavioral
> Health Data Portal.[73]

Regarding the military's commitment to ensuring compliance with its own
clinical practice guidelines and treatment policies, the IOM concluded that the

> DoD lacks a mechanism for the systematic collection, analysis, and dissem-
> ination of data for assessing the quality of PTSD care. There are no specific
> DoD policies or procedures that stipulate the use of measurement-based
> care for PTSD and no consistent use of standardized outcome measures,
> before, during, or after treatment.[74]

The military also has failed to deliver on promise to improve access to
treatment. In 2015, congress mandated that the DoD "shall ensure that all
beneficiaries shall obtain an appointment within the health care access
standards."[75] A year later, the GAO was tasked with reassessing the DoD's
compliance.[76] The GAO's 2016 report title says it all: "DoD Lacks an Access
Standard for the Most Common Type of Direct Care Mental Health
Appointment." The GAO's condemnatory findings that the

> DoD lacks an important standard for follow-up appointments, which rep-
> resent nearly two-thirds of mental health care provided . . . without such a
> standard, DoD does not have a mechanism for holding MTFs or the services
> accountable for providing timely access to the most common mental health
> care provided.[77]

The extent to which the military relies on its strategy to delay, deceive, and delay in addressing the mental health dilemma is clear.

When pressed for a response, the military's explanation punctuates their stance only further: "an access standard for follow-up appointments was not established in regulation, and that follow-up appointments generally do not have an official access standard against which they are measured." In essence, the DoD ignored the need for follow-up appointment standards because they were not required by law to establish them. Subsequently, the GAO noted the effect of the military's delay strategy, saying "patients with more severe symptoms and diagnostic and clinical complexity reported higher rates of access problems."[78]

The military's half-hearted commitment toward mental health is only further evident when the DoD's legally mandated initial (intake) mental health appointment requirements were assessed by the GAO. "In the case of routine appointments—initial appointments for a new or exacerbated condition—data show that other than the Air Force, MHS (military health system) routine mental health appointments generally did not meet the 7-day access standard."[79] Even on legally required standards, the military engages in only partial compliance.

SUMMARIZING THE STATUS QUO

Seven years after the DoD TF-MH report, the IOM best summarized the military's current command and leadership structure pertaining to mental healthcare, reporting that implementing Assistant Secretary of Defense for Health Affairs directives had been left to the discretion of each branch. As a result,

> the committee recognizes that, in part, such stove pipping of responsibility is inherent in the organizational structure of DOD and serves a purpose, given the different mission and culture of each service branch, but these differences do not preclude a more systematic and integrated approach to PTSD management.[80]

The IOM reported a persistent lack of standardized and consistent PTSD programs without coordination across branches or installations.

As the U.S. Army's Combat Lesson Number Five says, "delay means more casualties."[81] Although no direct empirical evidence exists to test the

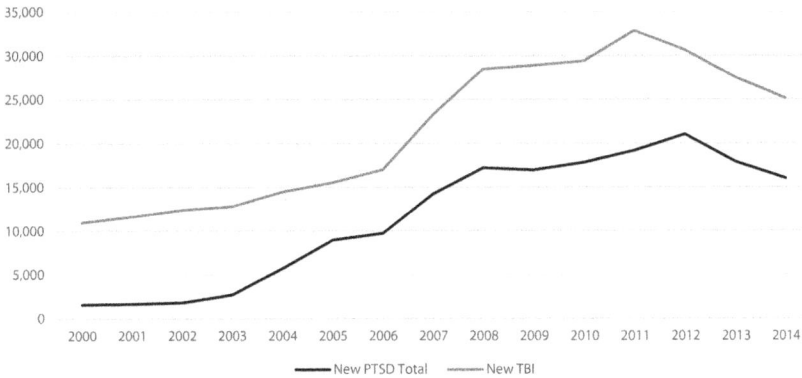

FIGURE 8.1 Annual prevalence of new cases of PTSD and TBI diagnosed by Military Medicine.

assertion that the military's delaying strategies have harmed war veterans and their families, anecdotally, 237 service members committed suicide during the nearly two years it took the DoD to complete its internal mental health review ordered by Congress[82] and to admit to a national crisis of its own creation.[83] Meanwhile, PTSD and TBI rates escalated (see figure 8.1). Without an infrastructure to support returning veterans and their families,[84] by 2007 the military had long missed a critical window to prevent a catastrophe.

In part, military researchers are strongly disincentivized to collect and report on clinical outcomes for service members receiving military mental healthcare, despite repeated implorations from various commissioned studies.[85] These reasons are many: a fear of military leader backlash if the actual prevalence and financial costs of war-stress injuries are tracked; a fear of public backlash caused by admitting a major mental health crisis; a diversion of financial resources from military missions to military healthcare treatment; and a fear of evacuation syndrome—large scale numbers of frontline personnel evacuated for treatment. One can simply look to U.S. military subject matter experts since WWI to know that the identification and treatment of war-stress injuries should be a critical wartime lesson learned, but the problem is institutional memory loss. In WWI, the military did not follow lessons learned simply in accordance with the best scientific practice to treat soldiers suffering with war neuroses as early and as effectively as possible. The military also learned that to do so was an important contribution toward the conservation of manpower and military morale.[86]

Writing in *War Neuroses in North Africa*, Grinker and Spiegel learned in WWII that although cases appear and disappear, without treatment, they will become a chronic psychiatric problem.[87]

During the first Gulf War, service members experienced unacceptably long waiting time for mental health clinic appointments, despite the anticipated mental health service needs, based on previous wars. The lessons were clear from past wars, as noted by the military's own investigations. The stressors inherent in military life make basic mental health services just as critical and time sensitive as basic medical care. The DoD TF-MH noted: "For individuals under stress, psychological health problems may quickly deteriorate. Stigma may cause active duty members to delay seeking help. As such, timely intervention is crucial."[88]

These facts represent a small sample of evidence that the military is cognizant of the importance of early identification and treatment of war-stress injuries. Therefore, strategies intended to avoid implementing this critical war trauma lesson through delay or deception rather than appropriate recognizing and responding to the mental health crises is harmful to veterans and their families.

9

FAULTY DIAGNOSIS AND BACKDOOR DISCHARGES

THE SEVENTH DARK-SIDE STRATEGY

Being diagnosed with a mental health condition is the leading reason for military administrative separations (ADSEP),[1] but proper diagnosis is also required for timely access to appropriate high-quality treatment.[2] Another tactic the military relies on to prevent psychiatric attrition, treatment, and disability pensions is avoiding accurate psychiatric diagnosis, rendering faulty and highly stigmatizing diagnoses (e.g., personality disorder, lacking moral fiber), and awarding diagnoses that allow for ADSEP that are devoid of service connection (e.g., post-traumatic stress disorder [PTSD]) and eligibility for Department of Veterans Affairs (VA) benefits, which are often called "backdoor" or "bad paper" discharges.

POLICIES TO AVOID DIAGNOSING WAR-STRESS INJURY

Thus, a solution was found for the excessive medical discharge of "psychoneurotic" cases, which consisted of both a change of psychiatric nomenclature and a tightening of the medical discharge process. The benefits of this hard-won lesson learned in World War II were continued during the Korean War and have become a permanent part of the policies and procedures of military psychiatry in the U.S. Armed Forces.

A. J. GLASS, "ARMY PSYCHIATRY BEFORE WORLD WAR II"

As illustrated here, the military regularly establishes policies that restrict psychiatric diagnosis of war-stress injury. Although some or many service members may benefit from policies that limit psychiatric diagnosis because of possible stigma, others are harmed by delaying appropriate diagnosis and treatment. Use of punitive and highly stigmatizing labels pertaining to cowardice (e.g., lacking moral fiber), desertion, malingering (e.g., gold-bricker, pension-seeking neuroses), and hysteria (e.g., not yet diagnosed neurotic [NYDN] in place of shell shock) as well as euphemisms convey-ing transient stress reactions expected to resolve rapidly with brief respite (e.g., combat fatigue, battle fatigue, combat exhaustion, flier's fatigue, com-bat stress reaction, combat and operational stress reactions) all represent military policies for avoiding psychiatric labeling with the explicit purpose of preventing psychiatric attrition, treatment, and pensions.[3]

Insight into the military's antagonistic view toward psychiatric diagnosis is gleaned from the U.S. Army Office of the Surgeon General's *Memoran-dum on Psychoneurosis (Combat Exhaustion)*.[4] The diagnosis of psycho-neurosis was the acceptable medical label at the time and is a precursor to modern-day diagnoses of anxiety disorders, PTSD, and somatoform disor-ders. The U.S. Army, however, has defined psychoneurosis as "a condition, not a disease, which results from an individual surrendering to an adverse situation. It manifests itself in many ways and varying degrees from a mild hypochondria to a severe anxiety neurosis."[5] In regard to etiology the army surgeon general reports: "The basic causes of psychoneurosis is insufficient courage."[6] In response to mass psychiatric attrition and disability discharges for psychoneurosis the surgeon general advises: "psychoneurosis is not a problem in the Russian Army. The Russians punish cowardice with death."[7] Fortunately, other senior medical leaders pushed back against this antidi-agnosis bias.

In March 1943, the U.S. Army abandoned its failed social experiment to purge weakness from its ranks using psychiatric screenings. Rather, it rein-stated World War I (WWI)-era frontline mental health services because "the problem of neuropsychiatric disabilities under modern battle conditions has been a serious one. Approximately 20 percent of all nonfatal casualties are psychiatric in origin."[8] In addition, the army mandated changes in diagnos-tic classification: "Hence, the only diagnosis permitted was 'exhaustion, in line with the policy established by General Bradley's directive in II Corps on 26 April 1943."[9]

Justification for the military dictating psychiatric diagnostic practices include concerns about the iatrogenic and stigmatizing effects of psychi-atric labels like psychoneurosis along with self-fulfilling prophecies of treating war-stressed soldiers as psychiatric patients.[10] Additionally, reports of successfully returning 60–98 percent of acutely emotionally injured soldiers to the frontlines after brief respite periods, coupled with anecdotal reports of significantly lower return-to-duty (RTD) rates when soldiers are medically evacuated and treated for psychiatric diagnosis, provided some face validity to the military's policy of avoiding psychiatric diagnoses as beneficial to the health and well-being of the troops.[11] The primary impetus for the military's heavy hand in dictating medical practice, however, is more straightforward:

> With the high rates of medical separations threatening to decimate the Army, concern reached the highest military authorities. On 11 November 1943, the War Department reversed the previous liberal discharge policy and established a policy of salvage and maximum utilization of marginal personnel. A prompt effect of this directive was a precipitous decline of the medical discharge rate.[12]

Importantly, some senior army psychiatry leaders disagreed with a headquarter-driven diagnostic doctrine:

> It has been suggested that cases of psychoneurosis should be designated by other terms in the hope of escaping the stigma attached to psychoneurosis. This office is strongly opposed to such a policy. There is ample evidence as to the unwisdom of employing euphemisms for well-established medical entities. The difficulty is not with the term, but rather with the attitude toward and understanding of the term.[13]

After World War II (WWII), publication of WD Technical Bulletin 203 significantly revised diagnostic nomenclature into two categories: (1) transient personality reactions that were divided into either combat exhaustion or acute situational maladjustments; and (2) immaturity reactions that could be applied to chronic symptoms and lead to ADSEP[14]— essentially eliminating psychiatric diagnoses that might result in medical discharge and disability pension. Predictably, the military's new diagnostic policies had the desired effect:

> The new diagnostic categories made unnecessary the widespread usage of the term "psychoneurosis" for situationally induced psychiatric disorders. As a result, the incidence of psychoneurosis, a distant cousin to PTSD, declined sharply and remained at low levels even during the Korean War.[15]

Importantly, the military's diagnostic policies meant that soldiers who were unable to RTD because of more chronic or severe stress reactions would be more susceptible to charges of cowardice, malingering, or predisposed weakness.[16]

CONTEMPORARY DIAGNOSTIC POLICIES

In the twenty-first century, the military's diagnostic policy has remained essentially unchanged, although the labels have evolved. For example, combat and operational stress control (COSC) personnel are required to defer making psychiatric diagnosis except under specific circumstances to preserve the soldier's expectations of normalcy and RTD, as well as to avoid the stigma associated with psychiatric labeling. According to the army, "It is both inappropriate and detrimental to treat Soldiers with COSR (combat and operational stress reaction) as if they are a BDP (behavioral disordered patient)."[17] Amid a plethora of negative publicity and congressional scrutiny over the military's use of backdoor discharges to manage its mental health problem the Department of Army published its policy on psychological assessment and diagnosis of war-stress injury:

> Military healthcare providers understand that caution is required in attributing current PTSD-like symptoms to certain diagnoses that can result in harmful clinical, occupational, or administrative consequences for the SM (service member), particularly malingering, personality disorders, or adjustment disorders. These conditions are often perceived as judgmental or pejorative, can result in administrative separation (or Uniform Code of Military Justice action in the case of malingering), and/or can influence how other medical care providers approach or treat patients when they see one of these diagnoses in the problem list. Patient-centered care within a culture of trust requires that care providers focus on patients' primary concerns, and these diagnoses, when inappropriately used, can damage therapeutic rapport and interfere with successful care.[18]

The Department of Defense's (DoD) commitment to its diagnostic policy, however, is best determined by the level of compliance and accountability of military personnel choosing to uncharacteristically disobey authority. To that end, the Government Accountability Office's (GAO's) reinvestigation of personality disorder discharges shows that "most of the services reported by fiscal year 2012 that they were not compliant with all eight requirements and many of the 20 reports contained incomplete and inconsistent information."

Moreover, in 2016, the secretary of army responded to congressional calls for investigating allegations of noncompliance with its discharge policies by wrongfully awarding 22,194 Operation Enduring Freedom/Operation Iraqi Freedom (OEF/OIF) soldiers diagnosed with war-stress injury (e.g., PTSD, traumatic brain injury [TBI]) an other-than-honorable (OTH) ADSEP for misconduct instead of considering treatment revealing:

> The Army remains confident in the administrative processes that define misconduct separation procedures. Although the Army was not always able to produce evidence that a mental health evaluation was considered by the separation authority, that finding alone does not mean the separation authority did not review it, or that the Army was non-compliant with 10 U.S.C. $1177.[19]

POTENTIAL HARM FROM THE MILITARY'S DIAGNOSTIC POLICIES

Although deferral of diagnosis may have merit in some or many cases, the military's diagnostic policies also can cause harm by compounding problems and delaying access to appropriate treatment. According to the U.S. Army: "Once mental disorder symptoms emerge, the most effective strategy for ensuring recovery lies in prompt application of evidence-based treatments."[20] In 2004, the VA and DoD published their joint practice guidelines for managing post-traumatic stress that included expert consensus recommendations for use of the identified evidence-based treatments.[21] The practice guidelines were updated in 2010 and explicitly state the necessity for timely PTSD treatment: "The clinically significant symptoms cause significant distress or impairment in social, occupational, or other important areas of functioning. The symptoms last more than 3 months after exposure to trauma. Chronic PTSD is unlikely to improve without effective treatment."[22] The military's RTD mandate coupled with restricting psychiatric evacuations for treatment outside war zones, however, inevitably results in delays in accessing effective treatment.[23] Consequently, returning veterans with unidentified or untreated war-stress injury are at high risk of a host of postdeployment readjustment problems that could result in legal involvement, family conflict, and suicide.[24]

FAULTY DIAGNOSING OF WAR-STRESS INJURY

A major concern for war veterans and their families is whether a potential or actual war-stress injury is intentionally not diagnosed, and instead the service member is given a label related solely to their misconduct or to a preexisting non-service-connected condition. For instance, drug use is frequently associated with war-stress injury like PTSD,[25] but it is also grounds for legal action and OTH ADSEP. War veterans can be given a diagnosis such as personality disorder, adjustment disorder, or schizophrenia that is not rated as a service-connected condition, and thus is subject to potential loss of VA benefits.[26] For instance, during the Vietnam War, relatively low rates (2 to 5 percent) of classic "combat exhaustion" or "combat fatigue" casualties were heralded by military leaders as a victory over combat stress and were attributed to a twelve-month rotation and frontline psychiatry policy intended to reduce attrition. At the same time, some three hundred thousand Vietnam veterans were diagnosed and discharged with non-service-connected disabilities in the context of exceedingly high incidence of "character and behavior disorders," including diagnoses such as personality disorder, substance abuse, and "indiscipline" (akin to misconduct stress behaviors) as well as to a dramatic increase in "psychosis" from 1.6 (1965) to 3.8 (1970) per one thousand veterans.[27]

CONTEMPORARY TRENDS OF FACULTY DIAGNOSING

Evidence does not support a broad military conspiracy to wrongfully alter diagnosis to reduce the cost of treatment and pensions. A string of media stories, however, have revealed that such unscrupulous behavior does exist. For instance, an army psychiatrist was audio-recorded disclosing to his army patient widespread pressure exerted on mental health clinicians to avoid giving PTSD diagnosis to war veterans: "Not only myself, but all the clinicians up here are being pressured to not diagnose PTSD and diagnose Anxiety Disorder Not Otherwise Specified instead."[28] A 2012 news story revealed a widely circulated army memo from medical leaders at Joint Base Lewis-McChord, Tacoma, Washington, advising mental health providers that a PTSD diagnosis costs $1.5 million over a service member's lifetime and warned doctors to be careful about "rubber-stamping" the diagnosis in the interest of saving taxpayer dollars.[29] An investigation by the *Seattle Times* and Sen. Patty Murray (D-WA) revealed unethical conduct by a forensic mental health team changing the postdeployment PTSD diagnoses of 285 soldiers to non-service-connected psychiatric conditions, such as personality disorder and adjustment disorder, leaving them potentially ineligible for medical disability compensation and VA benefits.[30]

Moreover, a recent anonymous survey of 543 army mental health providers reported clinical data for 399 service member patients, of whom 110 (28 percent) were reported to be suffering from PTSD.[31] An audit of the electronic health records, however, revealed that 41 percent of soldiers reported to have PTSD by their mental health provider were not actually given a PTSD diagnosis.[32] Instead, they were diagnosed with administrative situations (e.g., postdeployment related encounter) or lesser psychiatric conditions like adjustment disorder. The most common reason for not recording PTSD was reducing stigma or protecting the service. Whatever the rationalization, rendering a faulty diagnosis not only is considered unethical by professional mental health associations[33] but also is a violation of the military's own policies. For example, per Department of Army: "An adjustment disorder diagnosis should not be given if there is evidence that the individual has another specific Axis I disorder that explains the symptoms"[34] (e.g., PTSD). Such widescale misdiagnosing of war-stress injury like PTSD is problematic for a host of reasons: (1) it prevents military personnel from requesting service-connected disability benefits after they leave the military; (2) it can interfere with continuity of care and receiving appropriate PTSD treatment when service members change duty stations every two to four years; (3) it underestimates mental health demand and needed resources by distorting military prevalence statistics that are based entirely on electronic health record diagnoses; and (4) working around stigma serves only to reinforce stigma in the military.

BACKDOOR DISCHARGES COMING TO LIGHT

Typically, when military personnel are seriously injured in a physical manner (e.g., amputation) they go through a medical board process that determines whether their condition is "service-connected" and is something they warrants a medical disability pension as compensation given that they no longer can serve on active duty. The military's Medical Evaluation Board (MEB), also called Physical Evaluation Board (PEB) and medical disability pension policies also includes psychiatric conditions determined to be service-connected conditions. The MEB/PEB process is considered to be the most appropriate and fair means to discharge war veterans who can no longer serve on active duty because of injuries sustained in the military—that's the "front door."

An effective, albeit disturbing, strategy for the military to expeditiously get rid of or punish problematic service members with war-stress injuries and send an intimidating message to the remaining unit members—in addition to avoiding skyrocketing costs associated with psychiatric treatment, VA benefits, and disability pensions—is to administratively separate these veterans through backdoor discharges. In this case, the military forgoes the MEB/PEB process and instead, embarks on an effort to essentially get rid of service members who are no longer conforming. For instance, returning war veterans who are getting in trouble for alcohol abuse, who fail to show up to work on time, who are argumentative with their superiors, or who engage in a wide range of misbehavior and are labeled as "problem children"—regardless if they served with distinction before deployment. Backdoor discharges can originate through either legal or medical channels.

THE LEGAL BACKDOOR: BAD PAPER DISCHARGES

Service members convicted by courts-martial or administratively adjudicated for a pattern of misconduct (e.g., repeated minor rule violations) are subject to bad paper discharges, including bad conduct or dishonorable discharges, or an OTH ADSEP, resulting in forfeiture of military retirement pension, VA disability, and treatment benefits, as well as presenting significant barriers for future employment.[35] Frequent reasons for bad paper discharges include substance abuse (e.g., illicit drug use, wrongful prescription drug use, repeat driving under the influence), interpersonal violence (e.g., sexual assault, domestic violence, child abuse), absence without leave (AWOL, desertion), and patterns of misconduct (e.g., repeatedly being late to work, disrespectful conduct, minor rule violations).[36] Notably, these types of behavior are common sequelae of traumatic- and war-stress injuries[37] as well as misconduct stress behaviors.[38] Consequently, the majority of mentally ill or war-stress injured veterans discharged for misconduct traditionally are barred from receiving psychological health and substance abuse treatment both during and after military service.[39]

Commanders often use adverse or OTH ADSEP for patterns of misconduct or in lieu of courts-martial to expeditiously punish and get rid of problematic personnel, which is deemed necessary to maintain good order and discipline within the military.[40] The problem, however, is when military personnel are subject to bad paper discharges during or after deployments who otherwise have exemplary service records before deployment. We are not suggesting that war veterans who commit serious crimes (e.g., murder or rape) should not be held legally accountable for their actions. Most military leaders and legal personnel genuinely struggle to balance the legitimate circumstances of war veterans with the needs of the service and legal justice. As most who served in the military can attest, however, less scrupulous leaders may intentionally abuse their power to punish burdensome war veterans or may do so out of benign neglect, failing to consider mental health interventions before legal redress, when appropriate.[41]

CONCERNS OVER BACKDOOR AND BAD PAPER DISCHARGES

Multiple news media reports paint a tragic portrait of the military's wrongful use of the legal backdoor to deal with veterans with war-stress injury.[42] During WWII, a reported ninety thousand military personnel received OTH ADSEP for misconduct.[43] The military's bad paper stratagem for dealing with its mental health dilemma intensified during the Vietnam War. For instance, some 560,000 Vietnam veterans reportedly received discharges under conditions that were less than honorable, with 260,000 of those "bad paper" discharges—either OTH (also sometimes termed undesirable), bad conduct, or dishonorable discharges, raising the specter of backdoor discharges.[44] According to Rep. Maxine Waters (D-CA):

> Many bad-paper veterans are among the 250,000 ex-combat soldiers who suffer from post-traumatic stress disorder. They have a higher incidence of unemployment, violent behavior, alcohol and drug abuse, family problems and homelessness than other veterans. Yet we won't give them the treatment that could help them heal. They served their country and deserve treatment for their war wounds, physical and mental.[45]

In 2007, a high-ranking navy doctor sent a sobering warning to colleagues that the military was discharging marines and soldiers for misconduct, when in fact they were merely displaying symptoms of PTSD.[46] This was followed by a 2011 *Stars and Stripes* article describing multiple cases of previously deployed soldiers with prior clean records and diagnosed with war-stress injury (e.g., PTSD, TBI, depression, substance abuse) who reportedly were pressured by their commanders to accept OTH ADSEP instead of courts-martials for relatively minor misconduct, including ten cases of first-time drug use.[47] In June 2014, the army surgeon general launched an investigation into frequent complaints about army mental health clinicians conspiring with Fort Carson commanders to deny PTSD diagnosis of returning war veterans in favor of OTH ADSEP for misconduct.[48] On October 28, 2015, the army reportedly gave 22,194 war veterans OTH ADSEP for misconduct instead of treatment for postdeployment diagnosis of PTSD, TBI, or other psychiatric conditions.[49] Furthermore, on November 4, 2015, twelve U.S. senators tasked the army with investigating complaints of wrongful legal backdoor discharges.[50]

In response, on April 16, 2016, the secretary of army reported an internal audit of the 22,194 ADSEPs, revealing a total of 6,364 discharged soldiers were diagnosed with a potential war-stress injury, 4,837 soldiers with PTSD and 2,624 with TBI.[51] The remaining 15,830 discharged soldiers were excluded from review because of diagnoses other than PTSD or TBI, defying everything known about the spectrum of stress injury.[52] Rather than make a good-faith effort to investigate claims of improper backdoor discharges, the army proceeded to further eliminate cases to be reviewed by utilizing rigid case selection criteria (e.g., only soldiers diagnosed within two years of deployment). Consequently, the army's internal audit found that "only" 3,327 soldiers diagnosed with combat-related PTSD or TBI were ADSEP for misconduct, but that 2,933 of those received honorable discharges, with the remaining 324 soldiers receiving OTH.[53] Upon further scrutiny, however, the army reversed its reported findings and said that 96 percent of the 2,933 soldiers actually had received general, not honorable, discharges,[54] thus prohibiting certain VA benefits.[55] The army's in-depth analysis of the 324 OTH discharges determined that the army complied with its regulations in 64 percent (293) of the cases.[56] The army also reported additional audits of alleged wrongdoing were conducted and identified another 101 cases warranting further review. In the end, however, the army secretary reached the conclusion: "The Army does not routinely

TABLE 9.1 Misconduct ADSEP in U.S. Air Force

	2006	2007	2008	2009	2010	2011	2012
Misconduct administrative separations (other than honorable)	8,236	10,158	10,126	10,679	11,324	12,265	13,377

Source: S. Frizell, "U.S. Army Firing More Soldiers for Misconduct: Number Dismissed for Crime or Misconduct Doubled Between 2007 and 2013," Time, February 15, 2014."

separate soldiers for misconduct who have been diagnosed with PTSD or TBI to save time or resources."[57]

To our knowledge, this is first time the military has publicly been held accountable to explain its discharge policies of war veterans. Although it may be true that the majority of discharges have been fairly adjudicated, the army's response raises serious concerns. For example, the audit lacked independent outside review, selectively reviewing only the 22,128 cases identified in the news story rather than conducting a comprehensive fact-finding audit of all discharges and applying stringent administrative criteria to exclude cases from review—all of which perpetuates worry versus reassurance. In addition, it continues to make no sense to prohibit war veterans from accessing needed VA mental health treatment after being punished for their unlawful acts that is related or caused by a war-stress injury.[58] Fortunately, under intense congressional scrutiny, the VA now will consider granting treatment access to veterans with bad paper discharges.[59] Bad paper discharges are not only an army problem. For example, table 9.1 indicates the steady rise in air force misconduct ADSEP, which is an issue across all service branches.[60]

RECENT FINDINGS OF MILITARY COMPLIANCE WITH MISCONDUCT DISCHARGES

Given the level of news media and congressional scrutiny over the military's discharge policies, one might assume that it might at least temporarily abandon its use of this avoidant strategy. Not so.

In 2017, the GAO released its most recent survey of the DoD's compliance with legal and policy mandates to eliminate backdoor discharges. The GAO[61] found that 57,141 or 62 percent of the 91,764 service members

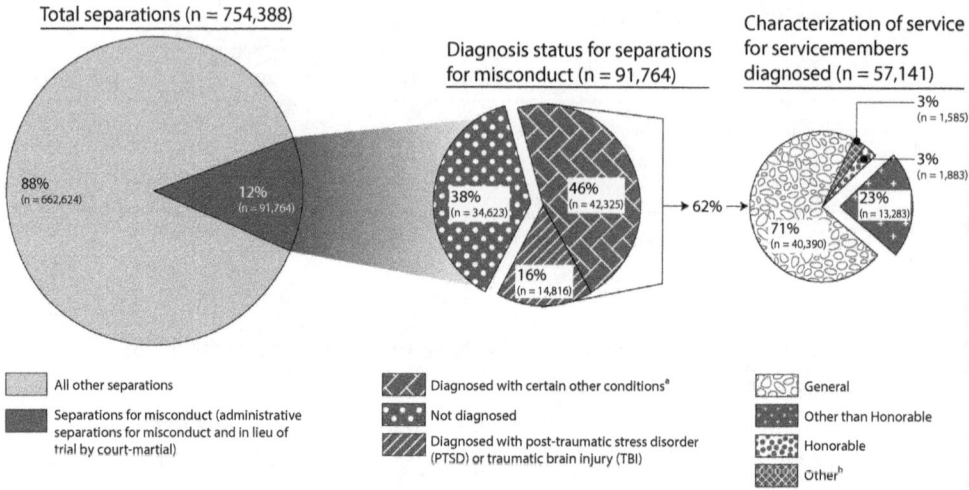

FIGURE 9.1 Diagnosis status and characterization of service for service members separated for misconduct, FY2011–2015.

SOURCE: GOVERNMENT ACCOUNTABILITY OFFICE, *DEFENSE HEALTH CARE: ACTIONS NEEDED TO ENSURE POST-TRAUMATIC STRESS DISORDER AND TRAUMATIC BRAIN INJURY ARE CONSIDERED IN MISCONDUCT SEPARATIONS*, GAO-17-260 (WASHINGTON, DC: GAO, 2017).

Notes: The data include data for active duty officers and enlisted servicemembers who were separated to civilian life. Other separations, such as those resulting from death, joining officer commissioning programs, or separating to the National Guard or Reserve, have been excluded. We defined separations for misconduct as administrative separations for misconduct and administrative separations in lieu of trial by courts-martial. We defined diagnoses of PTSD, TBI, or certain other conditions as diagnoses made within two years before a service member's separation date. The other conditions included in our study are adjustment disorders, alcohol-related disorders, anxiety disorders, bipolar disorders, depressive disorders, personality disorders, and substance-related disorders. This figure presents data on characterization of service for service members diagnosed with PTSD or TBI who received "general" discharge, but 23 percent received "other than honorable," 4 percent received "honorable," and 2 percent received other characterizations of service.

ᵃ This category does not include service members who were also diagnosed with PTSD or TBI. For our analyses, we included these service members only in the "diagnosed with PTSD or TBI" category.

ᵇ Other is defined as nonapplicable, uncharacterized, or unknown.

given an ADSEP for misconduct from fiscal years 2011 through 2015 had been diagnosed within two years before separation with PTSD, TBI, or other psychiatric conditions often associated with misconduct and postdeployment sequalae.⁶² Of the 57,141 service members, 23 percent or 13,283 received an OTH characterization of service (see figure 9.1). Importantly,

6,534 previously deployed personnel agreed to accept an OTH ADSEP in lieu of or instead of a courts-martial.[63] In Dave Phillipps's Pulitzer Prize–winning series on legal backdoors,[64] several service members featured accused the military of strongarming or threatening them with jail time, bad conduct discharge, and possible felony conviction through courts-martial, or to accept a quick less-than-honorable exit (ADSEP).

PSYCHIATRIC BACKDOOR DISCHARGES

The military utilizes improper or faulty psychiatric diagnosis and ADSEP to punish problematic personnel with war-stress injury, weaponize stigma, and/or reduce costs associated with psychiatric treatment, VA benefits, and pensions in two key ways: (1) diagnosis of mental health conditions considered to be preexisting or non-service-connected, and (2) diagnosis of a personality disorder.

Whether intentional, or thru incompetence, service members with war-stress injury can be misdiagnosed and ADSEP with a psychiatric condition whose etiological origin is not directly connected to military service or being deployed to war zones.[65] During WWII, an army brigadier general reported that "127,000 men with neuropsychiatric difficulties have been discharged on an administrative basis."[66] Today, such preexisting or non-service-connected conditions include, but are not limited to, ADHD, impulse control disorder, sleep-walking, specific learning disorder, adjustment disorder, or other conditions that typically originate in childhood or adolescence or are deemed "unsuitable" for further military service. Once diagnosed, service members can be ADSEP under the category of "Convenience to the Government," which typically is characterized as discharge as "General under Honorable, which is less than Honorable."[67] Essentially, those service members, regardless of time in service and deployment history who are given a general discharge typically are ineligible for any VA benefits or military retirement pensions unless they are also diagnosed with a service-connected disability. In addition, they also may experience difficulty obtaining certain civilian employment requiring an honorable discharge.[68]

To be certain, psychiatric backdoor discharges is not new to the twenty-first century. For example, during WWI, 6,196 army personnel were ADSEP for "character and behavior disorders," including 3,709 diagnosed as "constitutional psychopathic states" (akin to personality disorder), 455 for "alcoholism," 734 "bedwetting," 1,190 for "drug addiction," and two for "malingering."[69] In WWII, 163,119 soldiers were ADSEP for unsuitability due to neuropsychiatric reasons, including 2,930 for "character and behavior disorders," including chronic alcoholism and drug dependence.[70] Service members ADSEP for "psychopathic personality, chronic alcoholism, or sexual perversion including homosexuality, were discharged without honor."[71] Before 1982, Vietnam War veterans diagnosed with a preexisting mental health condition, such as schizophrenia, or other psychotic disorder, whether accurate or not, were often medically discharged or ADSEP without VA treatment benefits. This trend of backdoor discharges was reported to have notably increased during the Korean and Vietnam wars, but absolute numbers were never reported and thus are not available.[72]

PERSONALITY DISORDER

Although the military's classification of personality disorder (PD) has evolved over time, including constitutional psychopathy (WWI, WWII), asocial or psychopathic personalities (WWII), and PD (Korean War to present day), the general policies have not. Today, a PD is defined as follows:

> An enduring pattern of inner experience and behavior that deviates markedly from the expectations of the individual's culture, is pervasive and inflexible, has an onset in adolescence or early adulthood, is stable over time, leads to clinically significant distress or impairment in social or occupational functioning and is not better explained as a manifestation or consequence of another mental disorder, or the physiological effects of a substance (e.g., drug of abuse) or another medical condition [e.g., head trauma].[73]

Given its developmental nature, a PD is considered to be a preexisting (premilitary) and therefore non-service-connected condition. From the military's perspective, a PD diagnosis communicates an inherent difficulty adapting to social and occupational demands in adverse environments with the potential to become a substantial burden on the command or a safety risk to self or others. In other words, predisposed weakness, not exposure to war stress, is the underlying cause of one's postdeployment troubles. Therefore,

TABLE 9.2 Comparison of Personality Disorder Screening, Diagnosis, and Disposition

WAR	NUMBER SCREENED AND REJECTED	NUMBER DIAGNOSED IN THE MILITARY	NUMBER GIVEN DISABILITY DISCHARGES	NUMBER ADSEP	SOURCE
World War I	1,436 (army) for personality disorder alone	5,146 (army)	3,709 (army)	N/A	Bailey and Haber, 1929
World War II	716,000 (army) for mental or educational deficiency	5,599 (army per hospital admission)	N/A	21,000 (army) 64,000 (military-wide)	Karpinos and Glass, 1966; Ginzberg, 1959
Global War on Terror	Unknown		N/A		

Source: P. Bailey and R. Haber, "Analysis of Special Neuropsychiatry Reports," in *The Medical Department of the United States Army in the World War: Volume X Neuropsychiatry in the United States*, ed. P. Bailey, F. E. Williams, and P. O. Komora (Washington, DC: U.S. Government Printing Office, 1929), 157–269.

B. D. Karpinos and A. J. Glass, "Disqualifications and Discharges for Neuropsychiatric Reasons, World War I and World War II," in *Medical Department United States Army, Neuropsychiatry in World War II volume I: Zone of interior*, ed. A. J. Glass and R. J. Bernucci, (Washington DC: Office of the Surgeon General, Department of the Army, 1966), xiii–xiv.

E. Ginzberg, *The Lost Divisions: The Ineffective Soldier, Lessons for Management and the Nation* (New York: Columbia University Press, 1959).

service members with a PD diagnosis are routinely ADSEP for having a pre-existing condition that is incompatible and unsuitable for military service. By definition, a PD is not diagnosed in adulthood without substantial evidence of earlier maladjustment and only after excluding other psychiatric or physiological conditions.[74] A history of psychiatric hospitalization and legal conviction typically renders an individual as ineligible to join the military.[75] Since WWI, the military has psychiatrically screened and rejected volunteers and draftees because of possible PD or other psychiatric risk factors as reflected in table 9.2.

Once diagnosed, service members may be given an opportunity to remediate through counseling services with a formal written warning that further performance problems will result in ADSEP. The vast majority of personnel diagnosed with PD are recommended for ADSEP, however, and those with a history of suicidal ideation or attempts are often subject to "expeditious" ADSEP (figure 9.2).[76] In fact, Mark Russell has observed expeditious ADSEP occurring in as little as one week.

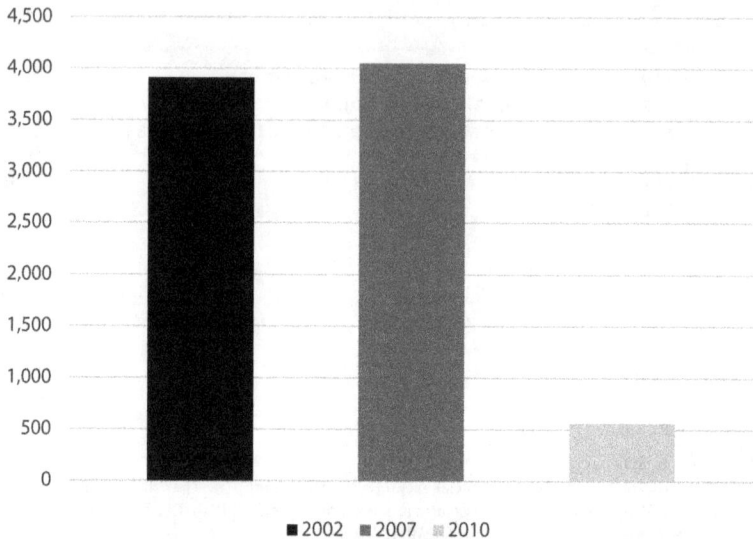

FIGURE 9.2 Number of military personality disorder administrative separations.

SOURCE: S. SIDIBE AND UNGER, "UNFINISHED BUSINESS: CORRECTING "BAD PAPER" FOR VETER-ANS WITH PTSD (VETERANS LEGAL SERVICES CLINIC, YALE LAW SCHOOL, 2016), HTTPS://LAW.YALE.EDU/SYSTEM/FILES/DOCUMENTS/PDF/UNFINISHEDBUSINESS.PDF.

Note: Data from U.S. Army, Air Force, Marine Corps, Navy, National Guard, and Coast Guard.

THE MILITARY'S WRONGFUL USE OF PD DIAGNOSIS AND BACKDOOR DISCHARGE

Anyway, given the fact that both the military and the VA heard this testimony, which is very, very shocking, that there is a systematic and a policy-driven misdiagnosis of PTSD as personality disorder to get rid of the soldier early, to prevent any expenditures in the future which are calculated in the billions of dollars, I would take that pretty seriously if I were you guys and say something about that.

B. FILNER, COMMITTEE OF VETERANS AFFAIRS, U.S. HOUSE OF REPRESENTATIVES

U.S. Army researchers surveyed psychiatrists deployed to Vietnam who reported that of all possible mental health diagnoses, PD was the most frequent (27 percent) followed by drug-dependence syndrome (15 percent) which is another ADSEP-qualifying condition.[77] An estimated three hundred thousand Vietnam veterans received general ADSEP's with an unknown condition, but a large number of those were subject to diagnostic abuses,[78] which carries a grave stigma and adverse effects on employment.

From 2000 through 2015, a total of 99,223 active-duty service members were diagnosed with PD by military healthcare.[79] It is unknown how many of the 81,223 service members were war veterans. In 2007, media reports surfaced alleging the army involuntarily ADSEP more than 40 percent or 28,000 soldiers for PD because of postdeployment adjustment problems.[80] On July 25, 2007, the U.S. House of Representatives conducted hearings on PD backdoor discharges, prompting the committee chair, Rep. Bob Filner (D-PA), to observe:

> My concern is that this country is regressing and again ignoring legitimate claims of PTSD in favor of the time and money saving diagnosis of Personality Disorder. Providing veterans with the correct medical diagnosis is key for a variety of reasons ranging from receiving proper treatment to eligibility for military and veterans' benefits. Once a service member is diagnosed with a Personality Disorder, he or she has a much more difficult time receiving benefits and treatment at the VA.[81]

In 2008, Congress charged the GAO to review the DoD's PD discharges amid widespread reports of wrongful backdoor discharges of war veterans. According to the GAO report, out of a sample of 31,000 personnel ADSEP for PD, 2,900 service members had deployed to OEF/OIF war zones.[82] Subsequently, Congress enacted several laws, and the DoD modified its ADSEP policies governing the military services' handling of PD and misconduct separations in cases involving PTSD and TBI.[83] Consequently, figures 9.2 and 9.3 reveal a dramatic reduction in military PD discharges since 2007 resulting from external pressure along with a corresponding increase in non-disability-related ADSEP for adjustment disorder diagnoses. In 2010, the GAO found the army, marine corps, and navy had remained noncompliant with the DoD's revised PD discharge regulations, which left open the possibility of backdoor discharges. In fact, as recent as 2015, the GAO cited problematic PD and other non-service-connected psychiatric discharges:

> DOD and three of the four military services—Army, Navy, and Marine Corps—cannot identify the number of enlisted service-members separated

for non-disability mental conditions because, for most separations, they do not use available codes to specifically designate the reason why service-members were separated.

Because the three military services are using the broad separation code "condition, not a disability" for most separations, the resulting data cannot be used to identify the number of service members separated for non-disability mental conditions. There is no other systematic way to track these separations.

In reply, the army justified its avoidance of specific separation codes needed to monitor possible backdoor discharges, citing concerns over the stigma and well-being of discharged soldiers. Most non-service-connected discharges are general discharges, under honorable conditions, however, and future civilian employers are more prone to discriminate against the absence of an honorable discharge. A more plausible reason for the military's approach is what the GAO asserts: "There is no other systematic way to track these separations." Case in point, figure 9.3 reveals a disturbing trend whereby the number of PD ADSEP significantly declined under the weight of immense external scrutiny, but the number of other non-service-connected psychiatric ADSEP (e.g., adjustment disorder) increased.

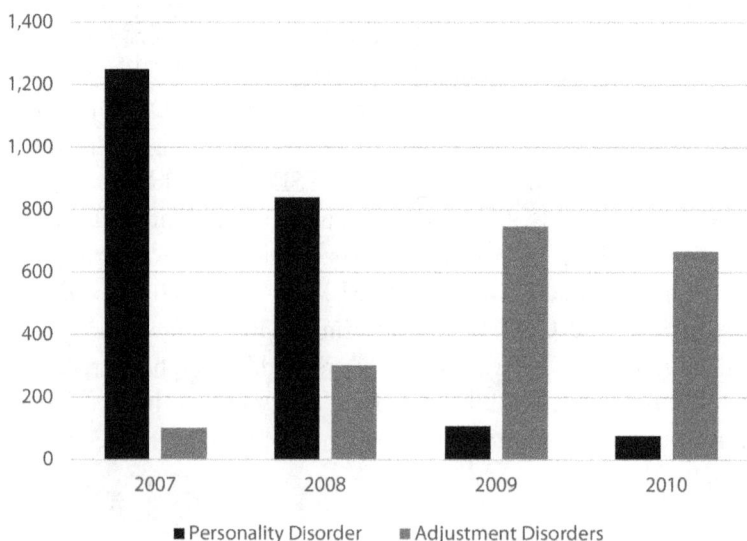

FIGURE 9.3 Nondisability personality and adjustment disorder separations, U.S. Air Force.

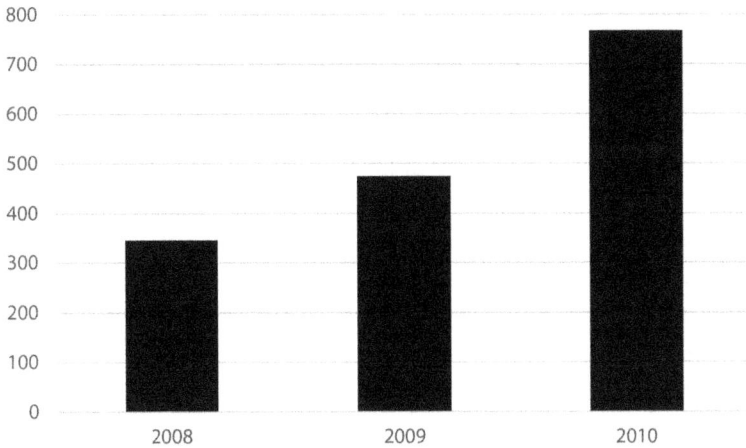

FIGURE 9.4 ADSEP for adjustment disorder, U.S. Army.

SOURCE: M. ADER, R. CUTHBERT, K. HOECHST, E. H. SIMON, Z. STRASSBURGER, AND M. WISHNIE, *CASTING TROOPS ASIDE: THE UNITED STATES MILITARY'S ILLEGAL PERSONALITY DISORDER DISCHARGE PROBLEM* (SILVER SPRING, MD: VIETNAM VETERANS OF AMERICA, 2012).

Specifically, since 2007, the number of PD discharges across all branches plummeted from an average of 3,849 service members per year in the period from 2001 to 2007 to only 907 from 2008 to 2010. During this same period, the number of non-service-connected psychiatric discharges significantly increased for conditions like adjustment disorder (see figure 9.3). For example, from 2008 to 2010, the army discharged a total of 6,492 service members for adjustment disorder with the number of deployed soldiers ADSEP for adjustment disorder increasing each year since 2008 (see figure 9.4). Furthermore, by 2010, 37 percent of the 2,033 soldiers ADSEP by the army for non-service-connected adjustment disorder had deployed to war zones, which again left open accusations of backdoor discharges.[84]

HOW DO BACKDOOR AND BAD PAPER DISCHARGES BENEFIT THE MILITARY?

The military benefits in a number of ways from awarding bad paper and backdoor discharges to war veterans rather than a medical discharge for conditions like PTSD or an honorable ADSEP to include the following:

(1) it can avoid increases in time and costs associated with medical boards and medical discharge; (2) it can avoid rewarding personnel with a honorable discharge whom the commander does not feel deserves it because of poor performance; (3) it can reflect resentment toward personnel who are choosing to act out or seek mental health rather than suck it up like "real warriors"; (4) it is a means to enact long-term retribution to someone the commander does not like or feels is unworthy of honorable discharge; (5) it saves a significant amount in cost and time to process personnel for ADSEP versus courts-martial or waiting for future legal violations to build a case; (6) it reflects the belief of "doing a favor" by granting a demoralized service member's request for expeditious ADSEP.

In regard to potential financial incentives, multiple news stories have reported that military medical leaders and mental health clinicians have circulated memoranda or verbally verified the top-down pressure to avoid spending millions of dollars associated with PTSD diagnosis and pensions.[85] In fact, during the 2007 congressional hearing on PD discharges, Rep. Filner notes:

> In addition, there is some indication that higher policy is leading to this or—policy made at higher levels. I have personally talked to a doctor psychiatrist who told me that his commander told him to make the diagnosis of personality disorder rather than PTSD which would lead to further cost and obligations by this Nation to our veterans.
>
> The doctor said, "You have the medical issues that call for a medical board, but the reason I am going to push this Chapter is because it will take care of both the needs of the Army and the needs of you. You will be able to receive all the benefits you would if you were going to go through a medical board, get out of the military, and focus on your treatment to get better. For the military, they can get a deploy-able body to fill your spot."[86]

To that end, it has been estimated that the DoD has saved $8 billion in disability compensation and $4.5 billion in medical care costs through its psychiatric backdoor discharges, but this excludes cost-savings from legal-related backdoors (e.g., OTH ADSEP for misconduct).[87] Regardless, the status quo harkens to German Army psychiatrist Robert Gaupp's declaration: "The most important duty of the neurologist and psychiatrist is to protect the Reich from proliferations of mental invalids and war pension recipients."[88]

Setting aside any potential financial incentives, perhaps the biggest payoff is to maintain control through fear and intimidation. Military psychiatrists and psychologists have long been called "wizards" not because of intellect, talent, or wit, but because they can make people disappear. As the military's designated specialists, all it takes is a diagnosis and recommendation to banish someone from the military kingdom. Within the military, especially among those seeking eventual retirement pension from military service, the inherent fear associated with backdoor discharges creates an oppressive organizational barrier to seeking mental healthcare. For instance, a deployed service member with eligibility for military retirement and lifetime pension after twenty years of active service, who is ADSEP with a bad paper discharge, forfeits that retirement pension and often their VA benefits. Therefore, backdoor discharges provide the military with a powerful, albeit unethical, deterrent against its mental health problem. Such weaponization of stigma explains the GAO's finding:

> The Army and Navy have made it clear that they do not wish to reduce attrition rates by trying to rehabilitate individuals who engage in misconduct. For example, the Navy has recently made its definition of "a pattern of misconduct" more stringent, changing the number of offenses constituting "a pattern" from three or more, to two or more. Also the Army's Director of military personnel management has emphasized to its major commands that two of the largest areas for separations, discharges for misconduct and discharges in lieu of courts martial, are "areas that are non-negotiable."[89]

In regard to the DoD's compliance with legal and discharge policy mandates, the GAO found that two of four service branches were noncompliant with counseling provision requirement and none of the branches tracked required training and screenings.[90] For example, 40 percent and 38 percent of deployed army and marine corps personnel, respectively, given OTH ADSEP were not screened for PTSD or TBI, as required. In conclusion, the GAO reported:

> DOD does not routinely monitor the military services' adherence to policies for screening service members for PTSD and TBI prior to separating them for misconduct, training officers on how to identify symptoms of TBI in the deployed setting, and counseling service-members on eligibility for VA benefits and services. Without monitoring adherence to these policies,

the military services cannot provide assurance that service members with PTSD and TBI are receiving adequate consideration of their conditions as well as the services DOD has established for them.[91]

In seeking an explanation as to *why* the military continues to defy its legal obligations with impunity, we must point to the inherent fragmentation and lack of leadership accountability in a dysfunctional mental health organizational structure.[92] Needless to say, the military's diffusion of responsibility is not by chance, but rather it represents yet another approach to avoid learning its war trauma lessons.

10

AVOIDING RESPONSIBILITY AND ACCOUNTABILITY

THE EIGHTH DARK-SIDE STRATEGY

> *In DoD and each service branch, unit commanders and leaders at all levels of the chain of command are not consistently held accountable for implementing policies and programs to manage PTSD effectively, including those aimed at reducing stigma and overcoming barriers to accessing care.*
> INSTITUTE OF MEDICINE, *TREATMENT FOR POSTTRAUMATIC STRESS DISORDER*

In their investigation into the treatment of post-traumatic stress disorder (PTSD) in the U.S. military, the Institute of Medicine (IOM), one of the most respected bodies of scientists in the world, addressed the core issue as to why so few members of the U.S. military with PTSD receive the help they need. In short, this reason is lack of accountability. We found that avoiding accountability and the always popular organizational plausible deniability were at the heart of this persistent failure to address mental health among members of the U.S. military. It is a subtler but no less effective strategy that the military relies on to avoid learning lessons from its soldiers' war trauma and managing its mental health dilemma. The popular government refrains "I can neither confirm or deny" and "It's not my department" both reflect a self-serving tendency to claim blissful ignorance and prevent accountability.

In the military vernacular, accountability often directly assigns blame to the leader of the unit, regardless of whether or not the leader is responsible for the error—navy captains are punished for major ship accidents even if they turned the helm over to another qualified officer; squadron commanders are sent packing for aircraft crashes despite previous safety records; and unit commanders are regularly stripped of their duties for negative publicity stemming from their subordinates' misconduct. Similarly, different leaders in the chain of command are accountable for those who are diagnosed with PTSD while serving on active duty. Directly or indirectly, these leaders are compelled to "fix the problem"—an impossible feat; an untrained commander cannot fix a soldier's diagnosis with a mental illness. Both the commanding officer and the subordinate know they need a mental health professional. So what is the practical impact of the military's neglect?

2007 MEDICAL BARRACKS SCANDAL AT WALTER REED

On February 18, 2007, the *Washington Post*'s Dana Priest and Anne Hull published the first of a series of damning revelations that erupted into a national scandal at Walter Reed National Military Medical Center—the U.S. military's flagship hospital. Unconscionable stories of neglect, indifference, and mistreatment shook the nation as images of wounded soldiers dealing with amputations, traumatic brain injuries (TBIs), and other serious physical and mental wounds living in neglected hospital quarters became publicly accessible. In keeping with the military's propensity to deny and deceive, army officials initially claimed to be surprised at these conditions despite news reports documenting the issues since 2004. Subsequent stories of suicide and avoidable accidental deaths of unmonitored wounded veterans made matters even worse, and subsequent heated congressional hearings revealed that Walter Reed was only the tip of the iceberg. The newly appointed defense secretary, Robert Gates, visited Walter Reed and sternly promised that those responsible would be "held accountable!" Yet, only some were.

On March 1, 2007, weeks after the first *Washington Post* story, Walter Reed's commanding officer was fired by the army secretary, even though the officer had been in charge of the hospital for only six months. But Congress's dissatisfaction resulted in the army secretary himself resigning the following day, followed by the army surgeon general (who cochaired the Department of Defense [DoD]Task Force on Mental Health [TF-MH]) on March 12. New leaders were appointed with strict congressional oversight to expeditiously and thoroughly correct the problems. This response is not usually fair, but the wheels of military accountability are swift and designed to send an intimidating message throughout the military establishment.

That same year, the nation was exposed to equally dishonorable and appalling revelations that additional victims of the military's negligence included mental health patients. On June 16, 2007, the DoD finally came clean after six years into the war in Afghanistan revealing a major public health crisis caused principally by chronic neglect and cataclysmic institutional deficiencies in staffing, training, research, public education (e.g., antistigma awareness), data collection, prevention, assessment, diagnosis, treatment, continuity of care, family support, and social reintegration.

The military's June 2007 pronouncement stood in direct contradiction to years of sworn congressional testimony and official public affairs guidance steadfastly denying a crisis as late as May 2007.[1] The congressionally mandated military task force urgently pleaded for urgent action. The task force called to mind the lessons in the wake of the Vietnam War and laid out prevention, early investment, and effective treatment as the military's responsibilities.[2]

It was not common knowledge, however, that senior military and congressional leaders were well informed on the mental health discrepancies and mandated corrective actions as early as 2005 to avoid predictable harm to veterans and their families.[3] The forewarning included a widely circulated DoD inspector's general grievance against military medicine in January 2006 for its failure to implement a century of documented mental health lessons.[4] The inspector general's complaint helped shape the investigatory lens of the DoD TF-MH.

The June 2007 announcement of these ignored mandates revealed that the lack of ceremonial firings or impassioned congressional hearings. In fact, the DoD was never challenged or investigated as to why the world's greatest superpower was so ineptly prepared to deal with predictable psychological outcomes of war or why it chose to delay recognition of an obvious public health crisis.[5] Not only was the military unprepared for and negligent of the crisis, it also deceived the U.S. Congress and the American public for more than six years, squandering an opportunity to address the issues in treatment and diagnosis and avert a mental health crisis.

Instead of accountability, the DoD task force's ninety-nine corrective actions—essentially a repetition of the military's documented "lessons learned"[6]—were heralded as a groundbreaking success.[7] Military leaders in positions of responsibility and accountability were congratulated. Subsequently, we have counted upward of 214 separate investigations into military mental healthcare since the Afghanistan invasion, most being government-commissioned studies at untold millions to taxpayers, essentially reidentifying the same problems and proposing the same corrective actions. We are unaware of a single high-ranking military official fired for negligent leadership—compared with the three senior leaders fired in March 2007 over the medical barracks scandal.

The costs from the military's dearth of due diligence to plan and prepare to meet basic mental health needs are relived every day by the nearly one million military personnel[8] and nearly seven hundred thousand veterans who served in Operation Iraqi Freedom (OIF), Operation Enduring Freedom (OEF), or Operation New Dawn and who were treated for psychiatric conditions by the DoD and Department of Veterans Affairs (VA), respectively.[9]

Whether by design or accident, the U.S. military has created (and more important chooses to sustain) a mental health system that, unlike military medicine, dentistry, and other organizational components within the military, is inherently fragmented and dysfunctional without an accountable chain of command or leadership structure.[10] Essentially, three major agencies are involved in providing mental health services: military medicine; family community counseling centers; and contractors, such as Mental Health Life Consultants, Educational Developmental and Intervention Services, and other civilian contractors.[11]

Each entity has its own separate chain of command, personnel, policies, recordkeeping, and data-collection procedures, with widely varying levels of collaboration with other mental health entities—this collaboration is referred to as stove-piping. Even worse, each mental health-related entity within the four military service branches has different policies and practices. Still, the DoD's organizational and leadership structure for mental healthcare has been reviewed extensively, and many reviews have identified required changes.[12]

Concerns over a deeply flawed organizational structure of military mental healthcare is far from new, however. Consider the World War II (WWII)–era chief army neuropsychiatric consultant's assertion that "certain factors within the Army—its organizations and system—further added to the difficulty for psychiatry."[13] Some have even proposed that "a separate corps within the Medical Department should have been created."[14]

THE ROLE OF MILITARY ORGANIZATIONAL STRUCTURE AND LEADERSHIP

Mental health organization, leadership, policies, and practices play a pivotal role of in causing or exacerbating behavioral health crises in the past and the present day.[15] According to the IOM, "providing uniform services within the DoD and VA healthcare systems across geographic locations, facilities, and providers should be a priority"[16] and "fragmentation of care diminishes continuity and coordination, often resulting in higher use of emergency departments, increased hospitalization, duplication of tests, and increased costs."[17]

In 2007, the DoD TF-MH conducted a year-long review of its pre-war planning and preparation and organizational capacity to meet the basic mental health needs of twenty-first century fighters and their families. The DoD TF-MH concluded that the military lacks the funding and personnel to support its service members in peace or war and called for urgent action.[18] These admissions are not unique and were reiterated in the wake of WWII as well.[19]

Consistent with a pattern we observed, we found further evidence of the DoD's significant delay in publicly acknowledging and proactively addressing a worsening tragedy. It was as if they were following a public relations playbook. The DoD significantly delayed publicly acknowledging responsibility of the crisis. Moreover, all would be forgiven if they had proactively addressed a worsening mental health crisis, a tragedy. Instead, they continued the years of contradictory pronouncements to the national media,[20] official military public affairs guidance,[21] and sworn congressional testimony.[22]

The extent of the military's organizational self-inflicted wound is exemplified in the DoD TF-MH's ninety-nine corrective actions for in every aspect of mental healthcare (i.e., staffing, training, stigma elimination, assessment, data collection, prevention, treatment, monitoring outcomes, family support, continuum of care, timely access, research, and social reintegration).[23] Each deficiency represents a failure to learn foundational lessons of war trauma documented by every war generation since World War I (WWI).[24]

The DoD TF-MH described the fragmented nature of the military mental healthcare system, reporting that psychological healthcare depends on military treatment facilities, specialty clinics, and third-party organizations, like counseling centers, religious programs, family services, and other organizations. The task force candidly reported that "the lack of an organized system for installation-level management of psychological health is paralleled by the lack of a DoD-Wide or Service-level strategic plan for the delivery of services to support psychological health."[25] The report also elucidated a lack of leadership, coordination, and accountability in the military's authority structures and funding streams, varying widely by the branch of service.

In short, the DoD acknowledged that no single organization or leadership structure was responsible or accountable for the provision of military mental healthcare. The lack of a single agency explains why the military consistently ignores the lessons it ostensibly has learned, perpetuating a cycle of preventable wartime behavioral health crises.[26]

ORGANIZING MILITARY HEALTHCARE

In 2013, of the estimated 9.66 million beneficiaries eligible for military medical services, 15.2 percent were active military personnel and 3.7 percent were reserves or National Guard members; in addition, 5.5 million military personnel were enrolled in TRICARE (the healthcare system for service members, retirees, and families).[27] The DoD's capacity to meet the physical and mental health needs of such a large and diverse population, in a variety of challenging environments, requires a straightforward, coherent, and efficient organizational structure with leaders at all levels who are held accountable for complying with policies and practices required to fulfill its healthcare mission. To fix the organizational and leadership deficiencies reported by the DoD TF-MH, it is essential to understand the critical differences in organizational structure between military's physical medicine and mental healthcare. There is no pattern of wartime military medical crises, unlike in mental healthcare. The military will fail to provide adequate mental healthcare by almost exclusively ensuring that physical health is maintained and ignoring mental health.

A civilian physician is appointed as head of the Military Health System with the positional title of assistant secretary of defense for health affairs whose responsibilities include maintaining the readiness of military personnel, providing emergency and long-term casualty care, and ensuring the delivery of healthcare to all service members.[28] The assistant secretary is supported by several deputy secretaries who divide up general oversight of their medical purviews. The essential management of military medicine, however, is the responsibility of a flag officer (a general or admiral) physician, assigned as the surgeon general to each respective service. The surgeon general is supported by flag officers who are accountable for managing their "corps" in carrying out medical policies and its mission.

CORPS

A corps provides professional identity and critical central management for a group of specialists, led by a flag officers who is accountable for tracking,

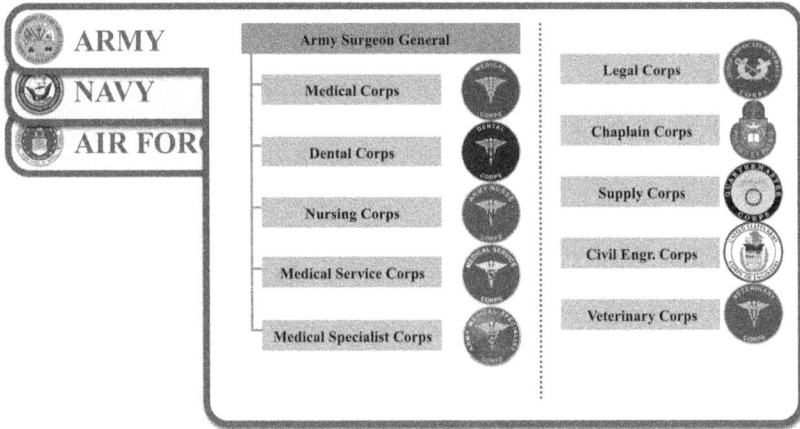

FIGURE 10.1 Existing military corps.

managing, and reporting on its manpower requirements (e.g., recruiting, retention, promotions), training, readiness, assignments, career progression, and implementation of lessons learned. Current military corps include Medical Corps (MC), Nursing Corps (NC), Dental Corps (DC), Legal Corps (JAG), Civil Engineering Corps (CEC), Chaplain Corps (CC), Supply Corps (SC), Medical Service Corps (MSC), and Veterinary Corps (VC) (see figure 10.1). The corps flag officers are supported by midlevel officers assigned as specialty leaders or assistants to the surgeon general who manage a specific discipline of specialists for their service branch (e.g., navy psychiatry specialty leader, army psychiatry specialty leader).

The Military Health System directly manages the physical needs of service members, their families, veterans, and DoD civilians. Each base or installation has a military hospital or military treatment facility or medical clinics. A unified, coherent chain of command is responsible for medical policies and the delivery of physical medicine, dentistry, and nursing. A single, centralized electronic recordkeeping and data-collection system is used across the DoD. These medical policies and practices across the service branches do not significantly vary. Other than outsourcing specific aspects of medical care through the TRICARE network to the private sector, no competing or alternative agencies are accountable for medical care within the DoD.

In contrast, the mental healthcare system is not so centralized. The IOM has reviewed the military mental health system and its vast array of programs and concluded that "PTSD management in DoD appears to be local, ad hoc, incremental, and crisis-driven with little planning devoted to the development of a long range, population-based approach for the disorder."[29] As an illustration of the inherent fragmentation of military mental healthcare, all prevention and resilience-building programs are the responsibility of the under-secretary of defense for manpower and readiness, not the assistant secretary of defense for health affairs, despite the recent creation of the Defense Health Agency to consolidate responsibility for healthcare.[30] This fragmented system inherently provides inadequate care that fails the service members affected.

Three major organizational components are involved in providing mental health services: (1) military medicine (i.e., the Military Health System), (2) family community counseling centers, and (3) other miscellaneous programs (see the text box). Each entity has its own chain of command, personnel, policies, recordkeeping, and data-collection procedures with varying levels of collaboration with other mental health entities. Complicating matters further is that each mental health–related entity within the four military service branches has different policies and practices.[31]

MILITARY MEDICINE AND THE MILITARY HEALTH SYSTEM

Active-duty and civilian psychiatrists, neurologists, psychiatric nurses, clinical psychologists, clinical social workers, and occupational therapists are assigned to inpatient hospitals at military treatment facilities, outpatient mental health clinics, and Wounded Warrior Programs. They also are embedded in combat units as well as operational platforms (e.g., combat and operational stress control units, aircraft carriers). According to the IoM, "Mental health staff in DoD increased from about 4,000 in 2007 to almost 6,500 in 2010," and the numbers of mental health staff have grown ever since.[32] Services include diagnostic evaluations, medication management, prevention activities, outreach, personnel-related functions, and individual and group psychotherapeutic treatments for mental health conditions.[33] Military-related clientele also may seek mental health services from civilian TRICARE network providers.

The organizational chain of command and policies are identical to those already described with regard to medical services, except at the corps level— that is, the military has no Mental Health Corps or Behavioral Health Corps. Instead, neurologists and psychiatrists are assigned to the MC; psychiatric nurses belong to the NC; and clinical psychologists, social workers, and occupational therapists are assigned to the MSC[34].

As an example of the significance of this dispersion of mental health professionals across corps, military officers who are responsible for the bulk of psychotherapy do not get promoted to the flag officer level and receive significantly smaller recruitment and retention bonuses than their medical mental health colleagues.[35] As a result, a senior military position is lacking to oversee military mental healthcare with the level of authority that the crisis demands. Moreover, each service corps varies in policy and practice, so staffing, training, assessment, diagnosis, prevention, and treatment services are not standardized among the same discipline types.[36]

The absence of a formal Behavioral Health Corps greatly affects the military's capacity to meet mental health needs. A clear example is evident in a February 2007 memorandum from the admiral responsible for managing the Navy's Medical Service Corps, announcing the elimination of all navy unformed social workers and occupational therapists. The navy quickly reversed its policy after the release of the June 2007 TF-MH report revealing a chronic, severe mental health staffing crisis within the navy and the DoD. The navy's misguided action is perhaps understandable given the twenty-two specialties lumped together in the Medical Service Corps. Additionally, all officers in these different specialties compete against one another for promotions. By military law, all eligible military officers who fail to promote to the next rank after two years are involuntarily discharged from the military. Therefore, every year, active-duty mental health providers are involuntarily discharged from the military regardless of the clinical competency and productivity, which aggravates staffing crises.[37] Moreover, military psychotherapists (clinical psychologists and social workers) cannot advance to the flag and general staff levels, relegating pre-war planning of psychotherapy provisions to a lower-ranked priority.[38] In short, the absence of a Behavioral Health Corps helps explain the 2007 DoD TF-MH finding that current military mental health staff are understaffed and lack the necessary resources to adequately treat those they serve.[39]

FAMILY AND COMMUNITY COUNSELING CENTERS

According to the IOM, "Family and community services play a critical role in supporting the psychological health of service members and their families."[40]

Although each branch of the military offers a slightly different mix of programs and services, they generally fall under four broad areas: (1) family support, (2) child and youth services, (3) counseling and advocacy support, and (4) morale, welfare, and recreation (see the text box).

Each of these four service branches employs thousands of civilian mental health professionals, including psychiatrist, psychologists, social workers, marriage and family counselors, and substance abuse counselors at centers funded and managed by the military service branch, independent of military medicine. For example, the Navy Fleet and Family Counseling Centers are accountable to regular navy fleet or line commanders, not to navy medicine or the navy surgeon general.[41] Additionally, each one of these centers—located at every military base—has separate headquarters, policics, budgcts, trainings, organizational chains of command, staff management requirements, recordkeeping systems, and databases. The base commander, not the base medical commander, is responsible for the military's community counseling centers, limiting the authority of the medical commander. Further complicating the situation, is that each service branches' community counseling center varies in its policies, programs, and data management from the other services, and the degree or coordination with other mental health organizations widely varies at each military base.[42]

COMPARISON OF MILITARY MENTAL HEALTH ORGANIZATIONAL STRUCTURE AND ACCOUNTABILITY

Current Organizations Providing Mental Health

MILITARY MEDICINE—SURGEON GENERAL

- Medical Corps
  - Neurology
  - Psychiatry
- Nursing Corps
  - Psychiatric Nursing
- Medical Service Corps (Medical Support Corps–Army)
  - Clinical Psychology
  - Social Work
  - Occupational Therapy
  - Physical Therapy

(Continued)

COMMUNITY COUNSELING SERVICES

- Marriage and Family Counseling
- Substance Abuse Counseling
- Vocational Counseling
- Others

MILITARY CIVILIAN CONTRACTORS

- Educational and Developmental Intervention Services
- Military Life Consultants
- Others

Integrated Behavioral Health Corps

BEHAVIORAL HEALTH CORPS—BH GENERAL

- Therapeutic Management and Reconditioning
- Prevention, Education, and Training
- Center for Behavioral Health Research and Lessons Learned
- Transition and Social Reintegration
- Operational
  - Neurology
  - Psychiatry
  - Psychiatric Nursing
  - Clinical Psychology
  - Social Work
  - Occupational Therapy
  - Physical Therapy
- Community Counseling Services
  - Marriage and Family Counseling
  - Substance Abuse Counseling
  - Vocational Counseling
  - Others
- Military Civilian Contractors
  - Educational and Developmental Intervention Services
  - Military Life Consultants
  - Others

OTHER MENTAL HEALTH ENTITIES

Outside of military medicine and the Military Health System and family community counseling center organizations, each service branch contracts for an array of mental health-related agencies, programs, and practitioners.

Some of these contractors include the Military and Family Life Consultants program, chaplains, suicide hotlines, web-based programs like the Real Warriors Campaign and Military OneSource, civilian mental health offered through the Educational and Developmental Intervention Services, and the TRICARE network that consists of more than three thousand hospitals and nearly one thousand behavioral health facilities.[43] Further complicating matters, a National Council for Community Behavioral Healthcare study reported 23 percent of veterans and active military currently are seeking mental healthcare in the private sector—that percentage had increased to 40 percent by 2014.[44] No single organization or leadership structure monitors and manages these diverse programs, each of which has a disparate database.[45]

Let us now look at an example of how these fragmentations contribute to behavioral health crises. On November 5, 2013, leaders of Navy Medicine and the Navy and Marine Corps Community Counseling Centers reissued a memorandum of understanding (MOU) reinforcing a long-standing agreement of how the agencies collaborate and coordinate mental health services. According to the Department of the Navy MOU, licensed civilian Navy and Marine Corps mental health staff are prohibited from assessing, diagnosing, or treating service members seeking help for potentially disabling conditions, such as depression, anxiety, eating disorders, PTSD, suicide, or other major mental health problems. Instead, all such military clients and their family members must be referred to mental health providers at military treatment facilities. In one case, a sole credentialed military mental health provider stationed at a rural overseas marine corps base of roughly six thousand personnel reported that, per navy and marine corps instruction, the cadre of licensed civilian mental health staff employed at the Marine Corps Community Counseling Services center were forced to refer marines experiencing PTSD, depression, or suicide symptoms to a military treatment facility with a month-long waiting list.[46] In the midst of a mental health crisis and severe staffing shortages, institutional policies reinforcing organizational fragmentation exacerbate the crisis. Moreover, family community counseling centers operated by the army and air force do not place such restrictions on the scope of practice for their clinical specialists, exemplifying an incoherent policy.[47]

Workload data from community counseling centers and other mental health entities are kept separate from military medicine's records. Therefore, this information is invisible in DoD prevalence statistics, resulting in the gross underestimations of mental health needs.[48]

DEPARTMENT OF DEFENSE RESPONSE TO TASK FORCE AND OTHER RECOMMENDATIONS

The 2007, DoD TF-MH identified four goals in its vision to transform military mental healthcare into a "world-class health system involved in supporting the psychological health of military members and their families," as follows:

1. A culture of support for psychological health wherein all service members and leaders will be educated to understand that psychological health is essential to overall health and performance, will be fostered. Early and non-stigmatizing psychological health assessments and referral to services will be routine and expected.

2. Service members and their families will be fully and psychologically prepared to carry out their missions. Service members and their families will receive a full continuum of excellent care in both peacetime and wartime, particularly when service members have been injured or wounded in the course of duty.

3. Sufficient and appropriate resources will be allocated to prevention, early intervention, and treatment in both the Direct Care and TRICARE Network systems, and will be distributed according to need.

4. At all levels, visible and empowered leaders will advocate, monitor, plan, coordinate, and integrate prevention, early intervention, and treatment.[49]

Subsequently, both the office of assistant secretary of defense for health affairs and each branch of the military have issued policy directives and instructions related to improving prevention, assessment, treatment, and management of PTSD.[50]

To transform monumental organizational and leadership deficits, the military established new directors of psychological health at the service headquarters and installation levels to "ensure visible leadership and advocacy for psychological mental health services." Those directors are responsible for assisting with strategic planning on psychological health and TBI; monitoring and reporting on the availability, accessibility, and quality of mental health services; monitoring the psychological health of service members and their families; and ensuring communication with the departments responsible for the provision of mental healthcare at relevant installations and military treatment facilities.[51] The military also formed a DoD-wide oversight committee—the DoD Psychological Health Council—including active duty, National Guard, and reserve directors and multiple high-level leaders. This committee's mission is to develop a vision and strategic plan to support the psychological health of service members and their families, provide policy and guidance, and develop standardized indicators for tracking and reporting outcomes.[52]

DoD Instruction 6490.09 "establishes policy, assigns responsibilities, and prescribes procedures to ensure visible leadership and advocacy for the psychological health and mental health disease and injury protection of the military service members" by designating specific roles of the DoD TF-MH recommended DPH positions and DoD Psychological Health Council.

By 2011, each service branch, the reserves, and the National Guard had established service-level directors. The new directors report directly to the surgeon general and medical officer of the marine corps, or equivalent, but they lack the authority to develop or enforce policies. It is unclear how the directors as consultants to the surgeon general differ from existing mental health specialty leaders assigned to advise the surgeon general, or how adding another midlevel advisor significantly enhances "visible leadership and advocacy for psychological health" in a transformative manner to accomplish the DoD's vision and goals.[53]

Per DoD instruction, these directors are assigned to each military base to consult with the installation commander, make recommendations on staffing and their ability to meet mental health needs, and ensure the coordination of services among the various programs providing support for psychological health. Despite appearances, the DoD's policy does not create a unified, single chain of command; establish standardized policies, procedures, or a centralized database; or grant installation directors the authority to enforce policies.[54] These installation and service branch directors have limited authority to realistically effect necessary changes in military mental healthcare.

As of 2019, nearly eighteen years after the invasion of Afghanistan and twelve years past the DoD's promised vision for reforming its mental health services, organizational and leadership fragmentation and dysfunction remain have remained as strong today as ever. There still is no centralized leadership structure accountable for ensuring proper access to the highest quality of mental health services possible. Since 2001, a total of 214 independent investigations have been conducted looking into the military's management of mental healthcare—all of which screams for congressional action. How can this be? What is the payoff for the military and the U.S. government for maintaining its fragmented and dysfunctional leadership structure?

THE MILITARY BYSTANDER EFFECT

One plausible rationale for maintaining the status quo can be drawn from a social psychology phenomenon known as the "bystander effect."[55] Briefly, the bystander effect arises when the presence of others discourages an individual from intervening in an emergency situation. The concept was sensationalized after the infamous 1964 Kitty Genovese murder in New York City, when Genovese was repeatedly and fatally stabbed outside her apartment despite screaming for help and multiple bystanders who saw the brutal assault but chose to not assist or call the police. Darley and Latané attributed the effect to the perceived diffusion of responsibility (e.g., onlookers are more likely to intervene if there are few or no other witnesses) and social influence (individuals in a group monitor the behavior of those around them to determine how to act). In Genovese's case, each onlooker concluded from their neighbors' inaction that their own personal help was not needed. Per Darley and Latané, the degree of responsibility a bystander may experience is dependent on three factors: (1) whether or not they feel the person is deserving of help, (2) the competence of the bystander to help, and (3) the relationship between the bystander and the victim.

Building on Darley and Latané's assertions, the three factors responsible for a bystander effect also can be found in relation to the military's inertia.[56] First is the question of whether or not the military believes that mentally ill or war-stressed personnel deserve help. If that were true, ample evidence should reveal the military's commitment to learn its war trauma lessons at the same level as battlefield medicine and war tactics, such as ensuring ready access to high-quality treatment and zero tolerance policy for stigma. We have not seen or discussed anything that suggests the upper echelon of military leaders as a group feels that mentally injured service members deserve to be helped. In regard to military leader competency to help, a surgeon general would have the authority to make changes only within their service branches' medical departments; thus, only civilian medical leaders at the DoD level could exercise authority across the different branches. Even the assistant secretary of defense for health affairs, however, does not have influence over mental health agencies outside military medicine's jurisdiction (e.g., community counseling centers, contractors).[57] Therefore, the absence of a centralized, integrated, and accountable leadership structure ensures that few military leaders will feel competent to fix military mental healthcare. Last, in terms of the relationship between top military officials and those suffering war-stress injury, it seems highly unlikely that senior war planners would have personal relationships with enlisted members and junior officers who do most of the warfighting. In sum, the status quo fulfills all three factors necessary to create a bystander effect.

Astute observers of human behavior, like B. F. Skinner, have long recognized that people engage in specific behavior when it serves them to either obtain something desirable or avoid something undesirable. That said, what is the evidence of a benefit for the military to maintain the conditions that foster the military bystander effect toward mental health? The service surgeons general are appointed as leaders for their respective medical departments and are held accountable for medical failures. For instance, when the Walter Reed Hospital scandal broke in 2006 depicting horrid treatment conditions for medically wounded soldiers, a number of military medical leaders, including the army surgeon general, were promptly fired.[58] No diffusion of responsibility or the bystander effect could save the army surgeon general.

In stark contrast, when the DoD TF-MH revealed the mental health crisis caused primarily by rampant organizational and leadership failure, certainly someone would be held accountable.[59] Military medicine's belated admission of a mental health crisis, however, actively concealed that it did not result in customary firings or congressional factfinding investigations.[60] Indeed, the task force chairs—the army and navy surgeons general—were congratulated, not rebuked, by Congress.[61]

Moreover, not even the recent publication of condemnable findings from multiple independent commissioned has have proven sufficient to spur any punitive actions for military officials or congressional investigations over the military's repeated failure.[62] Notably:

> Through its review, the committee found that PTSD management in DoD appear to be local, ad hoc, incremental, and crisis-driven with little planning devoted to the development of a long-range, population-based approach for this disorder by either the office of the Assistant Secretary of Defense for Health Affairs (OASD(HA)) or any of the service branches.[63]

The only plausible explanation for the inexplicable lack of vaunted military discipline and accountability is the effectiveness of the dysfunctional organizational status quo to avoid pursuing an alternative response to its mental health dilemma. Simply put, how can any military leader be held accountable for mental health problems when the IOM findings indict the entire system?[64]

Further evidence of the military's diffusion strategy and its effectiveness in avoiding implementation of war trauma lessons such as the need to eliminate stigma is provided by the GAO:

> Finally, GAO found that responsibilities for mental health care stigma reduction are dispersed among various organizations within DOD and the services, and some information sharing is hampered.
>
> No single entity is coordinating department-wide efforts to reduce stigma.
>
> Without a clear definition for "mental healthcare stigma" with goals and measures, along with a coordinating entity to oversee program and policy efforts and data collection and analysis, DOD does not have assurance that its efforts are effective and that resources are most efficiently allocated.[65]

WHY DOES THE MILITARY GO TO ALL THIS TROUBLE?

From all we have read and sorted through, we think the payoff for the military to maintain the current dysfunctional organizational and unaccountable leadership structure is that it works brilliantly. The trick is to diffuse responsibility and freely permit military leaders to act (or not act) with impunity when it comes to mental health. This might seem terribly shortsighted, but there is a discernible logic. If the DoD adopted the recommendation of establishing a Behavioral Health Corps with an accountable chain of command led by flag or general officers similar to existing corps services, then the military would need to divert resources, personnel, and finances toward mental health and away from weapon development and procurement and other valued expenditures.[66]

On the face of it, a Behavioral Health Corps makes practical sense given the enormity of the problems and costs associated with psychiatric casualties and attrition as well as the negative public attention given to the military's mental health problem.

The new accountability from a Behavioral Health Corps would mean high-ranking officers could be publicly prosecuted or fired for dereliction should the military repeat its neglect of war trauma lessons and inadequately plan, prepare for, and deliver needed mental health services. Such a public spectacle would invariably result in dragging the military establishment and its ambivalent bias toward mental health into the open. Indeed, the status quo provides ample diffusion of responsibility with little chance that upper echelon leaders will be held accountable. Removing the bystander effect would be disastrous for high-ranking officers. In truth, however, it is possible that fully committing to learning its war trauma lessons and establishing a Behavioral Health Corps with accountable leadership may in fact result in significant cost savings and improved military readiness.[67]

11

INADEQUATE, EXPERIMENTAL, OR HARMFUL TREATMENT

THE NINTH DARK-SIDE STRATEGY

After World War I (WWI), Sir Andrew MacPhail posited a seminal reason for the military's steadfast avoidance of providing psychiatric treatment despite acknowledging the necessity for early intervention to prevent chronic problems—specific treatment facilities foster hysteria around certain diseases.[1] A few years later, Major Thomas Salmon would similarly insist on the critical need for treatment provision before discharging veterans as a vital foundational war trauma lesson.[2] Moreover, the current official policy reflects these concepts: "Once mental disorder symptoms emerge, the most effective strategy for ensuring recovery lies in prompt application of evidence-based treatments."[3]

Despite a clear and consistent consensus on solutions to treat these mental illness symptoms, the military fails to follow through in the various sectors that control mental health quality and quantity. Despite the mental health leaders and policy makers present in the system, not enough people are trained to treat service members and their families. As a result, many people who need and want mental health treatment will not receive it on active duty or will receive grossly substandard or harmful care.[4]

The primary concern is the military's deep-seated fear that permitting access to mental health treatment will only encourage its development, (e.g., hysteria epidemics). From the military's perspective, the least desirable outcome of providing service members—those fighting the wars—access to well-staffed mental health treatment facilities would be an increase in catastrophic evacuation syndromes. Herein lies the genesis for the military's ninth strategy to manage a growing mental health dilemma by avoiding learning its war trauma lessons.

Most veterans have received grossly inadequate, harmful, or no mental health treatment throughout different eras—either in active duty or after it.[5] Aside from emergent or stabilizing medical interventions, the military traditionally has been reluctant, if not averse, toward treating traumatized personnel opting instead to defer that responsibility to the Department of Veterans Affairs (VA) or the private sector.[6]

The notable exception to the military's aversion toward treatment is its heralded frontline psychiatry or combat operational stress control programs.[7] Although some inaccurately refer to frontline psychiatry as a treatment, the military officially acknowledges that the primary purpose of these brief interventions is to preserve the fighting force by avoiding psychiatric evacuations; thus, it is not psychotherapy.

AVOIDING TREATMENT

The most straightforward proof of the military's deliberate avoidance of providing treatment is its explicit policies prohibiting or severely restricting treatment access. One such policy states that "individuals permanently unfit for Army service because of neuropsychiatric disturbances will not be retained for definitive treatment, but will be discharged and arrangements will be made for further care by the Veterans Administration if such is indicated."[8] The navy and marine corps has admitted its propensity to avoid treatment. In 2010, the navy acquiesced that treatment for injuries and illnesses in mental healthcare "have historically been shunned for stress-related problems occurring in operational settings for fear of drawing attention to them and fostering epidemics of stress casualties."[9]

In addition to these contemporary admissions, reports throughout different eras also have demonstrated systemic poor treatment or avoidance of treatment.[10] Although some service members may receive effective treatment, an organizational commitment to learn this critical war lesson is lacking. In WWI, Salmon reported that

> such patients could not be cared for in the individual American base hospitals scattered throughout France, partly because of the lack in some of them of medical officers, nurses, or enlisted personnel who had had experience in the actual care and treatment of patients suffering from acute mental disorders, but chiefly because of the absence of any special facilities for treatment.[11]

In World War II (WWII), Brill wrote that "from the beginning, there was a shortage of trained psychiatrists, neurologists, psychiatric nurses, attendants, aides, social workers, psychologists, occupational therapists, and recreational therapists."[12] Glass would report even more damningly that "facilities for the care and treatment of psychiatric cases were only barely sufficient for the small peacetime Army."[13]

Then, in the Vietnam War, the comparison between the efforts of the day and the historical lessons that were well known was explicitly called to attention as a failing of the military: "Particularly following WWI and WWII great gains were made in diagnosing and treating stress reactions. Sad to say, many of these lessons were forgotten and had to be relearned with Vietnam veterans."[14]

After WWII, the military took great pains to document the lessons it learned regarding mental health treatment provision; those lessons did not emerge until late in the war after President Roosevelt issued his 1944 executive order to the war department secretary (see chapter 10). The army's multidisciplinary reconditioning program was established on August 30, 1944, by *War Department Technical Bulletin* 80 and applied to "any patient who has even a remote chance for salvage for additional military service."[15] Similar to the War Department's 1863 General Order 212 establishing the Invalid Corps (a precursor of today's wounded warrior retention policy), the WWII-era program emphasized the philosophy of psychiatric reconditioning that followed several basic principles:

1. Regard every case as salvageable
2. Start treatment as early as possible,
3. Avoid the hospitalization of psychoneurotics,
4. Remove situational factors if possible and
5. An individual or group approach as indicated.[16]

MEMORANDUM FOR: THE ASSISTANT CHIEF OF STAFF, G-1

10 NOVEMBER 1944

Through: The Commanding General, Army Service Forces.

Subject: Psychoneuroses.

Treatment. The present policy provides for the treatment of all individuals with psychoneurosis. This is in contrast to previous policy which provided for the disposition of cases without benefit of treatment. In spite of this change in policy, however, the emphasis which can be placed on treatment depends upon the current policy regarding disposition and utilization of individuals with psychoneurosis.

(Continued)

a. Policy.

TREATMENT POLICY INCLUDES THE FOLLOWING POINTS:

(1) All cases of psychoneurosis will be treated. Those individuals to be discharged, however, will not be retained merely to receive maximum benefit of treatment except in the cases where the psychoneurosis has been incurred in combat.

(2) Each case will be regarded as a medical emergency requiring prompt treatment.

(3) Cases will be regarded as sick men needing medical treatment rather than disciplinary cases needing punishment or threats.

(4) Military discipline will be maintained.

(5) Treatment will be by or under the supervision of psychiatrists. Other personnel will be utilized including line officers, other medical officers, clinical psychologists, Red Cross, etc.

(6) Treatment facilities will be centralized in order to control policy and procedures and to compensate for the existing shortage of trained personnel.

(7) Patients will be segregated from nonpsychiatric cases in most instances.

(8) The majority of cases will be kept out of hospitals for treatment.

(9) Patients will be given a full-time program including training, education, orientation, physical reconditioning and occupational therapy.

(10) Full use will be made of accepted medical treatment methods including drugs, individual and group psychotherapy and adjuvant therapy.

(11) Every effort will be made to supply an incentive for recovery.

b. Procedures.

(1) Treatment in combat zones is conducted at battalion aid stations; division clearing stations; designated clearing companies known as "exhaustion centers" and evacuation hospitals at Army level.

(2) Treatment in base areas is conducted in dispensaries; training center mental hygiene clinics; hospital outpatient departments; station and general hospitals; neuropsychiatric centers; and the reconditioning programs at convalescent centers.

c. Results.

(1) Combat cases: 40 to 60 percent return to full combat duty, 80 to 90 percent to duty of some sort.

(2) Base area cases: Approximately 50 percent return to full or limited duty.

SOURCE: E. F. QUINN, "RECONDITIONING OF PSYCHIATRIC PATIENTS," IN *ZONE OF INTERIOR*, VOL. I OF *MEDICAL DEPARTMENT UNITED STATES ARMY, NEUROPSYCHIATRY IN WORLD WAR II*, ED. R. S. ANDERSON, A. J. GLASS, AND R. J. BERNUCCI (WASHINGTON DC: OFFICE OF THE SURGEON GENERAL, DEPARTMENT OF THE ARMY, 1966), 816.

In the wake of the initiation of the Afghanistan and Iraq Wars, no military treatment policies were in effect. In fact, it was not until 2012 that the army published policy guidance on mental health treatment. Unlike previous generations of military medical leadership, this generation had access to the proliferation of evidence-based therapies (EBTs) shown to provide effective treatment. In 2004, the VA published its first clinical practice guidelines for PTSD with expert consensus that clinicians be trained in one of four top trauma-focused EPTs (i.e., exposure therapy, stress inoculation, cognitive therapy, and eye movement desensitization and reprocessing [EMDR]).

A military psychologist surveyed more than one hundred uniformed mental health clinicians, however, and found that "90 percent of the providers indicated they had received no training or supervision in clinical practice guidelines for PTSD."[17] The training survey deficits resulted in a joint Department of Defense (DoD)/VA PTSD training program to bring in national trainers to provide more than 260 military therapists supervised clinical training on EMDR (one of the EBTs for PTSD) at no cost.[18] An analysis of archival chart reviews from nonrandomized completed treatments revealed significant changes in pre- and post-PTSD and depression symptoms after an average of four sessions in a group of forty-eight service members diagnosed with combat-PTSD.[19] These findings were repeatedly forwarded up the chain of command to surgeon generals from 2004 to 2007 to increase compliance with the DoD's own clinical training and treatment guidance,[20] but military leaders resisted.[21]

Despite this ostensible progress, multiple reports, including the 2007 Task Force on Mental Health[22] and the 2014 Institute of Medicine (IOM) reports, found that the military still failed to provide adequate resources, staffing, and treatments to its service members. With regard to PTSD, the IOM found that service members received no treatment.[23] The DoD's treatment provision continued to be insufficient and the DoD failed to learn any treatment lessons. Ultimately, the independent investigators concluded that

> the majority of SMs (service-members) with PTSD do not receive treatment for this condition. . . . In conjunction with the DVA, DOD has developed comprehensive evidence-based CPGs for assessment and treatment of key psychological disorders, including PTSD, depression, substance abuse and psychosis. These guidelines are not consistently implemented across the DOD and the Task Force was unable to find any mechanism that ensures

their widespread use. Furthermore, providers who were interested in utilizing evidence-based approaches complained during site visits that they did not have the time to implement them.[24]

After the DoD Task Force on Mental Health released its findings, the military instituted a variety of clinical training and treatment programs, including the DoD Centers for Excellence,[25]and the army issued its first treatment policy directive in the DoD in sixty-eight years. Despite these announcements and proclamations, another study two years after the 2014 IOM report found that issues persisted. RAND researchers defined "minimally adequate level of care" for patients entering a new treatment episode as receiving four psychotherapy visits or two evaluation and management visits within the initial eight weeks after being diagnosed. Even though most EBTs required ten or twelve sessions, researchers found that out of nearly fifteen thousand military patients diagnosed with PTSD, only 34 percent received the minimum of four sessions and only 24 percent of more than thirty thousand military patients diagnosed with depression received four sessions within eight weeks of being diagnosed.[26] RAND researchers concluded that, despite the significant risk that the sizeable number of cases of depression and PTSD posed to force readiness, little data were available about the care given, if any was given at all.[27] These findings strongly indicate that veterans with war-stress injuries and their families continue to face significant barriers to receive timely and appropriate mental healthcare. The delay of this treatment has been shown repeatedly to be harmful to the health and well-being of those involved.

The military avoids taking responsibility for mental health treatments for many reasons, including the following: (2) a staunch belief that war-stress injuries are primarily caused by personal weakness and predispositions and not military service;[28] (2) a general devaluation of mental health and its treatments; (3) a belief that most war-stress injuries are untreatable, so the injured must be discharged; (4) a fear that treatment referrals will increase evacuation syndromes;[29] (5) a fear that treatment is too costly and will divert funding away from other military expenditures;[30] (6) a desire to maintain cost efficiency—because few service members need treatment, they should be discharged instead;[31]; (7) concerns over warehousing large numbers of psychiatrically damaged personnel unfit to deploy;[32] and (8) a belief that the military is responsible only for brief interventions, whereas the VA is responsible for long-term treatment.[33]

EXPOSURE TO EXPERIMENTAL OR HARMFUL TREATMENTS

Service members have always been subject to the medical knowledge and technology of the day that would appear unethical by contemporary conventions (e.g., WWI-era electric shock), and they also have been historically susceptible to compulsory and experimental treatments, some of which have been proven to be harmful. Salmon famously said that war provides "medical scientists with thousands of natural experiments of the sort that they would rarely encounter in peacetime or more likely, would ordinarily encounter only in experimentation involving animals."[34]

Historian Eric J. Leed divided early military psychiatric treatments (e.g., persuasion therapy and aversion therapy) into two broad categories: (1) disciplinary approaches emphasizing aversion therapy, using practices like electric shock, seclusion, and dietary restriction to persuade the service members to prefer the frontlines to the hospital; and analytic or psychological approaches, emphasizing ventilation, uncovering, and abreaction of traumatic or emotionally laden experiences (e.g., hypnosis, narcosynthesis, brief psychodynamic therapy).

A third category of treatments can be described as somatic-based treatments; these focused on correcting neurophysiological imbalances in the brain (e.g., drug therapy, insulin-coma therapy). Military patients could receive any one or a combination of these approaches throughout the course of their treatment. The availability of treatment methods reflects how the medical officers conceive of war neuroses, a concept as true for Salmon as it is today.[35] These treatments have varied throughout the military's history. Today, the DoD still refuses to establish standardized mental healthcare services despite recommendations for such uniformed care since WWI.[36]

Electrotherapy was prominent in the military until the Vietnam War.[37] Although induced electrical currents had been used to treat hysteria in the private sector before WWI, the building frustration of military doctors overwhelmed with psychiatric casualties led some clinicians to use increasingly harsh and perhaps torturous methods rationalized by a "tough love" mentality to salvage the dignity of shell-shocked soldiers. Other disciplinary treatments included hydrotherapy—described as "a cold douche, either as a shower or an unbroken jet of water to obtain the crisis"[38]—seclusion, and barbiturate-induced sedation (two or three days or longer), called narcosis. For instance, one study reported twenty cases of war neuroses treated with continuous narcosis induced by sodium amytal and supplemented by paraldehyde and sodium phenobarbital. Despite sleeping from twenty-seven to more than one hundred hours, only three of twenty patients showed improvement.[39] Moreover, the study noted that "some patients were made worse by the treatment," were "loath to awaken," and experienced prolonged periods of delirium and "days of nightmare-like horror alternating with periods of relief."[40] Fortunately, the military stopped the use of disciplinary treatments after Vietnam War.

Psychodynamic approaches emphasizing abreaction (the expression and release of a previously repressed emotion through reliving the experience that caused it) have been commonplace since WWI. The psychodynamic approach dominated therapeutic practice in the United States, including in the VA. Many contemporary talk therapies, including trauma-focused EBTs for PTSD—like prolonged exposure, EMDR, and cognitive processing therapy—adopt a multistage approach that has been common since WWI.[41] Individual psychotherapy was standard until WWII when group therapy modalities were adopted because of acute staffing shortages, large treatment demand, and emerging evidence of curative social factors.[42] To expedite treatment, military clinicians often relied on hypnosis as an adjunctive technique to talk therapy, a temporarily effective practice that ran its course until the Vietnam War. Similarly, narcosynthesis—the use of powerful sedatives like sodium pentothal to induce hypnotic states—was widely employed through WWII and faded away after the Vietnam War,[43] apparently because of its time intensiveness and questionable durability of treatment gains once patients were returned to duty.

Massages, baths, and fever-induced treatment or pyrotherapies like malaria therapy represent a few somatic approaches used in WWI that often were either ineffective or potentially harmful. During WWII and the Korean War, insulin-coma therapy—the administration of small doses of insulin to induce hypoglycemia—reportedly improved appetite and weight gain.[44] A modified insulin-coma therapy was invented by U.S. Army psychiatrist Sargant, who reported rapid improvement of anxiety and depression symptoms in twenty-eight soldiers with war neuroses after inducing prolonged hypoglycemic coma, despite the risk of permanent coma and death. Even military observers like the American Psychiatric Association openly questioned the medical ethics of the practice:

> It is difficult to explain why doctors would adopt a risky treatment usually reserved for cases of schizophrenia to encourage weight gain in service

men suffering from post-combat disorders. Reflecting the absence of safe and reliable methods, this intervention was driven by a determination to do something.[45]

Experimentation with drugs also has been a frequent practice in the military's treatment of war-stress injuries. For example, sixteen WWII-era soldiers were given ergotamine tartrate to block sympathetic over-reactivity (e.g., exaggerated startle response), despite the knowledge that it could "damage the vascular endothelium, producing vascular stasis, thrombosis (blood clots), and gangrene."[46] The study found that thirteen soldiers developed toxic symptoms, three had phlebitis, and two experienced blood clots; only two patients exhibited improvement in tremors. The army also experimented with hyoscine hydrobromide, which had been used to treat tremors and extrapyramidal symptoms; however, the drug gave soldiers "a very high percentage of toxic reactions consisting mainly of vertigo, fatigue, lethargy, and nausea."[47] In the Korean and Vietnam Wars, military "experimental psychotherapists" injected more than seven hundred soldiers with lysergic acid diethylamide regardless of whether they had been diagnosed with a war-stress injury.

Narcotics also have a history of being overprescribed to service members. During the Civil War, the unlimited and unmonitored prescription of morphine, heroine, and cocaine to treat physical wounds and medically unexplained pain symptoms like functional rheumatism was widespread, leading to drug addiction in thousands of war veterans. This practice of narcotic over-prescription continues to this day. There are anecdotal accounts of similar iatrogenic effects in WWI. In the twenty-first century, however, reports of rampant intentional over-prescription of opioids within the VA for treating psychological problems, such as PTSD, appears to be in violation of the medical ethics of "physician do no harm."

On October 10, 2013, the House Committee on Veterans' Affairs heard testimony from VA physicians that narcotic prescriptions, especially opiates, are "renewed month after month, sometimes up to two years without examination," explaining that, "the problem is endemic in the VA because quick and cheap is rewarded over good and thorough."[48] According to the testimony, the worst part of this practice is the apparent knowledge of the practice without regard for the consequences. A VA physician working in a pain management clinic testified, "I was ordered by superiors to write large amounts of schedule two narcotics inappropriately. . . . I pointed out 10–20 percent of opioid users become addicted . . . we were creating addicts . . . all of this fell on deaf ears, copious, large amounts of opioids inappropriately prescribed for PTSD." The VA physician concluded, "I do not understand how any medical institution in good conscience can perpetuate a therapy that's harmful to the people they are supposed to serve."[49] Similarly disturbing, over-prescription of opiates and pain killer medications has been rampant in military populations, raising concerns by conscientious VA doctors of unethical practices of knowingly causing harm by nurturing drug addiction.

Perhaps one of the more disturbing practices was the use of psychosurgery. During WWII, American service members deemed as treatment resistant or having an "obsessional neurosis" were sometimes recommended for prefrontal leucotomy—which resulted in favorable outcomes in 80 percent of cases.[50] Moreover, the VA's first major clinical trial for treating war-stress injury involved prefrontal lobotomies of WWII and Korean War veterans—from 1949 to 1959, fifteen hundred veterans received lobotomies. In one of the largest clinical trials conducted on lobotomies in the world, three hundred veterans were compared with two hundred controls; no significant differences were revealed—in fact the control group improved without the surgery.[51]

The explicit mission of the military's one-hundred-year-old frontline psychiatry doctrine is to ensure that upward of 95 percent of service members diagnosed with war-stress injuries or psychiatric disorders are kept in war zones until they are grossly incapacitated or pose imminent safety risks to themselves or others.[52] These programs, which are referred to as forward/combat/war psychiatry, combat stress control (CSC), or combat and operational stress control, originated in WWI as the military's primary weapon against evacuation syndromes and financial ruin from skyrocketing pension costs.[53] The military's sustained emphasis on its return-to-duty rate is based on claims that soldiers who receive psychiatric treatment and are evacuated from war zones experience significantly worse long-term health and social outcomes—including PTSD—than those who are returned to duty.[54]

U.S. GOVERNMENT STUDIES ON DOSAGE EFFECT FROM COMBAT STRESS

The military has known about the link between exposure to war stress and psychological injury for some time. Beebe and Appel conducted the first known U.S. government–sponsored study on the psychological tolerance to combat exposure to answer the research question: "How long will men last without breaking down psychologically?"[55] The National Academy of Science (NAS) researchers followed 3,500 U.S. Army infantry personnel from WWII units who fought in the European Theater of Operations (ETO; n = 1,000 and n = 500 replacement personnel) or Mediterranean Theater of Operations (MTO; n = 2,000 original personnel). According to NAS researchers, "The breaking point of the average man is reached after about 85 company days (one company day equals 7.8 calendar days for MTO and 3.6 calendar days for ETO)." Evidence of the cumulative effects of war-stress exposure are apparent in that "the chance of psychiatric breakdown per unit of stress is an increasing function of time; that is, the probability of breakdown in any week will give way to an even higher probability in succeeding weeks," and that during WWII, surveys showed that fear of battle increased with length of combat and that peak combat efficiency was reached in the interval of four to five calendar months for riflemen in infantry companies.[56]

Specifically, the author's algorithm revealed the following: "In all three samples attrition proceeded at a fast, fairly even rate such that half of the men had disappeared from their units by company day 18, 75 percent by day 34, and 83 to 92 percent by day 50."[57] The authors conceded, however, that "We must not forget . . . the fact that only 15.2 percent of the MTO originals actually broke down: other forms of attrition intervened too rapidly for psychiatric attrition to occupy a major role."[58]

Consequently, the government researchers noted that "men who left combat for non-psychiatric reasons would, had they remained, have become psychiatric casualties at the same rate as men with longer exposure."[59] In conclusion, Beebe and Appel reported:

> Our principal finding is that the breaking point of the average rifleman seems to have been reached at about 88 days of company combat (days in which a company casualty occurred). This estimate provides a measure of the average psychologic strength and endurance of human beings in the combat environments of World War II.[60]

They added: "It would appear that we are all more vulnerable than we may have wanted to admit."[61]

Similarly, after analyzing a host of pre-military (e.g., childhood trauma), military (e.g., combat), and post-military (e.g., level of social support) factors previously reported to be etiological factors in combat-PTSD, the authors of the National Vietnam Veterans Readjustment Study (NVVRS) concluded the following: "It is clear that exposure to war zone stress makes a substantial contribution to the development of PTSD in war veterans that is independent of a broad range of potential predisposing factors."[62] Moreover, an independent and scientifically more rigorous analysis of the NVVRS data was undertaken to address methodological limitations, including a substantially more thorough assessment of the etiologic role of combat exposure.[63]

Results of the reanalysis revealed that three measures of war-stress exposure (i.e., combat exposure, vulnerability, and personal involvement in harming civilians or prisoners) when combined reached 97 percent sufficiency for new onset Post-Traumatic Symptom Scale. According to Dohrenwend et al. the statistically significant results revealed "a clear dose-response relationship between the combat stress exposure severity scale and the risk of both PSS onset and current PSS."[64]

CONTEMPORARY REVIEWS OF SCIENTIFIC LITERATURE ON WAR-STRESS IMPACT ON HEALTH

After the Persian Gulf War, several large national scientific reviews were conducted on the long-term health effects of war-stress exposure.[65] According to the Institute of Medicine, "Although they generally dissipate over time, it is not uncommon for symptoms of psychological or bodily distress to persist for years."[66] Importantly, the IOM also attempted to answer why people deployed to a war zone may report more symptoms than people who are not deployed, regardless of whether they actually saw combat. The report found that the stress response stems from physiological changes, particularly in the brain, that affect multiple organ systems, resulting in greater physical and emotional symptoms: "The continuation of altered physiologic states over months and years can contribute to the accumulation of a chronic stress burden that has adverse long-term health consequences."[67] The report also found that memory and decision-making are dramatically affected, exacerbating individuals' symptoms of fear and anxiety and increasing the risk of substance use disorders.[68]

Additionally, the IOM cited empirical evidence linking excessive war-stress exposure and acute and long-term pathogenic changes in the endocrine system, affecting obesity rates, insulin resistance, and glucose intolerance; the immune and inflammatory response systems, affecting autoimmune and age-related diseases; the cardiovascular system, contributing to hypertension, atherosclerosis, and coronary heart disease; and the gastrointestinal system and brain-gut axis, leading to dyspepsia and irritable bowel syndrome. These findings resemble somatic symptoms historically referred to as "psychoso-matic illness," medically unexplained symptoms.[69]

In practice, the stated goal of the U.S. Army's frontline behavioral health treatment and restoration centers in Afghanistan continues to be "to maximize the return-to-duty rate of service members who are temporarily impaired or incapacitated by stress related conditions."[70] To that end, in 2010, the army reported a 98.7 percent return-to-duty rate of nearly two hundred war stressed soldiers after completing three to five days of behavioral health treatment in Afghanistan, including 20 percent of soldiers diagnosed with an adjustment disorder and 7 percent diagnosed with PTSD.[71] The military publicly posits that the health benefits of its return-to-duty policy include fewer PTSD and other psychiatric diagnoses, less stigma and shame, and increased post-traumatic growth.[72] Consequently, the military reasons that both service members and their units benefit from continued force sustain-ment and reduced stigma.[73] In fact, some military leaders adopt an even more strident moral stance toward frontline psychiatry policy insisting that "inappropriate evacuation may constitute medical malpractice."[74]

British researchers Jones and Wessely, however, were the only ones until 2017 to have reviewed the efficacy of the military's outdated programs; they raised serious concerns about the legitimacy of the military's data on return-to-duty and relapse rates. Moreover, the U.S. military has not conducted a single clinical trial comparing the health outcomes between soldiers return-ing to duty and those receiving psychiatric evacuations and treatment.[75] Instead, the DoD relies on three small longitudinal studies by the Israeli Defense Force (IDF) from the 1982 Lebanon War—the two most recent investigations reveal the harmful effects of repeated combat stress reactions.[76]

EVIDENCE THAT FRONTLINE PSYCHIATRY IS HARMFUL

According to the U.S. military, its frontline psychiatry doctrine, which emphasizes early intervention for combat stress reactions, combat and oper-ational stress reactions, or other behavioral health conditions in war zones and sets a clear expectation of returning to duty, is explicitly designed to prevent or mitigate the harmful dosage of war stress by avoiding stigmatizing psychiatric labeling, treatment, and evacuations.[77] Yet evidence is grossly insufficient to support the military's beneficial health claims of its war-zone mental health policies.[78] We asked whether the military's frontline psychiatry and combat operational stress control programs might actually be harmful to military personnel[79]

We found that since 1893, the U.S. military and its medical departments have established numerous research agencies to fulfill its force health protection mission, which includes mental health.[80] These agencies have been instrumental in medical breakthroughs like immunizations, disease prevention, diagnostics, triage, surgery, burn care, emergency medicine, and a host of other lifesaving advances.[81] Consequently, one might expect investigations of the military's frontline psychiatry clinical outcomes to support its claims that service members are able to withstand mental stress and recover quickly from stress-induced injuries.[82]

Table 11.1 provides the results from an exhaustive search for any investigation comparing any immediate or long-term health outcomes of deployed personnel returned to duty after receiving frontline psychiatry compared with those who were evacuated and treated outside the war zone.

U.S. MILITARY RESEARCH ON FRONTLINE PSYCHIATRY OUTCOMES

The U.S. military has not published a study comparing the immediate or long-term outcomes of deployed personnel returned to duty after receiving frontline psychiatry compared with those who were psychiatrically evacuated. Tragically, despite more than a hundred years of enforcing a controversial return-to-duty mental health policy that appears to starkly contradict mainstream science on the harmful effects of war-stress injuries, the U.S. military has failed to ask basic questions essential to accomplishing its force health protection mandate. In fact, the only U.S. studies reporting frontline psychiatry health outcomes were conducted by the National Research Council and Veterans Administration after WWII and a 2015 independent RAND report on the U.S. Marine Corps' version of frontline psychiatry and combat operational stress control, called the Operational Stress Control and Readiness program.[83] Neither investigation tested the core tenet of frontline psychiatry doctrine—that is, that return to duty and preventing psychiatric evacuations "promotes long-term health and well-being of individual Marines and Sailors and their family members."[84]

WWII OUTCOME STUDY

Brill and Beebe's five-year follow-up study involved an extensive examination of nearly fifteen hundred U.S. personnel diagnosed and treated for psychoneuroses while on active duty compared with control groups of veterans not diagnosed with psychoneuroses. The primary purpose of this research was to assess the long-term effects of treatment after psychiatric breakdown. Researchers reported 24 percent of veterans received final treatment through frontline psychiatry and 76 percent were eventually evacuated and treated at hospitals outside war zones. About 70.1 percent of combatants receiving hospitalized psychiatric treatment were returned to duty compared with 70.2 percent of those medically treated for physical wounds. In addition, data on length of hospitalized care reveals that only 9.6 percent of evacuees for psychoneuroses remained in hospitals for 120 days compared with 26.6 percent of those physically wounded. No direct comparisons were made between those returned to duty after receiving frontline psychiatry and those who were evacuated. Nonetheless, both findings appear to refute the principle of proximity underlying the military's repeated claim of harm caused by psychiatric evacuations and treatment.

2015 RAND OUTCOME STUDY ON FRONTLINE PSYCHIATRY

The second U.S. government-sponsored frontline outcome study was conducted eighty years after the WWII investigation. RAND researchers examined the health benefits from extensive predeployment Operational Stress Control and Readiness prevention or resilience training and peer support in a sample of more than two thousand five hundred U.S. Marines deployed to Iraq or Afghanistan who either received the supplemental frontline psychiatry services or did not. The independent investigators reported that the only significant benefit that the Operational Stress Control and Readiness program provided was an increase in personal help-seeking behaviors. More important, the researchers were taken aback that many clinical outcomes from the Operational Stress Control and Readiness group generally were worse than those in marines who did not receive the extra prevention intervention, including higher rates of PTSD, depression, and worse physical health. Although methodological limitations prevent extrapolating the

RAND's results to all of the military's frontline psychiatry programs, it is notable that both of these nonmilitary investigations into frontline psychiatry yielded evidence rebutting military claims of health benefits.

As shown in Table 11.1, only three IDF retrospective studies from the 1982 Lebanon War met inclusion criteria for head-to-head comparisons of deployed personnel returned to duty after receiving frontline psychiatry versus those evacuated and treated outside war zones.[85] Moreover, the IDF's research offers a direct assessment of the harm hypothesis from a longitudinal perspective at one year and twenty years after war.[86]

1986 STUDY OF CLINICAL OUTCOMES FROM FRONTLINE PSYCHIATRY

Solomon and Benbenshity's study was the first investigation directly comparing clinical outcomes of groups of deployed personnel returned to duty after receiving frontline psychiatry with those who were evacuated and treated at a general hospital. Researchers examined returned-to-duty and PTSD rates of an unspecified number of Israeli soldiers treated for combat stress reactions one year after the 1982 Lebanon War. Results indicated that being diagnosed with combat stress reactions was significantly related to developing PTSD, regardless of treatment group; however, veterans receiving frontline psychiatry were reported to have significantly lower PTSD rates than evacuees. The researchers also reported a positive dose response to applying frontline psychiatry proximity, immediacy, and expectancy (PIE) principles. For example, 71 percent of soldiers returned to duty reportedly receiving no PIE-related intervention developed PTSD within one year after the war compared with 40 percent PTSD of veterans who returned to duty after receiving all three principles. Consequently, the initial IDF findings appear to lend direct support for the military's health benefit claims and refutes the harm hypothesis.

Great caution is warranted, however, when drawing conclusions about the efficacy of PIE principles; the authors found no overall statistical significance. For instance, regarding the principle of expectancy of return-to-duty rates, there was no statistically significant difference in PTSD rates—some 52 percent of soldiers returned to duty were eventually diagnosed with PTSD. Moreover, the type and quality of hospitalized psychiatric treatment of evacuees was not reported, prohibiting any conclusion about the principle of proximity or comparing relative harm associated with returning to duty or evacuation. Most important, 52 percent of those returned to duty after receiving frontline psychiatry developed PTSD within a year compared with 66 percent of soldiers who were evacuated to a general, nonmilitary hospital. Obviously, a 66 percent PTSD rate in evacuees suggests a modest reduction in harm for those receiving frontline psychiatry. There was no control group, however, to assess outcomes of veterans who did not receive frontline psychiatry or were evacuated. Furthermore, evacuated veterans with combat stress reactions were sent to general civilian hospitals, not to specialized military treatment facilities, and no details of treatment were provided. In accordance with standard frontline psychiatry doctrine, typically deployed personnel with the most severe or debilitating combat stress reactions were evacuated out of war zones.[87] That said, a 55 percent PTSD rate for deployed personnel returned to duty after receiving frontline psychiatry greatly exceeds the rate reported in every epidemiological study conducted on combat-related PTSD. For example, national studies on Vietnam veterans reported a 30 percent lifetime prevalence of PTSD in combat veterans.[88] Importantly, Solomon and Benbenshity's results offer a glimpse into the relative clinical outcomes, in particular, PTSD rates, of deployed personnel returned to duty after receiving frontline psychiatry and what is known about PTSD prevalence in deployed populations. Given that combat stress reaction severity and inpatient treatment are two major unspecified variables for evacuees, the initial analysis from the IDF's seminal study raises legitimate concerns of the potential greater harm resulting from frontline psychiatry. Nevertheless, substantial methodological limitations exist prohibiting that any conclusions can be drawn (see table 11.1).

1987 IDF REANALYSIS OF FRONTLINE PSYCHIATRY OUTCOMES

The second IDF study conducted by Solomon, Weisenberg, Schwarzwald, and Mikulincer in 1987 compared outcomes from both frontline psychiatry and psychiatric evacuation of four hundred and seventy Israeli veterans one year after the 1982 Lebanon War against a control group. One hundred and fifty-five combat veterans who received frontline PIE treatment for combat stress reactions were compared with three hundred and fifteen veterans evacuated to rear hospitals for treatment of combat stress reactions and to a control group of three hundred and thirty-four veterans without a diagnosed

TABLE 11.1 Research Directly Comparing Outcomes for Deployed Personnel Returned to Duty Versus Evacuation

STUDY	WAR	SAMPLE	TREATMENT SETTING	ASSESSMENT	DEPLOYMENT OUTCOMES	POSTDEPLOYMENT AND LONG-TERM OUTCOMES	LIMITATIONS
Solomon and Benbenishty, 1986	1982 Israeli Lebanon War	N = "several hundred" Israeli soldiers diagnosed and treated for combat stress reactions. Sample size unspecified, only percentages reported: Divided into four groups: (1) Treated at frontline; (2) treated within border of war zone; (3) evacuated to general hospital in Israel; and (4) sought psychiatric help after deployment while on leave.	Frontline PIE treatment By groups: (1) 43 percent at front (2) 59 percent border (3) 21 percent evacuated (4) 28 percent on leave 151 percent total unexplained if relapses are included	One year after war proximity, immediacy, and expectancy (PIE), return to duty (RTD), and post-traumatic stress order (PTSD-1) assessed: Proximity: RTD rate; frontline treatment versus evacuated to rear hospital in Israel. Immediacy: queried if treatment received within hours, days, week, or after war. Expectancy: one year after ceasefire queried about perceptions of PIE treatment goals (e.g., RTD).	93 percent RTD No data for relapse	Overall, 34 percent of RTD diagnosed with PTSD 1 year after war versus 74 percent of those evacuated to rear or sought treatment after deployment; Proximity did not significantly reduce PTSD: 52 percent of RTD after frontline treatment developed PTSD versus 66 percent evacuated to rear; 59 percent of RTD after PIE treatment at border developed PTSD versus 66 percent evacuated to rear; Immediate treatment significantly reduced PTSD: 54 percent of 44 percent soldiers treated immediately developed PTSD; 73 percent of 26 percent soldiers treated within 1 day; 56 percent of 29 percent treated within 2 or more days; and 74 percent of 24 percent after the war; Expectancy did not significantly reduce PTSD, but lowered rates: 55 percent of 53 percent soldiers RTD at all cost developed PTSD; 62 percent of 40 percent RTD if capable; and 67 percent of 23 percent not-RTD; Trend of cumulative benefit of PIE reported, but not statistically significant:	No statistical data except %; Small sample size; Lack randomization and control group; Severity of not measured; Sampling bias of possible more severe CSR in evacuated group; Retrospective study with self-report and recall bias; Informal, unsystematic assessment of PIE principles; No data on relapse; Measurement error (e.g., all reported % total >100); No information on treatment by a general, non-military hospital

NUMBER OF PIE PRINCIPLES	RTD%	PTSD%
0	22	71
1	23	64
2	48	59
3	60	40

Study	War	Sample	Treatment	Assessment	RTD/Relapse	Results	Limitations
Solomon, Weisenberg, Schwarzwald, and Mikulincer, 1987	1982 Lebanon War	N = 470 Israeli soldiers with CSR: n = 155 received frontline treatment for CSR; n = 315 soldiers evacuated to rear hospital treatment for CSR, compared with control of n = 334 matched soldiers without CSR.	Frontline use of PIE principles; Unspecified treatment at rear hospitals.	One year postwar assessment of CSR and PTSD PTSD-I.	No data for RTD No data for relapse	Overall, 59 percent (n = 255) of soldiers experiencing CSR developed PTSD 1 year after war statistically significant compared with control; N = 53 (16 percent) of control group developed PTSD, but none sought treatment; Older veterans had higher PTSD rates and marital status was not significant; No report of significant difference between CSR group treated at frontline versus evacuated to rear hospital	Retrospective study; Self-report and recall bias; No data on hospital treatment; Severity of CSR or impairment not assessed.
Solomon, Shklar, and Mikulincer 2005	1982 Israeli Lebanon War	N = 79 Israeli soldiers who received frontline treatment for CSR; n = 156 soldiers with CSR evacuated for treatment in rear hospitals; matched with n = 194 soldiers not diagnosed with CSR.	Frontline PIE treatment and unspecified rear hospital treatment.	20-year postwar assessment of mental, physical, and social functioning.	No data for RTD	After 20 years, soldiers diagnosed with CSR and received frontline treatment had lower rates of PTSD, psychiatric symptoms, and post-war social functioning problems, but results were not statistically significant.	20-year retrospective self-report and recall bias; Unable to substantiate PIE principles applied;

(continued)

TABLE 11.1 (*Continued*)

STUDY	WAR	SAMPLE	TREATMENT SETTING	ASSESSMENT	DEPLOYMENT OUTCOMES	POSTDEPLOYMENT AND LONG-TERM OUTCOMES	LIMITATIONS
Solomon, Shklar, and Mikulincer 2005 (*continued*)				IES SCL-90R ULS PTSD-I Problems in Social Functioning Score Subjects asked what PIE principles they received and level of recovery before RTD.	No data for relapse	Cumulative trend of PIE treatment and PTSD rate reported, but was not statistically significant, revealing 25 percent PTSD rate when all three PIE principles applied; 32.6 percent with two principles; 38.5 percent one principle; and 49.7 percent no principles; No significant group difference in PTSD rate, occupational functioning for CSR casualties treated on frontlines or evacuated to hospitals; No statistically significant outcomes between CSR casualties RTD, and those not RTD; 50 percent more PTSD symptoms in CSR casualties who felt RTD was premature vs. those RTD who felt completely recovered.	No measures of CSR severity; Quasi-experimental design, lack random assignment; sampling bias. Small sample size in analysis of long term effects of frontline treatment in comparison group (n=27), CSR group receiving frontline treatment (n=24) as compared to CSR group receiving rear echelon treatment (n= 64); Unspecified hospital treatment

Sources:

Z. Solomon and R. Benbenishty, "The Role of Proximity, Immediacy, and Expectancy in Frontline Treatment of Combat Stress Reaction Among Israelis in the Lebanon War," *American Journal of Psychiatry* 143 (1986): 613–617.

Z. Solomon, M. Weisenberg, J. Schwarzwald, and M. Mikulincer, M., "Posttraumatic Stress Disorder Among Frontline Soldiers with Combat Street Reaction: The 1982 Israeli Experience," *American Journal of Psychiatry* 144, no. 4 (1987): 448–454.

Z. Solomon, R. Shklar, and M. Mikulincer, "Frontline Treatment of Combat Stress Reaction: A 20-year Longitudinal Study," *American Journal of Psychiatry* 162 (2005): 2319–2314.

M. C. Russell and C. R. Figley, "Is the Military's Century-Old Frontline Psychiatry Policy Harmful to Veterans and Their Families? Part Three of a Systematic Review," *Psychological Injury and Law* 10 (2017): 72–95.

combat stress reaction who received neither treatment. Results indicated there was no significant difference in clinical outcomes between the groups of veterans with combat stress reactions treated at the frontline or in rear hospitals—that is, experiencing combat stress reactions significantly increased a veteran's risk of subsequent PTSD diagnosis regardless of whether they were returned to duty or evacuated. Specifically, 59 percent (n = 255) of soldiers in the two combat stress reaction groups (frontline psychiatry and evacuees) and 16 percent (n = 53) of veterans in the control group went on to develop PTSD within a year after the war. Nearly identical scientific limitations exist in the previous IDF study prohibiting any firm conclusions about frontline psychiatry efficacy.[89]

We now can compare, however, the relatively low 16 percent PTSD rate of deployed veterans who did not receive frontline psychiatry (control group) with a 59 percent PTSD rate of those returned to duty after frontline intervention. A rate of 16 percent of PTSD in deployed veterans falls within the range of previous epidemiological investigations.[90]

Therefore, one should reasonably expect that if frontline psychiatry is effective in mitigating the adverse dosage effects of war stress as the military proclaims, then PTSD rates of frontline psychiatry group should be comparatively equal to the control group. A 59 percent PTSD rate from the frontline psychiatry group compared with the 52 percent reported earlier, however, represents a clear negative trend that substantially exceeds expectations even of the controversial 30 percent PTSD rate reported by the NVVRS.[91] Combined with the IDF's second and reportedly more rigorous study reporting no significant differences in clinical outcomes between the frontline psychiatry and evacuated treatment groups, the finding is even more troublesome for frontline psychiatry, particularly given the unknown status of combat stress reaction severity and inpatient treatment factors of evacuees.

2005 IDF 20-YEAR FOLLOW-UP ON LONG-TERM HEALTH OUTCOMES FROM FRONTLINE PSYCHIATRY

The final study is the IDF's twenty-year retrospective re-analysis of its 1987 study conducted by Solomon, Shklar, and Mikulincer in 2005.[92] Solomon et al. compared seventy-nine veterans diagnosed with combat stress reactions who returned to duty after receiving frontline intervention with one hundred and fifty-six veterans with combat stress reactions who were evacuated and treated at rear hospitals and one hundred and ninety-six veterans with no documented history of combat stress reactions in the war zone. Veterans returned to duty after receiving frontline psychiatry were asked to recall whether the frontline treatment they received included the PIE principles, replicating the 1986 study. In addition, veterans were asked to recall whether they felt recovered from their combat stress reactions before being returned to duty. Results of the analysis comparing veterans returned to duty after frontline psychiatry to those evacuated again revealed no significant differences in PTSD diagnoses; 30 percent (frontline psychiatry) and 41 percent (evacuated) of veterans were later diagnosed with PTSD, which was significantly higher than the 14 percent in the control group. Secondary analysis indicates that veterans in the frontline treatment group reported significantly more intrusion and hyperarousal symptoms than those evacuated. There were no significant differences, however, between frontline psychiatry and rear treatment on a diverse range of outcomes, including avoidance symptoms, global symptoms of distress, loneliness, perceived social support, interpersonal functioning, and occupational functioning. In their retrospective analysis of PIE principles, Solomon et al. concluded that "the percentages suggest a clear trend"—a repetition of earlier reports of a modest dose response relationship between lower rates of PTSD diagnosis and the number of PIE principles applied.[93] For instance, a 25 percent PTSD rate was found when all three PIE principles were applied, compared with 32.6 percent with two principles, 38.5 percent with one principle, and 49.7 percent with no principles. Importantly, combat stress reaction casualties who felt their return-to-duty rate was premature reported 50 percent more PTSD symptoms than those returned to duty after feeling completely recovered. The researchers, however, rightly reiterated the serious methodological flaws mentioned earlier, prohibiting any causal inferences associated with return-to-duty and evacuation statuses.

Looking at the evidence of potential harm from frontline psychiatry, we find the same trend of substantially greater PTSD rates in personnel returned to duty after frontline interventions (30 percent) than in veterans who remained in war zones (14 percent). Again, one may argue the group returned to duty (30 percent PTSD rate) enjoyed better clinical outcomes than those evacuated (41 percent PTSD rate). Combat stress reaction severity and absence of treatment information at general hospitals, however, prohibit further inferences about evacuees. For example, it is unclear whether the 41 percent PTSD rate in evacuees is a by-product of more severe combat stress reactions or inadequate treatment. More notably, the third IDF study found the two treatment groups to be relatively indistinguishable across the majority of clinical outcomes, including PTSD diagnosis. All things being equal, one would expect that if those returned to duty after receiving front-line psychiatry was more efficacious in ameliorating the adverse health impact from cumulative war stress as purported, then the clinical outcomes between veterans returned to duty should be roughly equal to the controls and significantly better than the evacuees. Neither situation was the case. Whereas 70 percent of veterans returned to duty after receiving frontline psychiatry did not develop PTSD, the IDF found significantly poorer clin-ical outcomes in veterans returned to duty (30 percent PTSD rate) than their nonfrontline psychiatry counterparts (14 percent PTSD rate) and insig-nificant differences between returned-to-duty and evacuated groups twenty years after the war.

CLASSIFIED REPORTS ON FRONTLINE PSYCHIATRY

Perhaps most telling about the durability of frontline psychiatry interventions to restore psychological equilibrium of soldiers returned to a combat environ-ment is the number of secret and classified military investigations from the WWII generation. For instance, a U.S. Army restricted report on frontline psychiatry outcomes concluded that "of patients returned to duty, how many go back combat? We have no figures with which to answer the question, but can make a fairly good estimate—*it is less than 2.0 per cent!*" (emphasis in original).[94] Although Grinker and Spiegel initially predicted that 98 percent of returned-to-duty combatants would be fully restored, in reality, they found that "a pitiful few are sufficiently recovered to enable us with clear conscience to order them back to the front" and added that "over 70 percent can be rehabilitated for selective non-combatant service, in quiet sectors." Additional classified studies by the British Army in WWII found similarly low restoration rates, including a restricted report citing full recovery rates that fluctuated between 16 and 32 percent and a secret report on the frontline treatment of battle exhaustion, indicating a 43 percent relapse rate.[95] Furthermore, a 1945 military commission sent to France to investigate combat exhaustion programs determined that only 40 percent of service personnel receiving PIE principles who were returned to duty actually fully recovered, leading to a consensus that recoveries from acute breakdowns was short-lived.[96]

What would explain the apparent contradiction in well-entrenched military doctrine positing the normative temporary nature of acute combat breakdown? Grinker and Spiegel's restricted analysis posits "one of the most frequently heard remarks in our wards was, 'I took it as long as I could; I can't take it any more,' "[97] leading the authors to conclude that "constitutional factors and the individual's life history, including the genetic background of his personality, are very important. Yet many observers have given these factors undue weight."[98] In light of the aforementioned IDF studies on the long-term adverse impact of combat stress reactions, the relapse findings are highly concerning. Specifically, serious health and safety implications exist for deployed personnel with even a mild level of impaired functioning in a war zone, raising considerable apprehension for the individual service member, their fellow unit members, and innocent noncombatants.

During WWII, senior military leaders held sufficient skepticism as to the veracity of return-to-duty claims made by frontline psychiatry proponents, which resulted in several classified investigations that essentially confirmed suspicions of an incomplete portrayal of fact. These high-level inquiries did not examine long-term health effects of service members returned to duty or evacuated and appeared to be concerned primarily with discrediting mental health services rather than effecting change in policy. Nevertheless after WWII, most Western militaries, including the United States, established a permanent frontline psychiatry doctrine undoubtedly for the clear benefit it provided to the military in terms of conserving the fighting force by preventing mass psychiatric attrition.[99] Subsequently, the military has not conducted any further high-level or classified investigations or even basic research into the effects of its return-to-duty policy.

Subsequently, we conducted the first comprehensive review of the military's frontline mental health policies, examining whether these policies are beneficial or harmful to veterans and their families, and addressing unanswered clinical, moral, and legal questions.[100] In 2003, the British High Court of Justice heard expert testimony from the military on both sides of the issue during an unprecedented class action law suit.[101] The plaintiffs were Falkland Island and Persian Gulf War British soldiers, and the defendant was the Ministry of Defense. The plaintiffs claimed that the ministry had failed to provide adequate treatment services, including CSC interventions that could have prevented their chronic PTSD. The Ministry of Defense asserted that "despite the general acceptance of the principles of forward psychiatry they have never been shown to be of therapeutic benefit to the individual,"[102] referring to the absence of scientific data that frontline intervention for acute breakdown does anything more than its intended design as expressed by American Army Medicine's motto of "conserving the fighting strength."[103]

After reviewing existing literature, the British High Court upheld the ministry's defense ruling, noting that "given this relative absence of reliable evidence as to their therapeutic effect there was a further question mark over whether or not it was even ethical to implement the principles of forward psychiatry at all."[104] This ruling left serious unasked questions regarding the neglected state of military research on frontline interventions despite standardized implementation since 1917.[105]

After reviewing empirical studies on the health effects from cumulative exposure to war stress; previously classified reports on frontline psychiatry, prevalence, and treatment of mental health conditions among deployed personnel; risk and protective factors of combat-related PTSD; and prospective deployment research on health outcomes, we legitimately reached several conclusions.[106]—there is overwhelming Specifically, evidence is overwhelming that (1) the military has significantly benefited from preventing psychiatric attrition, treatment, and evacuations maintaining averages of a 90–98 percent return-to-duty rate and a 3–5 percent rate of psychiatric evacuations;[107] (2) repeated exposure to war-stress injuries is significantly associated a variety of serious long-term adverse medical, psychiatric, and social outcomes for individual veterans and their families;[108] and (3) there is clear and convincing evidence that veterans and their families are substantially more likely to be harmed than helped by military's frontline policies and procedures.[109] Moreover in 2006, the DoD reversed its policy of preventing military personnel from deploying to war zones with known or suspected psychiatric diagnoses like PTSD,[110] while maintaining its adherence to frontline psychiatry principles that actively discourage psychiatric diagnosis and treatment in war zones.[111]

In short, the military's frontline psychiatry doctrine likely contributes to the generational cycle of self-inflicted wartime behavioral health crises. Yet, it remains the military's cornerstone policy for managing its mental health dilemma and is a major strategy used to avoid learning war trauma lessons.

HARMFUL DELAYS IN ACCESSING EVIDENCE-BASED TREATMENT FOR BEHAVIORAL HEALTH DIAGNOSES

In 2004, the VA and DoD published their joint-practice guidelines for managing post-traumatic stress that included expert consensus recommendations for the use of identified evidence-based treatments.[112] The practice guidelines were updated in 2010 and 2017 and explicitly state the necessity for timely PTSD treatment: "The clinically significant symptoms cause significant distress or impairment in social, occupational, or other important areas of functioning. The symptoms last more than 3 months after exposure to trauma. Chronic PTSD is unlikely to improve without effective treatment."[113] The military's return-to-duty mandate, coupled with its practice of restricting psychiatric evacuations for treatment outside war zones, inevitably results in delays in accessing quality effective treatment. What is the potential or foreseeable impact of systemic barriers that such treatment delay?

An IDF study examined clinical characteristics between delayed and immediate combat stress reaction responders in which one hundred and twenty-five combat veterans sought help for war-stress injuries eight years after the 1982 Lebanon War were compared with three hundred and seventy soldiers diagnosed with combat stress reactions who were treated a year after the war.[114] Findings indicate that veterans from the delayed help-seeking group suffered a significantly higher rate (92 percent compared with 59 percent) and a greater intensity of PTSD, as well as more intrusive symptoms and more general psychiatric symptoms than the immediate help-seeking group.[115]

DOD'S TREATMENT GUIDELINES FOR TRAUMATIC STRESS INJURIES

According to the VA and DoD's 2010 post-traumatic stress treatment guidelines,

> the following treatment recommendations should apply for all acutely traumatized people who meet the criteria for diagnosis of ASD (acute stress disorder), and for those with significant levels of acute stress symptoms that last for more than two-weeks post-trauma, as well as those who are incapacitated by acute psychological or physical symptoms.[116]

Importantly, the expert-based guidelines go on to state that

> there is insufficient evidence to recommend for or against the use of Psychological First Aid to address symptoms beyond 4 days following trauma [and that] survivors of trauma may not complain directly of ASD symptoms, such as re-experiencing or avoidance. Instead, they may complain of sleeping problems, pain, or other somatic concerns.[117]

Psychological first aid is a civilian term for military's frontline psychiatry PIE principles, which similarly strives to avoid psychiatric labeling or treatment and essentially consists of nonpsychotherapeutic interventions akin to frontline psychiatry and combat operational stress control.[118] Specific treatment recommendations by the VA and the DoD include psychotherapy and pharmacotherapy for acute stress and PTSD.

The joint VA/DoD *Clinical Practice Guideline* recommends early brief intervention (four to five sessions) of cognitive-based therapy (CBT) that includes exposure-based therapy, alone or combined with a component of cognitive restructuring therapy, for patients with significant early symptom levels, especially those meeting diagnostic criteria for ASD. No evidence, however, supports the recommendation for use of a pharmacological agent to prevent the development of acute stress disorder or PTSD.[119]

Regarding the use of psychotherapy for PTSD, the guidelines "strongly recommend that patients diagnosed with PTSD receive one of the evidence-based trauma-focused psychotherapies," such as "exposure-based therapy (e.g., Prolonged Exposure), cognitive therapy (e.g., Cognitive Processing Therapy) or Eye Movement Desensitization and Reprocessing (EMDR)."[120]

PSYCHOTHERAPY RESEARCH IN WAR ZONES

The military's century-old frontline psychiatry principle of simplicity requires clinicians in war zones to refrain from using traditional psychiatric labeling and treatments for deployed personnel exhibiting combat stress reactions or combat and operational stress reactions to avoid stigma and evacuations.[121] The DoD's deployment policy, however, ensures that thousands of deployed personnel already diagnosed with psychiatric conditions are sent to war zones, while others already in war zones are diagnosed with psychiatric conditions.[122] Consequently, it is essential for deployed personnel to have ready access to high-quality evidence-based treatments as recommended by the VA and the DoD.

A handful of case studies on psychiatric treatment have reported successful war-zone treatment using evidence-based psychotherapies for deployed U.S. service members diagnosed with PTSD as recommended by the DoD's clinical practice guidelines, such as prolonged exposure and virtual reality exposure therapy.[123] A review of these studies, however, uncovered a disturbing trend whereby treatment success was primarily defined as short-term symptom reduction and service members were returned to duty with no research looking at long-term outcomes of those service members.[124] For instance, both studies recorded a 100 percent return-to-duty rate coinciding with a substantial reduction in symptoms; however, no clinical follow-up beyond the war zone was assessed.[125]

The robust trend of reporting return-to-duty rates while ignoring long-term clinical outcomes extends to other military treatment record analyses.[126] For instance, Hung analyzed treatment records of nearly fifty thousand deployed U.S. personnel receiving frontline psychiatry, including more than eight thousand personnel treated for psychiatric disorders, such as depression disorders (n = 1,389), anxiety disorders (n = 928) and acute stress disorder and PTSD (n = 720) in war zones. The only treatment outcome reported was that 99 percent were returned to duty within the war zone. No information was provided about the type of treatment administered or whether treatments met the VA/DoD's clinical practice guidelines or postdeployment adjustment. In addition, another U.S. military study examined frontline mental health provider treatment recommendations for more than a thousand deployed personnel seeking psychiatric treatment in war zones.[127] Although 63 percent of military patients with a PTSD diagnosis were prescribed medications, only 40 percent had recommendations to receive psychotherapy or counseling,[128] which contradicts the DoD's practice guidelines. Moreover, the medical records of approximately 21 percent of deployers diagnosed with a psychiatric disorder (n = 245) did not contain any treatment plans other than referral to other providers in war zones.[129] The authors concluded that "further examination of post-deployment health outcomes may help to facilitate the development of more effective acute intervention strategies in theater."[130] The DoD, however, has yet to undertake such outcome-based research.[131] In fact, the primary outcome reported in Schmitz et al., as in nearly all previous war-zone treatment research, is high return-to-duty rates and low psychiatric evacuation rates.

Evidence is overwhelming that most deployed personnel diagnosed with a psychiatric condition either before or during deployment do not receive optimal treatment in accordance with the military's own clinical practice guidelines. Schmitz et al. stated that "the therapy recommendations were mainly for supportive counseling instead of a full course of trauma-focused psychotherapy due to the inhospitable environment and access-to-care."[132] Although this assertion appears to be contradicted by several multiple case studies employing evidence-based psychotherapies in war zones,[133] it does raise critical and unexplored clinical and ethical questions regarding the timing of trauma-focused treatment. Importantly, Schmitz and his team's finding that deployed personnel diagnosed with PTSD were treated with supportive counseling is in direct contravention with the VA/DoD's practice guidelines.

Unfortunately, a century of frontline psychiatry has not even scratched the surface in advancing our knowledge in this vital area. Until frontline mental health treatment is thoroughly researched, we can only deduce that the majority of mental-health-treatment-seeking deployed personnel do not have access to the recommended evidence-based treatments in war zones and that non-mental-health-treatment-seeking deployed personnel must endure extended delays to access optimal mental healthcare until they return from deployments because of the U.S. military's strict return-to-duty policy.

All things considered, we are left with the certain, albeit uncomfortable truth that a preponderance of clear and convincing evidence indicates that the military's frontline psychiatry doctrine is substantially more likely to harm service members and their families than to help.

The onus is squarely on the military to prove how its war-zone mental health policies that strive for a 95 percent return-to-duty rate is beneficial to individual well-being when such practices appear to be misaligned with medical science and military reports on the known cumulative adverse health impact from war-stress exposure. Moreover, we also found grossly insufficient evidence supporting military claims of individual health benefits from its frontline mental health policies.[134] Therefore, the combined evidentiary weight from both reviews establishes a burden of proof for the military that belies any plausible conclusions other than as stated—that is, frontline psychiatry as it currently exists is detrimental to the health and well-being of service members and their families. This well-being can be easy to gloss over when statistics and averages are used to set policy. But the individual details of those suffering from these mental health issues illustrate the true need for adequate mental healthcare.

In March 2007, a soldier tested positive for cocaine use. He was not required to enroll in an Army Substance Abuse Program (ASAP), and a Department of the Army Form 4833 was never completed. Despite fifteen negative urinalyses from October 2008 to January 2011, the soldier self-enrolled in the ASAP for cocaine abuse and marijuana and alcohol dependence. He was apprehended in July 2011 for assault consummated by a battery (domestic violence).

A review of law enforcement databases revealed that these offenses were not the beginning of this soldier's high-risk behavior; he had been arrested for criminal trespass, marijuana possession, and evading arrest in 2003—three years before his delayed-entry report date of August 2006. While driving on an interstate highway in November 2011, the soldier collided with another vehicle, killing himself and two others instantly and injuring two others. He had been driving the wrong way on the highway for two miles at the time of the accident. Although drug and toxicology results are unknown at this time, packets of a synthetic drug called Spice were found in the soldier's vehicle.[135] This is but one example of the preventable casualties of war born of military negligence to learn, not avoid, its war trauma lessons.

12

PERPETUATING NEGLECT, INDIFFERENCE, AND SELF-INFLICTED CRISES

THE TENTH DARK-SIDE STRATEGY

The Greatest Generation did not hold back from candid self-condemnation for neglecting to learn its war trauma lessons and contributing to a major public health crisis. In one report, World War I (WWI) was identified as a source of abundant evidence that combat would produce large numbers of psychiatric causalities."[1] Yet despite this knowledge, this same report laid out the severe lack of preparation for an active army. Two massive data-filled volumes were compiled by the World War II (WWII) cohort on lessons learned for every aspect of meeting wartime mental health needs. Consciously, these leaders strove to reflect on past mistakes (and successes) to avert future preventable wartime crises. For instance, U.S. Army Surgeon General Leonard D. Heaton gave this stern warning: "With this information so readily available, there can be little excuse for repetition of error in future wars, should they occur!"[2] The final strategy the military uses to avoid its mental health dilemma is a sustained indifference and neglect of mental healthcare, including indifference toward war trauma lessons to develop and maintain peak mental healthcare. As a result, once again, this strategy perpetuates the generational cycle of preventable or self-inflicted crises.

From an organizational perspective, indifference and neglect of mental health often naturally results from adopting one or more of the previous nine strategies. For instance, neglect of mental health services will arise when leaders are focused on weaponizing stigma or punishing service members to prevent evacuation syndromes. Similarly, maintaining a diffuse and fragmented leadership structure invites the bystander effect and neglect. Obviously, attempts to purge the military of predisposed weakness and psychiatry results in the neglect of mental health services, as do strategies to avoid psychiatric diagnosis and treatment. Assuredly, efforts to avoid transparency and delay the expenditure of resources are disincentives for investing in mental healthcare.

Despite the continual profession of war trauma lessons and the need to meet wartime mental health needs after each major conflict following WWII, the contemporary cohort of military leadership persists in its failure to care for the mental health needs of its service members. Consider that it has been seventy-three years since WWII, forty-five years since an all-volunteer professional military, and thirty-eight years after the post-traumatic stress disorder (PTSD) diagnosis was officially acknowledged and became the most frequently researched condition in psychiatric history. The 2007 congressionally mandated Department of Defense (DoD) Task Force on Mental Health found that "the Military Health System lacks the fiscal resources and the fully-trained personnel to fulfill its mission to support psychological health in PEACETIME (emphasis added) or fulfill the enhanced requirements imposed during times of conflict."[3]

The task force's revelation of chronic and severe deficiencies in every conceivable aspect of mental healthcare as a result of sustained gross negligence and moral abdication of the military's force protection duty is made all the more stunning by the fact that it occurred six years after invading Afghanistan. In stark contrast to the WWII generation, however, contemporary military leaders deflect all blame to the unprecedented nature of so-called signature wounds of PTSD and traumatic brain injury allegedly unique to the current conflicts, despite the commonality of war-stress injuries since the advent of artillery. The task force even calls on the historical knowledge following the Vietnam War as evidence that the issue will not be resolved without prevention, intervention, and treatment.[4]

Despite this repeated call, previous generations have continued to acknowledge a lack of preparation in meeting these needs. The military leadership following the First Gulf War admitted, "mental health personnel deployed to the Gulf War were often not adequately trained as individuals or units, they were not well equipped, in many cases doctrine was not followed."[5] In contrast to military medicine, after each major U.S. armed conflict since the twentieth century, well-documented psychiatric lessons of war have been routinely ignored,[6] causing or greatly exacerbating predictable crises of unmet mental health needs.[7] The neglect of the ten foundational lessons essential to meeting basic mental health and social needs of its service members has been systemically perpetuated. Even the introductory chapter in the U.S. Army's *Textbook of Military Medicine: War Psychiatry* summarizes the history of war-stress management with the table headers of "Lessons Learned/Relearned" and "Lessons Available but Not Learned,"[8] thus forming the genesis for preventable wartime crises.[9]

THE NATIONAL RESET

The latest research on the generational cycle of military mental health crises reveals another disturbing trend, what we call the National Reset. The National Reset is a disturbing trend not only because of its ruinous impact on millions of future war veterans and their families but also because of its predictability over time. Simply put, at the outset of every major American war since the U.S. Civil War, military mental healthcare has been in an impoverished, dilapidated state born out of abject indifference and neglect. As described throughout this book, the military has been forced to reluctantly relearn its war trauma lessons as a result of intense pressure from the news media, congress, and the president. Consequently, at the end of each conflict, the military's mental health services have significantly improved in resources, staffing, and treatment. Soon after this external scrutiny of the military fades, however, a pattern of indifference and neglect returns. In turn, we have found that this pattern automatically leads to the gradual deterioration of wartime mental healthcare resources and programs.

The clearest proof of actual lessons learned is the absence of forgetting or ignoring basic tenets for meeting wartime mental health needs and preventing crisis. Hundreds of psychiatric lessons of war are available through numerous retrospective analyses and official reports conducted by the military, historians, commissioned investigations, and memoirs by senior military leaders.

It is highly uncharacteristic for sophisticated armed forces like the United States to blatantly and repeatedly neglect the lessons of war. In stark contrast to well-defined military policies and dedicated "lessons learned" centers designed to incorporate tactical and medical lessons, no official policy or central repository exists wherein psychiatric lessons are explicitly collected, identified, reported, regularly incorporated into training, or monitored for compliance. Instead, each armed service relies on an ill-defined, fragmented patchwork of reports and Internet postings of "war trauma lessons" embedded within its extensive medical lessons learned systems.[10] The absence of dedicated policies and systems for learning war trauma lessons creates the high probability that psychiatric lessons will again be overshadowed by medical lessons, further perpetuating this generational crises. Even worse, post-WWII analyses commentary identified this exact issue and expressed surprise given the prevalence of psychiatric disorders following WWI, which suggested the experience would repeat itself.[11]

Every war generation has described similar problems associated with the gross disparity between medical and mental health. For instance, during the WWII era, the leading mental health officer noted that the mental casualties were so high they could no longer be ignored. Perhaps as a result, during the Vietnam War, it was assumed that a limited tour of duty would greatly limit mental health problems, but this assumption was incorrect.[12] Following the Persian Gulf War, military authors reported that "Operation Desert Storm demonstrated marked differences between policies and practice for managing physical casualties and those for managing stress casualties."[13] This changed with the introduction of the Operational Stress Control and Readiness (OSCAR) program during the wars in Iraq and Afghanistan a number of programs emerged within military mental health, including an emphasis on resilience and identify and acting on risks indicators for poor mental health. OSCAR had the backing of many inside and outside the military. Even the name was appealing as well as the role of the program: serve in combat, ensure the involvement of downrange (embedded) mental health military personnel (e.g., psychiatrists, psychologists, social workers), and use officers who are familiar with the needs of the units to lead the program. Applying the lessons learned, these teams of officers and noncommission officers were trained in the risk and protective factors of mental illness within a deployed context and were taught how best to intervene early to prevent negative outcomes and to increase use of mental health services.[14]

Thus, a National Reset following war both celebrates and is proud of the emergence of mental health services and resources with the military, including efforts to maintain Force Preservation within the military and to improve services through the Department of Veterans Affairs (VA) following military service. We fear, however, that the reset simply will reset to how it has been and will repeat all of the problems present before the war.

PREVENTABLE WARTIME BEHAVIORAL HEALTH CRISES AND THEIR CONSEQUENCES

The term "preventable" conveys the extent of unnecessary suffering, disability, and premature death resulting from organizational neglect to provide basic mental health and social services.[15] Preliminary investigations into present and past wartime behavioral health crises have revealed a clear pattern of self-inflicted or preventable crises caused primarily by the military's continual neglect and failure to learn from its own documented lessons of war trauma, despite the acknowledgment of the value of knowing the history of war-stress injuries.[16]

Each of the military medical departments (Air Force, Army, and Navy, which also provides for the Marine Corps) is responsible for providing mental health services to their respective service personnel and family members during times of peace as well as war.[17] Evidence of learning war trauma lessons is relatively straightforward. The clearest proof of actual lessons learned is the absence of forgetting or ignoring the basic tenets essential to meet wartime mental health needs and preventing crisis. The many psychiatric lessons of war are available through numerous retrospective analyses and official reports, including reports conducted by the military and historians, commissioned investigations, and memoirs by military leaders.[18]

The tragic measurable preventable harm from the military's reliance on neglect as a strategy to deal with its mental health dilemma is all around us. Throughout this book, we have reported the harmful effects of the military's negligence: More than 1.3 million active-duty have been diagnosed with a psychiatric disorder since 2001, and another million discharged war vets are being treated in the VA. More veterans of Operation Enduring Freedom, Operation Iraqi Freedom, and Operation New Dawn have died by suicide than in military action, and have faced legal incarcerations, bad paper discharges, divorce, drug addictions, homelessness, and on and on. More than two hundred government-sponsored investigations have looked into the DoD's mental health services over the span of sixteen war years. The endless litany of news stories depicting how the military's gross negligence has affected countless Americans, both those who served in the military and those who did not, is not difficult to find. For instance, multiple headlines indicate the high-level of mental health demand within the military population, and a spectrum of wartime needs far beyond a PTSD diagnosis, including "Long

Deployments Stress Military Families";[19] "A Deluge of Troubled Soldiers Is in the Offing, Experts Predict";[20] "Officer Sees 'Perfect Storm' Brewing in Military's Mental Health Care System";[21] "PTSD Reports Up 20,000 in a Year";[22] "Home From the War, Many Veterans Battle Substance Abuse";[23] and "Sexual Assaults in Military Raise Alarm in Washington."[24] Moreover, media reports convey a message of a mental health system at or near collapse, like "VA Sees Shortfall of Mental Health Specialists";[25] "Military Not Doing Enough to Curb Alcohol, Drug Abuse, IOM Concludes";[26] "Panel Says Pentagon Does Not Know If PTSD Programs Work";[27] "Recent War Vets Face Hiring Obstacle: PTSD Bias";[28] and "Army Orders Reforms for Mental Health Care Treatment."[29]

Eventually, the lack of mental health services, specialists, and resources leads to an increase in suicides within the military and among those recently released. In 2017, the DoD published its latest suicide report revealing that between 2012 and 2016, a total of 2,451 service members in active duty, the reserves, and the national guard had committed suicide. But the report is also quick to point out the most were not deployed. Military-related suicides have reportedly eclipsed the total number of combatants killed in action in Vietnam, Persian Gulf, Operation Enduring Freedom, and Operation Iraqi Freedom. In 2012, the VA estimated that twenty-two veterans die by suicide each day—that is, eight thousand annually or one hundred and thirty-six thousand during the current Afghanistan and Iraq wars. The suicide estimate was revised by the VA in 2016 to "only" twenty per day. The DoD and VA suicide studies consistently reveal that the majority of veteran and active-duty personnel who committed suicide never received mental health treatment either because it was unavailable or because individuals chose not to contact clinics. We conclude from this that the OSCAR program, shown to increase the use of behavioral and mental health services, should be extended to units that are in base camp and to the nondeployed.

Chronic DoD and VA mental health staffing shortages, extensive waiting times, substandard treatment quality, a lack of treatment outcome monitoring, inadequate family support, and other reasons all violate bedrock war trauma lessons. How many veterans and service members' lives could have been saved if military leaders had headed their predecessors' warnings?

How many military families affected by suicide in just the past seventeen years could have been spared? The long-term effects of neglecting fundamental war trauma lessons has produced an incalculable effect on those who serve our nation's military.

The systemic neglect of these trauma lessons has been consistent for multiple war generations, particularly in the disparity between medical and mental healthcare in their organization, leadership, and policies. For instance, WWII, the U.S. Army's chief neuropsychiatric consultant wrote, "In spite of the fact that the number of psychiatric casualties created a problem of such size that it could not be ignored, in too many instances psychiatrists were only tolerated very reluctantly; often they were resisted."[30] He later wrote, "Certain factors within the Army—its organizations and system—further added to the difficulty for psychiatry. Each of these contributed directly to the production of psychiatric casualties. All of this could be changed so that they would be much less of a menace to mental health."[31] Other senior WWII psychiatrists would echo his comments, "A frequent comment by frustrated and harassed psychiatrists during World War II was that responsible authorities failed to heed the lessons learned by psychiatry in World War I."[32] These observations were then only repeated roughly half a century later, "Operation Desert Storm demonstrated marked differences between policies and practice for managing physical casualties and those for managing stress casualties."[33]

WHY MILITARY LEADERS NEGLECT WAR TRAUMA LESSONS

What explains this neglect at the individual level? Perhaps after the first two world wars, some leaders may have been uninformed and thus through gross ignorance or incompetence unintentionally failed to learn the lessons of war trauma. Contemporary military officials, especially those involved in war planning, cannot claim the same lack of information. Instead, we posit three distinct and extreme sources for personalized indifference and neglect: (1) a callous, impersonal, and apathetic personality—a small number of leaders who genuinely do not care about the health and well-being of service members; (2) ardent believers of the antipsychiatry movement—a likely much larger group of leaders who care about their troops, but honestly believe that mental healthcare is harmful to individuals and should be avoided; and (3). as noted in chapter, structural disorganization and a constant flow of new military leaders with their own agenda, who likely have failed to take action because of this disorganization.

Individuals with excessive personality traits or disorders of a narcissistic, schizoid, or antisocial variety may exhibit the kind of cold, impersonal, and apathetic attitude toward military personnel and their families that could foster mental health issues. Their personal indifference is not likely relegated only toward neglecting mental healthcare but also toward individual well-being in general. The stereotypical "bad" general who callously orders multitudes to be slaughtered for their ego or the heartless bureaucrat concerned only with the bottom line and worker productivity may not be a common feature in the military ranks. In fact, it would be a fallacy and a great disservice to suggest many military leaders fit this category, but it is also naïve to suggest that is does not exist.

The antipsychiatry movement may be a much more plausible reality. David Cooper is credited with coining the term "antipsychiatry," but public skepticism, disbelief, and open antagonism toward the legitimacy of mental health as a profession, mental health providers, and their clientele is centuries old.[34] The contemporary antipsychiatry movement represents a generalized condemnation of the mental health field as a pseudo-science with dubious origins, history of oppressive and harmful practices, proclivity to over-pathologize, and a morally corrosive influence on society resulting in a culture of victims. A plethora of publications depict societies that are embroiled in impassioned "trauma-pension wars" (i.e., the battle to legitimize) since the nineteenth century. Vigorous attacks on post-traumatic stress conditions as being illegitimate, fraudulent injuries exacerbated by quackery and the desire for disability pensions have harmed veterans and society alike.[35]

> The Americans, for understandable reasons repeated many of the sociopolitical mistakes they had made in the 1920's. Just as many Great War veterans became chronic patients by the time the gleaning VA hospitals became available to treat them in 1922, so many Vietnam veterans had become irretrievably lost by the time Vet Centers were conjured upon earlier 1979.[36]

We also have medical explanations for normal mental health reactions: "The fact that the physician shows interest in the event can have the effect of further fixing the symptoms, by persuading the patient that they have a physical cause"[37]

And we have military tradition explanations:

> Others decry the effect of the compensation culture on the service ethos. One of the most liberal and intelligent of British generals, Lord Carver.

Lord Carver was a veteran of the Western Desert and of Normandy. Shepard suggests that he was unable to accept today's soldiers in his command, in contrast to traditional military culture. Those days in which soldiers sucked it up and endure the risks of war and view it as part of the job. Lord Carver has suggested that the new ethos was encouraged by reporters that "plays to a sentimental public, and . . . exploited by a certain type of lawyer." He is speaking specifically about a culture that includes and expects counselling and compensation are expected for any "adverse effect they claim results from their military service."[38]

These trauma-pension debates were greatly magnified with the 1980 adoption of the PTSD diagnosis. Both sides of the antipsychiatry debate accused the other of perpetuating unscientific, unethical, and harmful practices especially impacting war veterans.[39] The side of the debate depend on what was best for the military and other institutions, such as the U.S. military and the VA, or the injured veteran seeking relief from injuries. Like the general public, military leaders are bombarded by conflictual authoritative statements about the legitimacy of PTSD and the value of mental healthcare in general.[40] Credible sources undermining the authenticity of PTSD or extolling harm caused by psychiatric diagnosis, treatment, and disability compensations of war veterans have been written by notable military historians,[41] Princeton academics,[42] distinguished medical lecturers,[43] and Harvard and VA researchers.[44]

In sum, a sizable, yet uncertain number of military leaders are likely influenced by antipsychiatry propaganda. Some may believe it is their moral duty to prevent the military and its people from being harmed by the pseudoscience and cultural fiction that is mental health. But as chapter 13 will show, success indeed has been achieved in military mental health, thanks in large part to the dedicated service member practitioners despite inconsistent standards of practice between civilian standards and military policies and procedures. This success will be the reset required for significant, sustainable, and evidence-based practice of military mental health resilience.

13

TOWARD A RESILIENT AND MENTALLY HEALTHY MILITARY

Winning wars are lost if those who won the wars are broken. Force protection must be taken seriously by war planners, this includes mental health!
MARK C. RUSSELL

I n the preceding chapters, we have revealed some fairly condemning evidence of the military's complicity in perpetuating generational harm to millions of veterans and their families by its steadfast refusal to learn foundational war trauma lessons and deal openly with the inherent mental health dilemma posed by modern warfare. Admittedly, our portrayal of military mental healthcare up to this point is principally dark and stands in stark contrast to the picture painted by contemporary military officials.

That said, we have identified several positive aspects of military mental healthcare, including the military's recent efforts to apply its war trauma lessons. Much more needs to be said about the herculean efforts by uniformed and civilian mental health providers as well as about the many notable innovations and advancements that have had extraordinary benefit for the private sector.

U.S. CIVIL WAR

Even though the mental health professions did not exist during the U.S. Civil War, several Union Army physicians were instrumental in laying important foundation for meeting wartime mental health needs. For instance, the Union Army's Surgeon General William A. Hammond advocated his progressive "mind-body unitary theory," which professed equal treatment for physical and mental wounds. Under Hammond's leadership, the Union Army established the world's first dedicated military research and treatment facility for war-stress injury with the 1863 creation of Turner Lane Military Hospital. It was at Turner Lane that the world's first clinical trials for treating war-stress injury—called irritable heart, a precursor to modern-day post-traumatic stress disorder (PTSD)—was conducted by Union Army physician Jacob DaCosta, who published his clinical study in 1871. DaCosta teamed up with S. Weir Mitchell and utilized Mitchell's innovative "resting cure" treatment to return 33 percent of soldiers diagnosed with irritable heart back to full duty.[1]

Near the end of the Civil War, practitioners' emphasis on mental health rehabilitation, retention, and treatment before military discharge provided invaluable war trauma lessons that were ignored at the war's end. Mitchell's groundbreaking observations on traumatic brain injury (TBI) and other "nervous injuries" led to his distinction as the father of American neurology. Coincidentally, the father of American psychiatry and the American Psychiatric Association (1844) was another army surgeon general—Dr. Benjamin Rush who served in the American Revolution under General George Washington and wrote the first American textbook on psychiatry. Mitchell's "resting cure" would later evolve into the military's controversial World War I (WWI) frontline psychiatry programs, which emphasized brief respite, treatment near the frontlines, occupational therapy, and expectations of returning to duty. By 1865, both American psychiatry and neurology were put on the map—a clear societal contribution from military medicine.

WORLD WAR I

In 1917, as the Great War in Europe raged on, U.S. Army medicine initially adopted an unprecedented proactive stance toward managing its prospective mental health dilemma by sending Major Thomas Salmon to England and France to learn from their war trauma lessons. Military historians routinely cite Salmon's adoption of Western frontline psychiatry policies aimed at preventing psychiatric attrition as the principle accomplishment. Salmon's proposals formed the U.S. military's seminal one-hundred-year-old mental health policy that successfully preserved the fighting force by returning emotionally injured soldiers to the frontlines, which tremendously benefited the military and its war-fighting mission but only harmed its service members.[2]

Salmon's *The Care and Treatment of Mental Diseases and War Neuroses (Shell Shock) in the British Army*, however, provided overlooked, yet no less groundbreaking, lessons on the need for top-down destigmatizing of mental health, acceptance of the universal vulnerability and inevitability of psychiatric casualties regardless of predispositions, early identification and treatment for a broad spectrum of war-stress injuries, the need for transparent reporting, close collaboration between military and civilian treatment centers, adequate numbers of well-trained specialists, and policies advocating for mental and physical health parity. Salmon also advocated for definitive treatment before military discharge with an emphasis on rehabilitation and retention and on organizational commitment to learn its war trauma lessons and leadership accountability.[3]

When WWI started in 1914, a sum total of just nine American psychologists identified themselves as clinical or applied psychologists. The majority of American and European psychologists were academics or engaged in laboratory studies on human sensation, perception, and memory. In April 1917, U.S. Army Major Robert Yerkes, the president of the American Psychological Association (founded in 1892), convened a group of notable American psychologists, including G. Stanely Hall, Edward Thorndike, John B. Watson, and James McKeen Cattell, to help with the war effort.

At the outset of WWI, American psychologists were contracted by the army to develop psychometrically sound methods for group screening recruits to help prevent the scourge of war neuroses and pensions and to assign military vocations based on these tests. Consequently, they developed the first group of mental abilities or intelligence testing (Army Alpha for literate recruits and Beta for English illiterate), which became the precursors to modern intelligence testing. This team also developed the first standardized personality test (i.e., the Woodworth Personality Data Sheet). It was assumed that such tests would help to screen out unfit personalities. The military's efforts sparked great enthusiasm in standardized testing. This led to the widespread use of standardized tests in American schools, colleges, business, and other parts of government.

The advent of airplanes in WWI to deliver death and fear from above also led to the new field of Aviation psychology, which involved the screening and training of pilots that extended to commercial pilots and eventually astronauts. This generation also developed the well-known psychological construct of human response to fear and stress—the fight-or-flight response was coined by U.S. Army psychiatrist Walter B. Cannon to explain why even the strongest, bravest, and best-trained soldiers broke down in combat.

In 1930, Congress authorized the Veterans Administration (VA) to "consolidate and coordinate Government activities affecting war veterans."[4] The VA represents the nation's largest health system, composed of 171 medical centers; more than 350 outpatient, community, and outreach clinics; 126 nursing home care units; and 40 domiciliary.[5]

WORLD WAR II

Most historians of war stress emphasize the contributions of WWII-era military mental healthcare in terms of preserving the fighting force and the resulting benefits to the military and its government.[6] For instance, the U.S. Army's failed mass psychiatric screening program is notable because it led to the "relearning" of the WWI lesson of avoiding evacuation syndromes through permanent frontline psychiatry policies.[7] From the perspective of service members, however, the military screening debacle proved the limits of human endurance in the face to toxic war stress. Other, more discernable achievements included the advent of group therapy; research revealing the importance of morale, leadership, and social support in helping veterans cope; the proliferation of psychotherapy; and the 1943 introduction of the Minnesota Multiphasic Personality Inventory (MMPI), which has become the gold standard in personality assessment and is used regularly by governments to screen recruits for highly sensitive positions.[8]

As post–World War II (WWII) American society struggled with the fallout from its wartime behavioral health crisis, more than six hundred thousand psychiatrically discharged veterans rapidly overwhelming an inept VA system.[9] Legions of enlightened former military leaders became disillusioned with the fragmented, antiquated, dualistic mental healthcare policies in the private sector that emphasized social isolation, stigma, and institutionalization.[10]

Specifically, crucial paradigmatic changes gleaned from hard-won psychiatric lessons of WWII were tragically ignored in the public sector. This new military paradigm centered on the ability to treat traumatic stress injuries and the need for a coordinated continuum of holistic care focusing on prevention, early identification, and intervention. Critical social reintegration services were prioritized with clear expectations of recovery along well-defined, integrated echelons of community-based treatment aimed to support families and restore the individual to a maximal level of functioning and productivity.[11] These seasoned clinicians also knew that changing public perception of war-stress injuries would require a concerted effort and resources to generate the necessary public awareness, destigmatization, and social reintegration implemented by well-trained, knowledgeable practitioners informed by scientific investigation and innovation.[12] Military leaders were all too familiar with the consequences of neglecting psychiatric lessons of war, which resulted in many of these leaders becoming staunch reform advocates.[13]

As a result of this new military paradigm, on July 3, 1946, President Harry S. Truman signed into law H.R. 2550, the bipartisan National Neuropsychiatric Institute Act—known as the National Mental Health Act. This key piece of legislation created the National Institute of Mental Health (NIMH), which was intended to bring mental health on par with physical health and close the chasm in research, public education, treatment, and policy between the medical and psychological sciences.[14] In the spirit of parity, the VA created new clinical psychology internships in 1946, enrolling two hundred psychology interns and resulting in greater societal acceptance of psychologists not only as researchers but also as practitioners.

From our vantage point, however, the two biggest mental health contributions by the WWII cohort are a book and a film. The book, *Neuropsychiatry in World War II*, includes two massive volumes compiled by U.S. Army mental health officers. These officers exhibited a heartfelt commitment to transform mental healthcare in the military and private sector, and as such, they compiled detailed, data-driven lessons learned, resulting in a blueprint for what is required to effectively meet mental health needs during times of war and peace.[15] The volume covers lessons on staffing, training, centralized accountable organization and leadership, transparency, antistigmatization, family member support, proper diagnosis, definitive treatment before military discharge, and reintegration support. One of most significant results of the volume that crossed over to the private sector was recognition of the universal vulnerability of emotional breakdown as a result of stress exposure. Because of the acceptance of this concept in the private sector, early identification and intervention were adopted to prevent long-term disability, and mental illness became treatable.

The other significant contribution was the film *Let There Be Light*. In 1946, legendary Hollywood film director and Army Captain John Huston produced what remains the single-most-important documentary about mental illness and about war-stress injury, in particular. The U.S. Army commissioned Huston to document the army's pilot implementation of President Franklin D. Roosevelt's 1944 treatment mandate "to ensure all combatants returning from overseas receive maximum benefit from hospitalization" before discharge. The film follows the six to eight weeks of treatment of veterans with war-stress injuries from the time their transport ship docks to the time of discharge from Edgewood State Hospital, New York. It contains the most progressive and enlightened messages ever publicly stated by the military, then or now, unequivocally communicating a nonstigmatizing belief that war-stress injuries and physical wounds are both legitimate consequences of war.

> Here is human suffrage, the final result of all that fire and metal can do to violate human flesh. Some wear the badges of the pain, the crutches, the bandages, the splints, others show no outward signs . . . yet THEY TOO ARE WOUNDED!
>
> These are the casualties of the spirit, the troubled in mind, men who are damaged emotionally. Born and bred in peace, educated to hate war, they were overnight plunged into sudden and terrible situations.
>
> EVERY man has his breaking point! And these, in fulfillment of their duty as soldiers were forced beyond the limit of human endurance.[16]

The film also depicts the broad spectrum of stress injuries in a racially diverse group of service members, coinciding with today's diagnoses of PTSD, depression, traumatic or complicated grief, conversion disorder, medically unexplained physical symptoms, generalized anxiety disorder, and moral injury.

Just as important, the military's multidisciplinary and comprehensive approach is documented—veterans receive the highest quality of treatment available in that era, including medication, hypnosis, narco-synthesis, psychodynamic therapy, group therapy, art therapy, recreational therapy, and vocational retraining. While the pre- and post-treatment outcomes of the veterans are demonstrated, the percentage of "successful" cases and whether any long-term care was provided are not mentioned. And no female patients are featured. Despite the melodramatic movie scores and the propogandist depictions, invaluable lessons are still to be learned.

Unfortunately, at the New York theatrical premiere of *Let There Be Light*, military police officers entered the premises and confiscated the film. Senior military officials claimed concerns for the privacy of the veterans who had consented to be filmed, but more likely, they objected to the messages the film sent the American public and future service members. So, the army classified the film and locked it away until its 1981 resurrection by Army Secretary Clifford Alexander, Jr., on behalf of his friend Jack Valenti who requested the ban be lifted.[17]

The army then commissioned and released a second film, *Shades of Gray*, whose principle message is that the military should not be held accountable for failing to appropriately manage its mental health dilemma, deflecting all responsibility to the inherent weakness of predisposed individuals and the weakness of modern American culture. The military is depicted as doing its utmost to screen out the nation's weakest at induction centers, contradicting the army's official lesson regarding using screening to purge weakness.[18]

Let There Be Light is readily available on YouTube, Netflix, and other outlets. *Let There Be Light* poses two pivotal questions: What is the likelihood that most of the veterans depicted would have reached the same outcome if they had been discharged directly to the private sector without military intervention? And, if the military had maintained these policies of destigmatization, comprehensive rehabilitation, and reintegration services before military discharge, would the scope and breadth of the current mental health crisis be different?

KOREAN WAR

Military historians routinely refer to the military's rapid relearning of the value of frontline psychiatry as its main achievement to reduce attrition. During the Korean War, there were likely new treatment regimens developed, but we are aware of no major innovations. The Korean War marked the American military's abrupt move away from transparency evident during the previous two world wars. Consequently, little is recorded on military mental healthcare around this war and what lessons may be gleaned from that era are reflected in unpublished manuscripts by army psychiatrists. In 1952, a Bronze Star was awarded to a military psychologist, Richard H. Blum, for his role in a classified army unit's secret mandate to reduce psychiatric evacuations,[19] becoming the first-ever military psychologist so awarded. In addition, the air force and navy created research centers on human engineering, thus giving rise to the field of human factors engineering.[20]

Following the war, military mental health professionals and Korean War veterans joined their WWII counterparts to advocate for needed changes to the national mental health system. In 1955, Congress passed the Mental Health Study Act, establishing the Joint Commission on Mental Illness and Health (JCMIH).[21] The JCMIH was a first-of-its-kind, congressionally funded multidisciplinary team of national experts and leaders from the NIMH, American Psychiatric Association, American Medical Association, and Council of State Governments, as well as representatives from clinical psychology, psychiatric social work, nursing, and the VA.[22] The JCMIH mandate was to design an integrated comprehensive mental health system based on many of the psychiatric lessons born of war. In particular, the JCMIH was tasked with (1) studying the biopsychosocial and cultural etiological factors of mental illness; (2) identifying, developing, and applying appropriate assessment, diagnosis, treatment, and rehabilitation services; (3) evaluating the recruitment and training of mental health personnel; (4) conducting a national survey of mental healthcare to design a comprehensive program; and (5) disseminating the reported findings and public education.[23]

In 1961, the JCMIH's final report was submitted to Congress, state governors, and the general public. The report recommended a comprehensive integrated national program made up of the following four interrelated elements:

1. Greater investment in basic research to reduce the gap in scientific knowledge.
2. Adoption of national recruitment and training programs to increase the supply of well-trained mental health clinicians who would provide an integrated, continuum (echelon) of community-based mental health services reflecting previous wartime experiences.
3. A pressing need to destigmatize mental health needs by a national public education campaign.
4. A dramatic and progressive increase in federal funding of mental health resources to raise standards of care.

Unfortunately, political infighting among healthcare stakeholders and government officials resulted in greatly watered-down legislation. In 1963, President John F. Kennedy signed the Mental Retardation and Community Mental Health Centers Construction Act, which eventually led to deinstitutionalization and community mental health programs. Many wartime lessons like adequate resourcing, ending the stigma of mental health injuries, and disparity in treatment, however, were still ignored.

VIETNAM WAR

Similar to mental healthcare during the Korean War, military mental healthcare during the Vietnam War ignored war trauma lessons and produced few publications. It is difficult to find any lasting mental health "innovations" during this time period. Although some army psychiatrists may point to a greater use of frontline psychiatry and psychotropic medications in war zones, leading to historically low rates of combat stress casualties reported in the war zone as a major achievement, this low rate likely does not reflect the reality of those injured.

A few courageous healthcare providers have published ethical and moral reservations about the military's frontline policy. The military's attempted to reduce exposure to war stress by limiting deployment length to twelve months (reflecting a noteworthy attempt to implement a foundational war trauma lesson), but some healthcare providers advocated that twelve months is still excessive. Others have roundly critiqued the military's rotation policy whereby individuals are deployed and returned from war zones as individuals as opposed to units, negating the resiliency benefit from social support deemed critical in returning war veterans. The Vietnam War also saw the institution of the military's mandatory drug-testing program, which was necessitated because of an epidemic of drug abuse in Vietnam. Many researchers blame the rise in substance abuse, personality discharges, discipline problems, and non-service-connected psychotic disorder diagnoses to explain the reported historically low psychiatric casualty rate.

Ultimately, the military's attention given to mental health issues was so effective that it did not record its psychiatric "lessons learned" until 2017.[24] Despite this lack of documentation, mental health professionals did produce some lasting results. In 1978, the navy established a multidisciplinary mental health crisis response team—Special Psychiatric Raid Intervention Team (SPRINT)—composed of psychiatrists, psychologists, chaplains, nurses, and enlisted corpsmen to provide relief after training accidents, suicide, and natural disasters. SPRINT appears to be the first documented crisis response team of its kind. Subsequently, the American Red Cross Disaster Mental Health services have borrowed extensively from the military's experiences.

The majority of mental health contributions have occurred outside of the military. Recognizing that a significant number of Vietnam veterans were experiencing readjustment problems, Congress established community-based Vet Centers in 1979 to increase veteran access to free mental health treatment and peer-to-peer support programs like rap groups, substance use assessment, employment assistance, and outreach services. Today, three hundred Vet Centers are located in all fifty states, the District of Columbia, and U.S. territories. During fiscal year 2017, nearly three hundred thousand veterans, active-duty service members, and family members received mental health services from a Vet Center.

Although antipsychiatry advocates,[25] ivory tower academics,[26] and military historians[27] have the luxury of debating the status of mental health conditions, the official recognition of trauma-induced, service-connected, and compensable conditions, like PTSD, has been a significant positive outcome in the lives of millions of veterans and their families.[28] As noted in chapter 2, Vietnam veterans were not the only war cohort to experience chronic emotional problems, but the freshness of their combat narratives as recorded by treating mental health clinicians provided sufficient justification to codify the first post-traumatic stress diagnosis since traumatic neuroses in 1889. In 1989, the VA conducted the first-ever randomized controlled trials to treat combat-related PTSD with psychotherapy (imaginal exposure), thus beginning an era of evidence-based therapies.

PERSIAN GULF WAR

The shortest war in American history also has little documentation on mental healthcare associated with it. The few war trauma lessons learned that were documented appear in an edited commercial book.[29] A similar story is told, however—that is, extensive reliance on forward deployed mental health assets resulted in a low number of psychiatric battlefield casualties. An epidemic of suicide and PTSD in Gulf War vets raises questions, however, about the military's professed success.

Arising from the public backlash of one hundred thousand U.S. personnel complaining of a wide range of medically unexplained physical symptoms (Gulf War Syndrome or Gulf War Illness), a host of congressional mandates resulted in positive implications for service members and their families. In April 1991, Congress extended the eligibility to veterans who served during other periods of armed hostilities after the Vietnam era; in October 1996, Congress also extended the eligibility to include WWII and Korean combat veterans. This increase in eligibility led to large groups veterans seeking health and mental health services, and seeking compensation for their wounds. This was the first significant increase in services provided to veterans since WWII. This increase significantly addressed veteran's mental health and health services that had been insufficient or poor within the military.

In 1992, Congress established the Defense and Veterans Brain Injury Center to integrate specialized TBI care, research, and education across military and veteran medical care systems. As a result of this focus, military advancements in TBI screening and rehabilitation have been adapted by the private sector, most notably, within contact sports.

The Department of Defense (DoD) also established the first prescription privilege training of clinical psychologists in 1994 in response to a national shortage of psychiatrists. Despite military medical leaders pressuring the DoD to end the highly successful program in 1997, the groundbreaking program led to laws extending prescription privileges to psychologists in New Mexico, Louisiana, Illinois, Iowa, Idaho, and Guam; a host of other state legislatures are contemplating similar laws, providing American citizens access to psychotropic medications in underserved areas.[30]

Since 1998, every navy carrier and large amphibious ship has been assigned mental health officers to service an entire battlegroup. Although the military clearly benefits from reducing attrition, embedding mental health professionals also may decrease the stigma of mental health injuries, increase early access to care, and prevent crises or long-term problems. With a 12,000:1 ratio, however, the only clear data point is a reduction in the cost of psychiatric evacuations. Continued fallout from the Gulf Illness debacle led Congress in 1999 to mandate that the DoD use pre- and postdeployment health assessments, including mental health screenings. The military's screening program, when properly implemented, provides warfighters invaluable documentation for service-connected disabilities that otherwise would not exist and also helps the government effectively track the prevalence of war-stress injury.

GLOBAL WAR ON TERRORISM

We have roundly criticized contemporary military officials engaging in deception by grossly understating or flat out lying to Congress, the media, the American public, and service members and their families. Such criticism is deserving in that it causes harmful delays for millions of veterans and family members to get the help they are owed. That said, a great deal of substance can be found in the extensive list of new programs and initiatives within military mental healthcare that have been launched over the past sixteen years of war:

- Real-time army research on the prevalence of several war-stress injury, stigma, and barriers to care as early as 2004.[31] This was proactive research, not mandated by Congress, and it reflects a level of transparency not seen since the later years of WWII.
- VA/DoD Clinical Practice Guidelines. The first-ever clinical practice guidelines for PTSD in the United States was published by the VA/DoD.
- Annual Mental Health Assessment Teams (MHAT). This army research initiative assesses mental health issues in the war zones since 2003.
- Mandated postdeployment health reassessment screenings. In 2012, DD Form 2900 became required for all personnel after three to six months of redeployment.
- DoD Centers of Excellence (DCoE). In 2007, Congress established the DCoE to provide central guidance and leadership role on PTSD and TBI management across the DoD.
- National Intrepid Centers of Excellence (NICoE). In 2007, Congress mandated the DoD creation of NICoE to provide specialized multidisciplinary, comprehensive care of war-stress injury and TBI using evidence-based and complementary alternative approaches. The NICoE opened in 2010 with plans to expand to other regions and marks the return to Union Army specialty hospitals that operated during the U.S. Civil War.
- Improved access to mental health training. In 2006, Congress established the Center for Deployment Psychology (CDP) to provide critical mental health trainings, including training on evidence-based PTSD therapies.
- Expansion of military mental health workforce. In 2007, in response to the congressional mandate for the DoD to increase staffing and assess current and future mental health provider staffing needs, the DoD created the Psychological Health Risk-Adjusted Model for Staffing (PHRAMS). Although the Government Accountability Office (GAO) reported a 34 percent increase of military mental health clinicians from 4,608 providers in 2009 to 6,186 providers in 2013, they also found noncompliance with PHRAMS.[32]
- Collaborative research initiatives. The DoD has dramatically reduced its isolationist approach and reached out to the civilian sector and the VA for collaboration on a host of research and training initiatives, including suicide prevention and prospective studies to measure the pre- and post-effects from deployments.

- Centralized database for tracking and reporting military suicides. In 2011, the Defense Suicide Prevention Office (DSPO) was established to manage efforts to prevent suicide and to publish quarterly suicide reports.
- Unprecedented frontline mental health access. Mental health officers are now embedded in infantry units, navy ships, or airwings, the number of combat and operational stress control personnel within war zones has increased.
- Expanded access to Vet Centers and the VA. In 2003, active-duty and Operating Enduring Freedom/Operation Iraqi Freedom (OEF/OIF) veterans were granted Vet Center access as well as children and spouses to provide bereavement counseling.
- Increased investment in military clinical research. Before 2001, few research dollars went toward clinical research to assess and treat war-stress injury in the military.
- Improved family member support throughout deployment cycle. Each service branch and community counseling center has developed a number of deployment support programs (e.g., Family Readiness).
- Improved military recovery and reintegration support. In 2008, Congress mandated the DoD to proactively support wounded, ill, and injured service members by creating what is now called the Office of Warrior Care Policy (WCP).
- Numerous veteran and military nonprofits. In 2015, the VA reported there are more than forty-five thousand nonprofits devoted to veterans and their families had registered with the IRS (e.g., American Legion, Veterans of Foreign Wars, Wounded Warrior Project, Blue Star Family).
- Web-based programs. A plethora of programs, such as *Military One Source* and *After Deployment*, provide a wide range of information and resources for service personnel and families.
- National promulgation of veteran's courts. This court emphasizes legal problem-solving and treatment versus punishment for war-stress-injured veterans (see chapter 3).
- VA initiatives to eradicate veteran's homelessness. In 2010, the VA developed Opening Doors, the first-ever federal strategic plan to end homelessness. The VA has reported a 50 percent reduction in veteran homelessness since 2010.
- Creation of VA and DoD crisis hotlines. In 2007, the VA and DoD established a Veterans Crisis Line and Military Crisis Line, respectively, in response to media reports of veterans' suicide.
- National Center for Telehealth and Technology (T2). In 2007, Congress established T2 as a component of DCoE to provide innovation of health

technology solutions for psychological health and TBI and to deliver tested solutions.

- Resilience training. The army has developed a number of programs (e.g., Battle-mind, Comprehensive Soldier Fitness) emphasizing resilience training to prevent war-stress injury.
- Revamped transition assistance program (TAP). In 2011, DoD overhauled its TAP for service personnel and family members to address concerns about inadequate reintegration support. Unfortunately, however, the GAO has reported that the DoD "misstated the performance of the TAP."[33]
- Revised policies. The military has revised its policies on backdoor and bad paper discharges (see chapters 3 and 4).
- Organizational policies restructuring military medicine and mental health-care. In 2007, the DoD was required to established Directors of Psychological Health, and in 2017, Congress mandated the Defense Health Agency to consolidate its headquarters and standardized healthcare policies in DoD.
- Military media antistigma campaign. The Armed Forces Radio and Television networks frequently air messages against stigma and encourage personnel to seek treatment. A former high-ranking general publicly advocated for "PTS" without the "D" to reduce stigma.
- Legislation. Numerous legislation has been passed, including the Wounded Warriors Act (2007), the Military and Veterans Mental Health Provider Assessment Act (2015) to improve the provision of mental healthcare; and the Military Suicide Prevention Act (2014) to mandate universal annual mental health assessments.
- Revised VA eligibility policies. In 2017, eligibility policies were revised to include service members with bad paper discharges.
- Navy/Marine Corps openness toward war-stress injury. In 2010, the U.S. Navy/ Marine Corps revised their combat and operational stress control guidance to include a candid self-assessment of harmful policies (e.g., weaponizing stigma) in an effort to reverse trends.

FIXING MILITARY MENTAL HEALTHCARE: MISSION ACCOMPLISHED?

In black and white on congressional briefing documents, research papers, and editorials, and in commissioned study after study, the body of work on war-stress injury is impressive. It is obvious, however, that contemporary military leaders have not reviewed the lessons learned by their historical counterparts when they arrogantly boast about "unprecedented" mental health efforts. Despite the significant number of accomplishments, the constant need for investigations into the treatment of military service members and the number of injuries that continue to be reported reveal that valuable lessons have not been learned. Furthermore, we ask:

- Why does the military continue to avoid its war trauma lessons and why was it grossly negligent in preparing to meet the wartime mental health needs of yet another generation?
- Why is the military unwavering in employing its harmful strategies to avoid acknowledging the psychiatric realities of modern warfare, such as neglect, denial, deception, delay, legal prosecutions, bad paper discharges, faulty diagnoses, weaponizing stigma, preventing treatment access, and perpetuating an organizational structure that prohibits leadership accountability?
- Why the proliferation of scandals in veteran suicide, changing PTSD diagnoses, chronic staffing shortages, wrongful discharges, opioid addiction, inadequate treatment, family, and reintegration support, and veterans' courts?
- Why have the national news media, Congress, and the commanders-in-chief failed to even ask these basic questions and why are they ever so willing to accept the military's lengthy brag sheet as evidence of mission accomplished?

Despite the accomplishments of the past two decades, we must acknowledge the failures that have yet to be resolved to address the persistent mental health dilemma. While acknowledging the military's efforts and demonstrating respect and gratitude to U.S. service members, we have to accept both realities of military mental healthcare to adequality address the mental health dilemma. A modern, state-of-the-art military must both embrace and promote mental health more forcefully, systematically, and sustainably, embracing both the military's rich culture and the science of human factors and behavioral health.

The army's recent to-do list describes future changes needed—such as improving mental health utilization, substance abuse and chronic pain treatment, TBI research, and postdeployment support—and indeed these areas require reform.[34] Conspicuously absent in the military's congratulatory summary, however, is a steadfast refusal to admit culpability in perpetuating generational crises by ignoring foundational war trauma lessons from their predecessors. This reflects a striking lack of humility and candor compared with their WWII counterparts. Until the military directly confronts its harmful approach toward its mental health dilemma, true transformative change will remain elusive. A blueprint for meaningful reform of mental healthcare within and outside of the military could end the dishonorable cycle of preventable wartime crises. But what if the DoD elects to remain in the dark and ignore, deny, or refuse to correct the problems uncovered?

14

TRANSFORMING MILITARY
MENTAL HEALTHCARE

THREE OPTIONS FOR CHANGE

Individuals are said to resist change because of habit and inertia, fear of the unknown, absence of the skills they will need after the change, and fear of losing power.

Organizations are said to resist change because of inertia, sunk costs, scarce resources, threats to the power base of the old dominant coalition, values and beliefs, conformity to norms, and inability to perceive alternatives.

CAROL AGÓCS, "INSTITUTIONALIZED RESISTANCE TO ORGANIZATIONAL CHANGE"

Those who have served in the military routinely hear statements like, "Don't come to me bellyaching about how bad things are. You better have a solution; otherwise, you're just part of the problem!" This type of solution-focused, can-do attitude is a clear strength of military culture and often separates the U.S. military from other armed forces in the world. To that end, the previous fourteen chapters amounted to our collective bellyaching about the dark side of the military's approach to dealing with its mental healthcare dilemma.

In this final chapter, we examine three options to effect the change in military mental healthcare that is needed to end the immoral pattern of self-inflicted and largely preventable wartime behavioral health crises: (1) support the status quo of waiting for the military to internally institute incremental changes as it sees fit—the do-nothing option; (2) actively petition Congress and the commander-in-chief to externally mandate transformative changes by implementing all foundational war trauma lessons—the watchful waiting or hope and pray option; and (3) seek redress from the judicial branch that would compel the military to follow its own policies, lessons learned, and legal requirements—the class action option.

We examine the pros and cons for each option. For the second option, specific concrete changes are presented that, if the legislative or executive branches mandated with conviction, would end the generational cycle of preventable wartime behavioral health crises. Last, we offer a legal analysis for an unprecedented class action against the Department of Defense (DoD) to effect change. After briefly reviewing the history of tort law and the U.S. military's immunity from the *Feres* doctrine, we examine legal precedents both domestic and abroad.[1]

WHAT IS MEANT BY TRANSFORMATIVE CHANGE?

It is easy to say words like "transformation" or "overhaul" when it comes to proposing radical system changes, but these words are meaningless if not backed up by precise, practical, and justifiable solutions. Transformation is also highly subjective. Using a term like "war-stress injury" would be radical by itself for some leaders. We believe that transformative change has to completely alter the current approach. For instance, we can say that one transformative change for the military would be to stop avoiding learning its war trauma lessons. Although implementing these lessors would not end combat-related post-traumatic stress disorder (PTSD) or veteran suicide (in the same way that implementing battlefield medical lessons has not eradicated war-related deaths), implementing the ten foundational war trauma lessons would assuredly end the cycle of indifference, neglect, crisis, transient change, and national reset that plagues military mental healthcare and unnecessarily victimizes U.S. service members. In the remainder of this chapter, we describe twenty-four specific policies and organizational changes required to demonstrate the legitimate learning of war trauma lessons.

TWENTY-FOUR SPECIFIC CHANGES THAT WILL TRANSFORM MILITARY MENTAL HEALTHCARE

The following corrective actions are essential for transforming military mental healthcare and to guarantee an end to the generational cycle of mental health neglect and self-inflicted crises:

1. Conduct the first investigations by congressional committees on armed services into the preventable root causes of the current wartime crisis to

identify specific policies and practices requiring change. The U.S. government has never investigated or held hearings on the reasons *why* the military neglects its war trauma lessons and repetitively goes to war being unable to meet basic mental health needs in *peacetime*, yet alone war (see chapter 1).

2. Establish a Behavioral Health Corps (BHC) that integrates all three independent components of military mental healthcare (military medicine, family/community counseling centers, and DoD contractors) into a single, accountable chain of command equal in power, resources, and status that exists for military medicine (see chapter 10). The BHC critically raises the status and priority of mental health services and its providers within the DoD. The DoD-BHC would be led by flag or general officers, equal in status to the military surgeon general. The BHC director will be held accountable for ensuring compliance with the noted recommendations.[2]

3. Creation of a service-wide Behavioral Health Lessons Learned Center with dedicated policies, programs, and personnel equal to those that exist for military medicine. Require the DoD to ensure that all ten foundational lessons of war trauma are implemented, monitored, and reported for compliance on an annual basis (see chapter 12).

4. Publish a DoD-wide zero-tolerance policy for mental health stigma, disparity, and organizational barriers to seeking mental healthcare similar to existing military zero-tolerance policies intended to eliminate other forms of social injustice, such as discrimination based on race, gender, sexual orientation, sexual harassment, and other command climate issues (see chapter 5). The DoD's current annual command equal opportunity climate surveys should include measures of mental health stigma and barriers to care with commanders similarly held accountable for noncompliance.

5. Commission the Institute of Medicine (IOM) to investigate the efficacy and potential harm caused by the military's frontline psychiatry programs—such as the combat and operational stress control program (COSC)—and the DoD's policy of deploying service members with known existing untreated war-stress injury.[3]

6. Require the DoD and Department of Veterans Affairs (VA) to end the delay in implementing recommendations by government-commissioned studies, such as the IOM and RAND, to ensure a seamless transition to civilian life for veterans and their families (see chapter 8).[4]

7. Reinstate President Roosevelt's 1944 executive order mandating the military provide the maximum benefit of comprehensive, multidisciplinary treatment and reconditioning services before discharging military personnel, including

reconditioning, vocational training, family support, and peer mentoring (see chapters 10 and 11). For example, all service members serving in combat or operational zones should have access to treatment through the DoD's Center for Excellence programs before separation from combat with the goal of rehabilitation and retention. Legislation should be passed mandating that military be responsible and accountable for the provision of primary mental health services, including definitive treatment with evidence-based practice, before discharge. VA treatment should be a continuation of care rather than a primary or initial treatment source.

8. Develop a centralized, publicly accessible database to track and transparently report the full spectrum of war-stress injury prevalence and standardized program and treatment outcomes across the DoD and VA (see chapters 6 and 8).

9. Establish and maintain a service-wide National Reentry Program providing coordination among the DoD, VA, and nonprofit agencies consisting of peer mentors and a centralized, searchable database and coordination service covering the full spectrum of reentry needs for veterans and their families.[5]

10. Issue a deployment policy limiting deployment length to six months, similar to the UK's Ministry of Defense' Harmony Guidelines, and enact legislation requiring the institution of the military draft without any exemptions after the second deployment cycle to reduce the service gap within the United States. Currently, less than 1 percent of U.S. citizens have carried the burden for the entire country during the past eighteen-years of war.

11. Pass legislation prohibiting the military's use of backdoor or bad paper discharges of war veterans (see chapters 4 and 9), and task the Government Accountability Office (GAO) to monitor for annual compliance.

12. Issue legislation ensuring that all war veterans and their families, regardless of length of service or characterization of military discharge, have access to VA mental health services for perpetuity (see the appendix).

13. Issue legislation requiring the DoD and VA ensure they maintain adequate numbers of well-trained behavioral health specialists during times of peace and war, including a substantial increase in recruiting military personnel and family members to attend the Uniformed Health Services University, as well as hiring licensed marriage and family therapists or other graduate-level counselors per the IOM.[6]

14. Pass legislation for the DoD and VA to conduct research, train, and provide access to all evidence-based psychotherapies according to VA and DoD clinical practice guidelines, including eye movement desensitization and

reprocessing (EMDR) as well as complementary alternative medical services.[7] Specifically, end the political scientific bias within the DoD and VA that prevents researching EMDR and limits treatment access.[8]

15. Establish standardized assessment, diagnosis, and treatment measurements and procedures to be utilized across the DoD and VA (see chapter 9).

16. Eliminate the 203 DoD policies that the GAO[9] identified as being responsible for maintaining organizational sanctioned mental health stigma and barriers to seeking care (see chapter 5).

17. Pass legislation to amend the *Feres* doctrine by adding the exception under the Federal Tort Claims Act, allowing class action for medical and mental health negligence outside war zones to provide equal constitutional protection for citizen-soldiers.[10]

18. Pass legislation mandating the military publish publicly accessible, comprehensive, and accurate reporting of its compliance with the ten foundational war trauma lessons (see chapters 2 and 12).

19. Require the DoD to complete and publish a checklist ensuring readiness to meet wartime mental health needs before or shortly after entering war (see the appendix).

20. Reconstitute and maintain the military's veteran's court or rehabilitation-oriented, problem-solving legal system for veterans with war-stress injuries (see chapter 4).

21. Ensure that immediate and extended family members have access to quality mental health and social support services throughout the deployment cycle and post-military transition (see chapter 11).

22. Require the U.S. Army and Air Force to adopt the U.S. Navy and Marine Corps' COSC guidance, including an accurate portrayal of the military's weaponization of stigma.[11]

23. Require the DoD to adopt policies that end the disparity between mental and physical health, by (a) mandating routine annual mental health assessments to existing annual medical readiness exams for all and ensuring access to mental health services during business hours akin to medical services; (b) eliminating career repercussions for disclosing war-stress injuries and seeking mental health treatment; (c) eliminating the current promotion ceiling of military psychotherapists (clinical psychologists, social workers) from reaching the flag and general officer ranks; (d) providing equal recruitment and retention bonuses for mental health and physical health clinicians; and (e) expanding the army's integrative primary care practices to other service branches (chapters 5 and 12).

24. Establish a DoD/VA behavioral health oversight committee that includes veterans, family members, and key nonprofit organizations to track and report annually on implementation and compliance with these injunctions (see chapter 10).

OPTION 1. MAINTAINING THE STATUS QUO OF INTERNAL INCREMENTAL CHANGE

The first option for changing military mental healthcare is to maintain the current systems responsible for instituting incremental change. This option leaves changes to the discretion of the military with instruction from congress and the executive branch to effect piecemeal change to end the cycle of preventable crises. Consequently, change is inherently piecemeal, haphazard, and almost entirely reactive to the crisis of the day, as opposed to a proactive, coherent, long-term strategy. Of course, the major obstacle in this option is that neither the military, congress, or commander-in-chief view the current mental health crisis as a continuation of government failures from previous wars, nor do they appreciate that these crises are largely self-inflicted. This first option is entirely crisis driven, and when wars end and there are no public outcries or sensational news stories of mistreated service members, history shows we enter into a national reset phase.

ADVANTAGES OF PRESERVING THE STATUS QUO

As discussed in chapter 13, the military's only effort to be proactive in addressing its mental health dilemma occurred during World War I (WWI) when the U.S. Army sent Major Salmon to Europe before the U.S. entry into the war.[12] A recent *Time* magazine article by the Pentagon's chief psychiatric consultant *Military Mental Health's Wins and Losses Since the Iraq Invasion* describes several unprecedented accomplishments from this century, including extensive deployment health screenings, annual frontline assessments by Mental Health Advisory Teams (MHAT), a plethora of educational resources for service personnel and family members, greater emphasis on resilience training, and funding of treatment research.[13] Additional noteworthy initiatives include publication of the first PTSD practice guideline, the proliferation of VA/DoD treatment applications for smart phones, increased access to crisis services (e.g., Veterans Crisis Line), the roll out of standardized training and dissemination of evidence-based PTSD treatments, revamping military transition assistance programs, societal and media support of returning veterans, and an increase in the number of non-profit agencies filling the void in veterans' social reintegration services.[14] These accomplishments clearly demonstrate that this generation, as in past war generations, has responded to a wartime mental health crisis with the sense of urgency it deserves. Our focus on the causes of generational crises should not detract from the herculean individual efforts within military populations, government, and the private sector to respond to the crisis.

DISADVANTAGES OF PRESERVING THE STATUS QUO

Despite the impressive list of recent incremental changes, the IOM reviewed the DoD's progress in implementing its new vision, concluding that despite striving to understand the challenges to reintegrating to civilian life, their response often does not match the "magnitude of the problems, and many readjustment needs are unmet or unknown." Furthermore, the IOM warned that

> the urgency of addressing those issues is heightened by the sheer number of people affected, the rapid drawdown of personnel, . . . and the long-term effects that many of the issues might have not only on military personnel and veterans and their families, but on the country as a whole.[15]

What remains to be seen is whether the military's current organizational reforms are sufficient to meet wartime needs and end the cycle of preventable crises.

EVIDENCE OF THE STATUS QUO FAILING

Perhaps the most compelling argument against relying on internally generated, incremental mental health reform is the military's own acknowledgment of its repeated failure to provide basic mental healthcare during peace, let alone war. As mentioned earlier, the military candidly admits to neglecting its fundamental lessons of war trauma that have been linked to the generational cycle of preventable crises.[16] Moreover, investigation into these wartime crises reveals a clear pattern in which the military and congress is forced to react to the neglectful state of mental health services through a mass hiring of specialists and improvements in clinical training, treatment, prevention, research, monitoring, stigma, and reintegration.[17] Therefore, the vast majority of the military's recent mental health accomplishments can be described accurately as reactionary and driven by congressional and executive mandates as opposed to proactive policies pursued by enlightened military leaders.

Furthermore, after every major war since WWI, millions of dollars have been spent on commissioned studies and congressional legislation intended to address major mental health deficiencies.[18] Seven years after the DoD Task Force on Mental Health[19] published its recommended tweaking of military mental healthcare, multiple government-sponsored studies have been conducted on DoD's mental health system as a whole,[20] as well as on specific program components. These studies have included psychological health and traumatic brain injuries (TBIs),[21] PTSD assessment and treatment,[22] suicide prevention,[23] substance abuse,[24] and prevention, resilience, and reintegration services.[25] Since 2001, no less than 214 separate investigations, studies, and task forces have looked into military mental healthcare. Aside from the unknown taxpayer expense of these studies, the results have been limited. Russell, Butkus, and Figley conducted a systematic review of major independent investigations that, taken together, offer compelling evidence against pitting one's hope that internal reform will end the cycle of self-inflicted crises in the foreseeable future.[26]

Seven years after the DoD Task Force on Mental Health, a report from the IOM

> found that PTSD management in DoD appear[s] to be local, ad hoc, incremental, and crisis-driven with little planning devoted to the development of a long-range, population-based approach for this disorder by either the office of the Assistant Secretary of Defense for Health Affairs (OASDHA) or any of the service branches.[27]

Having neglected to develop a sufficient plan for mental health,[28] the ASDHA has failed to avert another preventable crisis.

The IOM aptly sums up the status quo:

> Although the ASD(HA) has issued some directives and instructions that apply to all service branches, implementation typically is at the discretion

of each service branch's surgeon general, installation commander, or even military treatment facility (MTF) leaders.

The committee recognizes that, in part, such stove pipping of responsibility is inherent in the organizational structure of DOD and serves a purpose, given the different mission and culture of each service branch, but these differences do not preclude a more systematic and integrated approach to PTSD management.

Standardization and consistency of PTDS programs and services among facilities and service branches are not evident, and they often appear to have been developed and sustained at the local level without coordination with similar programs on other installations.[29]

In conclusion, Evidence is clear and convincing from multiple objective and credible sources that the DoD's current organizational and leadership structure as it pertains to mental healthcare is critically flawed. Rampant fragmentation, inefficiency, and a lack of accountability prohibit the military from learning its psychiatric lessons of war, further perpetuating the tragic cycle of preventable wartime behavioral health crises.

OPTION 2. TRANSFORMATIVE CHANGES TO MILITARY MENTAL HEALTHCARE VIA EXTERNAL MANDATE

Given that the military's current structure clearly will not provide a suitable response to the mental health crisis taking place in its ranks, one must turn to other options to bring about the necessary changes. One such option is to change military mental healthcare through external mandates from congress or the president of the United States. This option defers primary responsibility to congress and commander-in-chief to compel the military to learn its war trauma lessons.

ADVANTAGES OF TRANSFORMATIVE CHANGES VIA EXTERNAL MANDATE

The U.S. Congress enjoys the constitutional responsibility for maintaining the armed forces. Congress has the ability to pass and enforce laws that implement all or most of the twenty-four specific changes outlined earlier, thus ensuring a greater likelihood of continuity or permanency of those changes. Military leaders cannot unilaterally disregard the law, or they risk prosecution. Congress is also in the best (if not only) position to provide effective monitoring or oversight of the military's implementation of transformative changes to mental health.

DISADVANTAGES OF TRANSFORMATIVE CHANGES VIA EXTERNAL MANDATE

Previous wars have shown that the U.S. Congress has not been effective in fixing military mental healthcare or ending the generational cycle of neglect and self-inflicted crises. Presidential intervention has shown slightly more progress in the past. In 1944, President Roosevelt mandated the War Department be held accountable for ensuring all returning service members received the "maximum benefit of treatment prior to discharge." He wrote:

> My dear Mr. Secretary: I am deeply concerned over the physical and emotional condition of disabled men returning from the war. I feel, as I know you do, that the ultimate ought to be done for them to return them as useful citizens-useful not only to themselves but to the community.
>
> The president went on to direct that
>
> it should be the responsibility of the military authorities to insure that no overseas casualty is discharged from the armed forces until he has received the maximum benefits of hospitalization and convalescent facilities which must include physical and psychological rehabilitation, vocational guidance, prevocational training, and resocialization.[30]

A successful prototype of this progressive approach was preserved in John Huston's (1946) film *Let There Be Light*. When Roosevelt died and War World II (WWII) ended, however, the public pressure on the military to sustain these programs faded. Whether by subsequent executive order or by benign neglect, the military has never since been compelled by the president to provide treatment of service members with war-stress injury. Traditionally, the president has deferred this responsibility almost entirely to the VA—until recently, that is, with the advent of military treatment centers. Nevertheless, the military currently has no treatment mandate.

SUMMARIZING THE CASE FOR TRANSFORMATIVE CHANGES VIA EXTERNAL MANDATE

The only viable way to institute transformative change in the military's mental healthcare system is for congress to pass legislation requiring alterations to the current structure. The president has the authority to issue executive privilege or petition congress to act on this issue, but no president has done so since WWII. The tragic absence of any congressional or presidential fact-finding hearings or investigations into the DoD's belated 2007 disclosure of rampant mental health neglect and another national self-inflicted crisis is a major point of concern, as is the failure of congress to execute its oversight of the military. The 214 commissioned studies all have called for the need for a major overhaul, and the lack of any action in response to those studies indicates that the responsible government authorities likely will not act to resolve this raging crisis. Perhaps only a national outcry for radical change to military mental healthcare would draw the attention of congress or the president to the issue. Yet, plenty of reports should have alarmed the public, such as the studies that show twenty-two veterans commit suicide a day or that reveal scandals like the army's dishonorable backdoor discharges or the alteration of PTSD diagnoses to save pension costs (see chapter 9). Until congress or the president starts asking the right questions and seeking the right answers, it is unlikely that either branch of government will be the source for systemic change.

OPTION 3. TRANSFORMATIVE CHANGE VIA CLASS ACTION

If the country deems the legislative and executive branches will not act, then the only other recourse is to invoke the judicial branch of government through class action. Russell, Zinn, and Figley conducted a preliminary exploration into the potential legal merits, precedents, and framework for a major class action against the DoD to make the required transformative changes.[31] Does the aforementioned scenario constitute a legal breach of duty, rendering the DoD culpable and vulnerable to mass civil litigation from hundreds of thousands of service members and their families harmed by its actions and inaction?

To date, we are not aware of any civil action against the DoD or government for failure to provide adequate mental health services to its beneficiaries. Indeed, significant legal barriers exist, like the *Feres* doctrine that protects the U.S. military from tort suits. Although the status quo suggests that the U.S. government and its military enjoy certain immunity from civil action for its complicit role in perpetuating a cycle of mental health neglect and crisis, a recent legal precedent may make this option plausible.

LEGAL PRECEDENT OF MILITARY MENTAL HEALTH TORT ACTION: *MULTIPLE CLAIMANTS V. MoD*

In 2003, a mostly invisible but landmark legal case was adjudicated by the British High Court of England and Wales.[32] More than two thousand British combat veterans serving before 1996 claimed negligence by the Ministry of Defense (MoD) for failing to utilize proper measures to prevent, detect, and treat predictable long-term adverse effects of war such as PTSD.[33] The judgment outlined the current state of knowledge of PTSD and its prevention and defined standards of management through the testimony of sixteen leading international experts in the field, with the glaring exception of the United States. For unknown reasons, the U.S. government forbade any of its experts from testifying in this landmark case, suggesting that they were concerned that testimony from U.S. military and VA authorities could be prejudicial in future legal proceedings. Regardless, eight experts provided instruction to each side and then subjected their evidence to scrutiny and cross-examination.

The claimants did not argue that the MoD was wrong for exposing them to the harmful effects of war, thus avoiding the government's assertion of "combat immunity" that prohibits military personnel from suing the military for exposing them to the dangers of war. In turn, the MoD did not dispute that military culture can make it difficult for people to admit to psychological disorders, which might be seen as an expression of weakness. Instead, the case was principally centered around the MoD's responsibility to provide a standard of care for those suffering from war-stress injuries.

Specifically, the claimants argued and the MoD contested eight charges of negligent conduct: (1) the MoD had demonstrated an inability to properly learn from its documented war trauma lessons to prevent or ameliorate war-stress injuries; (2) the MoD failed to effectively address the harmful effects of mental health stigma and organizational barriers to care; (3) the MoD failed to properly screen out recruits with known high-risk factors for PTSD; (4) the MoD failed to train all service personnel in the nature of the psychiatric consequences of combat stress and did not offer preventative resilience training; (5) the MoD failed to employ a system of early intervention based on the principles of forward psychiatry for those suffering from acute stress reactions; (6) the MoD failed to train commanders to use operational debriefing strategies after unit members were exposed to traumatic events; (7) the MoD failed to employ a system for early detection of war-stress injury, including the use of standardized diagnostic assessments; and (8) the MoD failed to employ a system of early, evidence-based treatment of war-stress injuries.[34]

The British High Court concluded "that combat can result in psychiatric injury was not at issue in this case as this was accepted by both sides. Nor was it argued that the MoD did not have a 'duty of care' to look after psychiatrically injured personnel."[35] The British High Court held the MoD defense against the landmark mass civil action, and several court rulings were used to successfully litigate four subsequent individual tort claims by service members.

Following the highly publicized tort cases, the MoD took concerted action to avoid repeating the mistakes of the past. It established the King's Centre for Military Health Research and the Academic Department of Military Mental Health, dedicated to acquiring and learning from the MoD's psychiatric lessons of war. The MoD pledged more than £7 million (or about US$9.8 million) toward combating mental health disorders and committed to ensuring that all service personnel receive treatment and other needed support services. It also established sixteen departments of community mental health across the United Kingdom, created additional centers overseas, and embarked on aggressive antistigma campaigns to encourage more veterans and active-duty personnel with PTSD to come forward.[36]

According to a 2015 *Guardian* news article, rates of PTSD, depression, TBI, substance abuse, interpersonal violence, homelessness, unemployment, incarcerations, and other predictable psychological outcomes of war among British Iraq and Afghanistan veterans have increased modestly each year during these protracted wars.[37] No further known class actions have been filed against the MoD, however, for neglecting its duty to care, nor have there been rampant suicide spikes amongst the UK's armed forces. The MoD reports a prevalence of PTSD diagnosis in about 3–7 percent of its veterans from Operation Enduring Freedom, Operation Iraqi Freedom, and Operation New Dawn,[38] compared with 20–50 percent in U.S. veterans.[39] In short, despite remaining imperfections, the British military appears to have taken seriously the need to learn its psychiatric lessons of war and implemented its foundational war trauma lessons.[40] Consequently, the MoD and its government stand a fighting chance to end their cycle of self-inflicted crises.

EMPIRICAL EVIDENCE OF THE POTENTIAL BENEFIT OF MILITARY CLASS ACTION

Empirical studies reinforce British news media reports. In 2010, UK researchers examined the consequences of deployment to Iraq and Afghanistan on the mental health of 9,900 (56 percent) of UK military active-duty service members and reservists from 2003 to 2009. The study specifically focused on the effects of multiple deployments and time since returning from deployment in light of public concerns over the impact of multiple deployments and escalating rates of PTSD, suicide, and other war-stress injuries in the U.S. military.[41] In adherence to one of the foundational lessons of war trauma, MoD researchers used a fairly comprehensive approach to assessing for war-stress injuries that went beyond PTSD diagnosis and included a broader range of psychiatric diagnoses, substance use disorders, and medically unexplained physical conditions. Notably, the latter has been generally neglected by U.S. researchers for decades.[42] Follow-up surveys were conducted with 6,429 randomly selected personnel, including those who left the military.[43] Overall, the results indicated that despite multiple deployments, the prevalence of mental disorders in the MoD remained stable between 2003 and 2009, with 4 percent of respondents reporting probable PTSD, 19.7 percent reporting some other mental disorder, and 13 percent reporting alcohol misuse. These percentages were significantly lower than those documented in U.S.-based reports.[44]

Efforts to explain the significant discrepancy between UK and U.S. military personnel despite roughly equivalent exposure to combat stress led MoD researchers to cite its Harmony Guidelines, adopted in 2003 in the aftermath of *Multiple Claimants v. MoD*, which outlines the recommended number of deployments and length of time between deployments for the MoD. Some of the differences between the U.S. and UK forces include younger troops, longer deployments, more reservists, a higher troop-to-leader ratio, and higher casualties and fatalities in Iraq, although not in Afghanistan.[45] Care also differed between the two forces—U.S. personnel have access to care from the VA for combat-related disorders for five years after leaving the armed forces.[46] UK ex-personnel have lifetime access to the National Health Service.[47] The MoD is also implementing more new measures that will need more time to take full effect, such as a few days of decompression in Cyprus before returning to family from active duty.[48]

Although it is certainly beyond this study to present a comprehensive analysis of the differential military mental healthcare policies and practices between the Unites States and other countries, it is difficult to doubt that the United Kingdom is making more substantial progress. Reports of a significant mental health needs in the United Kingdom, including thousands of incarcerated veterans, has led the British government to adopt programs like the American veterans' court system.[49] In relation to operations in Iraq and Afghanistan, however, it strongly appears that the UK's relative success in effectively managing its wartime behavioral health needs and avoiding a self-inflicted crisis is predominantly attributed to the 2003 and 2005 civil actions (e.g., *Multiple Claimants v. MoD*). It is exceedingly unlikely that these results would have occurred without these landmark cases. In fact, some U.S. legal scholars have asserted that the capacity to file tort claims against the military is instrumental in compelling military medicine to make critical changes that can prevent avoidable harm and save lives.[50]

SUMMARY OF TRANSFORMATIVE CHANGE VIA CLASS ACTION

Nearly seven years after the start of the longest armed conflict in U.S. history, the 2007 report by the congressionally mandated DoD Task Force on Mental Health acknowledged a largely self-inflicted crisis caused by chronic and cataclysmic neglect of mental health services rendered incapable of meeting peacetime or wartime needs. Moreover, occupational hazards of a military career routinely expose service members to potentially traumatic events beyond war, including training accidents, military sexual trauma, terrorism, and disaster relief missions. Therefore, the DoD is in a prime position to be the national, if not international, leader in understanding, research, assessment, treatment, and prevention of traumatic stress injuries. The U.S. military, however, has neglected this responsibility, and a crisis of mental health injuries in its service members has perpetuated as a result. Compounded with the negligence of U.S. Congress and the president to mandate lasting change, civil action may be the final recourse to forcing systemic change to military mental healthcare. Unlike the United Kingdom, which permits class actions, the United States lacks an equivalent vehicle.

Awareness of this vicious self-perpetuating cycle motivated WWII U.S. military leaders to painfully reflect on their failure to learn from previous generations of hard-won war trauma lessons, "In contrast to the endeavors of The Surgeon General in planning for the medical and surgical problems of mobilization, there was no comparable effort in the sphere of military psychiatry," leading to the conclusion that "such an omission is all the more surprising because the experience of even the peacetime Army after World War I had demonstrated the prevalence of psychiatric disorders of such magnitude as to be the subject of repeated comment in the Annual Reports of the Surgeon General since 1920."[51] Recognizing its culpability in replicating a generational crisis of unmet mental health and social needs of its warrior class, U.S. Army Surgeon General Leonard D. Heaton warned, "With this information so readily available, there can be little excuse for repetition of error in future wars, should they occur."[52]

Each subsequent American generation has repeated the same mistakes and acknowledged its culpability in ignoring the previous cohort's documented war trauma lessons, with impunity. As such, U.S. military's recent expressed intent to finally learn its war trauma lessons reflects smoke and mirrors:

> The time for action is now. The human and financial costs of un-addressed problems will rise dramatically over time. Our nation learned this lesson, at a tragic cost, in the years following the Vietnam War. Fully investing in prevention, early intervention, and effective treatment are responsibilities incumbent upon us as we endeavor to fulfill our obligation to our military service members.[53]

Proof is in the sage that "actions speak louder than words." To that end, we have to look only at the conclusions from the most recent commissioned study by the IOM seven years after the DoD task force report:

> In the DoD, there is no central leader who has sufficient responsibility and authority to ensure the quality and consistency of efforts to manage

PTSD in all service branches or at the national level; different PTSD services and programs are the responsibility of different commands and service branches.[54]

Additionally, "in each service branch, there is no overarching authority to establish and enforce policies for the entire spectrum of PTSD managements activities (prevention, screening, treatment, and rehabilitation)."[55]

These condemning findings and the successful progress demonstrated in the United Kingdom provide clear and convincing evidence that nothing short of class action by veterans of this and every U.S. war will compel the government to overhaul the military mental healthcare system to end the cycle of mental self-inflicted crises.

We have outlined three options for instituting mental health reforms in the DoD that will end the preventable aspects of wartime behavioral health crises. It is our conclusion that we are well beyond watchful waiting for the military's internal incremental changes and for responsible government authorities to overhaul the mental healthcare system. Therefore, this reality leaves us with only the third option—to petition the judicial branch—to effect systemic change. To that end, there appears to be ample legal justification, moral rationale, and economic motivations to seek injunctive relief from the courts to compel the DoD to act. The proposed tort action will require heavy lifting by impassioned attorneys willing to work pro bono or under strict financial caps who are similarly invested in correcting a social injustice for past, present, and future military veterans and their families who serve this country. The effort will require veterans of every American war and their families to be willing to come forward to once again serve their brothers and sisters in arms.

Similar to the U.S. military's pivotal role as lead social agent in integrating race, gender, and sexual orientation, transforming the military mental healthcare system (including the eradication of mental health stigma and disparity) will provide an invaluable working model to overhaul the private sector's mental health system. For those who entertain direct involvement or support of a future military class action, we can take pride in knowing that we lived up to Horace Mann's 1859 challenge, "Be ashamed to die until you have won some victory for humanity."

APPENDIX

PRE-WAR PLANNING CHECKLIST FOR BEHAVIORAL HEALTH SERVICES

Each military cohort since the First World War has documented its psychiatric "lessons learned." Ten foundational war trauma lessons have been identified across time as essential for meeting the mental health needs of warfighters and their families.[1] The subsequent neglect of such lessons has resulted in a generational pattern of a largely preventable wartime behavioral health crises—whereby war-stress casualties surpass the total number of military personnel both wounded and killed in action since the Second World War.[2]

Therefore, it is incumbent on military and government leaders to ensure adequate planning and preparation for meeting the behavioral health needs of military populations during times of peace and war.

"Military populations" include active and reserve military components, national guard, veterans, military retirees, family members, healthcare professionals, embedded journalists, Department of Defense–civilian contractors, law enforcement personnel, and homeland security.

Ending the tragic cycle of neglect and self-inflicted crisis requires the following checklist be completed and regularly monitored by responsible authorities to ensure that the behavioral health and social reintegration needs of military populations are properly met:

_____ 1. Is there evidence of a visible top-down leadership commitment toward a public awareness campaign that advocates cumulative exposure to chronic, severe, and potentially traumatic stress by itself, regardless of predisposition, morality, or lifestyle factors, inevitably causes a legitimate spectrum of war-stress injury beyond post-traumatic stress disorder (PTSD), which may include a wide range of psychiatric and medically unexplained physical conditions, substance abuse, traumatic brain injury, suicide/high-risk behaviors, post-traumatic anger, traumatic grief, moral injury, chronic fatigue/pain, and misconduct stress behaviors, as well as potential resilience and post-traumatic growth?

_____ 2. Is there clear evidence that behavioral health needs are given equal priority to medical services during times of peace and war, thus reflecting the reality of inevitable large numbers of war-stress casualties outnumbering the physical sacrifices of war?

_____ 3. Is there a sufficiently large cadre of well-trained behavioral health specialists and peer advisors during peace and war to provide the full range of high-quality behavioral health and reintegration services for military populations?

_____ 4. Is there a robust public health campaign on behavioral healthcare and war-stress injuries reflecting full mental health parity with medical services whereby behavioral health is viewed as a top military readiness issue reflected in leadership training and performance evaluations?

_____ 5. Does a coherent, centralized, comprehensive, searchable, and well-coordinated national social reintegration network exist linking the full-range of reintegration services across military, veterans affairs, government, nonprofit, and private sectors, including peer advising, behavioral health, pastoral, medical, housing, education, and employment services?

_____ 6. Do all military personnel regularly receive routine pre-military, military, and post-military health examinations at the same priority as medical and dental screenings?

_____ 7. Is there a centralized national database across all military, veterans, and private sector organizations that regularly provides accurate, transparent, comprehensive, real-time tracking, and reporting of behavioral health need, outcomes, suicide, and social reintegration services for military populations across the transition continuum?

_____ 8. Is there a robust, coherent, and coordinated behavioral health research program on prevention, etiology, stigma, assessment, treatment, families, post-traumatic growth, social reintegration, and program/treatment outcomes for military populations across the transition continuum?

_____ 9. Is compliance with a zero-tolerance policy targeting stigma, barriers to care, and mental health disparity evident at all leadership levels?

_____ 10. Do all beneficiaries have ready access to a full continuum of high-quality behavioral health services, including maximum benefit of definitive, comprehensive rehabilitation, and reintegration services before military discharge?

_____ 11. Do family members have ready access and receive high-quality behavioral health and social support services during and after military service?

_____ 12. Are dedicated behavioral health "lessons learned" policies and programs on par with medical and tactical or weapon programs, and is there adequate top-level monitoring of implementation of such lessons?

_____ 13. Is compliance with a policy prohibiting backdoor discharges, improper legal prosecution, and career reprisal for behavioral health issues being monitored and transparently reported?

_____ 14. Do war veterans convicted of misconduct stress-related crimes or who are administratively separated for "convenience of the government" have access to behavioral health and social reintegration services?

_____ 15. Are frontline psychiatry or combat and operational stress control programs robustly researched and transparently reported to evaluate the short- and long-term effects on personnel?

_____ 16. Is compliance with policies emphasizing behavioral health reconditioning, rehabilitation, and retention versus military discharge and disability compensation being adequately tracked and reported?

_____ 17. Have disability and compensation laws been revised to reflect lump-sum distribution and ongoing reintegration support services, including sheltered employment, rehabilitation, and housing, if necessary, to avoid lifelong dependency on disability pensions, except in extreme hardship?

_____ 18. Has Congress passed national security legislation limiting life-threatening effects of excessive cumulative exposure to war stress for the all-volunteer force, whereby after two military deployments during protracted armed conflict, a no-waiver civilian draft is automatically initiated?

_____ 19. Does a clearly identifiable organizational structure or Behavioral Health Corps (BHC) exist with an empowered and accountable leadership of equal status as military medicine, responsible for providing and monitoring the full continuum of behavioral health and social reintegration services as outlined here in a single, unified chain of command?

_____ 20. Are the BHC goals and outcomes regularly monitored and reported by congressional oversight committees and inspector generals?

_____ 21. Are responsible authorities properly held accountable for failure to adhere to these regulations?

_____ 22. Are the causes of wartime mental health crises properly investigated by Congress?

_____ 23. Are the intangible sacrifices of war-stress injury formerly recognized at the same level as tangible medical wounds?

NOTES

Preface

1. J. Appel and G. Beebe, "Preventive Psychiatry: An Epidemiologic Approach," *Journal of the American Medical Association* 131 (1946).

Introduction: The Genesis of the Military's Mental Health Dilemma

1. G. Santayana, *Reason in Common Sense*. Vol. 1 of *The Life of Reason* (New York: Scribner's, 1905).
2. See, among others, U.S. Army Military History Institute, *Combat Lessons Number 5: Rank and File in Combat—What They're Doing How They Do It* (EO-10501 Restricted Report, Washington, DC: Combat Analysis Section, Operations Division, War Department, 1944).
3. U.S. Army, Army Regulation (A.R.) 11–33, in *Army Lessons Learned Program: System Development and Application* (Washington, DC: Headquarters, Department of the Army, 1989), i.
4. U.S. Army, Army Regulation (A.R.) 11–33, 8.
5. Cited in F. A. Reister, *Battle Casualties and Medical Statistics: U.S. Army Experience in the Korean War* (Report of the War Office Committee of Enquiry into "Shell Shock, Washington, DC: Surgeon General, Department of the Army, 1922), f.
6. U.S. Army, Army Regulation (A.R.) 11–33, 2.
7. T. Tanielian and L. H. Jaycox, *Invisible Wounds of War: Psychological and Cognitive Injuries, Their Consequences, and Services to Assist Recovery* (Center for Military Health Policy Research MG-720-CCF, Santa Monica, CA: RAND, 2008).
8. R. A. Gabriel, *Between Flesh and Steel: A History of Military Medicine from the Middle Ages to the War in Afghanistan* (Washington, DC: Potomac Books, 2013).

9. Gabriel, *Between Flesh and Steel*.

10. For example, U.S. Army, Army Regulation (A.R.) 11-33; U.S. Department of Navy (1996).

11. Congressional Research Service (CRS), *American War and Military Operations Casualties: Lists and Statistics* (Washington, DC: CRS, February 26, 2010), http://fas.org/sgp/crs/natsec/RL32492.pdf.

12. Brill (1966); B. H. Chermol, "Wounds Without Scars: Treatment of Battle Fatigue in the U.S. Armed Forces in the Second World War," *Military Affairs: Journal of Military History, Including Theory and Technology* 49 (1985): 9–12.

13. A. J. Glass, "Lessons Learned," in *Zone of Interior*, Vol. 1 of *Medical Department United States Army, Neuropsychiatry in World War II*, ed. A. J. Glass and R. J. Bernucci (Washington, DC: Office of the Surgeon General, Department of the Army, 1966), 735–759.

14. CRS, *Post-traumatic Stress Disorder and Other Mental Health Problems in the Military: Oversight Issues for the Congress*, prepared by K. Blakeley and D. J. Jansen (7–5700: R43175, Washington, DC: CRS, August 8, 2013).

15. For example, Department of Veterans Affairs, *Analysis of VA Health Care Utilization Among Operation Enduring Freedom, Operation Iraqi Freedom, and Operation New Dawn Veterans, from 1st Qtr FY 2002 through 1st Qtr FY 2015* (Washington, DC: Epidemiology Program, Post-Deployment Health Group, Office of Public Health, Veterans Health Administration, 2015). No VA psychiatric data are available for 2016–2020

16. U.S. military casualty statistics, accessed March 10, 2020, www.defense.gov/news/casualty.pdf.

17. M. C. Russell and C. R. Figley, "Investigating Recurrent Generational Wartime Behavioral Health Crises: Part One of a Preliminary Analysis," *Psychological Injury and Law* 8, no. 1 (2015): 1.

18. Going back chronologically from the Persian Gulf War (1990–1991): "Gulf War Taking Toll at Home" (Jordan, 1991); Vietnam War (1965–1973): "Veterans Battle Emotional Strain: Vietnam Returnees Discuss Problems of Dislocation," *New York Times*, May 1, 1973; Korean War (1951–1953): Harrison, "Psychiatry Panel Scores VA Policy: Physicians at Parlay Say Incentives Are Lacking for Hospital Staff" (1957); WWII (1939–1945): "Bradley Demands Aid for Veterans: Says Community Must Help or Create Conditions That Can Breed Psychoneurotics," *New York Times*, 1945; WWI (1914–1919): "Insane War Veterans Reported Increasing: Legions Rehabilitation Body Told Number Exceeds Hospital Facilities," *New York Times*, 1934; the Spanish-American War (1898): "Suicide and Insanity in Army," *New York Times*, 1900; and even the American Civil War (1861–1865): "Suicide of an Army Officer," *New York Times*, 1874.

19. G. Zoroya, "Psychologist: Navy Faces Crisis," *USA Today*, January 17, 2007, 10; Philpott, "Military update: VA Fails to Meet Veterans PTSD Needs," *Gazette*, 2011; M. Thompson, "The Army's Continuing Dearth of Mental-Health Workers," *Military Mental Health*, March 20, 2012; American Forces Press Service, "Obama: Improve Mental Health Access, Care for Military, Veterans," *U.S. Defense Department*, August 31, 2012; and T. Williams, "Suicides Outpacing War Deaths for Troops," *New York Times*, June 8, 2012.

20. Russell and Figley, "Investigating Recurrent Generational Wartime Behavioral Health Crises."

21. M. C. Russell and C. R. Figley, "Generational Wartime Behavioral Health Crises: Part Two of a Preliminary Analysis," *Psychological Injury and Law* 8, no. 1 (2015): 132–152.

22. F. D. Jones, "Psychiatric Lessons of War," in *Textbook of Military Medicine: War Psychiatry*, ed. F. D. Jones, L. R. Sparacino, V. L. Wilcox, J. M. Rothberg, and J. W. Stokes (Washington, DC: Office of the Surgeon General, U.S. Army Borden Institute, 1995), 1–34.

23. M. C. Russell, C. R. Figley, and K. R. Robertson, "Investigating the Psychiatric Lessons of War and Pattern of Preventable Wartime Behavioral Health Crises," *Journal of Psychology and Behavioral Science* 3, no. 1 (2015): 1–16.

24. Jones, "Psychiatric Lessons of War."

25. Jones, "Psychiatric Lessons of War," 5.

26. T. W. Salmon, *Recommendations for the Treatment of Mental and Nervous Diseases in the United States Army* (New York: National Committee for Mental Hygiene, 1917).

27. T. W. Salmon, "General View of Neuropsychiatric Activities," in *The Medical Department of the United States Army in the World War*, Vol. X of *Neuropsychiatry in the American Expeditionary Forces*, ed. T. W. Salmon and N. Fenton, prepared under the direction of Maj. Gen. M. W. Ireland, Surgeon General (Washington, DC: U.S. Government Printing Office, 1929), 273–302, http://history.amedd.army.mil/booksdocs/wwi/Neuropsychiatry/default.htm.

28. Glass (1966), 989.

29. Glass, "Army Psychiatry Before World War II," in Glass and Bernucci, *Zone of Interior*, 18.

30. A. J. Glass, "The North Korean Invasion (25 June 1950–15 September 1950)," chapter 6 in *Psychiatry in the U.S. Army: Lessons for Community Psychiatry*, ed. A. J. Glass, F. D. Jones, L. R. Sparacino, and J. M. Rothberg (Bethesda, MD: Uniformed Services University of the Health Sciences, 2005), 5.

31. R. A. Kulka et al., *Trauma and the Vietnam War Generation: Report of Findings from the National Vietnam Veterans Readjustment Study* (New York: Brunner/Mazel, 1990), 286.

32. J. A. Martin and W. R. Cline, "Mental Health Lessons from the Persian Gulf War," in *The Gulf War and Mental Health: A Comprehensive Guide*, ed. J. A. Martin, L. R. Sparacino, and G. Belenky (Westport, CT: Praeger, 1996), 176.

33. Department of Defense Task Force on Mental Health (hereafter DoD TF-MH), *An Achievable Vision: Report of the Department of Defense Task Force on Mental Health* (Falls Church, VA: Defense Health Board, 2007), ES-2.

34. DoD TF-MH, *An Achievable Vision*, 63.

35. Russell, Figley, and Robertson, "Investigating the Psychiatric Lessons of War."

36. Russell and Figley, "Investigating Recurrent Generational Wartime Behavioral Health Crises"; Russell and Figley, "Generational Wartime Behavioral Health Crises."

37. Plymouth Colony Records, as cited in W. M. Burke, *History and Functions of Central Labor Unions* (New York: MacMillan, 1899).

38. Institute of Medicine (hereafter IOM), 2007.

39. L. J. Bilmes, "Current and Projected Future Costs of Caring for Veterans of the Iraq and Afghanistan Wars" (unpublished manuscript, Department of Economics, Harvard University, Cambridge, MA, 2011).

40. IOM (2007).

41. IOM (2007).

42. IOM (2007).

43. See, for example, IOM (2007).

44. IOM (2007).

45. IOM (2007), 45.

46. Veterans Administration, Office of Inspector General, "Review of State Variances in VA Disability Compensation Payments" (report no. 05-00765-137, VA OIG, Washington, DC, 2005).

47. Veterans Benefits Administration, *Annual Benefits Report FY2018* (Washington, DC: U.S. Department of Veterans Affairs, 2019).

48. IOM (2007), 20.

49. IOM *Posttraumatic Stress Disorder: Diagnosis and Assessment* (Washington, DC: National Academies Press, 2006).

50. Congressional Budget Office (CBO), *Veterans' Disability Compensation: Trends and Policy Options* (Washington, DC: CBO, August 2014).

51. CBO, *Veterans' Disability Compensation*.

52. Bilmes, *Current and Projected Future Costs of Caring for Veterans*.

53. CBO, *The Veterans Health Administration's Treatment of PTSD and Traumatic Brain Injury Among Recent Combat Veterans* (Washington, DC: CBO, 2012).

54. VA (2017).

55. CBO, *The Veterans Health Administration's Treatment of PTSD and Traumatic Brain Injury*.

56. Veterans Benefits Administration, *Annual Benefits Report FY2015* (Washington, DC: U.S. Department of Veterans Affairs, 2015).

57. Bilmes, *Current and Projected Future Costs of Caring for Veterans of the Iraq and Afghanistan Wars*, 5.

58. Veterans Benefits Administration, *Annual Benefits Report FY2015*.

59. Bilmes, *Current and Projected Future Costs of Caring for Veterans of the Iraq and Afghanistan Wars*.

60. Jones, "Psychiatric Lessons of War"; Russell and Figley, "Investigating Recurrent Generational Wartime Behavioral Health Crises"; Russell and Figley, "Generational Wartime Behavioral Health Crises."

61. E. Jones and S. Wessely, *Shell Shock to PTSD: Military Psychiatry from 1900 to the Gulf War* (New York: Psychology Press, 2005).

62. B. Shepard, *A War of Nerves: Soldiers and Psychiatrists in the Twentieth Century* (Cambridge, MA: Harvard University Press, 2001).

63. Glass, Glass and Bernucci, "Army Psychiatry Before World War II," 736

64. D. Harper, *Online Etymology Dictionary*, 2017, www.etymonline.com/index.php?term=dilemma.

65. For example, Russell and Figley (2015)..

66. Jones, "Psychiatric Lessons of War," 10.

67. Jones, "Psychiatric Lessons of War," 10.

68. F. D. Jones, "Disorders of Frustration and Loneliness," in *Textbook of Military Medicine: War Psychiatry*, ed. F. D. Jones, L. R. Sparacino, V. L. Wilcox, J. M. Rothberg, and J. W. Stokes (Washington, DC: Office of the Surgeon General, U.S. Army, Borden Institute, Walter Reed Army Institute of Research, 1995), 37–38.

69. W. Holden, *Shell Shock: The Psychological Impact of War* (London: Macmillan, 1998).

70. Cited in Holden, *Shell Shock*, 84.

71. E. C. Ritchie, "Military Mental Health's Wins and Losses Since the Iraq Invasion," *U.S. Time*, March 19, 2013.

72. Department of Veterans Affairs and Department of Defense, *VA/DoD Clinical Practice Guideline for the Management of Post-Traumatic Stress* (Office of Quality and Performance Publication 10Q-CPG/PTSD-04, Washington, DC: Veterans Health Administration, Department of Veterans Affairs and Health Affairs, Department of Defense, 2004).

73. J. Dao, "Military Study Finds Benefits in Mental Health Screening," *New York Times*, January 18, 2011, http://www.nytimes.com/2011/01/19/us/19military.html?_r=0.

74. S. Vogel, "Senate Approves Amendment to Expand Military Mental Health Care," *Washington Post*, November 29, 2012, http://www.washingtonpost.com

/blogs/federal-eye/wp/2012/11/29/senate-approves-amendment-to-expand
-military-mental-health-care-2.

75. J. Dao, "Study Seeks Biomarkers for Invisible War Scars," *New York Times*, February 6, 2013, http://www.nytimes.com/2013/02/07/us/study-seeks-biomarkers -for-ptsd-and-traumatic-brain-injuries.html?_r=0.

76. T. Rosenberg, "For Veterans, a Surge of New Treatments for Trauma," *New York Times*, September 26, 2012, http://opinionator.blogs.nytimes.com/2012/09/26 /for-veterans-a-surge-of-new-treatments-for-trauma.

77. S. Basu, "Army Seeks to Improve Troop Resilience as Suicides Increase," *U.S. Medicine*, March 2013, http://www.usmedicine.com/psychiatry/army-seeks-to -improve-troop-resilience-as-suicides-increase.html.

1. A War to Die For: Casualty Trends of Modern Warfare

1. Department of Defense (DoD), "Our Story," https://www.defense.gov/About.

2. DoD, "Our Story."

3. Carl von Clausewitz, *On War* (Harmondsworth, UK: Penguin, 1968).

4. R. A. Gabriel, *Man and Wounded in the Ancient World: A History of Military Medicine from Sumer to the Fall of Constantinople* (Washington, DC: Potomac, 2012).

5. R. A. Gabriel, *Between Flesh and Steel: A History of Military Medicine from the Middle Ages to the War in Afghanistan* (Washington DC: Potomac, 2013).

6. Gabriel, *Man and Wounded in the Ancient World*.

7. Gabriel, *Man and Wounded in the Ancient World*, 2.

8. Gabriel, *Between Flesh and Steel*.

9. Gabriel, *Man and Wounded in the Ancient World*.

10. American Psychiatric Association (APA), *Diagnostic and Statistical Manual of Mental Disorders, Third Edition* (Washington, DC: APA, 1980).

11. E. Jones and S. Wessely, "A Paradigm Shift in the Conceptualization of Psychological Trauma in the 20th Century," *Journal of Anxiety Disorders* 21 (2007): 65.

12. W. H. McCann, "Nostalgia: A Review of the Literature," Psychological Bulletin 38, no. 3 (1941): 165.

13. Hoffer, cited in McCann, "Nostalgia," 165.

14. McCann, "Nostalgia."

15. McCann, "Nostalgia."

16. P. Wanke, *Russian/Soviet Military Psychiatry: 1904–1945* (London: Frank Cass, 2005).

17. Wanke, *Russian/Soviet Military Psychiatry*.

18. W. C. Maclean, "Diseases of the Heart in the British Army, the Cause and the Remedy. *British Medical Journal* 1 (1867):161–164..

19. Wanke, *Russian/Soviet Military Psychiatry*.

20. Wanke, *Russian/Soviet Military Psychiatry*.

21. Wanke, *Russian/Soviet Military Psychiatry*.

22. E. T. Dean, *Shook Over Hell: Post-Traumatic Stress Vietnam and the Civil War* (Cambridge, MA: Harvard University Press, 1997).

23. Dean, *Shook Over Hell*.

24. J. M. Da Costa, "On Irritable Heart: A Clinical Study of a Form of Functional Cardiac Disorder and Its Consequences," reprinted in 1951 *American Journal of Medicine* (November 1871): 559–567.

25. Dean, *Shook Over Hell*.

26. F. D. Jones, "Psychiatric Lessons of War" in *Textbook of Military Medicine: War Psychiatry*, ed. F. D. Jones, L. R. Sparacino, V. L. Wilcox, J. M. Rothberg, and J. W. Stokes (Washington, DC: Office of the Surgeon General, U.S. Army, Borden Institute, Walter Reed Army Institute of Research 1995), 1–34; Russell, Figley, and Robertson, "Investigating the Psychiatric Lessons of War."

27. P. Lerner, *Hysterical Men: War, Psychiatry, and the Politics of Trauma in Germany, 1890–1930* (London: Cornell University Press, 2003); Wanke, *Russian/Soviet Military Psychiatry*.

28. H. Oppenheim, *Die traumatischen neurosen* (Berlin: Hirschwald, 1889).

29. J. Brunner, "Trauma in Court: Medico-Legal Dialectics in the Late Nineteenth-Century German Discourse on Nervous Injuries," *Theoretical Inquiries in Law* 4, no. 2 (2003): 697–727.

30. Brunner, "Trauma in Court"; T. R. Glynn, "The Traumatic Neuroses," *Lancet* (November 5, 1910): 1332–1336.

31. Lerner, *Hysterical Men*.

32. Brunner, "Trauma in Court."

33. Lerner, *Hysterical Men*, 38.

34. M. I. Finucane, "General Nervous Shock, Immediate and Remote, After Gunshot and Shell Injuries in the South African Campaign," *Lancet* 156, no. 4020 (September 1900): 807.

35. Finucane, "General Nervous Shock," 807.

36. E. Jones, "LMF: The Use of Psychiatric Stigma in The Royal Air Force During the Second World War," *Journal of Military History* 70 no. 2 (2006): 439–458.

37. A. G. Kay, "Insanity in the Army During Peace and War, and Its Treatment," *Journal of the Royal Army Medical Corps* 18 no. 1 (1912): 153.

38. T. W. Salmon, *Recommendations for the Treatment of Mental and Nervous Diseases* (New York: National Committee for Mental Hygiene, 1917), 14.

39. Jones, "Psychiatric Lessons of War," 10.

40. Jones, "Psychiatric Lessons of War," 10.

41. F. D. Jones, "Disorders of Frustration and Loneliness," in *Textbook of Military Medicine: War Psychiatry*, ed. F. D. Jones, L. R. Sparacino, V. L. Wilcox,

J. M. Rothberg, and J. W. Stokes (Washington, DC: Office of the Surgeon General, U.S. Army, Borden Institute, Walter Reed Army Institute of Research, 1995), 37–38.

42. Cited in Lerner, *Hysterical Men*, 67.

43. R. Gaupp, *Uber den Begriff der hysterie*. ZgNP 5 (1911): 457–466, cited in Lerner, *Hysterical Men*, 38.

44. B. Shepard, *A War of Nerves: Soldiers and Psychiatrists in the Twentieth Century* (Cambridge, MA: Harvard University Press, 2001).

45. M. C. Russell and C. R. Figley, "Do the Military's Frontline Psychiatry/Combat and Operational Stress Control Doctrine Help or Harm Veterans? Part One: Framing the Issue," *Psychological Injury and Law* 10 (2017): 1–23.

46. Russell and Figley, "Do the Military's Frontline Psychiatry/Combat and Operational Stress Control Doctrine Help or Harm Veterans? Part One: Framing the Issue."

47. M. C. Russell and C. R. Figley, "Do the Military's Frontline Psychiatry/Combat and Operational Stress Control Doctrine Help or Harm Veterans? Part Two: Systematic Review of the Evidence," *Psychological Injury and Law* 10 (2017): 24–71.

48. M. C. Russell and C. R. Figley, "Is the Military's Century-Old Frontline Psychiatry Policy Harmful to Veterans and Their Families? Part Three of a Systematic Review," *Psychological Injury and Law* 10 (2017): 72–95.

49. W. Holden, *Shell Shock: The Psychological Impact of War* (London: Macmillan, 1998).

50. Jones and Wessely, "A Paradigm Shift in the Conceptualization of Psychological Trauma"; Shepard, *A War of Nerves*.

51. Brunner, "Trauma in Court."

52. Lerner, *Hysterical Men*.

53. Department of Navy and U.S. Marine Corps, *Combat and Operational Stress Control*, U.S. Navy, NTTP 1–15M; U.S. Marine Corps, MCRP 6–11C (Washington, DC: Pentagon, December 2010), 1–3.

54. Jones and Wessely, "A Paradigm Shift in the Conceptualization of Psychological Trauma."

55. Holden, *Shell Shock*; Russell and Figley, "Do the Military's Frontline Psychiatry/Combat and Operational Stress Control Doctrine Help or Harm Veterans? Part One: Framing the Issue."

56. Holden, *Shell Shock*.

57. Russell and Figley, "Do the Military's Frontline Psychiatry/Combat and Operational Stress Control Doctrine Help or Harm Veterans? Part One: Framing the Issue,"

58. Jones, "Psychiatric Lessons of War," 10.

59. Lerner, *Hysterical Men.*
60. Holden, *Shell Shock*, 94.
61. Russell and Figley, "Do the Military's Frontline Psychiatry/Combat and Operational Stress Control Doctrine Help or Harm Veterans? Part One: Framing the Issue,"
62. Congressional Research Service (CRS), *American War and Military Operations Casualties: Lists and Statistics* (Washington, DC: CRS, February 26, 2010), http://fas.org/sgp/crs/natsec/RL32492.pdf.
63. B. D. Karpinos and A. J. Glass, "Disqualifications and Discharges for Neuropsychiatric Reasons, World War I and World War II," in *Zone of Interior*, Vol. I of *Medical Department United States Army, Neuropsychiatry in World War II*, ed. A. J. Glass and R. J. Bernucci (Washington DC: Office of the Surgeon General, Department of the Army, 1966), xiii–xiv.
64. T. W. Salmon and N. Fenton, "Neuropsychiatry in the American Expeditionary Forces," in *Neuropsychiatry: The Medical Department of the United States Army in the World War*, Vol. 10, ed. P. Bailey, F. E. Williams, P. A. Komora, T. W. Salmon, and N. Fenton (Washington, DC: Office of the Surgeon General, US Army, 1929), 271–474.
65. Institute of Medicine (IOM), (Washington, DC: National Academies Press, 2007).
66. Salmon and Fenton, "Neuropsychiatry in the American Expeditionary Forces."
67. Salmon, *Recommendations for the Treatment of Mental and Nervous Diseases in the United States Army.*
68. Salmon, *Recommendations for the Treatment of Mental and Nervous Diseases in the United States Army.*
69. Salmon and Fenton, "Neuropsychiatry in the American Expeditionary Forces."
70. IOM (2007), 39.
71. IOM (2007).
72. "400 Ex-Soldiers New York Suicides: Dr. Salmon So Charges in Testimony of Lack of Care on Mentally Disabled Veterans." *New York Times*, July 7, 1921.
73. "26,000 Veterans Now in Hospital: Alarming Increase Is Reported in Neuro-Psychiatric and Tuberculosis Cases. Seek Relief from Congress," *New York Times*, September 9, 1923.
74. P. Bailey, "Provisions for Care of Mental and Nervous Cases," in *The Medical Department of the United States Army in the World War: Vol. 10, Neuropsychiatry in the United States*, ed. P. Bailey, F. E. Williams, and P. O. Komora (prepared under the direction of Maj. Gen. M. W. Ireland, Surgeon General; Washington, DC: U.S. Government Printing Office, 1929), 39–55.
75. "Colonel Paul V. McNutt, National Commander of the American Legion: Declared That the Needs of Disabled Veterans Were Becoming an Increasingly

Difficult Problem Because of the Failure of Congress to Provide Adequate Funding," *New York Times*, 1929; "Insane War Veterans Reported Increasing: Legions Rehabilitation Body Told Number Exceeds Hospital Facilities," *New York Times*, June 24, 1934.

76. "Veteran's Claims Cut by 57 Percent: Reviewing Boards Disallow 29,995 of 51,213 Disability Cases Nervous Diseases Found More Frequent in Cities," *New York Times*, January 2, 1934.

77. "400 Ex-Soldiers New York Suicides."

78. "Says Veterans Lack Psychiatric Relief: McNutt Declares Disabled Men Are in Jails, As Hospitals Are Not Available," *New York Times*, May 26, 1929.

79. IOM (2007).

80. R. L. Swank and W. E. Marchand, "Combat Neuroses: Development of Combat Exhaustion," *Archives of Neurology and Psychiatry* 55 (1946): 236–247.

81. Cited in IOM (2007), 41.

82. Salmon, *Recommendations for the Treatment of Mental and Nervous Diseases in the United States Army*, 28.

83. T. W. Salmon, "General View of Neuropsychiatric Activities," in *The Medical Department of the United States Army in the World War: Vol. X, Neuropsychiatry in the American Expeditionary Forces*, ed. T. W. Salmon and N. Fenton (prepared under the direction of Maj. Gen. M. W. Ireland, Surgeon General (Washington, DC: U.S. Government Printing Office, 1929), 279.

84. I. C. Berlien and R. W. Waggoner, "Selection and Induction," in *Zone of Interior*, Vol. I of *Medical Department United States Army, Neuropsychiatry in World War II*, ed. A. J. Glass and R. J. Bernucci (Washington, DC: Office of the Surgeon General, Department of the Army, 1966), 153–191.

85. C. S. Myers, "Contributions to the Study of Shell Shock: Being an Account of Certain Disorders of Speech, with Special Reference to Their Causation and Their Relation to Malingering," *Lancet* (September 1916): 461–467.

86. C. S. Myers, *Shell Shock in France 1914–1918* (London: Cambridge, 1940).

87. Myers, "Contributions to the Study of Shell Shock."

88. Myers, *Shell Shock in France*.

89. Myers, *Shell Shock in France*.

90. Holden, *Shell Shock*.

91. Salmon, *Recommendations for the Treatment of Mental and Nervous Diseases in the United States Army*.

92. K. L. Artiss, "Human Behavior Under Stress: From Combat to Social Psychiatry," *Military Medicine* 128 (1963): 1011–1015.

93. Jones, "Psychiatric Lessons of War"; E. A. Strecker, "Experiences in the Immediate Treatment of War Neuroses," *American Journal of Insanity* (July 1919): 45–69.

94. N. Jones et al., "Long-Term Military Work Outcomes in Soldiers Who Become Mental Health Casualties When Deployed on Operations," *Psychiatry: Interpersonal and Biological Processes* 73, no. 4 (2010): 352–364.

95. W. Johnson and R. G. Rows, "Neurasthenia and the War Neuroses," in *History of the Great War*, Vol. 2 (London: HMSO, 1923), 1–67.

96. Johnson and Rows, "Neurasthenia and the War Neuroses."

97. Department of Navy and U.S. Marine Corps. *Combat and Operational Stress Control*, 1–3.

98. Department of Navy and U.S. Marine Corps. *Combat and Operational Stress Control*, 1–3.

99. IOM (2007).

100. *Report of the War Office Committee of Enquiry Into "Shell Shock"* (London: Imperial War Museum, 1922).

101. A. J. Glass, "Army Psychiatry Before World War II," in *Zone of Interior*, Vol. I of *Medical Department United States Army, Neuropsychiatry in World War II*, ed. A. J. Glass and R. J. Bernucci (Washington, DC: Office of the Surgeon General, Department of the Army, 1966), 7.

102. Shepard, *A War of Nerves*.

103. Berlien and Waggoner, "Selection and Induction."

104. N. Q. Brill and H. I. Kupper, "Problems of Adjustment in Return to Civilian Life," in *Zone of Interior*, Vol. I of *Medical Department United States Army, Neuropsychiatry in World War II*, ed. A. J. Glass and R. J. Bernucci (Washington, DC: Office of the Surgeon General, Department of the Army, 1966), 721–733; B. H. Chermol, "Wounds Without Scars: Treatment of Battle Fatigue in the U.S. Armed Forces in the Second World War," *Military Affairs: Journal of Military History, Including Theory and Technology* 49 (1985): 9–12.

105. Jones, "Psychiatric Lessons of War,", 1–34.

106. A. J. Glass, "Lessons Learned," in *Zone of Interior*, Vol. I of *Medical Department United States Army, Neuropsychiatry in World War II*, ed. A. J. Glass, and R. J. Bernucci (Washington, DC: Office of the Surgeon General, Department of the Army, 1966), 735–759.

107. Glass, "Lessons Learned," 1966.

108. Jones, "Disorders of Frustration and Loneliness."

109. Glass, "Lessons Learned."

110. U.S. Army Circular Letter No. 17, Neuropsychiatric Treatment in the Combat Zone

111. CRS, *American War and Military Operations Casualties*.

112. Berlien and Waggoner, "Selection and Induction."

113. N. Q. Brill, "Hospitalization and Disposition," in *Zone of Interior*, Vol. I of *Medical Department United States Army, Neuropsychiatry in World War II*:

Zone of Interior, ed. A. J. Glass and R. J. Bernucci (Washington, DC: Office of the Surgeon General, Department of the Army, 1966), 196–253.

114. Brill, "Hospitalization and Disposition."

115. Brill and Kupper, "Problems of Adjustment in Return to Civilian Life"; Chermol, "Wounds Without Scars."

116. "500,000 Discharged as Psychiatric Cases," *New York Times*, September 14, 1945.

117. N. Q. Brill and G. W. Beebe, "Psychoneurosis: Military Applications of a Follow-up Study," *U.S. Armed Services Medical Journal* 3 (1952): 15–33.

118. A. Glantz, "Suicide Rates Soaring Among WWII Vets," *New America Media*, November 11, 2010.

119. Warren, "U.S. Owes Veterans Better Psychiatric Aide," *Washington Post*, 1944.

120. S. Stavisky, "Thousands of GIs Temporarily Disabled During the War Now Stand to Become Permanently Crippled During the Peace . . . Is the Problem so Urgent? *Washington Post*, 1945, B3.

121. Stavisky, "Thousands of GIs Temporarily Disabled."

122. "Communities Held Failing Veterans: Social Service Experts Find a Lack of Help in Solving Readjustment Problems," *New York Times*, 1945.

123. "Plan Urged to Get New Psychiatrists: $100,000,000 for Training to Meet War Veteran Needs Asked by Dr. Kubie," *New York Times*, February 15, 1946.

124. L. Freeman, "Veterans Seeking Psychiatric Help: But Most Must Wait Months Even for Screening Tests Survey in City Shows," *New York Times*, March 1949.

125. R. R. Baker and W. E. Pickren, *Psychology and the Department of Veterans Affairs: A Historical Analysis of Training, Research, Practice, and Advocacy*, (Washington, DC: American Psychological Association, 2007), 7.

126. Baker and Pickren, *Psychology and the Department of Veterans Affairs*, 7.

127. Cited in N. Q. Brill, "Station and Regional Hospitals," in *Zone of Interior*, Vol. I of *Medical Department United States Army, Neuropsychiatry in World War II*, ed. A. J. Glass and R. J. Bernucci (Washington, DC: Office of the Surgeon General, Department of the Army, 1966), 291–292.

128. C. Hurd, "The Veteran: House Veterans Committee Deflects Inquiry on Medical Care of Soldiers," *New York Times*, April 1, 1945.

129. "Psychiatrists Ask Rise in VA Funds: Deterioration of Services to Veterans Is Alternative, Congress Is Warned." *New York Times*, May 22, 1947.

130. Baker and Pickren, *Psychology and the Department of Veterans Affairs*.

131. Glass, "Lessons Learned," 736.

132. Brill, "Hospitalization and Disposition," 262.

133. Baker and Pickren, *Psychology and the Department of Veterans Affairs*, 91.

134. Glass, "Lessons Learned."

135. Glass, "Lessons Learned."

136. APA, *Diagnostic and Statistical Manual of Mental Disorders* (Washington, DC: Author, 1952).

137. Jones, "Psychiatric Lessons of War."

138. E. C. Ritchie, "Psychiatry in the Korean War: Perils, PIES, and Prisoners of War," *Military Medicine*, November (2002): 1–11.

139. Glass, "Lessons Learned."

140. Ritchie, "Psychiatry in the Korean War," 900.

141. Ritchie, "Psychiatry in the Korean War."

142. CRS, *American War and Military Operations Casualties.*

143. CRS, *American War and Military Operations Casualties.*

144. A. J. Glass, "An Introduction to Psychiatry in the Korean War," Chapter 5 in *Psychiatry in the U.S. Army: Lessons for Community Psychiatry*, ed. A. J. Glass, F. D. Jones, L. R. Sparacino, and J. M. Rothberg (Bethesda, MD: Uniformed Services University of the Health Sciences, 2005), 2.

145. Glass, "An Introduction to Psychiatry in the Korean War," 5.

146. F. A. Reister, *Battle Casualties and Medical Statistics: U.S. Army Experience in the Korea War* (Washington, DC: Surgeon General, Department of the Army, 1973); *Report of the War Office Committee of Enquiry into "Shell Shock."*

147. Reister, *Battle Casualties and Medical Statistics.*

148. Reister, *Battle Casualties and Medical Statistics.*

149. Reister, *Battle Casualties and Medical Statistics.*

150. Reister, *Battle Casualties and Medical Statistics.*

151. Jones and Wessely, *Shell Shock to PTSD.*

152. A. Fontana and R. Rosenheck, "Traumatic War Stressors and Psychiatric Symptoms Among World War II, Korean, and Vietnam War Veterans," *Psychology and Aging* 9, no. 1 (1994): 27–33.

153. Veterans Administration, *Administrator of Veterans Affairs Annual Report for Fiscal Year Ending June 30, 1957* (Washington, DC: U.S. Government Printing Office, 1958).

154. Glass, "Army Psychiatry Before World War II."

155. "640,000 in WWII: Army All Out in Study of Psycho Cases," *Washington Post*, July 4, 1951.

156. "Korean Veterans Seek Homes," *New York Times*, September 16, 1951.

157. Freeman, "Rise in Neurotic Seamen Called Challenge to Merchant Marine,"1952.

158. "Korean Veterans Due for Benefits: 2000,000 Expected to Collect Unemployment Aide but Job Outlook Is Bright," *New York Times*, November 9, 1952.

159. E. Harrison, "Psychiatry Panel Scores VA Policy: Physicians at Parlay Say Incentives Are Lacking for Hospital Staff," *New York Times*, 1957.

160. Baker and Pickren, *Psychology and the Department of Veterans Affairs*, 88.

161. Baker and Pickren, *Psychology and the Department of Veterans Affairs*.
162. Glass, "An Introduction to Psychiatry in the Korean War," 4.
163. A. J. Glass, "The North Korean invasion (25 June 1950–15 September 1950)," in *Psychiatry in the U.S. Army: Lessons for Community Psychiatry*, ed. A. J. Glass, F.D. Jones, L. R. Sparacino, and J. M. Rothberg (Bethesda, MD: Uniformed Services University of the Health Sciences, 2005), 5.
164. W. L. Peltz, "Report to Surgeon General U.S Army on Tour of Medical Installations of Far East Command, November-December-1951" (1951), cited in Ritchie, "Psychiatry in the Korean War."
165. R. A. Kulka et al., *Trauma and the Vietnam War Generation: Report of Findings from the National Vietnam Veterans Readjustment Study* (New York: Brunner/Mazel, 1990).
166. CRS, *American War and Military Operations Casualties*.
167. N. M. Camp, *U.S. Army Psychiatry in the Vietnam War: New Challenges in Extended Counterinsurgency Warfare* (U.S. Army Medical Department Center and School, Fort Sam Huston, TX: Borden Institute, 2014).
168. Camp, *U.S. Army Psychiatry in the Vietnam War*.
169. Kulka et al., *Trauma and the Vietnam War Generation*.
170. M. C. Russell and C.R. Figley, "Generational Wartime Behavioral Health Crises: Part Two of a Preliminary Analysis," *Psychological Injury and Law* 8, no. 1 (2015): 132–152.
171. Shepard, *A War of Nerves*.
172. Dean, *Shook Over Hell*.
173. Camp, *U.S. Army Psychiatry in the Vietnam War*, ix.
174. Camp, *U.S. Army Psychiatry in the Vietnam War*, ix.
175. N. M. Camp, "Ethical Challenges for the Psychiatrist During the Vietnam Conflict," in *Textbook of Military Medicine, Military Psychiatry: Preparing in Peace for War*, ed. F. D. Jones, L. R. Sparacino, V. L. Wilcox, and J. M. Rothberg (Washington, DC: Office of the Surgeon General, U.S. Army. Borden Institute, 1994).
176. S. Neel, *Vietnam Studies: Medical Support of the U.S. Army in Vietnam 1965–1970* (Washington, DC: Department of the Army, 1991).
177. Dean, *Shook Over Hell*; Gabriel; D. H. Marlowe, *Psychological and Psychosocial Consequences of Combat and Deployment: With Special Emphasis on the Gulf War* (No. MR-1018/11-OSD) (Santa Monica, CA: RAND, 2001).
178. Marlowe, *Psychological and Psychosocial Consequences of Combat and Deployment*.
179. L. A. Palinkas and P. Coben, "Psychiatric Casualties Among U.S. Marines in Vietnam," *Military Medicine* 153, no. 10 (1988): 521–526.
180. Palinkas and Coben, "Psychiatric Casualties Among U.S. Marines in Vietnam."
181. Tiffany (1967), 1585.

182. Jones, "Psychiatric Lessons of War"; Shepard, *A War of Nerves*.

183. J. P. Wilson, *Identity, Ideology, and Crisis: The Vietnam Veteran in Transition*, Vol. 2 (Washington, DC: Disabled American Veterans, 1978).

184. A. Egendorf, "The Postwar Healing of Vietnam Veterans: Recent Research," *Hospital and Community Psychiatry* 33, no. 11 (1982): 901–908.

185. Dean, *Shook Over Hell*.

186. Jones (2005).

187. Neel, *Vietnam Studies*.

188. Neel, *Vietnam Studies*, 47.

189. Neel, *Vietnam Studies*, 47.

190. R. A. Roffman and E. Sapol, "Marijuana in Vietnam," *International Journal of Addictions* 5, no. 1 (1970): 1–42.

191. M. D. Stanton, "Drugs, Vietnam, and the Vietnam Veteran: An Overview." *American Journal of Drug and Alcohol Abuse* 3, no. 4 (1976): 557–570.

192. S. L. Baker Jr., "Drug Abuse in the United States Army," *Bulletin of the New York Academy of Medicine* 47, no. 6 (1971): 541–549.

193. E. Jones and S. Wessely, *Shell Shock to PTSD: Military Psychiatry from 1900 to the Gulf War*. New York: Psychology Press, 2005 (2005), 19.

194. Dean, *Shook Over Hell*.

195. Shepard, *A War of Nerves*.

196. Neel, *Vietnam Studies*.

197. Dean, *Shook Over Hell*.

198. Neel, *Vietnam Studies*.

199. Department of the Army, *Field Manual 4–02.51: Combat and Operational Stress Control (FM 8–51)* (Washington, DC: Headquarters, Department of the Army, 2006).

200. Jones and Wessely, *Shell Shock to PTSD.*.

201. Jones and Wessely, *Shell Shock to PTSD*.

202. Marlowe, *Psychological and Psychosocial Consequences of Combat and Deployment*.

203. E. Linden, "The Demoralization of an Army: Fragging and Other Withdrawal Symptoms," *Saturday Review* 8 (1972): 12–17.

204. Jones and Wessely, *Shell Shock to PTSD*.

205. Neel, *Vietnam Studies*, 100.

206. Neel, *Vietnam Studies*, 42.

207. IOM (2008).

208. W. F. Caveness et al., *National Institutes of Health Vietnam Head Injury Study* (1979).

209. Veterans Administration, *Administrator of Veterans Affairs Annual Report for Fist Year Ending June 30, 1972*, (Washington, DC: U.S. Government Printing Office, 1973).

210. Kulka et al., *Trauma and the Vietnam War Generation*, xxiii

211. Kulka et al., *Trauma and the Vietnam War Generation*.

212. Kulka, et al., *Trauma and the Vietnam War Generation*.

213. Dohrenwend et al. (2007).

214. J. Nordheimer, "Postwar Shock Besets Veterans of Vietnam," *New York Times*, August 28, 1972.

215. Nordheimer, "Postwar Shock Besets Veterans of Vietnam."

216. B. Rensberger, "Delayed Trauma in Veterans Cited," *New York Times*, May 3, 1972; "Addiction in Vietnam Spurs Nixon and Congress to Take Drastic New Steps" (Schmidt 1971); "Delayed Trauma in Veterans Cited"

217. B. Weinraub, "Angry Vietnam Veterans Charging Federal Policies Ignore Their Needs: They See Neglect and Inaction by the Administration in Jobs, Education, Healthcare and Counseling," *New York Times*, 1979.

218. "Aid Urged for Vietnam Veterans," *New York Times*, January 28, 1979.

219. Baker and Pickren, *Psychology and the Department of Veterans Affairs*.

220. Baker and Pickren, *Psychology and the Department of Veterans Affairs*.

221. President's Commission on Mental Health, *Report of the Special Working Group: Mental Health Problems of Vietnam Era Veterans* (Washington, DC: U.S. Government Printing Office, February 15, 1978).

222. *Veterans Health Care Amendments of 1979*, Pub. L. 96–22, 93 Stat. 47 (1979).

223. Baker and Pickren, *Psychology and the Department of Veterans Affairs*.

224. A. Egendorf, *Legacies of Vietnam: Comparative Adjustment of Veterans and Their Peers: A Study* (Washington, DC: U.S. Government Printing Office, 1981).

225. IOM, *Veterans and Agent Orange: Health Effects of Herbicides Used in Vietnam* (Washington, DC: The National Academies Press, 1994).

226. Kulka et al., *Trauma and the Vietnam War Generation*.

227. Centers for Disease Control, "Vietnam Experience Study. Health status of Vietnam Veterans: I. Psychosocial Characteristics," *Journal of the American Medical Association* 259 (1988): 2701–2707.

228. Lerner, *Hysterical Men*.

229. J. A. Renner, "The Changing Patterns of Psychiatric Problems in Vietnam," *Comprehensive Psychiatry* 14, no. 2 (1973): 169–180.

230. Jones and Wessely, *Shell Shock to PTSD*.

231. Frueh (2000).

232. Jones and Wessely, "A Paradigm Shift in the Conceptualization of Psychological Trauma"; Shepard, *A War of Nerves*.

233. Lerner, *Hysterical Men*.

234. R. E. Huffman, "Which Soldiers Break Down: A Survey of 610 Psychiatric Patients in Vietnam," *Bulletin Menninger Clinic* 34, no. 6 (1970): 344.

235. Jones and Wessely, *Shell Shock to PTSD*.

236. Kulka et al., *Trauma and the Vietnam War Generation*, 286.

237. Jones and Wessely, *Shell Shock to PTSD*

238. APA, *Diagnostic and Statistical Manual of Mental Disorders.*

239. Dean, *Shook Over Hell.*

240. Jones and Wessely, "A Paradigm Shift in the Conceptualization of Psychological Trauma," 165.

241. Dean, *Shook Over Hell*; Shepard, *A War of Nerves.*

242. Jones, "Disorders of Frustration and Loneliness, 416.

243. Jones, "Disorders of Frustration and Loneliness, 417.

244. http://history.amedd.army.mil/booksdocs/AMEDDinODS/ameddODS.html.

245. Office of Inspector General, Department of Defense (IG DoD), (Washington, DC: Pentagon, 2000).

246. IOM, *Health Consequences of Service During the Persian Gulf War: Initial Findings and Recommendations for Immediate Action* (Washington, DC: National Academies Press, 1995).

247. (RAND, 2000).

248. IOM (Washington, DC: National Academies Press, 2006).

249. IOM (2006).

250. H. K. Kang, *Surveillance of Health Outcomes of Gulf War Veterans Environmental Epidemiology Service and War-Related Illness and Injury Study Center* (Gulf War Advisory Committee Meeting, November 20, 2008, Washington DC: VA Medical Center, 2008).

251. IOM (2006).

252. IOM (2006), 3.

253. IOM (2006).

254. Figley (1993).

255. IG DoD, "Evaluation Report on the Management of Combat Stress Control in the Department of Defense" (report no. 96–079, Pentagon, Washington, DC, February 29, 1996), 19.

256. IG DoD, "Evaluation Report on the Management of Combat Stress," 4.

257. IG DoD, "Evaluation Report on the Management of Combat Stress," 5.

258. E. Schmitt, "Stress Follows Troops Home from Gulf, *New York Times*, July 16, 1991.

259. Jordan, "Gulf War Taking Toll at Home," 1991.

260. S. Evans, "Gulf Veterans Still Paying the Price," *Washington Post*, January 17, 1992.

261. GAO, *Gulf War Illnesses: Basic Questions Unanswered* (February 2000-GAO/T -NSIAD-00-79; Washington, DC: GAO, 2000), 3.

262. IOM, *Health Consequences of Service During the Persian Gulf War: Initial Findings and Recommendations for Immediate Action* (Washington, DC: National Academies Press, 1995), 9.

263. GAO, *Gulf War Illnesses.*

264. GAO, *Monitoring of Clinical Progress and Reexamination of Research Emphasis Are Needed Gulf War Illnesses* (June 1997-GAO/NSIAD-97-163; Washington, DC: GAO, 1997); GAO, *Gulf War Illnesses*; IG DoD, "Evaluation Report on the Management of Combat Stress"; IOM *Health Consequences of Service During the Persian Gulf War*; IOM, *Gulf War and Health:* Vol. 6, *Physiologic, Psychologic and Psychosocial Effects of Deployment-Related Stress* (Washington, DC: National Academies Press, 2008); IOM, *Gulf War and Health:* Vol. 7, *Long-Term Consequences of Traumatic Brain Injury* (Washington, DC: National Academies Press, 2008); Marlowe, *Psychological and Psychosocial Consequences of Combat and Deployment.*

265. *Persian Gulf Service and PTSD*, Pub. L. 102–25, 105 Stat. 110 (1991).

266. *National Defense Authorization Act*, Pub. L. 102–190, 105 Stat. 1290 (1991).

267. *Persian Gulf War Veterans' Health Status*, Pub. L. 102–585, 106 Stat. 4943 (1992).

268. Presidential Advisory Committee on Gulf War Veterans' Illnesses (1996).

269. *Persian Gulf War Veterans Act*, Pub. L. 105–277, 112 Stat. 2681 (1998).

270. *Veterans Programs Enhancement Act of 1998*, Pub. L. 105–368, 112 Stat. 3315 (1998).

271. J. W. Stokes, "U.S. Army Mental Health System: Divisional and Corps Level Mental Health Units," In *The Gulf War and Mental Health: A Comprehensive Guide*, ed. J. A. Martin, L. R. Sparacino, and G. Belenky (Westport, CT: Praeger, 1996), 3–18.

272. J. A. Martin, "Combat Psychiatry: Lessons from the War in Southwest Asia," *Journal of the U.S. Army Medical Department*, PB 89-2-1/2 (1992): 40–44.

273. J. A. Martin and W. R. Cline, "Mental Health Lessons from the Persian Gulf War," in *The Gulf War and Mental Health: A Comprehensive Guide*, ed. J. A. Martin, L. R. Sparacino, and G. Belenky (Westport, CT: Praeger, 1996), 161–178.

274. Martin and Cline, "Mental Health Lessons from the Persian Gulf War."

275. IOM (2008).

276. IOM (2008).

277. Department of the Army, *Field Manual 4–02.51: Combat and Operational Stress Control.*

278. Jones, 1995.

279. Gabriel, *Man and Wounded in the Ancient World*, 17.

280. D. Harper, "Dilemma," *Online Etymology Dictionary*, 2017, www.etymonline.com/index.php?term=dilemma.

281. M. C. Russell and C. R. Figley, "Investigating Recurrent Generational Wartime Behavioral Health Crises: Part One of a Preliminary Analysis," *Psychological Injury and Law* 8, no. 1 (2015): 106–131.

282. See Russell and Figley, "Do the Military's Frontline Psychiatry/Combat and Operational Stress Control Doctrine Help or Harm Veterans? Part One: Framing the Issue"; Russell and Figley, "Do the Military's Frontline Psychiatry/Combat and Operational Stress Control Doctrine Help or Harm Veterans? Part Two: Systematic Review of the Evidence"; Russell and Figley, "Is the Military's Century-Old Frontline Psychiatry Policy Harmful to Veterans and Their Families? Part Three of a Systematic Review,"

2. The Dark Side of Military Mental Health: A History of Self-Inflicted Wounds

1. E. T. Dean, *Shook Over Hell: Post-Traumatic Stress Vietnam and the Civil War* (Cambridge, MA: Harvard University Press, 1997).
2. "26,000 Veterans Now In Hospital: Alarming Increase Is Reported in Neuro-Psychiatric and Tuberculosis Cases. Seek Relief from Congress," *New York Times*, September 9, 1923.
3. A. D. Mancini, "A Postwar Picture of Resilience," *New York Times*, February 5, 2012.
4. Department of Defense Task Force on Mental Health (DoD TF-MH), *An Achievable Vision: Report of the Department of Defense Task Force on Mental Health* (Falls Church, VA: Defense Health Board, 2007), ES-2.
5. Armed Forces Health Surveillance Center (AFHSC), *Medical Surveillance Monthly Reports* 24, no. 2 (2017).
6. Defense Manpower Data Center, Office of the Secretary of Defense, https://www.dmdc.osd.mil/dcas/pages/faq.xhtml.
7. For example, Congressional Research Service (2011).
8. Institute of Medicine (IOM) (Washington, DC: National Academies Press, 2006).
9. I. C. Berlien and R. W. Waggoner, "Selection and Induction," in *Zone of Interior*, Vol. 1 of *Medical Department United States Army, Neuropsychiatry in World War II*, ed. A. J. Glass and R. J. Bernucci (Washington, DC: Office of the Surgeon General, Department of the Army, 1966), 153–191.
10. IOM (Washington, DC: National Academies Press, 2007).
11. R. Sobel, *Combat Psychiatry: Experiences in the North African and Mediterranean Theaters of Operation, American Ground Forces, World War II*, ed. F. R. Hanson, U.S. Army Medical Department, U.S. Army Medical Department (Honolulu, HI: University Press of Pacific, 1949).
12. See, for example, E. A. Brusher, "Combat and Operational Stress Control," in *Textbooks of Military Medicine: Combat and Operational Behavioral Health*, ed. E. C. Ritchie (Falls Church, VA: Office of the Surgeon General, Department of the Army, 2011).
13. Joint Mental Health Advisory Team-7 (Joint MHAT-7), *Operation Enduring Freedom 2010 Afghanistan (22 February 2011)* (Office of the Surgeon General

United States Army Medical Command and Office of the Command Surgeon HQ, USCENTCOM and Office of the Command Surgeon U.S. Forces Afghanistan (USFOR-A), 2011).

14. *Joshua Omvig Veterans Suicide Prevention Act*, H.R. 327, 110th Congress (2007).

15. *Clay Hunt Act*, H.R. 203, 114th Congress (2015–2016).

16. "400 Ex-Soldiers New York Suicides: Dr. Salmon So Charges in Testimony of Lack of Care on Mentally Disabled Veterans," *New York Times*, July 7, 1921.

17. "Veterans Suicides Average Two a Day," *New York Times*, 1922.

18. Army Medical Bulletin, *Causes of Death: U.S. Army Compared with the C.C.C. Deaths Through Injury* (Washington, DC: War Department, 1940), 101–108.

19. A. Glantz, "Suicide Rates Soaring Among WWII Vets, Records Show," *New American Media*, November 11, 2010.

20. F. A. Reister, *Battle Casualties and Medical Statistics: U.S. Army Experience in the Korean War* (Washington, DC: Surgeon General, Department of the Army, 1973).

21. R. R. Baker and W. E. Pickren, *Psychology and the Department of Veterans Affairs: A Historical Analysis of Training, Research, Practice, and Advocacy* (Washington, DC: American Psychological Association, 2007), 88.

22. Baker and Pickren, *Psychology and the Department of Veterans Affairs*.

23. "Suicide Risk Double for Viet Veterans," *Chicago Tribune*, 1986.

24. Centers for Disease Control, *Post-service Mortality Among Vietnam Veterans: A Study Journal of the American Medical Association* (Atlanta, GA: Centers for Disease Control and Prevention, 1987).

25. See Dean, *Shook Over Hell*.

26. H. K. Kang, *Surveillance of Health Outcomes of Gulf War Veterans Environmental Epidemiology Service and War-Related Illness and Injury Study Center*, Gulf War Advisory Committee Meeting November 20, 2008 (Washington DC: VA Medical Center, 2008).

27. AFHSC (March 2012).

28. E. C. Ritchie, "Military Mental Health's Wins and Losses Since the Iraq Invasion," *U.S. Time*, March 19, 2013, http://nation.time.com/2013/03/19/military-mental-healths-wins-andlosses-since-the-iraq-invasion.

29. AFHSC (February 2012).

30. R. H. Pietrzak, A. R. Russo, Q. Ling, Q., and S. M. Southwick, "Suicidal Ideation in Treatment-Seeking Veterans of Operations Enduring Freedom and Iraqi Freedom: The Role of Coping Strategies, Resilience, and Social Support," *Journal of Psychiatric Research* 45 (2011): 720–726.

31. Joint Mental Health Advisory Team-7, *Operation Enduring Freedom*.

32. A. J. Mansfield, R. H. Bender, L. L. Hourani, and G. E. Larson, "Suicidal or Self-Harming Ideation in Military Personnel Transitioning to Civilian Life," *Suicide and Life-Threatening Behavior* 41, no. 4 (2011): 392–405.

33. Mansfield et al., "Suicidal or Self-Harming Ideation in Military Personnel."

34. Department of Veterans Affairs, *Analysis of VA Health Care Utilization Among Operation Enduring Freedom, Operation Iraqi Freedom, and Operation New Dawn Veterans, from 1st Qtr FY 2002 Through 3rd Qtr FY 2012* (Washington, DC: Author, 2012).

35. H. K. Kang and T. A. Bullman, *The Risk of Suicide Among U.S. War Veterans: Vietnam War to Operation Iraqi Freedom* (2010 DOD/VA Suicide Prevention Conference January 10–14, 2010, Washington DC: Department of Veterans Affairs, 2010).

36. J. Harris, "Pentagon Sends in Psychiatrists After 3 Suicides Among Troops in Haiti," *Washington Post*, October 19, 1994 (article refers to military personnel deployed on peace-keeping operations).

37. Department of Veteran's Affairs and Department of Defense (VA/DoD), *VA/DoD Clinical Practice Guideline for the Management of Post-Traumatic Stress* (Washington, DC: Veterans' Health Administration, Department of Veterans Affairs and Health Affairs, Department of Defense, 2010).

38. Department of Veterans Affairs, *Analysis of VA Health Care Utilization Among Operation Enduring Freedom, Operation Iraqi Freedom, and Operation New Dawn Veterans, from 1st Qtr FY 2002 Through 1st Qtr FY 2015*, Epidemiology Program, Post-Deployment Health Group, Office of Public Health, Veterans Health Administration (Washington, DC: Department of Veterans Affairs, 2015), www.publichealth.va.gov/epidemiology.

39. M. J. Roy, P. A. Koslowe, K. Kroenke, and C. Magruder, "Signs, Symptoms, and Ill-Defined Conditions in Persian Gulf War Veterans: Findings from the Comprehensive Clinical Evaluation Program," *Psychosomatic Medicine* 60 (1998): 663–668.

40. IOM, *Gulf War and Health:* Vol. 6 of *Physiologic, Psychologic and Psychosocial Effects of Deployment-Related Stress* (Washington, DC: National Academies Press, 2008), 59.

41. W. C. Menninger, *Reactions to Combat: Psychiatry in a Troubled World* (New York: MacMillan, 1948); E. Jones and S. Wessley, *Shell Shock to PTSD: Military Psychiatry from 1900 to the Gulf War* (New York: Psychology Press, 2005).

42. For example, Jones and Wessely, *Shell Shock to PTSD*.

43. U.S. Army, *The Medical and Surgical History of the War of the Republic: Part III*, Vol. I (Washington, DC: Government Printing Office, 1888).

44. IOM (2007).

45. U.S. Army, *The Medical and Surgical History of the War of the Republic*.

46. T. W. Salmon and N. Fenton, "Neuropsychiatry in the American Expeditionary Forces," in *Neuropsychiatry: The Medical Department of the United States*

Army in the World War: Vol. 10, ed. P. Bailey, F. E. Williams, P. A. Komora, T. W. Salmon, and N. Fenton (Washington, DC: Office of the Surgeon General, US Army, 1929), 271–474.

47. N. Q. Brill and G. W. Beebe, "Psychoneurosis: Military Applications of a Follow-up Study," *U.S. Armed Services Medical Journal* 3 (1952): 15–33.

48. Menninger, *Reactions to Combat.*

49. E. D. Palmer, "Military Experience with Ulcer Disease: A Review," *Military Medicine* 135 (1970): 871–877.

50. Reister, *Battle Casualties and Medical Statistics.*

51. Department of Veterans Affairs, "Medically Unexplained Physical Symptoms," War Related Illness and Injury Study Center, http://www.warrelatedillness .va.gov/education/healthconditions/medically-unexplained-syndrome.asp.

52. IOM (2007).

53. C. W. Hoge, A. Terhakopian, C. A. Castro, S. C. Messer, and C. C. Engel, "Association of Posttraumatic Stress Disorder with Somatic Symptoms, Health Care Visits, and Absenteeism Among Iraq War Veterans," *American Journal of Psychiatry* 164 (2007): 150–153.

54. S. M. Frayne, C. Y. Chiu, S. Iqbal, E. A. Berg, K. J. Laungani, R. C. Cronkite, J. Pavao, and R. Kimerling, "Medical Care Needs of Returning Veterans with PTSD: Their Other Burden," *Journal of General Internal Medicine* 26, no. 1 (2010): 33–39.

55. K. A. Babson and M. T. Feldner, "Temporal Relations Between Sleep Problems and Both Traumatic Event Exposure and PTSD: A Critical Review of the Empirical Literature," *Journal of Anxiety Disorders.* 24 (2010): 1–15.

56. Hoge et al., "Association of Posttraumatic Stress Disorder with Somatic Symptoms."

57. T. A. Mellman, V. Bustamante, A. I. Fins, W. R. Pigeon, and B. Nolan, "REM Sleep and the Early Development of Posttraumatic Stress Disorder," *American Journal of Psychiatry* 159, no. 10 (2002): 1696–1701.

58. Armed Forces Health Surveillance Center (AFHSC), "Hospitalizations Among Members of the Active Component, U.S. Armed Forces, 2010," *Medical Surveillance Monthly Report* 18, no. 4 (April 2011): 8–15.

59. AFHSC, "Hospitalizations Among Members of the Active Component, U.S. Armed Forces, 2010," 7.

60. For example, B. Shepard, *A War of Nerves: Soldiers and Psychiatrists in the Twentieth Century* (Cambridge, MA: Harvard University Press, 2001).

61. U.S. Army, *The Medical and Surgical History of the War of the Republic.*

62. N. Q. Brill, "Hospitalization and Disposition," in *Zone of Interior,* Vol. 1 of *Medical Department United States Army, Neuropsychiatry in World War II,* ed. A. J. Glass and R. J. Bernucci (Washington, DC: Office of the Surgeon General, Department of the Army, 1966), 196–253,

63. Institute of Medicine, *Treatment of Posttraumatic Stress Disorder: An Assessment of the Evidence* (Washington, DC: National Academies Press2008), 60, 66.

64. Institute of Medicine (IOM), *Returning Home from Iraq and Afghanistan: Assessment of Readjustment Needs of Veterans, Service Members, and Their Families* (Washington, DC: National Academies Press, 2013).

65. R. Hirsch, "World in a Jar: War and Trauma," *Historical Sociology* 22, no. 3 (2009): 291–311.

66. Salmon and Fenton, "Neuropsychiatry in the American Expeditionary Forces."

67. A. J. Glass and R. J. Bernucci, *Zone of Interior*, Vol. 1 of *Medical Department United States Army. Neuropsychiatry in World War II* (Washington DC: Office of the Surgeon General, Department of the Army, 1966).

68. A. J. Glass and F. D. Jones, *Psychiatry in the U.S. Army: Lessons for Community Psychiatry* (Bethesda, MD: Uniformed Services University of the Health Sciences, 2005).

69. Government Accountability Office (GAO), *Defense Health Care: Status of Efforts to Direct Lack of Compliance with Personality Disorder Separation Requirements* (GAO-10-1013T: Washington, DC: GAO, 2010).

70. D. Grossman, *On Killing: The Psychological Cost of Learning to Kill in War and Society* (New York: Back Bay, 1996).

71. B. T. Litz, N. Stein, E. Delaney, L. Lebowitz, W. P. Nash, C. Silva, and S. Maguen, "Moral Injury and Moral Repair in War Veterans: A Preliminary Model and Intervention Strategy," *Clinical Psychology Review* 29 (2009): 700.

72. A. Fontana and R. Rosenheck, "Traumatic War Stressors and Psychiatric Symptoms," *Psychology and Aging* 9, no. 1 (1994): 27–33.

73. R. Yehuda, S. M. Southwick, and E. J. Giller, "Exposure to Atrocities and Severity of Chronic Posttraumatic Stress Disorder in Vietnam Combat Veterans," *American Journal of Psychiatry* 149 (1992): 333–336.

74. L. Y. Zaidi and D. W. Foy, "Childhood Abuse Experiences and Combat-Related PTSD," *Journal of Traumatic Stress* 7 (1994): 33–42.

75. J. C. Beckham, M. E. Feldman, and A. C. Kirby, "Atrocities Exposure in Vietnam Combat Veterans with Chronic Posttraumatic Stress Disorder: Relationship to Combat Exposure, Symptom Severity, Guilt, and Interpersonal Violence," *Journal of Traumatic Stress* 11, no. 4 (1998): 777–785.

76. A. Fontana, R. Rosenheck, R., and E. Brett, "War Zone Traumas and Posttraumatic Stress Disorder Symptomatology," *Journal of Nervous and Mental Disease* 180 (1992): 748–755.

77. Joint MHAT-7, *Operation Enduring Freedom 2010 Afghanistan.*

78. C. W. Hoge, C. A. Castro, S. C. Messer, D. McGurk, D. I. Cotting, and R. I. Koffman, "Combat Duty in Iraq and Afghanistan, Mental Health Problems, and Barriers to Care," *New England Journal of Medicine* 351 (2004): 13–22.

79. S. Maguen, D. D. Luxton, N. A. Skopp, G. A. Gahm, M. A. Reger, T. J. Metzler, and C. R. Marmar, "Killing in Combat, Mental Health Symptoms, and Suicidal Ideation in Iraq War Veterans," *Journal of Anxiety Disorders* 25 (2011): 563–567.

80. Department of Veterans Affairs, *Iraq War Clinician Guide*, 2nd edition (Washington, DC: National Center for Post-Traumatic Stress Disorder, 2004), 75.

81. J. Shay, "Learning About Combat Stress from Homer's Iliad," *Journal of Traumatic Stress* 4 (1991): 561–579.

82. I. L. Pivar and N. P. Field, "Unresolved Grief in Combat Veterans with PTSD," *Anxiety Disorders* 18 (2004): 745–755.

83. I. Pivar, "Traumatic Grief: Symptomology and Treatment for Iraq War Veterans," in *Iraq War Clinician Guide*, 2nd edition (Washington, DC: National Center for Post-Traumatic Stress Disorder, 2004), 75.

84. Pivar and Field, "Unresolved Grief in Combat Veterans with PTSD."

85. Labatte, L. A., and M. P. Snow. "Post-Traumatic Stress Syndrome Among Soldiers Exposed to Combat in the Persian Gulf," Hosp Commun Psych, 43 (1992): 831–833.

86. C. W. Hoge, C. A. Castro, and K. M. Eaton, "Impact of Combat Duty in Iraq and Afghanistan on Family Functioning: Findings from the Walter Reed Army Institute of Research Land Combat Study," in *Human Dimensions in Military Operations—Military Leaders' Strategies for Addressing Stress and Psychological Support* (meeting proceedings RTO-MP-HFM-134, Paper 5. Neuilly-sur-Seine, France: RTO, 2006), 5.1–5.6.

87. Joint MHAT-7, *Operation Enduring Freedom 2010 Afghanistan*.

88. Hoge et al., "Combat Duty in Iraq and Afghanistan, Mental Health Problems, and Barriers to Care."

89. R. A. Kulka, W. E. Schlenger, J. A. Fairbank, R. L. Hough, B. K. Jordan, C. R. Marmar, D. S. Weiss, and D. A. Grady, , *Trauma and the Vietnam War Generation: Report of Findings from the National Vietnam Veterans Readjustment Study* (New York: Brunner/Mazel, 1990).

90. R. Blaine Everson and C. R. Figley, *Families Under Fire* (New York: Routledge, 2011).

91. R. Dekel and H. Goldblatt, "Is There Intergenerational Transmission of Trauma? The Case of Combat Veterans' Children," *American Journal of Orthopsychiatry* 78, no. 3 (2008): 281–289.

92. DoD TF-MH, *An Achievable Vision*, 36.

93. Dekel and Goldblatt, "Is There Intergenerational Transmission of Trauma?"

94. Dekel and Goldblatt, "Is There Intergenerational Transmission of Trauma?"

95. J. C. Beckham, M. E. Feldman, and A. C. Kirby, "Atrocities Exposure in Vietnam Combat Veterans with Chronic Posttraumatic Stress Disorder:

Relationship to Combat Exposure, Symptom Severity, Guilt, and Interpersonal Violence," *Journal of Traumatic Stress* 11, no. 4 (1998): 777–785.

96. M. J. Peebles-Kleiger and J. H. Kleiger, "Re-integration Stress for Desert Storm Families: Wartime Deployments and Family Trauma," *Journal of Traumatic Stress* 7 (1994): 173–194.

97. B. K. Jordan, C. R. Marmar, J. A. Fairbank, W. E. Schlenger, R. A. Kulka, and R. L. Hough, "Problems in Families of Male Vietnam Veterans with Post-Traumatic Stress Disorder," *Journal of Consulting and Clinical Psychology* 60, no. 6 (1992): 916–926.

98. AFHSC, "Mental Disorders and Mental Health Problems, Active Component, U.S. Armed Forces, 2000–2011."

99. Joint MHAT-7, *Operation Enduring Freedom 2010 Afghanistan.*

100. Mansfield et al., "Suicidal or Self-Harming Ideation in Military Personnel Transitioning to Civilian Life," *Suicide and Life-Threatening Behavior* 41, no. 4 (2011): 392–405.

101. Government Accountability Office (GAO), *DOD Mild Traumatic Brain Injury* (GAO-12-27R, Washington, DC: GAO, 2011).

102. IOM, *Gulf War and Health:* Vol. 7 of *Long-Term Consequences of Traumatic Brain Injury* (Washington, DC: National Academies Press, 2008).

103. Jones and Wessely, *Shell Shock to PTSD.*

104. C. S. Myers, *Shell Shock in France 1914–1918* (London: Cambridge, 1940).

105. Salmon and Fenton, "Neuropsychiatry in the American Expeditionary Forces."

106. Brill, "Hospitalization and Disposition."

107. Reister, *Battle Casualties and Medical Statistics.*

108. IOM, *Gulf War and Health:* Vol. 7.

109. Department of Veterans Affairs, *Analysis of VA Health Care Utilization Among Operation Enduring Freedom, Operation Iraqi Freedom, and Operation New Dawn Veterans, from 1st Qtr FY 2002 Through 1st Qtr FY 2015.*

110. IOM, *Gulf War and Health:* Vol. 7.

111. GAO, *DOD Mild Traumatic Brain Injury.*

112. IOM, *Returning Home from Iraq and Afghanistan: Assessment of Readjustment Needs of Veterans, Service Members, and Their Families.* Washington, DC: National Academies Press, 2013.

113. AFHSC, "Malingering and Factitious Disorders and Illnesses, Active Component, U.S. Armed Forces, 1998–2012," *MSMR* 20, no. 7 (2013): 20–24.

114. IOM, "Substance Use Disorders in the U.S. Armed Forces" (Report Brief, September 2012, Washington, DC: National Academies Press, 2012).

115. U.S. Army, *The Medical and Surgical History of the War of the Republic*, 890.

116. Salmon and Fenton, "Neuropsychiatry in the American Expeditionary Forces."

117. Glass and Bernucci, *Medical Department United States Army.*

118. Jones and Wessely, *Shell Shock to PTSD*.

119. M. D. Stanton, "Drugs, Vietnam, and the Vietnam Veteran: An Overview," *American Journal of Drug and Alcohol Abuse* 3, no. 4 (1976): 557–570.

120. A. J. Ognibene, "General Medicine," in *General Medicine and Infectious Diseases*, Vol. II of *Medical Department, United States Army, Internal Medicine in Vietnam*, ed. A. J. Ognibene and B. O'Neill, Jr. (Washington, DC: Office of the Surgeon General and Center of Military History, Washington, DC: United States Army, 1982).

121. S. L. Baker, Jr., "Drug Abuse in the United States Army," *Bulletin of the New York Academy of Medicine* 47, no. 6 (1971): 541–549.

122. Jones and Wessely, *Shell Shock to PTSD*, 19

123. IOM, *Returning Home from Iraq and Afghanistan*.

124. IOM, "Substance Use Disorders in the U.S. Armed Forces," 2.

125. I. Burnett-Zeigler, M. Ilgen, M. Valenstein, K. Zivin, L. Gorman, A. Blow, S. Duffy, and S. Chermack, "Prevalence and Correlates of Alcohol Misuse Among Returning Afghanistan and Iraq Veterans," *Addictive Behaviors* 36 (2011): 801–806.

126. Mental Health Advisory Team-IV (MHAT-IV), *Mental Health Advisory Team (MHAT-IV) Operation Iraqi Freedom 05–07, 17 November 2006* (Washington, DC: Office of the Surgeon Multinational Force-Iraq & Office of the Surgeon General, United States Army Medical Command, 2006).

127. IOM, *Returning Home from Iraq and Afghanistan*.

128. J. Pizarro, R. Cohen Silver, and J. Prause, "Physical and Mental Health Costs of Traumatic War Experiences Among Civil War Veterans," *Archives of General Psychiatry* 63, no. 2 (2006): 193–200.

129. D. Noble, D. C. Washington, M .E. Roudebush, and D. Price, "Studies of Korean War Casualties. Part I: Psychiatric Manifestations in Wounded Men," *American Journal of Psychiatry* 108, no. 7 (1952): 495–499.

130. Kulka et al., *Trauma and the Vietnam War Generation*; R. M. Scurfield and S. Tice, *Acute Psycho-Social Intervention Strategies with Medical and Psychiatric Evacuees of "Operation Desert Storm" and Their Families* (Operation Desert Storm Clinician Packet. White River Junction, VT: National Center for PTSD, 1991).

131. D. Desmond and M. MacLachlan, "Psychological Issues in Prosthetic and Orthotic Practice: A 25 Year Review of Psychology in *Prosthetics and Orthotics International*," *Prosthetics and Orthotics International* 26, no. 3 (2002); R. A. Sherman, C. J. Sherman, and L. Parker, "Chronic Phantom and Stump Pain Among American Veterans: Results of a Survey," *Pain* 18, no. 1 (1984): 83–95.

132. J. C. Beckham et al., "Chronic Posttraumatic Stress Disorder and Chronic Pain in Vietnam Combat Veterans," *Journal of Psychosomatic Research* 43, no. 4 (1997): 379–389.

133. M. Russell, D. Shoquist, and C. Chambers, "Effectively Managing the Psychological Wounds of War," *Navy Medicine*, Apr–Mar (2005): 23–26.

134. Department of the Army, *Field Manual 4–02.51: Combat and Operational Stress Control (FM 8–51)* (Washington, DC: Headquarters, Department of the Army, 2006).

135. F. D. Jones, "Psychiatric Lessons of War," in *Textbook of Military Medicine: War Psychiatry*, ed. F. D. Jones, L. R. Sparacino, V. L. Wilcox, J. M. Rothberg, and J. W. Stokes (Washington, DC: Office of the Surgeon General, U.S. Army, Borden Institute, Walter Reed Army Institute of Research 1995), 198.

136. F. Drimmer, F., *Until You Are Dead: The Book of Executions in America* (New York: Pinnacle Books, 1992).

137. For example, Jones and Wessely, *Shell Shock to PTSD*.

138. Reister, *Battle Casualties and Medical Statistics*.

139. S. H. Choe, C. J. Hanley, and M. Mendoza, "GI'S Tell of a US Massacre in Korean War," Associated Press, *New York Times*, 1999.

140. E. Linden, "The Demoralization of an Army: Fragging and Other Withdrawal Symptoms," *Saturday Review* 8 (1972): 12–17.

141. S. Neel, *Vietnam Studies: Medical Support of the U.S. Army in Vietnam 1965–1970* (Washington, DC: Department of the Army, 1991).

142. D. Nelson, *The War Behind Me: Vietnam Veterans Confront the Truth About U.S. War Crimes* (New York: Basic Books, 2008).

143. For example, the 2004 Abu Ghraib atrocity.

144. L. C. Baldor, "Misconduct Forces More Soldiers Out," Associated Press, February 17, 2014.

145. Mental Health Advisory Team-V (MHAT-V), *Mental Health Advisory Team (MHAT-V) Operation Enduring Freedom 06–08, 14 February 2008* (Washington, DC: Office of the Surgeon Multinational Force-Iraq & Office of the Surgeon General, United States Army Medical Command, 2008).

146. R. M. Highfill-McRoy, G. E. Larson, S. Booth-Kewley, and C. F. Garland, "Psychiatric Diagnosis and Punishment for Misconduct: The Effects of PTSD in Combat-Deployed Marines," *BMC Psychiatry* 10, no. 1 (2010): 88.

147. D. Forbes, R. Parslow, M. Creamer, N. Allen, T. McHugh, and M. Hopwood, "Mechanisms of Anger and Treatment Outcome in Combat Veterans with Post-traumatic Stress Disorder," *Journal of Traumatic Stress* 21, no. 2 (2008): 142–129.

148. C. T. Taft, D. S. Vogt, A.D. Marshall, J. Panuzio, and B. L. Niles, "Aggression Among Combat Veterans: Relationships with Combat Exposure and Symptoms of Posttraumatic Stress Disorder, Dysphoria, and Anxiety," *Journal of Traumatic Stress* 20, no. 2 (2007): 135–145.

149. A. Egendorf, "Legacies of Vietnam: Comparative Adjustment of Veterans and Their Peers: A Study" (Washington, DC: U.S. Government Printing Office, 1981)

150. Jordan et al., "Problems in Families of Male Vietnam Veterans with Post-Traumatic Stress Disorder."

151. K. Klostermann, T. Mignone, M. L. Kelley, S. Musson, and G. Bohall, "Intimate Partner Violence in the Military: Treatment Considerations," *Aggression and Violent Behavior* 17, no. 1 (2012): 53–58.

152. R. H. Pietrzak, M. B. Goldstein, J. C. Malley, A. J. Rivers, and S. M. Southwick, "Structures of Posttraumatic Stress Disorder and Psychosocial Functioning in Veterans of Operation Enduring Freedom and Iraqi Freedom," *Psychiatry Research* 178, no. 2 (2010): 323–329.

153. A. L. Teten, L. A. Miller, M. S. Stanford, N. J. Petersen, S. D. Bailey, R. L. Collins, M. J. Dunn, and T. A. Kent, "Characterizing Aggression and Its Association to Anger and Hostility Among Male Veterans with Post-Traumatic Stress Disorder," *Military Medicine* 175, no. 6 (2010): 405–410.

154. C. T. Taft, R. P. Weatherill, H. E. Woodward, L. A. Pinto, L. E. Watkins, M. W. Miller, and R. Dekel, R., "Intimate Partner and General Aggression Perpetration Among Combat Veterans Presenting to a Posttraumatic Stress Disorder Clinic," *American Journal of Orthopsychiatry* 79, no. 4 (2009): 461–468.

155. Cited in Klostermann et al., "Intimate Partner Violence in the Military."

156. D. Sontag and L. Alvarez, "Iraq Veterans Leave a Trail of Death and Heartbreak in U.S," *New York Times*, January 13, 2008.

157. M. E. Noonan and C. J. Mumola, *Bureau of Justice Statistics Special Report: Veterans in State and Federal Prison, 2004* (Washington, DC: U.S. Department of Justice Office of Justice Programs, 2007).

158. R. Stuart, "Jailed Veterans Case Brings Post-Vietnam Problem into Focus," *New York Times*, February 26, 1982.

159. Pizarro, Cohen-Silver, and Prause, "Physical and Mental Health Costs of Traumatic War Experiences Among Civil War Veterans."

160. R. E. Eberly and B. E. Engdahl, B.E., "Prevalence of Somatic and Psychiatric Disorders Among Former Prisoners of War," *Hospital Community Psychiatry* 42 (1991): 807–813.

161. VA/DoD, *VA/DoD clinical practice guideline for the management of post-traumatic stress*, 2010.

162. Joint MHAT-7, *Operation Enduring Freedom 2010 Afghanistan*.

163. VA/DoD, *VA/DoD Clinical Practice Guideline for the Management of Post-Traumatic Stress*, 2010.

164. G. Ozakinci, W. K. Hallman, and H. M. Kipen, "Persistence of Symptoms in Veterans of the First Gulf War: 5-Year Follow-Up," *Environmental Health Perspectives* 114, no. 10 (2006): 1553–1557.

165. Frayne, et al., "Medical Care Needs of Returning Veterans with PTSD."

166. Dean, *Shook Over Hell*.

167. Baker and Pickren, *Psychology and the Department of Veterans Affairs*.

168. M. J. Friedman and P. P. Schnurr, "The Relationship Between Trauma, PTSD, and Physical Health," in *Neurobiological and Clinical Consequences of stress: From Normal Adaptation of PTSD*, ed. M. J. Friedman, D. S., Charney, and A. Y Deutch (New York: Lippincott-Raven, 1995), 506–524.

169. C. Irwin, S. A. Falsetti, R. B. Lydiard, J. C. Ballenger, C. D. Brock, and W. Brener, "Comorbidity of Posttraumatic Stress Disorder and Irritable Bowel Syndrome," *Journal of Clinical Psychiatry* 57, no. 12 (1996): 576–578.

170. H. K. Kang, B. H. Natelson, C. M. Mahan, K. Y. Lee, and F. M. Murphy, "Post-Traumatic Stress Disorder and Chronic Fatigue Syndrome-Like Illness Among Gulf War Veterans: A Population-Based Survey of 30,000 Veterans," *American Journal of Epidemiology* 157, no. 2 (2003): 141–148.

171. J. Poundja, D. Fikretoglu, and A. Brunet, "The Co-Occurrence of Posttraumatic Stress Disorder Symptoms and Pain: Is Depression a Mediator?" *Journal of Stress Trauma* 19, no. 5 (2006): 747–751.

172. J. C. Beckham et al., "Health Status, Somatization, and Severity of Posttraumatic Stress Disorder in Vietnam Combat Veterans with Posttraumatic Stress Disorder," *American Journal of Psychiatry* 155, no. 11 (1998): 1565–1569.

173. Hoge et al., "Association of Posttraumatic Stress Disorder with Somatic Symptoms, Health Care Visits, and Absenteeism Among Iraq War Veterans."

174. Hoge et al., "Association of Posttraumatic Stress Disorder with Somatic Symptoms, Health Care Visits, and Absenteeism Among Iraq War Veterans."

175. L. W. McCray, P. F. Cronholm, H. R. Bogner, J. J. Gallo, and R. A. Neill, "Resident Physician Burnout: Is There Hope?" *Family Medicine* 40, no. 9 (2008): 626–632.

176. R. Rosenheck and P. Nathan, "Secondary Traumatization in Children of Vietnam Veterans," *Hospital and Community Psychiatry* 36, no. 5 (1985): 538–549.

177. Mental Health Advisory Team-II (MHAT-II), *Operation Iraqi Freedom-II, Mental Health Advisory Team (MHAT-II), 20 January 2005* (Washington, DC: U.S. Army Surgeon General, 2005).

178. P. J. Linnerooth, B. A. Moore, and A. J. Mrdjenovich, "Professional Burnout in Clinical Military Psychologists: Recommendations Before, During, and After Deployment," *Professional Psychology: Research and Practice* 42 (2011): 87–93.

179. H. C. Levy, L. M. Conoscenti, J. F. Tillery, B. D. Dickstein, and B. T. Litz, "Deployment Stressors and Outcomes Among Air Force Chaplains," *Journal of Traumatic Stress* 24, no. 3 (2011): 342–346.

180. J. Tyson, "Compassion Fatigue in the Treatment of Combat-Related Trauma During Wartime," *Clinical Social Work Journal* 35 (2007): 183–192.

181. S. H. Lynch and M. L. Lobo, "Compassion Fatigue in Family Caregivers: A Wilsonian Concept Analysis," *Journal of Advanced Nursing* 68, no. 9 (2012): 2125–2134.

3. Cruel and Inhumane Handling: The First Dark-Side Strategy

1. Department of the Army, *Field Manual 4–02.51: Combat and Operational Stress Control (FM 8–51)* (Washington, DC: Headquarters, Department of the Army, 2006), 1–6.
2. Memorandum issued by P. Mitchell, Captain, Assistant Adjutant 1st Special Services Force of 13 November 1944, Headquarters First Special Service Force (Washington, DC: U.S. Army, 1944).
3. Memorandum issued by P. Mitchell.
4. Department of the Army, *Combat and Operational Stress Control.*
5. P. von Zielbauer, 2007, "Marines' Trials in Iraq Killings Are Withering," *New York Times*, August 30, 2007.
6. von Zielbauer, "Marines' Trials in Iraq Killings Are Withering."
7. U.S. Army, Army Regulation (A.R.) 600–20, in *Army Command Policy*, 24 July 2020 (Washington, DC: Department of Army, 2020).
8. Anon, "This Is Gonna Hurt: Military Punishment Throughout the Ages," *Military History Now*, June 2012, http://militaryhistorynow.com/2012/06/29 /this-is-gonna-hurt-military-punishment-throughout-the-ages.
9. Anon, "This Is Gonna Hurt."
10. Anon, "This Is Gonna Hurt."
11. G. Sheffield, "World War One: Military Discipline and Punishment," *The British Library*, January 29, 2014, www.bl.uk/world-war-one/articles/military -discipline.
12. M. I. Finucane, "General Nervous Shock, Immediate and Remote, After Gunshot and Shell Injuries in the South African Campaign," *Lancet* 156, no. 4020 (September 1900): 807–809.
13. E. T. Dean, *Shook Over Hell: Post-Traumatic Stress Vietnam and the Civil War.* (Cambridge, MA: Harvard University Press, 1997).
14. Dean, *Shook Over Hell.*
15. D. H. Marlowe, "Psychological and Psychosocial Consequences of Combat and Deployment: With Special Emphasis on the Gulf War" (no. MR-1018/11-OSD, Santa Monica, CA: RAND, 2001).
16. M. Hastings, *Military Anecdotes* (New York: Oxford University Press, 1985), 18.
17. M. P. Manson and H. M. Grayson, "The Psychological Clinic at the MTOUSA Disciplinary Training Center," *American Psychologist* 1, no. 3 (1946): 91–94.

18. R. Sobel, R., "Anxiety-Depressive Reactions After Prolonged Combat Experience: The 'Old Sergeant Syndrome,' " in *Combat psychiatry: Experiences in the North African and Mediterranean theaters of operation American ground forces, World War II*, ed. F. R. Hanson (U.S. Army Medical Department; Honolulu, HI: University Press of Pacific, 1949), 137–146.

19. J. M. Da Costa, "On Irritable Heart: A Clinical Study of a Form of Functional Cardiac Disorder And Its Consequences," reprinted in 1951 *American Journal of Medicine, November* (1871): 559–567.

20. Sobel, "Anxiety-Depressive Reactions After Prolonged Combat Experience," 137.

21. Sobel, "Anxiety-Depressive Reactions After Prolonged Combat Experience."

22. B. H. Chermol, "Wounds Without Scars: Treatment of Battle Fatigue in the U.S. Armed Forces in the Second World War," *Military Affairs: The Journal of Military History, Including Theory and Technology* 49 (1985): 9–12.

23. *Twelve O'Clock High* (Hollywood, LA: Twentieth Century Fox, 1949).

24. M. Hing, J. Cabrera, C. Barstow, and R. Forsten, "Special Operations Forces and Incidence of Post-Traumatic Stress Disorder Symptoms," *Journal of Special Operation Medicine* 12, no. 3 (2012): 23–35.

25. H. M. Ward, *George Washington's Enforcers: Policing the Continental Army* (Carbondale, IL: Southern Illinois University Press, 2006).

26. H. Marshall, *On the Enlisting, Discharging, and Pensioning of Soldiers: With the Official Documents on These Branches of Military Duty* (Philadelphia, PA: A. Waldie, 1840), 30.

27. K. A. Baker, *The Effect of Post-traumatic Stress Disorder on Military Leadership: An Historical Perspective* (Fort Leavenworth, KS: U.S. Army Command and General Staff College, School of Advanced Military Studies, 2011).

28. Marshall, *On the Enlisting, Discharging, and Pensioning of Soldiers*, 132.

29. Marshall, *On the Enlisting, Discharging, and Pensioning of Soldiers*, 132.

30. W. Holden, *Shell Shock: The Psychological Impact of War* (London: Macmillan, 1998).

31. W. C. Menninger, *Reactions to Combat: Psychiatry in a Troubled World* (New York: MacMillan, 1948).

32. M. M. Kessler, "Troops in Transit," in *Zone of Interior: Vol. I of Medical Department United States Army. Neuropsychiatry in World War II*, ed. A. J. Glass, and R. J. Bernucci (Washington DC: Office of the Surgeon General, Department of the Army, 1966), 336.

33. Kessler, "Troops in Transit."

34. Kessler, "Troops in Transit," 336.

35. Kessler, "Troops in Transit," 337.

36. Kessler, "Troops in Transit."

37. Kessler, "Troops in Transit."
38. Kessler, "Troops in Transit," 338.
39. Kessler, "Troops in Transit."
40. T. W. Salmon and N. Fenton, "Neuropsychiatry in the American Expedition-ary Forces," in *Neuropsychiatry: The Medical Department of the United States Army in the World War*, Vol. 10, ed. P. Bailey, F. E. Williams, P. A. Komora, T. W. Salmon, and N. Fenton (Washington, DC: Office of the Surgeon General, U.S. Army, 1929), 40.
41. Kessler, "Troops in Transit."
42. J. Kors, "Disposable Soldiers: How the Pentagon Is Cheating Wounded Vets," *The Nation*, April 26, 2010.
43. Kors, "Disposable Soldiers."
44. Kors, "Disposable Soldiers."
45. C. Maslach and P. C. Zimbardo, "Dehumanization in Institutional Settings," (technical report Z-10, Arlington, VA: Office of Naval Research, 1973).
46. Maslach and Zimbardo, "Dehumanization in Institutional Settings," 1.
47. Maslach and Zimbardo, "Dehumanization in Institutional Settings," 2.
48. Maslach and Zimbardo, "Dehumanization in Institutional Settings," 2.
49. Maslach and Zimbardo, "Dehumanization in Institutional Settings," 3.

4. Legal Prosecution, Incarceration, and Executions of Mental Illness: The Second Dark-Side Strategy

1. M. P. Manson and H. M. Grayson, "The Psychological Clinic at the MTOUSA Disciplinary Training Center," *American Psychologist* 1, no. 3 (1946): 91–94.
2. E. R. Seamone, "Reclaiming the Rehabilitative Ethic in Military Justice The Suspended Punitive Discharge as a Method to Treat Military Offenders with PTSD and TBI and Reduce Recidivism," *Military Law Review.* 208, no. 1 (2011): 1–212.
3. Government Accountability Office (GAO), *Defense Health Care: Actions Needed to Ensure Post-Traumatic Stress Disorder and Traumatic Brain Injury Are Considered in Misconduct Separations* (GAO-17-260, Washington, DC: GAO, 2017).
4. R. Izzo, "In Need of Correction: How the Army Board for Correction of Mili-tary Records is Failing Veterans with PTSD," *Yale Law Journal* 123, no. 5 (2014): 1118–1625.
5. Institute of Medicine (IOM), "Substance Use Disorders in the U.S. Armed Forces" (Report Brief, September 2012, Washington, DC: National Academies Press, 2012).
6. U.S. Army, *The Medical and Surgical History of the War of the Republic: Part III*, Vol. I (Washington, DC: Government Printing Office, 1888), 890.

7. T. W. Salmon and N. Fenton, "Neuropsychiatry in the American Expedition-ary Forces," in *Neuropsychiatry: The Medical Department of the United States Army in the World War*, Vol. 10, ed. P. Bailey, F. E. Williams, P. A. Komora, T. W. Salmon, and N. Fenton (Washington, DC: Office of the Surgeon General, U.S. Army, 1929).

8. A. J. Glass and R. J. Bernucci, *Zone of Interior*, Vol. I. of *Medical Department United States Army: Neuropsychiatry in World War II* (Washington, DC: Office of the Surgeon General, Department of the Army, 1966).

9. E. Jones and S. Wessely, *Shell Shock to PTSD: Military Psychiatry from 1900 to the Gulf War*. New York: Psychology Press, 2005.

10. IOM, "Substance Use Disorders in the U.S. Armed Forces," 2.

11. Armed Forces Health Surveillance Center, "Substance Use Disorders in the U.S. Armed Forces, 2000–2011," *Medical Surveillance Monthly Report* 19, no. 11 (November 2012): 11–16.

12. Department of Veterans Affairs (VA), *Analysis of VA Health Care Utilization Among Operation Enduring Freedom, Operation Iraqi Freedom, and Operation New Dawn Veterans, from 1st Qtr FY 2002 through 1st Qtr FY 2015* (Epidemiology Program, Post-Deployment Health Group, Office of Public Health, Veterans Health Administration. Washington, DC: VA), 2015.

13. Department of Navy, *OPNAV Instruction 5350.4D: Navy Alcohol and Drug Abuse Prevention and Control of 4 Jun 2009* (Washington, DC: Office of the Chief of Naval Operations, 2009), 5.

14. D. Zwerdling, "Army Dismissals for Mental Health, Misconduct Rise," *NPR*, November 15, 2007.

15. S. Frizell, "U.S. Army Firing More Soldiers for Misconduct: Number Dismissed for Crime or Misconduct Doubled Between 2007 and 2013," *Time*, February 15, 2014.

16. D. Forbes et al, "Mechanisms of Anger and Treatment Outcome in Combat Veterans with Posttraumatic Stress Disorder," *Journal of Traumatic Stress* 21, no. 2 (2008): 142–129.

17. C. T. Taft, D. S. Vogt, A. D. Marshall, J. Panuzio, and B. L. Niles, "Aggression Among Combat Veterans: Relationships with Combat Exposure and Symptoms of Posttraumatic Stress Disorder, Dysphoria, and Anxiety," *Journal of Traumatic Stress*. 20, no. 2 (2007): 135–145.

18. K. Klostermann, T. Mignone, M. L. Kelley, S. Musson, and G. Bohall, "Intimate Partner Violence in the Military: Treatment Considerations," *Aggression and Violent Behavior*. 17, no. 1 (2012): 53–58.

19. R. H. Pietzrak, M. B. Goldstein, J. C. Malley, A. J. Rivers, and S. M. Southwick, "Structures of Posttraumatic Stress Disorder and Psychosocial Functioning in Veterans of Operation Enduring Freedom and Iraqi Freedom," *Psychiatry Research* 178, no. 2 (2010): 323–329.

20. A. L. Teten et al, "Characterizing Aggression and Its Association to Anger and Hostility Among Male Veterans with Post-Traumatic Stress Disorder," *Military Medicine*. 175, no. 6 (2010): 405–410.

21. C. T. Taft et al., "Intimate Partner and General Aggression Perpetration Among Combat Veterans Presenting to a Posttraumatic Stress Disorder Clinic," *American Journal of Orthopsychiatry*. 79, no. 4 (2009): 461–468.

22. B. Hiley-Young et al., "Warzone Violence in Vietnam: An Examination of Premilitary, Military, and Postmilitary Factors in PTSD Inpatients," *Journal of Traumatic Stress* 8, no. 1 (1995): 125–141.

23. S. Booth-Kewley et al., "Psychosocial Predictors of Military Misconduct," *Journal of Nervous Mental Disease* 198, no. 2 (2010): 91–98.

24. Booth-Kewley et al., "Psychosocial Predictors of Military Misconduct."

25. Booth-Kewley et al., "Psychosocial Predictors of Military Misconduct."

26. E. Jones and S. Wessely, *Shell Shock to PTSD: Military Psychiatry from 1900 to the Gulf War* (New York: Psychology Press, 2005).

27. F. A. Reister, *Battle Casualties and Medical Statistics: U.S. Army Experience in the Korean War*. Washington, DC: Surgeon General, Department of the Army, 1973.

28. S. H. Choe, C. J. Hanley, and M. Mendoza, "GI'S Tell of a US Massacre in Korean War," Associated Press, *New York Times*, 1999.

29. S. Neel, *Vietnam Studies: Medical Support of the U.S. Army in Vietnam 1965–1970* (Washington, DC: Department of the Army, 1991).

30. D. Nelson, *The War Behind Me: Vietnam Veterans Confront the Truth About U.S. War Crimes* (New York: Basic, 2008).

31. - H. S. Resnick et al., , "Antisocial Behavior and Post-Traumatic Stress Disorder in Vietnam Veterans," *Journal of Clinical Psychology* 45, no. 6 (1989): 860–866.

32. J. C. Beckman, M. E. Feldman, and A. C. Kirby, "Atrocities Exposure in Vietnam Combat Veterans with Chronic Posttraumatic Stress Disorder: Relationship to Combat Exposure, Symptom Severity, Guilt, and Interpersonal Violence," *Journal of Traumatic Stress*. 11, no. 4 (1998): 777–785.

33. L. C. Baldor, "Misconduct Forces More Soldiers Out," Associated Press, February 17, 2014.

34. *Manual of Courts-Martial (MCM)*, United States (Washington, DC: Joint Service Committee on Military Justice, 2012), i-1.

35. *Manual of Courts-Martial*, United States.

36. Manual of Courts-Martial, United States.

37. *Stapp v. Resor* (1970), 314 F. Supp. 475 (S.D.N.Y. 1970).

38. M. G. Mullen, *Letter from Admiral Michael G. Mullen, Chairman of the U.S. Joint Chiefs of Staff*, to Hon. Eric K. Shinseki, Secretary of the Department of Veterans Affairs (Washington, DC: Pentagon, February 15, 2011).

39. Department of the Army, *Field Manual 6–22.5: Combat and Operational Stress Control Manual for Leaders and Soldiers* (Washington, DC: Headquarters, Department of the Army, 2009); Institute of Medicine (IOM), 2008; M. C. Russell and C. R. Figley, "Investigating Recurrent Generational Wartime Behavioral Health Crises: Part One of a Preliminary Analysis," *Psychological Injury and Law* 8, no.1 (2015): 106–131.; M. C. Russell and C. R. Figley, "Generational Wartime Behavioral Health Crises: Part Two of a Preliminary Analysis," *Psychological Injury and Law* 8, no. 1 (2015): 132–152.

40. IOM, *Gulf War and Health:* Vol. 6, *Physiologic, Psychologic and Psychosocial Effects of Deployment-Related Stress* (Washington, DC: National Academies Press, 2008), 62.

41. Mental Health Advisory Team-V, *Mental Health Advisory Team (MHAT-V) Operation Enduring Freedom 06–08, 14 February 2008* (Washington, DC: Office of the Surgeon Multinational Force-Iraq and Office of the Surgeon General, U.S. Army Medical Command, 2008).

42. R. M. Highfill-McRoy et al., "Psychiatric Diagnosis and Punishment for Misconduct: The Effects of PTSD in Combat-Deployed Marines," *BMC Psychiatry* 10, no. 1 (2010): 88.

43. R. J. Bernucci, "Forensic Military Psychiatry," in *Zone of Interior*, Vol. I of *Medical Department United States Army: Neuropsychiatry in World War II*, ed. A. J. Glass and R. J. Bernucci (Washington, DC: Office of the Surgeon General, Department of the Army, 1966), 475–488.

44. Highfill-McRoy et al., "Psychiatric Diagnosis and Punishment for Misconduct."

45. E. R. Seamone, "Reclaiming the Rehabilitative Ethic in Military Justice: The Suspended Punitive Discharge as a Method to Treat Military Offenders with PTSD and TBI and Reduce Recidivism," *Military Law Review* 208, no. 1 (2011): 1–212

46. Seamone, "Reclaiming the Rehabilitative Ethic in Military Justice," 18.

47. Seamone, "Reclaiming the Rehabilitative Ethic in Military Justice," 18.

48. Seamone, "Reclaiming the Rehabilitative Ethic in Military Justice."

49. *Porter v. McCullum* (2009), 130 S. Ct. 447, 455, n.8.

50. R. T. Russell, "Veterans Treatment Court: A Proactive Approach," *New England Journal on Crime and Civil Confinement* 35 (2009): 364.

51. J. G. Holbrook, "Veterans' Courts and Criminal Responsibility: A Problem Solving History and Approach to the Liminality of Combat Trauma" (Widener Law School Legal Studies Research Paper No. 10-43, Widener University School of Law, Wilmington, DE, 2010), 1.

52. P. Bailey, "Provisions for Care of Mental and Nervous Cases," in *The Medical Department of the United States Army in the World War:* Vol. X, *Neuropsychiatry in the United States*, ed. P. Bailey, F. E. Williams, and P. O.

Komora (prepared under the direction of Maj. Gen. M. W. Ireland, Surgeon General, Washington, DC: U.S. Government Printing Office, 1929), 39–55.

53. Bailey, "Provisions for Care of Mental and Nervous Cases," 131

54. G. V. Strong, "The Administration of Military Justice at the United States Disciplinary Barracks, Fort Leavenworth, Kansas," *Journal of American Institute of Crime and Criminology* 8, no. 3 (1917): 8.

55. Seamone, "Reclaiming the Rehabilitative Ethic in Military Justice."

56. G. V. Strong, "The Administration of Military Justice at the United States Disciplinary Barracks, Fort Leavenworth, Kansas," *Journal of American Institute of Crime and Criminology* 8, no. 3 (1917): 420–421.

57. H. L. Freedman, "The Mental-Hygiene-Unit Approach to Reconditioning Neuropsychiatric Casualties," *Mental Hygiene* 269, no. 2 (1945): 269–302.

58. L. Knapp and F. Weitzen, "A Total Psychotherapeutic Push Method as Practiced in the Fifth Service Command Rehabilitation Center, Fort Knox, Kentucky," *American Journal of Psychiatry* 102, no. 3 (1945): 362–363.

59. A. H. MacCormick and V. H. Evjen, "The Army's Rehabilitation Program for Military Prisoners," *Social Correctives for Delinquency* 1 (1945): 8–11.

60. Seamone, "Reclaiming the Rehabilitative Ethic in Military Justice," 94.

61. MacCormick and Evjen, "The Army's Rehabilitation Program for Military Prisoners."

62. R. A. Chappell, "Naval Offenders and Their Treatment," *Federal Probation* 9 (1945): 3–5.

63. MacCormick and Evjen, "The Army's Rehabilitation Program for Military Prisoners."

64. Seamone, "Reclaiming the Rehabilitative Ethic in Military Justice," 91.

65. H. L. Freedman and M. J. Rockmore, "Mental Hygiene Frontiers in Probation and Parole Services," *Social Correctives for Delinquency* 44 (1945): 44.

66. Seamone, "Reclaiming the Rehabilitative Ethic in Military Justice."

67. Seamone, "Reclaiming the Rehabilitative Ethic in Military Justice."

68. N. M. Camp, *U.S. Army Psychiatry in the Vietnam War: New Challenges in Extended Counterinsurgency Warfare* (U.S. Army Medical Department Center and School, Fort Sam Huston, TX: Borden Institute, 2014).

69. Seamone, "Reclaiming the Rehabilitative Ethic in Military Justice."

70. F. Drimmer, *Until You Are Dead: The Book of Executions in America* (New York: Pinnacle, 1992).

71. W. Holden, *Shell Shock: The Psychological Impact of War* (London: Macmillan, 1998); T. Iacobelli, *Death or Deliverance: Canadian Courts Martial in the Great War* (Vancouver, BC: UBC Press, 2013).

72. Holden, *Shell Shock*, 84)

73. Iacobelli, *Death or Deliverance.*

74. U.S. Army, *The Army Lawyer: A History of the Judge Advocate General's Corps*, 1775–1975 (Honolulu, HI: University Press of the Pacific, 1975).

75. U.S. Army, *The Army Lawyer*.

76. W. B. Huie, *The Execution of Private Slovik* (Yardley PA: Westholme Publishing, 1954).

77. U.S. Army, *The Army Lawyer*.

78. U.S. Army, *The Army Lawyer*, 193.

79. U.S. Army, *The Army Lawyer*.

80. Seamone, "Reclaiming the Rehabilitative Ethic in Military Justice," 3.

81. Annual Report of the Adjutant General, *War Department Annual Reports* 1910 (Washington, DC: War Department, 1910).

5. Humiliate, Ridicule, and Shame into Submission: The Third Dark-Side Strategy

1. J. D. Acosta et al., *Mental Health Stigma in the Military* (prepared for the Office of the Secretary of Defense Center for Military Health Policy Research, Santa Monica, CA: RAND, 2014).

2. Acosta, et al., *Mental Health Stigma in the Military*.

3. E. T. Dean, *Shook Over Hell: Post-Traumatic Stress Vietnam and the Civil War*. (Cambridge, MA: Harvard University Press, 1997); W. Holden, *Shell Shock: The Psychological Impact of War* (London: Macmillan, 1998).

4. Dean, *Shook Over Hell*.

5. W. C. Menninger, *Reactions to Combat: Psychiatry in a Troubled World* (New York: MacMillan, 1948), 20.

6. Acosta et al., *Mental Health Stigma in the Military*, 27.

7. C. R. Figley. "Catastrophes: An Overview of Family Reactions." In *Stress and the family, Vol. II: Coping with Catastrophe*, edited by C. R. Figley and H. I. McCubbin, 3–20. New York: Brunner/Mazel. 1983..

8. M. C. Russell and C. R. Figley, "Generational Wartime Behavioral Health Crises: Part Two of a Preliminary Analysis," *Psychological Injury and Law* 8, no. 1 (2015): 132–152.

9. P. Bailey, "Provisions for Care of Mental and Nervous Cases," in *The Medical Department of the United States Army in the World War: Vol. X, Neuropsychiatry in the United States*, ed. P. Bailey, F. E. Williams, and P. O. Komora (prepared under the direction of Maj. Gen. M. W. Ireland, The Surgeon General, Washington, DC: U.S. Government Printing Office, 1929), 42–43.

10. Menninger, *Reactions to Combat*, 163

11. C. W. Hoge et al., "Combat Duty in Iraq and Afghanistan, Mental Health Problems, and Barriers to Care," *New England Journal of Medicine* 351 (2004): 21.

12. Department of Defense Task Force on Mental Health (DoD TF-MH), *An Achievable Vision: Report of the Department of Defense Task Force on Mental Health* (Falls Church, VA: Defense Health Board, 2007), 15.

13. Department of Navy and U.S. Marine Corps, *Combat and Operational Stress Control, U.S. Navy,* NTTP 1-15M; U.S. Marine Corps, MCRP 6-11C (Washington, DC: Pentagon, December 2010), 1–6.

14. Department of Navy and U.S. Marine Corps, *Combat and Operational Stress Control*, 1–6.

15. Department of Navy and U.S. Marine Corps, *Combat and Operational Stress Control*, 1–6.

16. E. Jones, "LMF: The Use of Psychiatric Stigma in the Royal Air Force During the Second World War," *Journal of Military History* 70, no. 2 (2006): 439–458.

17. Holden, *Shell Shock*.

18. Jones, "LMF: The Use of Psychiatric Stigma."

19. Jones, "LMF: The Use of Psychiatric Stigma," 444.

20. Holden, *Shell Shock*, 110.

21. B. Shepard, *A War of Nerves: Soldiers and Psychiatrists in the Twentieth Century* (Cambridge, MA: Harvard University Press, 2001).

22. Jones, "LMF: The Use of Psychiatric Stigma."

23. Jones, "LMF: The Use of Psychiatric Stigma," 454.

24. Owen, 2003, cited in Jones, "LMF: The Use of Psychiatric Stigma," 455.

25. Jones, "LMF: The Use of Psychiatric Stigma," 455–456.

26. W. C. Menninger, "Public Relations," in *Zone of Interior*, Vol. I of *Medical Department United States Army, Neuropsychiatry in World War II*, ed. A. J. Glass, and R. J. Bernucci (Washington DC: Office of the Surgeon General, Department of the Army, 1966), 132.

27. M. C. Russell and C. R. Figley, "Do the Military's Frontline Psychiatry/ Combat and Operational Stress Control Doctrine Help or Harm Veterans? Part One: Framing the Issue," *Psychological Injury and Law* 10 (2017): 1–23.

28. R. A. Cardona and E. C. Ritchie, "U.S. Military Enlisted Accession Mental Health Screening: History and Current Practice," *Military Medicine* 172, no. 1 (2007): 12.

29. M. C. Russell and C. R. Figley, "Do the Military's Frontline Psychiatry/Combat Operational Stress Control Programs Benefit Veterans? Part Two: Systematic Review of the Evidence," *Psychological Injury and Law* 10 (2017): 24–71.

30. Russell and Figley, "Do the Military's Frontline Psychiatry/Combat and Operational Stress Control Doctrine Help or Harm Veterans? Part One: Framing the Issue."

31. *Report of the War Office Committee of Enquiry Into "Shell Shock"* (London: Imperial War Museum, 1928), 128.

32. R. Sobel, "The Battalion Surgeon as Psychiatrist," in *Combat Psychiatry: Experiences in the North African and Mediterranean Theaters of Operation, American Ground Forces, World War II*, ed. F. R. Hanson, U.S. Army Medical Department (Honolulu, HI: University Press of Pacific, 1949), 40.

33. A. O. Ludwig, "Psychiatry at the Army Level," in *Combat Psychiatry: Experiences in the North African and Mediterranean Theaters of Operation, American Ground Forces, World War II*, ed. Hanson, F. R., U.S. Army Medical Department (Honolulu, HI: University Press of the Pacific, 1949), 95.

34. J. A. Shaw, "Psychodynamic Considerations in the Adaptation to Combat," in *Contemporary Studies in Combat Psychiatry*, ed. G. Belenky (Westport, CT: Greenwood Press, 1987), 131.

35. U.S. Army, *Circular No. 24 American Expeditionary Forces, France* (NATOUSA: Office of Surgeon, Headquarters, NATOUSA, April 23, 1918), 297.

36. M .K. Wells, *Aviators and Air Combat: A Study of the U.S. Eighth Air Force and RAF Bomber Command (No. AFIT/CI/CIA-92-136)* (London: Department of War Studies, King's College, University of London, 1992).

37. U.S. Army Air Force, *Eighth Air Force Policy Letter 200.9x373 of 29 October* (London: AFHRA, October 29, 1942).

38. Wells, *Aviators and Air Combat.*

39. Wells, *Aviators and Air Combat.*

40. U.S. Army Eighth Air Force, *The reclassification of Personnel Failures in the Eighth Air Force of 16 October 1944, 520.742–4* (London: AFHRA, October 16, 1944), 339.

41. Wells, *Aviators and Air Combat.*

42. Wells, *Aviators and Air Combat*, 306.

43. M. C. Russell and C. R. Figley, "Is the Military's Century-Old Frontline Psychiatry Policy Harmful to Veterans and their Families? Part Three of a Systematic Review," *Psychological Injury and Law* 10 (2017): 72–95

44. Hoge et al., "Combat Duty in Iraq and Afghanistan, Mental Health Problems, and Barriers to Care."

45. C. W. Hoge, C. A. Castro, and K. M. Eaton, "Impact of Combat Duty in Iraq and Afghanistan on Family Functioning: Findings from the Walter Reed Army Institute of Research land Combat Study," in *Human Dimensions in Military Operations—Military Leaders' Strategies for Addressing Stress and Psychological Support* (meeting proceedings RTO-MP-HFM-134, paper 5; Neuilly-sur-Seine, France: RTO, 2006), 5.1–5.6.

46. DoD TF-MH, *An Achievable Vision*, 4–5.

47. M. C. Russell, S. Butkus, and C. R. Figley, C. R., "Contribution of Military Organization and Leadership Factors in Perpetuating Generational Cycle of Preventable Wartime Mental Health Crises: Part One," *Psychological Injury and Law* 9, no. 1 (2016): 55–72.

48. Russell, Butkus, and Figley, "Contribution of Military Organization and Leadership Factors," 6.

49. Government Accountability Office (GAO), *Human Capital: Additional Actions Needed to Enhance DoD's Efforts to Address Mental Health Care Stigma* (GAO-16-404; Washington, DC: GAO, 2016), i.

50. GAO, *Human Capital*; J. D. Acosta et al., *Mental Health Stigma in the Military.*

51. GAO, *Human Capital*, i.

52. GAO, *Human Capital*, i.

53. GAO, *Human Capital*, i.

54. See Russell and Figley, "Do the Military's Frontline Psychiatry/Combat and Operational Stress Control Doctrine Help or Harm Veterans? Part One: Framing the Issue."

55. Acosta et al., *Mental Health Stigma in the Military.*

56. Department of Defense (DoD), *Department of Defense Directive Number 1020.02: Diversity Management and Equal Opportunity (EO) in the Department of Defense* (Washington, DC: Pentagon, 2009).

57. DoD, *Department of Defense Directive 1020.02*, 2.

6. Denying the Psychiatric Reality of War: The Fourth Dark-Side Strategy

1. "Denial," *Merriam-Webster*, www.merriam-webster.com/dictionary/denial.

2. A. Freud, *The Ego and the Mechanisms of Defense*: Vol. 2, *The Collected Works of Anna Freud* (New York: International Universities Press, 1936).

3. S. C. Thompson and S. A. Ting "Reaction to the Threat of Future Cardiovascular Disease," *Health Educ Behav* 39, no. 5 (2012): 620–29.

4. Thompson and Ting, "Reaction to the Threat of Future Cardiovascular Disease."

5. M. C. Russell and C. R. Figley, "Generational Wartime Behavioral Health Crises: Part Two of a Preliminary Analysis," *Psychological Injury and Law* 8, no. 1 (2015): 132–152.

6. A. G. Kay, "Insanity in the Army During Peace and War, and Its Treatment," *Journal of the Royal Army Medical Corps*. 18 no. 1 (1912): 153.

7. Cited in E. Jones and S. Wessely, *Shell Shock to PTSD: Military Psychiatry from 1900 to the Gulf War* (New York: Psychology Press, 2005), 13.

8. R. Gaupp, *Uber den Begriff der hysterie*, ZgNP 5 (1911): 457–466, cited in P. Lerner, *Hysterical Men: War, Psychiatry, and the Politics of Trauma in Germany, 1890–1930* (London: Cornell University Press, 2003), 40.

9. Oppenheim (1914), cited in Lerner, *Hysterical Men*, 67.

10. Oppenheim (1914), cited in Lerner, *Hysterical Men*, 67; J. Appel and G. Beebe, "Preventive Psychiatry; An Epidemiologic Approach," *Journal of the American Medical Association* 131 (1946): 1469–1475.

11. T. W. Salmon, *Recommendations for the Treatment of Mental and Nervous Diseases in the United States Army* (New York: National Committee for Mental Hygiene, 1917), 14.

12. A. J. Glass, "Lessons Learned," in *Zone of Interior*, Vol. I. of *Medical Department United States Army, Neuropsychiatry in World War II*, ed. A. J. Glass, and R. J. Bernucci (Washington, DC: Office of the Surgeon General, Department of the Army, 1966), 736.

13. Jones and Wessely, *Shell Shock to PTSD*, 165.

14. Salmon, *Recommendations for the Treatment of Mental and Nervous Diseases in the United States Army*, 65.

15. W. Casscells, "Rising to the Challenges of PTSD" (Pentagon news release by Assistant Secretary Health Affairs, Washington, DC: Pentagon, August 18, 2008), 2.

16. Department of Defense Task Force on Mental Health (DoD TF-MH), *An Achievable Vision: Report of the Department of Defense Task Force on Mental Health* (Falls Church, VA: Defense Health Board, 2007), 6.

17. Institute of Medicine (IOM) (Washington, DC: National Academies Press, 2014), 5.

18. A. J. Glass, "Army Psychiatry before World War II," in *Zone of Interior*, Vol. I. of *Medical Department United States Army, Neuropsychiatry in World War II*, ed. A. J. Glass and R. J. Bernucci (Washington, DC: Office of the Surgeon General, Department of the Army, 1966), 17.

19. Glass, "Army Psychiatry Before World War II," 18.

20. Glass, "Army Psychiatry Before World War II," 18.

21. U.S. Army Surgeon General, cited in L. D. Heaton, "Forward," in *Zone of Interior*, Vol. I of *Medical Department United States Army, Neuropsychiatry in World War II*, ed. A. J. Glass and R. J. Bernucci (Washington, DC: Office of the Surgeon General, Department of the Army, 1966), xiv.

22. J. A. Martin, "Combat Psychiatry: Lessons from the War in Southwest Asia," *Journal of the U.S. Army Medical Department*, PB 89-2-1/2 (1992): 40–44.

23. DoD TF-MH, *An Achievable Vision*, ES-2.

24. DoD TF-MH, *An Achievable Vision*.

25. M. C. Russell, B. Zinn, and C. R. Figley, "Exploring Options Including Class Action to Transform Military Mental Healthcare and End the Generational Cycle of Preventable Wartime Behavioral Health Crises," *Psychological Injury and Law* 9 (2016): 166–197.

26. Glass, "Lessons Learned," 739.

27. Glass, "Army Psychiatry Before World War II," 22.

28. Institute of Medicine (IOM), *Gulf War and Health*: Vol. 6, *Physiologic, Psychologic and Psychosocial Effects of Deployment-Related Stress* (Washington, DC: National Academies Press, 2008), 62.

29. Glass, "Army Psychiatry Before World War II," 387.

30. F. D. Jones, L. R. Sparacino, V. L. Wilcox, J. M. Rothberg, and J. W. Stokes, eds., *Textbook of Military Medicine: War Psychiatry* (Washington, DC: Office of the Surgeon General, U.S. Army, Borden Institute, Walter Reed Army Institute of Research 1995).

31. M. C. Russell and C. R. Figley, "Investigating Recurrent Generational Wartime Behavioral Health Crises: Part One of a Preliminary Analysis," *Psychological Injury and Law* 8, no.1 (2015): 106–131.

32. S. K. Ogden and A. D. Biebers, *Psychology of Denial* (New York: Nova Publishing, 2011).

33. N. Q. Brill, "Station and Regional Hospitals," in *Zone of Interior*, Vol. I of *Medical Department United States Army, Neuropsychiatry in World War II*, ed. A. J. Glass and R. J. Bernucci (Washington, DC: Office of the Surgeon General, Department of the Army, 1966), 255–295.

34. Cited in Brill, "Station and Regional Hospitals," 291–292.

35. Brill, "Station and Regional Hospitals"; W. C. Menninger, *Reactions to Combat: Psychiatry in a Troubled World* (New York: MacMillan, 1948).

36. T. W. Salmon and N. Fenton, "Neuropsychiatry in the American Expeditionary Forces," in *Neuropsychiatry: The Medical Department of the United States Army in the World War*, Vol. 10, ed. P. Bailey, F. E. Williams, P. A. Komora, T. W. Salmon, and N. Fenton (Washington, DC: Office of the Surgeon General, U.S. Army, 1929), 147.

37. Executive Order No. 13625, Federal Register, 77(172). *Improving Access to Mental Health Services for Veterans, Service Members, and Military Families*, 2012, www.gpo.gov/fdsys/pkg/FR-2012-09-05/pdf/2012-22062.pdf.

38. Government Accountability Office (GAO), *Post-traumatic Stress Disorder: DoD Needs to Identify the Factors Its Providers Use to Make Mental Health Evaluation Referrals for Service Members*, GAO-06-397 04 (Washington, DC: GAO, 2006), i.

39. GAO (2006).

40. p. 31

41. p. 31

42. T. W. Salmon, "Introduction," in *The Medical Department of the United States Army in the World War: Vol. X, Neuropsychiatry in the American Expeditionary Forces*, ed. T. W. Salmon and N. Fenton (prepared under the direction of Maj. Gen. M. W. Ireland, The Surgeon General. Washington, DC: U.S. Government Printing Office, 1929), i.

43. Joint Mental Health Advisory Team (J-MHAT), (2010), 78.

44. Department of Veterans Affairs and Department of Defense (VA/DOD), "VA/DoD Clinical Practice Guideline for the Management of Post-traumatic

Stress" (publication 10Q-CPG/PTSD-04, Washington, DC: Veterans Health Administration, Department of Veterans Affairs and Health Affairs, Department of Defense, Office of Quality and Performance, 2004).

45. VA/DoD, "VA/DoD Clinical Practice Guideline for the Management of Post-traumatic Stress," 24.

46. IOM (2014).

47. Russell, Zinn, and Figley, "Exploring Options Including Class Action to Transform Military Mental Healthcare."

48. C. Agócs, "Institutionalized Resistance to Organizational Change," *Journal of Business Ethics* 16 (1997): 918.

49. M. Russell "The Future of Mental Health Care" testimony before Congree (Washington, DC: Defense Health Board, 2006).

50. U.S. Navy, *Mental Health Public Affairs Guidance of 23 January* 2007 (unpublished document, Washington, DC: U.S. Navy Medical Department, Navy Medicine West, Bureau of Medicine and Surgery, January 23, 2007).

51. DoD TF-MH, *An Achievable Vision.*

52. G. Zoroya, *USA Today*, 2007.

7. Purging Weakness: The Fifth Dark-Side Strategy

1. F. D. Jones, in *Textbook of Military Medicine: War Psychiatry*, ed. F. D. Jones, L. R. Sparacino, V. L. Wilcox, J. M. Rothberg, and J. W. Stokes (Washington, DC: Office of the Surgeon General, U.S. Army, Borden Institute, Walter Reed Army Institute of Research 1995), 416.

2. Jones (1995), 417.

3. Jones (1995), 417.

4. Oppenheim, 1914, cited in P. Lerner, *Hysterical Men: War, Psychiatry, and the Politics of Trauma in Germany, 1890–1930* (London: Cornell University Press, 2003), 67.

5. B. Shepard, *A War of Nerves: Soldiers and Psychiatrists in the Twentieth Century* (Cambridge, MA: Harvard University Press, 2001).

6. T. W. Salmon, *Recommendations for the Treatment of Mental and Nervous Diseases in the United States Army* (New York: National Committee for Mental Hygiene, 1917), 23.

7. Salmon, *Recommendations for the Treatment of Mental and Nervous Diseases,* 27.

8. Salmon, *Recommendations for the Treatment of Mental and Nervous Diseases,* 47.

9. Salmon, *Recommendations for the Treatment of Mental and Nervous Diseases,* 23.

10. M. C. Russell and C. R. Figley, "Do the Military's Frontline Psychiatry/ Combat and Operational Stress Control Doctrine Help or Harm Veterans? Part One: Framing the Issue," *Psychological Injury and Law* 10 (2017): 1–23.

11. T. W. Salmon and N. Fenton, "Neuropsychiatry in the American Expeditionary Forces," in *Neuropsychiatry: The Medical Department of the United States Army in the World War*, Vol. 10, ed. P. Bailey, F. E. Williams, P. A. Komora, T. W. Salmon, and N. Fenton (Washington, DC: Office of the Surgeon General, U.S. Army, 1929)

12. Institute of Medicine (IOM), (Washington, DC: National Academic Press, 2007).

13. I. C. Berlien and R. W. Waggoner, "Selection and Induction," in *Zone of Interior*, Vol. I of *Medical Department United States Army, Neuropsychiatry in World War II*, ed. A. J. Glass and R. J. Bernucci (Washington, DC: Office of the Surgeon General, Department of the Army, 1966), 153–191.

14. Salmon and Fenton, "Neuropsychiatry in the American expeditionary forces," chapter 3.

15. Oppenheim (1914), cited in Lerner, *Hysterical Men*, 67.

16. *Report of the War Office Committee of Enquiry Into "Shell Shock"* (London: Imperial War Museum, 1922).

17. *Report of the War Office Committee of Enquiry Into "Shell Shock,"* 144.

18. Shepard (1999), 509–510.

19. F. D. Jones, "Disorders of Frustration and Loneliness," in *Textbook of Military Medicine: War Psychiatry*, ed. F. D. Jones, L. R. Sparacino, V. L. Wilcox, J. M. Rothberg, and J. W. Stokes (Washington, DC: Office of the Surgeon General, U.S. Army, Borden Institute, Walter Reed Army Institute of Research, 1995), 63–83.

20. R. Dekel, Z. Solomon, K. Ginzburg, and Y. Neria, "Combat Exposure, Wartime Performance, and Long-Term Adjustment Among Combatants," *Military Psychology* 15, no.2 (2003): 117–131

21. M. Hing et al., "Special Operations Forces and Incidence of Post-Traumatic Stress Disorder Symptoms," *Journal of Special Operation Medicine* 12, no. 3 (2012): 23–35

22. G. L. Belenky, C. F. Tyner, and F. J. Sodetz, *Israeli Battle Shock Casualties: 1973 and 1982* (Washington, DC: Walter Reed Army Institute of Research, 1983), 22.

23. Z. Solomon, M. Mikulincer, and M. Waysman, "Delayed and Immediate Onset Posttraumatic Stress Disorder: II. The Role of Battle Experiences and Personal Resources," *Social Psychiatry and Psychiatric Epidemiology* 26 (1991): 8–13.

24. D. Horesh, Z. Solomon, G. Zerach, and T. Ein-Dor, "Delayed-Onset PTSD Among War Veterans: The Role of Life Events Throughout the Life Cycle," *Social Psychiatry and Psychiatric Epidemiology* 46, no. 9 (2011): 863–870.

25. Zohar et al. (2008).

26. N. M. Camp, *U.S. Army Psychiatry in the Vietnam War: New Challenges in Extended Counterinsurgency Warfare* (Fort Sam Huston, TX: U.S. Army Medical Department Center and School, Borden Institute, 2014); R. A. Kulka et al., *Trauma and the Vietnam War Generation: Report of Findings from the National Vietnam Veterans Readjustment Study* (New York, NY: Brunner/ Mazel, 1990).

27. C. R. Brewin, B. Andrews, and J. D. Valentine, "Meta-analysis of Risk Factors for Posttraumatic Stress Disorder in Trauma-Exposed Adults," *Journal of Consulting and Clinical Psychology* 68, no. 5 (2000): 748–766; E. J. Ozer et al., "Predictors of Posttraumatic Stress Disorder and Symptoms in Adults: A Meta-Analysis," *Psychology Bulletin* 129, no. 1 (2003): 52–73; C. J. Phillips et al., "Risk Factors for Posttraumatic Stress Disorder Among Deployed US Male Marines," *BMC Psychiatry* 10 (2010): 1–11.

28. J. Du Preez et al., "Unit Cohesion and Mental Health in the UK Armed Forces," *Occupational Medicine* 62, no. 1 (2012): 47–53.

29. P. Armistead-Jehle et al., "Posttraumatic Stress in U.S. Marines: The Role of Unit Cohesion and Combat Exposure," *Journal of Counseling and Development.* 89 (2011): 81–88; R. H. Pietrzak et al., "Psychosocial Buffers of Traumatic Stress, Depressive Symptoms, and Psychosocial Difficulties in Veterans of Operations Enduring Freedom and Iraqi Freedom: The Role of Resilience, Unit Support, and Post-Deployment Social Support," *Journal of Special Operations Medicine.* 9, no. 3 (2009): 74–78.

30. A. A. Whitesell and G. P. Owens, "The Impact of Patriotism, Morale, and Unit Cohesion on Mental Health in Veterans of Iraq and Afghanistan," *Traumatology* 18, no. 1 (2012): 1–7.

31. S. C. Han et al. "Military Unit Support, Postdeployment Social Support, and PTSD Symptoms Among Active Duty and National Guard Soldiers Deployed to Iraq," *Journal of Anxiety Disorders*, 28 (2014): 446–453.

32. R. Ramchand et al., "Prevalence of, Risk Factors for, and Consequences of Posttraumatic Stress Disorder and Other Mental Health Problems in Military Populations Deployed to Iraq and Afghanistan," *Current Psychiatry Report* 17 (2015): 1–11.

33. A. J. Glass, "Army Psychiatry Before World War II," in *Zone of Interior*, Vol. I of *Medical Department United States Army, Neuropsychiatry in World War II*, ed. A. J. Glass and R. J. Bernucci (Washington, DC: Office of the Surgeon General, Department of the Army, 1966), 7.

34. Shepard, *A War of Nerves*.

35. D. W. Orr, "Objectives of Selective Service Psychiatric Classification," *Bulletin of Menninger Clinic* 5 (1941): 131–133.

36. Cited in Berlien and Waggoner, "Selection and Induction," 156.
37. Berlien and Waggoner, "Selection and Induction," 162.
38. Berlien and Waggoner, "Selection and Induction."
39. Glass, "Army Psychiatry Before World War II."
40. N. Q. Brill and H. I. Kupper, "Problems of Adjustment in Return to Civilian Life," in *Zone of Interior: Vol I. Medical Department United States Army. In Neuropsychiatry in World War II*, ed. A. J. Glass and R. J. Bernucci (Washington, DC: Office of the Surgeon General, Department of the Army, 1966), 721–733; B. H. Chermol, "Wounds Without Scars: Treatment of Battle Fatigue in the U.S. Armed Forces in the Second World War," *Military Affairs: The Journal of Military History, Including Theory and Technology* 49 (1985): 9–12.
41. Glass, "Army Psychiatry Before World War II."
42. R. A. Cardona and E. C. Ritchie, "U.S. Military Enlisted Accession Mental Health Screening: History and Current Practice," *Military Medicine* 172, no. 1 (2007): 31–35.
43. A. J. Glass, R. J. Bernucci, and R S. Anderson, eds., *Medical Department United States Army. Neuropsychiatry in World War II* (Washington, DC: Office of the Surgeon General, Department of the Army, 1966).
44. R. H. Eanes, "Standards Used by Selective Service and a Follow-up on Neuropsychiatric Rejectees in World War II," *Selection of Military Manpower: A Symposium* (1951): 149–156.
45. Berlien and Waggoner, "Selection and Induction."
46. Berlien and Waggoner, "Selection and Induction"; Cardona and Ritchie, "U.S. Military Enlisted Accession Mental Health Screening."
47. J. A. Plag and R. J. Arthur, "Psychiatric Re-examination of Unsuitable Naval Recruits: A Two-Year Follow-Up Study," *American Journal of Psychiatry* 122, no. 5 (1965): 534–541.
48. Cardona and Ritchie, "U.S. Military Enlisted Accession Mental Health Screening."
49. E. C. Ritchie, "Update on Combat Psychiatry: From the Battle Front to the Home Front and Back Again," *Military Medicine* 172, no. 2 (2007): 35.
50. Brewin, Andrews, and Valentine, "Meta-analysis of Risk Factors for Posttraumatic Stress Disorder."
51. Kulka et al., *Trauma and the Vietnam War Generation*; Xiu et al. (2015).
52. Ozer et al., "Predictors of Posttraumatic Stress Disorder and Symptoms in Adults."
53. Kulka et al., *Trauma and the Vietnam War Generation*, 85.
54. B. P. Dohrenwend et al., "The Roles of Combat Exposures, Personal Vulnerability, and Involvement in Harm to Civilians or Prisoners in Vietnam War-Related Posttraumatic Stress Disorder," *Clinical Psychology Science* 1, no. 3 (2013): 223–238.

55. Beebe and Appel (1958), 164.
56. IOM (2008); Kulka et al., *Trauma and the Vietnam War Generation.*
57. Solomon, *Combat Stress Reaction.*
58. Kulka et al., *Trauma and the Vietnam War Generation.*
59. K. Klostermann et al., "Intimate Partner Violence in the Military: Treatment Considerations," *Aggression and Violent Behavior* 17, no. 1 (2012): 53–58.
60. Ramchand et al., "Prevalence of, Risk Factors for, and Consequences of Posttraumatic Stress Disorder and Other Mental Health Problems."
61. T. McGeorge, J. H. Hughes, and S. Wessely, "The MoD PTSD Decision: A Psychiatric Perspective," *Occupational Health Review* 122 (2006): 21–28.
62. W. P. Nash et al., "Posttraumatic Stress in Deployed Marines: Prospective Trajectories of Early Adaptation," *Journal of Abnormal Psychology* 124, no. 1 (2015): 155–171; T. C. Smith et al., "Postdeployment Hospitalizations Among Service Members Deployed in Support of the Operations in Iraq and Afghanistan," *Annals of Epidemiology* 19, no. 9 (2009): 603–612; P. McCutchan et al., "Deployment, Combat, and Risk of Multiple Physical Symptoms in the US Military: A Prospective Cohort Study," *Annals of Epidemiology* 26, no. 2 (2016), DOI:10.1016/j.annepidem.2015.12.001; A. D. Seelig et al., "Sleep and Health Resilience Metrics in a Large Military Cohort," *Sleep* 39, no. 5 (2010): 1111–1120.

8. Delay, Deceive, and Delay Again: The Sixth Dark-Side Strategy

1. Department of Defense Task Force on Mental Health (DoD TF-MH), *An Achievable Vision: Report of the Department of Defense Task Force on Mental Health* (Falls Church, VA: Defense Health Board, 2007).
2. M. Russell, *The Future of Mental Health Care in the Department of Defense, Invited Testimony Before the Congressionally Mandated Department of Defense Task Force on Mental Health*, October 19–20, 2006 (San Diego, CA. Washington, DC: Defense Health Board, 2006).
3. M. Russell, M., "Mental Health Crisis in the Department of Defense: DoD Inspector General Hotline Investigation #98829 submitted by Commander Mark Russell, USN on 05JAN2006" (Washington, DC: Pentagon, 2006); G. Zoroya, *USA Today*, 2007.
4. A. J. Glass, "Lessons Learned," in *Zone of Interior*, Vol. I of *Medical Department United States Army, Neuropsychiatry in World War II*, ed. A. J. Glass, and R. J. Bernucci (Washington, DC: Office of the Surgeon General, Department of the Army, 1966), 735.
5. M. C. Russell and C. R. Figley, "Do the Military's Frontline Psychiatry/ Combat and Operational Stress Control Doctrine Help or Harm Veterans? Part One: Framing the Issue," *Psychological Injury and Law* 10 (2017): 1–23.

6. W. C. Menninger, "Education and Training," in *Zone of Interior*, Vol. I of *Medical Department United States Army, Neuropsychiatry in World War II*, ed. A. J. Glass and R. J. Bernucci (Washington, DC: Office of the Surgeon General, Department of the Army, 1966), 53–66; M. C. Russell, B. Zinn, and C. R. Figley, "Exploring Options Including Class Action to Transform Military Mental Healthcare and End the Generational Cycle of Preventable Wartime Behavioral Health Crises," *Psychological Injury and Law* 9 (2016): 166–197.

7. M. C. Russell and C. R. Figley, "Investigating Recurrent Generational Wartime Behavioral Health Crises: Part One of a Preliminary Analysis," *Psychological Injury and Law* 8, no. 1 (2015): 106–131; M. C. Russell and C. R. Figley, "Generational Wartime Behavioral Health Crises: Part Two of a Preliminary Analysis," *Psychological Injury and Law* 8, no. 1 (2015): 132–152.

8. M. C. Russell, S. Butkus, and C. R. Figley, "Contribution of Military Organization and Leadership Factors in Perpetuating Generational Cycle of Preventable Wartime Mental Health Crises: Part One," *Psychological Injury and Law* 9, no. 1 (2016): 55–72; M. C. Russell, S. Butkus, and C. R. Figley, "Ending the Generational Cycle of Preventable Wartime Mental Health Crises: Part Two: Establishing a Behavioral Health Corps and Other Constructive Solutions," *Psychological Injury and Law* 9 no. 1 (2016): 73–86.

9. Russell and Figley, "Investigating Recurrent Generational Wartime Behavioral Health Crises: Part One of a Preliminary Analysis."

10. DCAS, Defense Manpower Data Center, https://www.dmdc.osd.mil/dcas /pages/casualties.xhtml.

11. Defense Manpower Data Center, 2017, https://www.dmdc.osd.mil/dcas/pages /casualties.xhtml.

12. M. C. Russell, S. R. Schaubel, and C. R. Figley, "The Darker Side of Military Mental Healthcare—Part One: Understanding the Military's Mental Health Dilemma" (manuscript submitted for publication, 2017).

13. W. C. Menninger, "Public Relations," in *Zone of Interior*, Vol. I of *Medical Department United States Army, Neuropsychiatry in World War II*, ed. A. J. Glass, and R. J. Bernucci (Washington, DC: Office of the Surgeon General, Department of the Army, 1966), 141 [emphasis ours].

14. Menninger, "Public Relations," 148.

15. Menninger, "Public Relations," 148.

16. Menninger, "Public Relations," 148.

17. Menninger, "Public Relations," 250.

18. http://www.pdhealth.mil/clinical/psychological-health-numbers/mental -health-disorder-prevalence-among-active-duty-service

19. Russell, Butkus, and Figley, "Contribution of Military Organization and Leadership Factors in Perpetuating Generational Cycle of Preventable Wartime Mental Health Crises: Part One."

20. Institute of Medicine (IOM), *Treatment for Posttraumatic Stress Disorder in Military and Veteran Populations: Final Assessment* (Washington, DC: National Academies Press, 2014), 84.

21. IOM, *Returning Home from Iraq and Afghanistan: Assessment of Readjustment Needs of Veterans, Service Members, and Their Families* (Washington, DC: National Academies Press, 2013), 472.

22. Russell and Figley, "Investigating Recurrent Generational Wartime Behavioral Health Crises: Part One of a Preliminary Analysis."

23. Russell and Figley, "Investigating Recurrent Generational Wartime Behavioral Health Crises: Part One of a Preliminary Analysis."

24. U.S. Army, "Final Public Affairs Guidance: OEF/OIF Communications Plan Mental Health of 23 May 2006" (unpublished document, Headquarters, Army Medical Department, Washington, DC, May 23, 2006), 1.

25. U.S. Army, *Final Public Affairs Guidance*, 1.

26. U.S. Army, *Final Public Affairs Guidance*, 2–3.

27. DoD TF-MH, *An Achievable Vision*, 63.

28. P. Bailey, "Provisions for Care of Mental and Nervous Cases," in *The Medical Department of the United States Army in the World War:* Vol. I, ed. C. Lynch, F. W. Weed, and L. McAfee (Surgeon General's Office, prepared under the direction of Maj. Gen. M. W. Ireland, M.D. Surgeon General of the Army, Washington, DC: Government Printing Office, 1923), 384–394; T. W. Salmon and N. Fenton, "Neuropsychiatry in the American Expeditionary Forces," in *Neuropsychiatry: The Medical Department of the United States Army in the World War*, Vol. 10, ed. P. Bailey, F. E. Williams, P. A. Komora, T. W. Salmon, and N. Fenton (Washington, DC: Office of the Surgeon General, U.S. Army, 1929), 271–474.

29. A. J. Glass, "Army Psychiatry Before World War II," in *Zone of Interior*, Vol. I of *Medical Department United States Army, Neuropsychiatry in World War II*, ed. A. J. Glass and R. J. Bernucci (Washington, DC: Office of the Surgeon General, Department of the Army, 1966), 3–23; Glass, "Lessons Learned."

30. Russell and Figley, "Generational Wartime Behavioral Health Crises: Part Two of a Preliminary Analysis."

31. L. D. Heaton, "Forward," in *Zone of Interior*, Vol. I of *Medical Department United States Army, Neuropsychiatry in World War II*, ed. A. J. Glass and R. J. Bernucci, xiii–xiv (Washington, DC: Office of the Surgeon General, Department of the Army, 1966), xiv.

32. Russell and Figley, "Investigating Recurrent Generational Wartime Behavioral Health Crises: Part One of a Preliminary Analysis"; Russell and Figley, "Generational Wartime Behavioral Health Crises: Part Two of a Preliminary Analysis."

33. Russell and Figley, "Generational Wartime Behavioral Health Crises: Part Two of a Preliminary Analysis."

34. S. Neel, *Vietnam Studies: Medical Support of the U. S. Army in Vietnam 1965–1970* (Washington, DC: Department of the Army, 1991).

35. Zoroya (2007).

36. M. E. Kilpatrick, *Force Health Protection and Readiness Programs, Department of Defense, Hearing Before the U.S. Congress House of Representatives Committee on Oversight and Government Reform*, First Session, May 24, 2007 (Statement by Michael E. Kilpatrick, MD, Deputy Director), Serial No. 110–111 (Washington, DC: U.S. Government Printing Office, 2007), 63–79.

37. Kilpatrick, *Force Health Protection and Readiness Programs*, 61.

38. DoD TF-MH, *An Achievable Vision*.

39. Kilpatrick, *Force Health Protection and Readiness Programs*, 114.

40. Kilpatrick, *Force Health Protection and Readiness Programs*, 114 [emphasis ours].

41. U.S. Navy, "Mental Health Public Affairs Guidance of 23 January 2007" (unpublished document, U.S. Navy Medical Department, Navy Medicine West, Bureau of Medicine and Surgery, Washington, DC, January 23, 2007), 1.

42. A. Batdorff, "Officer Sees 'Perfect Storm' Brewing in Military's Mental Health Care System," *Stars and Stripes Pacific*, September 22, 2006.

43. U.S. Navy, *Mental Health Public Affairs Guidance*.

44. U.S. Navy, *Mental Health Public Affairs Guidance*.

45. DoD TF-MH, *An Achievable Vision*.

46. DoD TF-MH, *An Achievable Vision*, ES-2.

47. U.S. Navy, *Mental Health Public Affairs Guidance*.

48. H. Bernton, "Madigan Team Reversed 285 PTSD Diagnoses, Sen. Murray Says," *Seattle Times*, March 8, 2012; H. Bernton, "40 percent of PTSD Diagnoses at Madigan Were Reversed," *Seattle Times*, March 12, 2012.

49. D. Phillips, "Other Than Honorable: Disposable Surge in Discharges Includes Wounded Soldiers," *The Gazette*, May 19, 2013.

50. Phillips, "Other Than Honorable."

51. Zoroya (2007).

52. *Dignified Treatment of Wounded Warriors Act*, 2009, S 16.06, 110th Congress (2007–2008).

53. B. A. Obama, Exec. Order No. 13625, "Improving Access to Mental Health Services for Veterans, Service Members, and Military Families," 3 C.F.R. 13625 (August 31, 2012), https://obamawhitehouse.archives.gov/the-press-office/2012/08/31/executive-order-improving-access-mental-health-services-veterans-service.

54. B. Boxer, "Boxer Amendment to Establish a Mental Health Task Force Included in Defense Department Appropriations Bill" (press release for Senator Boxer, October 6, 2005).

55. DoD TF-MH, *An Achievable Vision.*
56. DoD TF-MH, *An Achievable Vision.*
57. IOM, *Returning Home from Iraq and Afghanistan.*
58. R. M. Weinick et al., "Programs Addressing Psychological Health and Traumatic Brain Injury Among U.S. Military Service Members and Their Families" (prepared for the Office of the Secretary of Defense Center for Military Health Policy Research, Santa Monica, CA: RAND, 2011).
59. IOM, *Treatment for Posttraumatic Stress Disorder.*
60. IOM, *Returning Home from Iraq and Afghanistan.*
61. IOM, *Preventing Psychological Disorders in Service Members and Their Families: An Assessment of Programs* (Washington, DC: National Academies Press, 2014_.
62. Russell, Butkus, and Figley (2015).
63. Department of Veterans Affairs and Department of Defense (VA/DoD), "VA/DoD Clinical Practice Guideline for the Management of Post-traumatic Stress" (publication 10Q-CPG/PTSD-04, Washington, DC: Veterans Health Administration, Department of Veterans Affairs and Health Affairs, Department of Defense, Office of Quality and Performance, 2004).
64. Russell (2006); Zoroya (2007).
65. *National Defense Authorization Act for Fiscal Year 2008*, Pub. L. 110–181, 122 Stat. 3 (2008).
66. The VA and DoD were required to develop PTSD/TBI programs.
67. RAND, 2008.
68. Weinick et al., "Programs Addressing Psychological Health and Traumatic Brain Injury."
69. Weinick et al., "Programs Addressing Psychological Health and Traumatic Brain Injury," 73.
70. Obama, "Improving Access to Mental Health Services for Veterans."
71. IOM, *Returning Home from Iraq and Afghanistan.*
72. IOM, *Preventing Psychological Disorders in Service Members and Their Families.*
73. IOM, *Treatment for Posttraumatic Stress Disorder.*
74. IOM, *Treatment for Posttraumatic Stress Disorder.*
75. *National Defense Authorization Act for Fiscal Year 2016*, Pub. L. 114-92-Nov. 25, 2015, 129 Stat. 726 (2015).
76. GAO, *Human Capital: Additional Actions Needed to Enhance DoD's Efforts to Address Mental Health Care Stigma* (GAO-16-404. Washington, DC: GAO, 2016).
77. GAO, "DoD Lacks an Access Standard for the Most Common Type of Direct Care Mental Health Appointment" (Washington, DC: GAO, 2016).
78. GAO, "DoD Lacks an Access Standard."
79. GAO, "DoD Lacks an Access Standard."

80. IOM, *Treatment for Posttraumatic Stress Disorder*, 216.
81. U.S. Army Military History Institute, "Combat Lessons Number 5: Rank and File in Combat—What They're Doing How They Do It" (EO-10501 restricted report, Classified "Unrestricted" on August 5, 1986, Combat Analysis Section, Operations Division, War Department, Washington, DC, 1944), 13.
82. R. Ramchand, R. Rudavsky, S. Grant, T. Tanielian, and L. Jaycox, "Prevalence of, Risk Factors for, and Consequences of Posttraumatic Stress Disorder and Other Mental Health Problems in Military Populations Deployed to Iraq and Afghanistan," *Current Psychiatry Reports* 17, no. 5 (2015): 1–11.
83. DoD TF-MH, *An Achievable Vision*.
84. This included a neglected crisis in mental health staffing and less than 90 percent of clinicians trained to treat PTSD (M. Russell, 2006).
85. IOM, *Preventing Psychological Disorders in Service Members and Their Families*.
86. T. W. Salmon, "Introduction," in *The Medical Department of the United States Army in the World War*: Vol. X, *Neuropsychiatry in the American Expeditionary Forces*, ed. T. W. Salmon and N. Fenton (prepared under the direction of Maj. Gen. M. W. Ireland, Surgeon General; Washington, DC: U. S. Government Printing Office, 1929), i.
87. R. R. Grinker and J. P. Spiegel, "War Neuroses in North Africa: The Tunisian Campaign (January–May 1943)" (restricted report prepared for The Air Surgeon, Army Air Forces, Josiah Macy, Jr. Foundation, New York, 1943).
88. DoD TF-MH, *An Achievable Vision*, 43.

9. Faulty Diagnoses and Backdoor Discharges: The Seventh Dark-Side Strategy

1. C. W. Hoge et al., "The Occupational Burden of Mental Disorders in the U.S. Military: Psychiatric Hospitalizations, Involuntary Separations, and Disability," *American Journal of Psychiatry* 162, no. 3 (2005): 585–591.
2. Department of Veterans Affairs and Department of Defense (VA/DoD), "VA/DoD Clinical Practice Guideline for the Management of Post-traumatic Stress" (publication 10Q-CPG/PTSD-04, Washington, DC: Veterans Health Administration, Department of Veterans Affairs and Health Affairs, Department of Defense, Office of Quality and Performance, 2004)
3. M. C. Russell and C. R. Figley, "Do the Military's Frontline Psychiatry/ Combat and Operational Stress Control Doctrine Help or Harm Veterans? Part One: Framing the Issue," *Psychological Injury and Law* 10 (2017): 1–23.; M. C. Russell, S. R. Schaubel, and C. R. Figley, *The Darker Side of Military Mental Healthcare—Part Two: Five Harmful Strategies to Manage Its Mental Health Dilemma* (manuscript submitted for publication, 2017).

4. Memorandum issued by U.S. Army, Office of the Surgeon General, "Memorandum on Psychoneurosis (Combat Exhaustion)" (Washington, DC: U.S. Army, Office of the Surgeon General, 1944).

5. Memorandum issued by U.S. Army, Office of the Surgeon General, "Memorandum on Psychoneurosis (Combat Exhaustion)," 1031.

6. Memorandum issued by U.S. Army, Office of the Surgeon General, "Memorandum on Psychoneurosis (Combat Exhaustion)," 1031.

7. Memorandum issued by U.S. Army, Office of the Surgeon General, "Memorandum on Psychoneurosis (Combat Exhaustion)," 1033.

8. U.S. Army, *Circular Letter No. 17. Neuropsychiatric Treatment in the Combat Zone* (Office of Surgeon, Headquarters, NATOUSA, June 12, 1943), 11.

9. A. J. Glass, "Army Psychiatry Before World War II," in *Zone of Interior*, Vol. I of *Medical Department United States Army, Neuropsychiatry in World War II*, ed. A. J. Glass and R. J. Bernucci (Washington, DC: Office of the Surgeon General, Department of the Army, 1966), 11.

10. Russell and Figley, "Do the Military's Frontline Psychiatry/Combat and Operational Stress Control Doctrine Help or Harm Veterans? Part One: Framing the Issue"; Russell and Figley, "Do the Military's Frontline Psychiatry/ Combat and Operational Stress Control Programs Benefit Veterans? Part Two: Systematic Review of the Evidence."

11. Russell and Figley, "Do the Military's Frontline Psychiatry/Combat Operational and Stress Control Programs Benefit Veterans? Part Two: Systematic Review of the Evidence."

12. Glass, "Army Psychiatry Before World War II," 755.

13. Colonel Menninger, 1944, cited in App. E of Glass, "Army Psychiatry Before World War II," 1966), 814.

14. See, for example, "personality disorder" in Glass, "Army Psychiatry Before World War II."

15. Glass, "Army Psychiatry Before World War II," 756.

16. See, for example, "personality disorder"; P. Lerner, *Hysterical Men: War, Psychiatry, and the Politics of Trauma in Germany, 1890–1930* (London: Cornell University Press, 2003).

17. Department of Army, *Field Manual 4–02.51: Combat and Operational Stress Control (FM 8–51)* (Washington, DC: Headquarters, Department of the Army, 2006), 11–1.

18. Department of the Army, *Policy Guidance on the Assessment and Treatment of Post-Traumatic Stress Disorder (PTSD) OTSG/MEDCOM Policy Memo 12–035 of 10 April 2012* (Fort Sam Houston, TX: Headquarters, United States Army Medical Command, 2012), 4.

19. Memorandum issued by Secretary of the Army, "Memorandum: Special Review and Assessment of Soldiers with Mental Health Conditions Separated from Active Duty for Misconduct of 14 April 2016" (Washington, DC: Department of Army, Headquarters, 2016), 1.

20. Joint Mental Health Advisory Team-7 (Joint MHAT-7), *Operation Enduring Freedom 2010 Afghanistan (22 February 2011)* (Washington, DC: Office of the Surgeon General, U.S. Army Medical Command and Office of the Command Surgeon HQ, USCENTCOM and Office of the Command Surgeon U.S. Forces Afghanistan, 2011), 78.

21. DVA/DoD, "VA/DoD Clinical Practice Guideline for the Management of Post-traumatic Stress 2004."

22. DVA/DoD, "VA/DoD Clinical Practice Guideline for the Management of Post-traumatic Stress," 24.

23. M. C. Russell and C. R. Figley (2016).

24. DVA/DoD, "VA/DoD Clinical Practice Guideline for the Management of Post-traumatic Stress"; Russell and Figley (2016).

25. DVA/DoD, "VA/DoD Clinical Practice Guideline for the Management of Post-traumatic Stress."

26. Department of Defense (DoD), *DoD Instruction 1332.14, Enlisted Administrative Separations. Of February 27, 2017* (Washington, DC: Pentagon, 2017).

27. M. Ader et al., *Casting Troops Aside: The United States Military's Illegal Personality Disorder Discharge Problem* (Silver Spring, MD: Vietnam Veterans of America, 2012); M .C. Russell and C. R. Figley, "Generational Wartime Behavioral Health Crises: Part Two of a Preliminary Analysis," *Psychological Injury and Law* 8, no. 1 (2015): 132–152.

28. M. de Yoanna and M. Benjamin, "I Am Under a Lot of Pressure to Not Diagnose PTSD," *Salon*, April 8, 2009, www.salon.com/2009/04/08/tape.

29. H. Bernton, "Madigan Team Reversed 285 PTSD Diagnoses, Sen. Murray Says," *Seattle Times*, March 8, 2012, http://old.seattletimes.com/text/2017692555.html; H. Bernton, "40 Percent of PTSD Diagnoses at Madigan Were Reversed," *Seattle Times*, March 12, 2012, www.seattletimes.com/seattle-news/40-of-ptsd-diagnoses-at-madigan-were-reversed.

30. Bernton, "Madigan Team Reversed 285 PTSD Diagnoses"; H. Bernton, "Army Opens Wide Review of PTSD-Diagnosis System," *Seattle Times*, May 17, 2012 www.seattletimes.com/seattle-news/army-opens-wide-review-of-ptsd-diagnosis-system.

31. J. E. Wilk et al., "Diagnosis of PTSD by Army Behavioral Health Clinicians: Are Diagnoses Recorded in Electronic Health Records?" *Psychiatric Services* 67, no. 8 (2016): 878–882.

32. Wilk et al., "Diagnosis of PTSD by Army Behavioral Health Clinicians."

33. American Psychological Association, *Ethical Principles of Psychologists and Code of Conduct* (Washington, DC: APA, 2002), www.apa.org/ethics/code/ethics-code-2017.pdf.

34. Department of the Army, *Policy Guidance on the Assessment and Treatment of Post-Traumatic Stress Disorder*, 7.

35. See Russell, Schaubel, and Figley, *The Darker Side of Military Mental Healthcare — Part Two*.

36. H. Bernton, "20,000 Misconduct Discharges Since 2008 Saving DoD Billions in War-related Disability Compensation," *Seattle Times*, September 8, 2012, https://themilitarysuicidereport.wordpress.com/2012/09/09/20000-misconduct-discharges-since-2008-saving-dod-billions-in-war-related-disability-compensation; J. Kors, "Disposable Soldiers: How the Pentagon Is Cheating Wounded Vets," *The Nation*, April 26, 2010, www.thenation.com/article/disposable-soldiers; D. Phillips, "Other Than Honorable: Disposable Surge in Discharges Includes Wounded Soldiers," *The Gazette*, May 19, 2013, http://cdn.csgazette.biz/soldiers/day1.html; Russell, Schaubel, and Figley, *The Darker Side of Military Mental Healthcare — Part Two*.

37. DVA/DoD, "VA/DoD Clinical Practice Guideline for the Management of Post-traumatic Stress."

38. Department of Army, *Field Manual 4–02.51: Combat and Operational Stress Control*.

39. GAO, *Defense Health Care: Status of Efforts to Direct Lack of Compliance with Personality Disorder Separation Requirements* (GAO-10-1013T; Washington, DC: GAO, 2010).

40. GAO, *Defense Health Care.*; Kors, "Disposable Soldiers"; Phillips, "Other Than Honorable."

41. Phillips, "Other Than Honorable."

42. Kors, "Disposable Soldiers"; Phillips, "Other Than Honorable"; B. Murphy, "Critics: Fort Carson Policy Targeted Troubled, Wounded Soldiers." *Stars and Stripes*, November 15, 2011.

43. E. Ginzberg et al., *The Lost Divisions: The Ineffective Soldier, Lessons for Management and the Nation* (New York: Columbia University Press, 1959).

44. R. Izzo, "In Need of Correction: How the Army Board for Correction of Military Records Is Failing Veterans with PTSD," *Yale Law Journal* 123, no. 5 (2014): 1118–1625.

45. M. Waters and J. Shay, "Heal the 'Bad Paper' Veterans," *New York Times*, July 30, 1994, 1.

46. A. Carpenter, "Military Misconduct May Be Sign of PTSD," *Washington Times*, January 12, 2010.

47. Murphy, "Critics: Fort Carson Policy Targeted Troubled, Wounded Soldiers."

48. Phillips, "Other Than Honorable"; Memorandum issued by Secretary of Army, "Memorandum: Special Review and Assessment of Soldiers with Mental Health Conditions."

49. D. Zwerdling, "Missed Treatment: Soldiers with Mental Health Issues Dismissed for 'Misconduct,'" NPR, October 15, 2015.

50. Memorandum issued by Secretary of Army, "Memorandum: Special Review and Assessment of Soldiers with Mental Health Conditions."

51. Memorandum issued by Secretary of Army, "Memorandum: Special Review and Assessment of Soldiers with Mental Health Conditions."

52. Department of Navy and U.S. Marine Corps, *Combat and Operational Stress Control* (U.S. Navy, NTTP 1–15M; U.S. Marine Corps, MCRP 6–11C; Washington, DC: Pentagon, December 2010).

53. Memorandum issued by Secretary of Army, "Memorandum: Special Review and Assessment of Soldiers with Mental Health Conditions," 1.

54. D. Zwerdling, "Senators, Military Specialists Say Army Report on Dismissed Soldiers Is Troubling," NPR, December 1, 2016.

55. See Russell, Schaubel, and Figley, *The Darker Side of Military Mental Healthcare—Part Two.*"

56. Memorandum issued by Secretary of Army, "Memorandum: Special Review and Assessment of Soldiers with Mental Health Conditions."

57. Memorandum issued by Secretary of Army, "Memorandum: Special Review and Assessment of Soldiers with Mental Health Conditions," 1.

58. Ader et al., *Casting Troops Aside.*

59. GAO, *Defense Health Care.*

60. GAO, *Defense Health Care.*

61. GAO, *Defense Health Care.*

62. Department of the Army, *Field Manual 6–22.5: Combat and Operational Stress Control Manual for Leaders and Soldiers* (Washington, DC: Headquarters, Department of the Army, 2009).

63. GAO, *Defense Health Care.*

64. See, e.g., Dave Phillipps, "Left Behind," *Gazette* (Colorado Springs, CO), May 20, 2013, , https://cdn.csgazette.biz/soldiers/day2.html..

65. Wilk et al., "Diagnosis of PTSD by Army Behavioral Health Clinicians."

66. W. C. Menninger, "Public Relations." In *Zone of Interior*, Vol. I of *Medical Department United States Army, Neuropsychiatry in World War II*, ed. A. J. Glass, and R. J. Bernucci (Washington, DC: Office of the Surgeon General, Department of the Army, 1966), 144.

67. DoD, *DoD Instruction 1332.14.*

68. GAO (2011).

69. T. W. Salmon and N. Fenton, "Neuropsychiatry in the American Expeditionary Forces," in *Neuropsychiatry: The Medical Department of the United States*

Army in the World War, Vol. 10, ed. P. Bailey, F. E. Williams, P. A. Komora, T. W. Salmon, and N. Fenton (Washington, DC: Office of the Surgeon General, U.S. Army, 1929)

70. A. J. Glass and R. J. Bernucci, *Medical Department United States Army: Neuropsychiatry in World War II: Vol. I, Zone of Interior* (Washington, DC: Office of the Surgeon General, Department of the Army, 1966).

71. R. J. Bernucci, "Forensic Military Psychiatry," in *Zone of Interior*, Vol. I of *Medical Department United States Army, Neuropsychiatry in World War II*, ed. A. J. Glass and R. J. Bernucci (Washington, DC: Office of the Surgeon General, Department of the Army, 1966), 484.

72. A. J. Glass and F. D. Jones, *Psychiatry in the U.S. Army: Lessons for Community Psychiatry* (Bethesda, MD: Uniformed Services University of the Health Sciences, 2005).

73. American Psychiatric Association (APA), *Diagnostic and Statistical Manual of Mental Disorders—Fifth Edition*(Washington, DC: American Psychiatric Association, 2013), 645.

74. APA, *Diagnostic and Statistical Manual of Mental Disorders—Fifth Edition*

75. Government Accountability Office, *Military Attrition: Better Data, Coupled with Policy Changes Could Help the Services Reduce Early Separations* (NSIAD-98-213; Washington, DC: GAO, 1998).

76. DoD, *DoD Instruction 1332.14*.

77. N. M. Camp and C. M. Carney "U.S. Army Psychiatry in Vietnam: Preliminary Findings of a Survey, II. Results and Discussion." *Bulletin of Menninger Clinic* 51, no. 1 (1987): 19–47.

78. Izzo, "In Need of Correction."

79. Armed Forces Health Surveillance Center, "Mental Disorders and Mental Health Problems, Active Component, U.S. Armed Forces: 2000–2015," *Medical Surveillance Monthly Report* 19, no. 16 (June, 2012): 11–17.

80. J. Kors, "How Specialist Town Lost His Benefits: Wounded Soldiers Returning from Iraq Are Increasingly Being Wrongly Diagnosed by the Military, Which Prevents Them from Collecting Benefits," *The Nation*, March 29, 2007; Zwerdling, "Army Dismissals for Mental Health, Misconduct Rise," *NPR*, November 15, 2007.

81. B. Filner, *Post-traumatic Stress Disorder and Personality Disorders: Challenges for the U.S. Department of Veterans' Affairs, Hearing Before the Committee on Veterans' Affairs. U.S. House of Representatives*, 110th Congress first session on July 25, 2007 (Opening Statement of Chairman Filner), Serial No. 110–37 (Washington, DC: Government Printing Office, 2007), 1.

82. GAO (2008).

83. *National Defense Authorization Act for Fiscal Year 2010*, Pub. L. No. 111–84, § 512, 123. Stat. 2190, 2280–82 (2009) (codified, as amended, at 10 U.S.C. § 1177); DoD, Task Force on the Prevention of Suicide by Members of the Armed Forces.

The Challenge and the Promise: Strengthening the Force, Preventing Suicide, and Saving Lives (Falls Church, VA: Defense Health Board, 2010).

84. Ader et al., *Casting Troops Aside.*

85. Bernton, "20,000 Misconduct Discharges Since 2008"; Carpenter, "Military Misconduct May Be Sign of PTSD"; de Yoanna and Benjamin, "I Am Under a Lot of Pressure to not diagnose PTSD"; Kors, "How Specialist Town Lost His Benefits"; S. Sidibe and F. Unger, "Unfinished Business: Correcting 'Bad Paper' for Veterans with PTSD" (Veterans Legal Services Clinic, Yale Law School, 2016), https://law.yale.edu/system/files/documents/pdf/unfinishedbusiness .pdf; Zwerdling, "Missed Treatment."

86. Filner, *Opening Statement of Chairman Filner.*

87. Sidibe and Unger, "Unfinished Business."

88. R. Gaupp, *Uber den Begriff der hysterie.* ZgNP 5 (1911): 457–466, cited in Lerner, *Hysterical Men*, 38.

89. Russell, Schaubel, and Figley, *The Darker Side of Military Mental Healthcare — Part Two*, 40.

90. GAO, *Defense Health Care.*

91. GAO, *Defense Health Care*, 27.

92. Institute of Medicine, *Treatment for Posttraumatic Stress Disorder in Military and Veteran Populations: Final Assessment* (Washington, DC: National Academies Press, 2014); M. C. Russell, S. Butkus, and C. R. Figley, "Contribution of Military Organization and Leadership Factors in Perpetuating Generational Cycle of Preventable Wartime Mental Health Crises: Part One," *Psychological Injury and Law* 9, no. 1 (2016): 55–72.

10. Avoiding Responsibility and Accountability: The Eighth Dark-Side Strategy

1. U.S. Army, "Final Public Affairs Guidance: OEF/OIF Communications Plan Mental Health of 23 May 2006" (unpublished document, Headquarters, Army Medical Department, Washington, DC, May 23, 2006); U.S. Navy, "Mental Health Public Affairs Guidance of 23 January 2007" (unpublished document, U.S. Navy Medical Department, Navy Medicine West, Bureau of Medicine and Surgery, Washington, DC, January 23, 2007); G. Zoroya (2007); M. E. Kilpatrick, *Force Health Protection and Readiness Programs, Department of Defense, Hearing Before the U.S. Congress House of Representatives Committee on Oversight and Government Reform*, First Session, May 24, 2007 (Statement by Michael E. Kilpatrick, MD, Deputy Director), Serial No. 110–111 (Washington, DC: U.S. Government Printing Office, 2007).

2. Department of Defense Task Force on Mental Health (DoD TF-MH), *An Achievable Vision: Report of the Department of Defense Task Force on Mental Health* (Falls Church, VA: Defense Health Board, 2007), 63.

3. M. Russell (2006).

4. Russell (2006); Zoroya (2007).

5. Russell et al. (2015).

6. A. J. Glass, "Army Psychiatry Before World War II," in *Zone of Interior*, Vol. I of *Medical Department United States Army, Neuropsychiatry in World War II*, ed. A. J. Glass and R. J. Bernucci, (Washington, DC: Office of the Surgeon General, Department of the Army, 1966), 3–23.

7. M. C. Russell, C. R. Figley, and K. R. Robertson, "Investigating the Psychiatric Lessons of War and Pattern of Preventable Wartime Behavioral Health Crises," *Journal of Psychology and Behavioral Science* 3, no. 1 (2015): 1–16.

8. Congressional Research Service, *Post-Traumatic Stress Disorder and Other Mental Health Problems in the Military: Oversight Issues for the Congress* (prepared by K. Blakeley and D. J. Jansen, 7–5700: R43175, Washington, DC: CRS, August 8, 2013).

9. Department of Veterans Affairs (VA), *Analysis of VA Health Care Utilization Among Operation Enduring Freedom, Operation Iraqi Freedom, and Operation New Dawn Veterans, from 1st Qtr FY 2002 through 1st Qtr FY 2015* (Epidemiology Program, Post-Deployment Health Group, Office of Public Health, Veterans Health Administration. Washington, DC: VA, 2015).

10. Institute of Medicine, *Preventing Psychological Disorders in Service Members and Their Families: An Assessment of Programs* (Washington, DC: National Academies Press, 2014); M. C. Russell, S. Butkus, and C. R. Figley, "Contribution of Military Organization and Leadership Factors in Perpetuating Generational Cycle of Preventable Wartime Mental Health Crises: Part One," *Psychological Injury and Law*, 9, no.1 (2016): 55–72; M. C. Russell, S. Butkus, and C. R. Figley, "Ending the Generational Cycle of Preventable Wartime Mental Health Crises: Part Two: Establishing a Behavioral Health Corps and Other Constructive Solutions," *Psychological Injury and Law* 9, no. 1 (2016): 73–86.

11. Russell, Butkus, and Figley, "Contribution of Military Organization and Leadership Factors."

12. Russell, Butkus, and Figley, "Contribution of Military Organization and Leadership Factors"; Russell, Butkus, and Figley, "Ending the Generational Cycle of Preventable Wartime Mental Health Crises."

13. W. C. Menninger, *Reactions to Combat: Psychiatry in a Troubled World* (New York: MacMillan, 1948), 516.

14. M. A. Seidenfeld, "Clinical Psychology," in *Zone of Interior*, Vol. I of *Medical Department United States Army, Neuropsychiatry in World War II*, ed. A. J. Glass and R. J. Bernucci (Washington DC: Office of the Surgeon General, Department of the Army, 1966), 586.

15. M. C. Russell and C. R. Figley, "Investigating Recurrent Generational Wartime Behavioral Health Crises: Part One of a Preliminary Analysis," *Psychological*

Injury and Law 8, no. 1 (2015): 106–131; M .C. Russell and C. R. Figley, "Generational Wartime Behavioral Health Crises: Part Two of a Preliminary Analysis," *Psychological Injury and Law* 8, no. 1 (2015): 132–152.

16. Institute of Medicine (IOM), *Returning Home from Iraq and Afghanistan: Assessment of Readjustment Needs of Veterans, Service Members, and Their Families* (Washington, DC: National Academies Press, 2013), 426.

17. IOM, *Returning Home from Iraq and Afghanistan*, 424.

18. DoD TF-MH, *An Achievable Vision*, ES-2.

19. Glass, "Army Psychiatry Before World War II," 18; A. J. Glass and R. J. Bernucci, *Medical Department United States Army: Neuropsychiatry in World War II: Vol, I, Zone of Interior* (Washington, DC: Office of the Surgeon General, Department of the Army, 1966), xiv

20. Zoroya (2007).

21. U.S. Army, *Final Public Affairs Guidance*; U.S. Navy, *Mental Health Public Affairs Guidance of 23 January 2007*.

22. Kilpatrick, *Statement by Michael E. Kilpatrick*.

23. DoD TF-MH, *An Achievable Vision*.

24. Russell, Figley, and Robertson, "Investigating the Psychiatric Lessons of War," 1–16.

25. DoD TF-MH, *An Achievable Vision*, 53.

26. Russell, Figley, and Robertson, "Investigating the Psychiatric Lessons of War", 1–16.

27. IOM, *Treatment for Posttraumatic Stress Disorder in Military and Veteran Populations: Final Assessment* (Washington, DC: The National Academies Press, 2014).

28. IOM, *Returning Home from Iraq and Afghanistan*, 48.

29. IOM, *Returning Home from Iraq and Afghanistan*, 6.

30. IOM, *Treatment for Posttraumatic Stress Disorder in Military and Veteran Populations*.

31. Readers are referred to the IOM study, *Returning Home from Iraq and Afghanistan*, for more detailed description and organizational charting.

32. IOM, *Treatment for Posttraumatic Stress Disorder in Military and Veteran Populations*, 126.

33. IOM, *Returning Home from Iraq and Afghanistan*.

34. Twenty-two other non-mental health specialists are included in this corps.

35. M. Russell, "Mental Health Crisis in the Department of Defense: DoD Inspector General Hotline Investigation #98829 submitted by Commander Mark Russell, USN on 05JAN2006," available upon request via Freedom of Information Act (FOIA) at Department of Defense; Office of Freedom of Information, 1155 (Washington, DC: Pentagon, 2006).

36. M. Russell, *The Future of Mental Health Care in the Department of Defense, Invited Testimony Before the Congressionally Mandated Department of Defense Task Force on Mental Health*, October 19–20, 2006, San Diego, CA (Washington, DC: Defense Health Board, 2006); R. M. Weinick et al., "Programs Addressing Psychological Health and Traumatic Brain Injury Among U.S. Military Service Members and Their Families" (prepared for the Office of the Secretary of Defense Center for Military Health Policy Research; Santa Monica, CA: RAND, 2011).

37. DoD TF-MH, *An Achievable Vision*

38. Russell, "Mental Health Crisis in the Department of Defense."

39. DoD TF-MH, *An Achievable Vision*, 43.

40. IOM, *Returning Home from Iraq and Afghanistan.*

41. IOM, *Returning Home from Iraq and Afghanistan.*

42. IOM, *Returning Home from Iraq and Afghanistan.*

43. IOM (2014).

44. National Council for Community Behavioral Healthcare, *Meeting the Behavioral Health Needs of Veterans: Operation Enduring Freedom and Operation Iraqi Freedom: Operation Enduring Freedom and Operation Iraqi Freedom*, November 2002 (Washington, DC: National Council for Community Behavioral Healthcare, 2012).

45. IOM, *Returning Home from Iraq and Afghanistan* .

46. Russell, "Mental Health Crisis in the Department of Defense."

47. Smith, personal communication, 2010.

48. Russell and Figley, "Investigating Recurrent Generational Wartime Behavioral Health Crises."

49. DoD TF-MH, *An Achievable Vision*, 7–8.

50. Memorandum issued by Assistant Secretary of Defense for Health Affairs, "Clinical Policy Guidance for Assessment and Treatment of Post-traumatic Stress Disorder" (ASD-HA 2012).

51. Weinick et al., "Programs Addressing Psychological Health and Traumatic Brain Injury."

52. DoD TF-MH, *An Achievable Vision*.

53. DoD (2012).

54. DoD (2012).

55. J. M. Darley and B. Latané, "Bystander Intervention in Emergencies: Diffusion of Responsibility," *Journal of Personality and Social Psychology* 8, no. 4 (1968): 377–383.

56. Darley and Latané, "Bystander Intervention," 377–383.

57. Russell, Butkus, and Figley, "Contribution of Military Organization and Leadership Factors."

58. D. Priest and A. Hull, "System Ill Equipped for PTSD: Troops Returning with Psychological Wounds Confront Bureaucracy, Stigma," *Washington Post*, June 16, 2007.

59. DoD TF-MH, *An Achievable Vision*.

60. M. C. Russell, B. Zinn, and C. R. Figley, "Exploring Options Including Class Action to Transform Military Mental Healthcare and End the Generational Cycle of Preventable Wartime Behavioral Health Crises," *Psychological Injury and Law* 9 (2016): 166–197.

61. Russell, Zinn, and Figley, "Exploring Options Including Class Action."

62. Russell, Butkus, and Figley, "Contribution of Military Organization and Leadership Factors."

63. IOM, *"Treatment for Posttraumatic Stress Disorder in Military and Veteran Populations,"* 216.

64. IOM, *"Treatment for Posttraumatic Stress Disorder in Military and Veteran Populations."*

65. Government Accountability Office, *Human Capital: Additional Actions Needed to Enhance DoD's Efforts to Address Mental Health Care Stigma* (GAO-16-404. Washington, DC: GAO, 2016), i.

66. Russell, Butkus, and Figley, "Contribution of Military Organization and Leadership Factors."

67. Russell, Butkus, and Figley, "Contribution of Military Organization and Leadership Factors."

11. Inadequate, Experimental, or Harmful Treatment: The Ninth Dark-Side Strategy

1. A. Macphail, "Official History of the Canadian Forces in the Great War: 1914–1919" (Ottawa, Canada: Medical Services, FAACLAND, 2015), 278.

2. T. W. Salmon, "Introduction," in *The Medical Department of the United States Army in the World War: Vol. X, Neuropsychiatry in the American Expeditionary Forces*, ed. T. W. Salmon and N. Fenton (prepared under the direction of Maj. Gen. M. W. Ireland, Surgeon General; Washington, DC: U.S. Government Printing Office, 1929), i.

3. Joint Mental Health Assessment Team-7 (Joint MHAT-7), *Operation Enduring Freedom 2010 Afghanistan (22 February 2011)* (Washington, DC: Office of the Surgeon General, U.S. Army Medical Command and Office of the Command Surgeon HQ, USCENTCOM and Office of the Command Surgeon U.S. Forces Afghanistan, 2011), 78.

4. M. C. Russell and C. R. Figley, "Is the Military's Century-Old Frontline Psychiatry Policy Harmful to Veterans and Their Families? Part Three of a Systematic Review," *Psychological Injury and Law* 10 (2017): 72–95.

5. Department of Defense Task Force on Mental Health (DoD TF-MH), *An Achievable Vision: Report of the Department of Defense Task Force on Mental Health* (Falls Church, VA: Defense Health Board, 2007).

6. Before the spring of 1944, the official attitude of the Army "toward psychiatric illnesses was a mixture of fatalism and disinterest; treatment was discouraged." In fact, Army Regulation (A.R.) 615–360, November 26, 1942, specifically denied definitive treatment for psychiatric patients. E. F. Quinn, "Reconditioning of Psychiatric Patients," in *Zone of Interior*, Vol. I of *Medical Department United States Army, Neuropsychiatry in World War II*, ed. R. S. Anderson, A. J. Glass, and R. J. Bernucci (Washington DC: Office of the Surgeon General, Department of the Army, 1966), 968.

7. Department of the Army, *Field Manual 6–22.5: Combat and Operational Stress Control Manual for Leaders and Soldiers* (Washington, DC: Headquarters, Department of the Army, 2009); M. C. Russell and C. R. Figley, "Do the Military's Frontline Psychiatry/Combat and Operational Stress Control Doctrine Help or Harm Veterans? Part One: Framing the Issue," *Psychological Injury and Law* 10 (2017): 1–23.

8. N. Q. Brill, "Station and Regional Hospitals," in *Zone of Interior*, Vol. I of *Medical Department United States Army, Neuropsychiatry in World War II*, ed. A. J. Glass and R. J. Bernucci (Washington, DC: Office of the Surgeon General, Department of the Army, 1966), 275.

9. Department of Navy and U.S. Marine Corps, *Combat and Operational Stress Control*, U.S. Navy, NTTP 1-15M; U.S. Marine Corps, MCRP 6-11C (Washington, DC: Pentagon, December 2010).

10. WWI: "It was obvious at the outset that such patients could not be cared for in the individual American base hospitals scattered throughout France, partly because of the lack in some of them of medical officers, nurses, or enlisted personnel who had had experience in the actual care and treatment of patients suffering from acute mental disorders, but chiefly because of the absence of any special facilities for treatment." T. W. Salmon, "General View of Neuropsychiatric Activities," in *The Medical Department of the United States Army in the World War*: Vol. X, *Neuropsychiatry in the American Expeditionary Forces*, ed. T. W. Salmon and N. Fenton (prepared under the direction of Maj. Gen. M. W. Ireland, Surgeon General; Washington, DC: U.S. Government Printing Office, 1929), 279.

WWII: "From the beginning, there was a shortage of trained psychiatrists, neurologists, psychiatric nurses, attendants, aides, social workers, psychologists, occupational therapists, and recreational therapists." Brill, "Station and Regional Hospitals," 262.

"Facilities for the care and treatment of psychiatric cases were only barely sufficient for the small peacetime Army." A. J. Glass, "Army Psychiatry Before

World War II," in *Zone of Interior,* Vol. I of *Medical Department United States Army, Neuropsychiatry in World War II,* ed. A. J. Glass and R. J. Bernucci (Washington, DC: Office of the Surgeon General, Department of the Army, 1966), 17–18.

Vietnam War: "In addition to providing an impetus for accurate diagnosis, the demands for treatment of large numbers of traumatized veterans spurred the development of effective treatments both for reactions that occurred on the battlefield, as well as those that occurred outside the war zone."

"Particularly following WWI and WWII great gains were made in diagnosing and treating stress reactions. Sad to say, many of these lessons were forgotten and had to be relearned with Vietnam veterans." R. A. Kulka et al., *Trauma and the Vietnam War Generation: Report of Findings from the National Vietnam Veterans Readjustment Study* (New York: Brunner/Mazel, 1990), 286.

11. Salmon, "General View of Neuropsychiatric Activities," 279.

12. Brill, "Station and Regional Hospitals," 262.

13. Glass, "Army Psychiatry Before World War II," 17–8.

14. Kulka et al., *Trauma and the Vietnam War Generation,* 286.

15. Quinn, "Reconditioning of Psychiatric Patients." 692.

16. Quinn, "Reconditioning of Psychiatric Patients", 693.

17. DoD TF-MH, *An Achievable Vision,* 20.

18. M. Russell et al., "Responding to an Identified Need: A Joint DoD-DVA Training Program for Clinicians Treating Trauma Survivors," *International Journal of Stress Management* 14, no. 1 (2007): 61–71.

19. Russell et al., "Responding to an Identified Need."

20. Department of Veterans Affairs and Department of Defense (VA/DoD), "VA/DoD Clinical Practice Guideline for the Management of Post-traumatic Stress" (publication 10Q-CPG/PTSD-04; Washington, DC: Veterans Health Administration, Department of Veterans Affairs and Health Affairs, Department of Defense, Office of Quality and Performance, 2004).

21. Russell (2006).

22. DoD TF-MH, *An Achievable Vision,* 43.

23. Institute of Medicine (IOM), 33.

24. IOM, 33.

25. Institute of Medicine, *Preventing Psychological Disorders in Service Members and Their Families: An Assessment of Programs* (Washington, DC: National Academies Press, 2014).

26. VA/DoD, "VA/DoD Clinical Practice Guideline for the Management of Post-traumatic Stress."

27. K. A. Hepner et al., "Quality of Care for PTSD and Depression in the Military Health System: Phase I Report," *RAND Health Quarterly* 6, no. 1 (2016): xxiii.

28. Department of Navy and U.S. Marine Corps, *Combat and Operational Stress Control*.

29. F. D. Jones, "Disorders of Frustration and Loneliness," in *Textbook of Military Medicine: War Psychiatry*, ed. F. D. Jones, L. R. Sparacino, V. L. Wilcox, J. M. Rothberg, & J. W. Stokes (Washington, DC: Office of the Surgeon General, U.S. Army, Borden Institute, Walter Reed Army Institute of Research, 1995), 63–83; B. Shepard, *A War of Nerves: Soldiers and Psychiatrists in the Twentieth Century* (Cambridge, MA: Harvard University Press, 2001).

30. L. J. Bilmes, "Current and Projected Future Costs of Caring for Veterans of the Iraq and Afghanistan Wars" (unpublished manuscript, Department of Economics, Harvard University, Cambridge, MA, 2011); P. Lerner, *Hysterical Men: War, Psychiatry, and the Politics of Trauma in Germany, 1890–1930* (London: Cornell University Press, 2003).

31. A. J. Glass, "Lessons Learned," in *Zone of Interior*, Vol. I of *Medical Department United States Army, Neuropsychiatry in World War II*, ed. A. J. Glass, and R. J. Bernucci (Washington, DC: Office of the Surgeon General, Department of the Army, 1966), 735–759; Brill, "Station and Regional Hospitals."

32. Department of Navy and U.S. Marine Corps, *Combat and Operational Stress Control*; Russell et al. (2017).

33. Institute of Medicine (IOM), *Treatment for Posttraumatic Stress Disorder in Military and Veteran Population: Final Assessment* (Washington, DC: National Academies Press, 2014).

34. A. Young, *The Harmony of Illusions: Inventing Post-traumatic Stress Disorder* (Princeton, NJ: Princeton University Press, 1995), 84.

35. T. W. Salmon, "Recommendations for the Treatment of Mental and Nervous Diseases in the United States Army" (New York: National Committee for Mental Hygiene, 1917), 37.

36. Department of the Army, *Policy Guidance on the Assessment and Treatment of Post-Traumatic Stress Disorder (PTSD)*, OTSG/MEDCOM Policy Memo 12–035 of 10 April 2012 (Fort Sam Houston, TX: Headquarters, United States Army Medical Command, 2012); IOM, *Treatment for Posttraumatic Stress Disorder in Military and Veteran Population*.
   "And thus a uniform standard of excellence and the same general approach to problems of treatment assured in each special base hospital organized in France." Salmon, "Recommendations," 58.

37. G. Roussy and J. Lhermitte, "The Psychoneuroses of War," in *Military Medical Manuals*, ed. A. Keough (London: University of London Press, 1918), 168.

38. Roussy and Lhermitte, "The Psychoneuroses of War," 169.

39. R. R. Grinker and J. P. Spiegel, *Men Under Stress* (Philadelphia, PA: Blakiston, 1945).

40. Grinker and Spiegel, *Men Under Stress*, 409.
41. VA/DoD, "VA/DoD Clinical Practice Guideline for the Management of Post-traumatic Stress."
42. E. Jones and S. Wessely, *Shell Shock to PTSD Military Psychiatry from 1900 to the Gulf War* (New York: Psychology Press, 2005).
43. Grinker and Spiegel, *Men Under Stress*.
44. Grinker and Spiegel, *Men Under Stress*.
45. Department of Veterans Affairs and Department of Defense (VA/DoD), "VA/DoD Clinical Practice Guideline for the Management of Post-traumatic Stress" (publication 10Q-CPG/PTSD-10; Washington, DC: Veterans' Health Administration, Department of Veterans Affairs and Health Affairs, Department of Defense, Office of Quality and Performance, 2010), 73–74.
46. Grinker and Spiegel, *Men Under Stress*, 410
47. Grinker and Spiegel, *Men Under Stress*, 411
48. C. J. Bahorik, *Between Peril and Promise: Facing the Dangers of VA's Skyrocketing Use of Prescription Painkillers to Treat Veterans, Hearing Before the Subcommittee on Health of the Committee on Veterans' Affairs*, U.S. House of Representatives, 113th Congress first session on October 10, 2013 (Prepared Statement of Ms. Bahorik), Serial no. 113–39 (Washington, DC: U.S. Government Printing Office, 2013), 1.
49. P. J. Gray, *Between Peril and Promise: Facing the Dangers of VA's Skyrocketing Use of Prescription Painkillers to Treat Veterans, Hearing Before the Subcommittee on Health of the Committee on Veterans' Affairs*, U.S. House of Representatives, 113th Congress first session on October 10, 2013 (Prepared Statement of Ms. Gray), Serial no. 113–39 (Washington, DC: U.S. Government Printing Office, 2013), 1.
50. W. Sargant and E. Slater, *An Introduction to Physical Methods of Treatment in Psychiatry* (London: Edinburgh: E&S Livingstone, 1944).
51. R. R. Baker and W. E. Pickren, *Psychology and the Department of Veterans Affairs: A Historical Analysis of Training, Research, Practice, and Advocacy* (Washington, DC: American Psychological Association, 2007).
52. Department of Navy and U.S. Marine Corps, *Combat and Operational Stress Control*.
53. Shepard, *A War of Nerves*
54. M. C. Russell and C. R. Figley, "Do the Military's Frontline Psychiatry/Combat and Operational Stress Control Doctrine Help or Harm Veterans? Part Two: Systematic Review of the Evidence," *Psychological Injury and Law* 10 (2017): 24–71.
55. J. Appel and G. Beebe, "Preventive Psychiatry; an Epidemiologic Approach," *Journal of the American Medical Association* 131 (1946): 88.

56. Appel and Beebe, "Preventive Psychiatry; an Epidemiologic Approach," 152.

57. Appel and Beebe, "Preventive Psychiatry; an Epidemiologic Approach," 143.

58. Appel and Beebe, "Preventive Psychiatry; an Epidemiologic Approach," 92.

59. Appel and Beebe, "Preventive Psychiatry; an Epidemiologic Approach," 92.

60. Appel and Beebe, "Preventive Psychiatry; an Epidemiologic Approach," 163.

61. Appel and Beebe, "Preventive Psychiatry; an Epidemiologic Approach," 164.

62. Kulka et al., *Trauma and the Vietnam War Generation*, 85.

63. B. P. Dohrenwend et al., "The Roles of Combat Exposures, Personal Vulnerability, and Involvement in Harm to Civilians or Prisoners in Vietnam War-related Posttraumatic Stress Disorder," *Clinical Psychology Science* 1, no. 3 (2013): 223–238.

64. Dohrenwend et al., "The Roles of Combat Exposures, Personal Vulnerability, and Involvement in Harm," 14.

65. IOM (2008).

66. IOM (2008), 18.

67. IOM (2008), 65.

68. IOM (2008), 62.

69. M. C. Russell and C. R. Figley, "Generational Wartime Behavioral Health Crises: Part Two of a Preliminary Analysis," *Psychological Injury and Law* 8, no. 1 (2015): 132–152.

70. Joint MHAT-7, *Operation Enduring Freedom 2010 Afghanistan*, 90.

71. J-MHAT-7, *Operation Enduring Freedom 2010 Afghanistan*.

72. Russell and Figley, "Do the Military's Frontline Psychiatry/Combat and Operational Stress Control Doctrine Help or Harm Veterans? Part One: Framing the Issue."

73. Mental Health Advisory Team-I (MHAT-I), *MHAT Operation Iraqi Freedom 16 December 2003* (Washington, DC: U.S. Army Surgeon General, 2003), B-14.

74. J. A. Martin and W. R. Cline, "Mental Health Lessons from the Persian Gulf War," in *The Gulf War and Mental Health: A Comprehensive Guide*, ed. J. A. Martin, L. R. Sparacino, and G. Belenky (Westport, CT: Praeger, 1996), 164.

75. Russell and Figley, "Do the Military's Frontline Psychiatry/Combat and Operational Stress Control Doctrine Help or Harm Veterans? Part Two: Systematic Review of the Evidence."

76. Russell and Figley, "Is the Military's Century-Old Frontline Psychiatry Policy Harmful to Veterans and Their Families? Part Three of a Systematic Review."

77. Department of Army, 2006; Department of Navy and US Marine Corps, *Combat and Operational Stress Control*; Russell & Figley (2016).

78. Russell and Figley (2016).

79. To best address this question, we searched for any publication since WWI directly comparing the immediate or long-term outcomes for deployed

personnel either returning to duty after receiving frontline psychiatry or evacuated for psychiatric treatment outside war zones.

80. Russell and Figley (2016).

81. R. A. Gabriel, *Between Flesh and Steel: A History of Military Medicine from the Middle Ages to the War in Afghanistan* (Washington, DC: Potomac Books, 2013).

82. Department of Navy and U.S. Marine Corps, *Combat and Operational Stress Control*, 1–2.

83. N. Q. Brill and G. W. Beebe, "Psychoneurosis: Military Applications of a Follow-up Study," *U.S. Armed Services Medical Journal* 3 (1952): 15–33; C. A. Vaughan et al., *Evaluation of the Operational Stress Control and Readiness (OSCAR) Program* (Santa Monica, CA: RAND Corporation, 2015).

84. Department of Navy and U.S. Marine Corps, *Combat and Operational Stress Control*, 1–2.

85. Z. Solomon and R. Benbenishty, "The Role of Proximity, Immediacy, and Expectancy in Frontline Treatment of Combat Stress Reaction Among Israelis in the Lebanon War," *American Journal of Psychiatry* 143 (1986): 613–617; Z. Solomon, R. Shklar, and M. Mikulincer, "Frontline Treatment of Combat Stress Reaction: A 20-year Longitudinal Study," *American Journal of Psychiatry* 162 (2005): 2319–2314; Z. Solomon et al., "Posttraumatic Stress Disorder Among Frontline Soldiers with Combat Street Reaction: The 1982 Israeli Experience," *American Journal of Psychiatry*, 144, no. 4 (1987): 448–454.

86. Solomon et al., "Posttraumatic Stress Disorder Among Frontline Soldiers."

87. Department of the Army, *Field Manual 6–22.5: Combat and Operational Stress Control Manual*.

88. Kulka et al., *Trauma and the Vietnam War Generation*

89. These limitations include recall bias, the absence of data on the type, duration, or effectiveness of hospitalized treatment, and potential sampling bias—evacuated veterans may have had more severe combat stress reactions and impairment during triage than those retained in war zones.

90. C. W. Hoge, C. A. Castro, and K. M. Eaton, "Impact of Combat Duty in Iraq and Afghanistan on Family Functioning: Findings from the Walter Reed Army Institute of Research land Combat Study," in *Human Dimensions in Military Operations—Military Leaders' Strategies for Addressing Stress and Psychological Support* (meeting proceedings RTO-MP-HFM-134, Paper 5; Neuilly-sur-Seine, France: RTO, 2006), 5.1–5.6.

91. Solomon and Benbenishty, "The role of Proximity, Immediacy, and Expectancy"

92. Solomon, Shklar, and Mikulincer, "Frontline Treatment of Combat Stress Reaction," 2319–2314.

93. Solomon and Benbenishty, "The Role of Proximity, Immediacy, and Expectancy," 2312.

94. R. R. Grinker and J. P. Spiegel, "War Neuroses in North Africa: The Tunisian Campaign (January-May 1943)" (restricted report prepared for The Air Surgeon, Army Air Forces, Josiah Macy, Jr. Foundation, New York, 1943), 255.

95. Grinker and Spiegel, "War Neuroses in North Africa," 255.

96. L. H. Bartemeier et al., "Combat Exhaustion," *Journal of Nervous and Mental Disease* 104 (1946): 358–389.

97. Grinker and Spiegel, *War Neuroses in North Africa*, 140.

98. Grinker and Spiegel, *War Neuroses in North Africa*, 140.

99. Glass, "Lessons Learned"; Russell and Figley (2016).

100. Russell and Figley, "Do the Military's Frontline Psychiatry/Combat and Operational Stress Control Doctrine Help or Harm Veterans? Part One: Framing the Issue"; Russell and Figley, "Do the Military's Frontline Psychiatry/Combat and Operational Stress Control Doctrine Help or Harm Veterans? Part Two: Systematic Review of the Evidence"; Russell and Figley, "Is the Military's Century-Old Frontline Psychiatry Policy Harmful to Veterans and Their Families? Part Three of a Systematic Review."

101. T. McGeorge, J. H. Hughes, and S. Wessely, "The MoD PTSD Decision: A Psychiatric Perspective," *Occupational Health Review* 122 (2006): 21–28.

102. McGeorge, Hughes, and Wessely, "The MoD PTSD Decision," 25.

103. E. Jones and S. Wessely, "Forward Psychiatry in the Military: Its Origin and Effectiveness," *Journal of Traumatic Stress* 16 (2003): 411–419.

104. McGeorge, Hughes, and Wessely, "The MoD PTSD Decision," 25.

105. Russell and Figley, "Do the Military's Frontline Psychiatry/Combat and Operational Stress Control Doctrine Help or Harm Veterans? Part One: Framing the Issue"; Russell and Figley, "Do the Military's Frontline Psychiatry /Combat and Operational Stress Control Doctrine Help or Harm Veterans? Part Two: Systematic Review of the Evidence"; Russell and Figley, "Is the Military's Century-Old Frontline Psychiatry Policy Harmful to Veterans and Their Families? Part Three of a Systematic Review."

106. Russell and Figley, "Do the Military's Frontline Psychiatry/Combat and Operational Stress Control Doctrine Help or Harm Veterans? Part Two: Systematic Review of the Evidence"; Russell and Figley, "Is the Military's Century-Old Frontline Psychiatry Policy Harmful to Veterans and Their Families? Part Three of a Systematic Review."

107. Russell and Figley, "Do the Military's Frontline Psychiatry/Combat and Operational Stress Control Doctrine Help or Harm Veterans? Part Two: Systematic Review of the Evidence."

108. Russell and Figley, "Is the Military's Century-Old Frontline Psychiatry Policy Harmful to Veterans and Their Families? Part Three of a Systematic Review."

109. Russell and Figley, "Is the Military's Century-Old Frontline Psychiatry Policy Harmful to Veterans and Their Families? Part Three of a Systematic Review."

110. Memorandum issued by William Winkenwerder, Jr., MD, Assistant Secretary of Defense for Health Affairs, to Secretary of Army, Secretary of Navy, Secretary of Air Force, and Chairman of the Joint Chiefs of Staff, "Policy Guidance on Deployment-Limiting Psychiatric Conditions and Medications" (Washington, DC: Pentagon, 2006).

111. Whereas timely screening and treatment for injuries and illnesses have always been cornerstones of physical health protection, these same activities have historically been shunned for stress-related problems occurring in operational settings for fear of drawing attention to them and fostering epidemics of stress casualties. Department of Navy and US Marine Corps, *Combat and Operational Stress Control*, 1–2.

112. VA/DoD, "VA/DoD Clinical Practice Guideline for the Management of Post-traumatic Stress," 2010.

113. VA/DoD, "VA/DoD Clinical Practice Guideline for the Management of Post-traumatic Stress," 2010, 24.

114. Z. Solomon, Y. Singer, and A. Blumenfeld, "Clinical Characteristics of Delayed and Immediate-onset Combat-induced Post-traumatic Stress Disorder," *Military Medicine* 160 (1995): 425–430.

115. Solomon, Singer, and Blumenfeld, "Clinical Characteristics of Delayed and Immediate-onset Combat-induced Post-traumatic Stress Disorder."

116. VA/DoD, "VA/DoD Clinical Practice Guideline for the Management of Post-traumatic Stress," 45.

117. VA/DoD, "VA/DoD Clinical Practice Guideline for the Management of Post-traumatic Stress," 46.

118. VA/DoD, "VA/DoD Clinical Practice Guideline for the Management of Post-traumatic Stress," 2010.

119. VA/DoD, "VA/DoD Clinical Practice Guideline for the Management of Post-traumatic Stress," 2010, 103.

120. VA/DoD, "VA/DoD Clinical Practice Guideline for the Management of Post-traumatic Stress," 2010, 117.

121. Department of the Army, *Field Manual 6–22.5: Combat and Operational Stress Control Manual.*

122. Russell and Figley (2016).

123. J. A. Cigrang, A. L. Peterson, and R. P. Schobitz, "Three American Troops in Iraq: Evaluation of a Brief Exposure Therapy Treatment for the Secondary Prevention of PTSD," *Pragmatic Case Studies in Psychotherapy* 1, no. 2 (2005); R. N. McLay et al., "Exposure Therapy With and Without Virtual

Reality to Treat PTSD While in the Combat Theater: A Parallel Case Series," *Cyberpsychology, Behavior, and Social Networking* 13, no. 1 (2010): 37–42.

124. Russell and Figley (2016).

125. Cigrang, Peterson, and Schobitz, "Three American Troops in Iraq"; McLay et al., "Exposure Therapy With and Without Virtual Reality."

126. Russell and Figley (2016).

Hung (2008).

127. K. J. Schmitz et al., "Psychiatric Diagnoses and Treatment of U.S. Military Personnel While Deployed to Iraq," *Military Medicine* 177 (2012): 380–389.

128. Schmitz et al., "Psychiatric Diagnoses and Treatment of U.S. Military Personnel."

129. Schmitz et al., "Psychiatric Diagnoses and Treatment of U.S. Military Personnel."

130. Schmitz et al., "Psychiatric Diagnoses and Treatment of U.S. Military Personnel," 388.

131. See table 2a; Russell and Figley (2016).

132. Schmitz et al., "Psychiatric Diagnoses and Treatment of U.S. Military Personnel," 386.

133. McLay et al., "Exposure Therapy With and Without Virtual Reality."

134. Russell and Figley (2016).

135. IOM, "Substance Use Disorders in the U.S. Armed Forces" (Report Brief, September 2012, Washington, DC: National Academies Press, 2012), 189.

12. Perpetuating Neglect, Indifference, and Self-Inflicted Crises: The Tenth Dark-Side Strategy

1. A. J. Glass, "Army Psychiatry Before World War II," in *Zone of Interior*, Vol. I of *Medical Department United States Army, Neuropsychiatry in World War II*, ed. A. J. Glass and R. J. Bernucci (Washington, DC: Office of the Surgeon General, Department of the Army, 1966), 18.

2. Cited in A. J. Glass and R. J. Bernucci, *Medical Department United States Army: Neuropsychiatry in World War II: Vol. I, Zone of Interior* (Washington, DC: Office of the Surgeon General, Department of the Army, 1966), xiv.

3. Department of Defense Task Force on Mental Health (DoD TF-MH), *An Achievable Vision: Report of the Department of Defense Task Force on Mental Health* (Falls Church, VA: Defense Health Board, 2007), ES-2.

4. DoD TF-MH, *An Achievable Vision*, 63.

5. J. A. Martin and W. R. Cline, "Mental Health Lessons from the Persian Gulf War," in *The Gulf War and Mental Health: A Comprehensive Guide*, ed. J. A. Martin, L. R. Sparacino, and G. Belenky (Westport, CT: Praeger, 1996), 161–178.

6. F. D. Jones, "Psychiatric Lessons of War," in *Textbook of Military Medicine: War Psychiatry*, ed. F. D. Jones, L. R. Sparacino, V. L. Wilcox, J. M. Rothberg,

and J. W. Stokes (Washington, DC: Office of the Surgeon General, U.S. Army, Borden Institute, Walter Reed Army Institute of Research 1995), 1–34.

7. WWI: "Although the total number of American troops in France in January, 1918, was only approximately 203,000, the caring for mental patients had already become a problem.

It was obvious at the outset that such patients could not be cared for in the individual American base hospitals scattered throughout France, partly because of the lack in some of them of medical officers, nurses, or enlisted personnel who had had experience in the actual care and treatment of patients suffering from acute mental disorders, but chiefly because of the absence of any special facilities for treatment." T. W. Salmon, "General View of Neuropsychiatric Activities," in *The Medical Department of the United States Army in the World War: Vol. X, Neuropsychiatry in the American Expeditionary Forces*, ed. T. W. Salmon and N. Fenton (prepared under the direction of Maj. Gen. M. W. Ireland, Surgeon General, Washington, DC: U.S. Government Printing Office, 1929), 279.

WWII: "In retrospect . . . the concepts and practices as developed by combat psychiatry in World War II, generally, rediscovered, confirmed, and further elaborated upon the largely forgotten or ignored lessons learned by the Allied armies, including the American Expeditionary Forces in World War I. Thus, the lessons of World War II combat psychiatry . . . should be regarded as relearned and consolidated insights." A. J. Glass, "Army Psychiatry Before World War II," 989.

Korean War: "In sharp contrast to the prompt application of psychiatry at the division level, psychiatric efforts at the Army level were meager and ineffective. It was evident that a need to support division psychiatry by a second echelon of psychiatry at the Army level was not recognized although such a need was first demonstrated in World War I and in World War II." A. J. Glass, "The North Korean Invasion (25 June 1950–15 September 1950)," chapter 6 in *Psychiatry in the U.S. Army: Lessons for Community Psychiatry*, ed. A. J. Glass, F. D. Jones, L. R. Sparacino, and J. M. Rothberg (Bethesda, MD: Uniformed Services University of the Health Sciences, 2005), 4.

Vietnam War: "In addition to providing an impetus for accurate diagnosis, the demands for treatment of large numbers of traumatized veterans spurred the development of effective treatments both for reactions that occurred on the battlefield, as well as those that occurred outside the war zone. Particularly following WWI and WWII great gains were made in diagnosing and treating stress reactions. Sad to say, many of these lessons were forgotten and had to be relearned with Vietnam veterans." R. A. Kulka et al., *Trauma and the Vietnam War Generation: Report of Findings from the National Vietnam Veterans Readjustment Study* (New York: Brunner/Mazel, 1990), 286.

First Persian Gulf War: "What should we learn from mental health issues associated with the Gulf War? From a mental health perspective, the primary lesson we should derive from our Gulf War experience centers on preparation. Regardless of where on the spectrum of conflict we commit soldiers, war is traumatic, and mental health issues will always be important. Like other readiness issues, mental health resources need to be prepared today." Martin and Cline, "Mental Health Lessons from the Persian Gulf War," 176.

8. Jones, "Psychiatric Lessons of War," 5.

9. M. C. Russell, C. R. Figley, and K. R. Robertson, "Investigating the Psychiatric Lessons of War and Pattern of Preventable Wartime Behavioral Health Crises," *Journal of Psychology and Behavioral Science* 3, no. 1 (2015): 1–16.

10. Department of the Navy, "Credentials Review and Clinical Privileging of Clinical Practitioners/Providers in Department of the Navy Fleet and Family Support Program and Marine Corps Community Services" (SECNAVINST 1754.7A PERS-61 07 Nov 2005, Washington DC: Office of the Secretary of the Navy, 2004).

11. Glass, "Army Psychiatry Before World War II", 17–18.

12. C. R. Figley, *Stress Disorders Among Vietnam Veterans* (New York: Brunner/Mazel, 1978).

13. F. R. Kirkland, "Preface," in *The Gulf War and Mental Health: A Comprehensive Guide*, ed. J. A. Martin, L. R. Sparacino, and G. Belenky (Westport, CT: Praeger Publishers, 1996).

14. C. A. Vaughan, C. M. Farmer, J. Breslau, and C. Burnette, "Evaluation of the Operational Stress Control and Readiness (OSCAR) Program" (Santa Monica, CA: RAND Corporation, 2015).

15. M. C. Russell and C. R. Figley, "Investigating Recurrent Generational Wartime Behavioral Health Crises: Part One of a Preliminary Analysis," *Psychological Injury and Law* 8, no.1 (2015): 106–131.

16. Jones, "Psychiatric Lessons of War," 6; Russell and Figley, "Investigating Recurrent Generational Wartime Behavioral Health Crises."

17. Institute of Medicine (IOM), *Returning Home from Iraq and Afghanistan: Assessment of Readjustment Needs of Veterans, Service Members, and Their Families* (Washington, DC: The National Academies Press, 2013).

18. Russell and Figley, "Investigating Recurrent Generational Wartime Behavioral Health Crises."

19. K. S. Peterson, "Long Deployments Stress Military Families," *USA Today*, October 8, 2001, http://usatoday30.usatoday.com/life/2001-10-09-military-families.htm.

20. S. Shane, "Chemicals Sickened '91 Gulf War Veterans, Latest Study Finds," *New York Times*, October 15, 2004.

21. A. Batdorff, "Officer Sees 'Perfect Storm' Brewing in Military's Mental Health Care System," *Stars and Stripes Pacific*, September 22, 2006.

22. G. Zoroya (2007).

23. L. Alvarez, "Home from the War, Many Veterans Battle Substance Abuse," *New York Times*, July 8, 2008.

24. J. Steinhauer, "Sexual Assaults in Military Raise Alarm in Washington," *New York Times*, May 7, 2013.

25. G. Zoroya, "VA Sees Shortfall of Mental Health Specialists," *USA Today*, April 4, 2012, http://usatoday30.usatoday.com/news/military/story/2012-04-04/military-veteran-mental-health-psychiatrists/54009974/1.

26. B. A. Bowser, "Military Not Doing Enough to Curb Alcohol, Drug Abuse, IOM Concludes," *PBS Newshour*, September 17, 2012.

27. P. Kime, "Panel Says Pentagon Does Not Know If PTSD Programs Work," *USA Today*, July 15, 2012.

28. G. Zoroya, "Recent War Vets Face Hiring Obstacle: PTSD Bias," *USA Today*, April 9, 2013.

29. S. Vogel, "Army Orders Reforms for Mental Health Care Treatment," *Washington Post*, March 8, 2013.

30. W. C. Menninger, *Reactions to Combat: Psychiatry in a Troubled World* (New York: MacMillan, 1948), 20–21.

31. Menninger, *Reactions to Combat*, 516.

32. A. J. Glass, "Lessons Learned," in *Zone of Interior*, Vol. I of *Medical Department United States Army, Neuropsychiatry in World War II*, ed. A. J. Glass, and R. J. Bernucci (Washington, DC: Office of the Surgeon General, Department of the Army, 1966), 735.

33. F. R. Kirkland, "Preface," in *The Gulf War and Mental Health: A Comprehensive Guide*, ed. J. A. Martin, L. R. Sparacino, and G. Belenky (Westport, CT: Praeger Publishers, 1996), xxx.

34. D. Cooper, *Psychiatry and Anti-psychiatry* (London: Tavistock Publications, 1967).

35. C. R. Figley, et al. (2017).

36. B. Shepard, *A War of Nerves: Soldiers and Psychiatrists in the Twentieth Century* (Cambridge, MA: Harvard University Press, 2001), 395.

37. A. Young, *The Harmony of Illusions: Inventing Post-traumatic Stress Disorder* (New Jersey: Princeton University Press, 1995), 74.

38. Shepard, *A War of Nerves*, 398.

39. R. J. McNally and C. B. Frueh, "Why Are Iraq and Afghanistan War Veterans Seeking PTSD Disability Compensation at Unprecedented Rates?" *Journal of Anxiety Disorders* 27, no. 5 (2013): 520–526.

40. H. A. Nasrallah, "The Antipsychiatry Movement: Who and Why," *Current Psychiatry* 10, no. 12 (2011): 4–53.

41. Shepard, *A War of Nerves*

42. Young, *The Harmony of Illusions.*

43. D. Summerfield, "The Invention of Post-traumatic Stress Disorder and the Social Usefulness of a Psychiatric Category," *BMJ* 322, no.7278 (2001): 95–98.

44. See McNally and Frueh, "Why Are Iraq and Afghanistan War Veterans Seeking PTSD Disability Compensation at Unprecedented Rates?"

13. Toward a Resilient and Mentally Healthy Military

1. J. M. Da Costa, "On Irritable Heart: A Clinical Study of a Form of Functional Cardiac Disorder And Its Consequences," reprinted in 1951, *American Journal of Medicine, November* (1871): 559–567.

2. T. W. Salmon, "Recommendations for the Treatment of Mental and Nervous Disease in the United States Army" (New York: National Committee for Mental Hygiene, 1917).

3. Salmon, "Recommendations for the Treatment of Mental and Nervous Disease."

4. Armed Forces Health Surveillance Center, "Substance Use Disorders in the U.S. Armed Forces, 2000–2011," *Medical Surveillance Monthly Report* 19, no. 11 (November 2012): 11–16.

5. Armed Forces Health Surveillance Center, "Substance Use Disorders in the U.S. Armed Forces."

6. B. Shepard, *A War of Nerves: Soldiers and Psychiatrists in the Twentieth Century* (Cambridge, MA: Harvard University Press, 2001).

7. F. D. Jones, "Psychiatric Lessons of War," in *Textbook of Military Medicine: War Psychiatry*, ed. F. D. Jones, L. R. Sparacino, V. L. Wilcox, J. M. Rothberg, and J. W. Stokes (Washington, DC: Office of the Surgeon General, U.S. Army, Borden Institute, Walter Reed Army Institute of Research 1995), 1–34.

8. C. H. Kennedy and J. A McNeil, "A History of Military Psychology," in *Military Psychology: Clinical and Operational Applications*, ed. C. H. Kennedy and E. A. Zillmer (New York: Guilford Press, 2006), 1–17.

9. R. R. Baker and W. E. Pickren, *Psychology and the Department of Veterans Affairs: A Historical Analysis of Training, Research, Practice, and Advocacy.* Washington, DC: American Psychological Association, 2007.

10. W. C. Menninger, *Reactions to Combat: Psychiatry in a Troubled World* (New York: MacMillan, 1948).

11. A. J. Glass and R. J. Bernucci, *Medical Department United States Army: Neuropsychiatry in World War II*: Vol. I, *Zone of Interior* (Washington, DC: Office of the Surgeon General, Department of the Army, 1966).

12. Menninger, *Reactions to Combat.*

13. See A. J. Glass, "Army Psychiatry Before World War II," in *Zone of Interior*, Vol. I of *Medical Department United States Army, Neuropsychiatry in World War II*, ed. A. J. Glass and R. J. Bernucci (Washington, DC: Office of the Surgeon General, Department of the Army, 1966), 3–23; Menninger, *Reactions to Combat.*

14. G. N. Grob and H. H. Goldman, *Critical Issues in Health and Medicine. The Dilemma of Federal Mental Health Policy: Radical Reform or Incremental Change?* (Rutgers, NY: Rutgers University Press, 2006).

15. Glass and Bernucci, *Medical Department United States Army.*

16. *Let There Be Light*, dir. John Huston (1946).

17. A. J. Glass and F. D. Jones, *Psychiatry in the U.S. Army: Lessons for Community Psychiatry: Lessons for Community Psychiatry* (Bethesda, MD: Uniformed Services University of the Health Sciences, 2005).

18. *Shades of Gray*, U.S. Army (Washington, DC: U.S. Army, National Audiovisual Center, 1948).

19. Kennedy and McNeil, "A History of Military Psychology."

20. M. C. Russell and C. R. Figley, "Overview of the Affordable Care Act's Impact on Military and Veteran Mental Health Services: Nine Implications for Significant Improvements in Care," *Journal of Social Work in Disability and Rehabilitation* 13 (2014): 162–196.

21. Russell and Figley, "Overview of the Affordable Care Act's Impact."

22. Russell and Figley, "Overview of the Affordable Care Act's Impact."

23. Russell and Figley, "Overview of the Affordable Care Act's Impact."

24. Armed Forces Health Surveillance Center, "Substance Use Disorders in the U.S. Armed Forces".

25. T. Szasz, "The Myth of Mental Illness," *American Psychologist* 15 (1960): 113–118.

26. A. Young, *The Harmony of Illusions: Inventing Post-traumatic Stress Disorder* (New Jersey: Princeton University Press, 1995).

27. Shepard, *A War of Nerves.*

28. American Psychiatric Association, *Diagnostic and Statistical Manual of Mental Disorders–Third Edition* (Washington, DC: Author, 1980).

29. J. A. Martin, L. R. Sparacino, and G. Belenky, eds, *The Gulf War and Mental Health: A Comprehensive Guide* (Westport, CT: Praeger, 1996).

30. Kennedy and McNeil, "A History of Military Psychology."

31. C. W. Hoge et al., "Combat Duty in Iraq and Afghanistan, Mental Health Problems, and Barriers to Care," *New England Journal of Medicine* 351 (2004): 13–22.

32. Department of Veteran's Affairs and Department of Defense (VA/DoD), "VA/ DoD Clinical Practice Guideline for the Management of Post-traumatic Stress" (publication 10Q-CPG/PTSD-04 Washington, DC: Veterans Health

Administration, Department of Veterans Affairs and Health Affairs, Department of Defense, Office of Quality and Performance, 2004).

33. Government Accountability Office, *Defense Health Care: Status of Efforts to Direct Lack of Compliance with Personality Disorder Separation Requirements* (GAO-10-1013T, Washington, DC: Author, 2010).

34. J. E. Wilk, R. K. Herrell, A. L. Carr, J. C. West, J. Wise, and C. W. Hoge, "Diagnosis of PTSD by Army Behavioral Health Clinicians: Are Diagnoses Recorded in Electronic Health Records?" *Psychiatric Services* 67, no. 8 (2016): 878–882.

14. Transforming Military Mental Healthcare: Three Options for Change

1. *Feres v. United States.* 340 U.S. 135 (1950).

2. M. C. Russell, S. Butkus, and C. R. Figley, "Contribution of Military Organization and Leadership Factors in Perpetuating Generational Cycle of Preventable Wartime Mental Health Crises: Part One," *Psychological Injury and Law* 9, no. 1 (2016): 55–72; Russell, Butkus, and Figley, "Ending the Generational Cycle of Preventable Wartime Mental Health Crises, Part Two: Establishing a Behavioral Health Corps and Other Constructive Solutions," *Psychological Injury and Law* 9, no. 1 (2016): 73–86.

3. See Chapter 11; M. C. Russell and C. R. Figley, "Is the Military's Century-Old Frontline Psychiatry Policy Harmful to Veterans and Their Families? Part Three of a Systematic Review," *Psychological Injury and Law* 10 (2017): 72–95.

4. Institute of Medicine (IOM), *Returning Home from Iraq and Afghanistan: Assessment of Readjustment Needs of Veterans, Service Members, and Their Families* (Washington, DC: National Academies Press, 2013); IOM, *Preventing Psychological Disorders in Service Members and Their Families: An Assessment of Programs* (Washington, DC: The National Academies Press, 2014); Ramchand et al., Prevalence of, Risk Factors for, and Consequences of Posttraumatic Stress Disorder and Other Mental Health Problems in Military Populations Deployed to Iraq and Afghanistan," *Current Psychiatry Report* 17 (2015): 1–11; Weinick et al., "Programs Addressing Psychological Health and Traumatic Brain Injury Among U.S. Military Service Members and Their Families" (prepared for the Office of the Secretary of Defense Center for Military Health Policy Research. Santa Monica, CA: RAND, 2011).

5. Russell, Butkus, and Figley, "Ending the Generational Cycle of Preventable Wartime Mental Health Crises."

6. IOM (2010).

7. Department of Veteran's Affairs (VA) and Department of Defense (DoD), "VA/DoD Clinical Practice Guideline for the Management of Post-traumatic

Stress" (publication 10Q-CPG/PTSD-10, Washington, DC: Veterans' Health Administration, Department of Veterans Affairs and Health Affairs, Department of Defense Office of Quality and Performance, 2010).

8. M. C. Russell (2008).

9. Government Accountability Office (GAO), *Human Capital: Additional Actions Needed to Enhance DoD's Efforts to Address Mental Health Care Stigma* (GAO-16-404, Washington, DC: GAO, 2016).

10. M. C. Russell, B. Zinn, and C. R. Figley, "Exploring Options Including Class Action to Transform Military Mental Healthcare and Ends the Generational Cycle of Preventable Wartime Behavioral Health Crises," *Psychological Injury and Law* 9 (2016):, 166–197.

11. Department of Navy and U.S. Marine Corps, *Combat and Operational Stress Control* (U.S. Navy, NTTP 1-15M; U.S. Marine Corps, MCRP 6-11C, Washington, DC: Pentagon, December 2010).

12. T. W. Salmon, "Recommendations for the Treatment of Mental and Nervous Diseases in the United States Army," New York: National Committee for Mental Hygiene, 1917.

13. E. C. Ritchie, "Military Mental Health's Wins and Losses Since the Iraq Invasion." *U.S. Time*, March 19, 2013, http://nation.time.com/2013/03/19/military-mental-healths-wins-andlosses-since-the-iraq-invasion.

14. Department of Veterans Affairs and Department of Defense (VA/DOD), "VA/DoD Clinical Practice Guideline for the Management of Post-traumatic Stress" publication 10Q-CPG/PTSD-04 (Washington, DC: Veterans Health Administration, Department of Veterans Affairs and Health Affairs, Department of Defense, Office of Quality and Performance, 2004).

15. IOM, *Returning Home from Iraq and Afghanistan*, 472.

16. M. C. Russell and C. R. Figley, "Investigating Recurrent Generational Wartime Behavioral Health Crises: Part One of a Preliminary Analysis," *Psychological Injury and Law* 8, no.1 (2015): 106–131; Russell and Figley, "Generational Wartime Behavioral Health Crises: Part Two of a Preliminary Analysis," *Psychological Injury and Law* 8, no. 1 (2015): 132–152.

17. Russell and Figley, "Generational Wartime Behavioral Health Crises: Part Two."

18. Russell and Figley, "Generational Wartime Behavioral Health Crises: Part Two."

19. Department of Defense Task Force on Mental Health (DoD TF-MH), *An Achievable Vision: Report of the Department of Defense Task Force on Mental Health*. Falls Church, VA: Defense Health Board, 2007.

20. IOM, *Returning Home from Iraq and Afghanistan*.

21. Weinick et al., "Programs Addressing Psychological Health and Traumatic Brain Injury."

22. IOM, *Treatment for Posttraumatic Stress Disorder in Military and Veteran Populations: Final Assessment*. Washington, DC: The National Academies Press, 2014.

23. RAND; Ramchand et al. (2011).

24. IOM, *Returning Home from Iraq and Afghanistan*.

25. IOM, *Preventing Psychological Disorders in Service Members*.

26. Russell, Butkus, and Figley, "Contribution of Military Organization and Leadership Factors."

27. IOM, *Treatment for Posttraumatic Stress Disorder in Military and Veteran Populations*, 216.

28. IOM, *Treatment for Posttraumatic Stress Disorder in Military and Veteran Populations*, 216.

29. IOM, *Treatment for Posttraumatic Stress Disorder in Military and Veteran Populations*, 216.

30. N. Q. Brill, "Station and Regional Hospitals," in *Zone of Interior*, Vol. I of *Medical Department United States Army, Neuropsychiatry in World War II*, ed. A. J. Glass and R. J. Bernucci (Washington, DC: Office of the Surgeon General, Department of the Army, 1966), 291–292.

31. Russell, Zinn, and Figley, "Exploring Options Including Class Action," 166–197.

32. T. McGeorge, J. H. Hughes, and S. Wessely, "The MoD PTSD Decision: A Psychiatric Perspective," *Occupational Health Review* 122 (2006): 21–28.

33. American Psychiatric Association (Washington, DC: American Psychiatric Association, 2000); McGeorge, Hughes, and Wessely, "The MoD PTSD Decision," 21–28.

34. McGeorge, Hughes, and Wessely, "The MoD PTSD Decision," 21–28.

35. McGeorge, Hughes, and Wessely, "The MoD PTSD Decision," 21.

36. Slater Gordon Lawyers, "Army PTSD Figures Rise as Shell Shock Brain Injury Identified," *Slater Gordon*, January 23, 2015, https://www.slatergordon.co.uk /media-centre/blog/2015/01/army-ptsd-figures-rise-as-shell-shock-brain-injury -identified/#ixzz3xGPEuftp.

37. S. Hattenstone and E. Allison, "G4S, the Company with No Convictions—But Does It Have Blood On Its Hands?" *Guardian*, December 22, 2014.

38. Hattenstone and Allison, "G4S, the Company with No Convictions."

39. Russell and Figley, "Investigating Recurrent Generational Wartime Behavioral Health Crises."

40. M. C. Russell, C. R. Figley, and K. R. Robertson, "Investigating the Psychiatric Lessons of War and Pattern of Preventable Wartime Behavioral Health Crises," *Journal of Psychology and Behavioral Science* 3, no. 1 (2015): 1–16.

41. J. Du Preez, J. Sundin, and N. T. Fear, "Unit Cohesion and Mental Health in the UK Armed Forces," *Occupational Medicine* 62 (2012): 47–53.

42. N. T. Fear et al., "What Are the Consequences of Deployment to Iraq and Afghanistan on the Mental Health of the UK Armed Forces? A Cohort Study," *Lancet* 375 (2010): 1783–1797; Russell and Figley, "Investigating Recurrent Generational Wartime Behavioral Health Crises"; Russell and Figley, "Generational Wartime Behavioral Health Crises: Part Two"; Russell, Figley, and Robertson, "Investigating the Psychiatric Lessons of War."

43. N. T. Fear et al., "What Are the Consequences of Deployment to Iraq and Afghanistan on the Mental Health of the UK Armed Forces? A Cohort Study," *Lancet* 375 (2010): 1783–1797.

44. Fear et al., "What Are the Consequences of Deployment to Iraq and Afghanistan?" 1794.

45. Fear et al., "What Are the Consequences," 1794.

46. This policy has been in place since January 2008.

47. Fear et al., "What Are the Consequences," 1794.

48. Fear et al., "What Are the Consequences," 1795.

49. Hattenstone and Allison, "G4S, the Company with No Convictions," 2014.

50. M. Feldmeier, "At War with the *Feres* Doctrine: The Carmelo Rodriguez Military Medical Accountability Act of 2009," *Catholic University Law Review* 60, no. 1 (2010): 145–182.

51. A. J. Glass, "Army Psychiatry Before World War II," in *Zone of Interior*, Vol. I of *Medical Department United States Army. Neuropsychiatry in World War II*, ed. A. J. Glass, and R. J. Bernucci (Washington, DC: Office of the Surgeon General, Department of the Army, 1966), 17–18.

52. A. J. Glass and R. J. Bernucci, *Medical Department United States Army: Neuropsychiatry in World War II*: Vol. I, *Zone of Interior* (Washington, DC: Office of the Surgeon General, Department of the Army, 1966), xiv.

53. DoD TF-MH, *An Achievable Vision*, 63.

54. IOM, *Treatment for Posttraumatic Stress Disorder in Military and Veteran Populations*, 123.

55. IOM, *Treatment for Posttraumatic Stress Disorder in Military and Veteran Populations*, 218.

Appendix: Pre-War Planning Checklist for Behavioral Health Services

1. M. C. Russell, C. R. Figley, and K. R. Robertson, "Investigating the Psychiatric Lessons of War and Pattern of Preventable Wartime Behavioral Health Crises," *Journal of Psychology and Behavioral Science* 3, no.1 (2015): 1–16.

2. M. C. Russell and C. R. Figley, "Investigating Recurrent Generational Wartime Behavioral Health Crises: Part One of a Preliminary Analysis," *Psychological Injury and Law* 8, no.1 (2015): 106–131; M. C. Russell and C. R. Figley, "Generational Wartime Behavioral Health Crises: Part Two of a Preliminary Analysis," *Psychological Injury and Law* 8, no. 1 (2015): 132–152.

REFERENCES

"32 of 100 Veterans File for Disability." *New York Times*, September 14, 1944.

"400 Ex-Soldiers New York Suicides: Dr. Salmon So Charges in Testimony of Lack of Care on Mentally Disabled Veterans." *New York Times*, July 7, 1921.

"26,000 Veterans Now in Hospital: Alarming Increase Is Reported in Neuro-Psychiatric and Tuberculosis Cases. Seek Relief from Congress." *New York Times*, September 9, 1923.

"500,000 Discharged as Psychiatric Cases." *New York Times*, September 14, 1945. "640,000 in WWII: Army All Out in Study of Psycho Cases." *Washington Post*, July 4, 1951.

Acosta, J. D., A. Becker, J. L. Cerully, M. P. Fisher, L. T. Martin, R. Vardavas, M. E. Slaughter, and T. L. Schell. *Mental Health Stigma in the Military*. Prepared for the Office of the Secretary of Defense Center for Military Health Policy Research. Santa Monica, CA: RAND, 2014.

Ader, M., R. Cuthbert, K. Hoechst, E. H. Simon, Z. Strassburger, and M. Wishnie. *Casting Troops Aside: The United States Military's Illegal Personality Disorder Discharge Problem*. Silver Spring, MD: Vietnam Veterans of America, 2012. https://law.yale.edu/system/files/documents/pdf/Clinics/VLSC_CastingTroopsAside.pdf.

Adler, H. M. *Report to the Surgeon General of the Army of the Work of the Class in Disciplinary Psychiatry at the United States Disciplinary Barracks, Fort Leavenworth, Kansas*. Washington, DC: Historical Division, SGO, March 1, 1919.

Ahronson, A., and J. E. Cameron. "The Nature and Consequences of Group Cohesion in the Military Sample." *Military Psychology* 19, no. 1 (2007): 9–25.

"Aid Urged for Vietnam Veterans." *New York Times*, January 28, 1979.

Allerton, W. S. "Army Psychiatry in Viet Nam." In *The Psychology and Physiology of Stress: With Reference to Special Studies of the Viet Nam War*, ed. P. G. Bourne. New York: Academic Press, 1969.

Alvarez, L. "Home from the War, Many Veterans Battle Substance Abuse." *New York Times*, July 8, 2008. http://www.nytimes.com/2008/07/08/world/americas/08iht -vets.1.14322423.html?pagewanted=all.

American Forces Press Service. "Obama: Improve Mental Health Access, Care for Military, Vets." *U.S. Defense Department*. August 31, 2012. https://obamawhitehouse .archives.gov/the-press-office/2012/08/31/executive-order-improving-access -mental-health-services-veterans-service.

American Psychiatric Association. Washington, DC: American Psychiatric Association, 2000.

American Psychiatric Association. *Diagnostic and Statistical Manual of Mental Disorders*. Washington, DC: American Psychiatric Association, 1952.

American Psychiatric Association. *Diagnostic and Statistical Manual of Mental Disorders, Third Edition*. Washington, DC: American Psychiatric Association, 1980.

American Psychiatric Association. *Diagnostic and Statistical Manual of Mental Disorders, Fifth Edition*. Washington, DC: American Psychiatric Association, 2013.

American Psychiatric Association. *Practice Guidelines for the Treatment of Patients with Acute Stress Disorder and Posttraumatic Stress Disorder*. Arlington, VA: American Psychiatric Association, 2004.

American Psychological Association. *Ethical Principles of Psychologists and Code of Conduct*. Washington, DC: American Psychological Association, 2002. www.apa .org/ethics/code/ethics-code-2017.pdf.

American Psychological Association. *Presidential Task Force on Military Deployment Services for Youth, Families and Service Members, The Psychological Needs of U.S. Military Service Members and Their Families: A Preliminary Report*. Washington, DC: American Psychological Association, 2007. http://www.apa .org/about/governance/council/policy/military-deployment-services.pdf.

Anderson, R. C. "Neuropsychiatric Problems of the Flier." In *Overseas Theaters*, Vol. II of *Medical Department, United States Army. Neuropsychiatry in World War II*, ed. A. J. Glass, 881–891. Washington, DC: U.S. Government Printing Office, 1973.

Anon. "This Is Gonna Hurt: Military Punishment Throughout the Ages." *Military History Now*, June 2012. http://militaryhistorynow.com/2012/06/29/this-is-gonna -hurt-military-punishment-throughout-the-ages.

Annual Report of the Adjutant General. *War Department Annual Reports 1910*. Washington, DC: War Department, 1910.

Appel, J. W. "Preventive Psychiatry." In *Zone of Interior*, Vol. I of *Medical Department United States Army. Neuropsychiatry in World War II*, ed. A. J. Glass and R. J. Bernucci, 373–416. Washington, DC: Office of the Surgeon General, Department of the Army, 1966.

Appel, J., and G. Beebe. "Preventive Psychiatry; An Epidemiologic Approach." *Journal of the American Medical Association* 131 (1946): 1469–1475.

Archibald, H. C., D. M. Long, C. Miller, and R. D. Tuddenhan. "Gross Stress Reaction in Combat-a 15-Year Follow-up." *American Journal of Psychiatry.* 119 (1962): 317–322.

Armed Forces Health Surveillance Center "Health Care Experiences Prior to Suicide and Self-Inflicted Injury, Active Component, U.S. Armed Forces, 2001–2011." *Medical Surveillance Monthly Report* 19, no. 2 (February 2012): 2–6. http://www.afhsc.mil/viewMSMR?file=2012/v19_n06.pdf#Page=07.

Armed Forces Health Surveillance Center. "Hospitalizations Among Members of the Active Component, U.S. Armed Forces, 2010." *Medical Surveillance Monthly Report* 18, no. 4 (April 2011): 8–15.

Armed Forces Health Surveillance Center. "Hospitalizations Among Members of the Active Component, U.S. Armed Forces, 2011." *Medical Surveillance Monthly Report* 19, no. 4 (April 2012): 10–16.

Armed Forces Health Surveillance Center. "Hospitalizations for Mental Disorders, Active Components, U.S. Armed Forces, January 2000-December 2009." *Medical Surveillance Monthly Report* 17, no. 11 (November 2010): 14–16.

Armed Forces Health Surveillance Center. "Medical Evacuations from Operation Iraqi Freedom/Operation New Dawn, Active and Reserve Components, U.S. Armed Forces, 2003–2011." *Medical Surveillance Monthly Report* 19, no. 2 (February, 2012): 18–21. http://www.afhsc.mil/viewMSMR?file=2012/v19_n06. pdf#Page=07.

Armed Forces Health Surveillance Center. "Mental Disorders and Mental Health Problems, Active Component, U.S. Armed Forces, 2000–2011." *Medical Surveillance Monthly Report* 19, no. 16 (June 2012): 11–17. http://www.afhsc.mil /viewMSMR?file=2012/v19_n06.pdf#Page=07.

Armed Forces Health Surveillance Center. "Mental Disorders and Mental Health Problems, Active Component, U.S. Armed Forces: 2000–2015." *Medical Surveillance Monthly Reports. Annual MSMR Report* (2016). www.afhsc.mil.

Armistead-Jehle, P., S. L. Johnston, N. G. Wade, and C. J. Ecklund. "Posttraumatic Stress in U.S. Marines: The Role of Unit Cohesion and Combat Exposure." *Journal of Counseling and Development* 89 (2011): 81–88.

Army Medical Bulletin. *Causes of Death: U.S. Army Compared with the C.C.C. Deaths Through Injury.* Washington, DC: War Department, 1940.

"Army Nervous Disorders Few." *Washington Post*, April 26, 1919.

Arthur, R. J. "Reflections on Military Psychiatry." *American Journal of Psychiatry* 135 (1978): 2–7.

Artiss, K. L. "Human Behavior Under Stress: From Combat to Social Psychiatry," *Military Medicine* 128 (1963): 1011–1015.

Ayers, B. D. "Combat Fatigue in Vietnam Rare: Facilities at Front, Almost Eliminate It Doctors Say." *New York Times*, May 4, 1969, 7.

Babson, K. A., and M. T. Feldner. "Temporal Relations Between Sleep Problems and Both Traumatic Event Exposure and PTSD: A Critical Review of the Empirical Literature." *Journal of Anxiety Disorders* 24 (2010): 1–15.

Bahorik, C. J. *Between Peril and Promise: Facing the Dangers of VA's Skyrocketing Use of Prescription Painkillers to Treat Veterans. Hearing Before the Subcommittee on Health of the Committee on Veterans' Affairs.* U.S. House of Representatives, 113th Congress first session on October 10, 2013 (Prepared Statement of Ms. Bahorik). Serial no. 113–39. Washington, DC: U.S. Government Printing Office, 2013. https://ia601604.us.archive.org/34/items/gov.gpo.fdsys.CHRG-113hhrg85864/CHRG-113hhrg85864.pdf.

Bailey, P. "Division of Neurology and Psychiatry." In *The Medical Department of the United States Army in the World War:* Vol. I, ed. C. Lynch, F. W. Weed, and L. McAfee, 384–394. Prepared under the direction of Maj. Gen. M. W. Ireland, Surgeon General. Washington, DC: Government Printing Office, 1923. http://history.amedd.army.mil/booksdocs/wwi/VolISGO/frontmatter.html

Bailey, P. "Provisions for Care of Mental and Nervous Cases." In *The Medical Department of the United States Army in the World War:* Vol. X. *Neuropsychiatry in the United States,* ed. P. Bailey, F. E. Williams, and P. O. Komora, 39–55. Prepared under the direction of Maj. Gen. M. W. Ireland, Surgeon General. Washington, DC: U.S. Government Printing Office, 1929. http://history.amedd.army.mil/booksdocs/wwi/Neuropsychiatry/default.htm.

Bailey, P., and R. Haber, R. "Analysis of Special Neuropsychiatry reports." In *The Medical Department of the United States Army in the World War:* Vol. X. *Neuropsychiatry in the United States,* ed. P. Bailey, F. E. Williams, and P. O. Komora, 157–269. Prepared under the direction of Maj. Gen. M. W. Ireland, Surgeon General. Washington, DC: U.S. Government Printing Office, 1929. http://history.amedd.army.mil/booksdocs/wwi/Neuropsychiatry/default.htm.

Baker, K. A. *The Effect of Post-traumatic Stress Disorder on Military Leadership: An Historical Perspective.* Fort Leavenworth, KS: U.S. Army Command and General Staff College, School of Advanced Military Studies, 2011.

Baker Jr., S. L. "Drug Abuse in the United States Army." *Bulletin of the New York Academy of Medicine* 47, no. 6 (1971): 541–549.

Baker, R. R., and W. E. Pickren. *Psychology and the Department of Veterans Affairs: A Historical Analysis of Training, Research, Practice, and Advocacy.* Washington, DC: American Psychological Association, 2007.

Baldor, L. C. "Misconduct Forces More Soldiers Out." Associated Press, February 17, 2014.

Bartemeier, L. H., L. S. Kubie, K. A. Menninger, J. Romano, and J. C. Whitehorn. "Combat Exhaustion." *Journal of Nervous and Mental Disease* 104 (1946): 358–389.

Basu, S. "Army Seeks to Improve Troop Resilience as Suicides Increase." *U.S. Medicine*, March 2013. http://www.usmedicine.com/psychiatry/army-seeks-to-improve-troop-resilience-as-suicides-increase.html.

Batdorff, A. "Officer Sees 'Perfect Storm' Brewing in Military's Mental Health Care System." *Stars and Stripes Pacific*, September 22, 2006. http://www.stripes.com/news/officer-sees-perfect-storm-brewing-in-military-s-mental-health-care-system-1.54480.

Beckham, J. C., et al. "Chronic Posttraumatic Stress Disorder and Chronic Pain in Vietnam Combat Veterans." *Journal of Psychosomatic Research* 43, no. 4 (1997): 379–389.

Beckham, J. C., M .E. Feldman, and A. C. Kirby. "Atrocities Exposure in Vietnam Combat Veterans with Chronic Posttraumatic Stress Disorder: Relationship to Combat Exposure, Symptom Severity, Guilt, and Interpersonal Violence." *Journal of Traumatic Stress* 11, no. 4 (1998): 777–785.

Beckham, J. C., S. D. Moore, M. E. Feldman, M. A. Hertzberg, A. C. Kirby, and J. A. Fairbank. "Health Status, Somatization, and Severity of Posttraumatic Stress Disorder in Vietnam Combat Veterans with Posttraumatic Stress Disorder." *American Journal of Psychiatry* 155, no. 11 (1998): 1565–1569.

Belenky, G. L., C. F. Tyner, and F. J. Sodetz. *Israeli Battle Shock Casualties: 1973 and 1982*. Washington, DC: Walter Reed Army Institute of Research, 1983.

Benyamini, Y., and Z. Solomon. "Combat Stress Reactions, Posttraumatic Stress Disorder, Cumulative Life Stress, and Physical Health Among Israeli Veterans Twenty Years After Exposure to Combat." *Social Science and Medicine* 61 (2005): 1267–1277.

Berlien, I. C., and R. W. Waggoner. "Selection and Induction." In *Zone of Interior*, Vol. I of. *Medical Department United States Army. Neuropsychiatry in World War II*, ed. A. J. Glass and R. J. Bernucci, 153–191. Washington, DC: Office of the Surgeon General, Department of the Army, 1966.

Bernucci, R. J. "Forensic Military Psychiatry. In *Zone of Interior*, Vol. I of *Medical Department United States Army. Neuropsychiatry in World War II*, ed. A. J. Glass and R. J. Bernucci, 475–488. Washington, DC: Office of the Surgeon General, Department of the Army, 1966.

Brewin, C. R., B. Andrews, and J. D. Valentine. "Meta-analysis of Risk Factors for Posttraumatic Stress Disorder in Trauma-Exposed Adults." *Journal of Consulting and Clinical Psychology* 68, no. 5 (2000): 748–766.

Bernton, H. "40 percent of PTSD Diagnoses at Madigan Were Reversed." *Seattle Times*, March 12, 2012. www.seattletimes.com/seattle-news/40-of-ptsd-diagnoses-at-madigan-were-reversed.

Bernton, H. "20,000 Misconduct Discharges Since 2008 Saving DoD Billions in War-Related Disability Compensation." *Seattle Times*, September 8, 2012.

https://themilitarysuicidereport.wordpress.com/2012/09/09/20000-misconduct -discharges-since-2008-saving-dod-billions-in-war-related-disability-compensation.

Bernton, H. "Army Opens Wide Review of PTSD-Diagnosis System." *Seattle Times*, May 17, 2012. www.seattletimes.com/seattle-news/army-opens-wide-review-of-ptsd -diagnosis-system.

Bernton, H. "Madigan Team Reversed 285 PTSD Diagnoses, Sen. Murray Says." *Seattle Times*, March 8, 2012. http://old.seattletimes.com/text/2017692555.html.

Bilmes, L. J. "Current and Projected Future Costs of Caring for Veterans of the Iraq and Afghanistan Wars." Unpublished manuscript, Department of Economics, Harvard University, Cambridge, MA, 2011. http://costsofwar. org/sites/default /files/articles/52/attachments/BilmesVeteransCosts. pdf.

Booth-Kewley, S., R. M. Highfill-McRoy, G. E. Larson, and C. F. Garland. "Psychosocial Predictors of Military Misconduct." *Journal of Nervous Mental Disease* 198, no. 2 (2010): 91–98.

Bowser, B. A. "Military Not Doing Enough to Curb Alcohol, Drug Abuse, IOM Concludes." *PBS Newshour*, September 17, 2012. http://www.pbs.org/newshour /rundown/2012/09/militarys-care-for-addicts-outdated-major-study-concludes .html

Boxer, B. "Boxer Amendment to Establish a Mental Health Task Force Included in Defense Department Appropriations Bill." Press Release for Senator Boxer, October 6, 2005.

Brill, N. Q. "Hospitalization and Disposition." In *Zone of Interior*, Vol. I of *Medical Department United States Army. Neuropsychiatry in World War II*, ed. A. J. Glass and R. J. Bernucci, 196–253. Washington, DC: Office of the Surgeon General, Department of the Army, 1966.

Brill, N. Q. "Station and Regional Hospitals." In *Zone of Interior*, Vol. I of *Medical Department United States Army. Neuropsychiatry in World War II*, ed. A. J. Glass and R. J. Bernucci, 255–295. Washington, DC: Office of the Surgeon General, Department of the Army, 1966.

Brill, N. Q., and G. W. Beebe. *A Follow-up Study of War Neuroses*. Washington, DC: US Government Printing Office, 1955.

Brill, N. Q., and G. W. Beebe. "Psychoneurosis: Military Applications of a Follow-up Study." *U.S. Armed Services Medical Journal* 3 (1952): 15–33.

Brill, N. Q., and H. I. Kupper. "Problems of Adjustment in Return to Civilian Life." In *Zone of Interior*, Vol. I of *Medical Department United States Army. Neuropsychiatry in World War II*, ed. A. J. Glass and R. J. Bernucci, 721–733. Washington, DC: Office of the Surgeon General, Department of the Army, 1966.

Brunner, J. "Trauma in Court: Medico-Legal Dialectics in the Late Nineteenth-Century German Discourse on Nervous Injuries." *Theoretical Inquiries in Law* 4, no. 2 (2003): 697–727.

Brusher, E. A. "Combat and Operational Stress Control." In *Textbooks of Military Medicine: Combat and Operational Behavioral Health*, ed. E. C. Ritchie. Falls Church, VA: Office of the Surgeon General, Department of the Army, 2011.

Burke, W. M. *History and Functions of Central Labor Unions.* New York: MacMillan, 1899.

Burnett-Zeigler, I., M. Ilgen, M. Valenstein, K. Zivin, L. Gorman, A. Blow, S. Duffy, and S. Chermack. "Prevalence and Correlates of Alcohol Misuse Among Returning Afghanistan and Iraq Veterans." *Addictive Behaviors* 36 (2011): 801–806.

Camp, N. M. "Ethical Challenges for the Psychiatrist During the Vietnam Conflict." In *Textbook of Military Medicine, Military Psychiatry: Preparing in Peace for War*, ed. F. D. Jones, L. R. Sparacino, V. L. Wilcox, and J. M. Rothberg. Washington, DC: Office of the Surgeon General, U.S. Army. Borden Institute, 1994.

Camp, N. M. *U.S. Army Psychiatry in the Vietnam War: New Challenges in Extended Counterinsurgency Warfare.* Fort Sam Huston, TX: U.S. Army Medical Department Center and School, Borden Institute, 2014.

Cardona, R. A., and E. C. Ritchie. "U.S. Military Enlisted Accession Mental Health Screening: History and Current Practice." *Military Medicine* 172, no. 1 (2007): 31–35.

Carpenter, A. "Military Misconduct May Be Sign of PTSD." *Washington Times*, January 12, 2010. www.washingtontimes.com/news/2010/jan/12/misconduct-may-be -symptom-of-stress-disorder.

Casscells, W. "Rising to the Challenges of PTSD." Pentagon News Release by Assistant Secretary Health Affairs, August 18, 2008.

Caveness, W. F. "Onset and Cessation of Fits Following Craniocerebral Trauma." *Journal of Neurosurgery* 20 (1963): 570–583.

Caveness, W. F., et al. *National Institutes of Health Vietnam Head Injury Study.* (1979).

Centers for Disease Control and Prevention. *Post-Service Mortality Among Vietnam Veterans: A Study Journal of the American Medical Association.* Atlanta, GA: Centers for Disease Control and Prevention, 1987.

Centers for Disease Control and Prevention. "Vietnam Experience Study. Health Status of Vietnam Veterans: I. Psychosocial Characteristics." *Journal of the American Medical Association* 259 (1988): 2701–2707.

Chappell, R. A. "Naval Offenders and Their Treatment." *Federal Probation* 9 (1945): 3–5.

Chermol, B. H. "Wounds Without Scars: Treatment of Battle Fatigue in the U.S. Armed Forces in the Second World War." *Military Affairs: Journal of Military History, Including Theory and Technology* 49 (1985): 9–12.

Choe, S. H., C. J. Hanley, and M. Mendoza. "GI'S Tell of a US Massacre in Korean War." Associated Press, *New York Times*, 1999.

Cigrang, J. A., A. L. Peterson, and R. P. Schobitz. "Three American Troops in Iraq: Evaluation of a Brief Exposure Therapy Treatment for the Secondary Prevention of PTSD." *Pragmatic Case Studies in Psychotherapy* 1, no. 2 (2005).

Clay Hunt Act. H.R. 203. 114th Congress (2015–2016).

"Colonel Paul V. McNutt, National Commander of the American Legion: Declared That the Needs of Disabled Veterans Were Becoming an Increasingly Difficult Problem Because of the Failure of Congress to Provide Adequate Funding." *New York Times*, 1929.

"Communities Held Failing Veterans: Social Service Experts Find a Lack of Help in Solving Readjustment Problems." *New York Times*, November 21, 1945.

Congressional Budget Office. *Veterans' Disability Compensation: Trends and Policy Options.* Washington, DC: CBO, August 2014.

Congressional Budget Office. *The Veterans Health Administration's Treatment of PTSD and Traumatic Brain Injury Among Recent Combat Veterans. February 2012.* Washington, DC: CBO, February 2012.

Congressional Research Service. *American War and Military Operations Casualties: Lists and Statistics.* Washington, DC: CRS, February 26, 2010. http://fas.org/sgp /crs/natsec/RL32492.pdf.

Congressional Research Service. *Post-Traumatic Stress Disorder and Other Mental Health Problems in the Military: Oversight Issues for the Congress.* Prepared by K. Blakeley and D. J. Jansen. 7–5700: R43175. Washington, DC: CRS, August 8, 2013. https://fas.org/sgp/crs/natsec/R43175.pdf.

Cooper, D. *Psychiatry and Anti-Psychiatry.* London: Tavistock Publications, 1967.

"Coordination of Aid for Veterans Urges." *New York Times*, September 9, 1944.

Da Costa, J. M. "On Irritable Heart: A Clinical Study of a Form of Functional Cardiac Disorder and Its Consequences." Reprinted in 1951. *American Journal of Medicine* (November 1871): 559–567.

Dao, J. "Branding a Soldier with 'Personality Disorder.'" *New York Times*, February 24, 2012. www.nytimes.com/2012/02/25/us/a-military-diagnosis-personality-disorder -is-challenged.html.

Dao, J. "Military Study Finds Benefits in Mental Health Screening." *New York Times*, January 18, 2011. http://www.nytimes.com/2011/01/19/us/19military.html?_r=0.

Dao, J. "Study Seeks Biomarkers for Invisible War Scars." *New York Times*, February 6, 2013. http://www.nytimes.com/2013/02/07/us/study-seeks-biomarkers-for-ptsd-and -traumatic-brain-injuries.html?_r=0.

Dean, E. T. *Shook Over Hell: Post-Traumatic Stress Vietnam and the Civil War.* Cambridge, MA: Harvard University Press, 1997.

Dekel, R., and H. Goldblatt, "Is There Intergenerational Transmission of Trauma? The Case of Combat Veterans' Children," *American Journal of Orthopsychiatry* 78, no. 3 (2008): 281–289.

Dekel, R., Z. Solomon, K. Ginzburg, and Y. Neria. "Combat Exposure, Wartime Performance, and Long-Term Adjustment Among Combatants." *Military Psychology* 15, no. 2 (2003): 117–131

Department of the Army. *Field Manual 4–02.51: Combat and Operational Stress Control (FM 8–51).* Washington, DC: Headquarters, Department of the Army, 2006.

Department of the Army. *Field Manual 6–22.5: Combat and Operational Stress Control Manual for Leaders and Soldiers.* Washington, DC: Headquarters, Department of the Army, 2009.

Department of the Army. *Policy Guidance on the Assessment and Treatment of Post-Traumatic Stress Disorder (PTSD). OTSG/MEDCOM Policy Memo 12–035 of 10 April 2012.* Fort Sam Houston, TX: Headquarters, United States Army Medical Command, 2012. http://cdn.govexec.com/media/gbc/docs/pdfs_edit /042312bb1.pdf.

Department of Defense. *Department of Defense Directive Number 1020.02: Diversity Management and Equal Opportunity (EO) in the Department of Defense.* Washington, DC: Pentagon, 2009. www.deomi.org/DiversityMgmt/documents /DoD_Directive102002p.pdfwww.deomi.org/DiversityMgmt/documents/DoD _Directive102002p.pdf.

Department of Defense. *Department of Defense Instruction Number 1332.14: Enlisted Administrative Separations of February 27, 2017.* Washington, DC: Pentagon, 2017. www.dtic.mil/whs/directives/corres/pdf/133214p.pdf.

Department of Defense. "Our Story." https://www.defense.gov/About.

Department of Defense. *Suicide Event Report: Calendar Year 2017 Annual Report.* Washington, DC: Defense Health Agency, 2017. https://www.pdhealth .mil/sites/default/files/images/docs/TAB_B_DoDSER_CY_2017_Annual _Report_508_071619.pdf.

Department of Defense Task Force on Mental Health. *An Achievable Vision: Report of the Department of Defense Task Force on Mental Health.* Falls Church, VA: Defense Health Board, 2007.

Department of Defense, Task Force on the Prevention of Suicide by Members of the Armed Forces. *The Challenge and the Promise: Strengthening the Force, Preventing Suicide, and Saving Lives.* Falls Church, VA: Defense Health Board, 2010. www.health.mil/dhb/subcommittees-tfpsmaf.cfm.

Department of the Navy. "Credentials Review and Clinical Privileging of Clinical Practitioners/Providers in Department of the Navy Fleet and Family Support Program and Marine Corps Community Services." SECNAVINST 1754.7A PERS-61 07 Nov 2005. Washington, DC: Office of the Secretary of the Navy, 2004.

Department of Navy. *OPNAV Instruction 5350.4D: Navy Alcohol and Drug Abuse Prevention and Control of 4 Jun 2009.* Washington, DC: Office of the Chief of Naval Operations, 2009.

Department of Navy and U.S. Marine Corps. *Combat and Operational Stress Control.* U.S. Navy, NTTP 1-15M; U.S. Marine Corps, MCRP 6-11C. Washington, DC: Pentagon, December 2010.

Department of Veterans Affairs. *Analysis of VA Health Care Utilization Among Operation Enduring Freedom, Operation Iraqi Freedom, and Operation New Dawn Veterans, from 1st Qtr FY 2002 through 3rd Qtr FY 2012.* Washington, DC: Department of Veterans Affairs, 2012.

Department of Veterans Affairs. *Analysis of VA Health Care Utilization Among Operation Enduring Freedom, Operation Iraqi Freedom, and Operation New Dawn Veterans, from 1st Qtr FY 2002 through 1st Qtr FY 2015.* Washington, DC: Epidemiology Program, Post-Deployment Health Group, Office of Public Health, Veterans Health Administration, 2015.

Department of Veterans Affairs. *Iraq War Clinician Guide,* 2nd edition. Washington, DC: National Center for Post-Traumatic Stress Disorder, 2004.

Department of Veterans Affairs. "Medically Unexplained Physical Symptoms." War Related Illness and Injury Study Center. http://www.warrelatedillness.va.gov /education/healthconditions/medically-unexplained-syndrome.asp.

Department of Veterans Affairs and Department of Defense. "VA/DoD Clinical Practice Guideline for the Management of Post-traumatic Stress." Publication 10Q-CPG/PTSD-04. Washington, DC: Veterans Health Administration, Department of Veterans Affairs and Health Affairs, Department of Defense, Office of Quality and Performance, 2004.

Department of Veteran's Affairs and Department of Defense. "VA/DoD Clinical Practice Guideline for the Management of Post-traumatic Stress." Publication 10Q-CPG/PTSD-10. Washington, DC: Veterans Health Administration, Department of Veterans Affairs and Health Affairs, Department of Defense, Office of Quality and Performance, 2010.

Desmond, D., and M. MacLachlan. "Psychological Issues in Prosthetic and Orthotic Practice: A 25 Year Review of Psychology in *Prosthetics and Orthotics International.*" *Prosthetics and Orthotics International* 26, no. 3 (2002).

de Yoanna, M., and M. Benjamin. "I Am Under a Lot of Pressure to Not Diagnose PTSD." *Salon,* April 8, 2009. www.salon.com/2009/04/08/tape.

Dignified Treatment of Wounded Warriors Act, 2009. S.16.06, 110th Congress (2007–2008). www.congress.gov/bill/110th-congress/senate-bill/1606.

Dohrenwend, B. P., J. B. Turner, N. A. Turse, B. G. Adams, K. Koenen, and R. Marshall. "The Psychological Risks of Vietnam for U.S. Veterans: A Revisit with New Data and Methods." *Science* 18, no. 313 (2006): 979–982.

Dohrenwend, B. P., T. J. Yager, M. M. Wall, and B. G. Adams. "The Roles of Combat Exposures, Personal Vulnerability, and Involvement in Harm to Civilians or Prisoners in Vietnam War-Related Posttraumatic Stress Disorder." *Clinical Psychology Science* 1, no. 3 (2013): 223–238.

Drayer and Glass. Introduction. In *Neuropsychiatry in World War II*, Vol. 2: Overseas theaters, ed. A. J. Glass, pp,1-23. Washington, DC: Office of the Surgeon General, US Army.

Drimmer, F. *Until You Are Dead: The Book of Executions in America*. New York: Pinnacle Books, 1992.

Du Preez, J., J. Sundin, S. Wessely, and N. T. Fear. "Unit Cohesion and Mental Health in the UK Armed Forces." *Occupational Medicine* 62, no. 1 (2012): 47–53.

Eagan, J. R., L. Jackson, and R. H. Earnes. "A Study of Neuropsychiatric Rejectees." *Journal of American Medical Association* 145 (1951): 466–469.

Eanes, R. H. "Standards Used By Selective Service and a Follow-up on Neuropsychiatric Rejectees in World War II." *Selection of Military Manpower: A Symposium* (1951): 149–156.

Eberly, R. E., and B. E. Engdahl. "Prevalence of Somatic and Psychiatric Disorders Among Former Prisoners of War." *Hospital Community Psychiatry* 42 (1991): 807–813.

Eibner C., J. S. Ringel, B. Kilmer, R. L. Pacula, and C. Diaz. "The Cost of Post-Deployment Mental Health and Cognitive Conditions." In *Invisible Wounds of War: Psychological and Cognitive Injuries, Their Consequences, and Services to Assist Recovery*, ed. Terri Tanielian and Lisa H. Jaycox. MG-720-CCF. Santa Monica, CA: RAND Corporation, 2008.

Egendorf, A. "*Legacies of Vietnam: Comparative Adjustment of Veterans and Their Peers: A Study*. Washington, DC: U.S. Government Printing Office, 1981.

Egendorf, A. "The Postwar Healing of Vietnam Veterans: Recent Research." *Hospital and Community Psychiatry* 33, no. 11 (1982): 901–908.

Elbogen, E. B., S. C. Johnson, H. R. Wagner, V. M. Newton, C. Timko, J. J. Vasterling, and J. C. Beckham. "Protective Factors and Risk Modification of Violence in Iraq and Afghanistan." *Journal of Clinical Psychiatry* 73, no. 6 (2012): 767–773.

Evans, S. "Gulf Veterans Still Paying the Price." *Washington Post*, January 17, 1992.

Everson, R. Blaine, and C. R. Figley. *Families Under Fire*. New York: Routledge, 2011.

Executive Order No. 13625, Federal Register, 77(172). *Improving Access to Mental Health Services for Veterans, Service Members, and Military Families*, 2012. www.gpo.gov/fdsys/pkg/FR-2012-09-05/pdf/2012-22062.pdf.

Fear, N. T., M. Jones, D. Murphy, L. Hull, A. C. Iversen, B. Coker, L. Machell, J. Sundin, C. Woodhead, N. Jones, N. Greenberg, S. Landau, C. Dandeker, R. J. Rona, M. Hotopf, and S. Wessely. "What Are the Consequences of Deployment to Iraq and Afghanistan on the Mental Health of the UK Armed Forces? A Cohort Study." *Lancet* 375 (2010): 1783–1797.

Feldmeier, M. "At War with the *Feres* Doctrine: The Carmelo Rodriguez Military Medical Accountability Act of 2009." *Catholic University Law Review* 60, no. 1 (2010): 145–182.

Feres v. United States. 340 U.S. 135 (1950).

Figley, C. R. *Stress Disorders Among Vietnam Veterans*. New York: Brunner/Mazel, 1978.

Filner, B. *Post-traumatic Stress Disorder and Personality Disorders: Challenges for the U.S. Department of Veterans' Affairs. Hearing Before the Committee on Veterans' Affairs*. U.S. House of Representatives, 110th Congress first session on July 25, 2007 (Opening Statement of Chairman Filner). Serial no. 110–37. Washington, DC: Government Printing Office, 2007. www.gpo.gov/fdsys/pkg /CHRG-110hhrg37475/pdf/CHRG-110hhrg37475.pdf.

Finucane, M. I. "General Nervous Shock, Immediate and Remote, After Gunshot and Shell Injuries in the South African Campaign." *Lancet* 156, no. 4020 (September 1900): 807–809.

Fontana, A., and R. Rosenheck. "Traumatic War Stressors and Psychiatric Symptoms Among World War II, Korean, and Vietnam War Veterans." *Psychology and Aging* 9, no. 1 (1994): 27–33.

Fontana, A., R. Rosenheck, and E. Brett. "War Zone Traumas and Posttraumatic Stress Disorder Symptomatology." *Journal of Nervous and Mental Disease* 180 (1992): 748–755.

Forbes, D., R. Parslow, M. Creamer, N. Allen, T. McHugh, and M. Hopwood. "Mechanisms of Anger and Treatment Outcome in Combat Veterans with Post-traumatic Stress Disorder." *Journal of Traumatic Stress* 21, no. 2 (2008): 142–129.

Frayne, S. M., V. Y. Chiu, S. Iqbal, E. A. Berg, K. J. Laungani, R. C. Cronkite, J. Pavao, and R. Kimerling. "Medical Care Needs of Returning Veterans with PTSD: Their Other Burden." *Journal of General Internal Medicine* 26, no. 1 (2010): 33–39.

Freedman, H. L. "The Mental-Hygiene-Unit Approach to Reconditioning Neuropsychiatric Casualties." *Mental Hygiene* 269, no. 2 (1945): 269–302.

Freedman, H. L., and M. J. Rockmore. "Mental Hygiene Frontiers in Probation and Parole Services." *Social Correctives for Delinquency* 44 (1945): 52–53.

Freeman, L. "Psychiatric Care of G.I. Improved: Navy-Marine Chief on Mental Ills Says Men Kept at Front Today Top Last War's Ratio." *New York Times*, October 23, 1952.

Freeman, L. "Veterans Seeking Psychiatric Help: But Most Must Wait Months Even for Screening Tests Survey in City Shows." *New York Times*, March 1949.

Freud, A. *The Ego and the Mechanisms of Defense: Vol. 2. The Collected Works of Anna Freud*. New York: International Universities Press, 1936.

Friedman, M. J., and P. P. Schnurr. "The Relationship Between Trauma, PTSD, and Physical Health." In *Neurobiological and Clinical Consequences of Stress: From Normal Adaptation of PTSD*, ed. M. J. Friedman, D.S. Charney, and A. Y. Deutch, 506–524. New York: Lippincott-Raven, 1995.

Frizell, S. "U.S. Army Firing More Soldiers for Misconduct: Number Dismissed for Crime or Misconduct Doubled Between 2007 and 2013." *Time*, February 15, 2014. http://nation.time.com/2014/02/15/u-s-army-firing-more-soldiers-for-misconduct.

Gabriel, R. A. *Between Flesh and Steel: A History of Military Medicine from the Middle Ages to the War in Afghanistan*, Washington, DC: Potomac Books, 2013.

Gabriel, R. A. *Man and Wounded in the Ancient World: A History of Military Medicine from Sumer to the Fall of Constantinople*. Washington, DC: Potomac Books, 2012.

Ginzberg, E., J. K. Anderson, S. W. Ginsberg, and J. L. Herma, *The Lost Divisions: The Ineffective Soldier, Lessons for Management and the Nation*. New York: Columbia University Press, 1959.

Glantz, A. "Suicide Rates Soaring Among WWII Vets." *New America Media*, November 11, 2010.

Glass, A. J. "Army Psychiatry Before World War II." In *Zone of Interior*, Vol. I of *Medical Department United States Army. Neuropsychiatry in World War II*, ed. A. J. Glass and R. J. Bernucci, 989–1027. Washington, DC: Office of the Surgeon General, Department of the Army, 1966.

Glass, A. J. "An Introduction to Psychiatry in the Korean War." Chapter 5 in *Psychiatry in the U.S. Army: Lessons for Community Psychiatry*, ed. A. J. Glass, F. D. Jones, L. R. Sparacino, and J. M. Rothberg, 1–6. Bethesda, MD: Uniformed Services University of the Health Sciences, 2005.

Glass, A. J. "Lessons Learned." In *Zone of Interior*, Vol. I of *Medical Department United States Army. Neuropsychiatry in World War II*, ed. A. J. Glass, and R. J. Bernucci, 735–759. Washington, DC: Office of the Surgeon General, Department of the Army, 1966.

Glass, A. J. "Lessons Learned." In *Overseas Theaters:* Vol. II of *Medical Department, United States Army. Neuropsychiatry in World War II*, 989–1027, ed. A. J. Glass. Washington, DC: US Government Printing Office, 1973.

Glass, A. J. "The North Korean Invasion (25 June 1950–15 September 1950)." Chapter 6 in *Psychiatry in the U.S. Army: Lessons for Community Psychiatry*, ed. A. J. Glass, F. D. Jones, L. R. Sparacino, and J. M. Rothberg, 1–16. Bethesda, MD: Uniformed Services University of the Health Sciences, 2005.

Glass, A. J. "The United Nations Offensive (15 September–26 November 1950)." In *Zone of Interior*, Vol. I of *Medical Department United States Army. Neuropsychiatry in World War II*, ed. A. J. Glass and R. J. Bernucci. Washington, DC: Office of the Surgeon General, Department of the Army, 1966.

Glass, A. J., R. J. Bernucci, and R. S. Anderson, eds. *Medical Department United States Army. Neuropsychiatry in World War II*. Washington, DC: Office of the Surgeon General, Department of the Army, 1966.

Glass, A. J., and F. D. Jones. *Psychiatry in the U.S. Army: Lessons for Community Psychiatry*. Bethesda, MD: Uniformed Services University of the Health Sciences, 2005.

Glynn. T. R. "The Traumatic Neuroses." *Lancet* (November 5, 1910): 1332–1336.

Government Accountability Office. *Defense Health Care: Actions Needed to Ensure Post-Traumatic Stress Disorder and Traumatic Brain Injury are Considered in Misconduct Separations.* GAO-17-260. Washington, DC: GAO, 2017.

Government Accountability Office. *Defense Health Care: Status of Efforts to Direct Lack of Compliance with Personality Disorder Separation Requirements.* GAO-10-1013T. Washington, DC: GAO, 2010.

Government Accountability Office. *DoD Lacks an Access Standard for the Most Common Type of Direct Care Mental Health Appointment.* Washington, DC: GAO, 2016.

Government Accountability Office. *DoD Mild Traumatic Brain Injury.* GAO-12-27R. Washington, DC: GAO, 2011.

Government Accountability Office. *Gulf War Illnesses: Basic Questions Unanswered.* February 2000-GAO/T-NSIAD-00-79. Washington, DC; GAO, 2000.

Government Accountability Office. *Human Capital: Additional Actions Needed to Enhance DoD's Efforts to Address Mental Health Care Stigma.* GAO-16-404. Washington, DC: GAO, 2016.

Government Accountability Office. *Military Attrition: Better Data, Coupled with Policy Changes Could Help the Services Reduce Early Separations.* NSIAD-98-213. Washington, DC: GAO, 1998.

Government Accountability Office. *Monitoring of Clinical Progress and Reexamination of Research Emphasis Are Needed Gulf War Illnesses.* June 1997-GAO/NSIAD-97-163 Washington, DC: GAO, 1997.

Government Accountability Office. *Post-traumatic Stress Disorder: DoD Needs to Identify the Factors Its Providers Use to Make Mental Health Evaluation Referrals for Service Members.* GAO-06-397 04. Washington, DC: GAO, 2006.

Gray, P. J. *Between Peril and Promise: Facing the Dangers of VA's Skyrocketing Use of Prescription Painkillers to Treat Veterans. Hearing Before the Subcommittee on Health of the Committee on Veterans' Affairs.* U.S. House of Representatives, 113th Congress first session on October 10, 2013 (Prepared Statement of Ms. Gray). Serial no. 113–39. Washington, DC: U.S. Government Printing Office, 2013. https://ia601604.us.archive.org/34/items/gov.gpo.fdsys.CHRG-113hhrg85864/CHRG-113hhrg85864.pdf.

Grinker, R. R., and J. P. Spiegel. "War Neuroses in North Africa: The Tunisian Campaign (January–May 1943)." Restricted report prepared for The Air Surgeon, Army Air Forces. Josiah Macy, Jr. Foundation, New York, 1943.

Grinker, R. R., and J. P. Spiegel. *Men Under Stress.* Philadelphia, PA: Blakiston, 1945.

Grob, G. N., and H. H. Goldman. *Critical Issues in Health and Medicine. The Dilemma of Federal Mental Health Policy: Radical Reform or Incremental Change?* Rutgers, NY: Rutgers University Press, 2006.

Grossman, D. *On Killing: The Psychological Cost of Learning to Kill in War and Society.* New York: Back Bay Books, 1996.

Han, S. C., F. Castro, L. O. Lee, M. E. Charney, B. P. Marx, K. Brailey, S. P. Proctor, and J. J. Vasterling. "Military Unit Support, Postdeployment Social Support, and PTSD Symptoms Among Active Duty and National Guard Soldiers Deployed to Iraq." *Journal of Anxiety Disorders* 28 (2014): 446–453.

Harper, D. "Dilemma." *Online Etymology Dictionary*, 2017. www.etymonline.com /index.php?term=dilemma.

Harris, J. "Pentagon Sends in Psychiatrists After 3 Suicides Among Troops in Haiti." *Washington Post*, October 19, 1994.

Harrison, E. "Psychiatry Panel Scores VA Policy: Physicians at Parlay Say Incentives Are Lacking for Hospital Staff." *New York Times*, 1957.

Hastings, M. *Military Anecdotes.* New York: Oxford University Press, 1985.

Hattenstone, S., and E. Allison. "G4S, the Company with No Convictions—But Does It Have Blood On Its Hands?" *Guardian*, December 22, 2014.

Heaton, L. D. "Forward." In *Zone of Interior*, Vol. I of *Medical Department United States Army. Neuropsychiatry in World War II*, ed. A. J. Glass and R. J. Bernucci, xiii–xiv. Washington, DC: Office of the Surgeon General, Department of the Army, 1966.

Hepner, K. A., Sloss, E. M., Roth, C. P., Krull, H., Paddock, S. M., Moen, S., Timmer, M. J., and Pincus, H. A. "Quality of Care for PTSD and Depression in the Military Health System: Phase I Report." *RAND Health Quarterly* 6, no. 1 (2016): 14.

Highfill-McRoy, R. M., G. E. Larson, S. Booth-Kewley, and C. F. Garland. "Psychiatric Diagnosis and Punishment for Misconduct: The Effects of PTSD in Combat-Deployed Marines." *BMC Psychiatry* 10, no. 1 (2010): 88.

Hiley-Young, B., D. D. Blake, F. R. Abueg, V. Rozynko, and F. D. Gusman. "Warzone Violence in Vietnam: An Examination of Premilitary, Military, and Postmilitary Factors in PTSD Inpatients." *Journal of Traumatic Stress* 8, no. 1 (1995): 125–141.

Hing, M., J. Cabrera, C. Barstow, and R. Forsten. "Special Operations Forces and Incidence of Post-Traumatic Stress Disorder Symptoms." *Journal of Special Operation Medicine* 12, no. 3 (2012): 23–35.

Hoge, C. W., C. A. Castro, and K. M. Eaton. "Impact of Combat Duty in Iraq and Afghanistan on Family Functioning: Findings from the Walter Reed Army Institute of Research land Combat Study." In *Human Dimensions in Military Operations—Military Leaders' Strategies for Addressing Stress and Psychological Support*, 5.1–5.6. Meeting Proceedings RTO-MP-HFM-134, Paper 5. Neuilly-sur -Seine, France: RTO, 2006.

Hoge, C. W., C. A. Castro, S. C. Messer, D. McGurk, D. I. Cotting, and R. L. Koffman. "Combat Duty in Iraq and Afghanistan, Mental Health Problems, and Barriers to Care." *New England Journal of Medicine* 351 (2004): 13–22.

Hoge, C. W., A. Terhakopian, C. A. Castro, S. C. Messer, and C. C. Engel. "Association of Posttraumatic Stress Disorder with Somatic Symptoms, Health Care Visits, and Absenteeism Among Iraq War Veterans." *American Journal of Psychiatry* 164 (2007): 150–153.

Hoge, C. W., H. E. Toboni, S. C. Messer, N. Bell, P. Amoroso, and D. T. Orman. "The Occupational Burden of Mental Disorders in the U.S. Military: Psychiatric Hospitalizations, Involuntary Separations, and Disability." *American Journal of Psychiatry* 162, no. 3 (2005): 585–591.

Holbrook, J. G. "Veterans' Courts and Criminal Responsibility: A Problem Solving History and Approach to the Liminality of Combat Trauma." Widener Law School Legal Studies Research Paper no. 10-43. Widener University School of Law, Wilmington, DE, 2010.

Holden, W. *Shell Shock: The Psychological Impact of War*. London: Macmillan, 1998.

Horesh, D., Z. Solomon, G. Zerach, and T. Ein-Dor. "Delayed-Onset PTSD Among War Veterans: The Role of Life Events Throughout the Life Cycle." *Social Psychiatry and Psychiatric Epidemiology* 46, no. 9 (2011): 863–870.

Huffman, R. E. "Which Soldiers Break Down: A Survey of 610 Psychiatric Patients in Vietnam." *Bulletin Menninger Clinic* 34, no. 6 (1970): 343–351.

Huie, W. B. *The Execution of Private Slovik*. Yardley, PA: Westholme, 1954.

Hurd, C. "The Veteran: House Veterans Committee Deflects Inquiry on Medical Care of Soldiers." *New York Times*, April 1, 1945.

Iacobelli, T. *Death or Deliverance: Canadian Courts Martial in the Great War*. Vancouver, BC: UBC Press, 2013.

"Insane War Veterans Reported Increasing: Legions Rehabilitation Body Told Number Exceeds Hospital Facilities." *New York Times*, June 24, 1934.

Institute of Medicine. *Health Consequences of Service During the Persian Gulf War: Initial Findings and Recommendations for Immediate Action*. Washington, DC: National Academies Press, 1995.

Institute of Medicine. *Gulf War and Health*: Vol. 4. *Health Effects of Serving in the Gulf War*. Washington, DC: National Academies Press, 2006.

Institute of Medicine. *Gulf War and Health*: Vol. 6. *Physiologic, Psychologic and Psychosocial Effects of Deployment-Related Stress*. Washington, DC: National Academies Press, 2008.

Institute of Medicine. *Gulf War and Health*: Vol. 7. *Long-Term Consequences of Traumatic Brain Injury*. Washington, DC: National Academies Press, 2008.

Institute of Medicine. *Posttraumatic Stress Disorder: Diagnosis and Assessment*. Washington, DC: National Academies Press, 2006.

Institute of Medicine. *Preventing Psychological Disorders in Service Members and Their Families: An Assessment of Programs*. Washington, DC: National Academies Press, 2014.

Institute of Medicine. *PTSD Compensation and Military Service*. Committee on Veteran's Compensation for Posttraumatic Stress Disorder. National Research Council. Washington, DC: National Academies Press, 2007.

Institute of Medicine. *PTSD Treatments. Committee on Veteran's Compensation for Posttraumatic Stress Disorder.* National Research Council. Washington, DC: National Academies Press, 2007.

Institute of Medicine. *Report to Congress Section 1661 of the National Defense Authorization Act for Fiscal Year 2008 Phase 1 Supporting Adjustment and Readjustment of Active Military, Veterans, and Family Members: IOM's March 31, 2010, Returning Home from Iraq and Afghanistan: Preliminary Assessment of Readjustment Needs of Veterans, Service Members, and Their Families.* Washington, DC: National Academies Press, 2010.

Institute of Medicine. *Returning Home from Iraq and Afghanistan: Assessment of Readjustment Needs of Veterans, Service Members, and Their Families.* Washington, DC: National Academies Press, 2013.

Institute of Medicine. "Substance Use Disorders in the U.S. Armed Forces." Report Brief September 2012. Washington, DC: National Academies Press, 2012.

Institute of Medicine. *Treatment for Posttraumatic Stress Disorder in Military and Veteran Populations.* Washington, DC: National Academies Press, 2008.

Institute of Medicine. *Treatment for Posttraumatic Stress Disorder in Military and Veteran Populations: Final Assessment.* Washington, DC: National Academies Press, 2014.

Institute of Medicine. *Veterans and Agent Orange: Health Effects of Herbicides Used in Vietnam.* Washington, DC: National Academies Press, 1994.

Irwin, C., S. A. Falsetti, R. B. Lydiard, J. C. Ballenger, C. D. Brock, and W. Brener. "Comorbidity of Posttraumatic Stress Disorder and Irritable Bowel Syndrome." *Journal of Clinical Psychiatry* 57, no. 12 (1996): 576–578.

Izzo, R. "In Need of Correction: How the Army Board for Correction of Military Records Is Failing Veterans with PTSD." *Yale Law Journal* 123, no. 5 (2014): 1118–1625.

Johnson, W., and R. G. Rows. "Neurasthenia and the War Neuroses." In *History of the Great War*, Vol. 2, 1–67. London: HMSO, 1923.

Joint Mental Health Advisory Team-7. *Operation Enduring Freedom, 2010 Afghanistan, 22 February 2011.* Washington, DC: Office of the Surgeon General, United States Army Medical Command and Office of the Command Surgeon HQ, USCENTCOM and Office of the Command Surgeon U.S. Forces Afghanistan, 2011.

Joint Mental Health Advisory Team-8. *Operation Enduring Freedom, 2013 Afghanistan, 12 August 2013.* Washington, DC: Office of the Surgeon General, United States Army Medical Command and Office of the Command Surgeon HQ, USCENTCOM and Office of the Command Surgeon U.S. Forces Afghanistan, 2013.

Jones, E. "LMF: The Use of Psychiatric Stigma in the Royal Air Force During the Second World War." *Journal of Military History* 70, no. 2 (2006): 439–458.

Jones, E., and S. Wessely. "Forward Psychiatry in the Military: Its Origin and Effectiveness." *Journal of Traumatic Stress* 16 (2003): 411–419.

Jones, E., and S. Wessely. "A Paradigm Shift in the Conceptualization of Psychological Trauma in the 20th Century." *Journal of Anxiety Disorders* 21 (2007): 164–175.

Jones, E., and S. Wessely. *Shell Shock to PTSD: Military Psychiatry from 1900 to the Gulf War.* New York: Psychology Press, 2005.

Jones, F. D. "Disorders of Frustration and Loneliness." In *Textbook of Military Medicine: War Psychiatry*, ed. F. D. Jones, L. R. Sparacino, V. L. Wilcox, J. M. Rothberg, and J. W. Stokes, 63–83. Washington, DC: Office of the Surgeon General, U.S. Army, Borden Institute, Walter Reed Army Institute of Research, 1995.

Jones, F. D. "Psychiatric Lessons of War." In *Textbook of Military Medicine: War Psychiatry*, ed. F. D. Jones, L. R. Sparacino, V. L. Wilcox, J. M. Rothberg, and J. W. Stokes, 1–34. Washington, DC: Office of the Surgeon General, U.S. Army, Borden Institute, Walter Reed Army Institute of Research 1995.

Jones, F. D. "Traditional Warfare Combat Stress Casualties." In *Textbook of Military Medicine: War Psychiatry*, ed. F. D. Jones, L. R. Sparacino, V. L. Wilcox, J. M. Rothberg, and J. W. Stokes , 35–61. Washington, DC: Office of the Surgeon General, U.S. Army. Borden Institute, 1995.

Jones, F. D., L. R. Sparacino, V. L. Wilcox, J. M. Rothberg, and J. W. Stokes, eds. *Textbook of Military Medicine: War Psychiatry.* Washington, DC: Office of the Surgeon General, U.S. Army, Borden Institute, Walter Reed Army Institute of Research 1995.

Jones, N., N. T. Fear, M. Jones, S. Wessely, and N. Greenberg. "Long-Term Military Work Outcomes in Soldiers Who Become Mental Health Casualties When Deployed on Operations." *Psychiatry: Interpersonal and Biological Processes* 73, no. 4 (2010): 352–364.

Jordan, B. K., C. R. Marmar, J. A. Fairbank, W. E. Schlenger, R. A. Kulka, and R. L. Hough. "Problems in Families of Male Vietnam Veterans with Post-Traumatic Stress Disorder." *Journal of Consulting and Clinical Psychology* 60, no. 6 (1992): 916–926.

Joshua Omvig Veterans Suicide Prevention Act. H.R. 327. 110th Congress (2007). https://www.govtrack.us/congress/bills/110/hr327/text.

Kang, H. K. *Surveillance of Health Outcomes of Gulf War Veterans Environmental Epidemiology Service and War-Related Illness and Injury Study Center.* Gulf War Advisory Committee Meeting, November 20, 2008. Washington, DC: VA Medical Center, 2008.

Kang, H. K., and T. A. Bullman. *The Risk of Suicide Among U.S. War Veterans: Vietnam War to Operation Iraqi Freedom.* 2010 DOD/VA Suicide Prevention Conference, January 10–14, 2010. Washington, DC: Department of Veterans Affairs, 2010.

Kang, H. K., B. H. Natelson, C. M. Mahan, K. Y. Lee, and F. M. Murphy. "Post-Traumatic Stress Disorder and Chronic Fatigue Syndrome-Like Illness Among Gulf War Veterans: A Population-Based Survey of 30,000 Veterans." *American Journal of Epidemiology* 157, no. 2 (2003): 141–148.

Karpinos, B. D., and A. J. Glass. "Disqualifications and Discharges for Neuropsychiatric Reasons, World War I and World War II." In *Zone of Interior*, Vol. I of *Medical Department United States Army. Neuropsychiatry in World War II*, ed. A. J. Glass and R. J. Bernucci, xiii–xiv. Washington, DC: Office of the Surgeon General, Department of the Army, 1966.

Kay, A. G. "Insanity in the Army During Peace and War, and Its Treatment." *Journal of the Royal Army Medical Corps* 18 no. 1 (1912): 146–158.

Kennedy, C. H., and J. A McNeil. "A History of Military Psychology." In *Military Psychology: Clinical and Operational Applications*, ed. C. H. Kennedy and E. A. Zillmer, 1–17. New York: Guilford Press, 2006.

Kessler, M. M. "Troops in Transit." In *Zone of Interior*, Vol. I of *Medical Department United States Army. Neuropsychiatry in World War II*, ed. A. J. Glass and R. J. Bernucci, 320–348. Washington, DC: Office of the Surgeon General, Department of the Army, 1966.

Kilpatrick, M. E. *Force Health Protection and Readiness Programs, Department of Defense. Hearing Before the U.S. Congress House of Representatives Committee on Oversight and Government Reform*, First Session, May 24, 2007 (Statement by Michael E. Kilpatrick, MD, Deputy Director). Serial no. 110–111. Washington, DC: U.S. Government Printing Office, 2007.

Kime, P. "Panel Says Pentagon Does Not Know if PTSD Programs Work." *USA Today*, July 15, 2012. http://usatoday30.usatoday.com/news/military/story/2012-07-13/post-traumatic-stress-disorder-programs/56207754/1.

King, H., dir. *Twelve O'Clock High*. Hollywood, LA: Twentieth Century Fox, 1949.

Kirkland, F. R. "Preface." In *The Gulf War and Mental Health: A Comprehensive Guide*, ed. J. A. Martin, L. R. Sparacino, and G. Belenky. Westport, CT: Praeger, 1996.

Klostermann, K., T. Mignone, M. L. Kelley, S. Musson, and G. Bohall. "Intimate Partner Violence in the Military: Treatment Considerations." *Aggression and Violent Behavior* 17, no. 1 (2012): 53–58.

Knapp, L., and F. Weitzen. "A Total Psychotherapeutic Push Method as Practiced in the Fifth Service Command Rehabilitation Center, Fort Knox, Kentucky." *American Journal of Psychiatry* 102, no. 3 (1945): 362–363.

"Korean Veterans Due for Benefits: 2000,000 Expected to Collect Unemployment Aide but Job Outlook Is Bright." *New York Times*, November 9, 1952.

"Korean Veterans Seek Homes." *New York Times*, September 16, 1951.

Kors, J. "Disposable Soldiers: How the Pentagon Is Cheating Wounded Vets." *The Nation*, April 26, 2010. www.thenation.com/article/disposable-soldiers.

Kors, J. "How Specialist Town Lost His Benefits: Wounded Soldiers Returning from Iraq Are Increasingly Being Wrongly Diagnosed by the Military, Which Prevents Them from Collecting Benefits." *The Nation*, March 29, 2007. www .thenation.com/article/how-specialist-town-lost-his-benefits.

Kulka, R. A., W. E. Schlenger, J. A. Fairbank, R. L. Hough, B. K. Jordan, C. R. Marmar, D. S. Weiss, and D. A. Grady. *Trauma and the Vietnam War Generation: Report of Findings from the National Vietnam Veterans Readjustment Study*. New York: Brunner/Mazel, 1990.

Lerner, P. *Hysterical Men: War, Psychiatry, and the Politics of Trauma in Germany, 1890–1930*. London: Cornell University Press, 2003.

Lerner, P. "Psychiatry and Casualties of War in Germany, 1914–18." *Journal of Contemporary History*, 35, no. 1 (2000): 13–28.

Levy, H. C., L. M. Conoscenti, J. F. Tillery, B. D. Dickstein, and B. T. Litz. "Deployment Stressors and Outcomes Among Air Force Chaplains." *Journal of Traumatic Stress* 24, no. 3 (2011): 342–6.

Linden, E. "The Demoralization of an Army: Fragging and Other Withdrawal Symptoms." *Saturday Review* 8 (1972): 12–17.

Linnerooth, P. J., B. A. Moore, and A. J. Mrdjenovich. "Professional Burnout in Clinical Military Psychologists: Recommendations Before, During, and After Deployment." *Professional Psychology: Research and Practice* 42 (2011): 87–93.

Litz, B. T., N. Stein, E. Delaney, L. Lebowitz, W. P. Nash, C. Silva, and S. Maguen. "Moral Injury and Moral Repair in War Veterans: A Preliminary Model and Intervention Strategy." *Clinical Psychology Review* 29 (2009): 695–706.

Ludwig, A. O. "Psychiatry at the Army level." In *Combat Psychiatry: Experiences in the North African and Mediterranean Theaters of Operation, American Ground Forces, World War II*, ed. F. R. Hanson, 74–104. Honolulu, HI: University Press of the Pacific, U.S. Army Medical Department, 1949.

Lynch, S. H., and M. L. Lobo. "Compassion Fatigue in Family Caregivers: A Wilsonian Concept Analysis." *Journal of Advanced Nursing* 68, no. 9 (2012): 2125–2134.

MacCormick, A. H., and V. H. Evjen. "The Army's Rehabilitation Program for Military Prisoners." *Social Correctives for Delinquency* 1 (1945): 8–11.

Maclean W. C. "Diseases of the Heart in the British Army, the Cause and the Remedy." *British Medical Journal* 1 (1867): 161–164.

Macphail, A. "Official History of the Canadian Forces in the Great War: 1914–1919." Ottawa, Canada: Medical Services, FAACLAND, 2015.

Maguen, S., D. D. Luxton, N. A. Skopp, G. A. Gahm, M. A. Reger, T. J. Metzler, and C. R. Marmar. "Killing in Combat, Mental Health Symptoms, and Suicidal Ideation in Iraq War Veterans." *Journal of Anxiety Disorders* 25 (2011): 563–567.

Mancini, A. D. "A Postwar Picture of Resilience." *New York Times*, February 5, 2012, http://www.nytimes.com/2012/02/06/opinion/a-postwar-picture-of-resilience .html?_r=0.

Mansfield, A. J., R. H. Bender, L. L. Hourani, and G. E. Larson. "Suicidal or Self-Harming Ideation in Military Personnel Transitioning to Civilian Life." *Suicide and Life-Threatening Behavior* 41, no. 4 (2011): 392–405.

Manson, M. P., and H. M. Grayson. "The Psychological Clinic at the MTOUSA Disciplinary Training Center." *American Psychologist* 1, no. 3 (1946): 91–94.

Manual of Courts-Martial, United States. Washington, DC: Joint Service Committee on Military Justice, 2012.

Marlowe, D. H. "Psychological and Psychosocial Consequences of Combat and Deployment: With Special Emphasis on the Gulf War." No. MR-1018/11-OSD. Santa Monica, CA: RAND, 2001.

Marshall, H. *On the Enlisting, Discharging, and Pensioning of Soldiers: With the Official Documents on These Branches of Military Duty.* Philadelphia, PA: A. Waldie, 1840.

Martin, J. A. "Combat Psychiatry: Lessons from the War in Southwest Asia." *Journal of the U.S. Army Medical Department* PB 89-2-1/2 (1992): 40–44.

Martin, J. A., and W. R. Cline. "Mental Health Lessons from the Persian Gulf War." In *The Gulf War and Mental Health: A Comprehensive Guide*, ed. J. A. Martin, L. R. Sparacino, and G. Belenky, 161–178. Westport, CT: Praeger, 1996.

Martin, J. A., L. R. Sparacino, and G. Belenky, eds. *The Gulf War and Mental Health: A Comprehensive Guide.* Westport, CT: Praeger, 1996.

Maslach, C., and P. C. Zimbardo. "Dehumanization in Institutional Settings." Technical report no. Z-10, Office of Naval Research, Arlington, VA, 1973.

McCann, W. H. "Nostalgia: A Review of the Literature." Psychological Bulletin 38, no. 3 (1941): 165–182.

McCray, L. W., P. F. Cronholm, H. R. Bogner, J. J. Gallo, and R. A. Neill. "Resident Physician Burnout: Is There Hope?" *Family Medicine* 40, no. 9 (2008): 626–632.

McCutchan, P., X. Liu, C. A. LeardMann, T. Smith, E. Boyko, K. Gore, M. C. Freed, and C. C. Engel. "Deployment, Combat, and Risk of Multiple Physical Symptoms in the US Military: A Prospective Cohort Study." *Annals of Epidemiology* 26, no. 2 (2016), DOI:10.1016/j.annepidem.2015.12.001.

McGeorge, T., J. H. Hughes, and S. Wessely. "The MoD PTSD Decision: A Psychiatric Perspective." *Occupational Health Review* 122 (2006): 21–28.

McHugh, P. R., and G. Treisman. "PTSD: A Problematic Diagnostic Category." *Journal of Anxiety Disorders* 21 (2007): 211–222.

McLay, R. N., C. McBrien, M. D. Wiederhold, and B. K. Wiederhold. "Exposure Therapy With and Without Virtual Reality to Treat PTSD While in the Combat Theater: A Parallel Case Series." *Cyberpsychology, Behavior, and Social Networking* 13, no. 1 (2010): 37–42.

McNally, R. J., and C. B. Frueh. "Why Are Iraq and Afghanistan War Veterans Seeking PTSD Disability Compensation at Unprecedented Rates?" *Journal of Anxiety Disorders* 27, no. 5 (2013): 520–526.

Mellman, T. A., V. Bustamante, A. I. Fins, W. R. Pigeon, and B. Nolan, "REM Sleep and the Early Development of Posttraumatic Stress Disorder." *American Journal of Psychiatry* 159, no. 10 (2002): 1696–1701.

Memorandum issued by Assistant Secretary of Defense for Health Affairs. "Clinical Policy Guidance for Assessment and Treatment of Post-traumatic Stress Disorder" (ASD-HA 2012).

Memorandum issued by P. Mitchell, Captain, Assistant Adjutant 1st Special Services Force of 13 November 1944, Headquarters First Special Service Force. Washington, DC: U.S. Army, 1944.

Memorandum issued by Secretary of the Army. "Memorandum: Special Review and Assessment of Soldiers with Mental Health Conditions Separated from Active Duty for Misconduct of 14 April 2016." Washington, DC: Department of Army, Headquarters, 2016.

Memorandum issued by U.S. Army, Office of the Surgeon General. "Memorandum on Psychoneurosis (Combat Exhaustion)." Washington, DC: U.S. Army, Office of the Surgeon General, 1944.

Memorandum issued by William Winkenwerder, Jr., MD, Assistant Secretary of Defense for Health Affairs, to Secretary of Army, Secretary of Navy, Secretary of Air Force, and Chairman of the Joint Chiefs of Staff. "Policy Guidance on Deployment-Limiting Psychiatric Conditions and Medications." Washington, DC: Pentagon, 2006.

Menninger, W. C. *Reactions to Combat: Psychiatry in a Troubled World.* New York: MacMillan, 1948.

Menninger, W. C. "Education and Training." In *Zone of Interior*, Vol. I of *Medical Department United States Army. Neuropsychiatry in World War II*, ed. A. J. Glass and R. J. Bernucci, 53–66. Washington, DC: Office of the Surgeon General, Department of the Army, 1966.

Menninger, W. C. "Public Relations." In *Zone of Interior*, Vol. I of *Medical Department United States Army. Neuropsychiatry in World War II*, ed. A. J. Glass, and R. J. Bernucci, 129–151. Washington, DC: Office of the Surgeon General, Department of the Army, 1966.

Mental Health Advisory Team-I. *MHAT, Operation Iraqi Freedom, 16 December 2003.* Washington, DC: U.S. Army Surgeon General, 2003.

Mental Health Advisory Team-II. *Mental Health Advisory Team (MHAT-II), Operation Iraqi Freedom-II, 20 January 2005.* Washington, DC: U.S. Army Surgeon General, 2005.

Mental Health Advisory Team-III. *Mental Health Advisory Team (MHAT-III), Operation Iraqi Freedom 04–06, 29 May 2006.* Washington, DC: Office of the Surgeon

Multinational Force-Iraq and Office of the Surgeon General, United States Army Medical Command, 2006.

Mental Health Advisory Team-IV. *Mental Health Advisory Team (MHAT-IV), Operation Iraqi Freedom 05–07, 17 November 2006*. Washington, DC: Office of the Surgeon Multinational Force-Iraq and Office of the Surgeon General, United States Army Medical Command, 2006.

Mental Health Advisory Team-V. *Mental Health Advisory Team (MHAT-V), Operation Enduring Freedom 06–08, 14 February 2008*. Washington, DC: Office of the Surgeon Multinational Force-Iraq and Office of the Surgeon General, U.S. Army Medical Command, 2008.

Mental Health Advisory Team-VI. *Mental Health Advisory Team (MHAT-6), Operation Enduring Freedom 2009 Afghanistan, 6 November 2009*. Washington, DC: Office of the Command Surgeon U.S. Forces Afghanistan and Office of the Surgeon General, United States Army Medical Command, 2009.

Mullen, M. G. *Letter from Admiral Michael G. Mullen, Chairman of the U.S. Joint Chiefs of Staff*, to Hon. Eric K. Shinseki, Secretary of the Department of Veterans Affairs. Washington, DC: Pentagon, February 15, 2011.

Murphy, B. "Critics: Fort Carson Policy Targeted Troubled, Wounded Soldiers." *Stars and Stripes*, November 15, 2011. www.stripes.com/critics-fort-carson-policy -targeted-troubled-wounded-soldiers-1.160871.

Myers, C. S. "Contributions to the Study of Shell Shock: Being an Account of Certain Disorders of Speech, with Special Reference to their Causation and Their Relation to Malingering." *Lancet* (September 1916): 461–467.

Myers, C. S. *Shell Shock in France 1914–1918*. London: Cambridge, 1940.

Nash, W. P., A. M. Boasso, M. M. Steenkamp, J. L. Larson, R. E. Lubin, and B. T. Litz. "Posttraumatic Stress in Deployed Marines: Prospective Trajectories of Early Adaptation." *Journal of Abnormal Psychology* 124, no. 1 (2015): 155–171.

Nasrallah, H. A. "The Antipsychiatry Movement: Who and Why." *Current Psychiatry* 10, no. 12 (2011): 4–53.

National Council for Community Behavioral Healthcare. *Meeting the Behavioral Health Needs of Veterans: Operation Enduring Freedom and Operation Iraqi Freedom*. Washington, DC: National Council for Community Behavioral Healthcare, November 2002. http://www.thenationalcouncil.org/galleries /resourcesservices%20files/Veterans%20BH%20Needs%20Report.pdf.

National Defense Authorization Act. Pub. L. 102–190, 105 Stat. 1290 (1991).

National Defense Authorization Act for Fiscal Year 2008. Pub. L. 110–181, 122 Stat. 3 (2008).

National Defense Authorization Act for Fiscal Year 2010. Pub. L. 111–84, § 512, 123. Stat. 2190, 2280–82 (2009) (codified, as amended, at 10 U.S.C. § 1177).

National Defense Authorization Act for Fiscal Year 2016. Pub. L. 114-92-Nov. 25, 2015, 129 Stat. 726 (2015).

Neel, S. *Vietnam Studies: Medical Support of the U.S. Army in Vietnam 1965–1970.* Washington, DC: Department of the Army, 1991.

Nelson, D. *The War Behind Me: Vietnam Veterans Confront the Truth About U.S. War Crimes.* New York: Basic Books, 2008.

Noble, D., D. C. Washington, M. E. Roudebush, and D. Price. "Studies of Korean War Casualties. Part I: Psychiatric Manifestations in Wounded Men." *American Journal of Psychiatry* 108, no. 7 (1952): 495–499.

Noonan, M. E., and C. J. Mumola. *Bureau of Justice Statistics Special Report: Veterans in State and Federal Prison, 2004.* Washington, DC: U.S. Department of Justice Office of Justice Programs, 2007.

Nordheimer, J. "Postwar Shock Besets Veterans of Vietnam." *New York Times,* August 28, 1972.

Obama, B. H. Exec. Order No. 13625. "Improving Access to Mental Health Services for Veterans, Service Members, and Military Families." 3 C.F.R. 13625 (August 31, 2012). https://obamawhitehouse.archives.gov/the-press-office/2012/08/31/executive -order-improving-access-mental-health-services-veterans-service.

Office of the Inspector General, Department of Defense. "Evaluation Report on the Management of Combat Stress Control in the Department of Defense." Report no. 96–079. Pentagon, Washington, DC, February 29, 1996.

Ogden, S. K., and A. D. Biebers. *Psychology of Denial (1st ed.).* New York: Nova, 2011.

Ognibene, A. J. "General Medicine." In *General Medicine and Infectious Diseases: Vol. 2. Medical Department, United States Army, Internal Medicine in Vietnam,* ed. A. J. Ognibene and B. O'Neill, Jr. Washington, DC: Office of the Surgeon General and Center of Military History. Washington, DC: U.S. Army, 1982. http://history.amedd.army.mil/booksdocs/vietnam/GenMedVN/default.html.

Oppenheim, H. *Die traumatischen neurosen.* Berlin: Hirschwald, 1889.

Orr, D. W. "Objectives of Selective Service Psychiatric Classification." *Bulletin of Menninger Clinic* 5 (1941): 131–133.

Owen, J. *Multiple Claimants Versus Ministry of Defence (Part 1) EWHC* 113, May 2003.

Ozakinci, G., W. K. Hallman, and H. M. Kipen. "Persistence of Symptoms in Veterans of the First Gulf War: 5-Year Follow-up." *Environmental Health Perspectives* 114, no. 10 (2006): 1553–1557.

Ozer, E. J., S. R. Best, T. L. Lipsey, and D. S. Weis, "Predictors of Posttraumatic Stress Disorder and Symptoms in Adults: A Meta-Analysis," *Psychology Bulletin* 129, no. 1 (2003): 52–73.

Palinkas, L. A., and P. Coben. "Psychiatric Casualties Among U.S. Marines in Vietnam." *Military Medicine* 153, no. 10 (1988): 521–526.

Palmer, E. D. "Military Experience with Ulcer Disease: A Review." *Military Medicine* 135 (1970): 871–77.

Peebles-Kleiger, M. J., and J. H. Kleiger. "Re-integration Stress for Desert Storm Families: Wartime Deployments and Family Trauma." *Journal of Traumatic Stress* 7 (1994): 173–194.

Peltz, W. L. "Report to Surgeon General U.S Army on Tour of Medical Installations of Far East Command, November-December-1951" (1951), cited in E. C. Ritchie, "Psychiatry in the Korean War: Perils, PIES, and Prisoners of War." *Military Medicine* (November 2002): 1–11.

Persian Gulf Service and PTSD. Pub. L. 102–25, 105 Stat. 110 (1991).

Persian Gulf War Veterans Act. Pub. L. 105–277, 112 Stat. 2681 (1998).

Persian Gulf War Veterans' Health Status. Pub. L. 102–585, 106 Stat. 4943 (1992).

Peterson, K. S. "Long Deployments Stress Military Families." *USA Today*, October 8, 2001. http://usatoday30.usatoday.com/life/2001-10-09-military-families.htm.

Phillips, C. J., C. A. LeardMann, G. R. Gumbs, and B. Smith. "Risk Factors for Posttraumatic Stress Disorder Among Deployed US Male Marines." *BMC Psychiatry* 10 (2010): 1–11.

Phillips, D. "Other Than Honorable: Disposable Surge in Discharges Includes Wounded Soldiers." *The Gazette*, May 19, 2013. http://cdn.csgazette.biz/soldiers/day1.html.

Philpott, T. "Military Update: VA Fails to Meet Vets PTSD Needs." *The Gazette*, December 6, 2011.

Pietrzak, R. H., M. B. Goldstein, J. C. Malley, A. J. Rivers, and S. M. Southwick. "Structures of Posttraumatic Stress Disorder and Psychosocial Functioning in Veterans of Operation Enduring Freedom and Iraqi Freedom." *Psychiatry Research* 178, no. 2 (2010): 323–329.

Pietrzak, R. H., D. C. Johnson, M. B. Goldstein, J. C. Malley, A. J. Rivers, C. A. Morgan, and S. M. Southwick. "Psychosocial Buffers of Traumatic Stress, Depressive Symptoms, and Psychosocial Difficulties in Veterans of Operations Enduring Freedom and Iraqi Freedom: The Role of Resilience, Unit Support, and Post-Deployment Social Support." *Journal of Special Operations Medicine* 9, no. 3 (2009): 74–78.

Pietrzak, R. H., A. R. Russo, Q. Ling, and S. M. Southwick. "Suicidal Ideation in Treatment-Seeking Veterans of Operations Enduring Freedom and Iraqi Freedom: The Role of Coping Strategies, Resilience, and Social Support." *Journal of Psychiatric Research* 45 (2011): 720–726.

Pivar, I. "Traumatic Grief: Symptomatology and Treatment for Iraq War Veteran." In *Iraq War Clinician Guide*, 2nd edition, 75–78 Washington, DC: National Center for Post-Traumatic Stress Disorder, 2004.

Pivar, I. L., and N. P. Field. "Unresolved Grief in Combat Veterans with PTSD." *Anxiety Disorders* 18 (2004): 745–755.

Pizarro, J., R. Cohen Silver, and J. Prause. "Physical and Mental Health Costs of Traumatic War Experiences Among Civil War Veterans." *Archives of General Psychiatry* 63, no. 2 (2006): 193–200.

Plag, J. A., and R. J. Arthur. "Psychiatric Re-examination of Unsuitable Naval Recruits: A Two-Year Follow-up Study." *American Journal of Psychiatry* 122, no. 5 (1965): 534–541.

"Plan Urged to Get New Psychiatrists: $100,000,000 for Training to Meet War Veteran Needs Asked by Dr. Kubie." *New York Times*, February 15, 1946.

Porter v. McCullum. (2009). 130 S. Ct. 447, 455, n.8.

Poundja, J., D. Fikretoglu, and A. Brunet. "The Co-Occurrence of Posttraumatic Stress Disorder Symptoms and Pain: Is Depression a Mediator?" *Journal of Stress Trauma* 19, no. 5 (2006): 747–751.

President's Commission on Mental Health. *Report of the Special Working Group: Mental Health Problems of Vietnam Era Veterans.* Washington, DC: U.S. Government Printing Office, February 15, 1978.

"Psychiatrists Ask Rise in VA Funds: Deterioration of Services to Veterans Is Alternative, Congress Is Warned." *New York Times*, May 22, 1947.

Quinn, E. F. "Reconditioning of Psychiatric Patients." In *Zone of Interior*, Vol. I of *Medical Department United States Army. Neuropsychiatry in World War II*, ed. R. S. Anderson, A. J. Glass, and R. J. Bernucci, 687–699. Washington, DC: Office of the Surgeon General, Department of the Army, 1966.

Ramchand, R., R. Rudavsky, S. Grant, T. Tanielian, and L. Jayconx. "Prevalence of, Risk Factors for, and Consequences of Posttraumatic Stress Disorder and Other Mental Health Problems in Military Populations Deployed to Iraq and Afghanistan." *Current Psychiatry Report* 17 (2015): 1–11.

Reister, F. A. *Battle Casualties and Medical Statistics: U.S. Army Experience in the Korean War.* Washington, DC: Surgeon General, Department of the Army, 1973.

Renner, J. A. "The Changing Patterns of Psychiatric Problems in Vietnam." *Comprehensive Psychiatry* 14, no. 2 (1973): 169–180.

Rensberger, B. "Delayed Trauma in Veterans Cited." *New York Times*, May 3, 1972.

Report of the War Office Committee of Enquiry Into "Shell Shock." London: Imperial War Museum, 1922.

Resnick, H. S., D. W. Foy, C. P. Donahue, and E. N. Miller. "Antisocial Behavior and Post-Traumatic Stress Disorder in Vietnam Veterans." *Journal of Clinical Psychology* 45, no. 6 (1989): 860–866.

Ritchie, E. C. "Military Mental Health's Wins and Losses Since the Iraq Invasion." *U.S. Time*, March 19, 2013, http://nation.time.com/2013/03/19/military-mental -healths-wins-andlosses-since-the-iraq-invasion.

Ritchie, E. C. "Psychiatry in the Korean War: Perils, PIES, and Prisoners of War." *Military Medicine* 167, no. 11 (November 2002): 1–11.

Ritchie, E. C. "Update on Combat Psychiatry: From the Battle Front to the Home Front and Back Again." *Military Medicine* 172, no. 2 (2007): 11–14.

Roffman, R. A., and E. Sapol. "Marijuana in Vietnam." *International Journal of Addictions* 5, no. 1 (1970): 1–42.

Rosenberg, T. "For Veterans, a Surge of New Treatments for Trauma." *New York Times*, September 26, 2012. http://opinionator.blogs.nytimes.com/2012/09/26/for-veterans-a-surge-of-new-treatments-for-trauma.

Rosenheck, R., and P. Nathan. "Secondary Traumatization in Children of Vietnam Veterans." *Hospital and Community Psychiatry* 36, no. 5 (1985): 538–549.

Roussy, G., and J. Lhermitte. "The Psychoneuroses of War." In *Military Medical Manuals*, ed. A. Keough. London: University of London Press, 1918.

Roy, M. J., Koslowe, P. A., Kroenke, K., and Magruder, C. "Signs, Symptoms, and Ill-Defined Conditions in Persian Gulf War Veterans: Findings from the Comprehensive Clinical Evaluation Program." *Psychosomatic Medicine* 60 (1998): 663–668.

Russell, M. C. "After 214 Investigations Isn't It Time for a Department of Defense (DoD) Mental Health Accountability Act?" *Huffington Post*, June 28, 2017. http://www.huffingtonpost.com/entry/after-214-investigations-isnt-it-time-for-a-department_us_5955a3e7e4b0c85b96c6608a.

Russell, M. C. "Mental Health Crisis in the Department of Defense: DoD Inspector General Hotline Investigation #98829, Submitted by Commander Mark Russell, USN on 05JAN2006." Available upon request via Freedom of Information Act (FOIA) at Department of Defense; Office of Freedom of Information, 1155. Washington, DC: Pentagon, 2006.

Russell, M. C. *The Future of Mental Health Care in the Department of Defense. Invited Testimony Before the Congressionally mandated Department of Defense Task Force on Mental Health.* October 19–20, 2006, San Diego, CA. Washington, DC: Defense Health Board, 2006. www.ha.osd.mil/DHB/mhtf/meeting/2006oct.cfm.

Russell, M. C., D. Shoquist, and C. Chambers. "Effectively Managing the Psychological Wounds of War." *Navy Medicine* (April–March 2005): 23–26.

Russell, M. C., S. Butkus, and C. R. Figley. "Contribution of Military Organization and Leadership Factors in Perpetuating Generational Cycle of Preventable Wartime Mental Health Crises: Part One." *Psychological Injury and Law* 9, no. 1 (2016): 55–72.

Russell, M. C., S. Butkus, and C. R. Figley. "Ending the Generational Cycle of Preventable Wartime Mental Health Crises, Part Two: Establishing a Behavioral Health Corps and Other Constructive Solutions." *Psychological Injury and Law* 9, no. 1 (2016): 73–86.

Russell, M. C., and C. R. Figley. "Do the Military's Frontline Psychiatry/Combat and Operational Stress Control Doctrine Help or Harm Veterans? Part One: Framing the Issue." *Psychological Injury and Law* 10 (2017): 1–23.

Russell, M. C., and C. R. Figley. "Do the Military's Frontline Psychiatry/Combat Operational Stress Control Programs Benefit Veterans? Part Two: Systematic Review of the Evidence." *Psychological Injury and Law* 10 (2017): 24–71.

Russell, M. C., B. Zinn, and C. R. Figley. "Exploring Options Including Class Action to Transform Military Mental Healthcare and End the Generational Cycle of Preventable Wartime Behavioral Health Crises." *Psychological Injury and Law* 9 (2016): 166–197.

Russell, M. C., and C. R. Figley. "Generational Wartime Behavioral Health Crises: Part Two of a Preliminary Analysis." *Psychological Injury and Law* 8, no. 1 (2015): 132–152.

Russell, M. C., and C. R. Figley. "Investigating Recurrent Generational Wartime Behavioral Health Crises: Part One of a Preliminary Analysis." *Psychological Injury and Law* 8, no. 1 (2015): 106–131.

Russell, M. C., and C. R. Figley. "Investigating Recurrent Generational Wartime Behavioral Health Crises: Part Two of a Preliminary Analysis." *Psychological Injury and Law* 8, no. 2 (2015): 132–152.

Russell, M. C., and C. R. Figley. "Is the Military's Century-Old Frontline Psychiatry Policy Harmful to Veterans and Their Families? Part Three of a Systematic Review." *Psychological Injury and Law* 10 (2017): 72–95.

Russell, M. C., and C. R. Figley. "Overview of the Affordable Care Act's Impact on Military and Veteran Mental Health Services: Nine Implications for Significant Improvements in Care." *Journal of Social Work in Disability and Rehabilitation* 13 (2014): 162–196.

Russell, M. C., C. R. Figley, and K. R. Robertson. "Investigating the Psychiatric Lessons of War and Pattern of Preventable Wartime Behavioral Health Crises." *Journal of Psychology and Behavioral Science* 3, no. 1 (2015): 1–16.

Russell, M. C., S. R. Schaubel, and C. R. Figley. "The Darker Side of Military Mental Healthcare, Part One: Understanding the Military's Mental Health Dilemma." *Psychological Injury and Law* 11, no. 1 (2018): 22–36.

Russell, M. C., S. R. Schaubel, and C. R. Figley. "The Darker Side of Military Mental Healthcare, Part Two: Five Deadly Strategies to Manage its Mental Health Dilemma." *Psychological Injury and Law* 11, no. 1 (2018): 37–68.

Russell, M.C., S. R. Schaubel, and C. R. Figley. "The Darker Side of Military Mental Healthcare, Part Three: Five Deadly Strategies to Manage its Mental Health Dilemma." *Psychological Injury and Law* 11, no. 1 (2018): 69–104.

Russell, R. T. "Veterans Treatment Court: A Proactive Approach." *New England Journal on Crime and Civil Confinement* 35 (2009): 357–364.

Sabo et al. v. United States. 08-899, 102 Fed. Cl. 619 (2016). http://www.uscfc .uscourts.gov/conferences/2012/materials/Military%20Pay%20Claims/Sabo%20v .%20US.pdf.

Salmon, T. W. "General View of Neuropsychiatric Activities." In *The Medical Department of the United States Army in the World War*: Vol. X. *Neuropsychiatry in the American Expeditionary Forces*, ed. T. W. Salmon and N. Fenton, 273–302. Prepared under the direction of Maj. Gen. M. W. Ireland, Surgeon General. Washington, DC: U.S. Government Printing Office, 1929. http://history.amedd .army.mil/booksdocs/wwi/Neuropsychiatry/default.htm

Salmon, T. W. "Introduction." In *The Medical Department of the United States Army in the World War*: Vol. X. *Neuropsychiatry in the American Expeditionary Forces*, ed. T. W. Salmon and N. Fenton. Prepared under the direction of Maj. Gen. M. W. Ireland, Surgeon General. Washington, DC: U.S. Government Printing Office, 1929. http://history.amedd.army.mil/booksdocs/wwi /Neuropsychiatry/default.htm

Salmon, T. W. *Recommendations for the Treatment of Mental and Nervous Diseases in the United States Army*. New York: National Committee for Mental Hygiene, 1917.

Salmon, T. W., and Fenton, N. "Neuropsychiatry in the American Expeditionary Forces." In *Neuropsychiatry: The Medical Department of the United States Army in the World War*, Vol. 10, ed. P. Bailey, F. E. Williams, P. A. Komora, T. W. Salmon, and N. Fenton, 271–474. Washington, DC: Office of the Surgeon General, U.S. Army, 1929.

Sargant, W. "Physical Treatment of Acute War Neurosis: Some Clinical Observations." *British Medical Journal* 2, no. 4271 (1942): 574–576.

Sargant, W., and E. Slater. *An Introduction to Physical Methods of Treatment in Psychiatry*. London: Edinburgh: Livingstone, 1944.

"Says Veterans Lack Psychiatric Relief: McNutt Declares Disabled Men Are in Jails, As Hospitals Are Not Available." *New York Times*, May 26, 1929.

Schmitt, E. "Stress Follows Troops Home from Gulf." *New York Times*, July 16, 1991. http://www.nytimes.com/1991/07/16/us/stress-follows-troops-home-from-gulf .html.

Scurfield, R. M., and S. Tice. *Acute Psycho-Social Intervention Strategies with Medical and Psychiatric Evacuees of "Operation Desert Storm" and Their Families.* Operation Desert Storm Clinician Packet. White River Junction, VT: National Center for PTSD, 1991.

Seamone, E. R. "Reclaiming the Rehabilitative Ethic in Military Justice: The Suspended Punitive Discharge as a Method to Treat Military Offenders with PTSD and TBI and Reduce Recidivism." *Military Law Review* 208, no. 1 (2011): 1–212.

Seelig, A. D., I. G. Jacobson, C. J. Donoho, D. W. Trone, N.C. Crum-Cianflone, and T. J. Balkin, "Sleep and Health Resilience Metrics in a Large Military Cohort," *Sleep* 39, no. 5 (2010): 1111–1120.

Shane, S. "Chemicals Sickened '91 Gulf War Veterans, Latest Study Finds." *New York Times*, October 15, 2004, http://www.nytimes.com/2004/10/15/politics/15gulf .htm.

Shaw, J. A. "Psychodynamic Considerations in the Adaptation to Combat." In *Contemporary Studies in Combat Psychiatry*, ed. G. Belenky, 117–132. Westport, CT: Greenwood Press, 1987.

Sheffield, G. "World War One: Military Discipline and Punishment." British Library, January 29, 2014. www.bl.uk/world-war-one/articles/military-discipline.

Shepard, B. A *War of Nerves: Soldiers and Psychiatrists in the Twentieth Century*. Cambridge, MA: Harvard University Press, 2001.

Sherman, R. A., C. J. Sherman, and L. Parker. "Chronic Phantom and Stump Pain Among American Veterans: Results of a Survey." *Pain* 18, no. 1 (1984): 83–95.

Sidibe, S., and F. Unger. "Unfinished Business: Correcting 'Bad Paper' for Veterans with PTSD." Veterans Legal Services Clinic, Yale Law School, 2016. https://law .yale.edu/system/files/documents/pdf/unfinishedbusiness.pdf.

Slater Gordon Lawyers, "Army PTSD Figures Rise as Shell Shock Brain Injury Identified." Slater Gordon, January 23, 2015. https://www.slatergordon.co.uk /media-centre/blog/2015/01/army-ptsd-figures-rise-as-shell-shock-brain-injury -identified/#ixzz3xGPEuftp

Smith, T. C., C. A. LeardMann, B. Smith, I. G. Jacobson, and M. A. K. Ryan. "Postdeployment Hospitalizations Among Service Members Deployed in Support of the Operations in Iraq and Afghanistan." *Annals of Epidemiology* 19, no. 9 (2009): 603–612.

Sobel, R. "Anxiety-Depressive Reactions After Prolonged Combat Experience: The 'Old Sergeant Syndrome.' " In *Combat Psychiatry: Experiences in the North African and Mediterranean Theaters of Operation American Ground Forces, World War II*, ed. F. R. Hanson, 137–146. Honolulu, HI: University Press of Pacific, U.S. Army Medical Department, 1949.

Sobel, R. "The Battalion Surgeon as Psychiatrist." In *Combat Psychiatry: Experiences in the North African and Mediterranean Theaters of Operation, American Ground Forces, World War II*, ed. F. R. Hanson, 36–44. Honolulu, HI: University Press of Pacific, U.S. Army Medical Department. 1949.

Solomon, Z., and R. Benbenishty. "The Role of Proximity, Immediacy, and Expectancy in Frontline Treatment of Combat Stress Reaction Among Israelis in the Lebanon War." *American Journal of Psychiatry* 143 (1986): 613–617.

Solomon, Z., M. Mikulincer, and M. Waysman. "Delayed and Immediate Onset Posttraumatic Stress Disorder: II. The Role of Battle Experiences and Personal Resources." *Social Psychiatry and Psychiatric Epidemiology* 26 (1991): 8–13.

Solomon, Z., R. Shklar, and M. Mikulincer. "Frontline Treatment of Combat Stress Reaction: A 20-year Longitudinal Study." *American Journal of Psychiatry* 162 (2005): 2319–2314.

Solomon, Z., Y. Singer, and A. Blumenfeld. "Clinical Characteristics of Delayed and Immediate-onset Combat-induced Post-traumatic Stress Disorder." *Military Medicine* 160 (1995): 425–430.

Solomon, Z., M. Weisenberg, J. Schwarzwald, and M. Mikulincer. "Posttraumatic Stress Disorder Among Frontline Soldiers with Combat Street Reaction: The 1982 Israeli Experience." *American Journal of Psychiatry* 144, no. 4 (1987): 448–454.

Sontag, D., and L. Alvarez. "Iraq Veterans Leave a Trail of Death and Heartbreak in U.S." *New York Times*, January 13, 2008. http://www.nytimes.com/2008/01/13/world/americas/13iht-vets.1.9171147.html?pagewanted=all

Stanton, M. D. "Drugs, Vietnam, and the Vietnam Veteran: An Overview." *American Journal of Drug and Alcohol Abuse* 3, no. 4 (1976): 557–570.

Stapp v. Resor. 314 F. Supp. 475 (S.D.N.Y. 1970).

Stavisky, S. "Thousands of GIs Temporarily Disabled During the War Now Stand to Become Permanently Crippled During the Peace . . . Is the Problem so Urgent? *Washington Post*, 1945, B3.

Stokes, J. W. "U.S. Army Mental Health System: Divisional and Corps Level Mental Health Units." In *The Gulf War and Mental Health: A Comprehensive Guide*, ed. J. A. Martin, L. R. Sparacino, and G. Belenky, 3–18. Westport, CT: Praeger, 1996.

Strecker, E. A. "Experiences in the Immediate Treatment of War Neuroses." *American Journal of Insanity* (July 1919): 45–69.

Strong, G. V. "The Administration of Military Justice at the United States Disciplinary Barracks, Fort Leavenworth, Kansas." *Journal of American Institute of Crime and Criminology* 8, no. 3 (1917): 420–421.

Stuart, R. "Jailed Veterans Case Brings Post-Vietnam Problem into Focus." *New York Times*, February 26, 1982. http://www.nytimes.com/1982/02/26/us/jailed-veteran-s-case-brings-post-vietnam-problem-into-focus.html.

Summerfield, D. "The Invention of Post-traumatic Stress Disorder and the Social Usefulness of a Psychiatric Category." *British Medical Journal* 322, no. 7278 (2001): 95–98.

Swank, R. L., and W. E. Marchand, W. E. "Combat Neuroses: Development of Combat Exhaustion." *Archives of Neurology and Psychiatry* 55 (1946): 236–247.

Szasz, T. "The Myth of Mental Illness," *American Psychologist* 15 (1960): 113–118.

Taft, C. T., D. S. Vogt, A. D. Marshall, J. Panuzio, and B. L. Niles. "Aggression Among Combat Veterans: Relationships with Combat Exposure and Symptoms of Posttraumatic Stress Disorder, Dysphoria, and Anxiety." *Journal of Traumatic Stress* 20, no. 2 (2007): 135–145.

Taft, C. T., R. P. Weatherill, H. E. Woodward, L. A. Pinto, L. E. Watkins, M. W. Miller, and R. Dekel. "Intimate Partner and General Aggression Perpetration Among Combat Veterans Presenting to a Posttraumatic Stress Disorder Clinic." *American Journal of Orthopsychiatry* 79, no. 4 (2009): 461–468.

Teten, A. L., L. A. Miller, M. S. Stanford, N. J. Petersen, S. D. Bailey, R. L. Collins, M. J. Dunn, and T. A. Kent. "Characterizing Aggression and Its Association to

Anger and Hostility Among Male Veterans with Post-Traumatic Stress Disorder." *Military Medicine* 175, no. 6 (2010): 405–410.

Thompson, M. "The Army's Continuing Dearth of Mental-Health Workers." *Time USA*, March 20, 2012. http://nation.time.com/2012/03/20/the-armys-continuing -dearth-of-mental-health-workers/#ixzz2LsjVcemW.

Tyson, J. "Compassion Fatigue in the Treatment of Combat-Related Trauma During Wartime." *Clinical Social Work Journal* 35 (2007): 183–192.

U.S. Army. *The Army Lawyer: A History of the Judge Advocate General's Corps, 1775–1975.* Honolulu, HI: University Press of the Pacific, 1975.

U.S. Army. Army Regulation (A.R.) 11–33. In *Army Lessons Learned Program: System Development and Application.* 10 October 1989. Washington, DC: Headquarters Department of the Army, 1989.

U.S. Army. Army Regulation (A.R.) 600–20, In *Army Command Policy. 24 July 2020.* Washington, DC: Department of the Army, 2020.

U.S. Army. *Circular Letter No. 17. Neuropsychiatric Treatment in the Combat Zone.* Office of Surgeon, Headquarters, NATOUSA, June 12, 1943.

U.S. Army. *Circular No. 24. American Expeditionary Forces, France.* Office of Surgeon, Headquarters, NATOUSA, April 23, 1918.

U.S. Army. "Final Public Affairs Guidance: OEF/OIF Communications Plan Mental Health of 23 May 2006." Unpublished document, Headquarters, Army Medical Department, Washington, DC May 23, 2006.

U.S. Army. *The Medical and Surgical History of the War of the Republic: Part III*, Vol. I. Washington, DC: Government Printing Office, 1888.

U.S. Army Air Force. *Eighth Air Force Policy Letter 200.9x373 of 29 October.* London: AFHRA, October 29, 1942.

U.S. Army Eighth Air Force. *The Reclassification of Personnel Failures in the Eighth Air Force of 16 October 1944, 520.742–4.* London: AFHRA, October 16, 1944.

U.S. Army Military History Institute. "Combat Lessons Number 5: Rank and File in Combat: What They're Doing How They Do It." EO-10501 Restricted Report, Classified "Unrestricted" on August 5, 1986. Combat Analysis Section, Operations Division, War Department, Washington, DC, 1944.

U.S. Navy. "Mental Health Public Affairs Guidance of 23 January 2007." Unpublished document, U.S. Navy Medical Department, Navy Medicine West, Bureau of Medicine and Surgery, Washington, DC, January 23, 2007.

Vaughan, C. A., C. M. Farmer, J. Breslau, and C. Burnette, "Evaluation of the Operational Stress Control and Readiness (OSCAR) Program." Santa Monica, CA: RAND Corporation, 2015.

Veterans Administration. *Administrator of Veterans Affairs Annual Report for Fiscal Year Ending June 30, 1957.* Washington, DC: U.S. Government Printing Office, 1958.

Veterans Administration. *Administrator of Veterans Affairs Annual Report for Fiscal Year Ending June 30, 1972.* Washington, DC: U.S. Government Printing Office, 1973.

Veterans Administration, Office of Inspector General. "Review of State Variances in VA Disability Compensation Payments." Report no. 05-00765-137, VA OIG, Washington, DC, 2005. www.va.gov/oig/52/reports/2005/VAOIG-05-00765–137.pdf.

Veterans Benefits Administration. *Annual Benefits Report FY2015.* Washington, DC: U.S. Department of Veterans Affairs, 2015.

"Veteran's Claims Cut by 57 Percent: Reviewing Boards Disallow 29,995 of 51,213 Disability Cases Nervous Diseases Found More Frequent in Cities." *New York Times,* January 2, 1934.

Veterans Health Care Amendments of 1979. Pub. L. 96–22, 93 Stat. 47 (1979).

Veterans Health Care Amendments of 1983. Pub. L. 98–160, 97 Stat. 993 (1983).

Veterans Programs Enhancement Act of 1998. Pub. L. 105–368, 112 Stat. 3315 (1998).

"Veterans' Suicide Average Two a Day," *New York Times,* 1922.

Vogel, S. "Army Orders Reforms for Mental Health Care Treatment." *Washington Post,* March 8, 2013. http://www.washingtonpost.com/blogs/federal-eye/wp/2013/03/08/army-orders-reforms-for-mental-health-care-treatment.

Vogel, S. "Senate Approves Amendment to Expand Military Mental Health Care." *Washington Post,* November 29, 2012. http://www.washingtonpost.com/blogs/federal-eye/wp/2012/11/29/senate-approves-amendment-to-expand-military-mental-health-care-2.

von Clausewitz, Carl. *On War.* Harmondsworth, England: Penguin, 1968.

Wanke, P. *Russian/Soviet Military Psychiatry: 1904–1945.* London: Frank Cass, 2005.

Ward, H. M. *George Washington's Enforcers: Policing the Continental Army.* Carbondale, IL: Southern Illinois University Press, 2006.

Warren, H. C. "U.S. Owes Veterans Better Psychiatric Aide." *Washington Post,* 1944.

Waters. M., and J. Shay. "Heal the 'Bad Paper' Veterans." *New York Times,* July 30, 1994. www.nytimes.com/1994/07/30/opinion/heal-the-bad-paper-veterans.html.

Weinick, R. M., E. B. Beckjord, C. M. Farmer, L. T. Martin, E. M. Gillen, J. D. Acosta, M. P. Fisher, J. Garnett, G. C. Gonzalez, T. C. Helmus, L. H. Jaycox, K. A. Reynolds, N. Salcedo, and D. M. Scharf. "Programs Addressing Psychological Health and Traumatic Brain Injury Among U.S. Military Service Members and Their Families." Prepared for the Office of the Secretary of Defense Center for Military Health Policy Research. Santa Monica, CA: RAND, 2011.

Weinraub, B. "Angry Vietnam Veterans Charging Federal Policies Ignore Their Needs: They See Neglect and Inaction by the Administration in Jobs, Education, Healthcare and Counseling." *New York Times,* 1979.

Wells, M. K. *Aviators and Air Combat: A Study of the U.S. Eighth Air Force and RAF Bomber Command.* No. AFIT/CI/CIA-92-136. London: Department of War Studies, King's College. University of London, 1992.

Whitesell, A. A., and G. P. Owens. "The Impact of Patriotism, Morale, and Unit Cohesion on Mental Health in Veterans of Iraq and Afghanistan." *Traumatology* 18, no. 1 (2012): 1–7.

Wilk, J. E., R. K. Herrell, A. L. Carr, J. C. West, J. Wise, and C. W. Hoge. "Diagnosis of PTSD by Army Behavioral Health Clinicians: Are Diagnoses Recorded in Electronic Health Records?" *Psychiatric Services* 67, no. 8 (2016): 878–882.

Williams, T. "Suicides Outpacing War Deaths for Troops." *New York Times*, June 8, 2012. http://www.nytimes.com/2012/06/09/us/suicides-eclipse-war-deaths-for -us-troops.html?_r=0).

Wilson, J. P. *Identity, Ideology, and Crisis: The Vietnam Veteran in Transition.* Vol. 2. Washington, DC: Disabled American Veterans, 1978.

Xue, C., Y. Ge, B. Tang, Y. Liu, P. Yang, M. Wang, and L. Zhang. "A Meta-Analysis of Risk Factors for Combat-Related PTSD Among Military Personnel and Veterans." *PLOS One* 10, no. 3 (2015): 1–11.

Yehuda, R., S. M. Southwick, and E. J. Giller. "Exposure to Atrocities and Severity of Chronic Posttraumatic Stress Disorder in Vietnam Combat Veterans." *American Journal of Psychiatry* 149 (1992): 333–336.

Young, A. *The Harmony of Illusions: Inventing Post-traumatic Stress Disorder.* Princeton, NJ: Princeton University Press, 1995.

Zaidi, L. Y., and D. W. Foy. "Childhood Abuse Experiences and Combat-Related PTSD." *Journal of Traumatic Stress* 7 (1994): 33–42.

Zoroya, G. "Navy Psychologist: Navy Faces Crisis." *USA Today*, January 16, 2007. http://usatoday30.usatoday.com/news/health/2007-01-16-ptsd-navy_x.htm.

Zoroya, G. "Officer Accuses Military of Trying to Silence Him." *USA Today*, June 21, 2007. http://usatoday30.usatoday.com/news/washington/2007-06-21-officer -accusation_N.htm.

Zoroya, G. "Psychologist: Navy Faces Crisis," *USA Today*, January 17, 2007.

Zoroya, G. "Recent War Vets Face Hiring Obstacle: PTSD Bias." *USA Today*, April 9, 2013, http://www.usatoday.com/story/news/nation/2013/04/06/recent-war -vets-face-hiring-obstacle-ptsd-bias/2057857.

Zoroya, G. "VA Sees Shortfall of Mental Health Specialists." *USA Today*, April 4, 2012, http://usatoday30.usatoday.com/news/military/story/2012-04-04/military-veteran -mental-health-psychiatrists/54009974/1.

Zwerdling, D. "Army Dismissals for Mental Health, Misconduct Rise." *NPR*, November 15, 2007. www.npr.org/templates/story/story.php?storyId=16330374.

Zwerdling, D. "Missed Treatment: Soldiers with Mental Health Issues Dismissed for 'Misconduct.'" *NPR*, October 15, 2015. www.npr.org/2015/10/28/451146230/missed -treatment-soldiers-with-mental-health-issues-dismissed-for-misconduct.

Zwerdling, D. "Senators, Military Specialists Say Army Report on Dismissed Soldiers Is Troubling." *NPR*, December 1, 2016. www.npr.org/2016/12/01/498557687/army -contests-npr-investigation-of-dismissed-soldiers-in-misleading-report.

INDEX

Page numbers in *italics* represent figures or tables.

GPSR Authorized Representative: Easy Access System Europe, Mustamäe tee 50, 10621 Tallinn, Estonia, gpsr.requests@easproject.com